Financial Management

Second Edition

Financial Management

Second Edition

Robert W. Kolb
University of Miami

Ricardo J. Rodríguez
University of Miami

First published 1996

Blackwell Publishers, Inc.
238 Main Street
Cambridge, Massachusetts 02142

Blackwell Publishers Ltd.
108 Cowley Road
Oxford OX4 1JF
UK

Library of Congress Cataloging-in-Publication Data

Kolb, Robert W.
    Financial management / Robert W. Kolb, Ricardo J. Rodríguez. – 2nd ed.
        p.   cm.
    Includes bibliographical references and index.
    ISBN 1-55786-843-3 (HC). ISBN 1-55786-844-1 (PB).
    1. Business enterprises—Finance. 2. Corporations—Finance. 3. Finmaster. 4. Corporations—Finance—Computer-assisted instruction. I. Title.
HG4026.K633   1996
658.15—dc20   95-45436
                                                                              CIP

British Library Cataloguing in Publication Data

A CIP catalogue record for this book is available from the British Library.

Commissioning Editor: Rolf Janke
Production Manager: Jan Leahy

Typeset by AM Marketing

Typeset in Janson on 10 pt. by AM Marketing

This book is printed on acid-free paper

Financial Management, Second Edition, is intended for a beginning or intermediate course in corporate finance. Throughout the book, finance is approached from the standpoint of shareholder wealth maximization, even in the discussion of such traditional topics as ratio analysis and financial planning. The book's financial orientation toward the subject matter is consistent with the emphasis on share price maximization. This contrasts with the accounting orientation of many introductory texts.

While the text avoids complicated mathematical exposition where possible, emphasis is placed on developing a sound conceptual framework. The concept of shareholder wealth maximization is emphasized by showing the cost/benefit trade-offs that the financial manager constantly confronts. This orientation is evident throughout the book, even in such traditionally descriptive areas as working capital management. For example, the working capital discussion emphasizes issues such as the comfort of liquidity versus the opportunity loss of idle funds, and the ease of managing with excess inventories versus the cost incurred in holding those inventories. The trade-off between risk and expected return is emphasized within a value maximization framework.

Pedagogical Features of the Text

The text always keeps two ideas in focus:

- the goal of financial management is to maximize shareholder wealth; and
- persistent trade-offs confront financial managers as they attempt to maximize shareholder wealth.

In addition to these two guiding principles, the following features are stressed:

- completely worked sample problems are integrated throughout the text;
- exceptionally detailed coverage is given to the time value of money;
- numerous questions and problems are found at the ends of the chapters;

Organization of the Text

Financial Management is organized into 23 chapters in a way that makes alternative sequencing easy. Chapter 1 sets the tone of the book by discussing the goals of the firm and the role of the financial manager in helping the firm meet those goals. This chapter also discusses alternative forms of business organization and taxation.

The next four chapters are devoted to the time value of money and its application to bonds and stocks. Chapter 2 is devoted to the time value of single payments, while chapter 3 discusses the time value of a series of payments, including annuities and perpetuities. This two-chapter approach to the foundations of the time value of money concepts allows detailed coverage of these essential issues. From our experience teaching corporate finance, it is clear that many students leave their first course with a poor grasp of time value concepts. Because of the crucial importance of this conceptual background, this text places extremely heavy emphasis on these topics. These chapters include many completely worked sample problems and extensive end-of-chapter questions and problems.

Chapter 4 focuses on bond valuation, stressing the recently acquired time value of money concepts. Similarly, chapter 5 applies time value concepts to stock valuation. These chapters approach stock and bond valuation from within the framework provided by the shareholder wealth maximization criterion.

Chapters 6 and 7 focus on the capital budgeting decision. The basic techniques of capital budgeting are introduced in chapter 6. Chapter 7 extends the discussion of capital budgeting to frequently encountered special problems, such as mutually exclusive projects, multiple internal rates of return, capital rationing, and the machine replacement problem.

Chapters 8 and 9 introduce the important concepts of risk and return. Chapter 8 deals with the problem of defining, identifying, and measuring the risk of a portfolio of assets. This chapter also explains the techniques for managing risk that have grown out of portfolio theory. After discussing the simple two-asset case, the book considers multiple-asset portfolios. This section stresses the fact that any portfolio imaginable can be discussed in terms of its covariance matrix. Chapter 9 stresses the trade-off between expected return and risk, and presents a step-by-step derivation leading to the important concept of beta risk.

The key financing issues facing the firm are considered in chapters 10 through 13. One of the major strategic decisions faced by the financial manager is the use of leverage, and this issue is addressed in chapter 10. After introducing the concepts of operating and financial leverage in chapter 10, chapter 11 addresses the question of how much financial leverage a firm should use. Chapter 12 discusses dividend policy, emphasizing the share price maximization criterion. The capital structure and dividend policies of the firm depend in part on the firm's ability to acquire long-term funds in the capital markets. Sources of long-term financing are discussed in chapter 13.

Chapters 14 through 18 discuss working capital management, treating it as a problem in capital budgeting and emphasizing the wealth maximization orientation. Chapter 14 focuses on inventory and cash management, placing emphasis on the fact that holding cash is equivalent to an inventory of money. As a result, the general approach of inventory management can also be applied in managing cash. Not surprisingly, under certain assumptions, finding the optimal amounts of inventory and cash requires using essentially the same formula. Chapter 15 considers accounts receivable management. Chapter 16 considers the issue of financing working capital. It is customary to finance seasonal working capital with short-term financing sources. To manage these sources, the firm must anticipate both the amount needed and the times at which they will be required. Chapter 17 focuses on financial analysis of financial statements, which is useful in determining the current situation of the firm. To avert problems in the future, the use of financial planning techniques is essential, and these techniques are considered in chapter 18.

The last five chapters are devoted to special topics. Chapter 19 discusses the issue of market efficiency, a topic that has become increasingly important since the market crash of October 19, 1987, and the mini-crash of October 13, 1989. Chapter 20 discusses leasing, a special form of financing that is becoming important for many consumers. Chapter 21 considers some special financing vehicles known as options. Mergers and acquisitions are the topic of chapter 22, and chapter 23 considers the international dimension of corporate finance.

The Instructional Package

Financial Management, Second Edition, is accompanied by a complete instructional package. The *Instructor's Manual* contains answers to all the questions and detailed step-by-step solutions to all the problems found at the end of each chapter. The *Instructor's Manual* is also accompanied by a test bank with more than 1,000 multiple-choice questions. Many of these questions are problem-oriented.

STUDY!, a computerized and dynamic study guide, includes a bank of multiple-choice questions created specifically for *Financial Management*. The student begins the program by selecting any combination of chapters for study. The program loads all available questions for those chapters in a random order and begins to present them to the student. If the student answers correctly, the program updates the student's score on screen and moves to the next question. If the student's answer is wrong, the program gives the correct answer and updates the score. By using the *STUDY!* program, students can cover all of the essential conceptual issues in any set of chapters that they choose.

In addition to the *Instructor's Manual* and the *STUDY!* software package, the text is accompanied by a set of transparency masters to aid instructors in the classroom.

Acknowledgments

Writing this textbook was only one of many steps in the complex process of bringing *Financial Management* to life. Many colleagues have contributed greatly by reading and commenting on various sections of the book. We have benefited from the comments and criticisms provided by the following colleagues: Paul J. Bolster, Northeastern University; Simon Hakim, Temple University; Reza Rahgozar, University of Wisconsin–River Falls; K. G. Viswanathan, Hofstra University; and Brian A. Mans, Northern Arizona University. The following colleagues suggested revisions to an earlier version of this manuscript: Seth C. Anderson, University of Alabama at Birmingham; Laurey R. Berk, University of Wisconsin–Green Bay; Tom Berry, De Paul University; Joe B. Copeland, University of North Alabama; David T. Crary, Louisiana State University; David Distad, University of San Francisco; Charles Edwards, University of South Carolina; Crumpton Farrell, St. Cloud State University; Eurico J. Ferreira, Clemson University; Hung-Gay Fung, North Dakota State University; and David S. Rystrom, Western Washington University.

In addition, Robert Zimmer helped develop the *Finmaster* software, Debbie MacInnes developed much of the ancillary material, Ana Vazquez helped in the creation of many of the "Finance Today" and "International Perspectives" boxes, and Kumar Venkataramany was brave enough to tackle the laborious and delicate task of checking the accuracy of the mathematical aspects of the text. Kateri Davis, Valerie Rubler, and Diane Rubler provided valuable help in the various stages of the manuscript's production.

Before a text is written, it is difficult to imagine the numerous steps involved. The staff at Blackwell Publishers has been instrumental in this process. We would like to thank Rolf A. Janke for his help and encouragement in this project. Jan Leahy was very helpful in managing the production of the book. In addition, Andrea Coens gave the book a thorough editing and made our work much easier. Many other people at Blackwell contributed to the publication of this book – from the artists to the permissions staff. To all of them, our profound gratitude.

Robert W. Kolb

Ricardo J. Rodríguez

.

ntents

■ *Chapter 4*   **Bond Valuation**   54

■ *Chapter 5*   **Stock Valuation**   69

■ *Chapter 6*   **Capital Budgeting**   85

■ *Chapter* 7   **Special Problems in Capital Budgeting**   **106**

■ *Chapter* 8   **Risk and the Required Rate of Return**   **123**

Chapter 1

Financial Management and the Business Environment

OVERVIEW

This chapter introduces the academic discipline of finance and its role in business. Finance is closely related to other disciplines such as accounting and economics, and has three major divisions: corporate finance (the topic of this book), financial institutions, and investments.

The financial manager requires a clear view of the goals of the firm. Many goals are possible, but the firm should maximize the price of its stock, which is equivalent to maximizing shareholder wealth. Thus, the goal of financial management must be to assist in maximizing share price by making decisions that increase the firm's value.

The three major types of business organizations are sole proprietorships, partnerships, and corporations. Each has advantages and disadvantages. This book deals primarily with corporate financial management, but we must understand the major characteristics of the other types of organizations as well.

Every business firm in the United States, no matter what its organizational form, is subject to taxation. Business taxation differs depending on the firm's organization. This chapter also discusses the taxation of businesses, with an emphasis on corporate taxation.

The government also taxes individuals on their personal income. The income from a sole proprietorship is considered personal income. In a corporation, however, the government taxes corporate profits. If a corporation pays some of its after-tax profits as dividends, the dividends received are taxed again. Thus, dividends are subject to double taxation.

FINANCE AND THE FINANCIAL MANAGER

Compared to disciplines such as chemistry or mathematics, modern finance has a short history, originating in the 1950s. At that time, finance grew out of economics as a discipline focusing on a special set of problems arising from activities relating to financial markets.

Essentially, there are two kinds of markets: financial markets and markets for real goods. A **real good** is a physical or tangible product, such as gold or wheat. A **financial**

asset is a good that promises future benefits in the form of cash payments, such as a bond. A **financial market** is a market in which financial assets are traded. For example, a share of stock is a financial asset representing partial ownership of a firm, and it entitles the owner to receive periodic payments from the issuing firm. The stock market, in which shares of stocks are traded, is an example of a financial market.

Finance has close ties to other disciplines, principally economics and accounting. For instance, economics studies the general problem of allocating scarce resources, such as labor and capital, whereas finance is solely concerned with allocating scarce financial resources, making it a special field of economics. The decisions facing the financial manager require information that the firm's accounting system must supply. However, the information is not always in the appropriate form. Therefore, the financial manager must be able to interpret the reports supplied by the accountant.

AN OVERVIEW OF FINANCE AS A DISCIPLINE

The finance discipline has three distinct divisions. The first is the financial management of corporations, which addresses the central question of how to acquire and employ funds. A **corporation** is a business firm with many stockholders.[1] The second division of finance focuses on financial markets and institutions, and the third on investments.

In the typical corporation, the financial manager acquires funds in the financial market and invests them in a real good. For example, the financial manager of a construction company might borrow money (a transaction in a financial market) to buy a bulldozer (an investment in a real good). In financial institutions, however, the financial manager acquires funds in the financial market and invests those funds in financial assets. For example, a bank's financial manager might receive a deposit (borrowing in a financial market) and lend those newly acquired funds to a customer who wants to purchase a house (another transaction in a financial market).

In addition to the financial management of corporations and the study of financial institutions and markets, finance includes investments. This area deals with finding the best collection, or portfolio, of financial assets and focuses on allocating funds once they have been acquired. It addresses questions such as whether people should put all their money into one stock, or hold portfolios of stocks and bonds.

The three areas of finance are complementary. Financial managers must deal with financial institutions such as banks and may also wish to sell the firm's shares in the stock market. This means they must make the firm's stock attractive to investors. Thus, the study of one area of finance involves the study of the others. This book focuses on the financial management of corporations, but we will also deal with financial markets and institutions and with investments.

THE CREATION OF FINANCIAL VALUE

Broadly speaking, financial value is created through the influence of just a few variables. The most important of these are **cash flow**, **time**, and **risk**. If all other variables are held

---

[1] Later in the chapter we explain the different forms of business organization in detail.

constant, the higher the cash flow produced by a financial decision, the more value the decision will create. Similarly, value is greater when the cash flows are received sooner. Value also increases as the risk associated with the cash flows decreases.

In practice, these three principal variables leading to the creation of value are interrelated, so they should be considered simultaneously when assessing the value of a financial decision. It is a potentially grave mistake to emphasize one variable to the detriment of the others. For example, it is a common fallacy to argue that one investment is better than another because it is expected to produce a greater cash flow. Such a statement is meaningless if one does not consider both the timing and the riskiness of the expected cash flows.

THE GOAL OF THE FIRM

In light of the discussion thus far, it should be clear that the general objective of the firm is to maximize its value. This is accomplished by making decisions in which the benefits exceed the costs. Although this is intuitive and clear, the actual means of maximizing firm value are less obvious. Nevertheless, we have already noted that any strategy leading to the creation of value for the firm must simultaneously take into account the three main variables involved: cash flow, time, and risk. We should keep this in mind when evaluating the desirability of various potential goals for the corporation.

Let us consider three possible goals for corporations: maximizing size, maximizing accounting profits, and maximizing the stock price.[2]

Maximizing Size

Some firms may not be able to operate efficiently if they are small. For example, a small firm may be unable to buy raw materials in large enough quantities to get the cheapest price. It is also true that if some firms are too large they can suffer from inefficiencies, as happens when managers cannot obtain information in time to act effectively. Furthermore, firms that grow too quickly may suffer "growing pains," and may eventually fail. That is, rapid growth may lead to excessive risk.

The goal of maximizing firm size is at least intuitively consistent with maximizing the firm's cash flow, one of the components in the creation of value. As the discussion makes clear, however, maximizing for size disregards both the time and the risk components. Thus, maximizing firm size cannot by itself be the main goal for corporations.

Maximizing Accounting Profits

By accounting profits we mean the earnings reported in the income statement of the firm following a set of accounting rules. However, accounting profits are not always the most

---

[2] Others could be proposed, such as social or environmental goals. While these are certainly desirable goals, they may be included as part of other more general goals. For example, a firm that donates to charity is presumably acquiring some goodwill, which it hopes will eventually translate into more sales and more profits, and a higher stock price.

economically meaningful measure of firm performance and value. In particular, they are not the same as cash flow, which is one of the essential components in the creation of financial value. In fact, a firm reporting accounting losses may have a positive cash flow if it has a sufficiently high depreciation expense, since this expense reduces profits even though it involves no direct cash outflow.[3]

In contrast to accounting profits, which depend on the application of a set of rules, cash flow refers to the actual receipt or payment of cash. The financial manager cares more about cash flow than profits, because cash is necessary to pay dividends to stockholders, wages to employees, and suppliers for raw materials. Since profits usually differ from cash flow, maximizing accounting profits does not take into account one of the essential variables involved in creating financial value.

The goal of maximizing accounting profits also does not consider the time dimension of value creation. For example, which period's accounting profits should we maximize? Maximizing short-run accounting profits can often be accomplished by hurting the firm's future prosperity. For instance, pharmaceutical firms typically spend heavily in research and development of new drugs and could easily increase this year's accounting profits by significantly reducing their current R&D expenses. Since R&D expenses usually help increase future, not current, sales, the firms would appear to benefit now only to suffer later, perhaps irrevocably. Smart investors will not be fooled by such tricks.

Furthermore, maximizing accounting profits is an unsuitable goal because it does not consider risk, the third component in the creation of value. In every period, the manager faces different projects with different risk levels. In most circumstances, the projects with the highest expected accounting profits possess the greatest risk. (As we will see in a later chapter, high profits and high risk tend to go together.) If we simply try to maximize expected accounting profits, we will ordinarily choose the riskiest projects. However, we have seen that high risk leads to a lower firm value. Therefore, failing to consider risk is a serious flaw in the strategy of maximizing accounting profits.

Maximizing the Stock Price

The third possible goal of the firm takes into account all of the essential variables involved in value creation. Thus, we argue that the corporation should be managed to maximize the price of its stock, which is equivalent to maximizing shareholders' wealth.

As discussed previously, investors focus mostly on the cash flows generated by a firm. If they perceive that the firm will generate substantial cash flow in the future, they will demand the stock in greater quantities, thus increasing its price. Furthermore, if the cash flow is to be received sooner rather than later, the stock price will also increase, because a dollar today has a greater value than the same dollar tomorrow. Thus, the goal of stock price maximization takes into account the time component of value creation. Finally, it takes account of risk. If investors think that the firm's strategy is too risky for the expected rewards, investors will sell their shares and the price of the stock will fall.

---

[3] Nevertheless, depreciation may affect cash by reducing taxes, as discussed later in the book.

In the remainder of this book we take maximizing shareholder wealth, which is equivalent to maximizing stock price, as the proper goal of the firm because it incorporates all of the components of financial value creation: cash flow, time, and risk.

THE FINANCE FUNCTION IN THE FIRM

The financial manager's job is to contribute to the firm's overall objective of maximizing the wealth of the shareholders. The head of the finance function is usually a vice president for finance, or the chief financial officer, who normally reports directly to the president, or the chief executive officer. Normally, the vice president for finance draws support mainly from the treasurer and the controller. Figure 1.1 shows how the main areas of finance are divided between the treasurer and the controller. The controller bears prime responsibility for those areas usually associated with accounting, such as preparing the firm's financial statements and budgets, paying and planning taxes, and managing the payroll operation. The treasurer manages the acquisition of funds in the capital markets by selling stock or by borrowing and ensures that those funds are employed effectively. Both activities require a great deal of financial analysis and planning. The basic task of the finance function is to acquire and employ funds. By making wise decisions in these areas, the financial manager adds to the wealth of the firm's shareholders.

The firm raises funds by selling ownership interest to stockholders or by borrowing money. However, raising money is costly since the suppliers of funds must be compensated.

FIGURE 1.1
The Organization of the Finance Function Within a Corporation

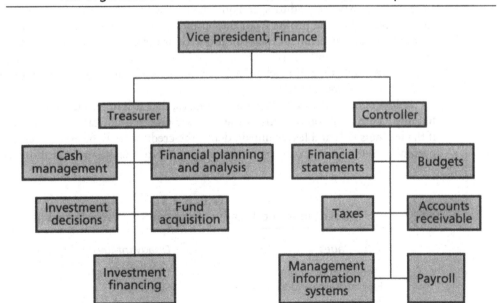

The funds raised in this way become the pool of investable funds, which are committed to the attractive investment projects through which the firm expects to increase its value.

If the investment projects are successful, they generate more funds, and these can be used in only two ways. First, the firm must return a portion of them to those who contributed the original investable funds as payment for committing their resources to the company. Second, the firm retains the remaining funds to increase the amount of investable funds available for future projects. The chief goal of this book is to explain how to evaluate financial decisions involving the acquisition and employment of funds.

FORMS OF BUSINESS ORGANIZATIONS

The three major forms of business organizations are **sole proprietorship**, **partnership**, and **corporation**. Each has advantages and disadvantages.

Sole Proprietorship

A sole proprietorship is a business owned by a single individual, for example, a gardening service firm. Only the wealth of the owner limits the size of a sole proprietorship, but most tend to be small. Sole proprietorships make up the vast majority of the businesses in existence in the United States. Because of their small size, however, they account for only a small fraction of sales by U.S. businesses.

A sole proprietorship has several special advantages and disadvantages, as summarized in table 1.1. One advantage is that the control of the business rests in the hands of a single individual. This makes it easy to set a course for the firm and to avoid disagreements. In addition, a sole proprietorship is easy to create and to dissolve: the owner may simply close the firm, pay the creditors, and quit the firm with all remaining proceeds. The owner also receives all of the profits from the business, which leads to the final advantage. For tax purposes the government treats all proceeds as the personal income of the owner, thus taxing these profits only once at the personal level. By contrast, corporations pay taxes at the level of the firm, and stockholders pay taxes on dividends from corporations as part of their personal income tax.

Sole proprietorships also have disadvantages, the most important of which is **unlimited liability**. That is, all obligations of the firm are personal obligations of the owner. Thus, if the business fails and leaves unpaid debts, the creditors may be able to seize the owner's personal assets. This seizure can occur even if the owner never used those assets in the

TABLE 1.1
Advantages and Disadvantages of Sole Proprietorships

Advantages	Disadvantages
Ownership of all profits	Unlimited liability
Easy to create and to dissolve	Small size
Tax savings	Difficulty of acquiring new funds

business. Other disadvantages of a sole proprietorship are its small size and the difficulty it faces in growing. For example, the sole proprietor of a single restaurant might wish to establish a second restaurant, but that might take too much money. The only source of additional funds is probably loans, and many lenders are unwilling to lend much to a single individual, even if that person owns a successful business.

Partnership

A partnership is an organization of two or more persons engaging in some line of business. Although it is a common form of business organization for a small business, such as a garage, some very large businesses are partnerships. For example, some accounting and investment banking firms often have more than 100 partners.

In a partnership, every partner is either a **general partner** or a **limited partner**. A **limited partnership** has at least one limited partner. In contrast to a general partner, who bears unlimited liability for the performance of the firm, a limited partner has limited liability and usually takes no active role in the management of the partnership. Every partnership must have at least one general partner, so there is always some individual who has unlimited liability for its performance.

The partnership has several advantages and disadvantages, summarized in table 1.2. It can bring the committed talents and wealth of more than one individual to the business. Partners often have complementary skills that enable them to work better together than they could work alone. The likelihood of a committed effort from partners is greater than it would be from someone who was an employee. In addition, banks and other potential creditors may be more willing to lend money to the partnership than to a sole proprietor. Finally, partnerships may expand by offering partner status to other individuals, generally to valuable employees. This provides partnerships with a way to grow and is an excellent way to motivate employees.

One disadvantage is that when a partner dies, the partnership is legally dissolved. This can be especially troublesome when the organization consists of only two people. It is also often difficult to withdraw funds from the partnership. Finally, antagonistic disputes over the contribution of the various partners often arise, giving credence to the television image of once-friendly partners at each others' throats.

TABLE 1.2
Advantages and Disadvantages of Partnerships

Advantages	*Disadvantages*
Easy to attract talent and wealth	The firm dissolves with the death
Incentive of future ownership to	of a partner
outstanding employees	Hard to withdraw wealth
Easy to grow and expand	Opportunity for dispute and ill will
Chance for better credit standing	among partners

The Corporation

A corporation is a business that is owned by stockholders and has a legal status similar to that of a person: it can make contracts, own property, sue, and be sued. As such, it is a legal entity created by a state willing to issue a corporate charter. Most important, a corporation has a legal existence that is separate from its owners, which has important implications for the liability of the owners. Although only a small percentage of businesses in the United States are corporations, they make the vast majority of all sales. There is no limit to the size of a corporation. Table 1.3 presents the largest corporations in the United States in terms of annual sales.

Ultimate control of a corporation rests with the stockholders. They elect a **board of directors** that is responsible for operating the firm. An **inside director** is a member of the board of directors who is also a top manager of the company, usually the president. An **outside director** is a member of the board who is not employed by the corporation's management but is paid a fee for services rendered. Usually, leading citizens are chosen as outside directors.

The board of directors appoints the officers of the firm, including the president, and is responsible for the overall conduct of the corporation. Because directors have sometimes been sued for the actions of the firm, corporations must often provide them with insurance against suits from dissatisfied stockholders.

The corporate form of business organization offers important benefits, chief among which is the **limited liability** of its owners. Stockholders may lose the full value of their stock, but they cannot lose more, a fact which becomes extremely important in case of

TABLE 1.3
The Largest U.S. Industrial Corporations

Rank	Name	Sales ($ billions)	Profits ($ billions)
1	General Motors	155.0	5.9
2	Ford Motor	128.4	5.3
3	Exxon	101.1	5.1
4	Wal-Mart Stores	82.5	2.7
5	AT&T	75.1	4.7
6	Mobil	67.1	1.8
7	IBM	64.1	3.0
8	General Electric	60.1	5.9
9	Sears, Roebuck	53.9	1.3
10	Philip Morris	53.8	4.7
11	Chrysler	52.2	3.7
12	Du Pont	39.3	2.7
13	Chevron	35.8	1.6
14	KMart	34.0	0.3
15	Texaco	33.4	1.0

Source: Business Week, March 27, 1995.

bankruptcy. A second advantage arises from a corporation's status as a separate legal entity with an indefinite life. It may operate through many generations of investors without suffering the problems associated with the death of a partner or sole proprietor.

Another major benefit is the ease with which one can enter and withdraw investment from the firm. For large firms, corporate shares can be traded in the stock market. Any current stockholder may sell shares and a new investor can become an owner by buying shares. Since transferring ownership is simple, corporations find it relatively easy to attract capital. Investors may confidently buy the firm's shares, since the commitment is not permanent. When they wish to sell their investment, they can easily do so in the stock market. Because ownership is through shares of stock, the publicly owned corporation may expand with relative ease. It raises new funds by issuing new shares of stock, which brings in new investment funds.

It is not surprising that some disadvantages exist in corporations. First, each corporation must have a charter granted by a state government. Thus, creating a corporation is almost certain to be more expensive and difficult than creating a sole proprietorship or a partnership. For very small businesses, these expenses can be large enough to make incorporation impractical.

Corporations also face considerable government regulation. Those with widely held or publicly traded securities are subject to rigorous reporting standards. They must make public annual reports of their business activities each year, and these can be quite voluminous. Also, the requirement of public reporting makes privacy difficult. Privacy of investment activities and plans can be very important for some firms, particularly those involved in research and development of new products. Compared with sole proprietorships and partnerships, in which the managers tend to be owners, corporations often have difficulty motivating their employees. When workers are compensated only through wages, their commitment to the success of the firm can wane.

Another big disadvantage to the corporate form of organization stems from its tax treatment. Investors in corporations face **double taxation**. This refers to the fact that the government taxes corporate earnings at the corporate level, and also at the individual level by taxing the dividends paid to stockholders. Relative to a sole proprietorship or a partnership, this can be a serious tax disadvantage. Table 1.4 shows the effect that double

TABLE 1.4
The Effect of Double Taxation of Corporate Profits

	Sole Proprietorship or Partnership	Corporation
Profits before business taxes	$100.00	$100.00
Corporate tax at 30%	N/A	−30.00
Profits after business taxes	100.00	70.00
Personal income tax at 28%	−28.00	−19.60
After-tax receipts by owners	72.00	50.40

Note: The calculations assume that all after-tax profits are paid to the owners. The corporate tax rate is 30 percent and the individual tax rate is 28 percent.

taxation can have on the after-tax profits paid to the owners of the firm. Consider before-tax profits of $100 earned by either a sole proprietorship or a partnership and the same profit made by a corporation. If the corporate income tax rate is 30 percent, this leaves only $70 of the original $100 to pay to the shareholders, compared with the full $100 that a sole proprietorship or partnership can pay to its owners.

If all after-tax profits are distributed to the owners, the individual owners of the firms must then pay their personal income tax, assumed to be 28 percent. On an after-tax basis, the sole proprietorship or the partnership delivers $72 of the $100 original profit to its owners. In comparison, the corporation delivers only $50.40 to its owners. Consequently, double taxation can be a serious problem for the corporate form of ownership.

Since double taxation may be particularly troublesome for small corporations, there is a provision open only to small corporations that escapes double taxation. A **subchapter S corporation** is a corporation with no more than 35 stockholders that chooses to be treated as a partnership for tax purposes. It enjoys the limited liability feature of a regular corporation and the government taxes earnings from the corporation only as personal income. Table 1.5 summarizes the advantages and disadvantages of the corporate form of organization.

BUSINESS TAXATION

For the financial manager, tax consequences have a strong effect on many operating decisions. Some tax rules affect all forms of business organizations, while others affect corporations particularly. The following discussion focuses on the major aspects of business taxation, while retaining as much generality as possible. Nevertheless, keep in mind that tax laws change constantly, and that some of these provisions may not be applicable in the future.

Adjustments to Income

Not all proceeds from a business are subject to taxation, so we have to understand several important adjustments to business income that have a significant effect on tax payments. The most important of these is depreciation.

TABLE 1.5
Advantages and Disadvantages of Corporations

Advantages	Disadvantages
Limited liability	More expensive form of organization
Potentially long life	Increased regulatory burden
Easy transferability of ownership	Lack of secrecy
Ease of attracting new capital	Double taxation
Ability to grow	

Depreciation   Depreciation is a reduction in taxable income that reflects the decrease in value of an item used to produce income. Consider a company that buys a new ship for use in its passenger cruise business. The firm invests funds and expects that investment to generate income over the next ten years. Each year the ship sails, it faces normal wear and tear. Therefore, the ship's value falls. After ten years, the firm expects the ship will no longer be suitable as a passenger liner, and it will sell the ship for its salvage value. The **salvage value** of an asset is the amount for which the firm can sell an asset at the end of its useful life.

The tax laws assume that the value of assets, such as the ship, decreases over time. To reflect this decrease, accounting rules allow the firm to reduce the value of each asset by a certain amount each year. This reduction can be subtracted from the firm's income as a depreciation expense for that year. The ability to treat the normal deterioration of an asset as an expense has major tax consequences for firms.

There are two basic ways to calculate the depreciation expense: the straight-line depreciation method and the Modified Accelerated Cost Recovery System (MACRS). The straight-line depreciation method begins by calculating the **depreciable** value of the asset, which equals the cost minus the expected salvage value. The depreciation expense is the depreciable value divided by the number of years in the depreciation period. If the initial cost of the ship in the example is $10 million and if it is expected to have a salvage value of $1 million after its ten years of service, then the ship's depreciable value is $9 million. With a ten-year life, the straight-line depreciation expense would be $900,000 for each year.

In general, if an asset has an initial cost of $$I$, a salvage value of $$SV$, and will be depreciated over a period of n years, the yearly depreciation, D, using the straight-line depreciation method is given by the following formula:

$$D = \frac{I - SV}{n} \tag{1.1}$$

Applying equation 1.1 to the ship example, we obtain the same yearly depreciation as before:

$$D = \frac{\$10,000,000 - \$1,000,000}{10}$$

$$= \$900,000$$

The modified accelerated cost recovery system classifies each kind of equipment by its useful life. It does not consider salvage value. The federal government stipulates the percentage of the value to take as depreciation each year. Current law assumes that firms place assets in service at mid-year, regardless of the actual date this occurs.

Computing depreciation expenses for an asset requires knowledge of the depreciable life of the asset, the depreciable value of the asset, and the appropriate MACRS percentage for each year of its life. It is customary to assume that the asset is acquired in period 0. We will assume that the first depreciation expense is at period one. The rules allow the owner to switch to straight-line depreciation at any time. The depreciable life of assets other than buildings can be three, five, seven, ten, fifteen, or twenty years. Table 1.6 gives the depreciation percentages for each class of property that we will consider and reflects a switching to straight-line at the time that makes the depreciation as fast as possible.

TABLE 1.6
Depreciation Rates Under MACRS

| | Recovery Period | | |
Year	3-Year	5-Year	7-Year
1	33.33	20.00	14.29
2	44.45	32.00	24.49
3	14.81	19.20	17.49
4	7.41	11.52	12.49
5		11.52	8.93
6		5.76	8.93
7			8.93
8			4.46

Note: This table is for illustration purposes. Other categories also exist.

EXAMPLE 1

A contractor buys a pick-up truck for $17,000. If this asset is classified as five-year property, what are the depreciation expenses generated by the truck for each year?

We calculate the depreciation as follows:

Year	MACRS Percentage	Depreciation Expense	Accumulated Depreciation
1	20.00	3,400.00	3,400.00
2	32.00	5,440.00	8,840.00
3	19.20	3,264.00	12,104.00
4	11.52	1,958.40	14,062.40
5	11.52	1,958.40	16,020.80
6	5.76	979.20	17,000.00

Loss Carry-Forward and Carry-Back   Another important adjustment to taxable income comes from loss carry-forwards and carry-backs. A firm with negative earnings in one year can carry that loss forward up to fifteen years later, and use the previous loss to reduce future taxable earnings. This is a **tax loss carry-forward**. The firm can also apply a loss in one year to positive earnings in previous years, for up to three years in the past. By getting credit for the reduction in earnings due to this **tax loss carry-back**, the firm reduces the taxes due for those previous years.

Dividends Received from Other Corporations   We have already noted that before the earnings from a corporation reach the pocket of the shareholder, the corporation pays taxes on them at the corporate level and the shareholder pays at the personal level. This is double taxation. A partial exception to this policy applies to dividends received by a corporation that owns the stock of another corporation, in which case 80 percent of the dividends received are free of corporate taxation. The government taxes the remaining 20 percent as ordinary corporate income.

EXAMPLE 2 _____

HAL, Inc., owns stock in IBM. If the corporate tax rate on profits from operations is 34 percent, what is the effective tax rate HAL pays on each $100 in dividends received from IBM?

Since 80 percent of the dividends are exempt from corporate taxes, HAL pays taxes only on the remaining $20. Thus, HAL must pay $20 × 0.34 = $6.80 in taxes on the original $100 it received. This means that the effective tax rate on dividends received by HAL is $6.80/$100 = 0.068, or 6.8 percent.

Business Taxes

Except for the dividend exclusion just discussed, which applies only to corporations, the adjustments to income and tax credits considered thus far apply equally to sole proprietorships, partnerships, and corporations. For proprietorships and partnerships, the business income is subject only to personal taxation (personal taxes are discussed later in this chapter). Corporations, however, must pay federal income taxes.

After all adjustments to income, the corporation's taxable income is obtained. Taxable income is subject to federal income tax at rates which generally increase with the amount of income. Nevertheless, in recent years the tax schedule has allowed for a tax rate reduction for the highest taxable income bracket. Table 1.7 illustrates such a corporate tax rate schedule. If the tax rates increase as income gets larger, the federal tax structure is said to use progressive tax rates. A **progressive tax rate** is a rate that increases as income increases. A **marginal tax rate** is the tax rate that applies to the next dollar of income. Thus, from table 1.7, if a corporation has profits of $25,000, its marginal tax rate is 15 percent. If the firm's profits are $50,000, however, its marginal tax rate becomes 25 percent, since the next dollar of profits would belong in the 25 percent tax bracket. For example, a corporation with $120,000 of taxable income would have a tax bill computed as seen in table 1.8.

TABLE 1.7
A Federal Tax Rate Schedule for Corporations

Taxable Income		Tax Rate (%)	Starting Tax ($)
From ($)	To ($)		
0	50,000	15	0.00
50,000	100,000	25	7,500.00
100,000	200,000	34	20,000.00
200,000	480,000	39	54,000.00
480,000		34	163,200.00

TABLE 1.8
Calculation of a Corporation's Tax Burden

| Taxable Income | | | | | |
From ($)	To ($)		Tax Rate (%)		Tax*
0	50,000	×	0.15	=	7,500
50,000	100,000	×	0.25	=	12,500
100,000	120,000	×	0.34	=	6,800
	Total Tax			=	26,800

*These values are calculated by taking the difference of the values in the To and From columns and multiplying by the appropriate tax rate. For example, (100,000 − 50,000) × 0.25 = $12,500.

In addition, we can compute average tax rates. The **average tax rate** equals the total amount of tax the firm must pay divided by the firm's taxable income. The average tax rate for this firm is 22.33 percent ($26,800/$120,000). Its marginal tax rate, however, is 34 percent, because, according to table 1.7, it must pay 34 percent on the next dollar of income it earns.

In general, the average tax rate is given by the following expression:

$$\text{Average Tax Rate} = \frac{\text{Total Tax}}{\text{Taxable Income}} \tag{1.2}$$

Figure 1.2 shows how the marginal and average tax rates change with taxable income, for the tax rate schedule presented in table 1.7.

Personal Income Tax and Its Effect on Corporations

Because investors are sensitive to taxes, corporations must know how their activities affect the after-tax income of investors. Investing in securities generates taxable income from two major sources: cash flows from owning the securities (dividends and interest payments) and changes in the value of the securities (capital gains or losses). This section briefly considers some of the more important ways that securities investing affects personal taxes.

The Taxation of Interest   Interest received by individuals or corporations is taxable income. This applies to interest on long-term bonds, money market accounts, and bank accounts. An important exception is the interest received on tax-exempt municipal debt. **Municipal debt** is debt issued by a town, state, or some other local government that is normally free of federal income taxation. Except for interest from municipal bonds, both individuals and corporations simply add any interest income to other taxable income to compute taxes.

Capital Gains and Losses   Changes in the value of a security give rise to tax obligations and benefits. An increase in the price of a security is a capital gain, while a decrease in its price is a capital loss. Capital gains and losses may be either realized or unrealized. In

FIGURE 1.2

Marginal and Average Tax Rates at Various Levels of Taxable Income

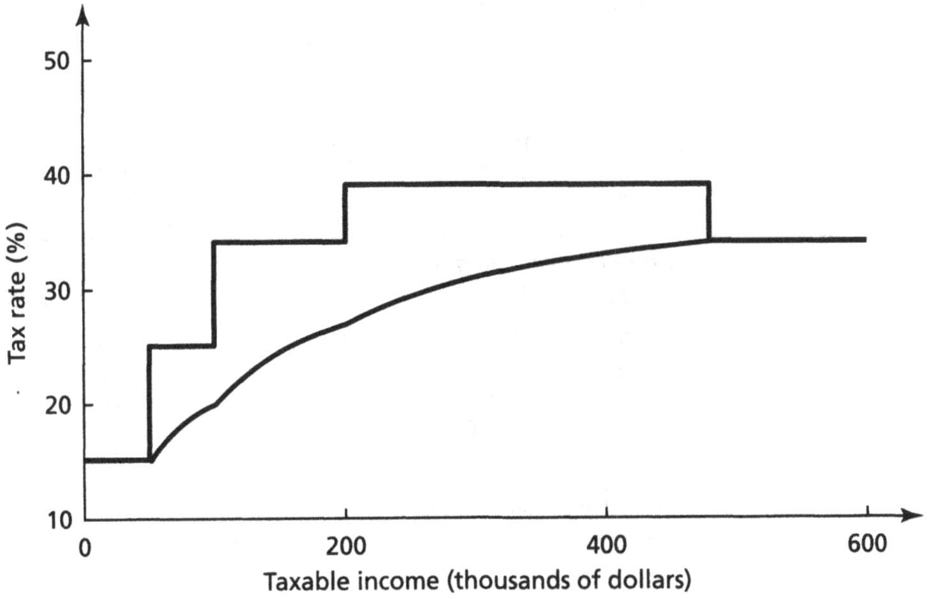

most cases, realizing a capital gain or loss occurs when an investor sells a security. With some exceptions, only realized capital gains and losses give rise to tax consequences. Capital gains are added to taxable income while capital losses are subtracted from taxable income. In essence, capital gains or losses are treated as additions to, or subtractions from, income. Since the 1940s, the capital gains tax rate has fluctuated between a low of 20 percent (1981) and a high of 35 percent (1972). The Revenue Reconciliation Act of 1993 left the maximum capital gains tax rate at 28 percent.

INDIVIDUAL TAX RATES

Taxable personal income consists of all income, including wages and investment income, adjusted for various factors. For instance, interest paid on a home mortgage and certain allowances for dependents are subtracted from income in the computation of taxable income. The final result is known as **adjusted gross income**, or AGI.

Once the adjusted gross income is determined, we can compute the tax using table 1.9, which contains tax rates for single individuals and married couples filing jointly. Suppose a couple is filing jointly and has a taxable income of $60,000. Using the table, the tax would be $5,700.00 plus 28 percent of all income between $38,000 and $60,000. The tax computation is given below.

TABLE 1.9
A Personal Federal Income Tax Schedule

Unmarried Taxpayers

From ($)	To ($)	Tax Rate (%)	Minimum Tax ($)
0	22,750	15	0.00
22,750	55,100	28	3,412.50
55,100	115,000	31	12,470.50
115,000	250,000	36	31,039.50
250,000	—	39.6	79,639.50

Married Couples Filing Jointly

From ($)	To ($)	Tax Rate (%)	Minimum Tax ($)
0	38,000	15	0.00
38,000	91,850	28	5,700.00
91,850	140,000	31	20,778.00
140,000	250,000	36	35,704.50
250,000	—	39.6	75,304.50

Note: This table is for illustration purposes only.

$$\text{Tax} = \$5,700 + 0.28(\$60,000 - \$38,000)$$
$$= \$5,700 + \$6,160$$
$$= \$11,860$$

For this couple, the tax paid on the next dollar of income – the marginal tax rate – equals 28 percent. However, the couple's average tax rate is lower at 19.77 percent ($11,860/ $60,000).

SUMMARY

This first chapter began by considering the nature of the finance discipline and its relationship to other disciplines. We considered several goals that the firm might adopt and concluded that the appropriate one is to maximize shareholder wealth. The financial manager's role is to contribute to this goal. Essentially, this is done by making wise decisions regarding the acquisition and employment of funds.

We also explored the basic forms of business organizations and the tax environment faced by firms operating in the United States. The three basic kinds of business organizations are sole proprietorships, partnerships, and corporations. A sole proprietorship is a business owned by a single individual who controls all aspects of the firm and receives all the profits. A partnership is a business organization owned by two or more individuals. Partners may be either limited partners or general partners. Corporations are entities owned by a group of stockholders. Corporations, like persons, can enter contracts. One of their most important features is the limited liability of their stockholders, who cannot lose more than the amount they invest.

Corporate income tax follows on a generally progressive schedule, which means that the greater the corporation's income, the greater its tax rate. There are various adjustments to corporate taxable income, however, such as the depreciation expense and loss carry-forward and carry-back. These adjustments help reduce the corporation's taxable income.

At the personal income level, investors pay tax on interest and dividends received. The tax law treats these amounts as ordinary income. In addition, investors may have capital gains or losses if the selling price of their investments is higher or lower, respectively, than the purchase price.

QUESTIONS

1. What is the goal of financial management?
2. What is the difference between a real and a financial asset?
3. What are the three traditional divisions of finance?
4. Comment on the following statement by a financial manager: "The stockholders in my firm look at the income statement I generate. Naturally, they want to see large earnings. Because my job is pleasing the stockholders, I give them what they want – I strive to maximize net income."
5. Explain the differences, if any, between maximizing shareholder wealth and maximizing the price of the stock.
6. Comment on the following claim: "Attempting to maximize stock price is a very nice goal, except it neglects risk. The true goal of financial management should be to maximize stock price, subject to a given level of risk."
7. Why is the acquisition and employment of funds the main decision made by the financial manager? To what does this decision owe its special importance?
8. How does a limited partner differ from a general partner?
9. What is the difference between limited and unlimited liability?
10. What kinds of investors have limited liability?
11. What kinds of investors have unlimited liability?
12. What is an inside director?
13. Explain the concept of double taxation.
14. What kinds of business firms are subject to double taxation?
15. What is a Subchapter S corporation? What tax advantages does it have over a regular corporation?
16. How does depreciation generate cash flow?
17. What two methods are permitted for depreciation?
18. How is interest taxed?
19. How does the taxation of dividends differ between corporations and individuals?
20. What is a capital gain?

PROBLEMS

1. A corporation has $100 in before-tax income that it plans to use to pay dividends. Assume that the corporation is in the 34 percent tax bracket and the investor

receiving the dividend is in the 28 percent tax bracket. How much after-tax income does the investor receive?

2. An investor receiving dividends from Debussy, Inc., retains $4 per share after paying personal taxes. The investor is in the 28 percent tax bracket. If the corporate tax rate is 34 percent, and Debussy pays out all of its profits as dividends, how much pre-tax profit did Debussy make per share?

3. A three-year property item costs $1,500. What is the depreciation schedule for this property under both the straight-line and MACRS methods?

4. A seven-year property item costs $150,000. Under MACRS, what is the depreciation expense allowed for this item in year three?

5. A firm in the 34 percent tax bracket has a depreciation expense of $150. What effect does this have on the firm's tax bill? What cash flow, if any, does this depreciation expense generate?

6. A firm in the 34 percent tax bracket just purchased a seven-year piece of equipment for $250,000. What is the effect of depreciation on the firm's tax bill in year six under both straight-line and MACRS depreciation?

7. Compute the tax bill for a corporation with $350,000 taxable income.

8. Compute the average corporate tax rate corresponding to the upper limit income of each corporate tax bracket, and compare it to the corresponding marginal tax rate.

9. Using the straight-line method, find the annual depreciation of a piece of equipment with a five-year useful life, an initial cost of $8,000, and an expected salvage value of $1,500.

10. An asset has a salvage value equal to its annual depreciation. If the asset's cost is $2,000 and it has an eight-year life, find the annual depreciation using the straight-line method.

11. An industrial compressor has a current book value of $2,000. Four years from now its book value will be $800. If the compressor initially costs $4,100, how many years has it been in use? Assume straight-line depreciation.

12. Consider a hypothetical individual tax schedule in which the amount of tax paid is proportional to the square of the taxable income. Show that the average tax rate is proportional to taxable income.

Chapter 2

The Time Value of Money: Single Payments

OVERVIEW

This chapter introduces the most important concept in finance – the time value of money. The **time value of money** refers to the principle that $1 received today has a greater value than $1 received in the future. This simple idea is the driving force for many financial decisions.

In this chapter we analyze the time value of single payments. For example, we want to understand how $1,000 deposited in a bank account grows to a greater sum in the future. In the next chapter we will study the time value of a series of payments. The ideas developed there will depend heavily on a thorough understanding of the concepts discussed in this chapter.

SIMPLE INTEREST

Suppose a customer walks into a bank and deposits $1,000 in a savings account that earns an interest rate of 6 percent per year. How much will this depositor have in two years if the account earns simple interest? We compute **simple interest** by assuming that interest does not itself earn interest. Equivalently, to compute the amount of interest earned during any period, we must always use the same base amount, or principal. The original deposit of $1,000 is the **principal**. The depositor receives this principal again at the end of the investment period, plus all interest earned. For this deposit, the value of the account after two years will be equal to the sum of the principal and the interest earned over the two years. The interest earned in the first year is $1,000 × 0.06 = $60. Similarly, in the second year the account earns another $60, since with simple interest the principal never changes. Consequently, the value of the account at the end of two years is $1,000 + $60 + $60 = $1,120.

In general, if P is the principal, r is the rate of interest, and n is the amount of time the principal earns interest, then the total dollar amount of interest (i) is calculated with the following formula:

$$i = P \times r \times n \qquad (2.1)$$

The total amount the depositor has at the end of n years equals the original deposit (P) plus the interest earned (i). Since the total interest earned can be found by using equation 2.1, the value of the account after n years of earning simple interest is:

$$\text{Value after } n \text{ years} = P + i$$
$$= P + P \times r \times n \tag{2.2}$$
$$= P(1 + r \times n)$$

In the example, the bank account earns simple interest for two years. After this two-year period the value of the bank account equals the principal plus the simple interest. This gives a total of $1,000 (1 + 0.06 \times 2) = $1,120$, the same result we had obtained.

COMPOUND INTEREST

In most cases, we calculate interest as **compound interest**, not simple interest. In computing compound interest, the principal and interest received earn interest in later periods. Equivalently, the accumulated amount at the beginning of a period becomes the principal used to compute the interest earned over the next period.

In the bank deposit example, suppose the account pays interest in the second year on both the principal and the first year's interest. Since we know that the account earns $60 interest during the first year, the value of the account at the end of the first year is $1,060. This $1,060 becomes the new principal for the second year, which will earn 6 percent interest over that year. Thus, the value of the account after two years is:

$$\text{Value after 2 years} = \text{Value after 1 year} + \text{Interest in year 2}$$
$$= \$1,060 + \$1,060 \times 0.06$$
$$= \$1,060(1.06)$$
$$= \$1,000(1.06)(1.06)$$
$$= \$1,000(1.06)^2$$
$$= \$1,123.60$$

Consider a deposit of P dollars. If this deposit is held for n years and earns r percent per year, it will be worth:

$$\text{Value after } n \text{ years} = P(1 + r)^n \tag{2.3}$$

Comparing the two ways of computing interest, we see that the value of the account after two years of simple interest is $1,120.00. With annual compounding, the value of the account after two years is $1,123.60. The difference of $3.60 between the two methods is due to the 6 percent interest earned in the second year on the first year's $60 interest when using compound interest: $3.60 = 60×0.06. This highlights the difference between simple interest and compound interest. In simple interest, interest earned previously does not itself earn interest. With compound interest, interest earned in previous periods becomes part of the principal that earns interest in later periods.

EXAMPLE 1

An investor deposits $500 in a bank account. What will be the value of the account after three years if it earns 9 percent simple interest?

$$\text{Value after 3 years} = P(1 + r \times n)$$
$$= \$500(1 + 0.09 \times 3)$$
$$= \$635$$

What will be the value of the account after three years if it earns 9 percent interest, compounded annually?

$$\text{Value after 3 years} = P(1 + r)^3$$
$$= \$500(1.09)^3$$
$$= \$647.51$$

PRESENT VALUE AND FUTURE VALUE

The **present value** of a future payment is the value of that payment if it were made immediately. The **future value** of a payment made today is the value of that payment if it were made at some point in the future.

The present value of the bank account is $1,000. If the owner deposits the funds at 6 percent for two years, compounded annually, we have seen that the account will be worth $1,123.60 after two years. This is the future value of the $1,000 deposit in two years and with an interest rate of 6 percent.

The interest rate and the amount of time between the present and the future payment tie the present values and future values together mathematically. Let the present value be denoted by PV, and the future value by FV. Then, the general relationship between future values and present values is:

$$FV = PV(1 + r)^n \tag{2.4}$$

EXAMPLE 2

A bank customer deposits $150 in an account for five years with an interest rate of 12 percent. What is the future value of this $150 at the end of the five years?

Using the basic relationship in equation 2.4, we have:

$$FV = PV(1 + r)^n = \$150(1.12)^5 = \$264.35$$

Equation 2.4 is the basic relationship of the time value of money. We will use this equation throughout this book to compute a multitude of extremely important relationships. It is truly a fundamental equation in finance.

EXAMPLE 3

Evelyn goes to a loan shark and borrows $1,000 for five years at an interest rate of 80 percent per year with annual compounding. What is the future value of the loan after five years?

$$FV = PV(1 + r)^n = \$1,000(1.80)^5 = \$18,895.68$$

Obviously, Evelyn has a problem waiting for her in five years, particularly if she does not understand how compound interest works or how a loan shark works.

Evelyn is a tough negotiator, however. What will Evelyn owe if she convinces the loan shark to forget the annual compounding and to lend her the $1,000 for five years at 80 percent simple interest?

$$\text{Total debt after 5 years} = P(1 + r \times n)$$
$$= \$1,000(1 + 0.80 \times 5)$$
$$= \$5,000$$

In this case, Evelyn will owe only $5,000 in five years. All of the difference between the $18,895.68 and the $5,000 debt is due to the interest earned on interest with annual compounding.

FUTURE VALUE AND THE FREQUENCY OF COMPOUNDING

The more frequently interest is compounded, the faster a present value grows. To illustrate this principle, let us compute the future value after one year for an initial investment of $1,000 at 12 percent annual interest, compounded semiannually. With semiannual compounding, we add the interest earned in the first half-year to the principal, and the total becomes the new principal that will earn interest in the second half-year. Since the annual interest rate is 12 percent, the interest rate for one-half year is 6 percent. This means that the value of the account after the first half-year is $1,060 = $1,000 (1 + 0.12/2). When this amount of $1,060 earns interest for the second half-year, it grows to be $1,123.60 = $1,060 (1 + 0.12/2). We can see that the value of the $1,000 initial investment with semiannual compounding is $1,123.60 after one year.

A more direct way to calculate this future value is to reason that the $1,000 is being invested for two periods of six months each, and that the rate of interest per period is 6 percent. Thus stated, this problem becomes a future value problem where the interest rate is 6 percent per period and the number of periods is 2. More generally, if there are m compounding periods per year, the value of PV dollars at the end of n years, with an r percent annual interest rate, is given by:

$$FV = PV\left(1 + \frac{r}{m}\right)^{mn} \tag{2.5}$$

Table 2.1 shows how the frequency of compounding affects the future value of $1,000 at the end of one year for an interest rate of 12 percent. Notice that the difference between

TABLE 2.1
Future Values and the Frequency of Compounding
(Nominal Annual Rate = 12%)

Frequency	m	Future Value of $1,000
Annual	1	$1,120.00
Semiannual	2	$1,123.60
Quarterly	4	$1,125.51
Monthly	12	$1,126.83
Daily	365	$1,127.47
Continuous*	∞	$1,127.50

*With continuous compounding the value of m is infinite, so we cannot use equation 2.5. Instead, the formula for continuous compounding is $FV = PVe^{rn}$, where $e = 2.718281828$ . . . is the base of the natural logarithms.

the daily and continuous compounding of $1,000 is only three cents after one year. This is a rather surprising result, in view of the fact that continuous compounding occurs every single instant. In contrast, daily compounding occurs just once every 86,400 seconds.

Figure 2.1 illustrates the effect of compounding over a ten-year period with a 12 percent annual interest rate. With simple interest, the $1,000 grows to $2,200, because $2,200 = $1,000(1 + 0.12 × 10). Figure 2.1 also shows the future value of the $1,000 assuming annual compounding and monthly compounding. With annual compounding and an annual interest rate of 12 percent, the future value of the $1,000 is $3,105.85 after ten years. With monthly compounding, the $1,000 grows to $3,300.39 over the same ten years.

THE EFFECTIVE RATE OF INTEREST

As we have already noted, the more frequently we compound, the faster the present value grows. The **effective rate of interest (r_e)** is the annually compounded rate of interest that is equivalent to an annual interest rate compounded more than once per year. This last annual rate is also known as the **nominal rate of interest**. The effective rate and the nominal, or stated, rate of interest are equivalent whenever they both generate the same future value. This indicates that in order to find the effective rate of interest, all we need do is solve the following equation:

$$(1 + r_e) = \left(1 + \frac{r}{m}\right)^m \tag{2.6}$$

We can interpret equation 2.6 as follows. The left side of the equation represents the future value after one year of a present value of $1 earning the effective rate of interest, whereas the right side is the future value of $1 compounded for m periods at a rate of r/m per period. Since m periods constitute one year, the equation expresses the requirement that both of these future values must be equal.

FIGURE 2.1
The Effects of Compounding on Future Value

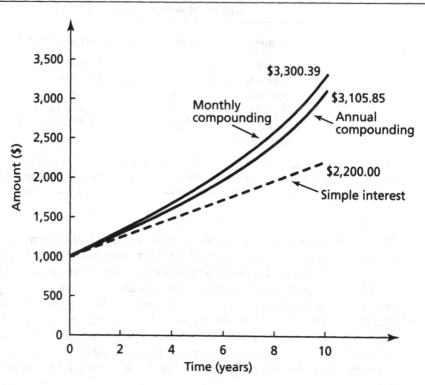

The effective rate of interest is very useful for comparing investment alternatives having different interest rates and different compounding intervals. By comparing the effective rate of interest of each alternative, we can determine the best investment.

EXAMPLE 4

You plan to invest $10,000 for one year and you have the chance to invest it at 12 percent annual interest, compounded monthly. Alternatively, you could invest the funds at an annual rate of 12.25 percent compounded semiannually. What is the effective rate of interest of each alternative?

For the investment at 12 percent annual rate compounded monthly, the monthly rate of interest is 1 percent. An investment of $1 at 1 percent per period over 12 periods will have a future value of:

$$FV = \$1(1.01)^{12} = \$1.1268$$

We invested $1 at the beginning and got back $1.1268 at the end of the year. Therefore, the effective rate of interest of 12 percent nominal interest, compounded monthly, is 12.68 percent. We could also obtain the effective rate by directly solving equation 2.6. Substituting the values in the example and solving for r_e gives 12.68 percent also.

Using equation 2.6 for the investment at 12.25 percent compounded semiannually, we have:

$$(1 + r_e) = \left(1 + \frac{0.1225}{2}\right)^2 = 1.1263$$

Solving for r_e gives an annual effective rate of interest of 12.63 percent.

FUTURE VALUE TABLES

As an alternative to the calculations of future values of single payments with the future value formula, this book includes a future value table in the Appendix. Table 2.2 reproduces a portion of the future value table to indicate how it should be used.

Suppose you want to know the future value of $2,000 three months from now, with an interest rate of 2 percent per month. Table 2.2 indicates that the future value of $1 invested at 2 percent per period for 3 periods is 1.0612. This is the future value factor for 2 percent and 3 periods. Since we are concerned with the future value of $2,000, and not of $1, we simply multiply by $2,000 the future value factor. The desired future value is $2,000 × 1.0612 = $2,122.40.

Note that the interest rate used in the tables is not necessarily an annual rate of interest. Similarly, the number of periods is not necessarily expressed in years. In our example, we used monthly rates and periods expressed in months. The important rule to remember is that the time periods should always be expressed in units consistent with the interest rate. For example, if each period is one month, the interest rate must be expressed as a monthly rate.

It will be useful to develop some shorthand notation for the future value factors. We will use the notation $FV(r, n) = (1 + r)^n$. With this notation, we can write the future value factor for 2 percent per period and 3 periods as $FV(2, 3) = (1 + 0.02)^3 = 1.0612$.

Note that while the future value table can be useful, it cannot solve all future value problems. This is because the table only has integer interest rates and integer periods, so

TABLE 2.2
Future Value of $1

n	1%	2%	3%	4%
1	1.0100	1.0200	1.0300	1.0400
2	1.0201	1.0404	1.0609	1.0816
3	1.0303	1.0612	1.0927	1.1249
4	1.0406	1.0824	1.1255	1.1699
5	1.0510	1.1040	1.1593	1.2167

it cannot solve a problem involving an interest rate of 8.5 percent per period for 7.3 periods. In such cases, the formulas discussed previously must be used.

PRESENT VALUE

As there are future values of sums invested now, payments scheduled for the future have a present value. By an algebraic manipulation of equation 2.4, we can derive an expression for the present value:

$$PV = \frac{FV}{(1 + r)^n} \qquad (2.7)$$

As an example, assume that a wealthy uncle promises to give you a gift of $1,000 in one year. Current interest rates are 10 percent. The $1,000 you will receive has a present value lower than $1,000 because you could invest less than $1,000 today at 10 percent and end up with $1,000 one year from now. This argument is the essence of the time value of money. In essence, money has a time value, because we can use money to earn interest.

The present value for the payment the uncle promised is the sum that would make you exactly as well off today as the $1,000 payment to be received in one year. So, the present value of next year's $1,000 payment is the amount you need to invest now in order to have $1,000 in one year. We can compute the present value of a $1,000 payment in one year with a 10 percent interest rate by using equation 2.7. In this case, the future value is $1,000, the interest rate is 10 percent, and the time until the future payment is one year. The present value is then:

$$PV = \frac{\$1,000}{1 + 0.10} = \$909.09$$

With interest rates at 10 percent per year, the present value of next year's $1,000 payment is $909.09. We can verify this conclusion by showing that $909.09 invested for one year at 10 percent has a future value of $1,000: $909.09(1.10) = $1,000.

Note that future values and present values are really two sides of the same coin. This is clear from considering the very close relationship between equation 2.4 for future values and its rearrangement to give equation 2.7 for present values.

EXAMPLE 5

If interest rates are 13 percent per year, what is the present value of $1,630.47 to be paid in four years?

$$PV = \frac{\$1,630.47}{(1 + 0.13)^4} = \$1,000.00$$

Thus, we see that $1,000 is exactly the amount we would need to invest now, at an annual interest rate of 13 percent, to generate a future value of $1,630.47 in four years.

PRESENT VALUE TABLES

As there are tables of future values, there are also tables of present values. Like the future value table, the present value table reflects values of $1. Table 2.3 presents a portion of the present value table found in the Appendix.

Let the notation $PV(r, n)$ represent the present value factor for an interest rate of r percent per period and n periods. For example, $PV(3, 4)$ is the present value factor for 3 percent and 4 periods. From table 2.3, $PV(3, 4) = 0.8885$. Notice that future value factors are always greater than 1 and present value factors are always less than 1. When using the present value tables, remember that the present value factors assume a future value of $1. When the future value is an arbitrary amount FV, the present value is given by $PV = FV \times PV(r, n)$.

EXAMPLE 6

Compute the present value of $3,500 to be received in four periods, for an interest rate of 3 percent per period.

We have already seen that the present value factor is $PV(3, 4) = 0.8885$. Since this is the present value of $1, we multiply this factor by $3,500 to find the total present value, so $PV = \$3,500 \times 0.8885 = \$3,109.75$.

SOLVING FOR AN UNKNOWN INTEREST RATE

On occasion, financial managers and investors must deal with a time value of money problem in which the present and future values are known, as well as the time between them, but not the interest rate that connects those values. For example, many bonds require a payment now and return a specified larger payment at some future date, but the implicit interest rate the bond earns is not stated, so it must be computed separately.

There are several ways to solve such problems. Today, financial calculators can easily do the job. A second technique is to solve the problem directly. We can also use the present value or future value tables to solve the same problem. To solve the problem directly, we need to find the interest rate from the present value equation. If the time

TABLE 2.3
Present Value of $1

n	1%	2%	3%	4%
1	0.9901	0.9804	0.9709	0.9615
2	0.9803	0.9612	0.9426	0.9245
3	0.9706	0.9424	0.9151	0.8889
4	0.9610	0.9239	0.8885	0.8547
5	0.9515	0.9058	0.8625	0.8218

between the present and future values is n, this requires essentially isolating the term containing r and taking the n-th root on both sides of the equation. The expression for r is then:

$$r = \left(\frac{FV}{PV}\right)^{1/n} - 1$$

EXAMPLE 7

Mr. Willie Himan, a fast-talking salesman, comes into your office and offers you a great deal. Willie offers to pay you $10,000 in six years. He says that the price you must pay today is only $8,375. To know whether this is an attractive deal, you would like to calculate the annual interest rate that your investment would earn.

We may solve this problem directly by applying equation 2.8:

$$r = \left(\frac{\$10,000}{\$8,375}\right)^{1/6} - 1 = 0.03$$

Thus, we see that the fantastic deal earns 3 percent on your investment.

EXAMPLE 8

Before you can throw Mr. Himan out the door, he improves the offer. Now Willie says he will give you the $10,000 six years from now for only $7,677.50 today. What interest rate does the deal represent?

We will solve this problem using the future value tables. We first find the future value factor. Since the future value is $10,000 for an investment of $7,677.50, the future value factor is:

$$FV(r, 6) = \frac{\$10,000}{\$7,677.50} = 1.3025$$

This factor is not found in the future value table in the Appendix. The value we seek lies between $FV(4, 6) = 1.265$ and $FV(5, 6) = 1.340$. Therefore, the interest rate is between 4 percent and 5 percent. Because our future value factor is about half-way between, the interest rate on the deal must be about 4.5 percent. The exact interest rate is 4.5033 percent, so interpolation gave us an excellent approximation in this case.

SOLVING FOR THE NUMBER OF PERIODS

Sometimes the financial manager needs to know how long it will take for a certain amount invested today to grow to a certain value, given that it earns a known rate of interest. For example, a pension fund manager may have $300 million to invest today to meet future pension needs. The manager might want to know how long it would take for that money to grow to the $1 billion needed to meet the firm's obligations. The analytical solution is derived from the relationship between present and future value, equation 2.4. Solving that expression for *n* gives:

$$n = \frac{\ln\left(\frac{FV}{PV}\right)}{\ln(1 + r)}$$

In this formula we use the natural logarithm, but any logarithm measure, such as base 10 logarithms, would work equally well. The only restriction is that the logarithms used in the numerator and denominator must use the same base.

EXAMPLE 9

If you earn an annual rate of interest of 10 percent compounded annually, how many years will it take for your money to double?

Since you wish to double your money, we can assume that you start out with $1, and after *n* years you will have $2. Substituting these numbers and the 10 percent interest rate in equation 2.9, we compute the value of *n*:

$$n = \frac{\ln\left(\frac{\$2}{\$1}\right)}{\ln(1 + 0.10)} = \frac{0.69315}{0.09531} = 7.27 \text{ years.}$$

To approximate the time required to double money, we can use the "**72 rule**." This rule states that the approximate time required to double money at an interest rate *r* is given by the ratio 72/*r*, where *r* is expressed as a percentage. In the example, the rule would give 72/10 = 7.2 years, for a very good approximation. Notice, however, that this rule cannot be applied when the exact doubling time is sought.

SUMMARY

This chapter has introduced the time value of money. The central idea is that $1 received today is worth more than $1 received in the future because we can invest money to earn an interest rate.

We can calculate interest in many ways. We began by considering simple interest and then learned how to calculate compound interest. With compounding, we add interest earned in one period to the principal, and this total becomes the new principal for the following period. In other words, with compound interest, interest earns interest. We also noted that the more often we compound interest, the greater will be the effective rate of interest.

We have seen how to calculate present values and future values. We can compute these values directly through the use of formulas, using a financial calculator, or by using present value and future value tables. Further, we have learned how to move cash flows through time and to value a present or future cash flow at any other moment in time. Finally, we learned how to compute an unknown interest rate if we know the present value, the future value, and the length of time between the two.

This chapter has considered only individual payments. In many finance applications, an investment involves a series of payments. The next chapter explores the present and future values of series of payments.

QUESTIONS

1. For a present value today, will the future value be greater or smaller the higher the rate of interest? Why?
2. For a present value today, will the future value be greater or smaller the longer the time until the future value is to be received? Why?
3. For a given future payment, will the present value be greater or smaller the higher the rate of interest? Why?
4. For a given future payment, will the present value be greater or smaller the longer the time until the future payment is to be made? Why?
5. Would you rather earn 10 percent for a year or an effective interest rate of 10 percent? Explain.
6. If you are borrowing $10,000, would you rather pay 10 percent simple interest or 10 percent interest compounded daily? Why?
7. If you are lending $10,000, would you rather receive 10 percent simple interest or 10 percent interest compounded daily? Why?
8. If you are investing funds, would you prefer a longer or a shorter compounding interval? Why?
9. Can you compute all possible future values using a future value table?
10. Explain what it means to find a present value for a future date.

PROBLEMS

1. For a $10,000 investment, what is the future value if it earns 10 percent simple interest for one year?
2. For a $10,000 investment, what is the future value if it earns 15 percent simple interest for two years?
3. For a $10,000 investment, what is the future value if it earns 10 percent simple interest for five years?
4. For a $10,000 investment, what is the future value if it earns 10 percent interest, compounded quarterly, for one year?
5. For a $25,000 investment, what is the future value if it earns 15 percent interest, compounded quarterly, for six quarters?
6. Using the future value table, compute the future value of an investment of $30,000 invested for three years at 12 percent simple interest.
7. Using the future value table, compute the future value of $30,000 invested for three years at 12 percent, compounded semiannually.

8. Using the future value table, compute the future value of $30,000 invested for three years at 12 percent, compounded quarterly.
9. Using the future value table, compute the future value of $30,000 invested for three years at 12 percent, compounded monthly.
10. What is the present value of a payment of $50,000 to be received in four years if the discount rate is 15 percent? What discounting period should be used for this computation? Why?
11. What is the present value of a payment of $50,000 to be received in four years if the discount rate is 15 percent, assuming semiannual discounting?
12. What is the present value of a payment of $50,000 to be received in four years if the discount rate is 15 percent, assuming quarterly discounting?
13. What is the present value of a payment of $50,000 to be received in four years if the discount rate is 15 percent, assuming discounting every two months?
14. Using the present value table, compute the present value of a payment of $100,000 to be received in eight years if the discount rate is 16 percent.
15. Using the present value table, compute the present value of a payment of $100,000 to be received in eight years if the discount rate is 16 percent, assuming semiannual discounting.
16. Using the present value table, compute the present value of a payment of $100,000 to be received in eight years if the discount rate is 16 percent, assuming quarterly compounding.
17. What is the effective rate of interest on a loan if the stated rate is 14 percent and the principal is compounded monthly?
18. What is the effective rate of interest on a loan if the stated rate is 14 percent and the principal is compounded semiannually?
19. You want to borrow money to be repaid in two years. Moon Bank offers you a loan rate of 13 percent with annual compounding. Venus Bank offers you the same two-year loan at a stated rate of 12.284 percent, but with monthly compounding. Which loan would you prefer?
20. Amerilast Bank uses quarterly compounding for its loans and offers you a nominal rate of 12 percent. What simple interest rate on a one-year loan could you get that would be equivalent to the quarterly loan?
21. Using the future value table, make the best estimate that you can for the future value of $10,000 in ten periods with an interest rate of 4.5 percent. Compute the same problem by calculator. How close were you to the exact answer when you used the table?
22. Using the present value table, make the best estimate that you can for the present value of $10,000 in ten periods with an interest rate of 4.5 percent. Compute the same problem by calculator. How close was the answer from the table?
23. Your Uncle Buck will pay you $1,000 in five years if you are a good boy or girl. What will be the present value of that future payment in two years, assuming an 11 percent discount rate?
24. One year from now, you tell your Uncle Buck, who was going to pay you the $1,000 in the preceding question, that you don't want to be a good boy or girl, because you are already a man or woman and that he should keep his lousy $1,000. In present value terms, how much did that rashness cost you?

25. Your Uncle Buck realizes that he shouldn't be treating you as a child and gives you a choice of $500 now or $1,000 in four years. What interest rate would make you indifferent between this present value and future value?

26. You are a hard bargainer and convince your Uncle Buck to agree to change the terms to $1,200 in three years or $600 now. What interest rate does this imply? Which would you choose if you can invest at 20 percent?

27. You can pay a tax of $150 now or $175 in one month. What interest rate does this choice imply? What choice should you make if you can earn 11 percent for one month in your savings account?

28. Suppose you can skip your $150 tax payment now and pay tax of $200 in one year, plus a penalty of $20. What interest rate must you earn to make it worthwhile to skip paying your tax now?

29. Your company is excited about a new research project. The project will take eight years to complete. At that time, the created technology should be worth $1,000,000. By the end of year 4, the value of the technology will be obvious, as will the ultimate success of the research. Consequently, your firm plans to sell rights to the technology at that time. If interest rates are 12 percent, what should the present value of the technology be at year 4?

30. Exactly how long does it take for money to double if you earn 5 percent annual interest? What if you earn 15 percent? Compare the exact answers to those given by the "72 rule."

31. How long does it take for money to triple if you earn 7 percent annual interest?

32. Wonderland, Inc., offers an investment with a 100 percent annual interest rate. If Alice decides to invest, how long will it take for her money to grow to 64 times her initial investment?

33. In the previous problem, suppose Alice has a goal of achieving a certain amount of money at the end of seven years. How long will it take Alice to reach half of her goal?

34. Investment A will quadruple your money in the same amount of time that investment B will triple it. Find the functional relationship between the two implicit interest rates. (For example, the relationship might be expressed as $r_A = 2r_B$.)

35. Many people like to complain about how expensive mailing a letter has become. They cite, for example, that in 1939 a first-class letter cost only three cents, whereas in 1996 an equivalent letter costs 32 cents – over ten times more! Find the average annual postal inflation rate over that 57-year period. Are those complaints really justified?

36. In 1654, Archbishop James Ussher of Ireland announced the results of his quest to pinpoint the moment of Creation. Somehow, he concluded that the event took place on October 26, in the year 4004 B.C., at precisely 9:00 A.M. Assuming that Ussher's estimation is correct, what has been the average annual population growth rate throughout the history of humankind? To simplify, assume that exactly 6,000 years have gone by since the creation, that the first two people – Adam and Eve? – were created at that time, and that the current world population is 5.5 billion.

37. The overall global population growth rate is 1.74 percent per year, and the world's population is 5.5 billion people. How many years will it take for the population to double? To triple?

38. Continuing with our population analysis, is the current population growth rate of 1.74 percent high or low by historical standards? (Hint: When would our earliest ancestors have lived?)

39. Nigeria's annual population growth rate is 3.4 percent. At this rate, how long will it take for the number of Nigerians to double?

40. Assume that Nigeria currently has a population of 120 million and a population growth rate of 3.4 percent. While the rest of the world grows at 1.7 percent, how many years would it take for the population of Nigeria to equal half the world's population? Recall that the entire world currently has a population of 5.5 billion people.

41. In a nutshell, what does population growth have to do with the time value of money anyway?

42. According to legend, Peter Minuit, the first director general of New Netherland province, bought Manhattan Island from the local Canarsee Indians in 1626. The price was 60 guilders, or about $24. It is often alleged that the Indians got the worst part of the deal. To investigate this question, compute the value of the original $24 in the year 2000, assuming annual interest rates of 2, 4, 6, 8 and 10 percent. Had that money been invested during that 374-year period, was the sale price reasonable?

43. There is a colorful legend surrounding the invention of chess. It is said that in those days, the local ruler became enamored with the new game and allowed its inventor to choose any prize, no matter how expensive. Without hesitating, the inventor humbly requested that a single grain of wheat be put on the first of the chess board's 64 squares, two grains of wheat on the next square, four grains on the third square, and so on, doubling the number of grains on each successive square. Once the board had been filled with the grains of wheat according to this procedure, the inventor would consider the prize paid in full. Was the inventor of chess really humble?

44. Over the 12-year period between 1979 and 1991, the number of Nicaraguan cordobas required to buy one U.S. dollar grew from ten to 25,000,000. What was the average annual "growth rate" of the cordoba during that period?

Chapter 3

The Time Value of Money: Series of Payments

OVERVIEW

In the previous chapter we introduced the principles of the time value of money and studied their application to single payments. This chapter shows how we can value a stream of payments by extending the time value of money concepts for single payments. We begin by analyzing an infinite stream of equal payments. Paradoxically, this is the easiest stream of all to value. We then proceed with the valuation of a finite stream of payments.

Many finance applications focus on a series of payments. For example, the typical home mortgage runs for 360 equal monthly payments. The typical car loan requires monthly payments for four or five years. We study how to deal with problems such as these in this chapter.

PERPETUITIES

A **perpetuity** is an infinite stream of equal cash flows occurring at regular intervals. For example, if a savings account has a current balance of $20,000 and earns an interest rate of 12 percent compounded annually, then the depositor, and the depositor's heirs, can enjoy a yearly cash flow of $2,400 forever, as long as the original $20,000 is left in the account and interest rates do not change.

An infallible rule in valuing any stream of payments is to value each of the component cash flows and then add all the individual values. Given that with perpetuities we must value an infinite number of cash flows, it is perhaps surprising that perpetuities are the easiest stream of cash flows to value.

We assume that the first payment of the perpetuity occurs one year from today. In principle, to find the present value, PV, of a perpetuity paying C each period with an interest rate of r percent per period, we must evaluate the sum of the individual present values:

$$PV = \frac{C}{(1 + r)} + \frac{C}{(1 + r)^2} + \frac{C}{(1 + r)^3} + \cdots$$

Fortunately, this infinite summation adds up to the following simple formula:[1]

$$PV = \frac{C}{r} \qquad (3.1)$$

It is very important to note that in the perpetuity formula in equation 3.1, the present value is located one period before the first payment. Thus, to find the present value of a perpetuity at time $t = 0$, the first payment must occur at time $t = 1$. Similarly, if the first payment of a perpetuity occurs at time $t = 19$, then equation 3.1 is still valid, but it gives the present value of the perpetuity as of time $t = 18$.

EXAMPLE 1

Find the present value of an investment that promises to pay \$2,500 each year, forever, when the interest rate is 12 percent.

Using equation 3.1, the present value is:

$$PV = \frac{\$2,500}{0.12}$$

$$= \$20,833.33$$

The following section shows that by using the perpetuity formula, we can easily value other types of cash flow streams.

ANNUITIES

An **annuity** is a finite series of equal cash flows made at regular intervals. For example, a car loan with 48 equal monthly payments is a typical annuity. As with perpetuities, finding the value of an annuity requires valuing the individual payments and adding up those values.

Calculating the value of an annuity is a common problem in finance. For example, consider an individual who decides to save \$1,000 per year for the next three years and makes the first payment one year from today. Taking the present time as time 0, the payment stream appears as follows:

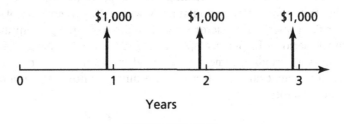

Years

---

[1] Finding the value of the infinite summation requires knowledge of geometric series. A geometric series, S, is a summation of the form $S = 1 + x + x^2 + x^3 + \ldots$, which adds up to $S = 1/(1 - x)$. Such summations are useful in finance and many other disciplines. The formula tells us, for example, that in the limit the sum $1 + 1/2 + 1/4 + 1/8 + \ldots$, adds up to 2.

Notice that in this three-year annuity the first payment occurs one year from today. An annuity in which the first payment takes place one period from now is called a **simple annuity**. If the individual were to make the first payment immediately, this would be an **annuity due**. In this book, if we speak of an "annuity" without qualification, we are discussing a simple annuity. As we will see, once we know how to value an ordinary annuity, it is easy to value an annuity due.

The Present Value of an Annuity

Often we can pay for a service now, or pay installments over time. For example, a two-year contract for a service might allow the buyer to pay $1,500 now. Alternatively, the buyer might pay $850 one year from now and another $850 two years from today. Which payment plan is better? When we must pay for a service, the basic rule is to choose the payment with the lowest present value.

We can calculate the present value of an annuity by treating it as a collection of individual payments. With this approach, we simply compute the present value of the individual payments in the annuity and add them to find the present value of the annuity. To see how this works, let us calculate the present value of an annuity of $850 for two years with a 12 percent rate of interest.

$$PV = \frac{\$850}{1.12} + \frac{\$850}{1.12^2}$$

$$= \$850\left(\frac{1}{1.12} + \frac{1}{1.12^2}\right)$$

$$= \$850(1.6900)$$

$$= \$1,436.54$$

With a present value of $1,436.54, the purchaser of the service should take the deferred payment plan and invest the $1,500 freed by this decision at 12 percent.

Although this was a simple calculation, we would not be so anxious to compute the present value of a 50 payment annuity. Accordingly, it is convenient to have a table of present value factors for annuities. This calculation requires three pieces of information: payment, interest rate, and number of periods. Table 3.1 provides some present value factors for annuities. A more complete table is found in the Appendix.

The final term in parentheses in the previous numerical calculation is the present value factor for a two-period annuity with a 12 percent rate of interest. We define $PA(r, n)$ as the present value factor for an annuity with an r percent interest rate per period and with n periods. In our example, $PA(12, 2) = 1.6900$. Note that the present value factor assumes a periodic payment of $1, so if we want to find the present value of an annuity with a payment different from $1, we simply multiply the amount of the payment by the annuity factor:

$$PV = C \times PA(r, n) \tag{3.2}$$

EXAMPLE 2

Your rich Aunt Julia knows that you are a finance student and decides to test your knowledge. She offers you a choice of a $1,100 gift right now or the payment

TABLE 3.1
The Present Value of an Annuity of $1, PA(r, n)

Period (n)	Interest Rate (r)			
	1%	2%	3%	4%
1	0.9901	0.9804	0.9709	0.9615
2	1.9704	1.9416	1.9135	1.8861
3	2.9410	2.8839	2.8286	2.7751
4	3.9020	3.8077	3.7171	3.6299
5	4.8534	4.7135	4.5797	4.4518

of $100 per month for 12 months beginning one month from now. If interest rates are 1 percent per month, which should you choose?

To decide, you must compare the present values of the two alternative gifts. Clearly, the present value of the lump-sum payment is $1,100, so we only need to find the present value of the 12 monthly payments. These constitute an annuity of 12 periods, with an interest rate of 1 percent per period. Therefore, the present value of the annuity is:

$$PV = C \times PA(1, 12) = \$100 \times 11.2551 = \$1,125.51$$

Because the present value of the stream of payments is greater, you would prefer the monthly payments – assuming Aunt Julia is reliable.

As an alternative to the use of the present value table, we can also find an explicit formula for calculating the present value of an annuity. This could be accomplished in essentially the same way as was done for perpetuities. However, rather than using brute-force mathematics, we will derive the annuity formula by using some financial intuition along with our knowledge of the perpetuity formula.

Figure 3.1 shows that an n-year annuity is just the difference of two perpetuities: one perpetuity with the first cash flow at time $t = 1$ and the other perpetuity with the first cash flow at time $t = n + 1$. It follows that the present value of an annuity is just the difference of the present values of its two component perpetuities. Thus, using equation 3.1 we have:

$$PV = \frac{C}{r} - \frac{C}{r}(1 + r)^{-n}$$

The n-year discount factor in the second term arises because, for the perpetuity that starts at time $t = n + 1$, equation 3.1 gives the present value at time $t = n$. Thus, it is necessary to bring the present value of the second perpetuity down to time $t = 0$. Rearranging gives the formula for the present value of an annuity:

$$PV = C\frac{1 - (1 + r)^{-n}}{r} \qquad (3.3)$$

FIGURE 3.1
An Annuity as the Difference of Two Perpetuities

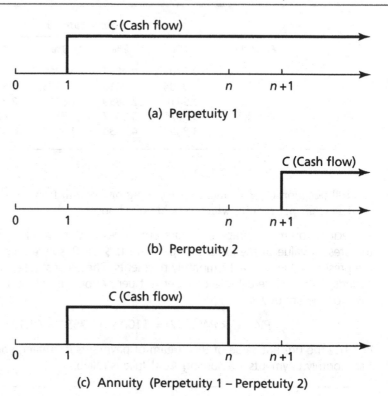

(a) Perpetuity 1

(b) Perpetuity 2

(c) Annuity (Perpetuity 1 – Perpetuity 2)

Comparing equation 3.3 to equation 3.2, it is clear that the present value annuity factor for r percent and n periods, $PA(r, n)$, is equal to:

$$PA(r, n) = \frac{1 - (1 + r)^{-n}}{r} \tag{3.4}$$

EXAMPLE 3

Find the present value annuity factor for an interest rate of 12.73 percent and nine years.

Note that it is not possible to compute this annuity factor using the present value table, since the table only contains integer values for r. Nevertheless, using equation 3.4 we can easily solve this problem:

$$PA(12.73, 9) = \frac{1 - (1.1273)^{-9}}{0.1273}$$

$$= 5.1836$$

The Future Value of an Annuity

A saver who places $1,000 into a savings account for each of the next three years, starting one year from now, might wonder how much the account will be worth just after making the third deposit. Assume that the account earns 10 percent, compounded annually.

We can compute the value of the account by considering each of the single payments and the interest they will earn by year 3. This treats the annuity as a collection of single payments. The graph on the following time line shows the essence of the calculation.

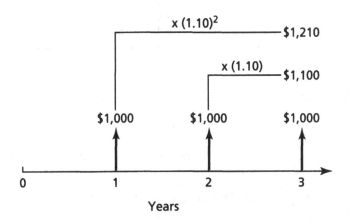

In the graph, the $1,000 at time $t = 1$ earns interest for the next two years at 10 percent. The cash flow at $t = 2$, however, can only earn interest for one year, and the final $1,000 does not earn any interest. We can now calculate the future value of the three payments by simply adding the individual future values.

$$FV = \$1,000(1.10)^2 + \$1,000(1.10) + \$1,000$$
$$= \$1,000[(1.10)^2 + (1.10) + 1]$$
$$= \$1,000(3.3100)$$
$$= \$3,310$$

Just as we did with the present value of an annuity, we can construct a table for the future value of an annuity. Notice from our example that the future value at year 3 of a three-year simple annuity with a 10 percent rate of interest would be 3.3100 times the $1,000 payment. The 3.3100 in the example is the future value factor of the three-year annuity at 10 percent. We can collect all of these future value factors for annuities and put them into a table. Table 3.2 presents a small table for the future value of an annuity of $1. A more extensive future value of an annuity table is found in the Appendix.

We will use the notation $FA(r, n)$ to denote the future value factor of an annuity with a periodic interest rate of r percent and with n periods. Thus, in our example, $FA(10, 3) = 3.3100$.

The general expression for the future value of an annuity is:

$$FV = C \times FA(r, n) \tag{3.5}$$

TABLE 3.2
The Future Value of an Annuity of $1, *FA(r, n)*

Period (n)	Interest Rate (r)			
	1%	2%	3%	4%
1	1.000	1.000	1.000	1.000
2	2.0100	2.0200	2.0300	2.0400
3	3.0301	3.0604	3.0909	3.1216
4	4.0604	4.1216	4.1836	4.2465
5	5.1010	5.2040	5.3091	5.4163

EXAMPLE 4

An investor plans to save $1,500 per year for 25 years as a retirement fund, starting one year from now, and she expects to earn 12 percent per year on all invested funds. Using the table for the future value of an annuity, calculate how much the investor will have at the end of 25 years.

The problem calls for the future value of a simple annuity. To calculate the solution using the table, we need to find the factor and multiply it by the periodic contribution. The future value table in the Appendix shows that the factor is *FA*(12, 25) = 133.3339. The complete solution is:

$$FV = \$1{,}500 \times FA(12, 25)$$
$$= \$1{,}500 \times 133.3339 = \$200{,}000.85$$

Immediately after making the last deposit in 25 years, the investor will have $200,000.85 in the retirement fund.

Just as we did with the present value of a simple annuity, we can find a formula for the future value of an annuity. This can be done in several ways. One way is to realize that the future value of an annuity at time n can be calculated by finding the present value of the annuity at $t = 0$ and compounding that present value for n periods. In other words:

FV of an annuity = *PV* of an annuity × $(1 + r)^n$

Since we already know the formula for the present value of an annuity, we simply multiply that expression by the n-year compound factor. Assuming the periodic payment is C and the interest rate is r, we have:

$$FV = C\frac{(1 + r)^n - 1}{r} \tag{3.6}$$

Equation 3.6 provides more flexibility than the future value table, since it is also valid for fractional interest rates and periods.

EXAMPLE 5

Find the future value of a five-year simple annuity with a $375 yearly payment, if the interest rate is 7.4 percent per year.

Using the formula for the future value of an annuity, equation 3.6, we have:

$$FV = \$375 \frac{(1.074)^5 - 1}{0.074}$$

$$= \$375(5.7968) = \$2,173.81.$$

SOLVING FOR AN UNKNOWN INTEREST RATE

Many life insurance companies sell annuities, particularly to retirees. For instance, we can pay a lump-sum now to receive an annuity. As an example, consider an annuity of $10,000 for ten years, with the first of the ten payments to be received one year from today. If the price you must pay for this annuity today were $61,450, would it be attractive? The answer depends on the interest rate implied by the annuity. This section shows how to find the interest rate in such situations.

We start from the basic relationship for the present value of an annuity, equation 3.2, which is reproduced here:

$$PV = C \times PA(r, n) \tag{3.2}$$

In our example, we know all the variables in this equation except the interest rate. Rearranging terms we have:

$$PA(r, n) = \frac{PV}{C} \tag{3.7}$$

Substituting the known values into equation 3.7 gives:

$$PA(r, 10) = \frac{\$61,450}{\$10,000}$$

$$= 6.1450$$

To find the interest rate this annuity implies, we need to find the 6.1450 factor in the ten-year row of the present value of an annuity table in the Appendix. In this case, it lies in the column for 10 percent. Therefore, the price charged for the annuity implies an interest rate of 10 percent.

This implied interest rate has a very specific meaning. If you could invest your funds at 10 percent per period, you would just be able to make the payments on the annuity and have nothing left at the end of the ten-year period.

EXAMPLE 6

A four-year annuity of $1,200 costs $3,700 today. What is the implied rate of interest?

To solve this problem, we substitute the known values into equation 3.7:

$$PA(r, 4) = \frac{\$3,700}{\$1,200} = 3.0833$$

To finish the problem, we need to look for the 3.0833 factor in the row for four periods in the present value of an annuity table in the Appendix, and then read the interest rate from the column heading. However, the value 3.0833 does not appear in the row for four periods. The closest values we find are $PA(11, 4) = 3.1024$ and $PA(12, 4) = 3.0373$. Therefore, the table cannot be used to determine the exact interest rate in this case. However, we can be sure that the rate lies between 11 and 12 percent.[2]

For an arbitrary annuity it is impossible to find a general formula that computes the value of the interest rate r when all other variables are known. All financial calculators can find the interest rate, but only because they use trial-and-error techniques to do the job. This is the reason that finding the interest rate in your calculator takes much longer than finding any of the other time value of money variables, as you can readily verify.

SOLVING FOR AN UNKNOWN ANNUITY PAYMENT

Suppose you want to consume $1,000,000 that you have in the bank by withdrawing equal annual amounts over a seven-year period. With an interest rate of 8 percent, how large will each of the seven annuity payments be? To find the size of the annuity payment, we can rearrange the terms in equation 3.2 to solve for the payment C:

$$C = \frac{PV}{PA(r, n)} \tag{3.8}$$

We can use equation 3.8 to find the annuity payment that the $1,000,000 will support. In our example, $PA(8, 7) = 5.20637$. Thus:

$$C = \frac{\$1,000,000}{5.20637} = \$192,072.40$$

The financial interpretation of this problem is as follows. If we invest the $1,000,000 in a savings account at 8 percent and withdraw $192,072.40 at the end of each of the next seven years, the last withdrawal will leave a zero balance in the account. Table 3.3 illustrates this solution in more detail. Each year some of the payment goes to pay the remaining principal, and some goes to pay interest. At the beginning, a large portion of the payment goes for interest, but that portion gets smaller as time progresses and principal is repaid. Since the sum of interest and principal totals $192,072.40, the principal portion of the annuity increases each year. Finally, at the end of the seventh year, the debt is completely paid, save for a negligible rounding error which may occur.

---

[2] Using a financial calculator, the actual rate is 11.29 percent.

TABLE 3.3
How $1,000,000 Supports an Annuity ($r = 8\%$; $n = 7$ years)

Time	Payment	Interest	Principal Reduction	Balance
0				1,000,000.00
1	192,072.40	80,000.00	112,072.40	887,927.60
2	192,072.40	71,034.21	121,038.19	766,889.41
3	192,072.40	61,351.15	130,721.25	636,168.16
4	192,072.40	50,893.45	141,178.95	494,989.21
5	192,072.40	39,599.14	152,473.26	342,515.95
6	192,072.40	27,401.28	164,671.12	177,844.83
7	192,072.40	14,227.59	177,844.81	0.02

EXAMPLE 7

Joe's parents have given him a lump-sum sufficient to generate 50 monthly payments of $500 for a college education, knowing that Joe can earn an interest rate of 1 percent per month in his savings account. However, Joe decides to spend $4,598 of that lump-sum on a used car right away. What monthly payment can the remaining amount generate over the next 50 months?

First, we find the required lump-sum payment, to the nearest dollar:

$$PV = C \times PA(1, 50)$$

$$= \$500 \times 39.1961 = \$19,598$$

After buying the car, Joe has $15,000 left in his savings account. We can now find the monthly payment using equation 3.8:

$$C = \frac{\$15,000}{PA(1, 50)}$$

$$= \frac{\$15,000}{39.1961} = \$382.69$$

Obviously, Joe is going to be living on a tighter budget and hoping the car does not break down.

THE NUMBER OF PERIODS OF AN ANNUITY

In some cases, both the amount available to fund an annuity and the size of the annuity payments are fixed. For example, assume a retiree has $85,000 and needs $10,000 per year to live. If annual interest rates are 9 percent, how long will the funds last? We can solve this kind of problem by using equation 3.2, the basic relationship for the present value of an annuity:

$$PV = C \times PA(r, n) \tag{3.2}$$

In this case, we have all the necessary values except the number of periods that the annuity will last. Substituting the known values gives:

$$\$85,000 = \$10,000 \times PA(9, n)$$

Isolating the unknown annuity factor, we obtain:

$$PA(9, n) = \frac{\$85,000}{\$10,000} = 8.5000$$

To find the solution, we consult the present value of an annuity table in the Appendix and search in the 9 percent column for the factor that equals 8.5000. In the table we find $PA(9, 16) = 8.3126$ and $PA(9, 17) = 8.5436$. Therefore, we conclude that funds will be available for 16 years, with a little money left over.

We can find the exact number of periods until money runs out by recalling that the present value of an annuity is also given by equation 3.3. Solving this expression for the number of periods, n, gives:

$$n = \frac{\ln\left(\dfrac{C}{C - PV \times r}\right)}{\ln(1 + r)} \tag{3.9}$$

Applying equation 3.9 to the retiree problem gives:

$$n = \frac{\ln\left(\dfrac{\$10,000}{\$10,000 - \$85,000 \times 0.09}\right)}{\ln(1 + 0.09)}$$

$$= \frac{1.44817}{0.8618}$$

$$= 16.80 \text{ years}$$

EXAMPLE 8

Returning to Joe, our college student who really wants a car, consider this possible solution to his lack of funds: purchase the car, leaving $15,000 in the college account, go to school spending $500 a month until the money runs out, and then beg his parents for more. By that time, graduation should be near and Joe hopes his parents will be willing to kick in some more money, albeit grudgingly. If interest rates are 1 percent per month, how long will this $500 annuity last?

Using equation 3.9 we have:

$$n = \frac{\ln\left(\dfrac{\$500}{\$500 - \$15{,}000 \times 0.01}\right)}{\ln(1 + 0.01)}$$

$$= \frac{0.35667}{0.00995}$$

$$= 35.85 \text{ months}$$

Joe can plan on using his persuasion skills in just less than three years.

VALUING AN ANNUITY DUE

We previously noted that an n-year ordinary annuity makes its first payment one year from the present, whereas an n-year annuity due makes its first payment immediately. However, both types of annuities have n payments. Thus, the last payment for the ordinary annuity occurs at time n, whereas for the annuity due the last payment occurs at time $n - 1$. This section shows how to value annuities due.

We could derive the formulas for an annuity due in a manner similar to what we did for ordinary annuities. Instead, we will use our knowledge of the formulas for ordinary annuities and some financial reasoning.

Suppose the first cash flow of the annuity due occurs now, at time $t = 0$. Then, the present value of an n-year annuity due of $\$C$ with an annual interest rate of r percent may be found by recognizing that an annuity due becomes an n-year ordinary annuity when viewed from time $t = -1$. This is shown in figure 3.2. Metaphorically, if you look into the future while standing at time $t = -1$, you see n equal payments, the first one at $t = 0$. This means that at time $t = -1$, the present value of the annuity due is equal to the present value of an n-year ordinary annuity. Since we are interested in the present value of the annuity due at time $t = 0$, not at $t = -1$, we must compound the value of the ordinary annuity for one period, from $t = -1$ to $t = 0$, to obtain the present value of the annuity due at time $t = 0$. All this means that:

$$PV_{n\text{-year annuity due}} = PV_{n\text{-year simple annuity}} \times (1 + r) \tag{3.10}$$

There is another way to find the expression relating the present values of both types of annuities. Consider the cash flows from $t = 1$ to $t = n - 1$ as an $(n - 1)$-year ordinary

FIGURE 3.2
An Annuity Due Starting at $t = 0$ Viewed as an Ordinary Annuity from $t = -1$

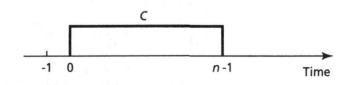

annuity. Find the present value of this annuity and add the payment at $t = 0$ to get the total value of the annuity due. The resulting expression is:

$$PV_{n\text{-year annuity due}} = PV_{(n-1)\text{-year simple annuity}} + C \tag{3.11}$$

It is left to the reader to show that equations 3.10 and 3.11 are equivalent expressions.

Once the present value at time $t = 0$ of an annuity due is found using either equation 3.10 or 3.11, its future value as of time $t = n$ can be found by compounding the present value for n periods. Thus, the future value of an n-year annuity due, at time $t = n$, is:

$$FV_{n\text{-year annuity due}} = PV_{n\text{-year annuity due}} \times (1 + r)^n \tag{3.12}$$

EXAMPLE 9

Compute the present and future values of a five-year annuity due, with 8 percent annual interest rate and $300 yearly payments.

First, we need to compute the present value of the equivalent ordinary annuity. Using the formulas derived previously, we have:

$$PV_{-1} = \$300 \times PA(8, 5) = \$300 \times 3.9927 = \$1,197.81$$

Since the present value of this ordinary annuity is located at $t = -1$, we can use equation 3.10 to find its value at $t = 0$:

$$PV_0 = \$1,197.81 \times 1.08 = \$1,293.63$$

We can now determine the future value of the annuity due at $t = 5$ using equation 3.12:

$$FV = \$1,293.63 \times (1.08)^5 = \$1,900.78$$

THE PRESENT VALUE OF A GROWING PERPETUITY

A growing perpetuity is an infinite stream of periodic cash flows which grow at a constant rate each period. If the cash flow growth rate is g percent per period, and the cash flow at time t is denoted by D_t, then we have the following relationship:

$$D_t = D_{t-1}(1 + g) \tag{3.13}$$

As with any cash flow stream, the present value of a growing perpetuity is just the sum of the present values of the individual cash flows. Thus, using equation 3.13 we have:

$$PV = \frac{D_1}{(1 + r)} + \frac{D_2}{(1 + r)^2} + \frac{D_3}{(1 + r)^3} + \cdots$$

$$= \frac{D_1}{(1 + r)} + \frac{D_1(1 + g)}{(1 + r)^2} + \frac{D_1(1 + g)^2}{(1 + r)^3} \cdots$$

$$= \frac{D_1}{(1 + r)}\left\{1 + \frac{1 + g}{1 + r} + \left(\frac{1 + g}{1 + r}\right)^2 + \cdots\right\}$$

The infinite summation in brackets is a geometric series of the form $1 + x + x^2 + \ldots$, where $x = (1 + g)/(1 + r)$, which adds up to $(1 + r)/(r - g)$. Using this expression and simplifying yields the formula for a growing perpetuity:

$$PV = \frac{D_1}{r - g} \tag{3.14}$$

Two important facts should be remembered when using the growing perpetuity formula. First, the cash payment to be used in the numerator is next period's payment, D_1. Second, the formula can only be used when the discount rate is strictly greater than the cash flow growth rate; that is, the formula is only valid when $r > g$.

EXAMPLE 10

The cash flow generated by Boone Enterprises is expected to grow at a rate of 5 percent per year, forever. Next year's cash flow is expected to be $45,000. If the annual discount rate appropriate for Boone is 14 percent, find Boone's current value.

We are given next year's cash flow and the discount rate is greater than the growth rate, so we can use the growing perpetuity formula. A direct application of equation 3.14 gives:

$$PV = \frac{\$45,000}{0.14 - 0.05} = \$500,000.$$

THE PRESENT VALUE OF A GROWING ANNUITY

A growing annuity is a finite stream of periodic cash flows which grow at a constant rate each period. Just as an annuity can be viewed as a truncated perpetuity, a growing annuity can be thought of as a truncated growing perpetuity. This fact links the valuation of a growing annuity to the value of a growing perpetuity. The derivation parallels the derivation of the annuity formula from the perpetuity formula.

The present value of an n-year growing annuity can be found by referring to figure 3.3. There we can see graphically that the growing annuity can be decomposed into the difference of two growing perpetuities: a growing perpetuity with the first cash flow at time $t = 1$, minus a growing perpetuity with its first cash flow at time $t = n + 1$. This means that the present value of the growing annuity at $t = 0$ is the difference of the present values of the two growing perpetuities:

$$PV = \frac{D_1}{r - g} - \frac{D_{n+1}}{r - g}(1 + r)^{-n}$$

Since cash flows grow at a rate of g percent per period, we have $D_{n+1} = D_1(1 + g)^n$. Using this result and rearranging gives the formula for a growing annuity:

$$PV = \frac{D_1}{r - g}\left[1 - \left(\frac{1 + g}{1 + r}\right)^n\right] \tag{3.15}$$

FIGURE 3.3
A Growing Annuity as the Difference of Two Growing Perpetuities

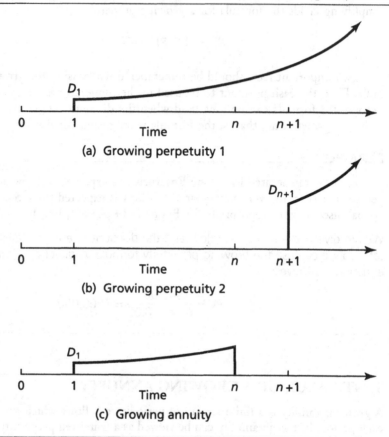

(a) Growing perpetuity 1

(b) Growing perpetuity 2

(c) Growing annuity

Equation 3.15 is valid not only when $r > g$, but also when $r < g$. This is in contrast to the growing perpetuity formula, which is valid only for $r > g$. However, equation 3.15 cannot be used in the special situation in which $r = g$.[3] In that case, to find the present value of the growing annuity we have to make use of the foolproof method of adding all the present values of the individual cash flows of the growing annuity. This gives:

$$PV = \frac{D_1}{(1+r)} + \frac{D_2}{(1+r)^2} + \ldots + \frac{D_n}{(1+r)^n}$$

$$= \frac{D_1}{1+r}\left[1 + \frac{1+g}{1+r} + \ldots + \left(\frac{1+g}{1+r}\right)^{n-1}\right]$$

[3] This is seen by noting that when $r = g$, we would have to divide by zero, which is never allowed. Alternatively, we would have an expression of the form 0/0, which is indeterminate. (0/0 is not necessarily 0, nor is it necessarily 1!)

Since $r = g$ by assumption, each term in brackets is equal to 1. Since there are n such terms within the brackets, the formula for a growing annuity when the discount rate equals the cash flow growth rate is:

$$PV = \frac{D_1 n}{1 + r} \qquad (3.16)$$

EXAMPLE 11

Ruth works at Rey Burger and expects her annual salary to grow steadily at 5 percent per year for the next ten years, when she expects to retire. Her current salary, which has just been paid, is $30,000. If Ruth can earn 12 percent on her investments, what is the present value of her remaining annual salaries?

First, we need to compute next year's salary. Since it will be 5 percent greater than this year's salary, then $D_1 = \$30,000 \times 1.05 = \$31,500$. Since $r > g$, to compute the present value of the growing annuity we use equation 3.15:

$$PV = \frac{\$31,500}{0.12 - 0.05}\left[1 - \left(\frac{1.05}{1.12}\right)^{10}\right] = \$213,992.79$$

What would be the present value of Ruth's future salaries if she can earn only 5 percent annually on her investments?

In this case $r = g$, so we must use equation 3.16:

$$PV = \frac{\$31,500 \times 10}{1.05} = \$300,000$$

We can interpret these present values as follows. If Ruth can earn 12 percent on her money, then with $213,992.79 invested today she could withdraw annual amounts equal to her future salaries and have nothing left after the tenth withdrawal. However, if Ruth can earn only 5 percent on her money, she needs to invest $300,000 today to be able to make annual withdrawals equal to her future salaries and have nothing left over at the end. In effect, the lower rate of interest must be overcome by investing a greater amount now.

SUMMARY

In this chapter we covered the time value of a series of payments. We began by calculating the present value of a perpetuity. Then we differentiated between ordinary annuities and annuities due, and we learned how to calculate the present value and future value of both types. We also discussed the techniques for determining how large an annuity a given lump-sum finances over a specified period. We then learned how to calculate the number of periods a given lump-sum lasts if it pays a specific annuity amount and showed how to find the required lump-sum payment necessary to generate a given annuity.

Finally, we discussed the valuation of growing perpetuities and growing annuities. Growing annuities are very useful in dealing with problems relating to the typical lifetime earnings pattern.

1. What happens to the present value of a perpetuity as the interest rate gets larger?
2. If the present value of a perpetuity at time $t = 0$ is $200, what is its present value at $t = 2$? At $t = 5$? At $t = 100$? Explain.
3. What happens to the present value of an annuity as the interest rate gets larger?
4. What happens to the future value of an annuity as the interest rate gets larger?
5. Consider two annuities for six periods with an interest rate of 11 percent. One annuity is for $100 and the other is for $200. What can you say about the present value of the two annuities?
6. Consider two annuities for six periods with an interest rate of 11 percent. One annuity is for $100 and the other is for $200. What can you say about the future value of the two annuities?
7. Which will have a greater present value, other things being equal, an annuity due or an ordinary annuity? Explain.
8. Which will have a greater future value, other things being equal, an annuity due or an ordinary annuity? Explain.
9. Explain how to find the present value of an annuity if you do not know any of the principles about valuing annuities.
10. Why is it absurd to use the formula for a growing perpetuity when the growth rate is greater than the discount rate?
11. Show that $PA(r, n) < n$ for any positive value of r.
12. Write the formula for a growing perpetuity in terms of the current cash flow, and not next year's cash flow.
13. We provided a formula for the present value of a growing annuity. However, no formula for the future value of a growing annuity was given. Nevertheless, the future value can be found by a simple adaptation of the present value formula. Explain how this may be done.

PROBLEMS

1. Find the future value of an annuity with a payment of $55 per period, 5 periods, and an interest rate of 7.5 percent.
2. Find the future value of an annuity with a payment of $20 per period, 4 periods, and an interest rate of 10.5 percent.
3. Find the present value of an annuity with a payment of $55 per period, 5 periods, and an interest rate of 7.5 percent.
4. Find the present value of an annuity with a payment of $515 per period, 2 periods, and an interest rate of 17.5 percent.

5. Find the future value of an annuity due at $t = 5$ with a payment of $55 per period, 5 periods, and an interest rate of 7.5 percent.
6. Find the future value of an annuity due at $t = 4$ with a payment of $20 per period, 4 periods, and an interest rate of 10.5 percent.
7. Find the present value of an annuity due with a payment of $55 per period, 5 periods, and an interest rate of 7.5 percent.
8. Find the present value of an annuity due with a payment of $515 per period, 2 periods, and an interest rate of 17.5 percent.
9. Calculate the present value of an annuity factor for 3 periods and an interest rate of 13.5 percent.
10. Calculate the future value of an annuity factor for 4 periods and an interest rate of 9.5 percent.
11. Would you prefer to make 4 annual payments of $100 or 5 annual payments of $85 if the interest rate is 12 percent?
12. Would you prefer to receive 4 annual payments of $100 or 5 annual payments of $85 if the interest rate is 12 percent?
13. Your life insurance agent offers you an annuity of $1,000 that you will receive every year for the next 12 years if you pay $3,498 now. What interest rate does this imply?
14. Your life insurance agent offers you an annuity of $1,000 to be paid every year for 12 years, but the first payment will be paid 4 years from today. If the interest rate is 7 percent, how much should this annuity cost today?
15. You received $100,000 as a signing bonus from your first employer. You plan to use this money to buy a 20-year annuity at a rate of 12 percent. How much will you receive each year?
16. For the same $100,000 with an interest rate of 12 percent, how long will your annuity run if you require $20,000 per year as your payment?
17. Consider the following cash flows:

Year	Cash Flow
1	$1,500
2	$ 900
3	$ 600
4	$ 600

Find the present value of this cash flow stream, assuming an interest rate of 8 percent.
18. A financial instrument with 10 years until maturity pays an annual cash flow of $90 and, in addition, pays $1,000 at maturity. What is the present value of the financial instrument if the interest rate is 11 percent?
19. A financial instrument with 10 years and 1 minute until maturity pays a cash flow at maturity of $1,000 and, in addition, pays an annual cash flow of $90, the

first to be paid 1 minute from now. What is the present value of the financial instrument if the interest rate is 11 percent?

20. If you put $2,000 every year in your savings account earning 12 percent each year, how long will it be before you have $50,000?

21. If you put $2,000 in your savings account every year and it earns 8 percent each year, how long will it be before you have $50,000?

22. Congratulations, you have just won $10 million in the lottery! However, the actual payment will be made in 20 equal annual installments, the first one to be received immediately. In present value terms, how much have you really won, assuming that you can earn 7 percent per year on your money?

23. Continuing with the lottery problem, suppose the lottery organization can invest its funds at an annual rate of 12 percent. How much money must the lottery set aside in order to pay your prize? In other words, how much money does the $10 million prize really cost them?

24. Jose Cangordo, a famous baseball player, has just signed a five-year contract for a total of $25 million. Cangordo will receive equal annual payments, starting one year from now. Included in the total figure is an immediate signing bonus of $2 million. If he can earn 10 percent on his money, how much is this deal worth today?

25. If you save 10 percent of your salary every year, and your salary increases by 6 percent annually, how many times your current salary will you have at the end of 20 years? Assume that you earn 8 percent annual interest over the entire period.

26. You currently have $20,000 in your savings account. One year from today you withdraw $2,000. Each year thereafter you withdraw 5 percent more than the previous year, for a total of 10 withdrawals. How much money is left in the savings account just after the final withdrawal? Assume a 10 percent interest rate.

27. By constructing a table, called an amortization schedule, determine the amount of interest and principal you will pay if you take out a $2,500 loan with your friendly banker. The annual interest rate on the loan is 15 percent, and it should be paid in four equal annual installments.

28. If you pay $300 per month on a loan with a 12 percent nominal annual interest rate, how many dollars of the very last installment go to pay the principal?

29. You make equal annual payments on a loan. If the interest portion of your last payment is one fifth of the entire payment, what is the interest rate on the loan?

30. Find an expression for the present value today of a perpetuity paying C each year, starting n years from today, if the discount rate is r percent.

31. Carmen Fleure wants to be remembered as a charitable person. To that effect, she wants to build a trust account by depositing $10,000 each year for the next few years, starting one year from now. The account is to pay $10,000 to charity in perpetuity, starting one year after her last annual contribution. Show that the only way in which this can be done is if the interest rate on the account (r) and the number of deposits she makes (n) are related as follows: $(1 + r)^n = 2$.

32. A gold mine is being depleted in such a way that the cash flow it generates each year is 4 percent lower than the previous year. If the mine is expected to generate $200,000 next year, how much is this mine worth today? Assume an interest rate of 13 percent.

33. Find an expression for the present value of a growing perpetuity with the first cash flow occurring n years from today.

34. A perpetual subscription to Newstimes magazine costs $250 (such subscriptions have actually been offered by some magazines in the past). A yearly subscription costs only $25. Whichever route you choose, you will subscribe immediately. If you are indifferent between the two alternatives, what is your annual rate of interest? Disregard inflation.

35. Insulating your home costs $5,000. On the other hand, insulating will save you 200 kilowatt-hours (kwh) of energy each month. Each kwh currently costs $0.10, but the cost per kwh is rising each month. If you earn 1 percent per month on your money, what is the minimum monthly inflation rate that makes insulating a smart investment? Assume the savings from insulating last forever.

36. A car dealer offers 0 percent financing on a new car with a price tag of $15,000. However, a down payment is required, and you must pay in 24 equal monthly payments. If the dealer can normally earn 1 percent per month on its money, how much down payment is needed so that the 0 percent financing gimmick is equivalent to a cash discount of $1,000 on the car?

37. Show that the present value of a growing perpetuity grows at the same rate as the cash flow growth rate, g. In other words, show that $PV_t = PV_{t-1} \times (1 + g)$.

Chapter 4

Bond Valuation

OVERVIEW

This chapter explains the most important kinds of bonds and their differences. When firms issue bonds, they make promises to the bondholders. The kinds of promises the firm makes affect the cost of borrowing from the bondholders.

The main concern for the corporation issuing the bond is to raise the funds with the lowest interest cost. To do this, the manager must understand how the market values bonds. This chapter applies the time value of money principles to the valuation of bonds. Because issuing a bond involves the promise to make a series of payments, present value techniques play a crucial role in bond valuation.

CORPORATE BONDS

Every corporate bond issuance includes an agreement between the issuing firm and the investor. The bond contract, or **bond indenture**, is a legal document that states the promises made by the issuer of a bond and the rights of the bondholders. The **trustee** for a bond issue protects the rights of the bondholders and monitors the performance of the issuer to assure that the issuer keeps its promises. The trustee is usually a bank and must be financially independent of the issuer. In addition to specifying the amount and timing of payments to the bondholders, the bond indenture also contains covenants. The **bond covenants** define the security that the issuer offers for the bonds and specifies how the issuer will retire the bonds.

Some issuing corporations offer bonds backed by mortgages on specific assets. For example, an issuer could offer a production plant as security for a bond issue. If the issuer defaults, the trustee can seize the mortgaged assets to recoup the investment of the bondholders. Such bonds may either be first mortgage bonds or have some inferior status, such as second or third mortgages. A **first mortgage bond** gives the bondholders first claim on the assets specified in the mortgage. In case of default, those assets provide funds to repay the bondholders. The first mortgage is the safest security available to bondholders.

A firm without enough physical assets to offer as security may pledge financial assets to secure the bond issue. Bonds secured by financial assets are called **collateral trust bonds**. Most corporate bonds, however, are not backed by any collateral. A bond with no specific pledge of particular assets is a **debenture**. Financially strong corporations often issue debentures instead of mortgage bonds. In addition to straight debentures, some firms issue **subordinated debentures**. These bonds are unsecured and have an inferior claim relative to other outstanding debentures.

The priority of claims, from highest to lowest, among the major securities of corporations is as follows: first mortgage bonds, second mortgage bonds, debentures, subordinated debentures, preferred stock, and common stock. First mortgage bondholders have the strongest claim on the assets, and debenture holders have the weakest. Common stockholders have the riskiest position. Typically, the weakest securities carry the highest rate of return. Without any specific security pledged to them, debentures may seem to be a very risky investment. However, this risk is controlled for both mortgage bonds and debentures through protective covenants that restrict the behavior of the issuer. For example, a covenant might require that the issuer maintain a minimal amount of cash. Another covenant might constrain dividend payments to common stockholders. These restrictions enhance the safety of the bond investment.

The bond contract also specifies how the issuer will retire the bond. There are many ways to pay off a bond, and many bonds are callable. The issuer of a **callable bond** has the option to call the bonds before maturity and repay them at a price the bond contract stipulates. Issuers have an incentive to call their bonds if the current interest rate in the market is sufficiently lower than the bond's coupon rate. Usually the issuer cannot call the bond for a certain period, say five years, after issue. Also, the price the issuer must pay to call the bond, the **call price**, usually gives a premium over the bond's par value to the bondholder.

Firms often retire callable bonds by using a sinking fund. The **sinking fund** provision of a bond contract provides for the orderly partial retirement of bonds before the maturity date. The sinking fund may operate in two basic ways. First, the trustee may use the resources of the sinking fund to buy bonds in the open market. Alternatively, the sinking fund may provide for retirement of a specific portion of the bonds on a certain date. The bonds to be retired are usually chosen at random.

Bondholders are told which bonds will be redeemed through a **notice of redemption**. This notice requires bondholders to surrender certain bonds in return for payment by the issuer. The accrual of interest on the selected bonds ceases on the redemption date. Some bond contracts schedule retirement of specific portions of the bond issue for predetermined dates. These bonds are **serial bonds**. This procedure allows the choice of the maturity date that best fits the investor's planning horizon. Another way to retire bonds is through conversion. A **convertible bond** gives the bondholder the option to exchange each bond for a specified number of shares of common stock.

BOND VALUATION

Firms issue bonds either as pure discount bonds or as coupon bonds. A **pure discount bond**, also known as **zero coupon bond** or simply **zero**, is a bond that makes no intermediate payments between its issue date and its maturity date. A **coupon bond** makes a series of equal periodic coupon payments throughout its life.

Pure Discount Bonds

A pure discount bond promises to pay a certain amount on its maturity date. The promised future payment is the **par value**, or **face value**, of the bond. The difference between the par value and the current selling price is the **bond discount**.

The price of any financial asset is always equal to the present value of all the future cash flows generated by the asset. Since a zero coupon bond generates only one future cash flow equal to its face value, its price (P) is the present value of the bond's face value (F). Figure 4.1 presents the cash flows for a pure discount bond. If the face value is to be received n years from now and investors require an annual rate of return of r percent on this bond, then the price of a pure discount bond is:

$$P = \frac{F}{(1 + r)^n} \qquad (4.1)$$

As an example, consider a pure discount bond that matures in five years and has a face value of $1,000. If the bond has an interest rate of 12 percent, then from equation 4.1 its price is $567.43, as shown below:

$$P = \frac{\$1,000}{(1.12)^5} = \$567.43$$

The Discount Yield

Money market securities are short-term securities that typically pay only at maturity. In this sense, they are financially equivalent to pure discount bonds. Many money market securities are quoted in terms of their "discount yield." Given this discount yield, the investor must calculate the dollar price of the money market instrument. The formula for the discount yield, d, is:

$$d = \frac{D}{F} \times \frac{360}{t} \qquad (4.2)$$

where: D = the dollar discount from the face value
F = the face value of the financial instrument
t = the number of days until the instrument matures

FIGURE 4.1
Cash Flows for a Pure Discount Bond

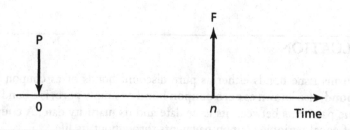

The first ratio in the discount yield formula given in equation 4.2 is the instrument's percentage discount from its face value. This ratio gives a measure of the rate of return the investor will get over the t days of the instrument's remaining life. The second ratio calculates the number of times that t days fit in 360 days (historically used as the "commercial" year). Multiplying the two ratios gives an annualized rate of return on the discount instrument. For example, if the face value is $F = \$100,000$, the dollar discount is $D = \$3,000$, and the discount instrument matures in 90 days, then from equation 4.2 the discount yield is:

$$d = \frac{\$3,000}{\$100,000} \times \frac{360}{90}$$

$$= 3\% \times 4 = 12\%$$

The actual dollar price, P, of the discount instrument depends on the face value and the amount of the dollar discount, D. The expression for D can be obtained from the discount yield formula. Since the price is $P = F - D$, the expression for the price of the instrument in terms of its discount yield, face value, and time to maturity is:

$$P = F\left(1 - \frac{d \times t}{360}\right) \tag{4.3}$$

Since money market instruments are quoted in terms of their discount yield, equation 4.3 can be used to calculate the price an investor must pay for the instrument. In our example of a 90-day money market instrument with a face value of $100,000 and a discount yield of 12 percent, the price of the instrument is:

$$P = \$100,000\left(1 - \frac{0.12 \times 90}{360}\right) = \$97,000$$

Although the discount yield is used extensively in the money market, it has several conceptual problems. First, it calculates the discount for each dollar of face value, instead of each dollar of the price paid by the instrument's buyer. In our example, the discount yield formula states that over a 90-day period the purchaser of the instrument receives a rate of return of $3,000/$100,000 = 3 percent, when in fact the investor receives a rate of return of $3,000/$97,000 = 3.09 percent on the $97,000 investment. Second, the discount yield formula assumes a year of 360 days, rather than 365 days.[1] Third, the discount yield disregards the time value of money, since equation 4.2 simply multiplies the t-day rate of return by the number of t-day periods in a year, without compounding it. As a result, the discount yield may differ considerably from the true yield of the instrument.

The first two problems associated with the discount yield are easily solved using an alternative expression known as the **equivalent bond yield** (EBY) formula:

$$\text{EBY} = \frac{D}{P} \times \frac{365}{t} \tag{4.4}$$

---

[1] Obviously, we are neglecting leap years. For you purists out there, the solar year has 365.242199 days, but who's counting?

By using equations 4.2 and 4.3 to solve for D and P, respectively, and substituting in equation 4.4, an equivalent expression is obtained for the equivalent bond yield in terms of the discount yield and the number of days to maturity:

$$EBY = \frac{365d}{360 - d \times t} \tag{4.5}$$

For the 90-day instrument example, the EBY using equation 4.5 is:

$$EBY = \frac{365 \times 0.12}{360 - 0.12 \times 90}$$

$$= 12.54 \text{ percent}$$

Of course, the same result would be obtained by using equation 4.4. Notice that the equivalent bond yield, while solving the first two problems discussed earlier, still disregards the time value of money, as equation 4.4 shows. Nevertheless, the EBY is closer to the true rate of return of the discount instrument than the discount yield.

The true annualized yield to maturity, r, that an investor receives when paying P today for a discount instrument that promises to pay F in t days can be found from the following general expression:

$$P(1 + r)^{\frac{t}{365}} = F \tag{4.6}$$

Equation 4.6 can be solved for r and be expressed in terms of the discount yield d and the number of days to maturity t. The resulting expression is:

$$r = \left(\frac{1}{1 - \frac{d \times t}{360}}\right)^{\frac{365}{t}} - 1 \tag{4.7}$$

For the 90-day pure discount instrument with a face value of $100,000 and a price of $97,000, the true annualized yield to maturity may be found directly by using equation 4.6 and solving for r:

$$\$97,000(1 + r)^{\frac{90}{365}} = \$100,000$$

$$r = \left(\frac{\$100,000}{\$97,000}\right)^{\frac{365}{90}} - 1$$

$$= 13.15\%$$

Thus, the true annualized yield to maturity is over one percentage point higher than the discount yield. This large difference is not unusual.

Coupon Bonds

Most corporate bonds are coupon bonds. Typically, these bonds make coupon payments semiannually and also pay the face value at maturity. However, since the semiannual payment of coupons makes the valuation of coupon bonds more cumbersome without adding any conceptual insight, we simplify by assuming that the coupon payments are annual, unless otherwise stated. Assume that the annual coupon is C and that the bond matures n years from now. Also assume that investors require a rate of return of r percent per year on the bond. Then, the price of the coupon bond is found by recalling that it must equal the sum of the present values of all the payments that the bond will make. This means that the price of the coupon bond is given by:

$$P = \frac{C}{(1 + r)} + \frac{C}{(1 + r)^2} + \cdots + \frac{C}{(1 + r)^n} + \frac{F}{(1 + r)^n}$$

Figure 4.2 shows the cash flow stream for coupon bonds and suggests that we can divide the promised payments on a coupon bond into two parts. First, the bond promises a series of n equal periodic coupon payments. Therefore, the coupon stream is an annuity. Second, the bond pays the par or face value at time n when the bond matures. We will assume a face value of $1,000, unless otherwise stated. Using the time value of money techniques, we can express the price of a coupon bond as follows:

$$P = C \times PA(r, n) + F(1 + r)^{-n} \tag{4.8}$$

EXAMPLE 1

Find the price of a newly issued 30-year coupon bond with a face value of $1,000 and an annual coupon payment of $80.

This bond promises 30 annual coupon payments of $80 and a $1,000 payment at the end of 30 years. Using the bond pricing formula in equation 4.8, we have:

$$P = \$80 \times PA(10\%, 30) + \$1,000(1 + 0.10)^{-30}$$
$$= \$754.15 + \$57.31$$
$$= \$811.46$$

When dealing with coupon bonds, we frequently refer to the **coupon rate** (CR). The coupon rate is the annual coupon payment for each dollar of face value. Thus, the coupon rate is given by:

FIGURE 4.2
Cash Flows for a Coupon Bond

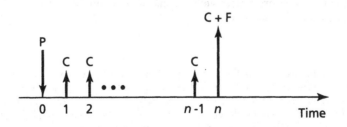

$$CR = \frac{C}{F} \qquad (4.9)$$

A related definition is the **current yield** (CY). The current yield of a coupon bond is the annual coupon payment for each dollar of the bond's current price:

$$CY = \frac{C}{P} \qquad (4.10)$$

Perhaps the most widely used measure for bonds is the **yield to maturity** (YTM). The yield to maturity of a bond is the discount rate that equates the present value of all the future payments of the bond to its current price. We can think of the yield to maturity as the annual rate of return that investors would earn if the bond were held to maturity. In other words, the YTM is r in the bond pricing formula of equation 4.8.

The Approximate Yield to Maturity Formula

Suppose we know the bond's price, coupon payments, face value, and maturity, and want to compute the bond's yield to maturity. Unfortunately, it is impossible to find a general formula for the yield to maturity of coupon bonds. Of course, we can always use a financial calculator to find the exact YTM of a bond. Because a general formula does not exist, all calculators rely on trial-and-error methods. Many such methods need a starting guess, obtained from an approximate YTM formula such as the one following. The formula is useful when programming a computer to calculate the exact YTM by iteration. The approximate yield to maturity formula is:

$$YTM \approx \frac{C + \frac{(F - P)}{n}}{\frac{(F + 2P)}{3}} \qquad (4.11)$$

EXAMPLE 2 _____

To evaluate the performance of the approximate YTM formula, consider a bond maturing in five years and paying a 10 percent annual coupon with a face value of $1,000. If the bond has a price of $1,059.12, its yield to maturity is exactly 8.50 percent. The approximate yield to maturity formula, equation 4.11, gives a close estimate of 8.48 percent:[2]

---

[2] Prior to the recent availability of this approximate formula, a similar formula was traditionally used. The only difference between the traditional yield approximation formula and the one given here is that the denominator of the traditional formula is $(F + P)/2$, rather than $(F + 2P)/3$. You can verify that the traditional formula gives a YTM of 8.56 percent for the example. The result of this example is typical, in that equation 4.11 provides a better estimate of the YTM in most realistic cases.

$$YTM \approx \frac{\$100 + \dfrac{(\$1,000 - \$1,059.12)}{5}}{\dfrac{(\$1,000 + 2 \times \$1,059.12)}{3}}$$

$$= \frac{\$100 - \$11.82}{\$1,039.41}$$

$$= 8.48\%$$

Important Bond Relationships

We can distinguish among bonds according to their price. For example, a **par bond** is a bond with a current market price equal to its face value, so for a par bond we have $P = F$. Most bonds sell at or near par value when they are issued. A **premium bond** is a bond with a current price exceeding its face value. A **discount bond**, on the contrary, is one that currently sells for less than its face value.

There is a set of useful relationships among the price of a bond, its coupon rate, and its yield to maturity. These relationships are:

If YTM > CR, then P < F

If YTM = CR, then P = F

If YTM < CR, then P > F

As an example, suppose that a bond has a coupon rate of 12 percent and a yield to maturity of 14 percent. Then, the first of these relationships tells us that the bond must sell at a discount. It should be noted that the relationships work in both directions. Thus, if a bond is selling for $900 and has a coupon rate of 12 percent, then the above relationships state that the bond's yield to maturity must be greater than 12 percent. While the inequalities don't give us the exact value of, say, the yield to maturity, they provide us with a quick estimate and may serve to check our results. Of special importance is the equality relationship, since it immediately tells us that if the bond is selling at par, we can be sure that the yield to maturity is identical to the coupon rate, without performing any calculation whatsoever. Notice that none of the three relationships requires knowledge of the bond's time to maturity, n; that is, they are always true regardless of the bond's maturity.

There is a corresponding, but better, set of relationships that compares the yield to maturity with the bond's current yield, as shown below:

If YTM > CY then P < F

If YTM = CY then P = F

If YTM < CY then P > F

The relationships using the current yield provide better information than the ones using the coupon rate. To see this, consider the example of the bond selling for $900 with a coupon rate of 12 percent. Using the first set of relationships we saw that the yield to maturity of this bond must be greater than 12 percent. With the latter set of relationships, we can say that the yield to maturity has to be greater than the bond's current yield; that is, we must have YTM > 13.33 percent ($120/$900). While both relationships are true, the one using the current yield is obviously closer to the true yield to maturity. The relationship between the yield to maturity, the coupon rate, and the current yield for premium, par, and discount bonds is shown in figure 4.3.

EXAMPLE 3

A ten-year, 10 percent coupon bond is currently selling for $800. Find the current yield and the exact YTM.

Since the coupon rate is 10 percent, the annual coupon payments are $100 (0.10 × $1,000). The current yield is then $100/$800 = 12.5 percent. Because the bond sells at a discount, we know that the YTM will be greater than the coupon rate of 10 percent. In fact, it will be greater than the current yield of 12.5 percent. Using a financial calculator we can see that the exact YTM is 13.81 percent. We verify that for this discount bond: CR < CY < YTM (10% < 12.5% < 13.81%), in agreement with figure 4.3.

Bond Risk, Bond Maturity, and the Cost of Debt

Corporations may sometimes fail to pay their financial obligations; therefore, bond investors are concerned with the chance that the issuing firm will not make its promised payments on a given bond. To aid bond investors in this task, there are services that rate the quality of bonds from different issuers.

FIGURE 4.3
Relationship Among the Coupon Rate, Current Yield, and Yield to Maturity

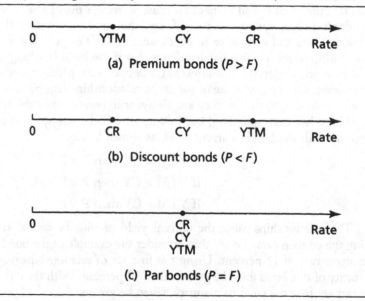

The ratings attempt to measure **default risk** – the chance that the issuer will defer or skip one or more payments on the bond. Table 4.1 shows the ratings systems of the two principal rating services, Moody's and Standard & Poor's. These two ratings systems follow each other very closely, with Standard & Poor's being quoted more often.

The cost of debt for a firm depends largely, but not exclusively, on its default risk. Other economic factors beyond the firm's control are important also. Higher risk bonds must pay a higher rate of interest, other things being equal. The differences in yields due solely to differences in default risk define the **risk structure of interest rates**.

The maturity of the bond may also affect the cost of debt. At any given moment, two bonds that are identical, except for their maturities, can have different yields. The **yield curve** is the graph of the relationship between yield and maturity for bonds that are similar in other respects. Yield curves have an upward slope when long maturity bonds have higher yields than short maturity bonds. Sometimes the yield curve may slope downward. In this case, short maturity bonds have higher interest rates. Another name for this relationship between maturity and yield is the **term structure of interest rates**.

THE YIELD CURVE AND FORWARD RATES

As discussed in the previous section, the yield curve may be flat, upward, or downward sloping. A **spot rate** is a yield prevailing at a given moment in time on a security. **Forward rates** of interest are rates for future time periods that are implied by currently available spot rates. From the yield curve, the analyst can infer implicit forward rates. Given a set of spot rates, we can calculate forward rates for any intervening time period.

Let us introduce the notation that a yield expressed as $r_{x,y}$ is the rate corresponding to the period beginning at time x and ending at time y. The present is always time $t = 0$. Therefore, a bond yield covering any time span beginning at time $t = 0$ is a spot rate. For example, $r_{0,5}$ would be the spot rate covering the period beginning now and ending five

TABLE 4.1
Bond Rating Categories

Moody's	Standard & Poor's
Aaa	AAA
Aa	AA
A	A
Baa	BBB
Ba	BB
B	B
	CCC-CC
Caa	
	C
Ca	
	DDD-D
C	

years from now. If the time covered by a particular rate begins after time $t = 0$, it is a forward rate. Thus, the forward rate covering a period beginning two years from now and extending three years to time $t = 5$ would be $r_{2,5}$ in our notation.

Forward rates are calculated on the assumption that returns over a given period of time are all equal, no matter which maturities of bonds are held over that span of time. Taking a five-year period as an example, this principle implies that we can compute forward rates by assuming that all of the following strategies earn the same return over the five years:

- Buy the five-year bond and hold it to maturity.
- Buy a one-year bond and, when it matures, buy more one-year bonds, following this procedure for the entire five years.
- Buy a two-year bond and, when it matures, buy three-year bonds and hold them to maturity.

According to the principle of calculation, holding bonds of any maturity over this five-year period must give the investor the same return. In our notation, we can express these three strategies as follows:

1. Hold a five-year bond for five years:
   total return $= (1 + r_{0,5})^5$
2. Hold a sequence of one-year bonds:
   total return $= (1 + r_{0,1})(1 + r_{1,2})(1 + r_{2,3})(1 + r_{3,4})(1 + r_{4,5})$
3. Hold a two-year bond followed by a three-year bond:
   total return $= (1 + r_{0,2})^2(1 + r_{2,5})^3$

As an example, assume we have the following spot rates:

$r_{0,1}$	$r_{0,2}$	$r_{0,3}$	$r_{0,4}$	$r_{0,5}$
0.080	0.088	0.090	0.093	0.095

This set of spot rates implies a number of forward rates to cover periods ranging from time $t = 1$ to $t = 5$. An investor with a five-year horizon might hold a five-year bond, with a yield of 9.5 percent. However, there are various alternative ways of holding a bond investment over the same time period. As an example of how to calculate forward rates, consider the third strategy above in which the investor holds a two-year bond followed by holding three-year bonds. Right now, at $t = 0$, we cannot know what the yield will be on the three-year bond to cover the time period from $t = 2$ to $t = 5$. At time $t = 0$, however, we can calculate a forward rate to cover the time span from time $t = 2$ to $t = 5$. The principle of calculation implies:

$$(1 + r_{0,5})^5 = (1 + r_{0,2})^2(1 + r_{2,5})^3$$

Using the spot rates given above, we have:

$$(1.095)^5 = (1.088)^2(1 + r_{2,5})^3$$

Since the only unknown is the forward rate, we can solve the equation to find $r_{2,5} = 0.0997$, or 9.97 percent.

Notice that nothing has been said about how the forward rates are to be interpreted. There are various theories of the term structure that interpret forward rates differently. However, all of the theories agree that forward rates give important information about the future course of interest rates.

CORPORATE BOND QUOTATIONS

The Wall Street Journal quotes New York Exchange Bonds, as figure 4.4 shows. The left column identifies the issuer of the bond. The second column shows the current yield on the bond. The next column shows the day's trading volume expressed as the number of bonds. Because most corporate bonds have a face value of $1,000, the volume figure gives a quick guide to the dollar volume of trading. The next three columns give the high, low, and closing prices for the trading in each bond, quoted as a percentage of par. For example, consider a bond with $1,000 face value and a price quoted as 80–3/8. The actual dollar price would be 80.375 percent of the $1,000 par value, or $803.75. The final column shows the change in the price from the preceding day's close to the current day's close.

SUMMARY

This chapter explored the characteristics and valuation of corporate bonds. When a firm needs a large amount of money or needs a very long commitment of funds, corporate bonds provide a useful financing vehicle. Maturities of 30 years are common, and the size of the bond issue can be very large. There are many different types of corporate bonds, ranging from first mortgage bonds which give the bondholders a claim on specific assets, to debentures, which the firm issues without any security.

In addition to differences in the security that bonds offer, they also have different payment structures. For example, zero coupon bonds, as the name implies, make no coupon payments. By contrast, most corporate bonds have regularly scheduled coupon payments. With callable bonds, the firm retains the option of redeeming the bonds. With convertible bonds, the bondholder has the option of converting the bonds into the common stock of the issuing firm. With both callable and convertible bonds, the redemption options are subject to certain restrictions stated in the bond covenants.

QUESTIONS

1. Why is a firm willing to place restrictions on its behavior through the bond contract?
2. If you were a prospective bond purchaser, what special kinds of restrictions not discussed in the text might you want to include in the bond indenture?
3. Is the right to call a bond a valuable right? Does the bondholder get paid for giving this right to the bond issuer? If so, how is this possible?

FIGURE 4.4
Corporate Bond Quotations

NEW YORK EXCHANGE BONDS

Quotations as of 4 p.m. Eastern Time
Tuesday, March 28, 1995

Volume $34,544,000

	Domestic		All Issues	
	Tue.	Mon.	Tue.	Mon.
Issues traded	376	350	385	359
Advances	136	197	141	204
Declines	164	86	167	87
Unchanged	76	67	77	68
New highs	9	11	9	11
New lows	2	3	2	3

SALES SINCE JANUARY 1
(000 omitted)

1995	1994	1993
$1,794,277	$2,004,852	$2,792,001

Dow Jones Bond Averages

–1994–		–1995–				---1995---			---1994--	
High	Low	High	Low			Close	Chg.	%Yld	Close	Chg.
105.61	93.56	98.06	93.63	20 Bonds		97.72	–0.34	7.57	101.19	–0.37
103.43	88.99	93.88	89.08	10 Utilities		93.51	–0.37	8.02	99.11	–0.42
107.93	97.93	102.25	98.08	10 Industrials		101.93	–0.32	7.11	103.28	–0.32

Source: *The Wall Street Journal*, March 29, 1995.

4. Coupon bonds may sell for more than their face value, whereas this is impossible for pure discount bonds. Why?

5. Explain the rationale behind the discount yield formula, equation 4.2.

6. Derive the true annual yield to maturity formula, equation 4.7 (Hint: solve for r in equation 4.6, and make use of equation 4.2 when appropriate.)

7. Explain why, over a two-year period, two one-year investments should give the same total return as a single investment that matures in two years.

8. If you knew the yields on a 5-year Treasury bond and a 15-year bond issued by an electric utility company, what could you tell about the term structure or the risk structure of interest rates from this information?

9. Two bonds are identical in all respects, except in their maturities. Each bond's coupon rate also happens to be equal to its yield to maturity. A friend of yours reasons that the bond with the larger maturity must have the greater price, simply because it will provide more coupon payments. What do you think?

10. Under what circumstances will the approximate yield to maturity formula give the exact YTM?

PROBLEMS

1. Consider a five-year pure discount bond with a face value of $1,000 that yields 10 percent compounded annually. What is its current price?

2. What will be the price of a five-year pure discount bond that pays $1,000 at maturity if interest rates suddenly rise to 11 percent?

3. What will be the price of a five-year pure discount bond that pays $1,000 at maturity if interest rates suddenly fall to 9 percent?

4. What is the price of a three-year 8 percent annual coupon bond yielding 11 percent and having a face value of $1,000?

5. For the bond of the previous problem, assume that interest rates suddenly rise to 13 percent. Compute the new price of the bond.

6. What is the price of a pure discount bond maturing in three years if the interest rate is 25 percent and the bond has a face value of $100,000?

7. A pure discount bond with a $1,000 face value and maturing in ten years is currently selling for $463.19. What will be its price in five years if interest rates do not change?

8. A pure discount bond with a $1,000 face value and maturing in five years is currently selling for $620.92. What was its price five years ago if interest rates have not changed?

9. A bond pays a coupon of 12 percent per annum on a face value of $1,000 and matures in three years. If it has a yield of 15 percent, what is its price?

10. A bond pays a coupon of 12 percent per annum on a face value of $1,000 and matures in three years. If it has a yield of 9 percent, what is its price?

11. A bond pays a coupon of 12 percent per annum on a face value of $1,000 and matures in three years. If it has a yield of 12 percent, what is its price?

12. Considering the last three problems, what can you say about the relationship between bond prices and bond yields? Be specific.

13. A bond with a coupon rate of 10 percent is currently selling at par. Find the bond's yield to maturity.

14. A bond with a current yield of 10 percent is currently selling at par. Find the bond's yield to maturity.

15. A bond with annual coupon payments of $120 has a yield to maturity of 12 percent. Find the bond's price.

16. A bond with annual coupon payments of $120 has a current yield of 12 percent. Find the bond's price.

17. If a bond sells at \$975 and has a coupon rate of 8 percent, what is the most you can say about the bond's yield to maturity? (For example, you might be able to say that the YTM of the bond is less than 40 percent.)

18. If a bond sells at \$1,200 and has a coupon rate of 11 percent, what is the most you can say about the bond's yield to maturity?

19. If a bond sells at \$1,000 and has a coupon rate of 15 percent, what is the most you can say about the bond's yield to maturity?

20. If the one-year spot rate is 8 percent and the two-year spot rate is 11 percent, what is the implicit forward rate between years 1 and 2?

21. If the one-year spot rate is 12 percent and the two-year spot rate is 7 percent, what is the implicit forward rate between years 1 and 2?

22. If the one-year spot rate is 10 percent and the two-year spot rate is 10 percent, what is the implicit forward rate between years 1 and 2?

23. Use the fact that forward rates, like any interest rate, must be positive, to show that the two-year discount factor must always be less than the one-year discount factor. In other words, show that $(1 + r_{0,2})^{-2} < (1 + r_{0,1})^{-1}$.

Chapter 5

Stock Valuation

OVERVIEW

This chapter covers the second major source of long-term funds for the corporation – financing with preferred and common stock. Preferred stock is a hybrid security, sharing features of both bonds and common stock. Common stock represents an ownership position in the firm.

This chapter begins with a discussion of preferred stock and then turns to a detailed consideration of common stock. The chapter concludes with a brief discussion of the relationship between the risk an investor bears with different securities and the return the firm must expect to pay for long-term financing.

PREFERRED STOCK

Firms usually issue preferred stock with a stated par value and promise to periodically pay a percentage of the par value as dividends. With a $100 par value and a 6 percent dividend, for example, the annual dividend on a share of preferred stock would be $6.

In many respects, the dividend on a preferred stock is similar to the coupon payment of a corporate bond. There are, however, important differences between preferred stock and corporate bonds. First, preferred stock never matures, so the purchaser is not promised a return of the par value by the issuing firm. Second, unlike a corporate bond, missing a scheduled payment on preferred stock does not put the firm in default.

Most preferred stock is cumulative. With **cumulative preferred stock**, if the firm omits any dividend, it must pay it later. In fact, the agreement between the firm and the preferred stockholders typically requires that it pay no dividends to the common stockholders until it makes all late payments to the preferred stockholders.

This cumulative feature of preferred dividends partially protects the preferred stockholders against missed payments. If a firm must temporarily suspend dividend payments to the cumulative preferred stockholder, it may make those payments later.

Like most coupon bonds, some preferred stocks are callable. The issuing firm can require the preferred stockholders to surrender their shares in exchange for a cash payment, the amount of which is the **call price**. The agreement between the preferred stockholders and the firm specifies what the call price will be.

Usually, preferred stockholders, like bondholders, cannot vote to determine corporate policy. By contrast, common stockholders have the right to vote on many important decisions. On occasion, the contract between the preferred stockholders and the firm allows the preferred stockholders to vote, but usually only when the firm is in serious financial difficulty.

Advantages and Disadvantages of Financing with Preferred Stock

Probably the greatest advantage of financing with preferred stock is flexibility. The firm may miss or delay a preferred dividend payment without being technically bankrupt. At worst, it has to make up such missed payments before it can pay dividends to its common stockholders. The second major advantage is that the firm can secure financing without surrendering voting control in the firm. Therefore, preferred stock both provides freedom from worry over bankruptcy when the firm misses a dividend, and maintains control of the firm for the common shareholders. These two features explain the attractions of preferred stock from the firm's perspective.

Preferred stock also has certain disadvantages. Interest payments on a bond come from the firm's before-tax income, thus lowering the firm's tax burden. Dividend payments to preferred stockholders come from the firm's after-tax earnings. This is a very important distinction, because it affects the actual after-tax cost of the two financing methods.

To see the importance of before-tax versus after-tax payments, consider a firm in the 34 percent tax bracket that must pay $1,000 interest to its bondholders and $1,000 in dividends to its preferred stockholders. The amount of before-tax earnings necessary to cover these two payments is very different. To make a $1,000 interest payment takes only $1,000 of before-tax earnings, because the interest expense is deductible for tax purposes. For the preferred stock, the firm must pay taxes on all earnings before paying the $1,000 in dividends. To generate $1,000 on an after-tax basis, the firm must have $1,515 = 1,000/ (1 − 0.34) in before-tax earnings. After the government takes its 34 percent tax, the firm has the $1,000 it will pay to the preferred stockholders. Therefore, the firm must weigh the advantage of the flexibility of preferred stock financing against its potentially higher cost.

The Valuation of Preferred Stock

As we know, the price of any security must equal the present value of all future cash flows that the security generates. Because the preferred stock is scheduled to make equal periodic payments forever, we may value it as a perpetuity.[1] If D is the dividend payment from the preferred share, and r is the appropriate discount rate, then the price P of the preferred share is:

$$P = \frac{D}{r} \tag{5.1}$$

EXAMPLE 1

Consider a share of preferred stock with a par value of $100 that pays an 8 percent annual dividend, or $8. If the discount rate for this share is 12 percent, the preferred stock would be worth:

---

[1] The valuation of perpetuities was discussed in chapter 3.

$$P = \frac{\$8}{0.12} = \$66.67$$

COMMON STOCK

Of the three major types of long-term financing – debt, preferred stock, and common stock – common stock is the most basic. No corporation can exist without common stock because it represents ownership interest. The firm's management bears the responsibility of advancing the interests of the common stockholders. This means that financial managers should maximize the price of the firm's common stock.

The owner of a share of common stock receives dividends, usually quarterly, as a compensation for investing in the firm. Like preferred stock, common stock never matures. In principle, a firm could continue in business forever, and shareholders could receive dividends forever. Dividends play a key role in determining the value of the shares of common stock. No law compels firms to pay dividends to common stockholders, however, and many firms, particularly new ones and those in financial distress, do not.

BENEFITS AND COSTS OF COMMON STOCK OWNERSHIP

Common stock has a **residual claim** on the assets and proceeds of the firm. The claim is residual because it is based on the value of the firm after satisfying all other claimants. For example, bondholders receive their promised payments before stockholders receive theirs. Although stockholders may be last in line to enforce their claims, they can justifiably claim everything that remains in the firm, once the firm meets the demands of all other claimants, including bondholders, employees, suppliers, and the government.

Although common stockholders have the riskiest position of all claimants, common stock also has important risk-limiting features. One of these is **limited liability**, which limits the potential losses of stockholders to the funds they have contributed to the firm. Stockholders cannot lose, for example, their home or car if the firm's assets are not sufficient to cover the claims made against it. In addition, common stockholders normally have a right to maintain their percentage of ownership in the corporation. That is, whenever the firm issues new stock, they have the **preemptive right** to buy new shares in proportion to their existing ownership, before any outsiders can buy those shares. For example, a stockholder who owns 5 percent of the old shares has the right to buy as much as 5 percent of the new shares before the firm offers the new shares to outside buyers.

Holders of common stock commit their funds and assume a residual claim on the value of the firm in the hope of securing profits. If they don't intend to sell the shares, the cash dividend is the only cash flow from those shares. Common stockholders also have the right to vote on major matters affecting the firm. Stockholders usually exercise these voting rights at the time of the annual meeting. Typically, however, shareholders vote on issues that management carefully defines with an eye toward securing the desired outcome. For example, management often asks shareholders to vote on new directors for the corporation, recommending its own slate of nominees.

On occasion, however, the right to vote can be very important. For example, stockholders may occasionally select new key management for the firm. In the normal event, management directs the course of most corporate elections. One important tool for doing so is the use of the **proxy** – a statement giving another party the right to vote one's shares. Since many shareholders do not attend the annual meeting to cast their votes, they empower someone else to vote for them by giving them a proxy. On occasion, real disputes arise that cause serious dissension and make voting rights important. Dissident shareholders might try to unseat management or try to change basic managerial policies. To do so, the dissident shareholders solicit proxies to acquire substantial voting power themselves. This leads to a **proxy fight**, the struggle to gain voting rights from shareholders who do not attend the annual meeting.

Some firms classify their common stock as class A and class B. Usually the difference between the two classes of stocks lies in their different voting rights. Normally, holders of class A stock have voting rights and those with class B stock do not. This difference can generate a premium for the price of class A stock.

Sometimes, owners of common stock receive stock dividends or stock splits. These generate no cash flows for the stockholders, so they are much less important than cash dividends. A stock dividend occurs when the firm prints additional shares and gives them to the current shareholders. A stock split is similar. With a **stock dividend**, the firm increases the number of shares by 25 percent or less. With a **stock split**, the percentage share increase is more than 25 percent. Sometimes, firms declare a **reverse stock split**. As the name implies, in a reverse stock split the shareholder ends up with fewer shares than before.

To see how this works, consider a stockholder who owns 100 shares of a stock trading at $80. Suppose the corporation declares a 20 percent stock dividend, after which the stockholder has 120 shares. How much are these new shares worth? Since a stock dividend generates no cash flow, it should not affect the firm's value. The original market value of the 100 shares was $8,000. Since the cash flow of the firm has not been affected by the stock dividend, the new total of 120 shares still has a total value of $8,000, or a price of $66.67. Therefore, the shares should fall in value by an amount proportional to the stock dividend.

In general, the relationship between the stock price before (P_b) and the stock price after (P_a) a stock dividend or a stock split of s percent is:

$$P_a = \frac{P_b}{1 + s} \tag{5.2}$$

We can use equation 5.2 in our example of the 20 percent stock dividend to obtain the same price as we found before:

$$P_a = \frac{\$80}{1 + 0.2} = \$66.67$$

Just as occurs with stock dividends, stock splits do not generate cash flow, so the value of the firm should not be affected. A stock split is usually spoken of as being, say, a two-for-one split; that is, the investor receives two shares to replace each original share. In this case, the share value should decrease by 50 percent just after the stock split.

The number of splits seems to fluctuate dramatically from year to year. There is a tendency for many firms to have very small stock dividends. It is not clear why stock splits and dividends continue to be so popular; roughly 8 to 10 percent of the firms listed on the New York Stock Exchange have a stock dividend or split each year. Several explanations are possible. First, stock dividends and splits might really matter due mostly to market imperfections. For example, when a stock dividend is paid, the stock price can only adjust in increments of $0.125 ($1/8). This may make it impossible for the share price to adjust to its exact theoretical value. Second, some observers think that stock splits are a useful way of bringing the stock price into a popular trading range. Some market observers believe that investors prefer stock prices in the $20 to $60 range. If a stock split puts the share price in the favored range, the increased popularity of the shares could make them more valuable. While there is no firm evidence in support of this view, intuition suggests that a share worth $40 should be easier to trade than a share with a price of $20,000. In the absence of stock splits or dividends, many shares would eventually reach such high prices.[2]

STOCK VALUATION

The stock prices reported in *The Wall Street Journal* emerge from the action of market traders, who continuously revise their opinions about how much stocks are worth. We know that the value of the stock depends on the amount and timing of the cash flows the stock generates. It also depends on the riskiness of the cash flows.

We have seen that bonds promise to make payments at certain times, so they are easy to predict. In contrast, the amount and timing of a stock's dividend payments are not always so clear. Some firms pay no dividends, but hope to do so in the future. Also, some firms that have paid dividends for a long time fall on hard times and reduce or eliminate these payments. Because of this greater speculative element in the amount and timing of dividend payments, risk assessment for equity securities is an important concern. The rate of discount applied to the firm's dividend stream reflects this risk assessment.

The value of a share of stock can be obtained by the following equation, which is called the **dividend valuation model**:

$$P_0 = \frac{D_1}{1 + r} + \frac{D_2}{(1 + r)^2} + \frac{D_3}{(1 + r)^3} + \cdots \tag{5.3}$$

where: P_0 = the price of the share at time 0
D_t = the expected dividend to be paid at time t
r = the risk-adjusted discount rate, or cost of equity capital

Equation 5.3 states that the current stock price (P_0) equals the present value of all future expected dividends (D_t), when we discount those dividends at the firm's cost of equity capital (r). Since it only considers dividends, equation 5.3 appears to neglect **capital gains** – profits that result from an increase in the price of an asset. Many investors have

---

[2] A few stocks do command very high prices. For example, the stock of Japan's telecommunication giant, Nippon Telegraph & Telephone Corp. (NTT), has traded around $17,000 per share in recent years.

a primary interest in capital gains when they buy stocks. Actually, this alleged problem is only apparent, as the following discussion shows.

The Dividend Valuation Model and Capital Gains

According to the dividend valuation model, the only cash flows that matter to a common stockholder are the expected dividends. Yet many investors buy stocks for the expected capital gains. In fact, many buy stocks that currently pay no dividends, with the plan to sell them later for a profit. Capital gains typically constitute a large part of the total returns for many stocks.

The dividend valuation model does not ignore capital gains. Instead, it treats them indirectly, through their relationship to dividends. To see how the dividend valuation model takes account of capital gains, consider a stock that pays a dividend annually. An investor might buy such a stock and plan to hold it for three years. In this case the cash flows would consist of the three annual dividends plus the value of the share when sold. It is at the time the stock is sold that the investor expects to earn the capital gains. In terms of the dividend valuation model, the value of such a share would be:

$$P_0 = \frac{D_1}{1 + r} + \frac{D_2}{(1 + r)^2} + \frac{D_3}{(1 + r)^3} + \frac{P_3}{(1 + r)^3} \tag{5.4}$$

In equation 5.4, P_3 is the value of the share three years after purchase, right after the third dividend payment is received. An investor with a three-year holding period would anticipate receiving three dividends and would hope for a capital gain in the stock over that period. This capital gain or loss equals $P_3 - P_0$.

At first glance, equation 5.4 appears to contradict the dividend valuation model of equation 5.3 because it contains a finite amount of dividend terms, after which we see a term for the price of the stock at the end of the third year, P_3. However, this is only an apparent discrepancy. The value of the share in three years depends on the future dividends that investors expect the shares to pay from that time forward. In other words, the value of the share in the third year (P_3) depends on the dividends to be paid in subsequent years:

$$P_3 = \frac{D_4}{1 + r} + \frac{D_5}{(1 + r)^2} + \frac{D_6}{(1 + r)^3} + \cdots \tag{5.5}$$

Notice that only the dividends after time $t = 3$ influence the price at time $t = 3$. If we substitute equation 5.5 into equation 5.4, we obtain the original version of the dividend valuation model, equation 5.3. This discussion shows that even if the dividend valuation model of equation 5.3 does not explicitly show capital gains, it reflects them implicitly.

Another way to show how the value of a share depends on the expected future dividends is to reflect upon the following question: how much is a share of stock worth, assuming that everyone knows it will absolutely never pay a dividend? In this case, investing in such a share would be investing in something that will never generate any cash flows. Thus, it has no value and its price should be 0. To this argument someone might object that the investor purchases the share for prospective capital gains, not dividends. The hope is to buy the stock now and sell it for a higher price to someone else. If the stock will never pay a dividend, however, and everyone knows it, no one should be willing to pay anything for the share, since it will never produce any dividends. In that case, its price will remain 0, and there will be no capital gains.

Actually, the hope of selling such a share for a capital gain depends on the "greater fool" theory. To pay something for a stock that promises never to pay a cent in dividends is very foolish. To try to make money by buying the stock and selling it for a profit to someone else depends upon finding someone who is a greater fool than the original purchaser.[3]

The Indefinite Future of Dividends

The dividend valuation model of equation 5.3 has a possibly infinite number of dividends that populate the right-hand side of the equation. If one wishes to apply the model in actual practice, how can the sum of the present values of all of those dividends be evaluated?

For preferred stock, the solution is simple because preferred dividends are normally constant. In this case, the preferred dividends are a perpetuity and, as equation 5.1 shows, the price merely equals the regular payment divided by the discount rate. However, if the dividends change over time, as typically happens with common stock, such a simple solution is not possible.

Even if dividends are not constant, there is still a way to apply the model and to avoid the pitfall of trying to add a potentially infinite number of dividends. Most firms that are successful hope to be able to pay increasingly larger dividends as time progresses. If the dividends grow at a constant rate, g, then we can simplify the dividend valuation model. The time line in figure 5.1 schematically illustrates a series of cash flows that grow at a constant rate, g. Under the constant dividend growth assumption, the dividend in the second year equals the dividend in the first year plus the growth in dividends, or:

FIGURE 5.1
Dividends Growing at a Constant Rate

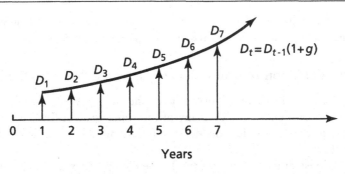

$$D_t = D_{t-1}(1+g)$$

Years

---

[3] Certain irrational behavior does appear to arise from time to time. A famous example is the tulip bulb craze that occurred in Europe in the early seventeenth century. At that time, investors bought tulip bulbs at prices that exceeded the price of gold, presumably because they expected to find another investor willing to pay even more. Such **speculative bubbles** are based on the greater fool theory and, like all bubbles, invariably burst after a while.

$$D_2 = D_1(1 + g)$$

Similarly, the dividend in the third year is:

$$
\begin{aligned}
D_3 &= D_2(1 + g) \\
&= [D_1(1 + g)](1 + g) \\
&= D_1(1 + g)^2
\end{aligned}
$$

In general, the dividend at time t can be expressed in terms of the dividend at time $t = 1$ through the following formula:

$$D_t = D_1(1 + g)^{t-1} \tag{5.6}$$

In this case, knowing the value of D_1 provides enough information to calculate the value of all subsequent dividends. For this special case of a constant growth rate in dividends, the dividend valuation model is:[4]

$$P_0 = \frac{D_1}{r - g} \tag{5.7}$$

This is the **constant growth model**. Two assumptions behind this simplification of the model are that (1) the dividends grow each year at the constant growth rate, g, forever, and (2) the growth rate, g, is less than the discount rate, r, $(g < r)$.

Equation 5.7 provides a practical way to deal with an infinite series of dividends. To see how to apply this version of the dividend valuation model, consider a stock that you expect will pay a dividend of $1.20 one year from now. Based on your assessment of the riskiness of the security, you believe that such an investment should have a return of 17 percent, and you expect that the long-term growth rate for the dividends of the company will be 3 percent. According to equation 5.7, the share should be worth $8.57:

$$P_0 = \frac{\$1.20}{0.17 - 0.03} = \$8.57$$

The value of a share of stock is highly sensitive to the discount rate, r, and the expected long-term growth rate in dividends, g. Table 5.1 reflects this sensitivity.

The Valuation of Stocks That Currently Pay No Dividends

Historically, many of the best buys in the stock market have been for shares that initially paid no dividends. In fact, many of the super-growth firms are unlikely to pay dividends early in their lives. The dividend valuation model has sufficient flexibility to handle such stocks.

Consider an imaginary firm, Prune Computer, with a current price of $15 and paying no current dividend. According to the dividend valuation model, the price of $15 must reflect the dividends that Prune is expected to pay in the future. After serious investigation, you expect that Prune will not pay any dividends for the next three years, as it reinvests all profits in new product development and in marketing existing products. At the end of

---

[4] The derivation of equation 5.7 follows the derivation of a growing perpetuity presented in chapter 3.

TABLE 5.1

Share Values for Stocks Paying $1 in Initial Dividends with Different Growth Rates and Different Discount Rates

g (%)	r (%)						
	8	10	12	14	16	18	20
0	12.50	10.00	8.33	7.14	6.25	5.56	5.00
2	16.67	12.50	10.00	8.33	7.14	6.25	5.56
4	25.00	16.67	12.50	10.00	8.33	7.14	6.25
6	50.00	25.00	16.67	12.50	10.00	8.33	7.14
8		50.00	25.00	16.67	12.50	10.00	8.33
10			50.00	25.00	16.67	12.50	10.00

the fourth year, however, you expect that Prune will be able to pay a dividend of $1.50 per share, and that this dividend will grow at a long-term annual rate of 10 percent. On an investment as risky as this, you demand a rate of return of 18 percent. You wonder if Prune is a good investment, given these assumptions.

To apply the dividend valuation model to Prune's stock, we need a two-step procedure. First, beginning with the fourth year, the dividend pattern of Prune Computer matches the requirements of the dividend valuation model. Viewed from the end of the third year, we estimate the dividend to be $1.50 for the next year, with a growth rate, g, of 10 percent, and to warrant a required rate of return of $r = 18$ percent. According to the dividend valuation model, the value of the shares at time 3 must be:

$$P_3 = \frac{D_4}{r - g}$$

$$= \frac{\$1.50}{0.18 - 0.10} = \$18.75$$

Given the assumptions, you estimate that the price of Prune in year 3 should be $18.75. However, we have to know what Prune is worth now, at time $t = 0$. Since no dividends will be paid in the next three years, to compute the current price according to the model we must discount the value of Prune Computer stock in year 3 back to the present:

$$P_0 = \frac{P_3}{(1 + r)^3}$$

$$= \frac{\$18.75}{(1.18)^3} = \$11.41$$

Since the estimate of Prune's value is lower than its market price of $15, this is not a good investment.

The Dividend Valuation Model and Earnings

Thus far in the discussion, we have emphasized dividends. Yet the reader of the financial press knows that market professionals analyzing a firm attend to its earnings reports and its earnings prospects. Not surprisingly, there is an intimate link between earnings and dividends and it is reflected by the dividend valuation model.

The after-tax earnings that a firm generates have only two outlets. They must be paid as dividends or retained in the firm. The dividend valuation model recognizes the very close relationship between earnings and dividends. Let y represent the proportion of earnings that the firm pays as a cash dividend. This proportion is known as the firm's **dividend payout ratio**. Firms that always pay a fixed percentage of their earnings follow a **constant dividend payout ratio** policy. For such firms, knowing the level of earnings is enough to know the level of dividends, since in a given year, t, the firm's earnings and dividends are related by the following expression:

$$D_t = yE_t \qquad\qquad (5.8)$$

For a firm following a constant dividend payout policy, estimating the dividend payments is the same problem as estimating the future earnings stream. For example, consider a well-established firm with a long-term growth rate of $g = 4$ percent. We expect next year's earnings to be \$3.60 per share and that the firm will pay 60 percent of its earnings in dividends. Furthermore, assume that the required rate of return for such a firm's shares is 14 percent. How much is the firm worth? The dividend valuation model, after incorporating equation 5.8, provides an easily calculated answer:

$$P_0 = \frac{yE_1}{r - g}$$

$$= \frac{0.6 \times \$3.60}{0.14 - 0.04} = \$21.60$$

Thus, the price of the shares should be \$21.60.

The price-earnings ratio (P/E) can also be analyzed using the dividend valuation model. More specifically, if dividends grow at a constant rate, we can use the constant growth model and equation 5.8 to express the P/E ratio as follows:

$$P_0/E_0 = \frac{y(1 + g)}{r - g}$$

This expression implies that, other things being equal, the P/E ratio of rapidly growing firms (high g) should be greater than for more mature firms (low g). Furthermore, the higher the dividend payout ratio, y, the higher the P/E ratio. Finally, the riskier the firm (high r), the lower the P/E ratio. However, we must be careful not to conclude that to increase a stock's P/E ratio all we have to do is, say, increase the dividend payout ratio. This is because the effects just mentioned occur only if other things are equal, but other things may not be equal. For example, if the dividend payout ratio is increased, the firm retains fewer earnings, which may result in fewer resources to invest for future growth. In other words, a high payout ratio may result in a lower growth rate. Since these effects counteract each other, their combined effect on the stock price is uncertain.

COMMON STOCK QUOTATIONS

The Wall Street Journal provides the most complete daily source of stock market quotations. Figure 5.2 shows a portion of the quotations for stocks listed on the New York Stock

FIGURE 5.2
Common Stock Quotations

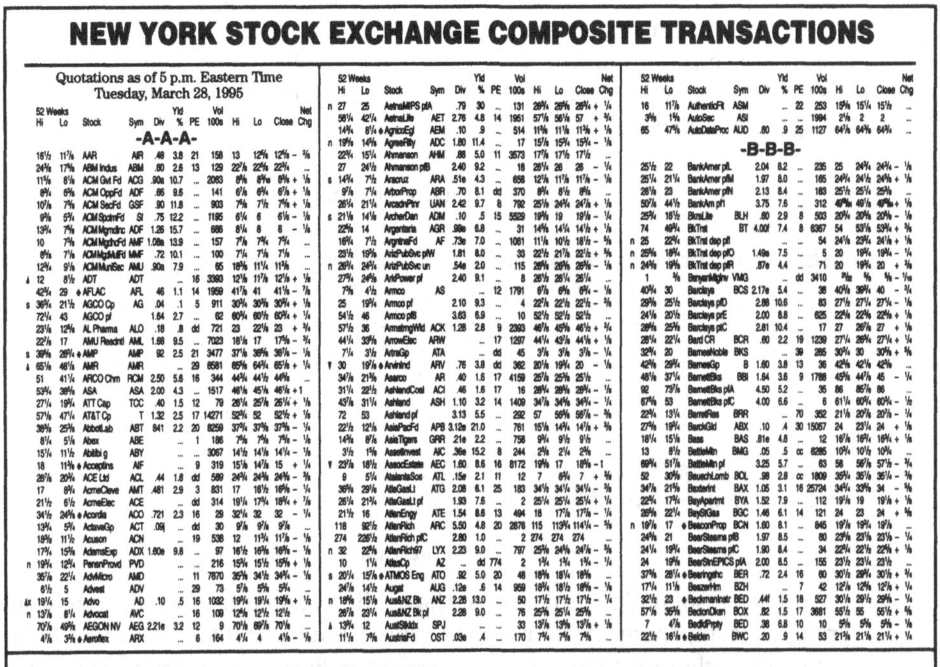

NEW YORK STOCK EXCHANGE COMPOSITE TRANSACTIONS

Quotations as of 5 p.m. Eastern Time
Tuesday, March 28, 1995

Source: *The Wall Street Journal*, March 29, 1995.

Exchange. The first two columns show the high and low prices over the last 52 weeks. Stock quotations appear in eighths of dollars, so a price of 20–3/8 is 20 and three-eighths dollars, or $20.375 per share. The third column contains the company's name, and the fourth shows its yearly dividend in dollars.

Column 5 shows the dividend yield on a share, which equals the annual dividend divided by the current price. Column 6 shows the P/E ratio, equal to the price divided by the year's earnings. This ratio is a widely used measure of the growth potential of the firm's stock price. Column 7 shows the number of shares traded, in hundreds. The next three columns are the high, low, and closing prices for the day. The final column is the change in the share's price from the close of trading on the preceding day to the close on the current day.

DIVIDEND YIELD AND CAPITAL GAINS YIELD

For common stock, much of its required return may come from its growth potential, in the form of a capital gains yield. This is seen by reorganizing the constant growth model to solve for the required rate of return:

$$r = \frac{D_1}{P_0} + g \tag{5.9}$$

The first term on the right-hand side of equation 5.9 is the dividend yield of the stock. We have seen that this ratio is quoted in *The Wall Street Journal* each day.[5] The second term, which is not quoted, is the capital gains yield. To see why the dividend growth rate is exactly the same as the capital gains yield, note that, by definition, the capital gains yield is given by the expression:

$$\text{Capital gains yield} = \frac{P_1 - P_0}{P_0} \tag{5.10}$$

Also, from the constant growth model, next year's price is equal to:

$$P_1 = \frac{D_2}{r - g} \tag{5.11}$$

$$= \frac{D_1(1 + g)}{r - g} = P_0(1 + g)$$

Thus, the stock's price grows at the same rate as dividends grow. Substituting equation 5.11 in 5.10 and simplifying, we have:

$$\text{Capital gains yield} = g$$

The reasoning presented here shows that, quoted or not, the firm's dividend growth rate is a component of the required rate of return on the stock. The higher the growth rate, the higher its relative importance to the firm's overall rate of return.

As an example, consider a firm that is expected to pay a dividend of $2 in one year, has a current price of $50, and is expected to experience a long-term growth rate of 6 percent each year. Then, the required rate of return on this stock is:

$$r = \frac{2}{50} + 0.06$$

$$= 0.04 + 0.06 = 10\%$$

In this example, most of the return of the stock is expected to come from capital gains, precisely the component that is not quoted in the financial press.

RISK AND THE REQUIRED RATE OF RETURN

We have now surveyed the principal instruments of the capital market and have discussed valuation principles for bonds, preferred stock, and common stock. One of the major differences among these different financing vehicles is the risk that investors take. We already know that risk, together with the level and timing of the cash flows, is one of the three essential variables in determining value.

---

[5] Actually, the dividend yield quoted is D_0/P_0. The error is usually not substantial.

Not surprisingly, investors demand compensation for bearing risk. For instance, we have noted that the owner of a first mortgage bond has a more secure position than the holder of the same firm's debentures. In general, all bondholders have a less risky position than preferred stockholders, and both of these bear less risk than common stockholders. The different rates of return these securities earn reflect differences in risk levels. Figure 5.3 presents this general relationship in a schematic form. The basic principle is clear – the greater the risk, the greater must be the required return if investors are to commit their funds.

SUMMARY

This chapter examined two major sources of long-term financing – preferred stock and common stock. Preferred stock is a hybrid security, having features of both corporate bonds and common stock. Preferred stock normally pays a fixed dividend rate, similar to the coupon rate on a corporate bond. However, unlike most corporate bonds, preferred stock usually has no maturity date, so the firm plans to pay preferred stock dividends forever. The firm has no contractual obligation to pay preferred dividends (as it does with most bonds) and preferred stockholders do not normally have voting rights (as do common stockholders).

Common stock is the one kind of financing common to all corporations, because it represents ownership in the corporation. The firm need not sell preferred stock or bonds,

FIGURE 5.3
Basic Relationship Between Risk and Return for Different Kinds of Securities

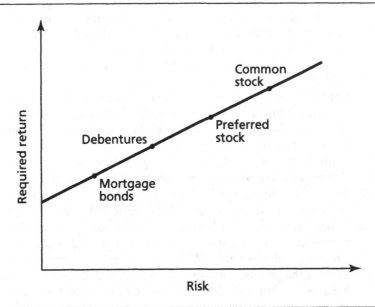

but there must be common stock. Common stockholders expect to receive dividends from the firm as a return on their investment. However, because dividends are received only after the firm satisfies other claimants, stockholders cannot be sure they will actually receive dividends. Common stock is the riskiest financing instrument. In exchange for that risk, stockholders have a voice in operating the company.

The value of any investment equals the sum of the present values of all of the future cash flows expected from the investment. Preferred stock pays a fixed annual dollar amount, so we may value it as a perpetuity. Common stock valuation is more complicated, because the firm may not pay dividends at the present or the amounts may vary each year. In the special case when dividends grow at a constant rate, we can value them with the constant growth model.

QUESTIONS

1. A new firm makes a totally believable commitment to never pay dividends. What should the price of the shares in that firm be?
2. Respond to the following claim: The dividend valuation model is worthless as a guide to stock prices because it completely neglects capital gains.
3. Why do many new firms pay no dividends? Does this imply that their share prices should be zero? Why or why not?
4. React to the following criticism: The dividend valuation model is not very useful, because it can only be applied to firms having smoothly growing dividends. For example, it cannot be applied to firms that might experience a period of rapidly and erratically growing dividends.
5. How would you respond to the following attack on the dividend valuation model: The dividend valuation model assumes that dividends grow at a rate g forever. This is obviously unrealistic, so the model cannot be applied in practice.
6. In terms of the dividend valuation model, why might a firm with a higher growth rate of dividends have a higher discount rate?
7. If a firm cuts its dividend, should its price fall according to the dividend valuation model?
8. Consider a firm that announces a very attractive new investment opportunity and also announces that it is eliminating its dividend in order to finance the new investment. What should happen to the stock price according to the dividend valuation model?
9. What similarities are there between preferred stock and a regular corporate bond?
10. What similarities are there between preferred stock and common stock?
11. Other things being equal, which kind of preferred stock should be more valuable, regular preferred stock or cumulative preferred stock? Explain.
12. A firm issues a bond with an infinite life having a par value of $100 and a 6 percent coupon and a share of preferred stock with a par value of $100 and a 6 percent dividend rate. Which should be more valuable? Explain.
13. What is the preemptive right held by the common stock owners?
14. What is the difference between a stock dividend and a stock split?
15. Why does the P/E ratio appear in the stock market quotations?

16. Explain how the P/E ratio is affected by the dividend payout ratio, the firm's growth rate, and the firm's required rate of return, other things being equal.

17. Explain how the firm's growth rate is likely to be related to its dividend payout policy. What does this explain about the payout policies of many high growth firms?

18. In 1993 IBM announced that it would cut its dividend payments. As a result, its stock price increased. How can this reaction be reconciled with the dividend valuation model?

19. *The Wall Street Journal* quotes the dividend yield of a stock. Is this the stock's required rate of return?

20. Why is a stock's dividend growth rate the same as its capital gains yield, according to the constant growth model?

PROBLEMS

1. Consider a firm that pays a dividend of $0.70 in the next period, and that has a growth rate of 11 percent for the next four years. What are the dividends for these periods? Assume that the firm will never pay any dividends beyond the fifth year. According to the dividend valuation model, what should be the price of this share? The discount rate is 15 percent.

2. For a share paying a dividend of $1.20 in the coming period, with a long-term growth rate of 4 percent, and a cost of equity capital of 10 percent, what is the share price according to the dividend valuation model?

3. For the previous share, what happens as the growth rate accelerates and other factors are held constant? Graph the share price as a function of the difference between the cost of equity capital (10 percent) and the growth rate.

4. You estimate that a firm will have the following dividends for the next three periods: $1.17, $1.44, $1.88. After these, you expect dividends to grow at their long-term growth rate of 3 percent. What is the share price according to the dividend valuation model? What would it be if the long-term growth rate were 5 percent rather than 3 percent? The discount rate is 10 percent.

5. A fully mature firm follows the policy of paying 60 percent of its earnings in dividends, and these earnings are expected to increase at 4 percent forever. If the earnings in the current period are $1.20 per share, what is the value of this share according to the dividend valuation model, assuming a 12 percent cost of equity capital?

6. For the firm in the preceding problem, assume that the payout ratio is 100 percent rather than 60 percent. What does this imply about the growth rate and what should be the value of the share?

7. For a share of preferred stock with a discount rate of 11 percent and an annual dividend of $6, what should its price be?

8. What should the price of a preferred share be if the appropriate discount rate is 13 percent and the annual dividend is $6?

9. Hard Times, Inc., is expected to skip its annual preferred dividend payments of $9 for the next three years. However, it is expected to resume its normal

payment pattern starting four years from now. At that time, the three delayed dividends will also be paid in full. If the required rate on the preferred stock is 12 percent, find the current price of the preferred stock.

10. In the previous problem, assume that Hard Times must pay 10 percent interest, compounded annually, on any delayed preferred dividends. What is the current preferred stock price in that case?

11. Assume now that Hard Times must pay 12 percent interest, compounded annually, on any delayed preferred dividends. What is the current preferred stock price in that case?

12. If you own 80 shares of Divisible Industries' common stock with a current price of $50 per share and the firm announces a three-for-two stock split, how many new shares will you have? What is the price of each share after the split?

13. A firm has a constant dividend payout policy of 40 percent of earnings, and next year's earnings are projected at $1.40. If the long-term growth rate in earnings is 6 percent and the firm's cost of capital is 11 percent, what should this share be worth?

14. If a stock will pay a $3 dividend in one year, is currently selling for $42, and has a long-term dividend growth rate of 3.5 percent, what is its required rate of return?

15. A share of common stock is currently worth $60. Dividend payments from this stock are expected to grow at 6 percent forever. What do you expect the price of this stock to be in five years?

16. The stock price of Lya's Creations is expected to double in five years. What is Lya's long-term dividend growth rate?

17. Microtech has decided not to pay any dividends on its common stock for the next six years, but instead to devote all its resources to research and development. In year seven it will pay a dividend of $4.50 per share, and each year thereafter it will increase its dividend by 3 percent. If the required rate on Microtech stock is 17 percent, what is its current stock price?

18. The Fortyniner gold mine is being depleted rapidly. In fact, each year it generates 10 percent fewer earnings for its common stockholders. Given this depressing state of affairs, all the earnings are paid to the stockholders. Earnings for the year just finished were $8 per share, and the corresponding dividends were just paid. If investors require 18 percent return from Fortyniner's stock, what is its current stock price? What will its price be in two years?

19. Yo-Yo Cellos, Inc., is experiencing a period of very fast growth. Yo-Yo expects to increase its dividends by 12 percent annually for the next 10 years. After that period, dividends will increase by 5 percent forever. Next year's dividends are expected to be $12 per share. If the annual discount rate is 10 percent, what is Yo-Yo's current price?

20. Mahler, Inc., expects its dividends to grow at 10 percent annually for the next ten years. After that, it expects them to decrease by 10 percent forever. If next year's dividends will be $10 per share and the annual discount rate is 10 percent, what is Mahler's current price?

Chapter 6

Capital Budgeting

This chapter introduces the basic principles for the key decision facing every firm – the capital budgeting decision. Capital budgeting is the allocation of investment funds to long-term real assets. For example, the decision to build or expand a factory is a typical capital budgeting project.

Any decision, financial or otherwise, involves an evaluation of the associated benefits and costs. In capital budgeting, the benefits consist of the future cash flows generated after undertaking a project, whereas the costs are mostly associated with the project's initial investment. We already know from the time value of money concepts that to measure the value of a future stream of cash flows, we must compute the present value of the stream. In capital budgeting, the manager tries to select a project with cash inflows that have a higher present value than the investment cost. The value created by sound selection is the difference between the present value of the cash inflows and the investment costs.

Various capital budgeting methods may be used to evaluate the desirability of a given project. Although consensus exists that the most appropriate one is the net present value technique discussed in the following section, other techniques remain in use. It is thus important for the financial manager to know both the strengths and weaknesses of each of the methods.

THE COST-BENEFIT PRINCIPLE OF VALUE CREATION

We all make decisions every day. Implicit in each one is the belief that the chosen course of action will be valuable. In general, we can say that value is created when the benefits of a decision exceed its costs. This **cost-benefit principle** applies to any type of rational endeavor. For example, it explains why some drivers deliberately exceed the maximum highway speed limit. For them, the benefits of speeding may include arriving at their destination earlier and spending less time driving, or perhaps showing off their 500 horse-power car. Of course, driving beyond the speed limit also has potential costs, including the possibility of being stopped by the police and receiving a ticket, paying a higher insurance premium, spending time in court, and the possibility of having an accident. Drivers violating the speed limit believe that the benefits exceed the costs. For many drivers, however, the expected costs of speeding are high compared to the benefits, which is why they decide to obey the speed limit.

The cost-benefit principle also applies in finance: a financial manager will proceed with a decision when the perceived benefits exceed its associated costs. For example, if an automobile firm invests in a new plant to build a new model, it must believe that the future benefits – revenues from sales – will exceed the cost of building and operating the new plant. This simple and intuitive principle will prove to be very powerful, and we will refer to it repeatedly. Whenever the benefits of a decision exceed its costs, we will say that value has been created by virtue of that decision. Thus, the decision to build a new automobile plant in the preceding example is expected to increase the overall value of the company.

THE NET PRESENT VALUE TECHNIQUE

If the firm invests in a project that generates cash flows with the same present value as the invested funds, the investment does not increase the firm's wealth. Such a decision merely exchanges funds in one form (a lump-sum amount today) for funds in another form of equal value (future cash flows). For such decisions, the benefits exactly offset the costs.

The entire goal of capital budgeting is to find projects with future cash inflows that have a present value greater than the initial investment cost. The difference between the present value of the future cash inflows and the initial investment is the project's **net present value** (NPV). If the initial investment is I dollars, the cash flow in period t is C_t, for $t = 1, \ldots, n$, and the appropriate discount rate for the project is r, then the net present value is:

$$\text{NPV} = -I + \sum_{t=1}^{n} \frac{C_t}{(1 + r)^t} \tag{6.1}$$

If the present value of a project's cash inflows exceeds the present value of the investment cost, the project has a positive net present value. Thus, it increases the firm's wealth by an amount equal to the positive net present value.

Because capital budgeting is so central to the creation of wealth, it is the most important financial decision in the management of the firm. The first obligation of the financial manager is to maximize the wealth of the current shareholders. The firm achieves this goal by undertaking projects with positive NPV.

To make our discussion concrete, assume that Medident, a medical and dental supplies company, is considering an expansion project. The cash flows are shown in table 6.1. We assume that the appropriate discount rate for this project is 20 percent.

Accepting this project adds $1,393.39 to the firm's wealth. If the project had a negative NPV, we would reject the project, since the firm's wealth would be reduced. The basic NPV rule is:

NPV RULE
**If the NPV is positive when the cash flows are discounted at the
appropriate discount rate, accept the project.**

Since a positive NPV simply means that the benefits of the project exceed the costs, the NPV rule is consistent with the cost-benefit principle of value creation.

TABLE 6.1
Yearly Cash Flows and Present Value for Medident's Expansion Project

Year	Cash Flow	Present Value at 20%	Present Value at 46.48%
0	−$2,500	−$2,500.00	−$2,500.00
1	1,500	1,250.00	1,024.03
2	1,700	1,180.56	792.30
3	1,000	578.70	318.17
4	1,000	482.25	217.21
5	1,000	401.88	148.29
Total		**$1,393.39**	**$0.00**

THE INTERNAL RATE OF RETURN

For any set of cash flows, the **internal rate of return** (IRR) is defined as the discount rate that makes the net present value of those cash flows equal to zero. In general, to find the IRR of a sequence of cash flows, we can use trial-and-error, a financial calculator, or a computer. Based on this definition, the formula used to solve for the IRR is:

$$0 = -I + \sum_{t=1}^{n} \frac{C_t}{(1 + IRR)^t} \tag{6.2}$$

To illustrate the IRR method, consider again the Medident project shown in table 6.1. We can find its IRR by forcing the NPV to equal zero and solving for the discount rate. The discount rate that produces a zero NPV is, by definition, the IRR. Table 6.1 shows that discounting the cash flows at 46.48 percent results in a zero NPV, so the IRR of the Medident project is 46.48 percent.

Notice that for the project just discussed there is a cash outflow in period 0, followed by a series of cash inflows. Thus, there is just one change of sign in this cash flow sequence. A project with only one sign change in its cash flow is called a **normal project**. Normal projects have only one positive IRR. If the sign changes more than once, there could be more than one positive IRR. In general, the maximum possible number of positive IRR's for a project is equal to the number of sign changes in the cash flows. The possibility of multiple IRRs is discussed in the next chapter. Here we will apply the IRR technique only to normal projects.

When the project is normal and the IRR is greater than the discount rate, the NPV will always be positive. Thus, we can use the IRR to decide whether to accept a project according to the following basic IRR rule:

IRR RULE
If the project is normal and the IRR exceeds the appropriate discount rate, accept the project.

Because the IRR of 46.48 percent in the Medident example exceeds the appropriate discount rate of 20 percent for this project, it should be accepted, according to the IRR rule. Note that following the IRR rule for normal projects gives the same accept or reject decision as the NPV rule. This fact is perhaps more easily noted by graphing the evolution of the NPV as the discount rate changes, as discussed in the following section.

THE NPV PROFILE

An extremely useful tool for analyzing capital budgeting problems is the **NPV profile**. The NPV profile is a graphical representation of the NPV of a project for various discount rates. For a normal project, the NPV profile is downward sloping, as shown in figure 6.1.

Several interesting features of the NPV profile should be noted. First, the NPV profile intercepts the NPV axis at a value equal to the simple sum of all the cash flows of the project. This is true because in that situation the discount rate is zero, so each of the denominators in the NPV equation becomes $(1 + 0)^t = 1$. Thus, we have:

$$NPV(r = 0) = -I + \sum_{n=1}^{n} C_t$$

Second, the discount rate at which the NPV profile crosses the horizontal axis (the discount rate axis) is exactly the IRR of the project. This follows from noting that at that discount rate, the NPV is precisely zero.

FIGURE 6.1
The NPV Profile

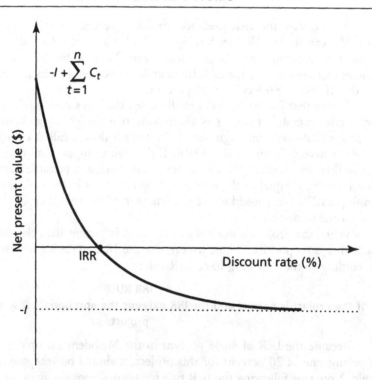

Third, for very high discount rates, the NPV profile approaches a value of $-I$, because as the discount rate increases more and more, the present value of each future cash flow is less and less. In the limit, the whole summation term in equation 6.1 vanishes. Thus:

$$NPV(r = \infty) = -I$$

The NPV profile in figure 6.1 provides a graphical confirmation of the IRR rule given earlier. Indeed, the figure shows that whenever the IRR is greater than the appropriate discount rate, r, the NPV of the project will be greater than zero. Consequently, for normal projects the NPV and IRR rules always produce the same accept or reject decision.

THE PAYBACK PERIOD

The payback period has long been a very popular capital budgeting decision criterion, mostly because of its simplicity. The **payback period** (PP) of a project is the time it takes for the future cash flows to equal the amount of the initial investment. Equivalently:

$$0 = -I + \sum_{n=1}^{PP} C_t \tag{6.3}$$

Equation 6.3 is easier to apply than it seems. For example, for the Medident project the payback period is the time until the sum of the positive cash flows equals the investment of $2,500. This does not happen within the first year since $1,500 < $2,500, but by the end of the second year the total operating cash flow received exceeds the initial investment: $1,500 + $1,700 = $3,200 > $2,500. Therefore, after two years the initial investment has already been repaid so the payback period falls between year 1 and year 2. Assuming that the cash flows occur evenly throughout the year, the payback period is 1.5882 years.[1] The payback rule is to prefer those projects with the shortest possible payback period.

There are serious drawbacks to the payback technique. First, the payback period neglects cash flows that occur after the payback period. This makes the payback period a myopic investment criterion. According to the payback period criterion, all of the following projects are equally desirable:

Year	Medident Project	Project A	Project B
0	−$2,500	−$2,500	−$2,500
1	1,500	1,500	1,500
2	1,700	1,700	1,700
3	1,000	0	0
4	1,000	0	0
5	1,000	1,000	3,000

[1] After one year we still need $1,000 to pay back the investment of $2,500. Since during the second year we will receive $1,700, the fraction of the second year required for the payback is $1,000/$1,700 = 0.5882. This is an example of a technique called **linear interpolation**.

Projects A and B have the same payback period as the Medident project, so they are equally desirable according to the payback criterion. However, any investor would prefer the Medident project to project A, because Medident provides an extra $1,000 in each of years 3 and 4 and the same cash flow in year 5. Clearly, the payback period criterion totally ignores cash flows beyond the payback period.

A second problem with the payback criterion is that it does not consider the timing of the cash flows. Consider the Medident project and project B. Although both projects have the same payback period, the Medident project is definitely better than project B. The cash flows of both projects have the same total, but Medident receives them earlier than project B. Due to the time value of money, we would always prefer the Medident project over project B.

Despite the shortcomings of the payback period, there is an important special case in which the payback period actually has a very specific financial meaning. Consider the project with an investment of I dollars whose cash flows constitute a perpetuity of $\$C$ per period. From equation 6.3, such a project has a payback period given by:

$$0 = -I + C \times PP$$

$$PP = \frac{I}{C}$$

Now note that, from equation 6.2, the IRR of this perpetuity is equal to:

$$IRR = \frac{C}{I}$$

It follows that the payback period for a project whose cash flows form a perpetuity is the inverse of the internal rate of return of the project:

$$PP = \frac{1}{IRR} \qquad (6.4)$$

Equation 6.4 may help us understand why the payback period is still often used as a substitute for other more sophisticated methods. For example, some investors refer to a project that is paid back in four years as an investment with a 25 percent rate of return, an intuition that is consistent with equation 6.4. However, we have shown that this equivalency is true only if the positive cash flows from the investment are a perpetuity. Otherwise, such a conclusion is usually false. Nevertheless, in practice equation 6.4 is *approximately* true for projects with a very long life, say 20 or 30 years, that are expected to generate roughly constant periodic cash flows.

THE DISCOUNTED PAYBACK PERIOD

We have seen that one of the major problems with the payback period is that it disregards the time value of money. The discounted payback period was created to address this shortcoming. The **discounted payback period** (DPP) is the time required for the present value of the future cash flows to equal the amount of the initial investment. The appropriate discount rate for the project is used to calculate the DPP. The DPP involves solving the following equation, which is the exact counterpart to equation 6.3:

$$0 = -I + \sum_{t=1}^{DPP} \frac{C_t}{(1+r)^t} \qquad (6.5)$$

For the Medident example of table 6.1, the discounted payback is slightly greater than two years, since after two years we have:

$$-69.44 = -2,500 + \frac{1,500}{1.20} + \frac{1,700}{1.20^2}$$

The DPP can be appreciated more clearly by graphically representing the process of searching for it. This is done by plotting the NPV of the project assuming that it is truncated after the first cash flow, the second cash flow, and so on. Figure 6.2 illustrates this process for the Medident project. There we see that if the project is truncated at $T = 0$, just after the initial investment is made, its NPV is –$2,500; and that if it is truncated at $T = 2$, its NPV is –$69.44. If the project is allowed to last until $T = 5$, its NPV is $1,393.39.

FIGURE 6.2
The Discounted Payback Period

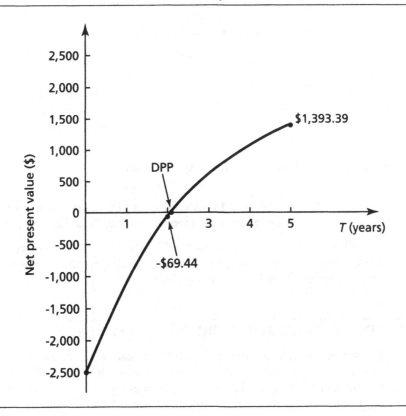

THE PROFITABILITY INDEX

The **profitability index** (PI) is another capital budgeting technique based on present value rules. The profitability index measures the ratio of present value benefits to cost:

$$PI = \frac{\sum_{t=1}^{n} \frac{C_t}{(1+r)^t}}{I} \tag{6.6}$$

We find the present value of the future cash flows by discounting them at the proper discount rate, as we did in our discussion of NPV.

As an example, consider the cash flows for Medident given in table 6.1, discounted at 20 percent. The present value of the inflows in years 1–5 is $3,893.39, while the present value of the investment is –$2,500. Thus, the profitability index for Medident is:

$$PI = \frac{\$3,893.39}{\$2,500}$$

$$= 1.5574$$

When the NPV is zero, the present value of the cash flows equals the investment cost. Consequently, a zero NPV corresponds to a PI of 1.0. If the PI is less than 1.0, the initial investment cost exceeds the present value of the future cash flows, so the NPV is negative. Finally, if the PI exceeds 1.0, the NPV is positive. Here is a table of these correspondences:

NPV	PI
negative	<1.0
zero	<1.0
positive	>1.0

Now we can formulate a profitability index rule:

PI RULE
If the PI exceeds 1.0 when the cash flows are discounted at the appropriate rate, then the project should be accepted.

The NPV rule, the IRR rule, and the PI rule give the same accept/reject decisions for normal capital budgeting projects. However, when projects are not normal, conflicts may occur. This possibility is discussed in the next chapter.

ACCOUNTING-BASED PROFITABILITY MEASURES

In essence, accounting-based profitability measures divide some measure of accounting profits by some measure of investment. For example, we usually calculate the return on investment (ROI) by dividing after-tax accounting profits by the investment. There are many other similar methods as well, all of which have serious flaws.

First, the methods focus on accounting profits, rather than on cash flows. The firm can spend or reinvest cash flows. It can do neither with accounting profits. Second, these accounting measures consider only the profits of one year. As a consequence, they are unable to deal with situations in which competing projects have different lives or with projects for which the profits change from period to period.

Since accounting-based methods cannot adequately consider the timing of cash flows or projects with uneven cash flows, they are greatly inferior to the present value techniques.

IDENTIFYING CASH FLOWS

So far we have assumed that we already know the cash flows to be discounted. In practice, a major part of capital budgeting analysis focuses on identifying the relevant cash flows. These cash flows are of two basic types: investment costs and incremental cash flows from operations.

Investment Costs

In most capital budgeting projects, the investment occurs at the outset of the project, with the project's cash inflows coming later. For example, if the project is the construction of an office building, the investment occurs during construction. Because the investment takes place at the beginning of most projects, it is relatively easy to identify the cash outlays for the investment. There are, however, several points that are worth noting.

Installation Costs   The investment includes the full cost of leaving the project in working order. For example, if you order a new lathe for a machine shop, the investment cost includes the price of the lathe, shipping and insurance charges incurred in getting the lathe to the work site, the cost of installing the machine, and any electrical work required to make the lathe operable.

Opportunity Costs   In many instances, managers overlook some of the cost of an investment. For example, assume the firm plans to construct an office building on land the firm already owns. Should the value of the land be included in the cost of the project? If the firm did not use the land it owns for the office building, it could sell the land or use it for some other purpose. Therefore, the land is an essential part of the investment and the firm should include the market value of the land as part of the investment. We say that the land has an opportunity cost because it could be put to uses other than the project. The market value of the land is the correct value to use because it is the amount that the firm could get for the land if it did not employ it in the investment.

To see this issue more clearly, assume that the firm acquired the land for the office building ten years ago for $100,000 and that is the value it has in the accounting books. You estimate that the land now has a market value of $350,000. In calculating the cost of the investment, we should value the land at $350,000, not $100,000, because the market value is the cash flow that the firm sacrifices by using the land for the office building. The amount originally paid for the land is irrelevant in calculating the cost of the investment.

Sunk Costs   This is a cost that the firm already incurred, but that has no current or future value. Consider again the project of a new office building on land the firm already owns. Assume that the firm paid $15,000 to install a fence around the property just before it thought about constructing the building. Suppose the fence must be removed before construction begins, at a cost of $4,000, and the fence is worthless as scrap. Which of these costs is part of the investment?

First, the $15,000 cost of installing the fence is irrelevant, because the existing fence has no use in the new project. By including the $15,000 already spent for the fence, we commit the **sunk cost fallacy**. Second, if the firm constructs the office building, it must remove the fence at a cost of $4,000. Since this is a cash outlay that the firm incurs only if it accepts the office building project, the fence removal is a relevant cost of the project.

Working Capital   Virtually every major project requires an investment in working capital, because projects typically require an increase in cash balances, inventory, or accounts receivable. If a firm undertakes a project, it needs funds to finance the increased working capital, so this is part of the investment.

For example, a toy manufacturer has a successful Poison Ivy Patch doll. Last year the firm was unable to meet demand for the doll, so it now considers building a new plant (no pun intended) to increase production. To meet the new demand the firm estimates it should increase its inventories by 100,000 units at a production cost of $5 per unit. This means that accepting the project will require an additional $500,000 investment in inventories.

The firm expects the itch for Poison Ivy dolls to last three years. After this time, the firm will deplete its doll inventory and it can recapture its investment in working capital. This recapture of working capital is typical. However, the firm will have to invest in inventory for the duration of the project. In the capital budgeting analysis, we therefore include the increase in working capital as part of the investment. We only recapture the working capital at the end of the project's life. The cash flow from recapturing that working capital investment is not taxed. Thus, we add the recaptured working capital to the final period's after-tax cash flow. This general situation is illustrated in figure 6.3.[2]

Incremental Cash Flows

In this section, we show that a capital budgeting analysis should consider only the incremental cash flows of an investment – those cash flows that differ if the firm undertakes a project. This principle of incremental cash flows is critical in proper capital budgeting analysis. Typically, the most important incremental cash flow is the after-tax operating cash flow generated by the project, as discussed below.

After-Tax Operating Cash Flows   The after-tax operating cash flows from the project are incremental cash flows because they would not exist if the project were not undertaken.

---

[2] This is a simplified account of the actual working capital cash flows. In practice, not all working capital is needed at time $t = 0$. Rather, it gradually increases over the initial years of the project, and gradually declines during its final years. Also, figure 6.3 assumes that all the investment in working capital is recaptured at the end of the project's life. In reality, some of the working capital is lost. For example, some of the inventory may become obsolete, and some accounts receivable may not be paid by customers.

FIGURE 6.3
Working Capital Cash Flows

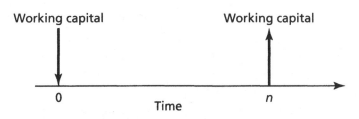

For example, consider a manufacturer that sells 100,000 widgets per year at $3 per widget. Total costs are $2.50 per widget. Furthermore, assume that the firm pays income taxes at the rate of 30 percent. With this information, we can calculate the firm's after-tax operating cash flows as shown in table 6.2.

In table 6.2 the general structure is very similar to an income statement, but each item pertains to the actual cash flow rather than accounting income or expenses. The difference arises from those cases when accounting rules do not recognize cash flows as they occur.

Depreciation   Depreciation is a reduction in accounting earnings intended to reflect the reduction in value of an income-producing asset. Even though depreciation is not itself a cash flow, it affects cash flow through taxes. As a result, every capital budgeting analysis must consider the **depreciation tax shield** – the reduction in taxes due to the depreciation charge. This depreciation tax shield is a cash flow, because it reduces the cash outlay for taxes by the amount of the depreciation tax shield.

The depreciation tax shield depends on the amount of the depreciation charge. In actual practice, firms prefer to use accelerated depreciation methods if possible. However, to simplify the discussion, we assume here that the firm uses straight line depreciation.

To understand exactly how the depreciation expense creates a tax shield, let us again consider our widget manufacturer. As we saw in table 6.2, the firm has an operating cash flow of $50,000. Table 6.3 examines the after-tax cash flow of the widget manufacturer with and without a depreciation expense of $15,000 for a widget compressor. Table 6.3 calculates the tax bill for the firm in each case. If the firm can deduct the $15,000 deprecia-

TABLE 6.2
Calculating After-Tax Operating Cash Flows

Cash from sales	$300,000
– Cash outlays to generate sales	–250,000
Operating cash flow	50,000
– Taxes	–15,000
After-tax cash flow	$35,000

TABLE 6.3
Effect of Depreciation on Cash Flow

	No Depreciation	With Depreciation
Total sales	$300,000	$300,000
– Cost of goods sold	–250,000	–250,000
Gross income	50,000	50,000
– Depreciation expense	–0	–15,000
Taxable income	50,000	35,000
– Taxes (30%)	–15,000	–10,500
Net income	35,000	24,500
After-tax cash flow*	35,000	39,500

*To obtain the firm's operating cash flow from its net income, just add back the depreciation expense.

tion expense, it pays $4,500 less tax. This $4,500 savings in the tax bill is the depreciation tax shield. The shield (S) equals the tax rate (T) times the amount of the depreciation (D):

$$S = T \times D \qquad (6.7)$$

For our example, we have $S = 0.30 \times \$15,000 = \$4,500$. This is the same result we obtained previously. Notice that in table 6.3 the after-tax cash flows with and without the effect of depreciation differ by $4,500 – the amount of the depreciation tax shield.

CALCULATING THE NET PRESENT VALUE

Earlier in this chapter we noted that the net present value of a project equals the present value of the future cash flows from a project minus the present value of the initial investment, as shown in equation 6.1, which is reproduced below:

$$NPV = -I + \sum_{t=1}^{n} \frac{C_t}{(1 + r)^t}$$

In our cash flow analysis, we consider all of the cash flows and convert them to an after-tax basis. As the final step in the capital budgeting procedure, we compute the net present value of all cash flows associated with the project. If the project has a positive NPV, the firm commits to the project. If the NPV is negative, the firm abandons it.

THE YUPPIE NOUGAT PROJECT

In this section we state a relatively complex capital budgeting problem and perform a complete analysis. This analysis provides a model for many capital budgeting problems that you might actually encounter.

The Loving Candy Co. has been studying an investment project calling for the manufacture and introduction of a new candy bar called Yuppie Nougat, targeted (you guessed it) for the yuppie market. As a consequence, Loving Candy expects to use the finest foreign chocolate and to price the candy very high relative to its cost; otherwise no self-respecting yuppie would even think of buying it. Part of the expense will consist of a vast marketing program, complete with endorsements by yuppie heroes.

The project is expected to last eight years, after which time yuppies will be more interested in dentures than candy bars. The introduction of the candy bar requires 400 new machines costing $10,000 each. Installing each machine costs $100. The machines will be depreciated on a straight line basis over five years. The production facility will be located at a site the company already owns. The company could rent the space that the candy facility will occupy for $500,000 per year.

Loving Candy expects to sell two million bars per year for the entire life of the project. The price will be $2.50 per candy bar, with a production cost of $0.50. The plan schedules the marketing expense per candy bar at $1.00. Outlets for the candy bar have been chosen with yuppies in mind, the aim being to have Yuppie Nougat "available wherever Perrier is sold." The firm expects to maintain an average inventory of about 500,000 bars, and expects no other increase in working capital. The appropriate after-tax discount rate for Yuppie Nougat is 18 percent. Should Loving Candy help sweeten the world with Yuppie Nougat?

We begin by breaking the problem into small steps. First, we determine the cash flows associated with the investment, the operating cash flows, and the terminal value. At first, we do not consider taxes, but merely note which flows are affected by taxes and which are not.

(1.) Determine the initial investment.

At the outset of the project, the firm buys 400 machines at $10,000 each plus an installation cost of $100 per machine. We treat the installation cost as part of the machine cost, so the investment for the machines is $4,040,000 (400 × $10,100). In addition, the firm must increase its investment in working capital in the form of inventory. For 500,000 bars at $0.50, the increased investment in working capital is $250,000. Therefore, the investment occurs according to the following schedule, where all of the flows are already on an after-tax basis.

	Year 0	Year 8
Investment	−$4,040,000	$250,000
Working Capital	$9,−250,000	$250,000

(2.) Determine the operating cash flows.

We estimate that the firm will sell two million bars per year. The use of the space for making Yuppie Nougat costs $500,000 a year because that is the opportunity cost of the rent we forego by using the space to produce the candy bar.

Sales	$5,000,000
Production Cost	–1,000,000
Marketing Expense	–2,000,000
Rent	–500,000
Gross Profit	$1,500,000

This gross profit will be subject to taxation. Before we can compute taxes, we must adjust the gross profit by the depreciation expense.

Depreciation Because the firm depreciates the machines for five years using the straight line method, and the depreciable amount is $4,040,000, the depreciation expense is $808,000 per year for five years.

	Years 1–5
Annual Depreciation Expense	$808,000

This depreciation expense will reduce the taxable income, and thus taxes, even though it is not itself a cash flow.

(3.) Identify the terminal cash flows.

Often the cash flow in the final year differs from the cash flow of regular years. The Yuppie Nougat project is no exception, because we must reflect the recovery of the additional working capital investment. If we recover the $250,000 increased investment in working capital, as assumed in Step 1, this amount will not be taxable. At the end of the final year the firm is also assumed to sell its machinery for its market value. We assume that the machinery has no value at the end of the project.

Having classified and identified the relevant cash flows, we now convert them to an after-tax basis. We proceed through each of the categories we have separated: the investment, the operating flows, and the terminal cash flows.

(4.) Identify the after-tax investment cash flows.

The firm uses after-tax funds to make the investment, so these cash flows are already expressed on an after-tax basis.

(5.) Identify the after-tax operating cash flows.

In table 6.4 we compute the after-tax cash flows for each year of the project. Notice that we compute net income and then add the depreciation expense to compute the operating cash flow. Because depreciation extends only through year 5, we treat years 1–5 and 6–8 separately. They differ by only the depreciation. We know from equation 6.7 that depreciation increases cash flow in an amount equal to the depreciation expense times the tax rate, because this is the depreciation tax

TABLE 6.4
After-Tax Operating Flows for Yuppie Nougat

	Years 1–5	Years 6–8
Sales	$5,000,000	$5,000,000
– Production	–1,000,000	–1,000,000
– Marketing	–2,000,000	–2,000,000
Net sales	2,000,000	2,000,000
– Facilities	–500,000	–500,000
– Depreciation	–808,000	0
Taxable income	$692,000	$4,500,000
– Tax (34%)	–235,280	–510,000
Net income	$456,720	$990,000
+ Depreciation	808,000	0
After-tax cash flows	$1,264,720	$990,000

shield. In our case, the depreciation tax shield is $808,000 × 0.34 = $274,720. Notice that this is exactly the amount by which the operating cash flows differ in table 6.4: $1,264,720 – $990,000.

(6.) Identify the after-tax terminal cash flows.

For the terminal cash flows in year 8 we add the nontaxable $250,000 recapture of the working capital investment for a total terminal after-tax cash flow of $990,000 + 250,000 = $1,240,000.

(7.) Compute the yearly after-tax cash flows.

Table 6.5 sets out the after-tax cash flows for each year, summarizing the results we have already obtained.

(8.) Compute the net present value and decide.

We compute the present value of the flows for years 1–8 from the final column of table 6.5, using the discount rate of 18 percent. The result is shown in table 6.6.

Thus, the total NPV of the project at a discount rate of 18 percent is $672,396. Because the Yuppie Nougat project increases the value of the firm by almost $700,000, we should accept it.

Using the after-tax cash flows, we also find that the IRR for this project is 23.09076 percent. The computation is presented in the final column of table 6.6.

TABLE 6.5
After-Tax Cash Flows for the Yuppie Nougat Project

Year	Investment Cash Flow	Operating Cash Flows	Working Capital	Total After-Tax Flows
0	−$4,040,000		−250,000	−$4,290,000
1		1,264,720		−$1,264,720
2		1,264,720		−$1,264,720
3		1,264,720		−$1,264,720
4		1,264,720		−$1,264,720
5		1,264,720		−$1,264,720
6		990,000		−$1,990,000
7		990,000		−$1,990,000
8		990,000	−$250,000	−$1,240,000

TABLE 6.6
Net Present Value for the Yuppie Nougat Project

Year	Total After-Tax Cash Flows	NPV (18%)	NPV (23.09076%)
0	−4,290,000	−4,290,000	−4,290,000
1	1,264,720	1,071,796	1,027,470
2	1,264,720	908,302	834,725
3	1,264,720	769,747	678,138
4	1,264,720	652,329	550,925
5	1,264,720	552,821	447,576
6	990,000	336,727	284,631
7	990,000	310,785	231,237
8	1,240,000	329,887	235,298
Total		**$672,396**	0

THE USE OF CAPITAL BUDGETING TECHNIQUES IN PRACTICE

There have been various surveys to investigate the use of the various capital budgeting techniques by firms. Harold Bierman, Jr., conducted the most recent survey in 1992, asking 74 of the largest industrial firms in the Fortune 500 listing.

Perhaps not surprisingly, 99 percent of the firms used the IRR or NPV method as either the primary or secondary capital budgeting method. The payback period is used by 84 percent of the respondent firms. However, no firm used only the payback period as its primary evaluation method.

Interestingly, more firms used the IRR (99%) than the NPV (85%). However, this percentage for the NPV method is a dramatic improvement over the barely 4 percent of firms that used that method in a similar study conducted in 1955. Clearly, the NPV method has come to be recognized as a premier capital budgeting technique. After reading this chapter, this recognition should not come as a surprise. In the next chapter, the advantages of the NPV over competing methods will be further established.

SUMMARY

This chapter introduced capital budgeting techniques. They are crucial because by making the correct capital budgeting decisions, the firm creates wealth for its shareholders.

We discussed the net present value (NPV) technique, by which the firm measures the benefits and the costs associated with undertaking a project. Because the NPV measures the additional wealth created by the investment decision, it should be used in capital budgeting analysis.

We also considered other capital budgeting techniques that have been historically important and are still widely used. Two of these are the internal rate of return and the profitability index, both based on present value concepts. Although they are useful, we must employ them with care because they can give erroneous decisions in some cases. When a project is normal, however, the NPV, IRR, and PI techniques give the same accept or reject decision.

The payback method and accounting-based techniques do not make use of present value concepts. Because they neglect either the timing of cash flows or the cash flows themselves, using them for capital budgeting analysis is risky. Even the discounted payback method, although it uses present value concepts, is inadequate for capital budgeting analysis, because it still disregards cash flows that occur after the payback period.

Usually the most difficult part of capital budgeting analysis is to estimate cash flows and convert them to an after-tax basis. Once we identify the after-tax cash flows, we discount them at the appropriate rate to determine the net present value of the project. If the NPV is positive, it adds to shareholder wealth and we should accept the project; otherwise, the project should be rejected.

QUESTIONS

1. How do good capital budgeting decisions create or destroy wealth?
2. In a successful capital budgeting decision, how much wealth will be created?
3. Assume that I am planning to sell an old electric motor for $200 but that I find I can use it in a new investment project. Does this use of the old machine affect the investment outlay for the new project? Explain.
4. Assume that your firm has invested $100,000 in a project for each of the last three years by paying a research firm. Also assume that there have been no cash flows from the project. Your firm is going to re-evaluate the viability of the project. If the project is dropped, all of the previous expenditures will have no future value. How should you treat these previous outlays?
5. If working capital is recaptured at the end of a project, why is there investment in working capital?
6. Your current widget-making process is generating positive cash flows of $150,000 each year on an after-tax basis. If you invest $500,000 to modernize your

widget process, the positive cash flows will increase to $250,000. Identify the cash flows that are relevant to making the modernization decision.

7. React to the following statement: $1 of depreciation expense reduces the firm's earnings by $1 just as does any other expense. Therefore, it should be treated as any other expense in a capital budgeting analysis.

8. What is the depreciation tax shield?

9. HAL, Inc., has a depreciation expense of $120,000 this year. Since the firm will sustain a net loss, it will not pay taxes. What is HAL's depreciation tax shield for this year?

10. ZIP, Inc., has very old equipment that is fully depreciated. The firm will have a net profit of $250,000 this year, and it is in the 34 percent tax bracket. What is ZIP's depreciation tax shield for this year?

11. At the end of a project, assume that you recapture $10,000 of invested working capital. Is this treated as an operating flow from the project? Explain.

12. If a ten-year project requires an initial working capital of $100,000 which will be completely recaptured in year 10, what is the NPV that the working capital contributes to the project? Assume a discount rate of 10 percent.

13. Evaluate the following assertion: The main thing you need to know in making an investment decision is how soon you will get your original investment out of the project. This is a question that is exactly answered by the best capital budgeting technique – the payback period.

14. Evaluate the wisdom of the following analysis: Investors in the firm are presented with the firm's annual report and other accounting data. Because that is what they see, they must make their investment decision on the basis of that information. Accordingly, the firm should choose those projects that will improve reported financial results. In particular, the firm should accept those projects that will give the greatest ROI.

15. The payback period technique is frequently maligned because it disregards the time value of money and neglects cash flows beyond the payback period. Is this an air-tight criticism?

16. The NPV and IRR methods are based essentially on the same formula. Despite this, they are radically different concepts. Explicitly state the differences between these methods.

17. Using the NPV profile technique, explain why the NPV and IRR rules will always result in the same accept or reject decision for a normal project.

18. Suppose that you have a ten-year project with an NPV of $100,000. You also find that the discounted payback period is 9.5 years. What does this say about the amount and timing of the cash flows of this project?

PROBLEMS

1. Your investment project will require a microcomputer with a sales price of $4,000. The sales tax is 5 percent. Delivery and setup is $150. Cables to connect the

machine to the existing printers will cost $50. A cabinet for the machine will cost $200. Which of these expenditures should be included in calculating the investment outlay? What is the investment?

2. In problem 1, assume that you have the needed cables on hand. Although used, these cables could be sold for $20. What effect does this have on the investment cost?

3. Your firm was considering raising alligators for the burgeoning specialty food market. Based on this plan, you snapped up 500 acres of swampland at $1,000 an acre in South Florida. Now your firm has abandoned that project and is considering a project to bring outdoor ice skating to Florida. You could sell the land for $100 an acre. If you go ahead with the ice skating project you may be on thin ice, but it would cost $1,000,000 to install the needed refrigeration equipment. Based on this information, what can you say about the investment in the ice skating rink?

4. You are trying to salvage a Spanish galleon laden with gold off the Florida Keys. In your efforts to date, one of your salvage boats worth $200,000 already sank and you are considering abandoning the project. If you go ahead, you estimate that the project will require an additional outlay of $350,000. What is the investment amount that is relevant to your decision now?

5. Everyone knows that chinchilla breed only in the presence of skunks. For your pelt business, you accordingly bought 1,000 skunks five years ago for $10 each. Now you have learned that chinchilla will breed even if there are no skunks present, so you want to sell the skunks, but, alas, the skunk market stinks, and each one will sell for only $1. What was the original investment for the chinchilla? (Beware of the skunk cost fallacy!)

6. Consider the following outlays necessary to open your hardware store and calculate the total investment. Land with building: $200,000; necessary renovations: $15,000; shelving: $10,000; inventory: $225,000; first year's property taxes: $5,000; one month's wages for the staff: $5,000; air conditioning service contract for three years: $1,500; neon sign: $750.

7. In your ice cream store, you expect to sell 15,000 scoops with cones per month at an average price of $0.75. You pay $0.40 per scoop and $0.02 per cone. What is your gross operating cash flow per month?

8. For the ice cream store of the previous problem, you will depreciate the building and equipment, and the depreciation expense will be $1,500 per month. If your tax rate is 35 percent, what will be your after-tax cash flow?

9. A firm buys a piece of capital equipment for an investment project at a price of $150,000 and pays $30,000 shipping, installation, and setup costs. What is the investment outlay?

10. In the previous problem, assuming straight line depreciation and a five-year life, what is the depreciation expense for the third year? What is the depreciation expense in the fifth year if the equipment is to be depreciated over a ten-year life?

11. A firm has $100,000 per year in sales, has a tax rate of 28 percent, has operating costs of $73,000, and shows a depreciation expense of $2,000 per year. Calculate the annual after-tax cash flow.

12. You are considering expanding your alligator wrestling show and have gathered the following data. The special alligator you need (with rubber teeth) costs $80,000. Annual receipts should be $150,000. Your operating expense will be $70,000 per year. (This includes fish for the alligator and hospital expenses for you.) You will have to buy a truck for $10,000. You can depreciate both the truck and the alligator on a straight line basis over five years. At the end of the five years, the project will terminate. You expect the alligator and the truck to be worthless at the end of the five years. If your tax rate is 30 percent, calculate all of the after-tax cash flows from the project.

13. If you could earn 18 percent in an investment of risk equal to that of the alligator project, should you wrestle or not?

14. Find the IRR of the alligator wrestling project.

15. If the cash flows from the alligator wrestling project are discounted at 12 percent, compute the profitability index.

16. Consider three projects. Project A requires an investment of $1,000 and pays $1,000 per year for two years. Project B also costs $1,000 and pays a single cash flow of $5,000 after five years. Project C costs $500 and pays a single cash flow of $3,000 after five years. Find the payback period, the NPV at 12 percent, and the IRR for each project, and choose the best one.

17. The ViVi Shampoo Company is considering a project that requires an immediate investment of $10,000 and is expected to generate a positive cash flow of $917 one year from today. Every year thereafter the project will generate a cash flow that is 5 percent greater than that of the previous year. This cash flow process will continue forever. Find the IRR of this project.

18. An investment project requires an immediate investment of $1,000 and will generate $80 each year (the first cash flow one year from today) from year 1 to year 19. In year 20, the project's last year, it will generate $1,080. Find the IRR of this project.

19. An investment project requires an immediate investment of $5,000 and will generate $650 each year (the first cash flow one year from today) from year 1 to year 10. In year 11, the project's last year, it will generate $5,650. If the appropriate discount rate for this project is 13 percent, find its NPV.

20. Clark Kant has decided to subscribe to the Daily Universe newspaper tomorrow. Clark has two alternatives: he can pay $530 for one full year or pay $175 for one quarter. Assuming that Clark will read the paper for an entire year, what is the IRR of subscribing yearly?

21. In the newspaper problem, find the IRR of subscribing yearly versus subscribing quarterly, assuming that Clark Kant will read the Daily Universe for the next two years.

22. We argued in the text that for normal projects the NPV and the IRR methods will always give the same accept or reject decision. Prove this assertion for any one-year project. (Hint: show that if IRR $> r$, then we must necessarily have NPV > 0.)

23. We showed in the text that for projects with perpetuity cash flows, the payback period, PP, is the inverse of the project's IRR. Find an expression for the

PP when the project's cash flows constitute an annuity. Assume that the life of the annuity exceeds the PP.

24. Projects A and B have the same single cash inflow, C, and the same IRR. However, their initial investments differ. Also, project A pays the cash inflow C one year from now, whereas C is received two years from now with project B. What is the relationship between the two investments? (For example, the relationship could be $I_A = I_B/C$.)

25. A ten-year project produces a final cash flow of $5,000 and has a discounted payback period of nine years. If the discount rate is 12 percent, what is this project's NPV?

26. A 20-year project produces annual cash flows of $12,000 from year 1 to year 20. At a discount rate of 10 percent, the discounted payback period is 12 years. What is the NPV of this project?

27. A project requires an initial investment at $t = 0$ and produces n equal annual cash flows starting at $t = 1$. Find an expression relating the investment, the annual cash flow, the discount rate, and the discounted payback period.

Chapter 7

Special Problems in Capital Budgeting

OVERVIEW

This chapter continues our exploration of capital budgeting principles. We consider various typical capital budgeting problems that deserve special attention. Although the basic concepts presented in the previous chapter are valid, their application may require more careful thought in the situations discussed here.

The first problem we consider relates to mutually exclusive projects. Capital rationing also presents special problems, since we must allocate the investment funds among a set of projects requiring more financing than is available. Next we consider the machine replacement problem, which considers the best time to replace an old machine with a new machine of the same type. Following is a discussion of projects with different lives, where the typical choice is between a high priced machine that lasts a long time and a cheap machine that wears out quickly. Finally, we discuss some special problems related to the IRR. First, a project may have more than one IRR. If multiple IRRs occur, the IRR rule presented in the previous chapter must be re-evaluated. Perhaps even more disturbing is the realization that some projects have no IRRs. However, even then we can provide a simple decision rule.

MUTUALLY EXCLUSIVE PROJECTS

Consider a firm that might consider a piece of land as a suitable location for a bakery or a service station, but not both. Because of this, the bakery and the service station projects are mutually exclusive – accepting one means rejection of the other. When considering mutually exclusive projects, the ranking given by the NPV and IRR techniques may differ. The ranking rules for mutually exclusive projects with each of these techniques are as follows:

NPV Ranking Rule
Of two mutually exclusive projects, choose the one with the higher NPV.

IRR Ranking Rule
Of two mutually exclusive projects, choose the one with the higher IRR.

Table 7.1 shows the cash flows for the service station and the bakery that are competing for the same land. At the bottom, the table shows the IRR and the NPV for a discount rate of 15 percent. At a discount rate of 15 percent both projects have a positive NPV, so both would be acceptable separately. Since only one can be accepted, we are forced to make a choice. The NPV ranking rule states that we should accept the service station because it has a higher NPV. According to the IRR ranking rule, however, we should accept the bakery because it has a higher IRR.

The reason for the conflicting ranking stems from the fact that the projects are of different scales. It is true that the bakery has a higher internal rate of return; however, because the service station requires a bigger investment, it has a greater NPV at the required return of 15 percent. Clearly, we have to determine which rule to follow when ranking mutually exclusive projects.

Figure 7.1 graphs the NPV of both projects. For low discount rates, the service station has a higher NPV, but for high discount rates, the bakery has a higher NPV. At a discount rate of 21.8 percent, the NPVs are equal at $912. Notice, however, that for discount rates greater than 21.8 percent, the NPV and IRR ranking methods would both favor the bakery project. For discount rates greater than 25.55 percent, the bakery's IRR, neither project should be chosen since they both would result in a negative NPV.

Firms should always follow the NPV ranking rule. The bakery requires an investment of $10,000, has an IRR of 25.55 percent, and increases the wealth of the firm by $2,985. The service station needs an investment of $25,000, has a 23.29 percent IRR, and an NPV of $5,809. Choosing the service station over the bakery adds more wealth to the firm. Because the goal of the firm is to increase the wealth of its stockholders, it should follow the NPV ranking rule. In this example, the firm should accept the service station and abandon the bakery project.[1]

TABLE 7.1
Service Station and Bakery Cash Flows

Year	Service Station	Bakery
0	−$25,000	−$10,000
1	8,141	3,431
2	8,141	3,431
3	8,141	3,431
4	8,141	3,431
5	8,141	3,431
6	8,141	3,431
IRR	23.29%	25.55%
NPV at 15%	$5,809	$2,986

---

[1] To further convince you that the scale difference can distort the IRR criterion, consider your own decision in the following simple experiment. Alice is feeling generous today and offers you two choices: give her $1 immediately, and she will give you $2 tomorrow; or give Alice $1,000 today and she will gladly pay you $1,200 tomorrow.

FIGURE 7.1
NPV Profiles for the Service Station and Bakery

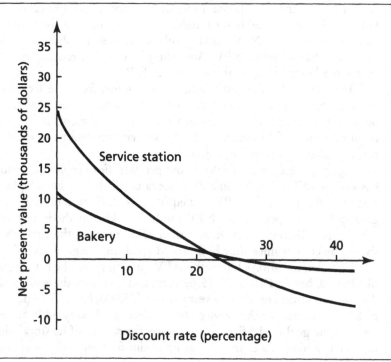

CAPITAL RATIONING

We saw that the firm should accept the service station and reject the bakery. An apparent difficulty with this line of reasoning is that the service station consumes $25,000 of the firm's investable funds. By contrast, the bakery uses only $10,000. Normally, this does not matter, because the firm should be able to obtain more investment funds from the capital markets if it has attractive projects. In the normal event, there should be no difficulty in raising new funds, as long as the firm has profitable investment opportunities.

Capital rationing deals with the case in which the firm has several attractive investment opportunities but limited funds, and is unable or unwilling to secure the additional funds needed to undertake all of the projects. The problem in this situation is to decide how to ration the available scarce capital among competing investment prospects.

To see the kinds of decisions financial managers must make under capital rationing, consider CapRat, Inc. CapRat has a total investment budget of $115,000 and uses a discount rate of 16 percent for the projects shown in table 7.2. CapRat must decide which projects

---

In the first case your IRR is 100 percent per day, whereas in the second your IRR is only 20 percent. Nevertheless, with the second scenario you will be a lot richer tomorrow than with the first choice. The relevant question is, do you prefer to be $1 or $200 richer by tomorrow?

TABLE 7.2
Ranking of Projects Available to CapRat, Inc.

Project	Investment	NPV	IRR
A	$10,000	$3,000. (3)	0.24 (1)
B	$30,000	$6,000.	0.18 (3)
C	$40,000	$10,000. (2)	0.22 (2)
D	$60,000	$15,000. (1)	0.16
E	$25,000	$5,000	0.17
F	$20,000	$4,000	0.16
G	$30,000	$6,500	0.18 (3)

to accept. While all of the projects in table 7.2 have positive NPVs and IRRs above 16 percent, the firm cannot accept all of them. The capital required to undertake all of the projects is $215,000, but CapRat has a total capital pool of only $115,000.

One possible strategy is to use the IRR to rank the projects. Then CapRat would accept the projects with the highest IRRs until it exhausts its investable funds. If the firm follows that procedure, it chooses projects A, C, B, and G. For these four projects, the investment totals $110,000 and the firm accepts no project with an IRR less than 18 percent. Furthermore, the total NPV of the four projects will be $25,500.

The IRR ranking rule may not give the best solution to the investment problem under capital rationing. Because the firm is striving to maximize the wealth of its stockholders, it should choose the set of projects that gives the highest NPV. With $115,000 available, the firm should choose projects D, C, and A. If it does this, its total investment will also be $110,000, but the total NPV will be $28,000. No other combination of the $115,000 investable funds creates as much wealth.

The IRR ranking technique fails once again. It misses the desirability of project D, which has a high NPV but a low IRR. Notice that project D also requires the highest investment of the set of projects. The problem arises once again due to the differences in investment size. In contrast to the IRR technique, the NPV focuses "like a laser beam" on the goal of wealth maximization.

The correct solution is to choose the subset of investment projects that has the highest total NPV. In the example of table 7.2, the firm can do this fairly easily, even by inspection. When matters become more complex, firms may use a computer technique called integer programming to ensure they find the subset of projects that meets their goal of maximizing wealth.

This technique of searching for the best subset of projects can be implemented even when some of the projects in the set are mutually exclusive. Assume that projects C and D in table 7.2 are mutually exclusive. Under this circumstance, what is the best combination of projects? By having the computer search across all possible combinations that do not include both C and D, and that do not exceed the total resources available, we can find the best subset of projects. The best combination that does not include both C and D is A, D, E, and F, with an investment of $115,000 and a total NPV of $27,000. Notice that in this case there are no idle funds, but the NPV is $1,000 less than when the choice of projects is unrestricted.

THE MACHINE REPLACEMENT DECISION

Firms buy machines, use them, and eventually replace them with new identical machines. Almost any machine can be kept in service a little longer by incurring a maintenance cost. As time goes on, however, the operating cost becomes increasingly higher. At some point, the operating cost becomes high enough to justify replacing the machine. The financial manager must determine when that point has been reached.

In making this decision, there are really no cash inflows to consider, even though the machine may be instrumental in generating positive cash flows. However, these do not form part of the decision about replacement because the new and old machines generate the same stream of positive cash flows. Instead, we have to consider only the costs, that is, the investment cost of a new machine and the operating cost of keeping it running. Therefore, the manager must choose the service life of the machine that minimizes the present value of the costs. By minimizing costs in present value terms, the decision contributes to the process of creating wealth. We will assume for simplicity that all machines in the replacement chain are identical.

To see the issues at stake with machine replacement, consider a machine that costs $10,000, and assume it has the following operating costs in each year:

Year	Operating Cost
1	$1,000
2	1,500
3	1,800
4	2,100
5	2,500
6	3,000
7	3,600
8	4,300
9	5,500
10	7,000
11	8,400

These operating costs include the general cost of running the machine and the maintenance expenses. We also assume that the firm discards worn out machines.

To see more exactly the choices the firm faces, consider a six-year period. Over that period, the firm can provide itself with a stream of machines by following several replacement strategies. For example, it can replace the machine every two years. Alternatively, it can replace the machine after three years, or it can keep it for the full six years. Table 7.3 shows the cash flows the firm will incur for each of these strategies. For example, if the

TABLE 7.3
Different Strategies for Machine Replacement Over a Six-Year Period

Year	Two-Year Cycle	Three-Year Cycle	Six-Year Cycle
0	$10,000	$10,000	$10,000
1	1,000	1,000	1,000
2	*11,500	1,500	1,500
3	1,000	*11,800	1,800
4	*11,500	1,000	2,100
5	1,000	1,500	2,500
6	1,500	1,800	3,000
PV($r = 18\%$)	$26,640	$20,945	$16,308

*Includes $10,000 for machine replacement.

firm replaces the machine every two years, it incurs an operating cost of $1,000 for the first year and $1,500 for the second year. In addition, it must pay the purchase price for the replacement.

Because each of these three strategies covers exactly the same six-year span, they are directly comparable. The firm can decide among these by choosing the strategy with the lowest present value of costs over the six-year period. Table 7.3 presents these present values assuming an 18 percent discount rate. Of the three strategies, keeping the machine for six years is the best plan because it has the lowest present value of costs.

MACHINE REPLACEMENT AND THE EQUIVALENT ANNUITY METHOD

Although we know that it is better to replace the machine every six years instead of every two or three years, we do not know if replacing every six years is the overall best available strategy. After all, we could replace the machine every five years, seven years, or some other amount of time. However, comparing the six-year strategy with the five- or seven-year replacement strategy is not so easy.

The three replacement strategies in the previous section were chosen as examples because at the end of the 6 years we would have to replace the machine under any of them. This allowed us to look at the present value of all the machine costs over 6 years. To analyze the 6-year versus the 7-year strategy in the same way, we would have to consider operating the machines over 42 years. While we could do this, it is a cumbersome procedure that we would rather avoid.[2]

---

[2] The period of analysis is the **least common multiple** (LCM) of the replacement strategies considered. For example, the LCM of 2, 3, and 6 is 6. This is why we chose a six-year period for the analysis. Similarly, to analyze the six- and seven-year strategies, we need to consider a period of 42 years, since the LCM of 6 and 7 is 42.

We can solve the machine replacement problem with an alternative strategy. The **equivalent annuity method** calculates the annuity that has the same present value as the present value of operating the actual machine over a given number of years.[3]

We can implement the equivalent annuity method by following these steps:

1. For each replacement strategy (two-year, three-year, etc.), calculate the present value of all costs incurred in operating a machine for that period.
2. For an annuity of the same length of time, find the periodic amount that results in the same present value found in step 1.
3. Because the equivalent annuity cost is effectively the annual cost of operating the machine, choose the strategy with the lowest equivalent annuity amount.

For example, consider the three-year replacement strategy, which involves the cash flows shown in table 7.3. Applying our three-step procedure we find:

1. The present value of the investment and operating costs for the first three years is:

$$PV = 10,000 + \frac{1,000}{1.18} + \frac{1,500}{1.18^2} + \frac{1,800}{1.18^3} = \$13,020$$

2. This present value of $13,020 will purchase an annuity of $5,989 for three years, assuming an 18 percent discount rate. The calculation is:

$$\$13,200 = C \times PA(18, 3)$$

$$C = \frac{\$13,020}{2.174} = \$5,989$$

Therefore, the annual cost of operating the machine with replacement every three years is $5,989.

3. We calculate the annuity amount for each replacement strategy as in steps 1 and 2. Table 7.4 shows these annuity amounts.

Each replacement strategy has its own equivalent annuity associated with it. In this case, the strategy that gives the lowest annuity cost is the best. The data from table 7.4 show that the effective annual cost reaches a minimum when the firm keeps the machine in service for eight years and then replaces it.

PROJECTS WITH DIFFERENT LIVES

The choice between price and quality is familiar in everyday life and in capital budgeting decisions. For example, the consumer must choose between an expensive refrigerator that will last more years and run on less energy, and the cheaper economy model that lasts fewer years and consumes more energy. Like the consumer, the financial manager faces

---

[3] The equivalent annuity may be known by different names. For example, some calculators call it the **net uniform series** (NUS).

TABLE 7.4
Effective Annual Costs of Operating a Machine
for Different Replacement Strategies

t (years)	C_t	PV_t	Equivalent Annual Cost
1	1,000	10,847	$12,792
2	1,500	11,925	7,615
3	1,800	13,020	5,989
4	2,100	14,103	5,243
5	2,500	15,196	4,860
6	3,000	16,308	4,662
7	3,600	17,438	4,575
8	4,300	18,582	*4,557
9	5,500	19,822	4,610
10	7,000	21,159	4,708
11	8,400	23,622	5,073

*Minimum equivalent annual cost.

a similar problem on a larger scale in choosing equipment for a plant. A given machine may cost more than another to buy, but the expensive one may have a lower maintenance cost and may last longer than the cheaper machine. This section shows how to apply capital budgeting techniques to problems involving projects with different lives.

Consider the cash flows for the two machines shown in table 7.5. The cheap machine costs $12,000, lasts for three years, and generates an after-tax cash flow of $7,000 per year. The quality machine costs $22,000, lasts five years, and generates after-tax cash flows of $8,000 per year. We assume that the discount rate is 15 percent.

We cannot simply determine which machine has the greater NPV in this case, due to the difference in lives. Comparing NPVs is meaningless because we do not know the cash flows from the cheap strategy for years 4 and 5. If we assume the firm replaces the cheap machine after three years, then that strategy would have cash flows for six years. By comparison, the quality machine would show cash flows for only five years. We could

TABLE 7.5
Cash Flows for the Cheap and Quality Machines

Year	Cheap Machine	Quality Machine
0	−$12,000	−$22,000
1	7,000	8,000
2	7,000	8,000
3	7,000	8,000
4	—	8,000
5	—	8,000

solve this problem by comparing a sequence of cheap and quality machines over a given time interval. For our example, the shortest such period would be the least common multiple of 3 and 5, or 15 years. At the end of the 15 years both machines would have to be replaced.

Working with 15 years of data is cumbersome. Fortunately, we can solve this type of problem by applying the equivalent annuity method. If we compare the present values of purchasing the two machines using a discount rate of 15 percent, we find that the present value of the cheap machine is $3,982 and that of the quality machine is $4,818. This suggests we should buy the quality machine. However, these NPVs are not directly comparable because they cover different periods. In particular, this comparison is not fair because it neglects the cash flows from the cheap strategy in periods 4 and 5. Consequently, a direct comparison of the two NPVs introduces a bias in favor of the project with the longer life.

To put the same point in a slightly different way, the net present value of the quality machine is the reward for operating that machine for five years. The NPV from the cheap machine is a reward the firm can reap every three years. Should the firm prefer an NPV of $4,818 every five years or an NPV of $3,982 every three years? The choice is not obvious, and to answer this question we turn to the equivalent annuity method.

By adopting the cheap machine, we achieve an NPV of $3,982. This present value of $3,982 buys a three-year annuity of $1,744, assuming a discount rate of 15 percent:

$$\$3,982 = C \times PA(15, 3)$$

$$C = \frac{\$3,982}{2.2832} = \$1,744$$

Because the firm will replace the cheap machine every three years, following the cheap machine strategy amounts to choosing a perpetuity of $1,744 per year.

The next task is to apply the equivalent annuity method to the five-year machine. Its net present value of $4,818 buys a five-year annuity of $1,437, assuming a 15 percent discount rate.

$$\$4,818 = C \times PA(15, 5)$$

$$C = \frac{\$4,818}{3.3522} = \$1,437$$

This is effectively a perpetuity as well, assuming the firm replaces the quality machine every five years.

Both machines are now on a comparable footing, because we consider the cash flow each one provides annually over the same infinite horizon. Comparing the two equivalent annuities, it is clear that the firm should prefer the cheap machine over the quality machine. Sometimes the price of quality is too high!

IRR COMPLICATIONS

We have already seen that if two projects are mutually exclusive, the IRR rule may lead to the wrong decision. The IRR has some additional problems. For example, some projects may have more than one positive and real IRR, and others may have none. The financial manager should be aware of these peculiarities to avoid making costly mistakes.

Projects with Multiple IRRs

We saw in the previous chapter that if a project has cash flows with only one change of sign, then we can be assured that the project has a single positive IRR. We defined such projects as normal. In practice, however, many projects have cash flow streams with multiple sign changes. When this happens, the project may have more than one positive IRR. The following important rule limits the possible number of positive IRRs that a project may have.[4]

The maximum possible number of positive and real IRRs equals the number of sign changes in the project's cash flow stream.

To illustrate, consider the following cash flow pattern with two sign changes.

Year	Cash Flow
0	−$2,000
1	+7,000
2	−6,000

For this cash flow stream, we can find the IRR by solving the following equation:

$$0 = -\$2,000 + \frac{\$7,000}{1 + IRR} - \frac{\$6,000}{(1 + IRR)^2}$$

Multiplying this expression by $(1 + IRR)^2$, we get:

$$0 = -2,000(1 + IRR)^2 + 7,000(1 + IRR) - 6,000$$

This quadratic equation can be solved using some algebra. The general solution to an equation of the form $ax^2 + bx + c = 0$ is found from equation 7.1 below:

$$x = \frac{-b \pm \sqrt{b^2 - 4ac}}{2a} \tag{7.1}$$

In our example, $a = -2,000$, $b = 7,000$, and $c = -6,000$. Also, in applying equation 7.1 to solve for the internal rate of return, the term $(1 + IRR)$ takes the place of x. Given this, we have:

---

[4] This is known as Descartes' rule, in honor of the seventeenth century French philosopher and mathematician.

$$(1 + \text{IRR}) = \frac{-7,000 \pm \sqrt{7,000^2 - 4 \times (-2,000) \times (-6,000)}}{2(-2,000)}$$

$$(1 + \text{IRR}_1) = 1.50$$

$$(1 + \text{IRR}_2) = 2.00$$

This computation shows that the two IRRs of this project are 50 percent and 100 percent. In this example, the project had two sign changes and produced two positive IRRs – the maximum allowed by the general rule.

Figure 7.2 shows how the NPV of this cash flow stream varies as a function of the discount rate. From the definition of the IRR we have NPV = 0 at discount rates of 50 and 100 percent. The NPV profile clearly shows that in this case it is erroneous to apply the IRR rule, which indicates that we should accept projects with an IRR greater than the appropriate discount rate. For example, if the discount rate is less than 50 percent, as is very likely in practice, then the IRR rule would lead to acceptance of the project, even though it has a negative NPV for discount rates less than 50 percent. In fact, this project should be accepted only when the appropriate discount rates are between 50 and 100 percent. Otherwise, the project should be rejected.

To better understand this conclusion, which may seem strange on first exposure, let us find the terminal value after two years that results from investing in the project, and compare it to the terminal value that would result from keeping the $2,000 in alternative

FIGURE 7.2
A Project with Multiple IRRs

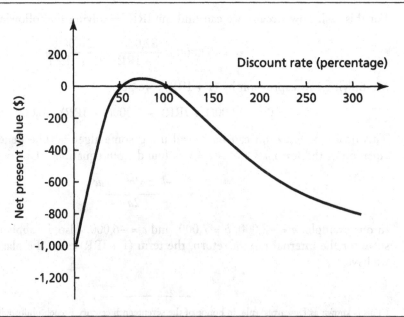

investments earning the appropriate discount rate. This appropriate discount rate is also known as the **opportunity cost of capital**.

Suppose the investor's opportunity cost of capital is less than 50 percent, say 30 percent. Then the terminal value (TV) the investor receives from keeping the $2,000 in alternative investments for two years is:

$$TV = \$2,000 \times (1 + 0.3)^2 = \$3,380$$

If the investor diverts the $2,000 from those alternative investments and places them in this project, the investor receives $7,000 at $t = 1$. The investor can then put these funds to work for one year at the opportunity cost of capital of 30 percent. Additionally, at time $t = 2$, the investor must sacrifice $6,000 by investing it in the project. As a result, the terminal value to the investor from moving the $2,000 into the project is:

$$TV = \$7,000 \times (1 + 0.3) - \$6,000 = \$3,100$$

Since alternative investments earning 30 percent result in a higher terminal value than investing in the project, the investor should reject the project. But this is exactly the conclusion already reached through the NPV profile of figure 7.2.

This terminal value approach can be used to show that for discount rates between 50 and 100 percent, the investor has a higher terminal value with the project than with alternative investments. For opportunity rates greater than 100 percent, the alternative investments are, once again, preferable, because they would result in higher terminal values.

Projects with No Real IRR

Consider a project with the following cash flows:

Year	Cash Flow
0	-$1,000
1	+1,500
2	-1,000

We can find the IRRs of this project using equation 7.1. In this example, $a = -1,000$, $b = 1,500$, and $c = -1,000$, so we have:

$$(1 + IRR) = \frac{-1,500 \pm \sqrt{1,500^2 - 4 \times (-1,000) \times (-1,000)}}{2(-1,000)}$$

$$(1 + IRR_1) = 0.75 + 0.66\sqrt{-1}$$

$$(1 + IRR_2) = 0.75 - 0.66\sqrt{-1}$$

The two solutions to this project involve the square root of −1, which does not exist as a real number. In other words, no real number multiplied by itself results in −1. The square root of –1 is the unit of the imaginary numbers and is symbolically written as i.[5] When we say that there is no real IRR, we mean that the IRR does not lie on the real number line. An important implication is that the NPV profile for the project will never cross the horizontal axis because, if it did, a real IRR would then exist, which is an obvious contradiction. Consequently, we have the interesting financial result that the NPV profile of a project with no real IRR remains either always above or always below the horizontal (discount rate) axis.

Since for projects with no real IRR the NPV is either always positive or always negative, regardless of the value of the discount rate used, the decision rule is extremely simple. Just determine the NPV for a convenient discount rate, say $r = 0$ percent, and if the NPV is positive, then accept the project; otherwise reject it. In the example, the NPV will always be negative since for $r = 0$ we have NPV = –\$1,000 + \$1,500 – \$1,000 = –\$500, so the project should be rejected regardless of the required discount rate.

The NPV profile for the project in our example is shown in figure 7.3. We verify that the NPV is always negative, so the project should be rejected without further ado.

FIGURE 7.3
A Project with No Real IRR

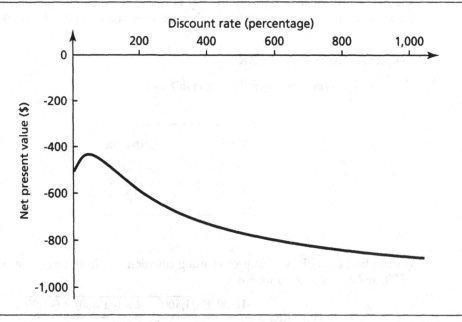

[5] The two IRRs found are complex numbers. Complex numbers consist of a real part and an imaginary part. Whenever a project has complex IRRs, it will always have an even number of them. Each pair of IRRs arises from the positive and negative signs in equation 7.1. As an application, if you have already found two complex IRRs for a three-year project, then the remaining IRR is necessarily a real number, since complex IRRs can only come in pairs.

Now that we have seen the possibility that a project may have IRRs that are not real numbers, we can state another important rule concerning the number of IRRs that a project may have:[6]

An *n*-year project has exactly *n* IRRs.

This rule says that, for example, a two-year project must have exactly two IRRs. These may be real or complex, and we have seen examples of both. The rule also states that even normal projects lasting *n* years, which we know can only have one positive real IRR, have (*n* − 1) additional IRRs. These additional IRRs can be a combination of negative and real IRRs and IRRs that are complex pairs.

SUMMARY

This chapter has examined some complex issues and common problems in capital budgeting. The problem of mutually exclusive projects complicates matters for the financial manager. In such a situation, using the IRR to rank the projects can lead to an erroneous decision.

Similar difficulties arise in choosing projects when the firm has a limited amount of investable funds. When the firm must ration capital, ranking projects by their IRR may lead to a less than optimal selection of projects. Instead, the manager should choose the subset of projects that has the largest NPV without exceeding the investment budget constraint.

The machine replacement problem requires choosing the best time to replace a machine with an identical new machine. This is essentially a cost minimization problem, and we developed methods to choose the correct time to replace. There is often a choice between a quality good and a cheap good. The two will typically differ in cost, performance, and useful life. This chapter showed how to evaluate such a choice.

The chapter concluded with a discussion of some problems associated with the internal rate of return method. Sometimes, projects may have more than one positive real IRR, and the IRR rule developed for normal projects may lead to the wrong decision. Also, there are projects with no real IRR. Although at first this appears to be a pathological case, we found that it is actually the easiest case for financial decision purposes, because when the project has no real IRR, the NPV of the project will always have the same sign, regardless of the discount rate used.

QUESTIONS

1. For projects that are mutually exclusive, why is there a need to rank projects?
2. What is the pitfall in ranking mutually exclusive projects by the IRR method?
3. If a firm does not face capital rationing, does it need to use IRR at all in ranking projects?

---

[6] This property is known as the **fundamental theorem of algebra**.

4. Explain why the firm should take the collection of projects with the highest combined NPV when the firm faces capital rationing.

5. What is the purpose of the equivalent annuity method as applied to the machine replacement problem?

6. In choosing between high and low quality machines, what is the main criterion for choosing one or the other?

7. Projects A and B are normal. If the sum of all the cash flows of project A is greater than the corresponding sum for project B, and if $IRR_A > IRR_B$, will the IRR and NPV techniques give the same ranking of the two projects?

8. You are considering a project in which the cash flows have a total of three sign changes. You wish to know all the real positive IRRs. You have already determined that, for $r = 0$, the NPV is –$2,000, and you have already found that $IRR_1 = 20$ percent and that $IRR_2 = 37$ percent. Should you continue to look for the third possible IRR? Explain.

9. In the previous question, suppose that for $r = 0$ the NPV is +$1,300. The two known IRRs are the same as before. Should you continue to search for the third possible IRR?

10. You are considering a project in which the cash flows have a total of four sign changes. You wish to know all the real positive IRRs. You have already determined that, for $r = 0$, the NPV is –$1,000, and you have already found that $IRR_1 = 10$ percent, $IRR_2 = 25$ percent, and $IRR_3 = 40$ percent. Should you continue to look for the fourth possible IRR? Explain.

11. In the previous question, suppose that, for $r = 0$, the NPV is +$1,000. The three known IRRs are the same as before. Should you continue to search for the fourth possible IRR?

12. You are considering a five-year project and wish to find all its real IRRs. You have already found two complex IRRs, which are $0.5 + 0.4i$ and $0.7 + 0.2i$, where i is the unit of the imaginary numbers. Of the three remaining IRRs, how many must be real?

13. You are considering a six-year project and wish to find all its positive real IRRs. You have already found three complex IRRs, which are $0.2 + 0.3i$, $0.9 + 0.8i$, and $0.5 + 0.4i$, where i is the unit of the imaginary numbers. Of the three remaining IRRs, how many must be real?

14. Two mutually exclusive projects have the same life, and their positive cash flows constitute annuities. If the project with the higher investment cost has a lower annuity cash flow, can the two NPV profiles cross at some positive discount rate?

PROBLEMS

1. You are considering opening a car dealership on a piece of land. The initial investment is $73 million and the cash inflows for years 1–5 are all equal to $26 million. What is the NPV for this project if the discount rate is 17 percent?

2. Compute the IRR for the car dealership project of problem 1.

3. Another project that interests you is building a shopping mall. For the mall the initial investment is $90 million and the cash inflows for years 1–5 are $30 million. What is the NPV of this project if the discount rate is 15 percent?
4. Compute the IRR for the shopping mall project of problem 3.
5. There is just one more problem with the two projects we have been considering. Both would use the same piece of land, so they are mutually exclusive. Which project should be chosen, if either? Explain.

Consider the following two projects. All cash flows shown are on an after-tax basis. Use these data to solve problems 6–9.

Year	Project A	Project B
0	–$75,000	–$55,000
1	–$30,000	–$22,000
2	–$18,000	–$13,200
3	–$50,000	–$36,667

6. If the discount rate is 18 percent, what is the NPV of Projects A and B?
7. Find the IRR of Projects A and B.
8. Which project should you prefer?
9. If the discount rate for Project A is 20 percent and the discount rate for Project B is still 18 percent, which project should you prefer?

You have analyzed the following projects and determined their NPVs, which are presented below. Use this information to solve problems 10–12.

Project	NPV	Required Investment
Alpha	$10,000	$50,000
Sigma	$20,000	$90,000
Gamma	$ 5,000	$10,000
Beta	$45,000	110,000
Epsilon	$ 9,000	$35,000
Nu	$ 7,000	$20,000
Tau	$12,000	$30,000
Phi	$30,000	$90,000

10. If you are limited to $70,000 in investable funds, which projects should you accept?

11. If you are limited to $130,000 in investable funds, which projects should you accept?

12. If you are limited to $250,000 in investable funds, which projects should you accept?

13. Machine A requires an investment of $100,000, has a five-year life, and produces equal annual cash flows of $50,000. Machine B requires an investment of $200,000, has a seven-year life, and produces equal annual cash flows of $60,000. The two machines are mutually exclusive. If the discount rate is 10 percent, which machine should be chosen?

14. Projects C and D are mutually exclusive. They have the same IRR and the same yearly cash flows. However, the life of project C is twice the life of project D. If project D is preferable to project C, how are the two investment amounts, the annual cash flow, and the life of project D related?

15. Consider projects A and B, where the positive inflows constitute annuities which start at time 1. Project A lasts for n_A years and project B lasts for n_B years. Show that if $NPV_A > NPV_B$ and $n_A < n_B$, then the equivalent annuity for project A is greater than the equivalent annuity for project B.

16. Machine X has an NPV of $20,000 and a life of five years. Machine Y has an NPV of $10,000 and a life of eight years. For both machines, the positive cash flows constitute annuities. Which machine should be chosen?

Chapter 8

Risk and the Required Rate of Return

OVERVIEW

In this chapter we introduce the concepts of risk and return. High risk almost always accompanies high expected returns. The investor must know how to measure both return and risk, and how to choose the investment with the most favorable combination. In this chapter, we learn to quantify expected return and risk.

Armed with these techniques for measuring risk and expected return, we can study how to combine securities to form portfolios. A portfolio is a collection of securities held by a single investor. As this chapter explains in detail, one of the main incentives for forming portfolios is diversification, which is the allocation of investable funds to a variety of securities in order to reduce risk.

PRINCIPLES OF RISK AND RETURN

This section introduces the basic concepts of risk and return. These concepts will be used extensively throughout this chapter and the next, and they constitute the foundation of all of portfolio theory.

Expected Return

Suppose you have the opportunity to invest $1 (or $1,000,000 if you enjoy dealing with larger numbers) in Bernoulli Research Corporation. This risky investment has two possible outcomes. If the outcome is favorable (F), you receive $4. If the outcome is unfavorable (U), the project generates no cash and you lose your entire $1 investment. Thus, the net payoff, or simply payoff, is either $3 or –$1. Assume the outcome occurs almost immediately, so you can disregard the time value of money. Because the payoff of this project is uncertain, the payoff is a **random variable**. Suppose the probability of each outcome is 50 percent. Before plunging into this investment, you want to know the expected payoff and the risk of the investment.

With the information given, we can obtain a probability distribution of the possible payoffs. A **probability distribution** is a list of all possible payoffs from the investment,

TABLE 8.1

Probability Distribution of Payoffs for Bernoulli Research Corporation

Outcome	Probability	Payoff
F	0.50	+$3
U	0.50	−$1

along with their respective probabilities. For this investment the probability distribution is given in table 8.1. This same information about the probability distribution of payoffs is presented graphically in figure 8.1.

Of course, if the investment is made only once, you will either win $3 or lose $1. Of more interest is knowing how much you can expect to earn or lose on average if you make a similar investment repeatedly. In this example, you expect to win $3 half the time and to lose $1 the other half. This suggests that the expected value of the payoff variable, E(Payoff), can be found as follows:

$$E(\text{Payoff}) = (\$3) \times 0.5 + (-\$1) \times 0.5 = \$1$$

In general, if a random variable r can have n possible outcomes r_i, where $i = 1, 2, \ldots,$ n, and each outcome has probability p_i, then the expected value of r is given by:

$$E(r) = r_1 p_1 + r_2 p_2 + \ldots + r_n p_n \tag{8.1}$$

We can write this summation more compactly using the following notation:

FIGURE 8.1

Probability Distribution of Payoffs for Bernoulli Research Corporation

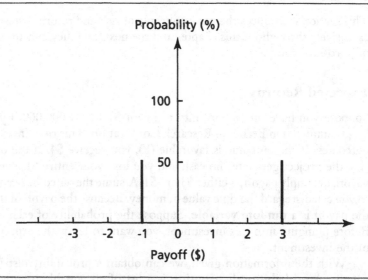

$$E(r) = \sum_{i=1}^{n} r_i p_i \qquad (8.2)$$

We also note the basic fact that the sum of all the probabilities must add to 1. This is true because we know with certainty that some outcome will be observed. In our notation, we have:

$$\sum_{i=1}^{n} p_i = 1 \qquad (8.3)$$

Variance and Standard Deviation

Now that we know how to compute the expected payoff of the investment, we need to quantify its risk. A casual definition of the riskiness of a random variable is the possibility that the outcome will differ from the expected outcome. In general, the more the outcome may differ from the expected outcome, the greater the riskiness of the random variable. Thus, the notion of risk is associated with the dispersion of possible outcomes.

A common way to measure the dispersion of any random variable, r, around its mean is to calculate its variance, σ^2, as follows:

$$\sigma^2 = [r_1 - E(r)]^2 p_1 + [r_2 - E(r)]^2 p_2 + \ldots + [r_n - E(r)]^2 p_n \qquad (8.4)$$

or, using the compact notation:

$$\sigma^2 = \sum_{i=1}^{n} [r_i - E(r)]^2 p_i \qquad (8.5)$$

For Bernoulli Research, the variance of the payoffs is equal to:

$$\sigma^2 = [3 - 1]^2 \times 0.5 + [-1 - 1]^2 \times 0.5 = 4$$

Notice that if the unit for the random variable is dollars, the unit for the variance is dollars squared, making the variance hard to interpret. Because of this difficulty, the standard deviation is often used as an alternative measure of risk. The **standard deviation** of a random variable is the square root of its variance, and is denoted by σ. Thus, the standard deviation is defined by the following relationship:

$$\sigma = \sqrt{\sigma^2} \qquad (8.6)$$

The standard deviation measures the dispersion of a random variable around its mean. For the $1 investment in Bernoulli, the standard deviation of the random payoffs is $2. The standard deviation gives a range of values around the mean that are likely to occur more frequently. Since Bernoulli has an expected payoff of $1, the standard deviation of $2 indicates that we can expect most payoffs to be between –$1 ($1 – $2) and $3 ($1 + $2). In fact, in this example the standard deviation gives the entire range of possible payoffs: –$1 and $3.[1]

To continue our example, suppose that another firm, Binomial Software, offers the same payoff distribution as Bernoulli Research, and you wonder if there is any benefit in

---

[1] This is not generally the case. For example, if the payoff probability distribution is normal, then the actual payoffs would fall within one standard deviation of the mean payoff about two thirds of the time.

TABLE 8.2
Probability Distribution of Payoffs from Combining Bernoulli and Binomial

Bernoulli Outcome	Binomial Outcome	Probability	Bernoulli Payoff	Binomial Payoff	Total Payoff
F	F	0.25	-$1.50	-$1.50	-$3.00
F	U	0.25	-$1.50	-$0.50	-$1.00
U	F	0.25	-$0.50	-$1.50	-$1.00
U	U	0.25	-$0.50	-$0.50	-$1.00

investing $0.50 in Bernoulli and the other $0.50 in Binomial. Because you invest half as much as before in each firm, you will receive a payoff of $1.50 from one of the firms if its outcome is favorable, and you will lose $0.50 for each firm with an unfavorable outcome.

Let us assume that Bernoulli and Binomial are **independent investments**. This means that the outcome of Bernoulli will not have any influence on the outcome of Binomial. Because the payoffs of the two firms are independent, the probability distribution of the combined investment consists of four equally likely outcomes, as shown in table 8.2.

Under the new probability distribution of returns there is a 50 percent chance of obtaining a payoff of $1 because two of the four possible outcomes have this payoff. Also, the probability of each extreme outcome has been reduced to 25 percent. Figure 8.2 depicts the probability distribution for this combined investment.

FIGURE 8.2
Probability Distribution of Payoffs from Combining Bernoulli and Binomial

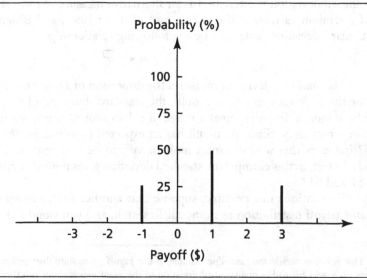

Knowing the probability distribution of this two-investment strategy, we can compute its expected payoff using equation 8.1:

$$E(\text{Payoff}) = \$3.00 \times 0.25 + \$1.00 \times 0.25 + \$1.00 \times 0.25 + (-\$1.00) \times 0.25$$
$$= \$1.00$$

We conclude that dividing money into two identical independent investments provides the same expected payoff as putting all the money into one of the investments. However, consider what happens to the risk of the combined investment. We compute the variance of the combined investment using equation 8.4:

$$\sigma^2 = [3 - 1]^2 \times 0.25 + [1 - 1]^2 \times 0.25$$
$$+ [1 - 1]^2 \times 0.25 + [-1 - 1]^2 \times 0.25$$
$$= 2.00$$

Notice that the variance from investing equally in Bernoulli and Binomial is half the variance of investing the entire \$1 in Bernoulli alone. Since the variance is a measure of risk, the combined investment is less risky than investing entirely in only one of the two firms.[2] Most importantly, there is no cost associated with this risk reduction because the expected payoff is unchanged.

Knowing the variance, we compute the standard deviation of the two-firm investment strategy using equation 8.6:

$$\sigma = \sqrt{2} = \$1.41$$

This simple example with two independent identical investments illustrates the following general result. By investing in equal proportions in n identical independent projects, the expected payoff will be the same as the expected payoff of investing all the money in only one of the projects. However, the overall standard deviation from the n project investment is lower than the standard deviation from the single project investment. If σ_1 is the standard deviation of each of the projects and σ_n is the standard deviation of the n project investment, then:

$$\sigma_n = \frac{\sigma_1}{\sqrt{n}} \tag{8.7}$$

In the case of Bernoulli and Binomial, there is no need to calculate the standard deviation of the combined investment directly from the definition. Rather, since we already know that it is \$2 for each of them, we can use equation 8.7 directly:

$$\sigma_2 = \frac{\$2}{\sqrt{2}} = \$1.41$$

This is exactly the same result we found before.

---

[2] Of course, this is not a surprising result if you believe in the saying: "Don't put all your eggs in one basket." Our real contribution lies in quantifying the different risks associated with any number of "baskets."

Covariance

The **covariance** (COV) measures the tendency of any pair of random variables to move together. Intuitively, the covariance measures the connection between two random variables. For example, because tall people tend to weigh more than short people, we can say that height and weight have a positive covariance. In finance, when interest rates increase unexpectedly, the stock market index tends to decrease. This is an example of two variables with a negative covariance. Knowledge of the behavior of one random variable helps predict the behavior of the other. Thus, higher future interest rates would likely lead to a decline in the stock market index, other things being equal. A further example is that of tossing two coins. We know from casual observation and intuition that the outcome of tossing one coin does not affect the outcome of the other coin toss. This is another way of saying that the coin tossing outcomes are independent. Therefore, for pairs of independent random variables we expect the covariance to be zero, since these variables are not connected.

To formalize these ideas, suppose two random variables, x and y, have n possible combined outcomes. When combined outcome i occurs, the value of x is x_i and the value of y is y_i. Assume that the probability that outcome i occurs is p_i. Let the expected values of x and y be $E(x)$ and $E(y)$, respectively. Then, the covariance between these two random variables is defined as follows:

$$COV(x, y) = [x_1 - E(x)][y_1 - E(y)]p_1 + \ldots + [x_n - E(x)][y_n - E(y)]p_n \qquad (8.8)$$

Using the compact notation, we can write:

$$COV(x, y) = \sum_{i=1}^{n} [x_i - E(x)][y_i - E(y)]p_i \qquad (8.9)$$

With this definition, we can compute the covariance between the payoffs of Bernoulli Research and the payoffs of Binomial Software, using the data in table 8.2:[3]

$$COV(x, y) = [1.50 - 0.5][1.50 - 0.5]0.25 + [1.50 - 0.5][-0.50 - 0.5]0.25$$
$$+ [-0.50 - 0.5][1.50 - 0.5]0.25$$
$$+ [-0.50 - 0.5][-0.50 - 0.5]0.25$$
$$= (1 - 1 - 1 + 1)0.25$$
$$= 0$$

This computation tells us that there is no covariance between the two identical firms. This should not be surprising, since we already know that the two investments are independent of each other and, therefore, do not covary.[4]

It is useful to note that the variance is just a special case of the covariance of an asset with itself. For example, the covariance of asset x with itself is, according to equation 8.9:

---

[3] Notice that while the expected payoff of the combined investment is $1, the expected payoff of each investment considered separately is $0.50.

[4] It is always true that if two random variables are independent, they have a zero covariance. However, a zero covariance does not necessarily imply independence of the random variables.

$$COV(x, x) = \sum_{i=1}^{n} [x_i - E(x)][x_i - E(x)]p_i = \sum_{i=1}^{n} [x_i - E(x)]^2 p_i \qquad (8.10)$$

$$= \sigma_x^2$$

Another useful property of the covariance is that the order of the variables is irrelevant in its computation. Thus:

$$COV(x, y) = COV(y, x) \qquad (8.11)$$

These properties of the covariance will be useful when we discuss multiple asset portfolios.

Correlation Coefficient

The covariance is a useful measure of the amount of connection between two random variables. However, it has two major disadvantages. First, the covariance is not bounded and may turn out to be any number, however large or small. Second, the numerical value of the covariance depends on the units used to measure the random variables. For example, the numerical value of the covariance between height and weight varies depending on whether the variables are measured in inches and pounds, or in centimeters and kilos. These problems make comparisons of different covariances difficult. For example, using only the covariance, it is impossible to say if the degree of connection between interest rates and the stock market index is stronger than the degree of connection between height and weight among people.

Fortunately, the problem of comparing the degree of connection between different pairs of random variables can be solved through the ingenious trick of dividing the covariance of two random variables by the product of their standard deviations. It is a remarkable fact that by performing this operation, the resulting number will always be between −1 and +1. This is true regardless of whether the variables are measured in pounds, kilos, dollars, annual rate of return, or any other unit. This number between −1 and +1 is called the **correlation coefficient** between the two random variables. That is, it measures their degree of connection. In general, the correlation coefficient between two random variables x and y is given by the following formula:[5]

$$\rho(x, y) = \frac{COV(x, y)}{\sigma_x \sigma_y} \qquad (8.12)$$

For the example of Bernoulli and Binomial, we found that the covariance between their payoffs is 0. It follows from equation 8.12 that their correlation coefficient is also 0, confirming that no connection exists between the payoffs.

The correlation coefficient is essentially a scaled covariance. The scaling means that the correlation must fall between −1 and +1. If the correlation coefficient exceeds zero, the two variables tend to move in the same direction. A negative value for the correlation coefficient indicates that the two variables tend to move in opposite directions. If the correlation between two variables equals zero, there is no connection between them.

---

[5] When there is no possible confusion, we will simply write ρ instead of $\rho(x, y)$.

RISK AND RETURN IN THE NEW YORK STOCK EXCHANGE

We now apply the concepts of risk and return to the history of the New York Stock Exchange. Figure 8.3 shows the yearly rate of return on common stocks for the period from 1926–1994. The largest return occurred in 1933 and was 53.99 percent, with the smallest, −43.44 percent, coming two years earlier in 1931. It is also clear from the figure that years of gains occurred more often than years of losses. But perhaps most striking is the great tendency for radical swings from one year to the next.

For these stocks, the historic mean rate of return has been around 12.5 percent and the standard deviation of the returns around 20 percent. These statistics provide a convenient way of summarizing a great deal of information.

PRINCIPLES OF PORTFOLIO ANALYSIS

For the discussion that follows, we make some simplifying assumptions about markets and investor psychology. While the assumptions themselves are not necessarily realistic, markets behave very much as if the assumptions were true.

First, we assume that the securities markets operate with no transaction costs, such as commissions and taxes. Second, we assume all investors have free access to all relevant information about securities. Third, we assume that investors appraise the available information similarly. With the same information and employing the same mode of analysis, investors have identical estimations about the risk and expected return of securities. Fourth, we assume that investors care about only the risk and expected return characteristics of securities, and that they seek higher expected returns and avoid risk. Finally, we assume that all of the investors in the marketplace have a one-period time horizon.

FIGURE 8.3
Yearly Rates of Return on Common Stocks

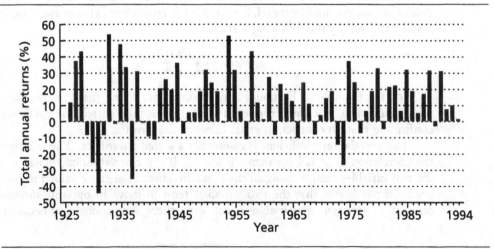

Source: Stocks, Bonds, Bills, and Inflation: 1994 Yearbook, Chicago: Ibbotson Associates, 1995.

While the assumptions are not realistic – for example, transactions costs are not zero – their lack of realism is more apparent than real. Relaxing the assumptions has the principal effect of making the mathematics much more complicated, but making them more realistic does not change the basic conclusions we will draw.

The Goals of Investing

We assume that investors desire only the monetary benefits of investing. For example, they do not value the many pleasures of tracking an investment portfolio on a daily basis. Second, we assume investors prefer more wealth to less. Finally, we assume they are risk averse. In other words, investors prefer to avoid risk where possible. This does not mean that they will refuse to undertake risk, but that they will demand greater expected returns for bearing increased risk.

These last two assumptions, which describe most people quite well, point out the essential tension that characterizes securities investment. The investment opportunities that seem to offer the greatest increase in wealth tend also to be the riskiest, so investors typically must trade off a benefit – higher return – against a cost – riskiness.

Given the fact that investors must struggle to secure high returns while trying to control risk, we can state the goal of investing in two equivalent ways:

1. For a given level of risk, to secure the highest expected return possible.
2. For a given expected return, to secure the smallest possible risk.

Risk/Expected Return Space

Table 8.3 presents data for two risky assets that we can use to illustrate the idea of a risk/ expected return space. Since we assume that we compute means and variances from past data, they are the historical mean and variance. According to our assumptions, however, investors focus on the *expected* return and variance.

It is customary to estimate future expected returns from past mean returns. For the two securities in table 8.3, we estimate the expected return of security A to be 7.8 percent

TABLE 8.3
Historical Returns for Securities A and B

Year	Security A	Security B
1	0.18	0.14
2	0.15	0.09
3	−0.13	0.02
4	0.05	−0.03
5	0.14	0.07
Mean	0.078	0.058
Variance	0.0127	0.0034
Standard deviation	0.1127	0.0582

and the expected return of security B to be 5.8 percent. Security B also has a smaller level of risk as measured by the variance or the standard deviation. An investor considering securities A and B faces a "risk/return trade-off."[6] The trade-off arises because the expected return of A is greater than that of B. However, to receive A's higher expected return, the investor must also accept its greater risk. Therefore, one trades a higher expected return against a lower risk. Given this fact, it is not clear whether all investors would prefer security A over security B.

When an investor can absolutely prefer asset X to asset Y, we say that asset X dominates asset Y. Figure 8.4 illustrates the idea of dominance by showing four securities in risk/return space. The arrow in the figure points to the preferred direction for all investors, because they like greater expected returns and wish to avoid risk. Given our assumptions, any investor would prefer security C to security E, because security C offers greater expected returns than security E, but they both have the same level of risk. Similarly, every investor prefers C to D, because, although they offer the same level of expected returns, C has less risk. Also, every investor would prefer C to F, because C offers both greater expected returns and less risk. By a similar reasoning, all investors prefer E to F and D to F.

FIGURE 8.4
Dominance in Risk/Expected Return Space

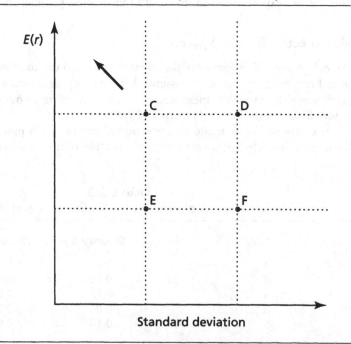

These preferences we have been observing help us to formulate a definition of dominance for any pair of securities:

Security X dominates Security Y if Security X has the same or greater expected return and the same or lower risk level than Security Y.

Note that the dominance relationship is transitive: because C dominates D and D dominates F, it follows that C dominates F.

Sometimes, however, it is not possible to say in advance that all investors would prefer one security to another. The choice between D and E in figure 8.4 depends on the individual investor's risk/return trade-off. For example, some are willing to accept the additional risk to capture more expected return. In this case, neither security dominates the other, because the dominance rule is not true for them.

TWO-ASSET RISKY PORTFOLIOS

We use a two-asset risky portfolio to illustrate diversification and the building of portfolios. The expected return of a two-asset portfolio depends on the expected returns of the individual assets and the relative percentage of funds invested in each.

The Expected Return of a Two-Asset Risky Portfolio

The expected return of a portfolio consisting of assets A and B is:

$$E(r_p) = w_a E(r_a) + w_b E(r_b) \tag{8.13}$$

where: w_i = percentage of funds, or weight, committed to asset $i = a, b$.

$E(r_i)$ = the expected return on asset i, where $i = a, b$, or P.

Notice also that, because all of the funds under consideration are committed to one asset or another to form the portfolio, we must have:

$$w_a + w_b = 1 \tag{8.14}$$

Equation 8.14 implies that we can express one of the weights in terms of the other.

To illustrate the central ideas behind two-asset risky portfolios, we use the data for securities A and B given in table 8.3. Suppose the proportions of assets A and B in the portfolio are 70 percent and 30 percent, respectively. Substituting the appropriate values in equation 8.13 gives:

$$E(r_p) = 0.7 \times 0.078 + 0.3 \times 0.058 = 0.072$$

As this calculation illustrates, the expected return of a two-asset portfolio is a simple weighted average of the expected returns of the individual assets.

The Risk of a Two-Asset Portfolio

The risk of a portfolio, like that of any asset, is measured by its variance and standard deviation. The same basic formula for the variance presented in equation 8.5 is also valid for a portfolio. After all, a portfolio may be viewed as just another asset. However, if we already have the expected return and the variance of each of the portfolio assets A and B, as well as the covariance between them and the weight of each asset in the portfolio, then equation 8.5 can be transformed into the following expression:

$$\sigma_p^2 = w_a^2 \sigma_a^2 + w_b^2 \sigma_b^2 + 2w_a w_b COV(r_a, r_b) \tag{8.15}$$

We previously discussed how to calculate the covariance in terms of the possible returns of each random variable and their associated probabilities. When dealing with returns, the past returns for each asset for each period are used to calculate their covariance. In this case, equal probability is assigned to each period. For example, if data from 20 past periods are used to calculate the covariance, each period is assigned a 5 percent probability. With this clarification, we use equation 8.9 to compute the covariance between assets A and B, which equals 0.0044. This covariance, in addition to our other information, is enough to compute the variance and standard deviation of a two-asset portfolio composed of securities A and B.

$$\sigma_p^2 = 0.7^2 \times 0.0127 + 0.3^2 \times 0.0034 + 2 \times 0.7 \times 0.3 \times 0.0044$$

$$= 0.0084$$

Using equation 8.6, the standard deviation of returns for this portfolio is 0.0915, or 9.15 percent. Recall that because the standard deviation is in the same units as the original variable, it is more intuitively meaningful than the variance.

We can also express the variance of a two-asset portfolio using the correlation coefficient, ρ. The formula is:[7]

$$\sigma_p^2 = w_a^2 \sigma_a^2 + w_b^2 \sigma_b^2 + 2w_a w_b \sigma_a \sigma_b \rho \tag{8.16}$$

Risk, Covariance, and Correlation

The risk of a portfolio depends mainly upon the covariance or correlation among the assets in the portfolio. We can illustrate this fact for a two-asset risky portfolio. Consider two securities A and B and assume they have the following risk/return characteristics.

Security	A	B
E(r)	0.10	0.18
σ	0.08	0.22
w	0.40	0.60

Notice that although the correlation between two assets affects the risk of a portfolio, it has no effect on the portfolio's return. This is clear from equation 8.13, the formula for

---

[7] To obtain this version of the formula, note that from equation 8.12 we have $COV(A, B) = \rho \sigma_a \sigma_b$.

the expected return of a portfolio. In the case of our portfolio made up of A and B, the expected return is:

$$E(r_p) = 0.4 \times 0.10 + 0.6 \times 0.18 = 0.148$$

To see how the correlation of returns determines the risk of a portfolio, we consider two special cases and examine the effect on the portfolio's risk. The first special case arises when the correlation between the assets equals 1. This is the case of perfect positive correlation. A second special case arises when the correlation equals −1. This is the case of perfect negative correlation.

Correlation = +1   If the correlation coefficient between the two assets equals 1, the last term in Equation 8.16 becomes $2w_a w_b \sigma_a \sigma_b$. In this special case, the expression for the variance is a perfect square:[8]

$$\sigma_p^2 = w_a^2 \sigma_a^2 + w_b^2 \sigma_b^2 + 2(w_a \sigma_a)(w_b \sigma_b)$$
$$= (w_a \sigma_a + w_b \sigma_b)^2$$

Taking the square root on both sides of this perfect square, we obtain:

$$\sigma_P = w_a \sigma_a + w_b \sigma_b \qquad (8.17)$$

When the correlation coefficient equals +1, the risk of the portfolio depends only on the risk of the individual assets and on the proportion of each asset in the portfolio. If assets A and B have perfect positive correlation, the standard deviation is:

$$\sigma_P = 0.4 \times 0.08 + 0.6 \times 0.22 = 0.164$$

Other portfolio weights would give portfolios of different risk levels. In fact, if we construct different portfolios of A and B by just choosing different weights, we can find the locus of all possible portfolios of A and B in risk/return space.

Figure 8.5 shows the position of A and B in risk/return space. It also shows portfolio P made up of 40 percent A and 60 percent B. Notice that when the correlation between A and B is $\rho = 1$, all possible portfolios lie on the straight line between A and B.

Correlation = −1   The second special case arises when the correlation coefficient between the two assets equals −1. In this case, the last term in equation 8.16 becomes $-2w_a w_b \sigma_a \sigma_b$. Once again, the expression for the variance is a perfect square:

$$\sigma_P^2 = w_a^2 \sigma_a^2 + w_b^2 \sigma_b^2 - 2(w_a \sigma_a)(w_b \sigma_b)$$
$$= (w_a \sigma_a - w_b \sigma_b)^2$$

Taking the square root on both sides of this expression gives:

$$\sigma_P = w_a \sigma_a - w_b \sigma_b \qquad (8.18)$$

For our portfolio of A and B, the standard deviation is:

$$\sigma_P = 0.6 \times 0.22 - 0.4 \times 0.08 = 0.10$$

---

[8] Recall that $(a + b)^2 = a^2 + b^2 + 2ab$.

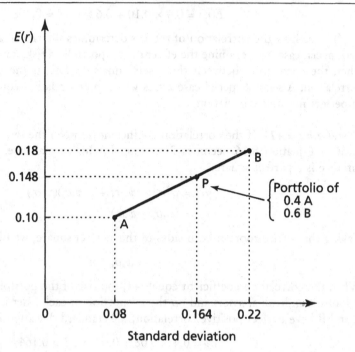

FIGURE 8.5
Possible Risk/Return Combinations of A and B when $\rho = 1$

Although the derivation of the two special cases considered thus far is very similar, the risk of the portfolios can be quite different. The most striking difference is that when two assets are perfectly negatively correlated, we can form a risk-free portfolio. This is because the two terms on the right side of equation 8.18 tend to cancel each other. By making an appropriate choice of the proportions of each asset in the portfolio, the two terms will cancel completely. This result is impossible when the assets are perfectly positively correlated.

To find the proportions of each asset that lead to a risk-free portfolio, we can see from equation 8.14 that $w_b = 1 - w_a$. Using this expression in equation 8.18 and solving for w_a we get:

$$w_a = \frac{\sigma_b}{\sigma_a + \sigma_b} \tag{8.19}$$

Similarly, the proportion of asset B required for a risk-free portfolio is:

$$w_b = \frac{\sigma_a}{\sigma_a + \sigma_b} \tag{8.20}$$

In our example, the proportion of asset A required to form a risk-free portfolio is:

$$w_a = \frac{0.22}{0.08 + 0.22} = 0.73$$

Since we require 73 percent of the investment in asset A, the other 27 percent should be allocated to asset B. In our example, these are the only weights that result in a risk-free portfolio of assets A and B.[9]

Figure 8.6 shows the possible portfolio combinations we can construct from assets A and B when $\rho = -1$. The line from B to the vertical axis and from there to A defines the risk/return possibilities, which include a risk-free portfolio, F.

Figure 8.6 also illustrates the idea of dominance introduced earlier. By combining A and B in the correct amounts, we can form a portfolio at point G on the line between B and F. Portfolio G dominates asset A because G has the same level of risk as A but offers greater expected return. In fact, some portfolio on the line from F to B will dominate any portfolio on the line from A to F. An immediate corollary is that because A is dominated, no investor should hold A in isolation.

FIGURE 8.6
Possible Risk/Return Combinations of A and B when $\rho = -1$

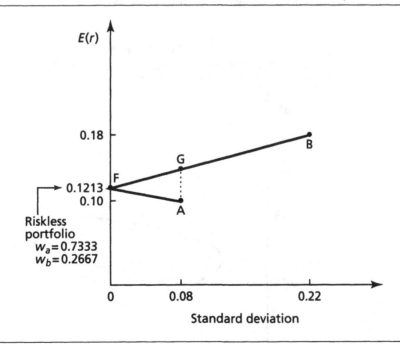

---

[9] We can check these proportions by calculating the standard deviation of the portfolio. The calculation is: $\sigma_p = 0.27 \times 0.22 - 0.73 \times 0.08 = 0.001$. The small discrepancy from zero is due to rounding error when computing the portfolio weights.

Correlation Between −1 and +1   Thus far we have considered two extreme cases, $\rho = +$ and $\rho = -1$. Because the correlation coefficient must lie within this range, these extremes define the entire realm of risk/return possibilities we can form using securities A and B. For most security pairs, however, the correlation of returns between them lies at neither extreme; rather, they are positively correlated.

Figure 8.7 shows the portfolio possibilities between A and B for a correlation of 0.7. This value is typical of the correlations between stocks in the marketplace.

MULTIPLE-ASSET PORTFOLIOS

All of the basic ideas introduced in the context of two-asset portfolios still hold when we allow investors to construct portfolios of many assets. The formulas for the expected return and risk of a portfolio with many assets are essentially the same as they were for the two-asset case, only somewhat lengthier. For example, the expected return for an n-asset risky portfolio is:

$$E(r_P) = \sum_{i=1}^{n} w_i E(r_i) \tag{8.21}$$

and the variance of an n-asset portfolio is given by:

FIGURE 8.7
Possible Risk/Return Combinations of A and B when $\rho = 0.7$

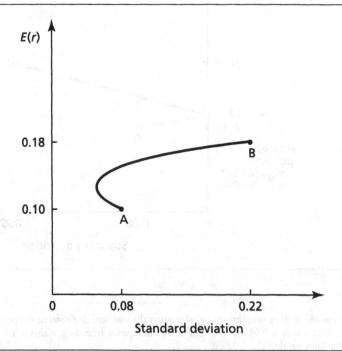

$$\sigma_P^2 = \sum_{i=1}^{n} \sum_{j=1}^{n} w_i w_j \text{COV}(i, j) \tag{8.22}$$

Although the expression for the variance of a multiple-asset portfolio seems menacing, do not despair, because there is a simple way to make it operational, using the so-called covariance matrix method. The **covariance matrix method** for finding the variance of an n-asset portfolio consists of forming an $n \times n$ matrix containing a total of n^2 cells.[10] Each cell is filled using the same simple general expression. Once the matrix is full, we can compute the variance of the portfolio by simply adding the values of all the cells in the matrix.

To illustrate, consider the two-asset portfolio discussed earlier. From equation 8.15, we know that the formula for the variance of a portfolio of assets A and B is:

$$\sigma_P^2 = w_a^2 \sigma_a^2 + w_b^2 \sigma_b^2 + 2 w_a w_b \text{COV}(r_a, r_b)$$

We can express the right-hand side of this expression differently using the covariance matrix method. The key is to realize that the last term of the above formula is really the sum of two equal terms (hence the 2 in that term), which means that there are really four terms in the variance formula. These four terms can be arranged in a 2×2 matrix, as follows:

	1	2
1	$(w_a \sigma_a)^2$	$w_a w_b \text{COV}(a, b)$
2	$w_b w_a \text{COV}(b, a)$	$(w_b \sigma_b)^2$

Each cell in the covariance matrix may be denoted by $c(i, j)$, where the index i indicates the row and the index j indicates the column in the matrix. In this two-asset example we have $c(2, 1) = w_b w_a \text{COV}(b, a)$, and $c(1, 2) = w_a w_b \text{COV}(a, b)$. Since we know from equation 8.11 that $\text{COV}(a, b) = \text{COV}(b, a)$, it follows that $c(2, 1) = c(1, 2)$. Whenever $c(i, j) = c(j, i)$, a matrix is said to be **symmetric**. A useful property to note is that any covariance matrix is symmetric.

Following the example of a 2×2 covariance matrix, we can now generalize these ideas to a matrix of arbitrary size. In the general case of an n-asset portfolio, each cell of the $n \times n$ covariance matrix can be filled using the following simple formula:

$$c(i, j) = w_i w_j \text{COV}(i, j) \tag{8.23}$$

It is important to note that equation 8.23 is also valid for the cells along the main diagonal. This is true because the covariance of any asset with itself is equal to the variance of that asset, as noted in equation 8.10. For example, in the two-asset case we can fill cell $c(1, 1)$ using the general formula in equation 8.23, as follows:

$$c(1, 1) = w_1 w_1 \text{COV}(1, 1) = (w_1 \sigma_1)^2$$

---

[10] In general, a matrix is nothing but a table of numbers, organized into rows and columns.

A similar computation gives $c(2, 2) = (w_2\sigma_2)^2$. Thus, equation 8.23 is the only expression needed to fill out any covariance matrix imaginable.

Summarizing, the variance of any n-asset portfolio can be calculated by performing the following two steps:

1. Calculate the value for each cell, $c(i, j)$, by using equation 8.23.
2. Once the n^2 cells have been filled, add up all the entries in the matrix. The resulting sum is the variance of the portfolio.

The Dramatic Effects of Diversification

The power of the covariance matrix method is revealed when we analyze the effects of diversification on the variance or standard deviation of a portfolio, as the number of assets in the portfolio increases. As a first example, consider the variance of a portfolio of n identical and independent assets. Equation 8.7 stated without proof that if the variance of each asset is σ_1^2, and the same amount is invested in each asset, so that $w_i = 1/n$ for each asset i, then the variance of that portfolio is:

$$\sigma_n^2 = \frac{\sigma_1^2}{n}$$

We can use the covariance matrix method to give a simple proof of this formula. Since there are n assets, we must fill an $n \times n$ matrix. Because the assets are independent, then $COV(i, j) = 0$ for $i \neq j$. Also, since the covariance of an asset with itself is the variance of that asset, we have $COV(i, i) = \sigma_1^2$. This reasoning means that the only non-0 cells in the $n \times n$ matrix are the n diagonal cells, each one equal to $(\sigma_1/n)^2$. The variance is equal to the sum of all the cells in the matrix:

$$\sigma_n^2 = n \times \left(\frac{\sigma_1}{n}\right)^2 = \frac{\sigma_1^2}{n}$$

This equation, which is the square of equation 8.7, shows that as the number of identical independent assets in the portfolio increases, the risk of the portfolio decreases. This is illustrated in figure 8.8. Notice that for a large number of independent assets, the portfolio variance eventually becomes negligible.

As a second application of the covariance matrix method, consider another portfolio of n stocks. As in the previous example, all stocks have the same variance, σ_1^2, and the same weight, $w_i = 1/n$. In this portfolio, however, all pairs of distinct assets have the same positive correlation, ρ. We are interested in computing the effect that the number of assets, n, has on the portfolio variance. In particular, is it possible to reduce the portfolio risk to a negligible amount by incorporating more and more stocks in the portfolio? To answer this question, we consider the covariance matrix for this portfolio.

Since all pairs of distinct assets have the same correlation, ρ, each of the $(n^2 - n)$ off-diagonal cells will have a value of:

$$c(i, j) = \left(\frac{1}{n}\right)\left(\frac{1}{n}\right) COV(i, j) = \left(\frac{\sigma_1}{n}\right)^2 \rho$$

FIGURE 8.8
The Variance of a Portfolio of n Independent Assets

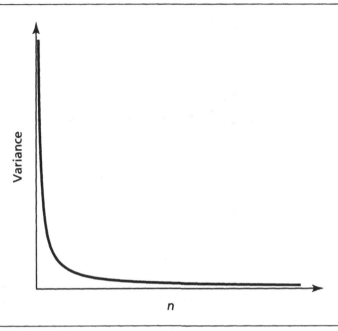

Similarly, since the correlation coefficient between an asset and itself is always $\rho = 1$, each of the n diagonal cells is equal to $c(i, i) = (\sigma_1/n)^2$. With this information, we can compute the variance of this portfolio by simply adding the off-diagonal and diagonal terms in the matrix. The sum of all these terms gives:

$$\sigma_n^2 = n \times \left(\frac{\sigma_1}{n}\right)^2 + (n^2 - n) \times \left(\frac{\sigma_1}{n}\right)^2 \times \rho \qquad (8.24)$$

$$= \frac{\sigma_1^2}{n}(1 - \rho) + \sigma_1^2 \times \rho$$

Equation 8.24 demonstrates the important result that, with n identical correlated assets, it is not possible to eliminate risk completely, except in the special case of $n = 2$ assets with perfect negative correlation ($\rho = -1$).[11] Indeed, since the second term of equation 8.24 is not affected by the number (n) of assets, the minimum possible variance of the portfolio is $\sigma^2\rho$. This shows that in many practical investment situations where pairs of assets are positively correlated, there is a limit to diversification. Try as we may, when pairs of assets have positive correlations, we will be unable to eliminate risk completely. Figure 8.9 graphs the variance for a portfolio of n stocks, where each pair of stocks has a

---

[11] This case has already been considered as one of the two extreme cases for two-asset portfolios.

FIGURE 8.9

The Variance of a Portfolio of *n* Correlated Assets ($\rho = 0.7$)

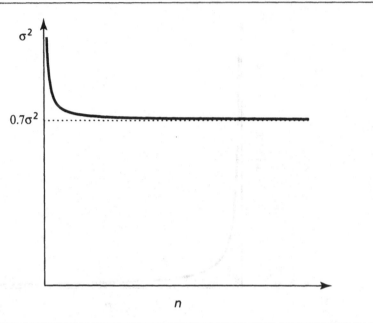

correlation coefficient of 0.7. In this example, an investor can avoid at most 30 percent of the risk of a single stock by diversifying.

The Efficient Set and the Efficient Frontier

In a market with many securities, the final result of portfolio building is likely to look like figure 8.10 in risk/return space. The points on the interior of the curve represent individual assets, while the curve running from L to H represents the ultimate portfolios that the investor can create from the many individual assets available in the marketplace. Certain portfolios on the curve from L to H are dominated, such as those on the curve from L to MR. However, all of the portfolios, including the single asset H, which lie on the line from H to MR, are not dominated. The **efficient set** is the set of all assets and portfolios that are not dominated, and the **efficient frontier** is its graphical representation. In figure 8.10, the efficient frontier is the line from H to MR.

The efficient set and the efficient frontier have a special significance for investors. Since all investors desire higher expected returns and wish to avoid risk, they will invest in portfolios that belong to the efficient set. This desire is reasonable, because any other portfolio that an investor might consider will be dominated by one on the efficient frontier.

FIGURE 8.10
The Efficient Frontier with Many Assets

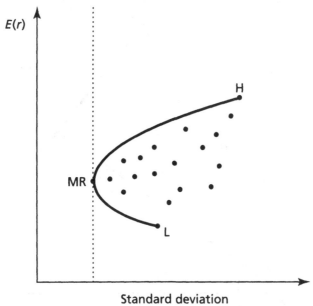

GRAPHICAL PORTFOLIO ANALYSIS

There is a very different way to analyze two-asset portfolios that can be very useful in solving risk and return problems. The essence of this graphical methodology is that it depicts the standard deviation of each asset as a vector in the plane, as shown in figure 8.11. There, the length of vectors OA and OB is proportional to the standard deviation of assets A and B, respectively. The vectors start at point O, and the angle θ between them is such that it satisfies the following equation:

$$\cos \theta = \rho \qquad (8.25)$$

As an example, if assets A and B are independent, so that $\rho = 0$, then the two vectors representing those assets form a right angle because cos (90°) = 0. If the assets are perfectly negatively correlated, so that $\rho = -1$, the vectors are colinear but facing in opposite directions; that is, they form a 180 degree angle because cos (180°) = −1.

The most important aspect of graphical portfolio analysis shown in figure 8.11 is the fact that any portfolio, P, that combines assets A and B will have a standard deviation described by the vector going from the origin, O, to point P on the line joining points A and B. Furthermore, the weights of assets A and B that produce portfolio P are given by $w_a = |BP|/|BA|$ and $w_b = |AP|/|BA|$, where the notation $|x|$ represents the length of vector x.

To illustrate the usefulness of this graphical technique, consider again the case of two perfectly negatively correlated assets A and B with standard deviations σ_a and σ_b, respec-

FIGURE 8.11
Combining Assets Using Graphical Portfolio Analysis

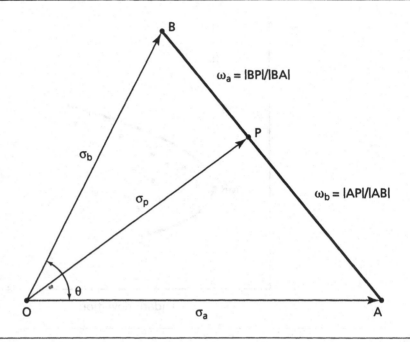

tively. Based on our discussion, these assets can be represented as shown in figure 8.12. Now let us use the technique to find the proportion to invest in each asset so that the resulting portfolio, P, has no risk. From figure 8.12, this implies that point P must coincide with the origin, O, because then $\sigma_p = |OP| = 0$. Using the rule just given for determining the weight of each asset, we have:

$$w_a = |BP|/|BA| = |BO|/|BA| = \sigma_a/(\sigma_a + \sigma_b)$$

Notice that this is the same result obtained in equation 8.19 through very different means.[12]

Other results that are cumbersome to obtain with traditional portfolio analysis can be obtained with ease using graphical portfolio analysis. For example, we can show that if we combine two independent and identical assets, A and B, in equal proportions, the resulting portfolio, P, has a correlation of 0.707 with each of the assets. In the graphical framework this occurs because the vector OP forms a 45 degree angle with each of the vectors OA and OB.[13] Substituting this angle in equation 8.25 gives cos (45°) = 0.707, and the desired result is obtained.

---

[12] Of course, we can also use figure 8.12 in a similar way to reproduce equation 8.20 for w_b.
[13] We leave the graphical proof of this fact to the reader.

FIGURE 8.12

Graphical Portfolio Analysis for Perfectly Negatively Correlated Assets

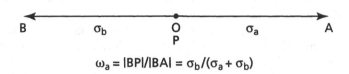

$$\omega_a = |BP|/|BA| = \sigma_b/(\sigma_a + \sigma_b)$$

SUMMARY

This chapter adopted the viewpoint that investors are concerned with achieving return and avoiding risk. Using simplifying assumptions, such as zero transaction costs, free access to information, and no taxes, this chapter also analyzed the effects of holding different securities in portfolios. Assuming that investors desire portfolios with high expected return and low risk, we saw the important benefits of diversification that arise from combining individual securities into portfolios.

The covariance or correlation of returns, both of which measure the tendency of returns on two investments to move together, are crucial in determining the risk of the portfolio. In fact, the tendency of returns to move together is the most important determinant of portfolio risk.

When returns are less than perfectly positively correlated, forming portfolios will reduce risk, but not completely. In a market with many risky assets, there will be many investment opportunities that are not dominated. The non-dominated investment opportunities constitute the efficient set and may be graphed in risk/return space as the efficient frontier. Individual investors may choose different risky portfolios according to their different attitudes toward risk. Risk-tolerant investors choose portfolios that offer high expected returns and high risk, and conservative ones choose portfolios with lower expected returns and lower risks.

QUESTIONS

1. In this book, we generally assume that investors dislike risk. If a particular investor liked both risk and high expected returns, what kinds of opportunities would that investor find in the financial marketplace?
2. In terms of risk and return, what are the goals of investing?
3. The standard deviation and variance consider outcomes that are both above and below the mean return. Someone might argue that this makes them poor measures of investment risk, because the only risk of concern to an investor is the chance that the result might be below the mean. How could you respond to this criticism?
4. Why do investors diversify?

5. Which is important to the investor's decision as we have defined it, return or expected return?

6. Security A has an expected return of 14 percent, while security B has an expected return of 12 percent. Is this enough information to determine whether A dominates B?

7. If Security A has an expected return of 14 percent and a standard deviation of returns of 20 percent, while security B has an expected return of 12 percent and a standard deviation of returns of 19 percent, does A dominate B? Why or why not?

8. If Security A has an expected return of 12 percent and a standard deviation of returns of 20 percent, while security B has an expected return of 14 percent and a standard deviation of returns of 19 percent, does A dominate B? Why or why not?

9. Your broker tells you that it is important to diversify because doing so will increase your expected returns, even if you diversify by randomly selecting stocks. What should you do?

10. Your broker tells you that the standard deviation of returns for a portfolio depends only on the standard deviations of the individual securities and the amount of funds invested in each. What should be your response? Why?

11. What is the relationship between the covariance of returns and the correlation of returns?

12. You already have a one-stock portfolio and, after reading this chapter, you are urgently considering adding a second. Your broker recommends against the one you are considering because it has a high covariance with the stock you already own. However, he does not know the standard deviation of either stock's returns. What should you do? Why?

13. Securities B and N have returns with a correlation of −0.9. Can you combine them to form a risk-free portfolio?

14. Securities E and L have returns with a correlation of −1. Can you combine them to form a risk-free portfolio?

15. Securities F and G have returns with a correlation of −1, with F having the lower expected return. Would any investor want to hold F in isolation?

16. Securities F and G have returns with a correlation of −1, with F having the lower expected return. Would any investor want to hold G in isolation?

17. In the case of many risky assets, why does the efficient frontier stop at the minimum risk investment opportunity?

18. Why is the covariance between assets A and B the same as the covariance between assets B and A?

19. If a and b are arbitrary numbers and X, Y, and Z are random variables, show that $COV(X, aY + bZ) = a \, COV(X, Y) + b \, COV(X, Z)$.

20. Why is the covariance a more general concept than the variance?

21. Can the variance of a random variable be computed without knowledge of the expected value of that random variable?

22. Comment on the following fact: The birthrate in Germany has been in a long decline recently, so a scientist suggested an explanation "that every child knows makes sense." He presented a curve depicting the number of newborn

babies, and another showing the number of pairs of brooding storks in Germany. The curves illustrate a remarkable correlation between the stork population and the number of newborn babies, as the decline in babies has closely followed the decline in storks. Haven't the Germans heard about the birds and the bees?

23. A student argues that it is ridiculous to define the variance by squaring every term in the summation, given that we usually take the square root afterwards to find the standard deviation. Might this be yet another attempt by professors to complicate the student's life?

24. Briefly explain how the insurance industry takes advantage of the diversification principles discussed in this chapter.

25. Briefly explain how the banking industry takes advantage of the diversification principles discussed in this chapter.

PROBLEMS

1. Over three years, an investor earns the following returns: 8 percent, 11 percent, and 15 percent. What is the arithmetic mean of these three annual returns?

2. An investor undertakes a series of one-year investments starting with $700. After the first year, the investment is worth $784.00; after two years, it is worth $878.10; after three years, it is worth $983.40; finally, after four years, it is worth $1,101.50. Calculate the annual arithmetic mean rate of return.

3. For a five-year period, a stock portfolio had the following rates of return: −15 percent, 23 percent, 11 percent, −3 percent, and 37 percent. What was the arithmetic mean rate of return and the variance of the returns?

4. Mr. Diversey held a portfolio with three stocks. He invested 20 percent of his funds in stock A, 45 percent in stock B, and 35 percent in stock C. The rate of return for stock A was 13 percent; for stock B, the rate of return was −5 percent; for stock C, the rate of return was 9 percent. What was the rate of return for the entire portfolio?

5. Security V has expected returns of 13 percent and a standard deviation of 20 percent, and security W has expected returns of 5 percent and a standard deviation of 13 percent. If the two securities are perfectly negatively correlated, how much money would you put in each to have a riskless portfolio? What would be the expected return of the portfolio?

6. Over three years, security Q had returns of 10 percent, 14 percent, and −3 percent. For the same three years, security R had returns of 12 percent, 10 percent, and 5 percent. What is the variance and standard deviation of returns for these two securities?

7. For securities Q and R, what is the covariance and the correlation of returns between them?

8. Consider a portfolio with 40 percent of the funds invested in security Q and 60 percent invested in security R of the previous problems. What is the variance of returns for this two-asset portfolio?

9. Show that if in the definition of the variance each term in the summation were of the form $[r_i - E(r)]$ instead of $[r_i - E(r)]^2$, then the summation would always add to 0, rendering the variance useless.

10. Starting with the compact definition of the variance of a random variable, show that the variance of a portfolio is given by equation 8.15.

11. Show that the correlation coefficient of an asset with itself is always 1.

12. You combine assets A and B, and the resulting portfolio is risk-free. The variance of asset B is four times larger than the variance of asset A. Also, the expected returns on A and B are 10 percent and 18 percent, respectively. Find the expected return on the portfolio.

13. You are considering investing $6 in two identical and independent projects with a probability p of a favorable outcome. Only one other outcome – unfavorable – is possible. If you invest all your money in one of the projects and the outcome is favorable, the payoff is $10, and if it is unfavorable, the payoff is –$6. On average, you expect the payoff from each project to be zero. What is the probability of a favorable outcome?

14. You combine two risky assets in equal proportions. If both assets have the same variance, and the resulting portfolio has a variance equal to one fourth the variance of each asset, what is the correlation between the assets?

15. Assets A, B, and C form a portfolio. The proportions in each are 25 percent, 25 percent, and 50 percent, respectively. The correlation is $\rho = 0.5$ for the three possible pairs of assets. The variances are equal to 100 for all three assets. Find the standard deviation of this portfolio.

16. Assets W, X, Y, and Z form a portfolio. The proportions in each are 10, 20, 30, and 40 percent, respectively. The correlation is $\rho = 0.7$ for the six possible pairs of assets. The variances are equal to 100, 200, 300, and 400, respectively. Find the variance of this portfolio.

Chapter 9

The Market Price of Risk

OVERVIEW

In the previous chapter we saw that investors seek high expected returns and avoid risk. This chapter continues the development of the model by introducing the risk-free asset, and shows how including it increases the investor's opportunities and improves the welfare of all investors.

The risk-free asset is also used to develop a market standard for risk and return against which we can compare the performance of any investment. We also examine the separation theorem, which states that all investors should hold the same portfolio of risky assets, no matter how risk tolerant or risk averse they may be. This leads to the capital asset pricing model, which expresses the expected rate of return of an asset as a function of its risk.

INTRODUCTION OF THE RISK-FREE ASSET

The risk-free asset is an asset with no default risk. As discussed in the previous chapter, the expected return of a two-asset portfolio is given by:

$$E(r_P) = w_a E(r_a) + w_b E(r_b) \tag{9.1}$$

where:

w_i = percentage of funds committed to asset $i = a, b$

$E(r_i)$ = the expected return on asset i, for $i = a, b, P$

We denote the return of the risk-free asset as r_f. The expected return of a portfolio composed of the risk-free asset and of risky asset j is just the weighted average of the two expected returns. As before, the weights are the percentage of funds committed to the two assets. Since the risk-free asset has no default risk, we have $E(r_f) = r_f$, and the expected return for the portfolio involving the risk-free asset is:

$$E(r_P) = w_f r_f + w_j E(r_j) \tag{9.2}$$

Likewise, our original equation for the variance of a two-asset portfolio still holds, so we have:

$$\sigma_P^2 = w_f^2 \sigma_f^2 + w_j^2 \sigma_j^2 + 2w_f w_j \text{COV}(f, j) \tag{9.3}$$

where $\text{COV}(f, j)$ is the covariance of returns between assets f and j, and we define the other terms as before. For the risk-free asset, $\sigma_f^2 = 0$ and $\text{COV}(f, j) = 0$. These facts simplify the evaluation of equation 9.3, since its first and third terms are zero. Consequently, the variance of a two-asset portfolio which includes the risk-free asset will be:

$$\sigma_P^2 = w_j^2 \sigma_j^2 \qquad (9.4)$$

From this, the standard deviation of the portfolio is:

$$\sigma_P = w_j \sigma_j \qquad (9.5)$$

To illustrate these principles, consider a portfolio made up of the risk-free asset f and a risky portfolio j. The table below gives the relevant data for assets f and j.

	f	j
Expected Return	0.10	0.17
σ	0.00	0.21
w	0.45	0.55
COV(f, j)	0.00	

In this case, the expected return for the portfolio is found using equation 9.2:

$$E(r_P) = 0.45 \times 0.10 + 0.55 \times 0.17 = 0.1385$$

and the standard deviation of the portfolio is found from equation 9.5:

$$\sigma_P = 0.55 \times 0.21 = 0.1155$$

Figure 9.1 shows the risk-free asset, f, the risky portfolio, j, and the combined portfolio, P, in risk/return space. We can achieve any point on the line between f and j by constructing a portfolio made up of just f and j. Each point along the line corresponds to a different weight combination.

As an alternative, we can combine equations 9.2 and 9.5 to express the expected return of a portfolio combining f and j as a function of its standard deviation:

$$E(r_P) = r_f + \frac{E(r_j) - r_f}{\sigma_j} \sigma_P$$

Thus, for a portfolio of f and j with a standard deviation of 11.55 percent, the expected return is:

$$E(r_P) = 0.10 + \frac{0.17 - 0.10}{0.21} 0.1155 = 0.1385$$

This is the same result obtained earlier.

CHOOSING THE BEST RISKY PORTFOLIO

In the example illustrated by figure 9.1, we combined risky portfolio j with the risk-free asset f to form portfolio P. However, investors may prefer to combine other risky portfolios

FIGURE 9.1
Combining the Risk-Free Asset with Risky Portfolio *j*

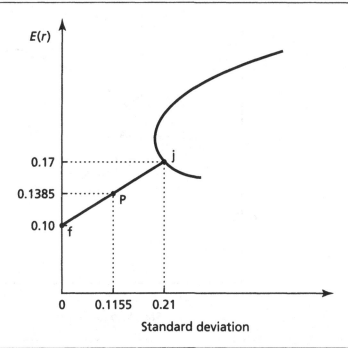

with *f*. In fact, this section shows that all rational investors will choose the same particular risky portfolio to combine with the risk-free asset.

No matter what an investor's risk preferences might be, investing in risky portfolio *j* is never optimal. To see why, consider figure 9.2, which shows *f* and another risky portfolio, *M*, chosen so that the line *fM* is tangent to the efficient frontier. Just as in figure 9.1 we could combine *f* and *j* to achieve portfolios on the line *fj*, we can now combine *f* and *M* to achieve portfolios on the line *fM*. Every portfolio on the line *fj* is dominated by another portfolio lying vertically above it on the line *fM*. This means that every investor would prefer to hold risky portfolio *M* rather than risky portfolio *j*.

Since the line from *f* to the risky portfolio *M* is just tangent to the efficient frontier, portfolios on the line *fM* cannot be dominated. Notice that introducing the risk-free asset changes the efficient frontier. Specifically, the curve from point *MR* (the Minimum Risk risky portfolio) to point *M* is no longer efficient. The new efficient frontier runs from *f* to *M* to Z. Any portfolio not lying on the line *fMZ* will be dominated.

BORROWING AND LENDING

Thus far we have determined that investors seek portfolios on the line *fMZ*. How can we trade to create such portfolios? To construct portfolios that lie on the curve from *M* to

FIGURE 9.2

Combining the Risk-Free Asset with the Optimal Risky Portfolio M

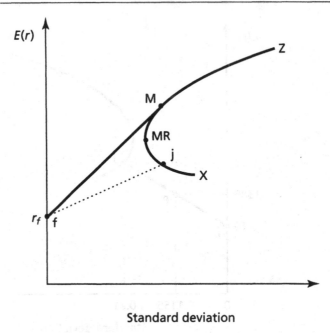

Z, the investor need only choose a risky portfolio on that curve and invest 100 percent of all funds in that portfolio. To build portfolios that lie on the line from f to M, the investor must hold the risky portfolio M, and also invest some money in the risk-free asset. We can think of this risk-free asset as a Treasury bill. Investing in Treasury bills is equivalent to lending to the government, so portfolios lying between f and M are **lending portfolios** since they involve some holding of stocks and some lending of funds to the government.

In addition to lending portfolios, there are also borrowing portfolios. We can construct **borrowing portfolios** by borrowing funds and investing those funds, in addition to our own capital, in a risky portfolio. Because we assume perfect markets, we can borrow and lend at the risk-free rate r_f.[1]

So far, we know that the investor could invest in any risky portfolio that lies on the curve from M to Z. Now, the chance to borrow at rate r_f improves the investor's opportunity set. To illustrate this improvement, consider the following example, using the data given below.

---

[1] Of course, in the real world individual investors cannot borrow at the risk-free rate. However, many institutional investors can borrow at rates very close to the risk-free rate.

Asset	f	M
E(P)	0.10	0.23
σ	0.00	0.18

Assume an initial wealth of $1,000. To create a borrowing portfolio, consider a situation in which the investor borrows $750 at the risk-free rate of $r_f = 10\%$. The borrowed funds plus the original capital are then invested in risky portfolio M. Table 9.1 shows the expected returns and standard deviations of portfolios combining f and M in various proportions. We computed these values using the formulas given earlier.

To better understand the borrowing portfolio, which has a negative weight in the risk-free asset, assume that risky portfolio M actually earns the expected return next period. Then the value of the portfolio combining f and M at the end of the period will be $1,750 × 1.23 = $2,152.50. After the investor repays the $750 loan with 10 percent interest, or $825, $1,327.50 remains. The investor has then earned $327.50 on the original capital of $1,000, or a 32.75 percent annual rate of return on the investor's capital. As this example shows, borrowing increases the expected return on the original capital, from 23 percent if the investor places all the funds in risky portfolio M to 32.75 percent when those funds plus the borrowed funds are placed in M.

Not only does borrowing at r_f to invest in a risky portfolio increase the expected return, it also increases the risk. To see how the risk increases, assume the risky portfolio M earns a return one standard deviation above or below its expected return. Under these assumptions we compute the returns on the borrowing portfolio.

If the risky portfolio M earns one standard deviation less than its expected return, it earns $0.23 - 0.18 = 0.05$, or 5 percent. In this situation, the borrowing portfolio will be worth $1.05 × $1,750 = $1,837.50. From this amount, the investor pays the debt of $825, leaving $1,012.50. This gives a return of 1.25 percent on the original capital. If the return on the risky portfolio is one standard deviation above the expected return, the risky portfolio will earn $0.23 + 0.18 = 0.41$, or 41 percent. The portfolio will then be worth $1.41 × $1,750 = $2,467.50 at the end of the period. From these proceeds, the investor repays $825, leaving $1,642.50, or a rate of return of 64.25 percent.

These results are summarized below:

TABLE 9.1
Portfolios Constructed from the Risk-Free Asset f and Risky Portfolio M

w_f	w_M	$E(r_P)$	σ_P
−0.5	0.5	0.165	0.09
−0.0	1.0	0.23	0.18
−0.75	1.75	0.3275	0.3150

	r_M	r_{borrow}
$E(r) + \sigma$	41.0%	64.25%
$E(r)$	23.0%	32.75%
$E(r) - \sigma$	5.0%	1.25%

As these data indicate, while investing only in portfolio M gives an expected return of 23 percent and a standard deviation of 18 percent ([41 − 23], or [23 − 5]), the borrowing portfolio has an expected return of 32.75 percent and a standard deviation of 31.50 percent ([64.25 − 32.75] or [32.75 − 1.25]). An alternative way of obtaining the same results is by using equations 9.2 and 9.5, as follows:

$$E(r_P) = -0.75 \times 10\% + 1.75 \times 23\% = 32.75\%$$

and

$$\sigma_P = 1.75 \times 18\% = 31.5\%$$

Figure 9.3 shows the relationship between the return on portfolio M and the return on the borrowing portfolio that combines f and M. The steeper slope of the borrowing portfolio indicates that it is riskier than investing all the funds in M. However, figure 9.3 also clearly shows that with the risk of the borrowing portfolio comes the opportunity of greater returns. Indeed, when the actual return on M is sufficiently high (greater than 10 percent in this example), the actual return on the borrowing portfolio will be greater. Of course, if the return on M is sufficiently low, the return on the borrowing portfolio will be even lower.

The use of borrowing, or leverage, increases both the expected return and the variability of returns. Figure 9.4 shows the result of borrowing funds at a rate r_f to invest in portfolio M in risk/return space. In the example just considered, we found that the expected return of the leveraged portfolio was 32.75 percent and the standard deviation of the portfolio was 31.50 percent. Figure 9.4 shows this leveraged portfolio, P. Notice that portfolio P falls on the straight line defined by f and M. In fact, all leveraged portfolios fall on that line.

Before we introduced borrowing to invest in a risky portfolio, the efficient frontier ran from f to M to Z, as shown in figure 9.2. Borrowing changes the efficient frontier. For example, consider portfolio V in figure 9.4, which lies on the curve between M and Z. Formerly, portfolio V was in the efficient set. Now a leveraged portfolio lying between M and P dominates V.

There is only one risky portfolio that is not dominated, and that is portfolio M. Therefore, all investors will hold M as their risky portfolio, although they may differ in the proportion of funds they choose to invest in M. Some will invest a portion of their funds in M and some in f, to form a lending portfolio. Such portfolios would fall on the line between f and M. Bolder investors might borrow funds at a rate r_f and invest the proceeds plus their original capital in M, to form a borrowing portfolio, which would fall beyond M on the line fMY. Whether investors form lending or borrowing portfolios, they will put all of their funds devoted to risky assets in portfolio M.

FIGURE 9.3
Returns on Portfolio M and on a Borrowing Portfolio

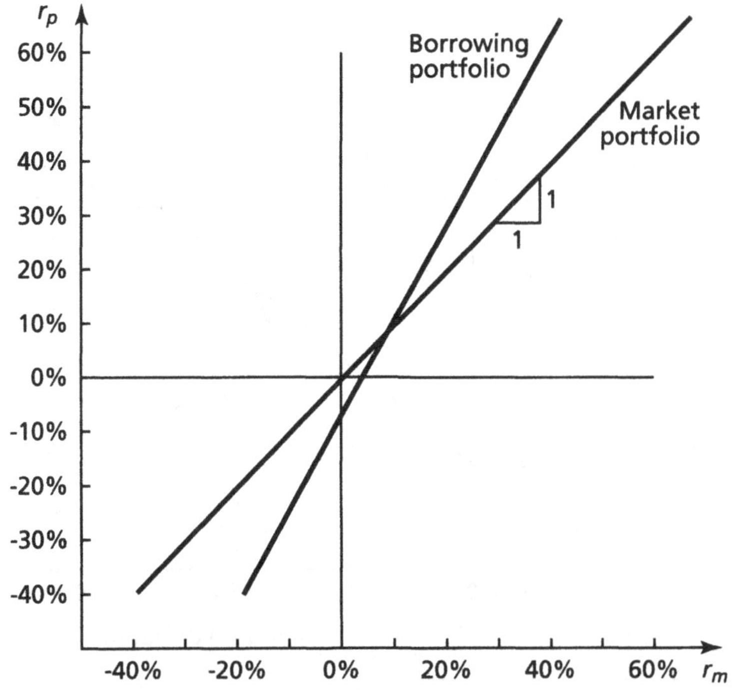

How well does this discussion of borrowing at the risk-free rate and investing the funds in M fit with reality? While some borrowers have very low borrowing costs that approximate the risk-free rate, they cannot borrow an unlimited amount of funds at that rate. Also, the Federal Reserve limits the amount of borrowing for securities investment through so-called margin requirements. In practice, then, investors cannot achieve unlimited leverage. In figure 9.4, there are practical limits to how far beyond M the investor can go on the line fMY. Within these practical limitations, however, figure 9.4 describes quite well the risk and expected return associated with borrowing and lending portfolios.

THE MARKET PORTFOLIO AND THE SEPARATION THEOREM

So far, we have seen that all investors who commit any funds to risky securities will do so by investing in portfolio M, shown in figure 9.4. Therefore, we need to understand the characteristics of this very important portfolio.

We now show that portfolio M is the **market portfolio**, that is, the portfolio of risky assets that includes every risky security in the marketplace, with each one having a weight proportional to its market value. For example, if the total market value of IBM's shares is

FIGURE 9.4
Portfolio Possibilities with Borrowing and Lending – The Capital Market Line

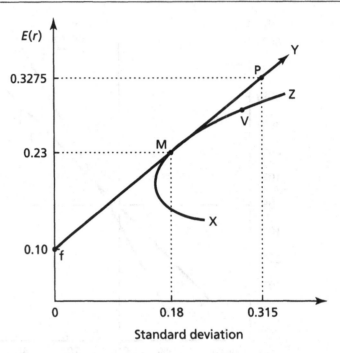

Standard deviation

$4 billion, and the combined market value of all securities in the market is $100 billion, then IBM would have a weight of 4 percent in the market portfolio. Accordingly, the market portfolio is a **value-weighted** portfolio.

We know that portfolio M must be the market portfolio from reflecting on the following two facts. First, we know all investors hold M as their risky portfolio. Second, we know that someone owns each security available in the market, since there are simply no securities floating around without owners. Since all investors hold M as their only risky portfolio, it follows that M must contain all possible securities. This is the same as saying that all investors hold the market portfolio.

Because all investors who hold any risky assets hold portfolio M, the choice of a risky portfolio is independent of the choice of a particular portfolio on the line fMY. This important result is known as the **separation theorem** – the investment decision is separate from the financing decision. Regardless of the degree of risk aversion each investor might have, everyone invests in risky portfolio M. The financing decision – whether to borrow or lend, and how much – is separate from the choice of investing in a portfolio of risky assets. The financing choice varies according to the degree of risk aversion of each investor.

To see this point in another way, note that the choice of risky portfolio M is separate from the decision about how much expected return to seek and how much risk to bear.

This is clear in figure 9.4, because the investor can attain any point along the line *fMY* while holding only portfolio *M* as the portfolio of risky assets.

THE CAPITAL MARKET LINE

As figure 9.4 shows, investors can attain any point on the line *fMY*. Each investor chooses a combination of the risky portfolio *M* and the risk-free asset *f*. Since investors can only move along the line *fMY*, that line represents the trade-off between risk and return available in the capital market. As such, it is the **capital market line** (CML). Because the CML slopes upward, it reveals graphically that the acquisition of greater expected return requires taking more risk. The slope of the CML is the rate of exchange between expected return and risk.

From algebra, we know that the equation of a straight line is $y = b + mx$, where y is the value on the vertical axis, m is the slope of the line, x is the value on the horizontal axis, and b is the intercept of the line on the y axis. Thus, in figure 9.4, line *fMY* intercepts the y axis at f, so $b = r_f$. Also, the slope of a line equals the change in vertical distance over the change in horizontal distance, or the rise over the run. In our case, the slope is found by noting that if the investor bears no risk, the return is r_f; if the investor accepts risk equal to σ_m, the expected return is r_m. Thus, if an investor increases risk from 0 to σ_m, the expected return increases from r_f to $E(r_m)$. From this information, the slope of the capital market line is:

$$\text{Slope of CML} = \frac{E(r_m) - r_f}{\sigma_m} \tag{9.6}$$

Now we can express the CML as an equation. Consider any portfolio j on the CML with an expected return of $E(r_j)$ and a risk of σ_j. Applying the equation of a straight line to portfolio j, we have:

$$E(r_j) = r_f + \frac{E(r_m) - r_f}{\sigma_m}\sigma_j \tag{9.7}$$

This equation is often written in the equivalent form:

$$E(r_j) = r_f + \frac{\sigma_j}{\sigma_m}[E(r_m) - r_f] \tag{9.8}$$

EXAMPLE 1

Consider a situation in which $r_f = 10$ percent, $E(r_m) = 17$ percent, $\sigma_m = 24$ percent, and $\sigma_j = 34$ percent. These values give us enough information to calculate the expected return of portfolio j lying on the CML:

$$E(r_j) = 0.10 + \frac{0.34}{0.24}[0.17 - 0.10] = 0.1992$$

The expected return of portfolio j (19.92 percent) exceeds the expected return of the market portfolio (17 percent) because portfolio j has higher risk. Investors will hold the riskier portfolio *j* instead of the market portfolio only if they receive a greater expected return for bearing the additional risk.

The CML is important because it expresses the relationship between the risk and expected return of a portfolio consisting of a mix of the market portfolio and the risk-free asset. The slope of the CML reveals how much extra return investors obtain for each extra unit of risk they bear. Therefore, the slope of the CML gives the market price of risk for fully diversified portfolios. Since every portfolio on the CML contains the market portfolio, each portfolio on the line is completely diversified.

RISK AND EXPECTED RETURNS FOR INDIVIDUAL SECURITIES

Another important relationship, the **security market line** (SML), expresses the expected return of an individual security as a function of its level of relevant risk. What is the relevant risk for each security in the market portfolio? We know it cannot be its variance, since part of that variance can be diversified away when the security is part of a portfolio. Since all investors hold the market portfolio of risky assets, the relevant risk of an individual security is the amount of risk it contributes to the variance of the market portfolio. We define this relevant risk of individual securities as their beta.

Beta

In the previous chapter we examined the behavior of multiple-asset risky portfolios. There we saw that the variance of a portfolio depended heavily on the correlation or covariance between all pairs of assets, and we introduced the covariance matrix method to facilitate the computation of the portfolio's variance. Using the same technique, we can also compute the variance of the market portfolio in terms of each of its component securities. This computation will reveal the **beta** of each security, since it will uncover the risk that each security contributes to the variance of the market portfolio.

If there are *n* risky assets in the market, and the proportion of the value of asset *i* relative to the value of the market is w_i, then the variance of the market portfolio, σ_m^2, is the sum of all the entries in the following covariance matrix:

	1	2	. . .	n
1	$(w_1\sigma_1)^2$	$w_1w_2\text{COV}(1, 2)$	. . .	$w_1w_n\text{COV}(1, n)$
2	$w_2w_1\text{COV}(2, 1)$	$(w_2\sigma_2)^2$	. . .	$w_2w_n\text{COV}(2, n)$
3	$w_3w_1\text{COV}(3, 1)$	$w_3w_2\text{COV}(3, 2)$	. . .	$w_3w_n\text{COV}(3, n)$
. . .	. . .	. . .	. . .	. . .
n	$w_nw_1\text{COV}(n, 1)$	$w_nw_2\text{COV}(n, 2)$	. . .	$(w_n\sigma_n)^2$

Now we will sketch the intermediate steps leading to the definition of beta. If we sum across each row of the covariance matrix, recall that $\text{COV}(i, i) = \sigma_i^2$, and note that for any random variables y, x_1, and x_2, and arbitrary numbers a_1 and a_2, the covariance can be expressed as:

$$COV(y, a_1x_1 + a_2x_2) = a_1COV(y, x_1) + a_2COV(y, x_2) \qquad (9.9)$$

then we eventually arrive at the following expression:

$$\sigma_m^2 = w_1COV(1, m) + w_2COV(2, m) + \ldots + w_nCOV(n, m) \qquad (9.10)$$

Finally, we multiply and divide the right-hand side of equation 9.10 by the variance of the market, σ_m^2, to get:

$$\sigma_m^2 = \sigma_m^2\left[w_1\frac{COV(1, m)}{\sigma_m^2} + w_2\frac{COV(2, m)}{\sigma_m^2} + \ldots + w_n\frac{COV(n, m)}{\sigma_m^2}\right] \qquad (9.11)$$

We now define the beta of asset i as the ratio of the covariance of that asset with the market, over the variance of the market:

$$\beta_i = \frac{COV(i, m)}{\sigma_m^2} \qquad (9.12)$$

With this definition of beta, we can rewrite equation 9.11 as follows:

$$\sigma_m^2 = \sigma_m^2[w_1\beta_1 + w_2\beta_2 + \ldots + w_n\beta_n] \qquad (9.13)$$

This is the expression we were seeking. It shows that the total risk of the market portfolio, σ_m^2, is the weighted average of the betas of the individual securities that it contains. It follows that a security's beta measures the risk it contributes to the risk of the market portfolio.

It is sometimes useful to express the beta of an asset in an alternative form, based on the identity $COV(i, m) = \sigma_i\sigma_m\rho_{i,m}$:

$$\beta_i = \frac{\sigma_i}{\sigma_m}\rho_{i,m} \qquad (9.14)$$

Notice that a direct consequence of equation 9.13 is that the weighted average of all the betas in the market portfolio is equal to 1:

$$\sum_{i=1}^{n}w_i\beta_i = 1 \qquad (9.15)$$

Equivalently, the beta of the market portfolio is $\beta_m = 1$. This fact provides a standard against which we can measure other securities or portfolios. A security or portfolio with a beta greater than 1 is **aggressive** because it has more risk than the market portfolio. A security or portfolio with a beta less than 1 is **defensive** because it has less risk than the market portfolio.

Figure 9.5 presents the actual distribution of betas for firms in the stock market, which has remained essentially unchanged for most of the century. The figure contains several interesting features. First, it shows that the distribution of betas is skewed to the right, indicating that most firms tend to be defensive. This is consistent with the notion that investors are risk-averse. Second, almost all firms have positive betas. A negative beta for an asset indicates a negative correlation between the asset and the market, and figure 9.5

FIGURE 9.5
The Distribution of Betas in the Stock Market

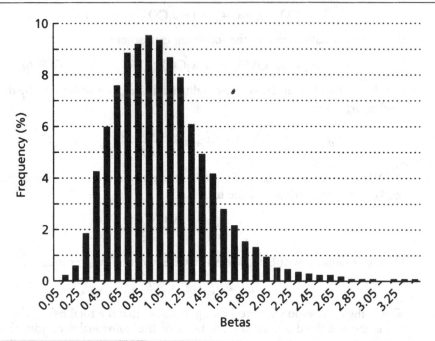

shows that such firms are extremely rare. Third, the figure confirms that the average risk of all firms in the market is 1. Notice that the graph peaks at a beta of 0.85, the mode of the beta distribution, and that the vast majority of firms has betas between 0.25 and 2.00.

Beta and the Characteristic Line

In practice, the beta of an asset is calculated by fitting a straight line between a set of points representing the returns on the asset and the market. Figure 9.6 shows the relationship between the returns of IBM and the market portfolio for 60 months. Each dot in the figure corresponds to the returns earned by IBM and the S&P 500 index, a proxy for the market portfolio, for a particular month. The line that best fits the pattern of points in figure 9.6 is called the **characteristic line**.

The slope of the characteristic line is the beta of the asset. For IBM, the measured beta during this period was 0.7037. We can interpret this as follows: when the market return increases by 1 percent, we expect the return on IBM to increase by 0.7037 percent. Similarly, when the market return decreases by 1 percent, we expect IBM's return to fall by 0.7037 percent. Therefore, IBM is less risky than the market, because we expect the return of IBM to fluctuate less than the market on a percentage basis.

The beta of any security or portfolio is a relative risk measure because it measures risk relative to the market portfolio. In particular, if we treat the market portfolio as a

FIGURE 9.6
The Characteristic Line for IBM

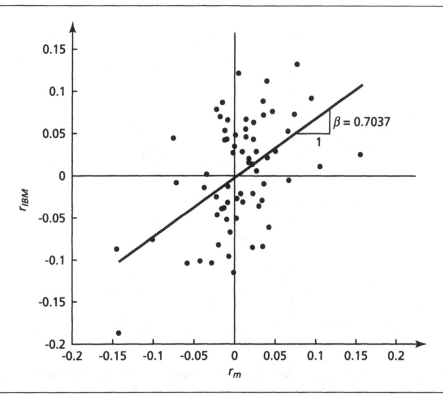

security and plot its returns against the market portfolio itself, we obtain an intercept of zero, and a slope of the characteristic line, or beta, of 1. This slope of 1 is consistent with our analytical finding that the market portfolio has a beta of 1. Figure 9.7 illustrates this result.

The Expected Return of a Security

What factors determine the expected returns of individual securities? We know that risk consists of two parts, systematic and non-systematic.[2] It is reasonable to suppose that the expected return of a security depends on its risk level. However, a single security has diversifiable risk remaining. If investors can diversify costlessly, only the systematic risk of the security will eventually remain, and this will be the only component of risk that is compensated in the market.

---

[2] The same holds true for portfolios that are not fully diversified. For this reason, although we will speak of single securities in this section, the argument holds equally well for portfolios that are not fully diversified.

FIGURE 9.7
The Characteristic Line for the Market Portfolio

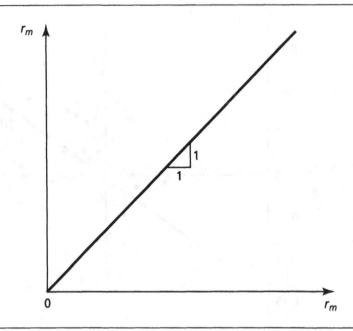

Another way to see this is to consider the risk-bearing function in society. Many benefits arise only after considerable risk taking. Drilling for oil is a clear example, since it involves considerable risk but, if successful, provides valuable energy for society. Investors who bear these risks deserve compensation for the service they render. However, there is no need to reward those investors who bear unnecessary risks, such as those who hold a single security, or who invest all their wealth in drilling a single oil well.

For an individual security, the expected return includes compensation for the passage of time, which is the risk-free rate. It also includes a reward for bearing systematic risk, as measured by beta. So the expected return of an individual security should equal the risk-free rate, plus an additional amount for bearing systematic risk. The security market line discussed in the next section expresses this relationship.

THE SECURITY MARKET LINE

The **security market line** (SML) expresses the central idea of the **capital asset pricing model** (CAPM): the expected return of a security increases linearly with risk, as measured by beta. This relationship is shown in figure 9.8.

We can construct the SML using the knowledge we have already acquired. By definition, the risk-free asset has 0 risk, and a return of r_f. We also know that the market portfolio has a beta of 1, and its expected return is $E(r_m)$. It is also clear from our previous discussion

FIGURE 9.8
The Security Market Line

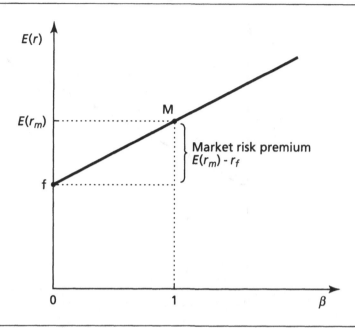

that $E(r_m) > r_f$, since bearing risk is compensated by the market. This means that the SML will slope upward and will pass through the points for the risk-free asset and the market portfolio. However, we still cannot guarantee that the SML will be a straight line, as the CAPM claims. For example, the SML could be a curve with an increasing slope. We now show why the SML must be a straight line.

Consider security A in figure 9.9, which lies below the SML and has a beta of 0.5. Security A is dominated by portfolio C on the SML, which combines the risk-free rate and the market portfolio in equal proportions. Since security A is dominated by C, no investor would hold security A. As a result, the return of security A would have to increase until it equals the return of C. Only then would security A become as attractive to investors as portfolio C. This shows that, in equilibrium, no security can lie below the SML.

Now consider security B located above the SML in figure 9.9. Combining security B with the risk-free security to achieve a beta of 1 generates portfolio D. Since portfolio D dominates the market portfolio, no investor would hold the market portfolio. But we already know that all investors hold the market portfolio. Consequently, the assumption that security B, or any other security, can lie above the SML cannot be true in equilibrium.

In equilibrium, each security or portfolio lies on the SML. The SML has its intercept at the risk-free rate, and the upward slope of the line indicates that greater expected returns accompany higher levels of beta.

Each security lying on the SML is receiving compensation for its level of beta risk, since only the systematic risk is rewarded in the marketplace. We can express the expected

FIGURE 9.9
Why the Security Market Line Is Straight

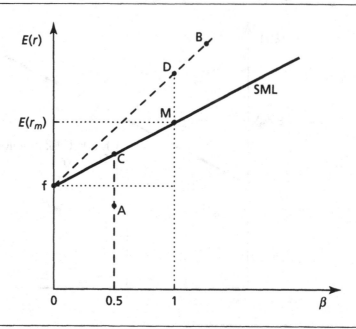

return for a security by the equation for the SML. To find this we use the basic equation for a straight line, $y = b + mx$, noting that for the SML the intercept is the risk-free rate and the slope of the line is found by comparing the coordinates of points M and f. We can then see that the basic equation of the capital asset pricing model is:

$$E(r_i) = r_f + [E(r_m) - r_f]\beta_i \qquad (9.16)$$

In equation 9.16, the market risk premium is $E(r_m) - r_f$. The **market risk premium** is the additional return the investor expects to earn by holding the market portfolio rather than the risk-free asset. It is also equal to the slope of the SML.

THE CAPITAL MARKET LINE AND THE SECURITY MARKET LINE

To complete our discussion of the capital asset pricing model, we compare the capital market line and the security market line to see how they are mutually consistent. Figure 9.4 presented the CML and figure 9.8 showed the SML. The two differ as follows:

1. The risk measure for the CML is the standard deviation, a measure of total risk. The risk measure for the SML is beta, a measure of systematic risk.
2. In equilibrium, only fully diversified portfolios lie on the CML, while individual securities will plot below the CML. For the SML, all securities and all portfolios fall exactly on the SML.

Because the graph of the CML measures risk by the standard deviation, it shows the total risk of the individual securities and portfolios in risk/return space. However, we know that some risk of a security is not relevant to determining its expected return. All individual securities embody some non-systematic risk. This portion of risk does not contribute to their expected return, so individual securities do not lie on the CML. Figure 9.8 used beta as the risk measure. Since beta measures only systematic risk, the expected returns of securities fully reflect that risk, so each security lies exactly on the SML when the market is in equilibrium. The graph of the SML reveals nothing about the total risk of the individual securities. It reflects only the systematic risk, as measured by beta. This is the only portion of the total risk relevant to determining the expected return of a security, assuming the security belongs to a well-diversified portfolio.

SUMMARY

In this and the preceding chapter, we traced the main outlines of capital market theory. In our discussion, we concentrated on the main argument. We assumed that security markets are perfect, that investors have full information about the pricing of securities, and that they all evaluate information similarly. Using these assumptions, we derived the main result of the capital asset pricing model. This result states that the expected return of any security or portfolio increases linearly with its risk, as measured by beta. This relationship is described by the security market line.

QUESTIONS

1. Why do the weights committed to different securities in a portfolio have to sum to 1?
2. Why should the firm consider risk from the point of view of the shareholder?
3. If we put $1,000 in an investment with a standard deviation of 0.2 and $1,000 in an investment with a standard deviation of 0.1, can the standard deviation of the resulting portfolio be found with the information provided? Explain.
4. On what factors does the risk of a two-asset portfolio depend?
5. Of all investment opportunities, assume that one has the highest expected return. Can it ever be dominated? Explain.
6. What is the difference between the efficient set and the efficient frontier?
7. Evaluate the following claim: "Diversification reduces risk, but only at the expense of reducing expected return."
8. If there is a risk-free asset available, why do all investors hold only the market portfolio as their risky portfolio?
9. Explain the separation theorem.
10. What types of investments must you make to have a lending portfolio?
11. What types of investments must you make to have a borrowing portfolio?
12. With a borrowing portfolio, are there practical limits to the amount of expected return you can have? Explain.

13. On any given year, can the risk-free rate be 10 percent and the actual return on the market portfolio be 5 percent?
14. Can the risk-free rate be 10 percent and the expected return on the market portfolio be 5 percent?
15. If the risk-free rate is 10 percent and the expected market rate is 20 percent, what is the expected return of an equally weighted portfolio of the two?
16. If the standard deviation of the market is 12 percent, what is the standard deviation of an equally weighted portfolio of the market and the risk-free asset?
17. What are aggressive stocks?
18. What are defensive stocks?
19. What interpretation does beta have for a stock with a beta equal to 1?
20. What interpretation does beta have for a stock with a beta equal to 0.5?
21. What interpretation does beta have for a stock with a beta equal to 2?
22. Why do some industries tend to have high betas or low betas?
23. For what factors do investors demand compensation?
24. What is the market risk premium?
25. You know that asset A has the same risk as the market. If the expected returns on A and the market are 12 percent, can you determine the risk-free rate? What's going on here?
26. If the risk of asset A is twice the risk of asset B, does it follow that the expected return of A is twice the expected return of B? Explain.
27. You know that the standard deviation of Generalized Motors is lower than the standard deviation of the market, and that GM has a positive correlation with the market. Can the stock of GM be aggressive? Explain.
28. If the risk-free rate increases 2 percent, and the market risk premium remains the same, what happens to the expected return of defensive and aggressive stocks?
29. If the risk-free rate increases by 3 percent, and the expected return on the market remains the same, what happens to the expected return of defensive and aggressive stocks?

PROBLEMS

1. Security X has an expected return of 0.25 and a standard deviation of returns of 0.20. Security Y has an expected return of 0.18 and a standard deviation of returns of 0.18. Plot the two securities in risk/return space. Does one dominate the other?
2. Find the expected return of a portfolio with 30 percent invested in security X of the preceding problem and with 70 percent invested in security Y.
3. For the portfolio created in problem 2, what would be the expected return if we put 50 percent of our funds in that portfolio and 50 percent in security Z, which has an expected return of 12 percent?
4. If we put $1,000 in an investment with a standard deviation of 0.2 and $1,000 in an investment with a standard deviation of 0.1, what is the standard

deviation of the resulting portfolio, if the covariance between the two investments is 0.3?

Security A has an expected return of 0.15 and a standard deviation of 0.2. Security B has an expected return of 0.1 and a standard deviation of 0.15. Use this information to solve problems 5–11.

5. If the correlation between securities A and B is 0.8, what is the expected return of a portfolio with half of the funds invested in each security?
6. What is the standard deviation of the portfolio in the previous problem?
7. If 30 percent of the funds are put in security A, what is the expected return of the portfolio composed of A and B?
8. What is the standard deviation of the portfolio in the previous problem?
9. The correlation between security C and the market is 0.8. If the standard deviation of security C is 0.2 and the standard deviation of the market is 0.17, what is the beta of security C?
10. Solve Problem 9, except assume that the standard deviation of security C is 0.14.
11. Solve Problem 9, except assume that the standard deviation of security C is 0.17.
12. The current risk-free rate is 12 percent, the expected return on the market is 18 percent, and security D has a beta of 1.2. According to the CAPM, what is the expected return on security D?
13. Security E has a beta of 1. If the risk-free rate of interest is 10 percent and the market risk premium is 8 percent, what is the required rate of return on security E, according to the SML equation?
14. A reputable firm, Muskrat Manor, is considering expanding its food franchising operation by opening another store to sell its smash hit food product, Muskrat Nuggets. Already operating 157 stores nationwide, the firm knows that the beta of these previous projects is 1.2. With the risk-free interest rate at 12 percent, and assuming a market risk premium of 8.9 percent, what required rate of return should be applied to the new store project?
15. If Muskrat Manor goes ahead with the new store, it expects sales of $1 million per year, with total costs of $800,000 per year, all stated on an after-tax basis. The project should last 20 years. Investment for the new store would be $800,000. Using the information from the previous problem, should they open the new store?
16. Muskrat Manor is considering a bold addition to the menu at its stores – hamburgers. Although this is a new product for them, the firm believes that it is relatively low risk and assigns a beta of 0.9 to the project. With a market risk premium of 8.9 percent and a risk-free rate of 11 percent, what should be the required rate of return for the hamburger project?
17. For Muskrat's hamburger project, considerable investment costs are involved, including market testing, promotion, and buying the necessary equipment. All of this investment should cost about $15 million. However, the firm believes that the hamburger might catch on. It estimates nationwide sales at $30 million per year, with total costs of $24 million, all after-tax. Assume the project

will last forever. Using the data from the previous problem, should Muskrat sell hamburgers?

Use these data to solve problems 18–20. The current risk-free interest rate is 11 percent. The market risk premium is 8.9 percent.

18. A firm is considering a project that will generate after-tax annual cash flows of $300,000 for five years. The beta of the project is 0.8. The investment cost for the project is $900,000. Should the firm undertake the project?
19. A firm is considering a project that will generate after-tax cash flows of $300,000 for five years. The beta of the project is 1.3. The investment cost for the project is $850,000. Should the firm undertake the project?
20. Draw a graph of the SML and locate the projects of the two previous problems on the graph.
21. If IBM has the same variance as the market, and the correlation between the two is 0.7, what is IBM's beta?
22. If GM has a beta equal to 1.5, and the standard deviation of GM is twice the standard deviation of the market, what is the correlation between GM and the market?
23. Asset A has a beta of 0.7, while asset B has a beta of 1.3. The expected rates of return are 10 percent and 14 percent, respectively. Find the risk-free rate of return.
24. Beatriz Foods, Inc., has a beta of 0.8 and an expected return of 13 percent. If Nadia's restaurant has twice the beta of Beatriz and the risk-free rate is 9 percent, what is the expected return on Nadia's restaurant? Under what circumstance would the answer be 26 percent? Is this a realistic circumstance?
25. You measure the return on Eli-Li, Inc., (el) as well as the return on the market (m) over 60 consecutive months. You notice that there is a peculiar relationship between the two returns, as follows: $r_{el} = 0.10 + 1.5\, r_m + \epsilon$, where ϵ represents a small random component, which over the 60 months averages zero. In other words, the linear relationship between the two returns is not a perfect fit, but it is very close to perfect. Given this information, what is your best estimate of Eli-Li's beta? Explain your reasoning.
26. You perform a linear regression of the returns of ER Mfg. against the return on the market using data from 60 consecutive months. The best fit to the data points is given by the regression equation $r_{er} = 0.03 + 0.5\, r_m$. What is your best estimate of ER's beta? Explain your reasoning.
27. In the example illustrated in figure 9.3, find the point where the return on the borrowing portfolio is equal to the return on portfolio M.
28. If the expected return on the market is 20 percent, the risk-free rate is 10 percent, and the standard deviation on the market is 15 percent, find the general relationship between the standard deviation and the expected return of a portfolio of these two assets.
29. If the risk-free rate is 8 percent, the expected return on the market is 15 percent, and the standard deviation on the market is 20 percent, find the equation of the capital market line.

30. If the risk-free rate is 8 percent, the expected return on the market is 15 percent, and the standard deviation on the market is 20 percent, find the equation of the security market line.

Chapter 10

Leverage and Risk

OVERVIEW

This chapter discusses commonly used techniques for analyzing the risk level associated with a firm's leverage. Firms use leverage to increase their expected returns. However, a higher expected return comes only by accepting higher risks.

A simple technique used to analyze the risk position of the firm is breakeven analysis. In breakeven analysis, the firm separates its costs into its fixed and variable components, and focuses on the sales level required to make a project profitable. The chapter also focuses on two different types of leverage and how they affect the risk level of the firm. Both types of leverage arise from the introduction of fixed charges into the firm's financial plan. Operating leverage results from the firm's fixed operating expenses, while financial leverage arises from the firm's fixed financing expenses. The interactions between operating and financial leverage are also important. Finally, the chapter integrates the perspectives of the financial manager and the firm's shareholder to form one consistent vision of firm risk.

BREAKEVEN ANALYSIS

The success of many projects depends upon producing a certain number of units of a given good or service. **Breakeven analysis** is a technique for analyzing profitability as a function of costs and sales. Virtually every project involves some fixed cost – the cost the firm incurs no matter how many units of a good it produces. Fixed costs include plant overhead, depreciation for equipment, and other expenses that do not vary with the level of production. For example, if a firm produces a pencil, the fixed costs include the facility and machinery for producing the pencil.

In addition to fixed costs, the firm also incurs variable costs – the direct cost incurred to produce each unit of the good. For the pencil manufacturer, the variable costs include the wood and graphite that go into each pencil and the labor and utility costs spent to produce a pencil. The total cost is the sum of the fixed and variable costs.

Breakeven analysis focuses on the relationship between sales and costs, fixed and variable. If the pencil manufacturer sells a pencil for $0.10 and the variable cost required to make the pencil is $0.07, then each pencil makes a $0.03 contribution toward paying its fixed costs. In spite of this, the firm may still lose money if it fails to sell enough pencils to recover all of its fixed costs.

Consider a firm that plans to manufacture computer switches to sell for $10 each. Assume the variable cost is $8 per switch. The fixed cost associated with this project will be $100,000. Figure 10.1 reflects these facts, showing the total cost and revenue lines. The firm incurs the $100,000 in fixed costs whether it manufactures one switch or one million. The total cost line reflects the fixed costs (F) plus the variable costs (V).[1] For example, if the firm manufactures a quantity (Q) of 10,000 switches, its total cost (TC) will be $180,000.

$$TC = F + V \times Q$$
$$= \$100,000 + \$8 \times 10,000$$
$$= \$180,000$$

Also, the firm's revenue (R) depends on the price (P) and quantity (Q) sold. Sales of 10,000 switches generate revenues of $100,000.

$$R = P \times Q$$
$$= \$10 \times 10,000$$

FIGURE 10.1
Breakeven Analysis with the Old Technology

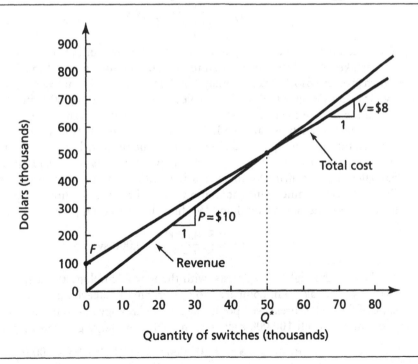

Quantity of switches (thousands)

---

[1] Since for each unit produced by the firm the total cost increases by V dollars, the slope of the total cost line is equal to V.

With production and sales of 10,000 switches, the company has total costs of $180,000 and revenues of $100,000, so the firm loses $80,000. Figure 10.1 shows that the total cost line lies above the revenue line at a production level of 10,000 switches; in fact, the firm loses money for any sales level below 50,000 switches.

If the firm produces and sells exactly 50,000 switches it has neither a profit nor a loss. This is the **breakeven point** – the level of sales at which total revenue equals total cost. If the firm sells more than 50,000 switches, it makes a profit.

To calculate the breakeven point, note that the project breaks even when total costs equal total revenues; that is, when $TC = R$. Equivalently, the project breaks even when the following equality holds:

$$F + V \times Q = P \times Q$$

Solving this expression for the number of units sold, Q, and denoting the breakeven quantity as Q^*, we have:

$$Q^* = \frac{F}{P - V} \tag{10.1}$$

For the switch example, we find the breakeven point by substituting values into equation 10.1:

$$Q^* = \frac{\$100,000}{\$10 - \$8} = 50,000 \text{ switches}$$

This value corresponds to the breakeven point shown in figure 10.1.

Breakeven analysis can be used to evaluate the likelihood of making a profit with the switch project. Also, breakeven analysis helps the financial manager see the loss or profitability for various levels of sales. If the projected sales level is 40,000 switches, the graph shows that there is little likelihood of making enough sales to earn an attractive profit.

Breakeven analysis can also help managers choose between different technologies or manufacturing techniques available for the same project. For example, the firm can make the same switch employing new technology. With this new technique, the fixed cost is $300,000, but the firm can make a switch with a variable cost of only $5, instead of $8. Because it is the same switch, it continues to sell for $10. Figure 10.2 presents a breakeven analysis with the new technology. We find the breakeven point (Q^*) using equation 10.1:

$$Q^* = \frac{\$300,000}{\$10 - \$5} = 60,000 \text{ switches}$$

Due to the higher fixed costs, with the new technology the firm needs to sell 60,000 switches to break even, compared to the original breakeven point of 50,000 switches. In spite of the higher breakeven point, the new technology has some advantages. For example, if the firm can sell 100,000 switches, the old technology generates a profit of $100,000:

$$\text{Profit}_{\text{old}} = \$10 \times 100,000 - (\$100,000 + \$8 \times 100,000)$$
$$= \$100,000$$

However, with the new technology, the same sales level of 100,000 switches produces a profit of $200,000:

FIGURE 10.2
Breakeven Analysis with the New Technology

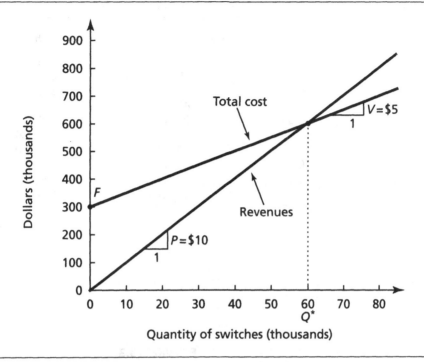

$$\text{Profit}_{\text{new}} = \$10 \times 100{,}000 - (\$300{,}000 + \$5 \times 100{,}000)$$
$$= \$200{,}000$$

Which technology should the firm choose? The answer depends on the firm's estimate of its sales and the confidence it attaches to that estimate. For example, if the firm is certain it will sell 55,000 switches, it should use the old technology. At that sales level, only the old technology shows a profit. Likewise, if the firm is sure it can sell 100,000 switches, it should employ the new technology because it produces the highest profit. If the firm is less confident about its sales forecasts, then the decision is murkier and the firm may want to engage in a more detailed analysis.

Table 10.1 shows the level of profit for different levels of sales under the two technologies, and figure 10.3 presents the same information graphically. If the firm sells 66,667 switches, figure 10.3 shows that the old and new technologies perform equally well. For any level of sales below 66,667 switches, the old technology strategy is better, making either a greater profit or a smaller loss; for higher levels of sales, the new technology is better. For example, we already noted that with sales of 100,000 switches the new technology strategy gives twice the profit of the old technology. By conducting a breakeven analysis, the financial manager can explore the trade-offs between the two processes.

Although breakeven analysis is a useful technique for examining the operating risk of a firm in a given period, it does not evaluate present values. In particular, it considers only

TABLE 10.1
Profits from the Switch Project for the Old and New Technologies
at Various Levels of Sales

Sales	Old Technology	New Technology
0	−$100,000	−$300,000
10,000	−80,000	−250,000
20,000	−60,000	−200,000
30,000	−40,000	−150,000
40,000	−20,000	−100,000
50,000	0	−50,000
60,000	20,000	0
70,000	40,000	50,000
80,000	60,000	100,000
90,000	80,000	150,000
100,000	100,000	200,000

FIGURE 10.3
Profits with the Old and New Technologies

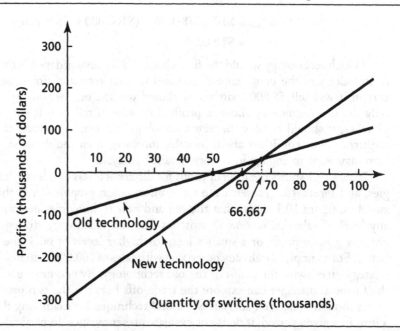

one period, and it does not reflect the present values of future cash flows. It also does not explicitly consider the investment outlay.[2] The next section discusses a modified version of the breakeven analysis technique that focuses on the net present value of the project.

DISCOUNTED BREAKEVEN ANALYSIS

We know from our study of capital budgeting that the financial manager should use the NPV technique to evaluate projects. Although traditional breakeven analysis focuses on the annual profits from a project, a similar analysis can be conducted by focusing on the project's NPV. Consider a project that requires an investment of I dollars. As in the previous section, let the price of each unit sold be P dollars, the variable cost per unit be V dollars, and the fixed annual costs be F dollars. These fixed costs contain the annual depreciation, D. The appropriate discount rate for the project is r percent, and the project has a life of n years. The firm estimates that it will sell Q units in each year of the project's life. For simplicity, suppose the firm does not pay taxes. This information is depicted graphically in figure 10.4.

The project has an outlay of I dollars at time $t = 0$ and generates annual cash inflows equal to:

$$\text{Annual Cash Flow} = PQ - (F - D + VQ)$$

These equal annual cash flows constitute an annuity. Notice that, to obtain the annual cash flow, it is necessary to subtract the depreciation, D, from the fixed costs, F, because depreciation is not a cash expense. We can now calculate the net present value of this project:

$$\text{NPV} = -I + [PQ - (F - D + VQ)]\text{PA}(r, n)$$

The project breaks even when its NPV equals zero. Let the breakeven quantity when using the NPV method be Q_d^*. Then, setting the preceding expression to zero and solving for the breakeven quantity, we obtain:

FIGURE 10.4
Cash Flows for Discounted Breakeven Analysis

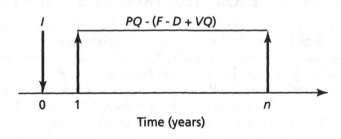

Time (years)

---

[2] Nevertheless, the investment is implicitly considered in the depreciation expense, which is part of the costs of the firm.

$$Q_d^* = \frac{F}{P-V} + \frac{I - D \times PA(r, n)}{(P-V)PA(r, n)} \tag{10.2}$$

Equation 10.2 shows that the discounted breakeven quantity will normally differ from the traditional breakeven quantity given in equation 10.1. Consequently, we should be careful in using the traditional breakeven quantity, as it is likely to give an erroneous estimate of the breakeven that results from using discounted cash flow techniques.

To illustrate the difference between the traditional and the discounted breakeven methods, let us return to the switch company and assume that it uses the old technology. In that case, annual fixed costs are $100,000, variable costs per switch are $8, and the price of each switch is $10. Given these data, we determined that the traditional breakeven quantity was 50,000 units.

To use the discounted breakeven technique, we must know the amount of initial investment for the project, the annual depreciation, the life of the project, and the appropriate discount rate. Assume that $I = \$500,000$, $D = \$50,000$, $n = 10$ years, and $r = 10$ percent.[3] Given this information, we calculate the discounted breakeven using equation 10.2:

$$Q_d^* = \frac{\$100,000}{\$10 - \$8} + \frac{\$500,000 - \$50,000 \times PA(10\%, 10)}{(\$10 - \$8)PA(10\%, 10)}$$

$$= 50,000 + 15,686$$

$$= 65,686 \text{ switches}$$

This calculation clearly illustrates that the traditional breakeven quantity may seriously underestimate the true breakeven quantity for the project given by the NPV technique. The discounted breakeven quantity of 65,686 switches is much greater than the traditional breakeven of 50,000 switches. If the firm believes it can sell 60,000 switches each year over the ten-year life of the project, then the traditional breakeven would indicate a profitable project. However, at that sales level the project has a negative NPV and should be rejected. Only with annual sales greater than 65,686 will the project generate wealth for the firm.

OPERATING LEVERAGE AND THE VARIABILITY OF EBIT

The proportion of fixed costs relative to variable costs is **operating leverage**. An operation with a high level of fixed costs relative to variable costs has high operating leverage. In our example of the switch company, the new technology strategy involves a higher measure of operating leverage than the old technology strategy.

We now examine the effect of operating leverage on the riskiness of the firm's operating cash profits. These operating profits are the firm's **earnings before interest and taxes** (EBIT). We focus on operating profits to separate the risk resulting from the firm's operations from the risk associated with its financing policy.

---

[3] These assumptions are consistent with straight line depreciation and a zero salvage value at the end of the project's life.

We define **business risk** as the variability in a firm's EBIT, and we show how operating leverage affects business risk. Table 10.2 shows the level of EBIT for different levels of sales for both the old and new technology strategies. In the table, the breakeven point is higher for the new technology strategy because of its higher fixed costs. This is consistent with our previous findings. In addition to the higher breakeven point, the table shows the greater variability of EBIT for the new technology. Indeed, for the annual sales range going from 10,000 units to 90,000 units shown in table 10.2, the EBIT for the old technology will vary between −$80,000 and $80,000, or a range of $160,000. For the new technology, EBIT fluctuates between −$250,000 and $150,000, or a range of $400,000.

To examine the effect of operating leverage more closely, assume the firm expects to sell 66,667 switches per year. At this sales level, the old and new technologies give the same EBIT of $33,334. Let us also assume that the standard deviation of sales is 10,000 units. If sales are normally distributed, this means that there is about a 68 percent chance that actual sales will fall somewhere between 56,667 and 76,667 units.

For the expected level of sales of 66,667, the two strategies have the same expected EBIT. However, as sales move away from the expected value of 66,667, EBIT varies as well. For the old technology the variability is not so great. In fact, as table 10.2 shows, a sales change of 10,000 units causes only a $20,000 change in EBIT for the old technology, compared with a $50,000 change for the new technology, so we reaffirm that the new technology strategy is much more susceptible to a variation in sales.

The relative variability of the EBIT for the two technologies can also be seen by comparing the analytic expressions for the EBIT of each process:

$$EBIT_{old} = 2Q - 100,000$$

and

$$EBIT_{new} = 5Q - 300,000$$

These expressions confirm the findings of table 10.2 that the EBIT of the new technology is 2.5 times more sensitive to changes in sales than the old technology.

TABLE 10.2
Revenue, Costs, and Profits for the Switch Company

Sales	Revenue	Old Technology		New Technology	
		Total Cost	EBIT	Total Cost	EBIT
10,000	100,000	180,000	−80,000	350,000	−250,000
20,000	200,000	260,000	−60,000	400,000	−200,000
30,000	300,000	340,000	−40,000	450,000	−150,000
40,000	400,000	420,000	−20,000	500,000	−100,000
50,000	500,000	500,000	0	550,000	−50,000
60,000	600,000	580,000	20,000	600,000	0
70,000	700,000	660,000	40,000	650,000	50,000
80,000	800,000	740,000	60,000	700,000	100,000
90,000	900,000	820,000	80,000	750,000	150,000

To measure the operating leverage, we compute the percentage change in EBIT resulting from a 1 percent change in sales. The **measure of operating leverage** (MOL) is:

$$MOL = \frac{\text{Percentage Change in EBIT}}{\text{Percentage Change in Unit Sales}} \tag{10.3}$$

It can be shown that an equivalent expression for the MOL is:

$$MOL = \frac{(P-V)Q}{(P-V)Q - F} \tag{10.4}$$

Equation 10.4 shows that the MOL will always be greater than 1 for any firm that has some fixed operating costs, F. If $F > 0$, the denominator in equation 10.4 is smaller than the numerator, and the entire fraction is greater than 1.

To explore the MOL further, consider again our example of an expected level of sales of 66,667 switches. With this sales level, and using the cost data for each strategy, we can compute the measure of operating leverage for each. For the old technology we have:

$$MOL_{old} = \frac{(\$10 - \$8)66,667}{(\$10 - \$8)66,667 - \$100,000} = 4$$

For the new technology we have:

$$MOL_{new} = \frac{(\$10 - \$5)66,667}{(\$10 - \$5)66,667 - \$300,000} = 10$$

Since both strategies have some fixed operating costs, both have MOL values greater than 1.0. However, using larger fixed operating costs increases the MOL significantly. The MOL of ten for the new technology means that for each 1 percent change in unit sales from the base level of 66,667, the EBIT will change by 10 percent. Such a big measure of operating leverage indicates that the firm will benefit greatly from an increased sales effort. The opposite is also true: if sales are expected to decline, the firm with the greatest MOL will suffer the most.

Notice that the MOL depends on the base sales level chosen. For example, at the breakeven quantity of sales, the MOL will be infinite. This is really not surprising, because it reflects the fact that at the breakeven point there are no operating profits, and any increase in sales will produce some operating profit, or EBIT. A change from no profit to some profit represents an infinite percentage increase.

Although operating leverage increases the business risk of the firm, we cannot conclude that the firm should minimize operating leverage. It merely means that the financial manager must choose the correct amount of operating leverage. As we have emphasized so many times, the financial manager must trade off the good (higher expected EBIT) against the bad (higher business risk).

FINANCIAL LEVERAGE AND THE VARIABILITY OF EPS

Financial leverage affects the firm in ways similar to operating leverage. The main difference is that whereas operating leverage results from fixed operating costs, financial leverage arises from fixed financing charges, which are the interest and principal payments on debt. Just as operating leverage increases the variability of EBIT, financial leverage increases the variability of the firm's **earnings per share** (EPS).

The operating leverage technique helps the manager choose the correct level of fixed operating costs. The financial leverage technique helps the manager choose how much debt financing to use. If the firm uses debt financing, it must make the promised debt payments no matter what level of EBIT it has, so the use of debt also represents an increased risk. However, debt financing may be cheaper than financing with equity because of its priority over stock in case of bankruptcy, and because interest payments are tax deductible, whereas dividends are not. As usual, the financial manager faces a trade-off between the benefits and costs of debt financing.

To see the effect of financial leverage on EPS, let us extend our consideration of the switch company. Assume the firm has decided to employ the old technology and requires $1 million to finance its operations. These funds may come from either debt or equity. Assume each share of stock trades in the market for $100. If the firm uses only stock, it will have 10,000 shares outstanding. We assume that it pays a 30 percent tax rate.

To begin the analysis, we assume the firm uses 100 percent stock financing, so the interest payment is $i = 0$. We consider different sales levels to examine the effect on the firm's EPS, using sales of 70,000 switches as our base case. Table 10.3 presents income statements for the firm at various sales levels.

Notice that if sales vary by 10,000 switches from the base level of 70,000 switches, EBIT changes by $20,000, or 50 percent. Net income and EPS also change by 50 percent in either direction. Indeed, if sales of switches drop from 70,000 units to 60,000 units, net income drops from $28,000 to $14,000 and EPS drops from $2.80 to $1.40, as shown in table 10.3. This illustrates the general fact that without financial leverage, a percentage change in EBIT causes the same percentage change in net income and EPS.

TABLE 10.3

Income Statement with No Debt for the Old Technology

| | Switches Sold | | |
	60,000	70,000	80,000
Sales	$600,000	$700,000	$800,000
Cost of goods sold	−480,000	−560,000	−640,000
Fixed operating costs	−100,000	−100,000	−100,000
EBIT	$20,000	$40,000	$60,000
Financing expenses	0	0	0
Earnings before taxes	$20,000	$40,000	$60,000
Taxes (30%)	−6,000	−12,000	−18,000
Net income	$14,000	$28,000	$42,000
Shares outstanding	10,000	10,000	10,000
EPS	$1.40	$2.80	$4.20

To see how financial leverage increases the variability of net income and EPS, assume now that the switch company gets 50 percent of its financing from stock and the remaining 50 percent from bonds that pay 4 percent interest. Because we assume the entire financing of the firm is $1,000,000, the firm has $500,000 in bonds outstanding. In addition, the firm has $500,000 in stock financing, or 5,000 outstanding shares with a market value of $100 per share.

For the case in which the firm uses 50 percent debt, table 10.4 presents the income statements for alternative levels of sales. Because changing financial leverage does not affect EBIT, we have the same EBIT as in table 10.3. Important changes emerge in the lower portions of the income statement. First, having borrowed $500,000 at 4 percent, the firm must make annual interest payments of $20,000. As a result, the firm's EPS becomes more variable. To see this, notice that at a level of sales of 70,000 switches, EPS is still $2.80. However, if the firm uses 50 percent, as in table 10.4, a sales level of 60,000 switches means EPS will drop to $0. This contrasts with an EPS of $1.40 without financing. Therefore, with financial leverage, a drop in sales causes EPS to fall more than it would if the firm used no debt.

Just as EPS drops more radically for a drop in sales, it increases more for an increase in sales, given the presence of debt. Tables 10.3 and 10.4 illustrate this principle. If the firm sells 80,000 switches instead of 70,000, and if it is using no financial leverage, EPS is $4.20. By contrast, with 50 percent debt financing, sales of 80,000 switches gives an EPS of $5.60.

Figure 10.5 highlights the relationship between EPS and sales for 0 percent and 50 percent debt financing. The greater the percentage of assets financed by debt, the more sensitive EPS is to any change in sales. In the graph, the higher the level of debt, the steeper the slope of the line relating EPS and sales. This shows that debt offers both greater potential for increased EPS, as well as greater risk.

TABLE 10.4

Income Statement with 50% Debt for the Old Technology

	Switches Sold		
	60,000	*70,000*	*80,000*
Sales	$600,000	$700,000	$800,000
Cost of goods sold	−480,000	−560,000	−640,000
Fixed operating costs	−100,000	−100,000	−100,000
EBIT	$20,000	$40,000	$60,000
Financing expenses	−20,000	−20,000	−20,000
Earnings before taxes	0	$20,000	$40,000
Taxes (30%)	0	−6,000	−12,000
Net income	$0	$14,000	$28,000
Shares outstanding	5,000	5,000	5,000
EPS	$0	$2.80	$5.60

FIGURE 10.5
The Variability in EPS as a Function of Sales
for Different Levels of Debt Financing

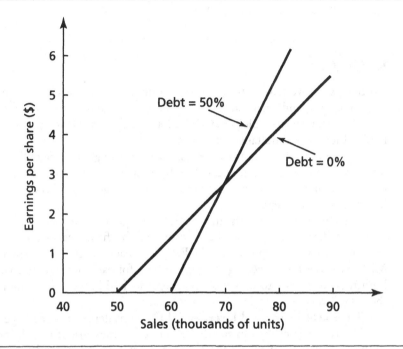

Just as there is a measure for the firm's operating leverage, there is a corresponding measure for financial leverage. We measured operating leverage by examining the percentage change in EBIT for a given percentage change in sales. For financial leverage we examine the percentage change in EPS for a given percentage change in EBIT. This is the **measure of financial leverage** (MFL) and is given by:

$$MFL = \frac{\text{Percentage Change in EPS}}{\text{Percentage Change in EBIT}} \qquad (10.5)$$

As was the case for measuring operating leverage, there is an equivalent formula for finding the MFL:

$$MFL = \frac{EBIT}{EBIT - i} \qquad (10.6)$$

In equation 10.6, i represents the firm's total interest payment. Note that the MFL, just as the MOL, will always be greater than 1 for any firm with some debt outstanding. The higher the financial leverage of the firm, the greater its measure of financial leverage.

To illustrate the computation of the MFL, consider a 50 percent financial leverage and a sales level of 70,000 switches, as shown in table 10.4. At this sales level, EBIT is $40,000. Using equation 10.6 we compute an MFL of 2:

$$MFL = \frac{\$40,000}{\$40,000 - \$20,000} = 2$$

Therefore, if the firm has a 50 percent financial leverage, a 1 percent change in EBIT induces a 2 percent change in EPS.

TOTAL LEVERAGE

To this point, we have considered operating and financial leverage individually. Because both operating and financial leverage affect the overall risk level of the firm in terms of its EPS, as shown in tables 10.3 and 10.4, the financial manager needs to consider both kinds of leverage simultaneously.

As we have discussed, the financial manager can greatly affect the riskiness of the firm by altering operating and financial leverage policies. In making such a decision, the financial manager must remember that high operating leverage magnifies the effect of high financial leverage, and vice versa.

We need a measure of the firm's total leverage because operating and financial leverage work together to determine the riskiness of the firm's earnings. Recall that the MOL measures the percentage change in EBIT for each percentage change in sales. Also, the MFL measures the percentage change in EPS for each percentage change in EBIT. Since both measures refer to percentage changes in EBIT, we can combine them to measure the total leverage.

The **measure of total leverage** (MTL) considers the percentage change in EPS for a unit percentage change in sales. We define the measure of total leverage as the product of the measures of operating and financial leverage. The general formula for the MTL is:

$$MTL = \frac{\text{Percentage Change in EPS}}{\text{Percentage Change in Sales}} \qquad (10.7)$$

If we multiply and divide the right-hand side of equation 10.7 by the percentage change in EBIT, then we can express the MTL in terms of the MOL and MFL defined previously:

$$MTL = MOL \times MFL \qquad (10.8)$$

As an example, we can find the measure of total leverage for the firm using the old technology, assuming a sales level of 70,000 switches and 50 percent debt, as in table 10.4. The MOL is 3.5, from equation 10.4:

$$MOL = \frac{(\$10 - \$8)70,000}{(\$10 - \$8)70,000 - \$100,000} = 3.5$$

Similarly, the measure of financial leverage is 2, from equation 10.6:

$$MFL = \frac{\$40,000}{\$40,000 - \$20,000} = 2$$

We now combine the operating and financial leverage to find the measure of total leverage. For the low leverage strategy:

$$MTL = MOL \times MFL = 3.50 \times 2 = 7$$

Thus, for the firm with the old technology and 50 percent debt financing, a 1 percent change in sales produces a 7 percent change in EPS.

SUMMARY

This chapter considered the effect of leverage on risk and introduced the breakeven analysis technique. Breakeven analysis examines the relationship between a firm's level of sales and the profit from a project. We defined the breakeven point as the level of sales that results in zero profit.

Although breakeven is a popular analysis technique, it has a few shortcomings, such as concentrating on a single year's profits. Also, it disregards the time value of money and focuses on accounting figures, not cash flows. The discounted breakeven technique is designed to overcome these problems. With discounted breakeven analysis, the problem is finding the sales level that leads to a zero NPV for a project. We illustrated how the traditional breakeven and the discounted breakeven may differ substantially for the same project. Consequently, although the traditional breakeven is easier to use, it must be used with caution.

The chapter then considered leverage and its effect on the risk level of the firm. We considered both operating and financial leverage and showed how both contribute to total risk. To gauge the extent of each one, we developed measures for each of them and a measure of total leverage.

QUESTIONS

1. How does breakeven analysis help the manager in assessing the firm's business risk?
2. In traditional breakeven analysis, what does the slope of the total cost line represent?
3. In traditional breakeven analysis, what does the intercept of the total cost line represent?
4. In traditional breakeven analysis, what does the slope of the revenue line represent?
5. Why does the revenue line start at the origin of the traditional breakeven graph?
6. How are the traditional and the discounted breakeven analyses related?
7. If the variable cost and price of each unit increase by the same dollar amount, what happens to the traditional breakeven quantity?
8. If the variable cost and price of each unit increase by the same percentage, what happens to the traditional breakeven quantity?
9. If the fixed cost and the unit contribution margin $(P - V)$ increase by the same dollar amount, what happens to the traditional breakeven quantity?
10. If the fixed cost and the unit contribution margin $(P - V)$ increase by the same percentage, what happens to the traditional breakeven quantity?
11. Does high operating leverage affect EPS or only EBIT? Explain.
12. Does financial leverage have any effect on EBIT? Why or why not?

13. Are dividend payments to common shareholders a kind of fixed financial charge? Explain.
14. Are interest payments to bondholders a kind of fixed financial charge? Explain.
15. What is business risk?
16. Explain how high operating leverage contributes to business risk.
17. What is the measure of operating leverage (MOL)?
18. If a firm has no fixed operating cost, what is its MOL?
19. What is the measure of financial leverage (MFL)?
20. If a firm has no financial leverage, what will be its measure of financial leverage?
21. If a firm has no financial leverage, what is the relationship between a change in EBIT and a change in EPS?
22. How do operating and financial leverage interact?
23. What is the measure of total leverage?

PROBLEMS

Use the following information to solve problems 1–15. Leporello Mfg. is expecting revenues next year of $100,000 if it sells 100 personal computers (PCs) at $1,000 each. If Leporello adopts technology A, it will have fixed operating costs of $40,000 and a variable cost per PC of $400. With technology B, the firm will have fixed costs of $20,000 and a variable cost per PC of $600. Leporello is subject to a 40 percent tax rate on its earnings.

1. For technology A, calculate the EBIT if sales are 80, 90, 100, 110, and 120 PCs.
2. For technology B, calculate the EBIT if sales are 80, 90, 100, 110, and 120 PCs.
3. For technology A, draw a graph showing the relationship between sales and EBIT.
4. For technology B, draw a graph showing the relationship between sales and EBIT.
5. What can you say about the choice of these two technologies? Can you confidently say which technology Leporello should choose?
6. Compute the EPS for technology A for a sales level of 90, 100, and 110 PCs, assuming that Leporello has no debt, and that the number of shares outstanding is 1,000.
7. Using 100 PCs as the base level of sales, compute the measure of operating leverage.
8. Compute the EPS for technology A for a sales level of 90, 100, and 110 PCs, assuming that Leporello has 500 shares outstanding, worth $100 per share, and that it has $50,000 of long-term debt on which it is paying 10 percent annual interest.
9. Using 100 PCs as the base level of sales, compute the measure of financial leverage.
10. Using 100 PCs as the base level of sales, compute the measure of total leverage.
11. Compute the EPS for technology B for a sales level of 90, 100, and 110 PCs, assuming that Leporello has no debt, and that the number of shares outstanding is 1,000.

12. Using 100 PCs as the base level of sales, compute the measure of operating leverage.

13. Compute the EPS for technology B for a sales level of 90, 100, and 110 PCs, assuming that Leporello has 500 shares outstanding, worth $100 per share, and that it has $50,000 of long-term debt on which it is paying 10 percent annual interest.

14. Using 100 PCs as the base level of sales, compute the measure of financial leverage.

15. Using 100 PCs as the base level of sales, compute the measure of total leverage.

16. Using the definition of the measure of operating leverage given in equation 10.3, and assuming a one unit change in sales, derive the expression for the MOL given in equation 10.4.

17. Using the definition of the measure of financial leverage given in equation 10.5, and assuming a $1 change in EBIT, derive the expression for the MFL given in equation 10.6.

18. Consider a project such as the one depicted in figure 10.4. Show that if the firm uses linear depreciation and the project has no salvage value, then the discounted breakeven quantity will always be greater than the traditional breakeven quantity.

19. Equation 10.4 expresses the MOL in terms of P, V, Q, and F. Find an equivalent expression for the MOL in terms of EBIT and F.

20. Using the result of the previous problem, find an expression for the measure of total leverage (MTL) in terms of EBIT, F, and the firm's annual interest payment (i).

21. Show that if a firm has no debt, its EPS is proportional to its EBIT. Assume that the firm has assets equal to A, that the price of each share is P, and that the tax rate is T.

22. For the firm of the previous problem, what is the slope of the line relating EPS to EBIT?

23. For the same firm, what happens to the EPS-versus-EBIT line if it incurs annual interest expenses equal to i? Assets are still A, and $i = Dr_D$, where D is the level of debt in the firm's capital structure and r_D is the annual interest rate.

24. Eli-Lili is selling twice as many units as it needs to break even. Determine the firm's profits in terms of the breakeven analysis variables F, P, V, and Q.

25. If Eli-Lili sells three times as many units as it needs to break even, what are its profits in terms of the breakeven analysis variables F, P, V, and Q?

Chapter 11

Capital Structure

OVERVIEW

In this chapter we consider the essential problem of capital structure, that is, the firm's division of the firm's total capital needs among equity and debt. In setting the firm's capital structure, the manager must determine which combination of financing sources maximize shareholder wealth.

The capital structure issue is one of the murkiest and most controversial problems in corporate finance. We begin our analysis by examining the role of capital structure in a world of zero taxes and perfect markets. A perfect market is a market with no transaction costs and free information. In such an idealized environment, capital structure policy does not affect the value of the firm. We then provide an added measure of realism to our discussion by including both taxes and market imperfections.

CAPITAL STRUCTURE WITH PERFECT CAPITAL MARKETS AND NO TAXES

This section explores the famous arguments Modigliani and Miller made in 1958,[1] in which they maintain that under special conditions the choice of capital structure has no effect on the value of the firm. The authors (MM) assume that capital markets are perfect and that there are no taxes. A perfect capital market is one in which all investors can borrow and lend funds at the same interest rate, and can move funds quickly from one place to another without incurring transaction costs.

Having shown that neither $V_L > V_U$ nor $V_L < V_U$ are equilibrium relationships, the only possible equilibrium result is to have $V_L = V_U$. Equivalently, in the absence of taxes, otherwise identical levered and unlevered firms must have the same value.

AN ILLUSTRATION OF CAPITAL STRUCTURE IRRELEVANCE IN THE ABSENCE OF TAXES

Consider a firm with assets worth $1 million that is studying two different plans for financing those assets. First, the firm can finance the assets with 100 percent common

---

[1] Modigliani, F. and M. H. Miller, "The Cost of Capital, Corporation Finance and the Theory of Investment," *American Economic Review*, 48, June 1958, pp. 261–97. This paper is generally considered to define the starting

TABLE 11.1
Alternative Financing Plans

	Unlevered	Levered
Stock	$1,000,000	$500,000
Debt (r_D = 10%)	0	500,000
Total financing	1,000,000	1,000,000

stock. Alternatively, it can finance 50 percent of the assets with stock and 50 percent with debt. The debt has an annual interest rate of 10 percent. Table 11.1 summarizes the two financing plans.

Throughout our discussion, we assume the investor has a total capital of $1,000,000 to invest. We also assume the firm's operating profit, or EBIT, is uncertain, but will be either $50,000 or $150,000. We will show that for each of these two possible EBIT outcomes, the investor receives the same total cash flow regardless of the capital structure employed.

Table 11.2 shows the earnings to the investor when the firm uses 50 percent stock and 50 percent debt to finance its assets. In this case the investor buys $500,000 in the firm's stock and also lends $500,000 to the firm at an interest rate of 10 percent. If the levered firm's operating income is $50,000, it earns exactly enough to pay the interest on the debt (10 percent of $500,000). This leaves no payment to the stock. Since the investor owns both the stock and the debt, the total cash flow to the investor is $50,000 + $0 = $50,000. Alternatively, if the operating income is $150,000, the firm pays $50,000 interest on the debt, leaving the other $100,000 as payment for the stock. In this case, the investor receives a total cash flow of $50,000 + $100,000 = $150,000. We see that no matter what the outcome, the investor holding both the debt and the stock of the levered firm receives the entire EBIT.

Table 11.3 shows the earnings to the investor when the firm uses only stock to finance its assets. In this case the investor buys $1,000,000 in the firm's stock. For this unlevered

TABLE 11.2
Investment of $1,000,000 in a Levered Firm

Operating income (EBIT)	$50,000	$150,000
Firm's interest expense	−50,000	−50,000
Earnings	0	$100,000
Total cash flow to investor	$50,000	$150,000

point of modern finance. Both Professors Modigliani and Miller received the Nobel Prize in Economics, in 1984 and 1989, respectively.

TABLE 11.3
Investment of $1,000,000 in an Unlevered Firm

Operating income (EBIT)	$50,000	$150,000
Firm's interest expense	0	0
Earnings	$50,000	$150,000
Total cash flow to investor	$50,000	$150,000

firm, its entire operating income, whether $50,000 or $150,000, is used as payment to the stock, so the total cash flow to the investor is the EBIT, just as in the case of the levered firm.

Tables 11.2 and 11.3 show that no matter what the capital structure of the firm may be, the investor can receive the entire EBIT. It follows that investors must assign the same value to both firms.

We have shown in the previous section that when two firms differ only in their capital structure, they must have the same value, and we have illustrated that result in this section. Therefore, the firm's leverage decision is irrelevant to the value of the firm. It is important to remember, though, that we reached this conclusion under the assumptions of perfect capital markets and no taxes. When we remove these assumptions, capital structure decisions may affect the value of the firm.

The argument runs as follows. Suppose there are two firms, U and L, that have identical assets producing the same cash flow every year.[2] The two firms differ only in their capital structure – firm U has financed its assets solely with stock, so it is unlevered, whereas firm L has financed its assets with a combination of debt and equity, so it is a levered firm.

If the value of firm L is greater than the value of firm U, the investor who owns the equity of firm L can take advantage of the difference in value by selling the shares in L, borrowing some additional funds, and using those funds to purchase the shares of firm U. These transactions will leave the shareholder who originally owns firm L better off. Since firm U itself is unlevered but the investor's position is levered, this is an example of investors trading to create **homemade leverage**, where investors can personally create any capital structure by transacting in the marketplace.

To make these ideas precise, let the value of the levered firm be $V_L = D + E_L$ where D and E_L are the market values of the firm's debt and equity, respectively. Similarly, for the unlevered firm, $V_U = E_U$ since it has no debt in its capital structure. Let EBIT represent the annual earnings before interest and taxes that each firm's assets generate.[3]

The investor owning the shares in the levered firm receives a cash flow, CF_L, equal to the firm's net income, so $CF_L = NI_L = \text{EBIT} - r_D D$. However, if $V_L > V_U$, this investor

---

[2] The cash flows of both firms may be uncertain, but they must be perfectly positively correlated.
[3] While EBIT can fluctuate from year to year, for simplicity we assume that it will always be greater than the interest payments the levered firm must make each year, $r_D D$.

can have a greater cash flow by performing the following transactions. First, the investor sells the equity in the levered firm and receives E_L dollars. Second, the investor borrows from a bank an amount equal to $(E_U - E_L)$ at an interest rate r_D, so the investor now has $E_L + (E_U - E_L) = E_U$ dollars available – exactly the amount needed to buy the unlevered firm's shares.

At the end of each year the investor who now owns the unlevered shares receives the firm's net income, which equals $NI_U =$ EBIT since the unlevered firm has no debt payments to make. However, the investor must pay interest equal to $r_D(E_U - E_L)$ on the personal debt of $(E_U - E_L)$. Thus, the investor obtains a net cash flow of $CF_U =$ EBIT $- r_D(E_U - E_L)$.

Comparing the annual cash flows to the investor under both scenarios depicted here, we find that:

$$CF_U - CF_L = [\text{EBIT} - (E_U - E_L)r_D] - [\text{EBIT} - Dr_D]$$
$$= [(D + E_L) - E_U]r_D$$
$$= [V_L - V_U]r_D$$
$$> 0$$

This shows that the investor who originally owns the levered firm and transacts as described will be better off selling the levered firm and buying the unlevered firm using some homemade leverage. However, since all investors realize this possibility, they will all perform the described transactions. The value of the levered firm will decrease due to its inferior cash flows and the value of the levered firm will increase because its cash flows will be desired by all investors. This adjustment process will continue until $V_L = V_U$. This shows that in equilibrium we cannot have $V_L > V_U$ for firms that only differ in their capital structure.

We now show that $V_L < V_U$ is also a disequilibrium situation. We use a procedure similar to the one already discussed. Consider an investor who owns the shares of the unlevered firm. The cash flow to this investor is $CF_U =$ EBIT. To take advantage of the differential in firm values, the investor sells the unlevered firm's shares and receives E_U dollars. With these funds the investor can now buy the shares and the debt of the levered firm, and still have some funds left over to keep in the bank. The excess funds are equal to $[E_U - (D + E_L)]$, or $(V_U - V_L)$. The various uses of the funds give the investor the following cash flow:

$$CF_L = (\text{EBIT} - r_D D) + r_D D + r_D(V_U - V_L)$$

Simplifying gives:

$$CF_L = \text{EBIT} + r_D(V_U - V_L)$$

The difference in cash flows to the investor from holding each of the firms is:

$$CF_L - CF_U = r_D(V_U - V_L) > 0$$

This expression shows that by performing the indicated transactions, the investor's cash flow will be greater with the levered firm than with the unlevered firm. As before, this is not an equilibrium situation, since all investors will try to sell their shares in the unlevered firm and buy the levered firm. Prices must adjust until the values of both firms are equal, or $V_U = V_L$. Thus, in equilibrium we cannot have $V_L < V_U$ for firms that only differ in their capital structure.

CAPITAL STRUCTURE IN THE PRESENCE OF TAXES

We begin our consideration of capital structure in the real world by analyzing the effect of taxes and the tax deductibility of the firm's interest payments. We continue to assume that capital markets are otherwise perfect.

Since firms may deduct all interest payments, it seems that firms should use a great deal of debt. To see why, we must recognize that there are three claimants to the firm's EBIT: stockholders, debtholders, and the government. Since the stockholders and the debtholders are the only investors in the firm, to increase its market value the firm should reduce the government's tax share whenever possible, thus delivering a greater portion of its EBIT to stockholders and debtholders. The firm can do this by choosing different capital structures. In effect, stockholders and debtholders can benefit from the firm's capital structure decisions at the expense of the government.

To illustrate the effect of taxes on the cash flows received by stockholders and debtholders, consider the previous example of a firm with $1,000,000 in assets that is trying to decide whether to use all-equity financing or to use 50 percent debt and 50 percent equity financing. Table 11.4 shows how the choice of capital structure can alter the allocation of funds to the three parties receiving funds from the firm, assuming a corporate tax rate of 30 percent.

If the firm has 0 percent debt, and the realized EBIT is $50,000, it pays $15,000 in taxes and the stockholders receive $35,000. If the firm has an EBIT of $150,000, it pays $45,000 in taxes and the stockholders receive $105,000.

TABLE 11.4
Capital Structure and the Division of a Firm's EBIT*

	Alternative Capital Structures			
	0% Debt		50% Debt	
EBIT	$50,000	$150,000	$50,000	$150,000
Interest expense	0	0	−50,000	−50,000
Earnings before tax	50,000	150,000	0	100,000
Tax (30%)	−15,000	−45,000	0	−30,000
Earnings to stockholders	35,000	105,000	0	70,000
Cash flow to debtholders and stockholders	$35,000	$105,000	$50,000	$120,000

*Assumptions: corporate tax rate = 30%; borrowing rate = 10%; assets = $1,000,000.

If the firm has some leverage in its capital structure, the tax bite becomes smaller for both possible EBIT outcomes. Indeed, with 50 percent of the assets financed by debt, table 11.4 shows that the firm pays no taxes when the EBIT is $50,000 and pays $30,000 in taxes when the EBIT is $150,000. Therefore, the use of leverage reduces the portion of the firm's EBIT lost to taxes. Equivalently, by using leverage, the two groups of investors that determine the firm's value – stockholders and debtholders – receive a larger share of the firm's EBIT. The last row of table 11.4 shows the cash flow available to debtholders and stockholders as a group: for an EBIT of $50,000 they receive $50,000, and for an EBIT of $150,000 they receive $120,000. Notice that for both possible EBIT values, they collectively receive a greater cash flow amount with leverage than without leverage. As we have said, it is at the expense of the government that the other two groups benefit, and this occurs because the government permits interest expenses to be tax-deductible.

The market value of the firm's outstanding securities increases with leverage because the cash available to stockholders and debtholders increases with the amount of leverage the firm uses. In general, the total amount of cash available to these two groups for a given EBIT depends on the amount available to stockholders when the firm uses no debt, CF_u, the corporate tax rate, T, the firm's borrowing rate, r_d, and the amount of debt the firm uses, D. The formula is:

$$\text{Cash to Debtholders and Stockholders} = CF_u + T \times r_D \times D$$

For example, when the firm of table 11.4 uses 50 percent debt (or $500,000) in its capital structure, and the EBIT is $150,000, the cash flow to debtholders and stockholders as a group is:

$$CF = \$105,000 + 0.30 \times 0.10 \times \$500,000 = \$120,000$$

Clearly, this expression for the cash flow to debtholders and stockholders shows that the more debt the firm uses, the greater the cash flow available to that group of investors. This suggests that the value of the firm should also increase in a similar fashion, as was shown by Modigliani and Miller in 1963.[4] Specifically, the value of the levered firm equals the value of the unlevered firm plus a component that increases with the use of debt:

$$V_L = V_U + T \times D \qquad (11.1)$$

Figure 11.1 shows how the value of the firm increases as leverage increases, in accordance with equation 11.1. Notice that this relationship implies that the firm should use virtually 100 percent debt financing. However, we must remember that we reached this conclusion assuming that markets are perfect, except for taxes. In the next section we consider other kinds of imperfections that also affect the capital structure decision. As a consequence, we should not assume that firm value increases in lock-step with leverage in the real world.

---

[4] Modigliani, F. and M. H. Miller, "Corporate Income Taxes and the Cost of Capital: A Correction," *American Economic Review*, 53, June 1963, pp. 433–43. The "correction" in the title refers to the fact that in their original 1958 article MM concluded, mistakenly, that taxes had no effect on firm value. This kind of error, while unfortunate, may occur to the best of researchers – it even happened to Einstein!

FIGURE 11.1

Debt and the Value of the Firm in the Presence of Corporate Taxes

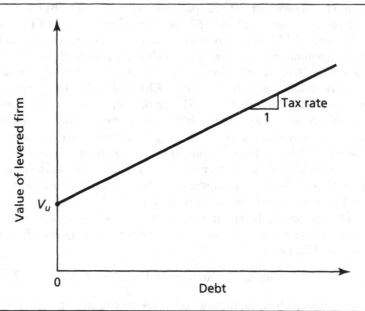

THE EFFECT OF CAPITAL STRUCTURE ON INVESTMENT PROJECTS

When investors are considering a new investment project, they can finance it entirely with equity or with a mixture of debt and equity. In this section we show how the NPV of a project changes when it is financed with debt.

Consider a project requiring an initial investment I and generating annual cash flows that constitute a perpetuity. Let the cash flow before interest and taxes be EBIT, the tax rate be T, and the discount rate for the equity be r_E. Then, if the project is financed solely with equity, its NPV is equal to:

$$NPV_E = -I + \frac{EBIT(1-T)}{r_E} \tag{11.2}$$

Now assume that the project is financed partially with an amount of debt, D, so the investors need only $I-D$ to finance the equity portion of the project. Under this scenario, and using the same cost of equity, r_E, the NPV to equityholders when there is some debt financing is:

$$NPV_D = -(I-D) + \frac{EBIT(1-T) - Dr_D(1-T)}{r_E}$$

$$= -I + \frac{EBIT(1-T)}{r_E} + D - D\frac{r_D(1-T)}{r_E}$$

Simplifying and noting that the first two terms on the right-hand side of this last expression are the NPV of the all-equity scenario in equation 11.2, we have:

$$NPV_D = NPV_E + D\left[1 - \frac{r_D(1 - T)}{r_E}\right] \tag{11.3}$$

Equation 11.3 shows that the NPV of the project using debt financing is greater than its NPV using solely equity, whenever the cost of equity is greater than the after-tax cost of debt. This assumption is normally innocuous, because equity is riskier than debt, so it must command a higher required rate of return.

There are two related corollaries to equation 11.3. First, the NPV profiles of the two scenarios cross at an equity discount rate equal to $r_E = r_D(1 - T)$, since at that discount rate the second term of equation 11.3 is zero, so $NPV_D = NPV_E$. Second, the internal rate of return when the project is financed partially with debt is greater than the all-equity internal rate of return. These results are graphically depicted in figure 11.2, which presents the NPV profiles for this project with and without debt financing.

CAPITAL STRUCTURE, RISK, AND FINANCIAL DISTRESS

In the preceding section we saw that firm value should increase with higher levels of leverage in the presence of taxes. We reached this conclusion by assuming that markets are perfect, except for taxes. In this section, we want to be more realistic and consider other market imperfections. In particular, we consider the risk of **financial distress**,

FIGURE 11.2
NPV Profiles With and Without Debt Financing

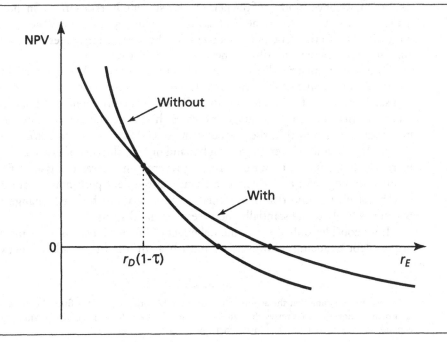

including **bankruptcy**. Financial distress arises when the financial obligations of the firm affect the firm's normal operations. For example, if a firm must sell productive equipment to meet its interest payments, the firm is in financial distress. In this situation, the financial obligations of the firm require the firm to alter its operating policy. There are many degrees of financial distress. The ultimate kind of financial distress is bankruptcy, a condition in which the firm is unable to meet its obligations.

By assuming that markets were perfect (except for taxes) in the previous section, we implicitly assumed that financial distress and bankruptcy were costless. For example, if markets were perfect, bankruptcy would be costless in the sense that, upon declaring bankruptcy, the firm could immediately sell its assets and transfer them to some other productive employment without loss. This would be possible in a perfect market, because there are no transaction costs or delays of any kind, even if bankruptcy were to occur. For example, there would be no lawyer fees! In the real world, however, financial distress can be very costly. The firm cannot sell and redeploy assets without a loss in efficiency. In bankruptcy proceedings, fees paid to accountants and lawyers are large, and the firm cannot employ these resources productively. Because we have assumed perfect markets, we have neglected the cost of financial distress. We must now include it as an important consideration.

In chapter 10 we saw how increasing financial leverage increases the riskiness of the firm's EPS. The higher the amount of leverage and the larger the promised debt payments, the greater the chance that the firm's EBIT will not be sufficient to make the promised payments to debtholders. For the stockholder, high financial leverage increases the chance that the firm will not be able to pay the debtholders. When this occurs, the stockholders receive nothing.

In spite of these dangers, we have seen that using debt reduces the firm's tax burden. As a result, we have another of the perpetual cost-benefit trade-offs in finance. The financial manager must weigh the benefit of saving on taxes by using leverage against the cost of increasing risk to the debt and stock owners. The financial manager must select the correct amount of leverage to maximize the value of the firm.[5]

The cost of financial distress rises as leverage increases. We measure this cost through its effect on the value of the firm. Low levels of leverage have little effect, because the use of a small amount of debt will not normally affect the probability of financial distress very much. As the amount of leverage increases, however, the cost of financial distress also increases. Because of this, the market value of the firm's debt and stock begins to fall.

As the amount of leverage gets higher and higher, the cost of expected financial distress increases dramatically, because increasing leverage increases the risk of financial distress at an increasing rate. For instance, a change in the debt percentage from 0 to 10 percent might not change the risk of financial distress very much, but a change from 70 to 80 percent is likely to substantially increase financial distress.

If we consider only the detrimental effect of financial distress, it seems the firm should use no debt financing. However, we must bear in mind the trade-off between the effect

---

[5] Here we are assuming that the action that maximizes the total value of the firm (the value of stock plus debt) is also the action that maximizes the value of the firm's stock. Remember that maximizing the value of the common stock is the true goal of the financial manager.

of a rising chance of financial distress and the tax savings generated by the use of debt. Figure 11.3 addresses those two offsetting effects explicitly by focusing on the changes in the firm's value as a function of financial leverage. Initially, the total effect of leverage is positive, because the tax savings greatly outweigh the financial distress effects. Eventually, however, the costs of financial distress become more important. At a debt level shown as $D_{optimal}$ in figure 11.3, the negative effect on firm value due to increasing financial distress exactly offsets the tax benefits, and this point represents the optimal capital structure for the firm. Beyond that point, the cost of financial distress is greater than the tax benefit of debt, and the value of the firm decreases.

We can summarize as follows: although capital structure had no effect on the value of the firm in the ideal world of no taxes and perfect markets, when the effect of taxes is considered, we reached the startling conclusion that a firm could always improve its position by using more debt. This happens because the firm reduces the government's tax bite, leaving more money to reward stockholders and debtholders. However, considering only taxes neglects another important kind of market imperfection – financial distress. Increasing leverage increases the risk of financial distress, and this has a negative effect on the value of the firm. The solution to this problem is to find the best trade-off between the benefit of saving taxes and the cost of an increasing risk of financial distress.

In the following section we discuss a model of the use of debt by the banking industry. This is an important example because banks abide by the implication of equation 11.1 – they use as much debt as possible. As discussed in this section, their great use of leverage

FIGURE 11.3

Debt and the Value of the Firm in the Presence
of Corporate Taxes and Financial Distress

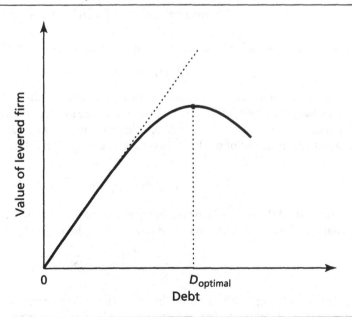

implies that financial distress costs are negligible for most banks, and we will show how banks achieve such a low risk of financial distress.

FINANCIAL DISTRESS, DIVERSIFICATION, AND BANK LEVERAGE

The banking industry is notorious for its heavy reliance on debt to finance its assets. It is normal for banks to have a leverage of over 90 percent. Since debt adds financial risk to any firm, how can banks operate safely with such high levels of debt? Indeed, most manufacturing firms would soon become bankrupt if they used the levels of debt considered normal in the banking industry.

In essence, a bank can operate with so much debt because most of its funds are invested in a well-diversified loan portfolio. Since most of a bank's revenues are in the form of interest from this loan portfolio, the risk of a drastic reduction in revenue is very small. Thus, banks can count on a stable income stream to pay their fixed debt burden.

To formalize this argument we can use the concepts of risk and return, introduced in chapter 8, in the following stylized example. Suppose the only asset of the Markowitz Bank is its loan portfolio, with a total of L dollars. The portfolio is financed with debt in the form of deposits, D, and equity, E, so that $L = D + E$. The portfolio consists of n identical and independent loans, each of which earns an interest rate r_L. Thus, the annual interest income from each paying customer is equal to $(L/n)r_L$. Also, the bank pays an interest rate r_D on its deposits; this is the only expense the bank has. There is a probability p that each of the n loans will be repaid. If a loan is not repaid, all of it, L/n, is lost and it becomes a loan loss expense for the period. Given these assumptions, and after some simplification, the expected revenue from each of the loans is given by the following expression:

$$E(\text{Revenue/Loan}) = \left(\frac{L}{n}\right)[(1 + r_L)p - 1]$$

Since there are n such loans, the total expected revenue for Markowitz Bank is:

$$E(\text{Revenue}) = L[(1 + r_L)p - 1] \tag{11.4}$$

Since the bank takes a risk with each of its loans, at the end of the year it may not actually have the revenues it expects. To measure the loan portfolio's risk, we must calculate its standard deviation, σ_n. To do this, calculate the risk associated with the hypothetical situation of putting all of the bank's assets into a single loan. After some algebra, the result is:

$$\sigma_1 = L(1 + r_L)\sqrt{p(1 - p)} \tag{11.5}$$

Since all of the bank's loans are independent of one another, we can use the techniques of chapter 8 to calculate the standard deviation of the entire loan portfolio, σ_n, as follows:

$$\sigma_n = \frac{\sigma_1}{\sqrt{n}} = \frac{L(1 + r_L)}{\sqrt{n}}\sqrt{p(1 - p)} \tag{11.6}$$

It is interesting to note that the bank's total expected revenue, shown in equation 11.4, is not affected by the number of loans outstanding, n. In contrast, the risk associated with those revenues depends critically on the number of loans. Equation 11.6 shows that the standard deviation of total revenues diminishes quite rapidly as the number of loans increases.

To illustrate these concepts, assume that L = $100 million, r_L = 10 percent, p = 0.99, and n = 1,000. Thus, this bank has 1,000 identical and independent loans of $100,000, each of which has a 1 percent probability of default. The expected total revenue for the bank, using equation 11.4, is equal to:

$$E(\text{Revenue}) = \$100,000,000[1.10 \times 0.99 - 1] = \$8,900,000$$

Thus, the bank expects an average revenue of $8,900 from each loan. This is because 99 percent of the loans are expected to generate $10,000 in interest revenue, and 1 percent of the loans are expected to default. With each default, the bank expenses the entire loan amount of $100,000.

We can now calculate the standard deviation for the bank under the assumption that it has a single loan of $100 million. Using equation 11.5, the standard deviation is over $10 million:

$$\sigma_1 = \$100,000,000 \times 1.1\sqrt{0.99 \times 0.01} = \$10,944,861.81$$

Of course, no banker would even think of putting all of the bank's funds into a single loan because that would be too risky, as the preceding calculation shows. By splitting its loanable funds into many independent loans, the bank can easily reduce the risk associated with its net revenues to a relatively small amount. If instead of having a single jumbo loan, the bank has 1,000 identical and independent loans, then from equation 11.6 the standard deviation of the revenues derived from the portfolio can be reduced to about $346,000:

$$\sigma_n = \frac{\$10,944,861.81}{\sqrt{1,000}} = \$346,106,92$$

These calculations show that Markowitz Bank can expect to have net revenues of $8.9 million next year, with a standard deviation of about $346,000. Thus, it faces relatively little risk. Indeed, assuming that the distribution of total revenues is essentially normal, there are only about 13 chances in 10,000 that revenues will be below the expected value by more than 3 standard deviations. In other words there is a 0.13 percent chance that revenues will not reach $8,900,000 − 3 × $346,106.92 = $7,861,679.24. As long as the bank's interest expenses are lower than $7.86 million, the bank will only have a 0.13 percent chance of losing any money in a given year. If the bank considers this to be the greatest risk it can accept, and if it pays an interest rate of 8 percent to its depositors (also known as the passive rate) the bank can support a level of deposits, D, equal to:

$$D = \frac{\$7,861,679.24}{0.08} = \$98,270,991$$

This calculation shows that Markowitz Bank may have a debt-to-asset ratio of 98.27 percent without taking undue risk.[6] Equivalently, the bank can operate with only 1.73

---

[6] This example suggests why the government feels it must impose minimum capital requirements for banks. Otherwise, some banks would indeed follow to the letter the implications of equation 11.1 and attempt to have 99.999 percent leverage.

percent equity and still face only 13 chances in 10,000 that its capital will be reduced in any given year. This is an extremely high level of comfort for any company, and it explains why banks can survive with such high leverage levels.

Needless to say, the preceding example is highly stylized. For example, we have disregarded the fixed costs that any bank must have. We have also assumed that loans are independent of one another. In reality, loans may be somewhat positively correlated since their repayment may be collectively affected by a recession, and many loans may be made to firms in the same industry. Nevertheless, the main conclusion of the example still holds, namely, that diversification is the tool that allows banks to reduce the risk of financial distress to negligible levels, even for extremely high leverage.

LEVERAGE AND THE FIRM'S COST OF CAPITAL

In the preceding section we discussed how the level of debt affects firm value in the presence of taxes. The firm's financing decision can also affect the required return on both debt and equity. For example, the higher the leverage, the higher the required return on both debt and equity, since both become riskier. As a consequence, the choice of leverage can affect the required return on all the assets of the firm. This overall required return for the assets of a firm is known as the **weighted average cost of capital** (WACC). It considers the after-tax cost of both debt and equity used by the firm and is a weighted average reflecting the proportions of both. Thus, we have:

$$\text{WACC} = \frac{D}{A} r_d (1 - T) + \frac{E}{A} r_e \tag{11.7}$$

where r_e is the market's required rate of return on the firm's shares, r_d is the market's required rate of return on the firm's debt, T is the company's tax rate, E is the market value of the equity in the firm, D is the firm's debt, and $A = D + E$ is the market value of the assets of the firm.

As an example, consider a firm in the 30 percent tax bracket, with a required rate of return on equity of 16 percent, and a required rate on its debt of 12 percent. If the firm's market value is composed of 30 percent debt and 70 percent equity, its WACC is:

$$\text{WACC} = 0.3 \times 12\% \times (1 - 0.3) + 0.7 \times 16\%$$

$$= 13.72\%$$

Derivation of the WACC Formula

To better understand the nature of the weighted average cost of capital concept, and how it can be applied, it is useful to derive equation 11.7 from concepts we have already learned. Suppose we wish to evaluate the NPV of a project that produces perpetual cash flows. The cost of the investment is I, and it will be financed with a combination of equity and debt, with market values of E and D, respectively. The tax rate is T, and the interest rate on debt is r_d. Given this information, there are two ways to find the NPV of the project. First, a straightforward approach is to find the shareholders' cash flow after deducting interest and taxes, and calculate the value of the equity by discounting this cash flow at the cost of equity (r_e). This gives the market value of the equity in the project (E). The NPV of the project is found by adding the value of the equity (E) to the value of the debt (D), and subtracting the cost of the investment (I). Thus, we have:

$$NPV = E + D - I \qquad (11.8)$$

Since the shareholders receive all the proceeds after paying the bondholders and the government, their cash flow is equal to $(\text{EBIT} - r_D D)(1 - T)$.[7] Thus, the market value of equity (E) is equal to:

$$E = \frac{(\text{EBIT} - r_d D)(1 - T)}{r_e} \qquad (11.9)$$

Substituting equation 11.9 into 11.8 we have:

$$NPV = \frac{(\text{EBIT} - r_d D)(1 - T)}{r_e} + D - I \qquad (11.10)$$

An alternative approach for computing the project's NPV is to find the value of the project by disregarding the effect of leverage in the cash flows, but incorporating it in the discount rate. With this technique, we compute the cash flows assuming the project is financed entirely with equity. Since we know that the project does include debt financing, however, we incorporate both the cost of equity and the cost of debt into a single discount rate, which is the WACC. This average rate is used to find the market value of the all-equity cash flows. To find the NPV, we subtract the amount of the investment from the value of the all-equity project.

Since, by design, interest is not considered in the cash flows of this alternative formulation, shareholders receive a cash flow equal to $\text{EBIT}(1 - T)$. Thus, the NPV of this all-equity project is:

$$NPV = \frac{\text{EBIT}(1 - T)}{\text{WACC}} - I \qquad (11.11)$$

Of course, if they are to be equivalent, both methods should yield the same NPV. With this requirement, we can find the expression for the average cost of capital by equating the NPVs in equations 11.10 and 11.11 and solving for the WACC. This yields:

$$\text{WACC} = \frac{r_e \text{EBIT}(1 - T)}{\text{EBIT}(1 - T) - r_d(1 - T) + r_e D} \qquad (11.12)$$

Now note that from equation 11.9 we have:

$$\text{EBIT}(1 - T) = E r_e + D r_d(1 - T) \qquad (11.13)$$

Substituting equation 11.13 into 11.12 and simplifying reduces to equation 11.7, which is the definition given for the WACC:

$$\text{WACC} = \frac{D}{A} r_d(1 - T) + \frac{E}{A} r_e \qquad (11.7)$$

---

[7] We assume that the firm pays out all its earnings as dividends.

The NPV and the WACC: An Example

The derivation given in the previous section shows that there are two equivalent ways of finding the NPV of a project that is financed with a mix of debt and equity. In essence, we may either incorporate the effect of debt in the cash flows, or we may incorporate it in the discount rate. We should be careful, however, not to incorporate debt in both the cash flows and the discount rate, as this would be double counting.

Consider a firm in the 30 percent tax bracket that is analyzing a new project with a cost of $1 million. The firm's required rate of return on equity is 16 percent, and its required rate on debt is 12 percent. The project is expected to generate an annual EBIT of $200,000 in perpetuity and will use debt with a market value of $300,000.

We can find the NPV of this project by computing separately the value of equity and debt. Using equation 11.10 we have:

$$\text{NPV} = \frac{(\$200,000 - 0.12 \times \$300,000)(1 - 0.03)}{0.16} + \$300,000 - \$1,000,000$$

$$= \$717,500 - \$700,000$$

$$= \$17,500$$

Alternatively, we can find the NPV of the project assuming that it is all-equity financed and using the WACC as the discount rate. We must be careful, however, to compute the WACC by using the market value of both equity and debt. We already know that the market value of debt is $300,000. The market value of equity can be found from equation 11.9 and is equal to $717,500. Also, the market value of the project is $717,500 + $300,000 = $1,017,500. Therefore, the WACC is equal to:

$$\text{WACC} = \frac{\$717,500}{\$1,017,500} \times 0.16 + \frac{\$300,000}{\$1,017,500} \times (1 - 0.3) \times 0.12$$

$$= 0.7051597 \times 0.16 + 0.2948403 \times 0.7 \times 0.12$$

$$= 0.1128256 + 0.0247666$$

$$= 0.1375922$$

Knowing that the WACC is equal to 13.75922 percent, we can use equation 11.11 to find the NPV of the project:

$$\text{NPV} = \frac{\$200,000(1 - 0.3)}{0.1375922} - \$1,000,000$$

$$= \$17,499.54$$

This result is the same as before, save for a small rounding error. It is interesting to note that the NPV is very sensitive to the way the WACC is calculated. For example, had we used book values rather than market values, the amount of equity would have been $700,000 and the WACC would have been equal to 13.72 percent, instead of 13.75922 percent. In that case, the project's NPV would have been equal to $20,408.16. Thus, using book values results in an NPV that is 16.62 percent over the correct value of $17,500. This sizable error underscores the importance of using market values when computing the weights for the costs of equity and debt in the WACC.

ALL ABOUT EVA

The **economic value added** (EVA) technique has recently gained popularity for analyzing the true performance of the firm. The EVA is simply the after-tax operating profit minus the total annual cost of capital of the firm. Let the firm's assets consist of investments with market value I that generate an annual operating profit denoted as EBIT. The firm's weighted average cost of capital is WACC, and the corporate tax rate is T. Then, the EVA is given by:

$$EVA = EBIT(1 - T) - WACC \times I \qquad (11.14)$$

To illustrate, consider the profits of Anheuser-Busch.[8] That firm had after-tax operating profits of $1,139 million. It also had a capital structure consisting of 67 percent equity and 33 percent debt, with after-tax costs of 14.3 percent and 5.2 percent, respectively. This results in a WACC of 11.3 percent:

$$WACC = 0.33 \times 5.2\% + 0.67 \times 14.3\% = 11.3\%$$

The assets of Anheuser had a market value of $8 billion, so its cost of capital for that year was $8 billion $\times$ 0.113 = $904 million. Using these data in equation 11.14 yields an EVA of $235 million.

$$EVA = \$1,139 - 0.113 \times \$8,000 = \$235 \text{ million}$$

This figure can be considered as the true profits of the firm after deducting the cost of capital that must be paid to debtholders and stockholders. An obvious implication is that a firm can have positive after-tax profits and yet result in a negative economic value added to the firm.

The EVA technique just described is really nothing new, although it must be said that it has been repackaged ingeniously. We will now show that the EVA is nothing but the old NPV concept in disguise. To see this, divide both sides of equation 11.14 by the firm's WACC, to get:

$$\frac{EVA}{WACC} = \frac{EBIT(1 - T)}{WACC} - I \qquad (11.15)$$

Now note that the right-hand side of equation 11.15 is exactly equal to the firm's NPV, as equation 11.11 shows. Therefore, equation 11.13 becomes, after a simple manipulation:

$$EVA = WACC \times NPV \qquad (11.16)$$

Since the WACC is necessarily positive, equation 11.16 shows that the EVA always has the same sign as the NPV. Equivalently, the EVA is proportional to the firm's NPV, and this explains why firms should strive to have a positive EVA – it simply means that the firm's management is using its projects to generate a positive NPV.

---

[8] The data for this example are taken from "The Real Key to Creating Wealth," *Fortune*, September 20, 1993, p. 27.

CAPITAL STRUCTURE PRACTICES

In real firms, financial managers invariably pay close attention to the capital structure decision. The decision is not merely a choice between issuing bonds or stocks. The firm must decide among a wide variety of different kinds of financing vehicles.

Even assuming that a firm has made a basic decision to use, say, 60 percent equity and 40 percent debt, it still must decide many issues. For example, what should be the maturity of the debt? Should any of it be callable and/or convertible? For the short-term debt, should the firm use bank financing or should it issue short-term notes in the money market? A similar array of questions confronts the financial manager in choosing the equity the firm plans to use. Should the firm issue preferred stock? If so, in what quantity and with what rate of preferred dividends?

While financial managers struggle with these issues, some underlying principles guide their conduct. For example, firms within a given industry have similar capital structures – firms in the electric utility industry use a great deal of debt financing, while firms in the chemical industry tend to use relatively less debt.

Table 11.5 illustrates the tendency for capital structure to vary across industries. By contrast, table 11.6 highlights the tendency of firms within a single industry to have similar capital structures. This table shows the debt-to-asset ratios for some of the nation's major electric utilities. Notice also that most of the firms have a high dividend yield (dividend/ share price). This combination is quite unusual for most industries, but is fairly normal for electric utilities. The steady demand for electrical power means that electric utilities have very regular cash flows. With low risk cash flows, electric utilities can safely use a high level of debt.

SUMMARY

This chapter has developed four main points. First, if there are perfect markets and no taxes, choose any capital structure. This is the world analyzed by Modigliani and Miller

TABLE 11.5
Variation in Capital Structure Across Industries

	Debt/Equity
Store, office, and bar equipment manufacturers	0.42
Wine and liquor distillers	0.38
Bakers	0.61
Clothing retailers	0.35
Restaurants, fast food retailers	1.31
Fuel retailers	0.46
Recreation clubs	0.53
Thread manufacturers	0.41
Drug wholesalers	0.36

TABLE 11.6

Similarities in Capital Structure Within the Electric Utility Industry

	Debt/Assets	Dividend Yield
Consolidated Edison	34.0%	6.8%
Duke Power	43.0	7.6
Delmarva Power	45.0	7.2
General Public Utilities	46.0	0.0
Potomac Electric	47.0	6.9
Carolina Power & Light	48.0	9.0
Long Island Lighting	48.0	0.0
Allegheny Power	49.0	8.6
Pennsylvania Power & Light	50.0	8.9
Boston Edison	51.0	7.5
FPL Group, Inc.	51.0	7.2
Philadelphia Electric	52.0	12.7
Dusquene Light	53.0	12.7
Southern Co.	53.0	9.3
New England Electric	55.0	7.7
Savannah Electric	55.0	7.7
Average across all utilities	48.0	8.0

Source: *Value Screen,* by Value Line Publishing, Inc.

in 1958. In this setting, the investor can alter leverage at no cost, so the choice of leverage by the firm is irrelevant.

Second, if interest expenses are tax deductible, the greater the amount of leverage, the greater the tax savings, other things being equal. Considering only the imperfection of taxes, higher leverage means lower taxes, giving the firm an incentive to use leverage. This scenario was also analyzed by Modigliani and Miller in 1963.

Third, the effect of financial distress reduces the value of leverage to a firm. Using more leverage gives greater tax benefits, but it increases the risk and expected cost of financial distress. The manager must consider the trade-off between them when using more financial leverage. In this case there will usually be an interior optimal amount of leverage for the firm.

Fourth, we discussed the concept of the weighted average cost of capital and several of its important uses. For instance, using this concept we were able to uncover the intimate relationship between the recently popular economic value added concept and the traditional net present value technique.

QUESTIONS

1. What is capital structure?
2. Why do different industries tend to have different capital structures?

3. What is the purpose of examining capital structure assuming that there are no taxes and that financial markets are perfect?
4. What is the importance of the capital structure decision in a world of no taxes and perfect capital markets? Explain.
5. What is homemade leverage?
6. If we add just a little bit of realism and assume that there are corporate taxes but still assume that there are perfect capital markets, what is the importance of the capital structure decision, if any? What kind of capital structure should firms adopt in this case?
7. With corporate taxes and perfect capital markets, does a firm with twice the financial leverage of another have twice the value, assuming they both have the same value when they are unlevered?
8. What is the importance of financial distress and bankruptcy if there are perfect capital markets? Explain.
9. If we acknowledge that there are corporate taxes and that capital markets are not perfect, does the capital structure decision affect firm value? Explain.
10. How does the cost of financial distress affect the value of increasing financial leverage?
11. What is the weighted average cost of capital (WACC)?
12. How can the WACC be used to evaluate projects?
13. Should the weights in the WACC formula use book values or market values?
14. Explain why most banks tend to use a great deal of financial leverage.
15. Explain why most insurance companies tend to use a great deal of financial leverage.
16. What is EVA?
17. How is the EVA technique related to the NPV?

PROBLEMS

Use this information to solve problems 1–10. A firm has a very simple capital structure of $50,000 of long-term debt with an interest rate of 10 percent. In addition, it has 1,000 shares outstanding with a market value per share of $50. This gives a total firm value of $100,000. Assume that capital markets are perfect and that any amount of new debt can be issued at 10 percent. Also assume that there are no corporate taxes and that you have $10,000 to invest.

1. Explain how to transact to create an investment in this firm that is 75 percent debt. Note that the capital structure of the company itself does not change, but you are to use homemade leverage to create your desired leverage.
2. Explain how to transact to create an investment in this firm that is 25 percent debt. Note that the capital structure of the company itself does not change, but you are to transact in a way that allows you to unwind the firm's leverage in order to have an investment that is 25 percent debt.
3. If the firm has EBIT of $20,000, what is the firm's net income, return on assets, and EPS?

4. If the firm has EBIT of $20,000 and you hold an investment in this firm that is 75 percent debt, what is your net income after all interest expense, and what is your return on assets?

5. If the firm has EBIT of $20,000 and you hold an investment in this firm that is 25 percent debt, what is your net income after all interest expense?

6. Assume now that the required rate of return for the firm's equity is 15 percent and that the corporate tax rate is 30 percent. What is the firm's WACC?

7. If the firm changed its capital structure to be 75 percent debt, what would its WACC be?

8. If the firm changed its capital structure to be 25 percent debt, what would its WACC be?

9. Based on problems 6–8, what appears to be the optimal capital structure for the firm in this case? (Remember that we are continuing to assume that financial distress is costless due to the existence of perfect capital markets.)

10. If we acknowledge that capital markets are not perfect and that financial distress is not costless, how does the conclusion of problem 9 change?

11. The firm is considering a new investment project costing $1,000,000 that is expected to generate an annual EBIT of $250,000 in perpetuity. The proportion of debt financing will be 50 percent. If the cost of equity is 15 percent, the cost of debt is 10 percent, and the tax rate is 30 percent, find the value of the equity of this project.

12. Find the NPV for the project of problem 11.

13. For the project of problem 11, find its NPV using the WACC.

14. For the project of problem 11, find its EVA.

Chapter 12

Dividend Policy

OVERVIEW

Our study of finance thus far has emphasized that the financial manager's primary goal is the maximization of shareholder wealth. We have also seen that the value of a share of stock equals the present value of the future cash dividends that flow from that share. The stock pricing relationships developed in chapter 5 emphasized the crucial role of dividends in share valuation. This chapter examines the role that dividend policy plays in maximizing the value of the firm's shares.

As in the preceding chapter, we begin by considering a world of zero taxes and perfect markets. In such an environment, neither capital structure nor dividend policy affects the value of the firm. After seeing why that is the case for dividends, we enrich our discussion to include both taxes and market imperfections.

DIVIDENDS IN A WORLD OF ZERO TAXES AND PERFECT MARKETS

Miller and Modigliani extended their capital structure arguments to dividends, maintaining that dividend policy is irrelevant to the value of the firm in a world with perfect markets and no taxes. Just as investors can create leverage, they can also create homemade dividends.

To concoct the recipe for homemade dividends, consider an all-equity firm with $1 million in assets that is considering paying a cash dividend. Assume also that the firm has 10,000 shares outstanding and that a particular shareholder holds 1,000 of them (10 percent). Throughout this chapter, we assume that book and market values are identical. The firm is considering two alternative dividend policies:

1. Pay $100,000 as a cash dividend, leaving the firm with assets of $900,000. After the dividend, each share will be worth $90.
2. Pay no dividend, keeping all $1,000,000 in assets. In this case, each of the 10,000 shares outstanding will be worth $100.

No matter which policy the firm follows, assume it earns a 10 percent return on its assets during the next year of operations, as figure 12.1 summarizes. If the firm pays $100,000 in dividends, the firm will be smaller as a result of the dividend decision, holding only $900,000 in assets. After the dividend, the stockholders will have $100,000 in cash. If the firm chooses not to pay a dividend, it will have $1,000,000 in assets.

We next consider the position of the firm under the two alternative scenarios after one year of operations, during which the firm earned 10 percent on its assets. After one

FIGURE 12.1
The Firm's Dividend Decision and Its Effects

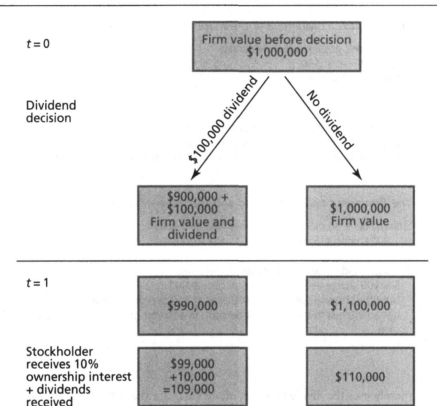

year, the firm will have a total value of $990,000 ($900,000 × 1.10) if it paid a dividend at time $t = 0$. If it paid no dividend it will have a total value of $1,100,000. The bottom panel of figure 12.1 shows both positions.

The stockholder with a 10 percent original interest will have stock worth $99,000 if the firm paid the dividend, plus the $10,000 in dividends received, for a total wealth of $109,000. We assume for convenience that the dividends were not invested. If the firm paid no dividends, the 10 percent ownership interest will be worth $110,000.

To show that the firm's dividend decision does not affect shareholder wealth, we need to see how the shareholder can undo the dividend policy of the firm by transacting in the marketplace. More exactly, if the firm chooses to pay a dividend, we show how the stockholder can achieve the same position as if the firm had not paid a dividend. Likewise, if the firm chooses not to pay a dividend, we show how the stockholder can achieve the same position as if the firm paid a dividend.

Table 12.1 shows the steps necessary for the stockholder to undo the firm's dividend decision. If the firm pays a dividend, as shown in the top panel of the table, the shareholder

TABLE 12.1

How to Undo the Firm's Dividend Policy

The firm pays a dividend and the shareholder doesn't want one.

Shareholder's position after dividend:

1,000 shares at $90.	$90,000
Cash dividend just received.	10,000
	$100,000

The shareholder transacts to offset the dividend:
   Buy 111.11 shares at $90 per share for $10,000.
   Now the shareholder owns 1,111.11 of 10,000 shares, or a 11.11 percent interest in the firm.

The firm doesn't pay a dividend and the shareholder wants one.

Shareholder's position after the no-dividend decision:

1,000 shares at $100.	$100,000

The shareholder transacts to create a dividend:
   Sell 100 shares at $100 for a total of $10,000.
   Now the shareholder holds 900 shares at $10 per share for a total value of $90,000 and has an interest in the firm of 9 percent. In addition, the shareholder has $10,000 in cash.

---

merely uses the dividend to buy more shares in the firm. With 10,000 shares outstanding and $900,000 in assets, each share sells for $90, so the shareholder can buy 111.11 shares with the $10,000 in dividends. This increases the shareholder's interest in the firm from 10 to 11.11 percent.

On the other hand, the firm may not pay a dividend, but the shareholder still desires a dividend. The bottom of table 12.1 shows the transactions to create a homemade dividend. In this case, the assets of the firm will be $1 million. With 10,000 shares outstanding, each share will be worth $100. To pay a $10,000 homemade dividend, the shareholder merely sells 100 shares. This leaves the shareholder with 900 shares at $100 per share, for an investment in the firm of $90,000.

Figure 12.2 summarizes the position of the shareholder who offset the firm's dividend policy. We assume the firm earns a 10 percent return on its assets, no matter what its dividend policy. If the firm paid a dividend, it has $900,000 in assets at the beginning of the year. These assets increase by 10 percent over the year to give a value of $990,000 at year end. With 10,000 outstanding shares, each share will be worth $99. Likewise, if the firm paid no dividend, its assets would be worth $1 million at the beginning of the year. After earning 10 percent, the firm will be worth a total of $1.1 million and each share will sell for $110.

Figure 12.2 also summarizes the position of the shareholder who did nothing to offset the firm's dividend policy. After the firm operates for a year, the shareholder's wealth will

FIGURE 12.2
Shareholder's Position Under Alternative Plans

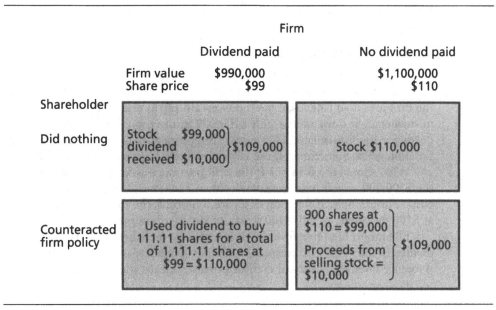

be either $109,000 or $110,000, depending on the firm's policy. If the firm paid a dividend and the shareholder counteracted the policy, the shareholder's position should be the same as if the firm had paid no dividend. This is exactly the case, as the figure confirms. The investor's wealth is identical in the southwest and northeast quadrants of figure 12.2. Similarly, if the firm paid no dividend and the shareholder created homemade dividends, the position should be the same as if the firm paid the dividend. The figure reflects these identical outcomes because the stockholder's position in the northwest and southeast quadrants is identical.

In this world of perfect markets and no taxes, the shareholder can transact to create any desired dividend policy. If the firm pays a dividend, the shareholder can transact to produce the same results as if no dividends are paid. Similarly, the shareholder can transact to create a dividend if the firm fails to provide one. This means that the firm's dividend policy can neither create nor destroy value. No matter what the firm does, it does not affect the options of the shareholder. The result of dividend irrelevance in these conditions is important, because it shows that the relevance of dividends in the real world depends on either taxes or imperfect markets.

DIVIDENDS IN A WORLD OF TAXES AND TRANSACTION COSTS

To consider dividends in a more realistic setting, we now discuss dividend policy in a world of income tax and transaction costs. For the moment, however, we continue to assume that everyone in the economy has the same information. The influences of taxes and transaction costs may mean that dividend policy can affect the value of the firm and the wealth of shareholders. We consider the problem from the point of view of both the firm and its shareholders.

The Firm's Transaction Costs

Consider again our firm with $1 million in assets that contemplates a $100,000 cash dividend. Now we assume that the firm's investment plan requires $1 million in assets. If the firm pays no dividends, it has the assets already in place. By contrast, if it pays $100,000 in dividends, it must raise a new $100,000 in the capital market to give it the capital it needs for its investments. However, raising capital is costly, because the firm must pay flotation costs. Sometimes, these costs may be as large as 8 percent of the capital raised.

What should the firm do? If the firm pays the dividend and sells new stock to replace the $100,000, it will have to sell more than 1,000 new shares to compensate for flotation costs. For example, if flotation costs are 6 percent, the firm will have to sell 1,064 shares at $100 per share, or $106,400 worth of stock, to raise the $100,000.

Flotation costs give firms an incentive to avoid dividends. In addition, by avoiding dividends the firm can escape the clerical expenses associated with paying dividends. Avoiding flotation costs and clerical expenses means the firm can preserve more wealth for its shareholders.

The Shareholder's Income Tax

Dividend payments to individuals are subject to personal income taxation in the year received. By contrast, capital gains on shares do not face taxation until the owner sells the shares. By paying dividends, a corporation forces its shareholders to pay taxes earlier. By not paying dividends and by allowing profits to accumulate in the value of the shares, the firm helps shareholders to postpone paying taxes. In many cases, shareholders can defer taxes for many years if the firm does not pay dividends.

The Shareholder's Transaction Costs

When a stockholder needs cash from a stock portfolio, there are two ways to receive it. First, the investor may receive dividends. Second, the investor may sell part of the portfolio shares for cash. We noted the tax consequences of receiving dividends. However, there are also disadvantages to selling part of the portfolio.

On selling stock an investor incurs transaction costs, which may be about 1 to 2 percent of the share's value. These transaction costs also diminish shareholder wealth. The firm may be able to provide investors with dividend income at a lower transaction cost than the investors can provide income for themselves. If the shares have increased in value, the investor must also pay a capital gains tax.

Dividend Clienteles

We have seen that the shareholders have some reasons to avoid dividends and some reasons to seek them. An investor mainly concerned about taxes on dividends will prefer firms that pay little or no dividends. By contrast, an investor concerned about obtaining a steady stream of income may well prefer firms with a generous dividend policy. This suggests that firms with different dividend policies will appeal to different investors. Each group of investors constitutes a different dividend clientele – a group of investors favoring a particular kind of dividend policy.

The Residual Theory of Dividends

As we have just seen, conflicting pressures on the dividend policy of the firm stem from taxation and transaction costs. The residual theory of dividends attempts to summarize the net impact of these conflicting influences. According to the residual theory, the firm should follow its investment policy of accepting all positive NPV projects, and paying out dividends if, and only if, funds are still available. In this way, the firm treats dividends as a residual – the amount remaining after the investment policy is satisfied. If the firm treats dividends strictly as a residual, the dividend can vary dramatically from period to period. The dividend will simply depend upon the investment plan and operating results of the firm.

When we couple the existence of dividend clienteles with the residual theory, firms may be wise to operate under a slightly modified residual theory. If firms attract investors falling into a particular dividend clientele, perhaps the firm should maintain a fairly stable dividend policy. For example, a firm that attracts investors seeking high dividends will keep those investors interested only if it consistently pays a fairly high level of dividends. If a firm lets its dividends oscillate radically, both investors that seek dividends and those that wish to avoid dividends may refrain from investing in the firm.

Dividend Management with Costly Information

Under the assumption of perfect markets and no taxes we found that dividends were irrelevant to shareholder wealth. Relaxing these strict assumptions, and considering the effect of taxes and transaction costs on the dividend decision, we found that firms were probably wise to manage their dividends to attract and keep a given dividend clientele. We reached this conclusion, however, under the assumption that all parties in the market have the same information about the firm. Here, we consider a more realistic situation that recognizes the superior information of some parties.

Thus far, we assumed that every investor has the same information about the firm. This is the same as saying that information is costless. In the real world, however, not everyone has the same information, and gathering it is expensive. This may give the dividend decision another dimension of importance that we have not yet considered.

When two parties possess information about the same subject and that information has different value, they have **asymmetric information**. Managers typically know much more about the firm than the typical investor. For instance, management may know today's sales figures, but the typical investor does not.

Let us assume that management has very favorable information about the firm, but this information is not available to investors. If management conveys this information to the marketplace accurately, it will increase the stock price. However, investors also know that managers may be tempted to signal falsely in their desire to maximize the price of the stock. In other words, why should the market believe any good news coming from a person with an incentive to deceive? This presents a problem, because the manager must find a way to make the market accept the truthful good news. This is a **signaling problem** – transmitting information so it is believed by those receiving it.

Within this asymmetric information context, dividends may have a special relevance because of their ability to act as a signal to the market. According to the **dividend signaling hypothesis**, dividend changes provide an effective way for management to convey believable information to the market about the firm's expected future cash flows. In essence, by raising the dividend, the management allows that to speak about the future cash flows of the firm. Thus, the dividend decision is an important managerial tool. By conveying the favorable information to the market in a believable way, the dividend decision may affect the value of the firm. Notice that simply announcing an increase in earnings is not as believable as an increase in dividends. This is because dividends are hard cash, whereas earnings are an accounting measure that depends on the accounting rules used to derive it.

OTHER CONSTRAINTS ON DIVIDEND POLICY

In addition to the considerations discussed earlier, other factors influence the dividend policy of the firm: cash flow, legal, and contractual constraints.

Cash Flow Constraints

Firms pay dividends in cash. Firms without available cash cannot pay dividends, no matter what their earnings. This emphasizes again the superiority of cash flow over earnings in most financial contexts. Even if firms do not have cash on hand, they may borrow funds to pay dividends. However, this requires incurring the costs of borrowing and, therefore, may be unwise.

Legal Constraints

Laws govern permissible dividend practices and may constrain the firm's dividend policy. To see why such laws exist, consider the firm Wealth Transfer, Unlimited, operating under the slogan "We move your wealth." Without any legal prohibitions, Wealth Transfer might be true to its slogan as follows. Suppose Wealth Transfer sells 10,000 shares for $10 each, for a total of $100,000 in common stock. In addition, the firm issues $900,000 in bonds. After these transactions start the firm, the balance sheet would appear as shown in the top panel of table 12.2.

Assume now that Wealth Transfer pays a dividend of $100 per share, leaving the firm with no cash. Each shareholder who paid $10 per share immediately gets $100 in dividends, leaving the firm an empty shell, as the bottom panel of table 12.2 shows. The firm has no assets and an equity of –$900,000. Because of the shareholder's limited liability, the bondholders cannot collect the missing $900,000. Now you can see how appropriately the firm is named, as it has transferred a considerable amount of wealth from the bondholders

TABLE 12.2
Balance Sheet of Wealth Transfer

When the firm is founded:

Assets		Liabilities	
Cash	$1,000,000	Debt	$900,000
		Equity	100,000
Total	$1,000,000	Total	$1,000,000

After paying a large dividend:

Assets		Liabilities	
Cash	$0	Debt	$900,000
		Equity	−900,000
Total	$0	Total	$0

to the stockholders. To the chagrin of the bondholders, the firm is suddenly out of business, and they are out of luck and money.

To protect bondholders against such sleazy maneuvers, laws regulate dividend payments, in essence prohibiting the **impairment of capital**. Capital is impaired when the firm strips itself of assets through a dividend payment. This is exactly what Wealth Transfer did. Usually, these laws prohibit dividends in excess of the retained earnings shown on the firm's balance sheet, the goal being to protect the bondholders from games such as this.

Contractual Constraints

Bondholders know fully well the bag of tricks that management might use to transfer their wealth to shareholders. To avoid this, **bond indentures** often restrict the kinds of dividends that firms can pay. The bond indenture is the contract between the firm and the bondholders that defines the firm's conduct with respect to bonds that it issues. It might typically restrict dividends to a certain percentage of earnings. In some cases, the bond indenture prohibits dividends altogether until the firm repays its debt. Another kind of constraint in the bond indenture might prohibit dividend payments unless the firm's current ratio (current assets / current liabilities) indicates a sufficiently large liquidity. All of these restrictions help ensure that the firm will have enough funds to meet its obligations to bondholders.

TYPES OF DIVIDEND POLICIES

Faced with the constraints on dividends and the reasons for managing dividends we have discussed, firms' dividend behavior generally falls into four kinds of policies: constant payout, regular dividend, multiple increases, and extras.

Constant Payout

In our discussion of stock price valuation models, we considered the possibility that some firms would pay dividends equaling a constant percentage of their earnings. For example, a firm with a 40 percent payout policy and earnings of $2 per share would pay a dividend of $0.80 per share. In fact, few firms follow such a policy because they generally have volatile earnings due to changes in the economy and their own special circumstances. When a firm follows a constant payout policy, the volatility in the dividends will match the volatility in earnings.

With different dividend clienteles, a constant payout policy is likely to be a disaster for most firms. Such a policy would result in wildly fluctuating dividends, which would scare away all investors seeking a particular level of dividends. Income seekers could not plan on a steady income from such a firm. Similarly, investors interested primarily in capital gains would never know when they might receive a large dividend and the large tax liability that goes with it. Consequently, very few firms follow such a policy.

Regular Dividend

The most popular policy is one that pays a regular steady dividend. For example, we can expect a firm that announces a dividend of $1.60 to maintain that dividend level for a fair amount of time. Further, if the firm establishes the dividend at $1.60, it is generally a signal to investors that the firm believes the dividend is sustainable. As a consequence, firms are generally careful to set the dividend at a sustainable level and to raise it only when the firm can sustain the higher level.

Figure 12.3 illustrates this policy. At the beginning of the period shown, the firm has a dividend of $1.60 per share. This amount is well below the maximum dividend that the firm believes it can sustain, giving the firm a cushion for error, in case its estimates were too optimistic. As shown, the firm prospers so its maximum sustainable dividend level increases; however, it does not raise the dividend immediately. When it does so eventually, it maintains a comfortable cushion between the actual dividend and its estimate of the maximum sustainable dividend.

Under this kind of regular policy, the firm tries to make sure that the dividend acts like a ratchet. It may go up, but the firm makes every effort to ensure it does not go down. Naturally, this kind of policy requires the conservatism shown in figure 12.3.

On occasion, a firm will err and must cut dividends. Although the firm may begin with a dividend well below its estimated maximum sustainable level, earnings may drop unexpectedly below the dividend level. Even so, the firm does not immediately cut its dividend because the desire to avoid a dividend cut is strong. However, the firm cannot pay a dividend greater than its earnings for very long, or it will exhaust its cash resources. Eventually the firm realizes that it cannot maintain its current dividend. Faced with this unhappy realization, the firm eventually cuts its dividend.

Firms abhor cutting dividends because of the extremely unfavorable news it conveys to the market. The most common cut, therefore, is total elimination of dividends when the point of reckoning is reached.

FIGURE 12.3
A Typical Regular Dividend Policy

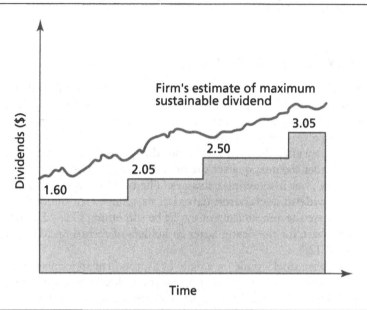

Multiple Increases

Some firms follow a policy of very frequent and very small dividend increases to give the illusion of movement and growth. The obvious hope behind such a policy is that the market rewards consistent dividend increases. At the very least, such a policy attracts some attention.

Instead of waiting for a considerable time as the firm in figure 12.3 did, the firm may announce frequent, but small, dividend increases. Some firms announce a dividend increase just about every year. As these examples show, firms can manage the same dividend potential in two quite different ways. Which tactic is better, or whether it makes any difference at all, is uncertain.

Extras

Some firms follow a policy of paying extra dividends. These firms consciously divide their announced dividends into two portions – a regular dividend and an extra dividend. The **regular dividend** continues at the announced level, and the **extra dividend** is made as circumstances permit. For example, a firm might have a regular dividend of $2 per year and may announce an extra dividend of $0.30 this year. In the next year, the stockholder can expect at least a $2 dividend and perhaps an extra one as well. However, the firm has not committed itself to an extra dividend and if it does pay one, it has already made clear that the amount may vary.

This policy allows the management of the firm to communicate with its shareholders very carefully. Also, the existence of such policies shows how seriously management takes the communication with shareholders through dividend announcements.

DIVIDEND PAYMENT PROCEDURES

Most firms pay dividends quarterly, no matter which policy they follow. There are some exceptions to this rule, however. Wrigley, Inc., the chewing gum company, has been in the habit of paying a monthly dividend, but this is very unusual. This section describes the normal payment system.

Shortly after the firm determines the quarter's earnings, the firm's board of directors meets to set the next quarter's dividend. In most cases, the new dividend will be the same as the old, but it sometimes changes. The time that the firm announces the new dividend is the **dividend declaration date**. Let us assume that the declaration date is February 3. In this case the announcement might be something like: "The firm will pay a dividend of $1 per share for the next quarter to holders of record on March 15, with a payment date of April 12."

Because stocks trade on a daily basis, the firm announces that the owner of the share, as shown on the books of the firm on the **holder-of-record date**, March 15, will receive the dividend. This still leaves a problem, because we cannot know how fast the transactions in the stock will reach the firm's books. For example, if you buy the share on March 12, will you be the holder of record on March 15 and get the dividend?

To resolve such nuisances, there is an ex-dividend date four business days before the holder-of-record date. The **ex-dividend date** is the date on which the stock begins trading without the right to receive the coming dividend. In our example, with a holder-of-record date of March 15, the ex-dividend date would be March 11.[1] If you bought the stock on the ex-dividend date or later, you will not get the dividend. It is customary to say that you bought the stock ex-dividend to avoid any ambiguity about who the dividend recipient is.

The final date in the process is the **payment date**, the date the firm actually mails the dividend checks. In our example, the payment date is April 12. Figure 12.4 shows the entire process for our example.

DIVIDEND SUBSTITUTES

So far we have focused on cash dividends. We conclude this chapter by considering stock repurchases.

Stock Repurchases

In a stock repurchase, a firm buys some of its own outstanding shares for cash. It can make a tender offer or it can buy shares on the open market. In a **tender offer**, the firm announces

---

[1] This is true only if the holder-of-record date is a Friday.

FIGURE 12.4
Dividend Payment Process

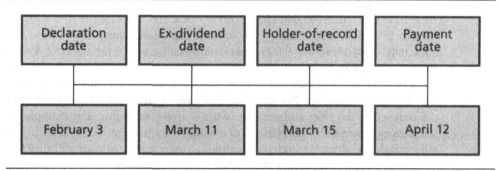

its intention to buy a certain number of shares at a stated price and allows shareholders to tender their shares at that price. In an **open market purchase**, the firm merely buys shares on the open market as any investor would.

Whichever method of repurchase is used, the result is essentially the same from the firm's point of view. Consider an all-equity firm with a market value of its stock of $1 million, and assume that there are 10,000 shares outstanding, each of which trades for $100. Assume also that the firm is considering a cash dividend of $10 per share. Alternatively, the firm might buy 1,000 shares.

The top section of table 12.3 shows the position of the firm before any dividend or share repurchase. The middle of table 12.3 shows the firm's position if it pays a dividend. If the firm pays a $10 per share dividend, it will distribute $100,000 in cash, so its assets will fall in value to $900,000. Correspondingly, each share must fall in value to $90. After

TABLE 12.3
Position of the Firm with Dividends or Stock Repurchase

Before the dividend or repurchase:

Assets	Liabilities
$1,000,000	10,000 shares at $100: $1,000,000

After a $10 per share dividend:

Assets	Liabilities
$900,000	10,000 shares at $90: $900,000

After the repurchase of 1,000 shares:

Assets	Liabilities
$900,000	9,000 shares at $100: $900,000

all, the share was worth $100 before the dividend, and then it paid $10, so the dividend merely changes the form in which the wealth is held.

The bottom section of table 12.3 shows the position of the same firm if it repurchases shares. Again, with $100,000 spent to buy stock, the value of the firm's productive assets falls to $900,000. Accordingly, the outstanding shares must now have a total value of $900,000. Now there are 9,000 shares outstanding and total assets of $900,000, so the shares continue to be worth $100 each.

From the point of view of the firm, these two alternatives are quite similar. Both leave the firm 10 percent smaller than before, with total assets of $900,000. The only real difference is in the price and number of the shares outstanding. For example, if you owned 500 shares before the repurchase, you would own 5 percent of the firm. If you kept them all through the share repurchase operation, you would now own 500 of 9,000 shares, or 5.56 percent of the firm. This shows that the main differences between cash dividends and share repurchases fall on the shareholders.

Advantages and Disadvantages of Stock Repurchases

A stock repurchase has certain advantages over a cash dividend, the most important being the tax effect for the shareholders. The stock repurchase strategy allows shareholders the option to take income now. If they want income now, they sell some fraction of their shares. If not, they merely hold their shares, receive no income, and incur no tax burden. Based on these considerations, firms should prefer stock repurchases to cash dividends. At the very least, share repurchases conserve taxes.

However, the Internal Revenue Service (IRS) knows about stock repurchases. Under the old tax law, with different rates for dividends and capital gains on stock sales, the IRS frowned on attempts by firms to help shareholders avoid taxes on dividends. As a consequence, firms could not follow the stock repurchase strategy on a consistent basis. Nevertheless, the IRS permitted occasional share repurchases without adverse tax effects.

DIVIDEND YIELDS ACROSS COUNTRIES

The importance of dividends in long-term investment performance is substantial. Over 40 percent of the average annual total return provided by U.S. equities over the last six decades was collected in the form of dividends.

Over the 20 years ending in December 1989, the contribution of dividends to the total return of U.S. equities was 35.6 percent. In contrast, global equity investors registered a lower dividend contribution over the same 20-year period, with dividend yields averaging 27.2 percent of the total return. The total return, capital gains yield, and dividend yield measures for selected countries over this 20-year period are shown in table 12.4.

SUMMARY

Most of the discussion in this chapter has focused on the concepts behind the dividend decision. First, we traced the dividend arguments of Miller and Modigliani in a world of

TABLE 12.4
Total Return, Capital Gains Yield, and Dividend Yield for Selected Countries
(December 31, 1969–December 31, 1989)

	Average Quarterly Return (%)	Average Quarterly Capital Gain (%)	Average Quarterly Dividend Yield (%)	Capital Gain in % of Total Return	Dividend Yield in % of Total Return
World index	3.97	2.89	1.08	72.8	27.2
Australia	3.42	2.34	1.08	68.4	31.6
Austria	3.12	2.35	0.77	75.3	24.7
Belgium	4.07	1.75	2.32	43.1	56.9
Canada	3.23	2.28	0.94	70.8	29.2
Denmark	4.19	3.12	1.07	74.4	25.6
France	4.05	2.78	1.26	68.8	31.2
Germany	2.61	1.55	1.06	59.5	40.5
Hong Kong	7.31	6.26	1.05	85.7	14.3
Italy	3.81	3.11	0.69	81.8	18.2
Japan	4.53	4.03	0.50	89.0	11.0
Netherlands	3.43	1.97	1.47	57.3	42.7
Norway	4.79	3.91	0.88	81.6	18.4
Singapore/Malaysia	4.90	4.27	0.63	87.2	12.8
Spain	3.55	1.83	1.73	51.4	48.6
Sweden	4.97	3.99	0.98	80.3	19.7
Switzerland	2.10	1.43	0.67	68.1	31.9
United Kingdom	4.50	3.22	1.28	71.5	28.5
United States	2.97	1.90	1.07	64.0	36.0

Source: A. Michael Keppler, "The Importance of Dividend Yields in Country Selection," *The Journal of Portfolio Management,* Winter 1991, pp. 24–25.

no taxes and no transaction costs. We found that the value of the firm was independent of the dividend level paid. Any impact of dividends on firm value depended on either market imperfections or taxes.

The existence of taxes creates an incentive for firms to avoid paying dividends. However, neither effect is absolute because of market imperfections in the form of transaction costs. For dividends, shareholders' transaction costs may provide a reason for the firm to pay dividends. In addition, we considered some of the practical procedures that managers actually follow in setting dividend policy.

QUESTIONS

1. What are the two outlets available for after-tax earnings?
2. What is the importance of the dividend decision in a world of perfect capital markets and no taxes?

3. If a firm pays too little in dividends for you, how could you remedy this problem? Assume no taxes and perfect capital markets.
4. If a firm pays dividends that are too large for you, how could you remedy this problem? Assume no taxes and perfect capital markets.
5. How do your answers to questions 3 and 4 change if there are taxes and imperfect capital markets?
6. Explain the reasoning that makes the residual theory of dividends attractive.
7. What is a dividend clientele? What kinds of clienteles would be attracted to utility stocks that normally pay very high dividends?
8. What kinds of dividend policies would you expect to be attractive to a Yuppie with a very high income?
9. How do dividends perform as a signal? Why doesn't management just announce the information it is trying to convey?
10. Explain the relationship between stock repurchases and the problem of asymmetric information.
11. What costs does a firm incur when it borrows to pay a dividend?
12. Why do bondholders place constraints on firms' dividend policies?

PROBLEMS

Use the following information to solve all of the following problems. A firm has earnings before tax of $100,000 and 10,000 shares of stock outstanding, with each share worth $100. Assume that you own 1,000 shares, that there are no taxes, and that capital markets are perfect.

1. What percentage of the firm do you own?
2. Assume that the firm pays no dividends. How could you transact on your own initiative to pay yourself a dividend of $5 per share?
3. After the transactions of problem 2 are completed, how many shares do you own, and what percentage of the firm do you now own?
4. Assume that the firm pays a dividend of $10 per share. How could you transact to avoid the dividend altogether?
5. After the transactions of problem 4, how many shares do you own and what percentage of the firm do you now own?

Forget all about the cash dividends from this firm now and assume that the firm will repurchase 10 percent of its shares.

6. After the repurchase, how many shares will be outstanding?
7. After the repurchase, what should be the value of each share?
8. If you do not sell any of your shares in the repurchase, what percentage of the firm do you now own?
9. If you do not participate in the share repurchase, how has your wealth been affected?

10. If you sell 50 percent of your shares in the share repurchase, what percentage of the firm do you now own?
11. If you sold 50 percent of your shares in the stock repurchase, how has the percentage of the firm that you own changed?
12. If you sold 50 percent of your shares in the stock repurchase, how has your wealth been affected?

Chapter 13

Sources of Long-Term Financing

OVERVIEW

This chapter examines the rights and obligations of common stock ownership and explores the organization of the stock and bond markets in the United States. Together the stock market and the bond market constitute the capital market – the market for long-term commitments of investable funds.

For most people, the stock market represents the focus of the securities markets. The nightly news frequently reports the day's developments in the stock market, but not other security markets on a regular basis. In particular, the bond market receives relatively little attention. This focus on the stock market arises because stocks trade much more actively than bonds. However, because the bond market is also a source of capital, the financial manager needs to understand both bond and stock market operations.

It is traditional to divide the debt market into two segments – the money market and the bond market. The money market includes those debt instruments that have a maturity of one year or less when issued. The maturity of a bond issue is the time until the bond makes its last payment. All debt instruments originally issued with maturities greater than one year are bonds. While this distinction is somewhat arbitrary, it is quite useful because money market instruments exhibit important family resemblances. This chapter discusses the stock market and the bond market – the market for debt obligations with original maturities of more than one year.

GENERAL ORGANIZATION OF THE STOCK MARKET

The stock market has developed several important new dimensions in the last 15 years. We can divide it into the **secondary market** for existing securities, and the **primary market** for new securities. Organized stock exchanges, such as the New York Stock Exchange (NYSE), the American Stock Exchange (AMEX), and a dealer market, called the over-the-counter market (OTC), make up the secondary market. In addition, third and fourth markets are informal trading arrangements used mainly by the largest traders. We discuss each division in turn.

THE SECONDARY MARKET

For many people, the stock market simply is the New York Stock Exchange. This largest of all of the world's organized exchanges dominates the market in certain respects. In addition, there are several organized stock exchanges in the United States and many foreign stock exchanges as well. A **stock exchange** is an exchange with a trading floor where stocks trade under rules created by the exchange. In the United States, the organized exchanges share many organizational features, largely because the smaller exchanges have patterned themselves after the NYSE. Figure 13.1 lists the world's largest stock exchanges, ranked by dollar volume of trading.

General Organizational Features

A stock exchange is a voluntary organization formed by a group of individuals to provide an institutional setting for trading securities. Usually, the stock exchange is a non-profit corporation that exists to further the financial interests of its members. Members of stock exchanges participate through the ownership of memberships, or seats, on the exchange. Certain rules govern trading on the exchange, and these rules are binding on the members. Only members of the exchange, or their representatives, can trade on the exchange. In

FIGURE 13.1

The World's Largest Stock Markets Ranked by Dollar Volume of Trading (1994)

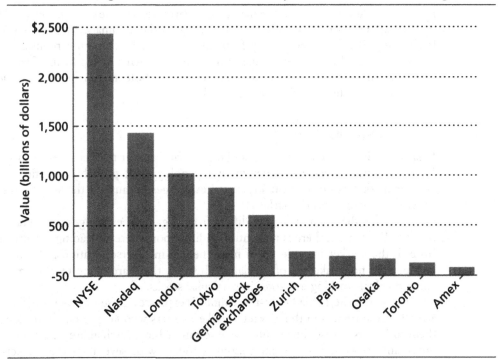

Source: NASDAQ Fact Book/Company Directory, 1995.

that sense, the members have a monopoly position, because all orders to buy or sell securities on a given exchange must flow through an exchange member. One of the key sets of regulations imposed by the exchange concerns restrictions on the place and time at which trading may occur. Each stock exchange allows trading only on the floor of the exchange and only during approved trading hours.

The floor of an exchange is an actual physical location – a trading floor – into which customers transmit orders for execution. The floor of the exchange has a vast array of electronic communications equipment to receive and transmit information concerning orders. In addition, participants on the floor of the exchange require a regular flow of information from the outside world. Since new information might affect share prices, the people on the floor need access to timely news about world and national events. They also need special information about business developments. The regular wire services, such as the Associated Press (AP), and special business news wire services, such as Reuters and Dow Jones, serve those needs. Some of the people working on the floor are exchange employees, while others trade stocks for themselves hoping to make a profit. In addition, there are brokers on the floor. A **broker** is an individual who receives orders from the public outside the exchange and executes the order. The order may be to buy or sell a given quantity of a specified security. The broker charges a commission for this service. Memberships on these exchanges are traded like other assets. Membership prices fluctuate through time and depend mainly on the volume of trading and the price level of stocks.

Organized Stock Exchanges

By far, the New York Stock Exchange dominates the stock exchanges in the U.S. and is the largest in the world. Within the United States, the dominance of the New York Stock Exchange is truly dramatic. Only firms meeting certain minimum requirements can be listed on the NYSE. The exchange imposes requirements in the form of earning power, total value of outstanding stock, and number of shareholders. Smaller firms trade on other exchanges or in the over-the-counter market.

The Over-the-Counter Market

Relative to the organized exchanges, the over-the-counter market receives little attention. However, future advances in computer technology will probably benefit the over-the-counter market more than the organized exchanges because of the structural differences between the two types of markets.

The over-the-counter market differs from organized exchanges in several ways. First, in the OTC market, there is no central trading floor where all trading activity takes place. Instead, the market is made up of many people in diverse locations. Second, the OTC market does not make use of specialists. Instead, there are many **market makers**, firms and individuals making a market in particular stocks.

In a sense, the name "over-the-counter" expresses these differences. This nickname arose because traders in the market are like retailers who keep a supply of shares and sell them to buyers across the counter, as one might buy merchandise in a general store. In important respects, this system continues today, with several market makers for each security. The National Association of Securities Dealers (NASD) grants the privilege of trading in the over-the-counter market, based on financial soundness and qualification examinations. This industry group plays a role analogous to the exchange as a regulator of market entry. In addition, the NASD plays an important self-regulatory role, as only its members can trade on the OTC market.

A distinction should be made between the OTC market and the National Association of Securities Dealers Automated Quotation (NASDAQ) market. The NASDAQ market, which originated from the over-the-counter market on February 8, 1971, requires that all of its securities be registered with the Securities and Exchange Commission (SEC) and that they meet qualification standards. In contrast, there are no qualification standards for OTC securities. NASDAQ is also a computerized market with some 60 percent of the trading done without telephone assistance, while the OTC market is mostly a telephone operation with some automation.

The NASDAQ market has been growing quite rapidly. Figure 13.2 shows the recent record of growth in share volume. The rate exceeds that of the organized exchanges in general, and the NYSE in particular.

THE BOND MARKET IN THE UNITED STATES

Three major issuers dominate the U.S. bond market: the U.S. government, corporations, and municipalities. Each of these types of issuers has special characteristics that make its

FIGURE 13.2
NASDAQ Share Volume

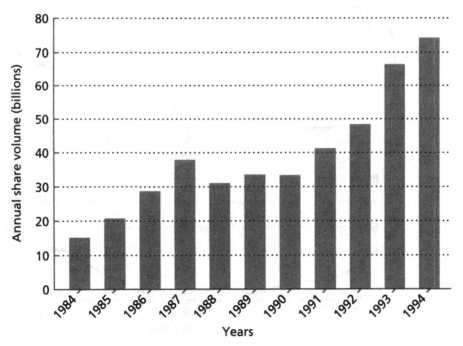

Source: NASDAQ Fact Book/Company Directory, 1995.

bonds different from those issued by members of the other groups. These characteristics include maturity, tax status, and risk level. Consequently, we will focus separately on the different segments of the market.

The Market for U.S. Government Bonds

The U.S. government is the world's single largest debtor, with new federal borrowing in the neighborhood of $250 billion each year in recent years. Borrowing by the U.S. government falls into two categories. First, the U.S. Treasury issues debt, such as Treasury bills, notes, and bonds. Second, various agencies of the U.S. government also borrow. Examples include the Government National Mortgage Association (GNMA), the Federal Housing Administration (FHA), and the Tennessee Valley Authority (TVA). Together, they are responsible for a tremendous amount of outstanding debt, as figure 13.3 shows. The amount of the outstanding government debt relative to GNP (Gross National Product) declined for many years, but it has recently begun to climb dramatically. Of this outstanding debt, the most important part is U.S. Treasury debt.

FIGURE 13.3
Net Federal Debt Outstanding

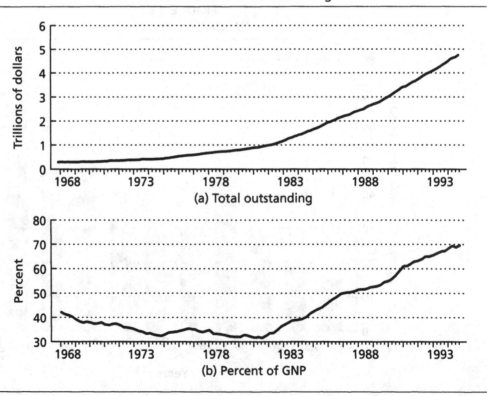

(a) Total outstanding

(b) Percent of GNP

Treasury Debt   The three principal kinds of U.S. Treasury obligations are Treasury bills, notes, and bonds. Treasury bills, or T-bills, are debt instruments issued by the U.S. Treasury with an initial maturity of one year or less. The focus here will be on the longer Treasury maturity issues – notes and bonds.

Treasury notes and bonds are alike in the structure of their payment streams and differ only in their maturity. Officially, a Treasury note (T-note) is an instrument having an original maturity lying in the range of 1–10 years. A Treasury bond (T-bond) has an original maturity in excess of 10 years. In practice, T-bonds have much longer maturities, usually in the range of 20–30 years. *The Wall Street Journal* and other major newspapers carry daily quotations for various federal issues.

Figure 13.4 presents the year-by-year percentage returns for both bills and bonds, and also shows the corresponding inflation rates. Notice that the Treasury bill investor has never had an actual loss in any year. This is due to the short maturity of T-bills, and to the fact that the government has always paid as promised. The investor in Treasury bonds, however, has been stung on occasion. Although T-bonds have also been paid as promised, an investor in T-bonds could still have a loss in a given year, if interest rates rise too much. The dollar return on holding a Treasury bond for a given year consists of the interest payments received plus any price change in the bond. In the years of losses, the fall in the bond price exceeded the interest income, resulting in a net loss on holding the Treasury bond.

To evaluate the success of an investment, it is also important to take inflation into account. **Inflation** is the change in the general price level over time. If we divide the terminal value of the investments by the change in the price level over the same period, the quotient indicates the change in purchasing power the investment generated. For example, assume you invest $100 for a year and earn 10 percent interest, but the price level goes up 10 percent during the year, so that items that originally cost $100 will cost $110 at the end of the year. In that case, you have the same purchasing power at the end of the year as at the beginning. Despite the nominal return of 10 percent on the investment, the real rate is actually 0 percent.

Federal Agency Debt   In addition to the Treasury debt, there are many federal and federally sponsored agencies that also issue debt. Among the federal agencies issuing debt we have the Export-Import Bank, the Tennessee Valley Authority, the Government National Mortgage Association, and the Postal Service. The federally sponsored agencies issuing debt include the Farm Credit banks, the Federal National Mortgage Association, and the Federal Home Loan banks. Most of this activity supports home mortgages and farm credit.

The Corporate Bond Market

The corporate bond market is smaller than either the home mortgage market or the municipal bond market. The issues of state and local governments make up the municipal bond market, which we examine in the next section. One of the best readily available sources for quotations on corporate bonds is *The Wall Street Journal*, which quotes New York Exchange bonds.

FIGURE 13.4
Year-by-Year Returns on Bonds, Bills, and Inflation

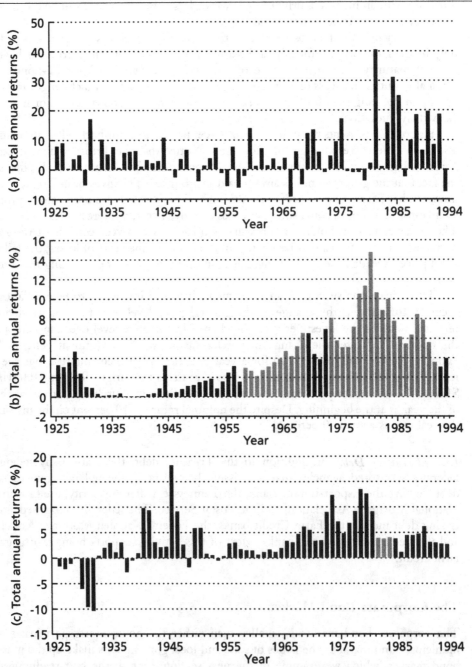

Source: Ibbotson Associates, *Stocks, Bonds, Bills and Inflation: 1994 Yearbook,* Chicago: Ibbotson Associates, 1995.

As we have already seen, the issuer of a bond promises to make a series of payments of a certain amount on specified dates. For bond investors, the chance that the issuer will pay as promised is extremely important. To help bond investors assess the future payment prospects of bonds, bond ratings are provided by Standard & Poor's and Moody's. The ratings attempt to measure **default risk** – the chance that one or more payments on the bond will be deferred or missed altogether. In general, the ratings systems used by Standard & Poor's and Moody's follow each other very closely, with Standard & Poor's being quoted more often than Moody's.

Returns on bond investments depend on other factors besides whether the bondholder pays as promised. An investor who holds a bond until it matures earns the yield to maturity on the bond, assuming the bond pays as promised. If the bond is held for a shorter time, the return on the investment is uncertain. Bond prices can change as a result of changes in interest rates and changes in the prospects of the issuing firm.

The Municipal Bond Market

A municipal bond is a debt security issued by government or quasi-government agencies, other than those associated with the federal government. These securities form a special segment of the bond market due to the special character of their issuers and to their special tax status. Almost without exception, municipal bonds are exempt from federal income taxation. This key feature distinguishes municipal bonds from the rest of the bond market. Because of their tax exemption, municipal bonds are of greater relative value to investors with high marginal tax rates. Such investors can obtain the same after-tax return from either a relatively low yield municipal bond or a higher yielding taxable bond.

For bonds of like risk and maturity, the rational investor should prefer the bond with the higher after-tax return. Table 13.1 presents taxable yields and their equivalent tax-exempt yield for investors in different tax brackets. As shown in the table, the higher the tax rate, the greater should be the preference for tax-exempt securities. Given the after-tax equivalences shown in the table, we should expect lower yields for tax-exempt securities than for taxable securities of the same risk. For example, an investor in the 40 percent

TABLE 13.1
Taxable and Tax-Exempt Equivalent Yields*

| | Marginal Tax Rate | | | |
Taxable Yield	20	30	40	50
8%	6.4%	5.6%	4.8%	4.0%
10%	8.0	7.0	6.0	5.0
12%	9.6	8.4	7.2	6.0
14%	11.2	9.2	8.8	7.0
16%	12.8	11.2	9.6	8.0

*The entries of the table show the equivalent tax-exempt yields.

marginal tax bracket would be equally happy with a taxable bond yielding 14 percent or a municipal bond yielding 8.8 percent, assuming both bonds have the same risk level.

Figure 13.5 shows the historical yield relationships among AAA tax-exempt and taxable securities. Although the rating systems for tax-exempt and taxable bonds are slightly different, AAA is the highest rating for both categories. Therefore, they are approximately equal in risk. The yield spread between the two kinds of bonds reflects the eagerness of investors for opportunities to escape taxation.

Although the municipal bond market is huge in total size and exceeds the size of the corporate bond market, it is not a very liquid market. A **liquid market** is one in which an investor can sell an asset easily for a price close to its true value. The low liquidity in the municipal bond market stems from the small size of many individual issues and the desire of investors to hold on to issues. As a consequence, it is somewhat difficult to acquire good information on the current prices of some issues. Two good information sources are *The Wall Street Journal* and the "blue list" of Standard & Poor's.

THE PRIMARY MARKET

The preceding sections have considered the secondary stock and bond markets. Before stocks and bonds reach the secondary market, firms or governments must issue them. This initial issuance takes place in the primary market.

We can distinguish new issues in the primary market by the type of issuer and the type of security being issued. The basic issuers of securities are governments and corpora-

FIGURE 13.5
AAA Industrials Versus AAA Municipal Yields

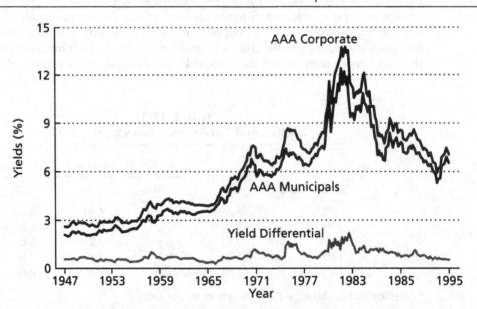

tions. The securities offered may be either bonds, common stock, or preferred stock. Of these three types of securities, only corporations issue common stock and preferred stock. Since stock, particularly common stock, represents an ownership claim on the issuing entity, governments cannot issue stock.

Private Placements Versus Public Offerings

There are two types of offerings – public and private. In a **public offering**, the issuer offers the security to the public at large, giving any investor the right to purchase a portion of the new issue. In a public offering, the entire process of issuance is governed by regulations of the Securities and Exchange Commission. As an alternative, many companies prefer to make a private placement. In a **private placement**, the issuer sells an entire bond issue to a single buyer, or to a small consortium of buyers. In a private placement the issuer never makes the bond available to the public. There are several advantages to private placements. If a corporation makes a private placement, the process of issuing the security escapes the attention of the SEC. Since the SEC imposes fairly rigorous and costly rules on the process of publicly issuing securities, it can be cheaper for the firm to engage in a private placement. Another advantage for the issuing firm is the chance to avoid too much public disclosure of its business plans. The SEC requires considerable disclosure in any public offering. For a firm engaged in an industry where protecting secrets is important, such as high technology firms in the computing or defense industries, making public disclosures can be very undesirable.

In private placements, the buyers of the securities tend to be large institutions with plenty of cash, such as insurance companies. For these buyers, there are certain advantages to participating in a private placement. Usually, privately placed bonds pay a little more interest than bonds sold in a public offering. The issuer can afford to pay a slightly higher interest rate because the cost of the private placement is lower than for a public offering.

For the buyer of a privately placed issue there is also an important disadvantage. The holder of a privately placed security cannot sell the bond, since it has never undergone the process of scrutiny required for a public offering. The buyer of a privately placed issue sacrifices liquidity to obtain the higher rate of interest paid on private placements.

Although common stocks generally attract more investor attention than the bond market, the primary stock market is really quite small compared to the primary bond market. However, stocks trade much more frequently than bonds on the secondary market. It is the degree of activity in stock trading in the secondary market that makes stocks the main focus of financial market analysts.

The largest issuer of securities in the world is the U.S. government. In addition to the U.S. government, state and local governments issue vast quantities of municipal bonds. The size of this market is also very large, almost equaling the total issuance of securities by corporations.

As mentioned earlier, all government securities are bonds, and the municipal market exceeds the corporate bond market in size by a wide margin. Considering the tendency of corporations to issue bonds rather than stocks, and considering the billions of dollars in bonds issued by governments, the huge size of the bond market becomes even more apparent.

The Process of Issuing Securities for a Corporation

The development of a good relationship with an investment banker is very important to the financial management of a firm. Most firms attempt to maintain a close working relationship with one or two investment bankers to whom they can turn when needed. Assuming the firm has established such a relationship, the corporation and the investment banker would be in regular contact as the financing needs of the firm develop. The investment banker will normally fulfill three functions for the corporation in the process of issuing a new security: consulting, forming a distribution network, and bearing the risk involved in the issuance of the new security.

As the firm prepares to issue the new security, it must resolve many questions, such as the timing of the issuance and the pricing of the security. In a public offering the issuer must meet many regulations of the SEC as well. The investment banker plays a critical role in helping the issuer with all of these matters.

The Investment Banker as Consultant

As a consultant to the firm planning to issue a security, the investment banker works in three main areas: preparation of the necessary registration and informational materials, timing of the issuance, and setting the sale price. One of the important requirements is the formal disclosure of the firm's financial condition and plans. This is done in a **prospectus**, a legal document required by the SEC. The investment banker will often play an important advisory role in creating the prospectus.

The information in a prospectus includes a report of the firm's financial condition, the names of the principal officers in the corporation, and an accounting of their holdings in the firm. The document must also give information about the firm's line of business and its plans for future expansion. This information must be detailed and highly accurate. Since the firm offers the securities for sale through the prospectus, any error in the prospectus could make the firm liable for investors' losses. Consequently, the prospectus is usually written by the legal staff in legal language. The authors of the prospectus usually include top management from the issuing firm, the legal staff of the issuing firm, and legal specialists in prospectus writing. Also, some of the expertise for the prospectus will usually come from the investment banker. Officially, only the prospectus can offer securities for sale. For that matter, only investors who have received a copy of the prospectus may buy the security anyway.

All firms prefer to issue their securities when they can receive a high price for them. For stocks, the ideal would be to issue securities when the secondary stock market is at a peak. For bonds, the ideal time to issue would be when interest rates are very low. Investment bankers often give firms advice on this issue of timing.

Pricing of the new securities is very important as well. Since investment bankers know the primary market, they should be in a good position to give advice on the proper pricing of the security. The goal of the pricing strategy is to set the highest price that will allow all of the issue to sell quickly.

The Distribution Network

Figure 13.6 shows the typical structure of the distribution network. The issuing corporation creates the security and passes it to the lead bank and the syndicate members. The **lead**

FIGURE 13.6
Organization of the Distribution Network

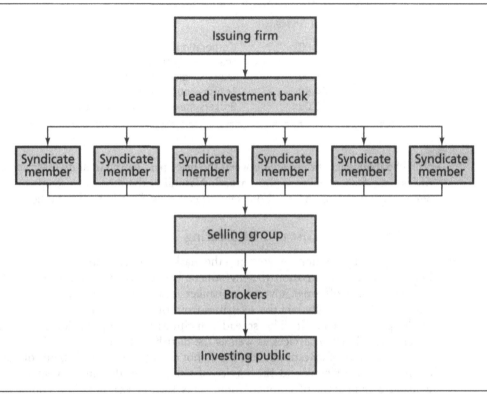

bank is the investment bank that has primary responsibility for the issuance of a particular security. The **syndicate members** are other investment banking firms that have committed themselves to helping float a given security. The **flotation** is the initial sale of the security.

From the several members of the syndicate, the securities go to members of the **selling group,** those investment houses that are participating to a smaller degree in the distribution process. Then the securities reach the brokers, and it is at this point that contact with the public is achieved. The brokers are in direct contact with their customers, the actual investors in the securities.

To illustrate this process of issuing a security, consider a firm making a fairly large issue ($20–50 million). Assume the corporation receives $100 per share of common stock, as table 13.2 shows. As the security flows through the network of intermediaries, each layer tacks on its profit. By the time the security reaches the members of the public, its final price may well be 6 percent or more above the amount the corporation receives. The prices shown in table 13.2 assume that the security flows through the entire chain. This will not be true of all the shares of stock in the issue, since the lead bank will also market the shares through its own internal distribution network.

TABLE 13.2
Typical Spreads in a Common Stock Issuance

Price per Share	Receiver
100.00	Corporation
101.25	Lead investment bank
103.00	Other syndicate members
104.50	Selling group members
106.00	Brokers making sales directly to the public

The total price difference between the price paid by the final investor and the amount the issuing firm receives is the **spread**. Naturally, the lead bank keeps a much greater percentage of the spread on those securities it sells directly to the public.

The Service and Cost of Risk Bearing

Creating the distribution network and the marketing of securities are parts of the retailing function. The compensation the investment banker receives is not only for acting as a retailer. In many offerings, investment bankers bear a great deal of risk. This is particularly true when they actually buy the securities from the issuing firm and then try to sell them to the public at a profit. The spread constitutes the compensation for the investment bankers' risk-bearing services as well as the distribution cost.

The services of investment bankers do not come cheaply. The talents of the employees of the investment bank and the service of risk bearing that investment bankers provide demand a high level of compensation. This section examines the compensation paid, directly or indirectly, to the investment banker. These flotation costs of issuing securities have a strong impact on the cost of acquiring funds and also on the desirability of new issues as investments.

Corporations pay their investment bankers in two ways. First, they typically pay out-of-pocket expenses for consulting services, legal fees, and document preparation. Second, the offering price of the security allows investment bankers and other members of the distribution network to make a profit. Of these two expense classes, the second is generally larger.[1]

When an investment banking syndicate actually buys the securities from the issuing corporation, the syndicate acts as an **underwriter**. The price the corporation receives must be low enough to allow the syndicate to distribute the securities to the public at a profit. The spread is the gross margin for the distribution network. In an issue that is underwritten, a large portion of the spread is compensation for bearing risk. Spreads are typically lower for debt issues than for common stock. Further, the spread is a smaller percentage of the

---

[1] Governments and their agencies operate somewhat differently. Many are required by law to offer securities under a process of competitive bidding, rather than through an underwriting system. The U.S. government issues securities through its own special media, including Federal Reserve Banks and U.S. government security dealers.

proceeds the larger the issue size. For very small issues, the flotation costs are prohibitively expensive.

In addition to the spread, the issuing firm also pays out-of-pocket expenses. While smaller than the spread, these expenses can add significantly to the total flotation costs. For small issues, total flotation costs can approach 20 percent; for the largest issues, they can be less than 3 percent.

REGULATION OF INVESTMENT BANKING IN THE SECURITIES MARKET

Important regulations affect the performance of the financial manager in the securities markets. This section discusses the most important laws and regulations governing the issuance of new securities and trading in the secondary market. Much of this legislation stems from the 1930s, as a response to the stock market panic of 1929 and the depression that followed.

Securities Act of 1933

The Securities Act of 1933 was the first major piece of legislation directed specifically toward the securities market itself. It is basically a "truth in securities" law. The law provides that issuers of new securities must provide truthful information about the securities to potential investors, and it prohibits fraud in security sales. This law requires that potential investors receive a prospectus before investing and specifies the information the prospectus must contain. As discussed earlier, the prospectus must contain information about the firm, its officers, the purpose of the issue, the financial position of the firm, and any pending legal actions against the firm.

Another major requirement of the law is that the prospective issuer must make a **registration statement**. The SEC conducts this registration. False statements in the SEC registration statement are subject to criminal penalties. Additionally, any purchaser of securities sold under a misleading registration statement may sue the issuer to recover funds lost.

The law covers long-term securities, such as stocks and bonds, and it specifically excludes certain securities from the requirement of registering and providing a prospectus. The law excludes short-term debt obligations with original maturities of 270 days or less, government securities, many debt obligations issued by commercial banks, and securities offerings of less than $500,000.

Trust Indenture Act of 1939

For bonds, the issuer normally appoints a trustee to protect the rights of the bondholders. Although appointed by the issuer, the trustee operates independently of the corporation. Large banks often act as trustees. Before passage of the Trust Indenture Act, there was no legal safeguard to make sure that the trustee could act independently and strongly on behalf of the bondholders. If the trustee is dependent on the corporation issuing the bonds, then the issuer may be able to break the terms of the indenture agreement and leave bondholders without any effective remedy.

The act requires that the trustee maintain financial independence from the issuing firm. This facilitates enforcement of the terms of the indenture by the trustee. Further, the act specifies more closely the kinds of information that the indenture agreement must include. The act also stipulates that the issuer must provide a list of the bondholders and semi-annual financial reports to the trustee.

Shelf Registration

Shelf registration allows firms to register with the SEC one time, and then to offer securities for sale through agents and through the secondary markets for two years following the registration. As shown earlier, issuing securities can be quite expensive. Regulators, notably the SEC, have thought these costs worthwhile, as regulations help protect the investing public and maintain a smoothly functioning primary market. As a cost reduction experiment, the SEC has instituted Rule 415 to allow shelf registrations. The rule applies to both stocks and bonds.

Corporations reap two chief advantages from Rule 415. First, a corporation can reduce its expense of offering securities by avoiding repeated registrations. Also, shelf registration allows firms to avoid the fixed price system of the investment bankers. Not surprisingly, the investment banking community lobbied very hard against the adoption of Rule 415. The second advantage to corporations arises from the greater flexibility the firm achieves in timing an offering. Before shelf registration, the issuer had to make a final decision on a security issuance about three to six weeks before the actual offering. Faced with security market fluctuations, firms can now take advantage of favorable market conditions by issuing quickly under the provisions of shelf registration. Shelf registration is one important example of the trend toward deregulating the securities industry.

Insider Trading

Officers of corporations, such as top financial managers, have special information about their firm's operations that is not available to the public. An **insider** is a person with special knowledge about the operation of a firm. Securities trading by such an individual is **insider trading**. For example, the officers of a corporation might know that the firm just won a particularly lucrative contract. If the officers traded on that private information, they would reap a profit through insider trading.

Believing that such trading impaired the performance of the securities markets, Congress passed the Securities Exchange Act of 1934. This law limited the trading of corporate insiders and required reports of insiders for transactions involving their firm's shares. The control of insider trading applies both to principals of the firm and to others who learn of material, nonpublic, information.

SUMMARY

The stock market is well developed and active, with trading taking place on organized exchanges and on the over-the-counter market. The presence of this well-organized secondary market means that firms that sell stock will have easier access to the capital market. Because the secondary market is so active, prospective investors need not fear that they are making a permanent commitment to a security when they purchase it. With the secondary market, one can always trade the stock.

Compared to the stock market, the bond market is not so active; however, it is sizable. Virtually every large size corporation has bond issues outstanding. Consequently, the prospective financial manager must anticipate the need to sell bonds for the firm to raise capital.

For most issues by corporations and municipalities, the investment banker acts as a distribution network. This is essentially a retailing function. In many cases, the investment banker also underwrites a new security issue. In an underwriting, an investment banking syndicate buys the securities from the issuer and tries to sell them at a profit. The difference between the amount the issuer receives and the amount the final investor pays is the spread. This spread is the gross profit margin and the investment banking syndicate takes this spread as compensation for its retailing and risk-bearing services.

Only by issuing securities in the primary market can the corporation obtain the long-term capital commitments it needs to undertake its investment plans. Further, corporate participation in the primary market is usually a continuing process, because successful corporations are growing and need new investment funds.

There are also important regulations that govern the conduct of firms in the issuance of new securities. The SEC regulates the market behavior of corporate insiders as they trade their own securities. Normally, these regulations apply to top financial managers.

QUESTIONS

1. Why is stock ownership a "residual claim" on the firm?
2. Can a securities market function without a specialist?
3. What are the main differences between the OTC market and an organized securities exchange?
4. Assume that you own 130 shares of a stock trading at $14. If the firm has a 4 percent stock dividend, how many shares would you expect to own after the dividend? How has your wealth changed?
5. Which entity is the largest issuer of securities in the world?
6. What information is found in a prospectus?
7. How might the fees charged by investment bankers for risk bearing be related to the creditworthiness of the issuer, the issuer's general reputation, and the current stability of financial markets?
8. Why does the federal government issue only debt and no equity?
9. How much cash does IBM receive if an investor buys a share of IBM on the secondary market?
10. Will a small or a large issue of securities have higher percentage flotation costs? Why?

11. In the United States, which is larger, the bond market or the stock market?
12. If you were the president of a software firm trying to raise funds for the introduction of a revolutionary product for personal computers, what considerations would be important to you in choosing between a public offering and a private placement? Why?

Chapter 14

Inventory and Cash Management

OVERVIEW

Inventories are assets of the firm, and as such they represent an investment. Because such investment requires a commitment of funds, managers must ensure that the firm maintains inventories at the correct level. If they become too large, the firm loses the opportunity to employ those funds more effectively. Similarly, if they are too small, the firm may lose sales. Thus, there is an optimal level of inventories. This chapter considers the economic order quantity model for determining the correct level of inventory.

In essence, cash is an inventory of money. Like inventory, holding some cash is essential to operating the firm, but holding too much is costly, because cash does not earn any explicit return. As with the management of inventories, the central question of cash management is determining the optimal amount to have on hand. This chapter also focuses on cash management.

Because money has a time value, the firm will want to collect cash owed to it as quickly as possible. Similarly, it wants to pay its obligations as slowly as possible. Naturally, the desire to collect cash quickly and to pay cash slowly is subject to some constraints. For example, failure to make payments within a reasonable time may damage the firm's credit rating. The cash manager must know the techniques for speeding collections and slowing payments that are acceptable business practice.

TYPES OF INVENTORIES

There are three basic types of inventories: **raw materials, work-in-process**, and **finished goods**. The raw materials inventory consists of the basic commodities that a firm purchases to use in its production process. Work-in-process inventory consists of goods in the production process, for example, partially assembled cars in an automobile firm. The finished goods inventory consists of completed items that are ready for sale.

BENEFITS AND COSTS OF HOLDING INVENTORIES

The benefits of holding inventories differ depending on the type of firm. A manufacturer must have some inventory of raw materials; otherwise, production would grind to a halt.

Similarly, it cannot avoid some work-in-process inventory, because the production process takes time. Finally, an inventory of finished goods allows the firm to fill sales orders quickly.

Firms in the retailing industry may hold their entire inventory in finished goods because they generally purchase the goods in finished form from manufacturers and sell them to the public. Service industry firms are likely to have virtually no inventory, except those items used in creating their service. For example, a janitorial firm might hold only cleaning supplies. These items are not to be resold, but used to provide the janitorial service.

Given the benefits of holding inventories and the costs of running out of them, it might seem that firms should hold the greatest amount possible. That is costly, too, however, because funds invested there cannot earn a return elsewhere. Therefore, firms must manage their inventories carefully to get the best return from their capital. They must measure the benefit of holding an item in inventory against the opportunity cost. The major inventory costs are carrying costs and ordering costs.

Carrying Costs

Two basic costs are associated with holding an item in inventory. First, there is the cost of storage. For example, bulky items like wheat can have substantial storage costs, and the same is true of items requiring special treatment, such as refrigeration. The second cost is that involved in financing the inventory. For example, if interest rates are 12 percent, holding an item costing $100 in inventory for one year entails a $12 annual financing cost. Together, the storage and opportunity costs of employing the funds elsewhere make up the total **carrying cost** of an item in inventory.

Ordering Costs

Management must also consider the cost of ordering new items. For example, a bicycle manufacturer requires an inventory of spokes for the wheels. The benefit of a supply of spokes is clear, since without them the firm cannot build bicycles. Holding too many spokes is wasteful, however, because the funds invested in them could be earning a return elsewhere.

To avoid holding too many spokes, the firm could order smaller quantities. At the extreme, it could buy them for each bicycle individually. This extreme strategy has two obvious drawbacks. First, placing an order costs money. This **ordering cost** is the fixed expense in the preparation and execution of an order for goods, including paperwork and communication with the supplier. For the bicycle manufacturer, ordering spokes each time it produces a bicycle would generate very large annual ordering costs.

A second problem with this extreme strategy is with delays in receiving spokes. If the firm receives some orders late, it cannot complete bicycles according to schedule. Ideally, it would like to receive each new shipment as it exhausts the old supply; however, it runs a high risk of running out of spokes if shipments are delayed or if it uses spokes faster than anticipated. Therefore, inventory management requires planning for safety stocks.

The **safety stock** is the amount of an item the firm plans to have when it receives new inventory. It provides the firm enough of an item with which to keep going if shipment delays occur or if the sales rate increases unexpectedly. Thus, it is designed to be available when unforeseen contingencies occur.

INVENTORY MODELS

Inventory models vary from very simple to sophisticated computerized ones, from the "look-and-see" approach to systems that record every sale and report it automatically and instantaneously to a computerized inventory-control program.

The Red Line Method

Imagine a bin full of spokes at the bicycle plant, from which workers withdraw the spokes as needed. As the level of spokes decreases, a red line painted on the inside of the bin becomes visible. When the level reaches the red line, the firm orders more spokes. In this case, the red line indicates the **reorder point**, the level of inventory at which the firm reorders the item. Of course, the line should be drawn at a level that allows enough time for the new shipment to arrive before the current inventory is depleted.

This is one of the simplest inventory-control techniques we can imagine. Unfortunately, it has definite limitations. For example, it works only for items that are all stored in one place. In addition, although the position of the red line may reflect a good deal of thought and experience, the reorder point may not realistically reflect the expected rate of usage, the safety stock, or the time for processing and transporting the order.

The ABC System

Because managerial time and effort are scarce and because some items in stock are more important than others, many firms use a system of priorities to manage their inventories. For example, it seems foolish to devote the same amount of managerial time to monitoring the inventory of a small item with annual sales of $1,000, as to an item with sales of $1,000,000 annually. The ABC system explicitly recognizes that some items are more important than others, and allocates management efforts in proportion to that importance.

The **ABC system** classifies the various inventory items into three separate sets or classes. The most important items are classified as class A, those of intermediate importance as class B, and the least important as class C. Managers monitor the items accordingly. For example, they might review class A items monthly or even weekly, whereas class B items might be reviewed quarterly, and class C items only twice a year.

To illustrate in more detail how the ABC inventory system works, consider Hammerhead, Inc., a very small hardware store. Hammerhead sells only nine items, and has decided to classify them according to the ABC system. The two most important items belong to class A, the following three items to class B, and the final four items belong to class C. In table 14.1, the firm classifies its inventory according to unit purchase cost. Lawn mowers are the most expensive to purchase ($110.00) and nails the least expensive ($1.60). Thus, management will devote most of its efforts to monitoring lawn mowers and so on down the line, with the least effort placed on monitoring nails.

TABLE 14.1

ABC Inventory for Hammerhead, Classified by Unit Cost

Item	Unit Cost	Unit Price	Units	Revenues	Profit
Lawn mowers	110.00	260.00	120	31,200	18,000
Pumps	60.00	145.00	200	29,000	17,000
Lumber	10.20	19.00	2,400	45,600	21,120
Paint	7.00	15.00	2,000	30,000	16,000
Plants	4.50	7.90	1,700	13,430	5,780
Flashlights	3.75	6.90	300	2,070	945
Batteries	1.75	3.00	1,000	3,000	1,250
Fertilizer	1.70	5.50	400	2,200	1,520
Nails	1.60	3.15	9,000	28,350	13,950

The major problem with the unit cost criterion is obvious by looking at the revenue and profit columns in table 14.1. Because nails are a class C item, they receive very little managerial attention. However, they provide much more revenue and profits than, say, plants, which are a class B item. This problem may be solved by classifying items according to the annual profits they are expected to generate. Using this criterion, a new ABC classification of the same nine items is obtained, as shown in table 14.2. Notice that now the most important item is lumber, despite its relatively small unit cost. Similarly, the importance of nails increases.

Other more sophisticated criteria can be used to classify items using the ABC method. For example, the firm might set up a system that assigns a numerical value to the items according to their shipping times or according to their strategic importance to the firm. Whatever the method, the principle remains the same: managerial time is scarce, and should be assigned to items in accordance with their relative importance to the firm.

TABLE 14.2

ABC Inventory for Hammerhead, Classified by Annual Profit

Item	Unit Cost	Unit Price	Units	Revenues	Profit
Lumber	10.20	19.00	2,400	45,600	21,120
Lawn mowers	110.00	260.00	120	31,200	18,000
Pumps	60.00	145.00	200	29,000	17,000
Paint	7.00	15.00	2,000	30,000	16,000
Nails	1.60	3.15	9,000	28,350	13,950
Plants	4.50	7.90	1,700	13,430	5,780
Fertilizer	1.70	5.50	400	2,200	1,520
Batteries	1.75	3.00	1,000	3,000	1,250
Flashlights	3.75	6.90	300	2,070	945

THE ECONOMIC ORDERING QUANTITY MODEL

This section introduces a formal model to help determine the optimal inventory level. The model is known as the **economic ordering quantity** (EOQ) model, because it establishes the most economic size of order to place. It depends on key variables such as the cost of carrying the item in inventory, its purchase and ordering costs, and its rate of usage.

Like all formal models, the EOQ model makes simplifying assumptions, the main one being that the inventory is used at a known constant rate, as shown in figure 14.1. With a constant level of usage, a starting level of Q units, and an ending level of 0 units, the average amount of inventory in stock will be $Q/2$ units.

The goal of the EOQ model is to choose the ordering amount, Q, that gives the lowest total annual cost of maintaining the inventory. The model ignores safety stocks, which we consider later. The total cost of inventory depends on the two separate factors that we identified earlier: ordering and carrying costs. An item that is ordered very infrequently has a low annual ordering cost. However, more items must be ordered each time, so the amount ordered, Q, will be larger. Also, because we assume the firm depletes its inventory at a constant rate, the average inventory, $Q/2$, will be larger the less frequently it is ordered. A policy of ordering only infrequently results in larger inventories and a higher carrying cost.

Figure 14.2 shows the impact of these two costs on the total inventory cost. The line for the ordering cost shows that the larger the order size, the smaller the ordering costs. This makes sense, because fewer orders will be placed. By contrast, the carrying cost increases with the order size. This also makes sense, because we have already seen that the larger the order size, the larger will be the inventory. The job of the EOQ model is

FIGURE 14.1
Inventory Level with a Constant Rate of Usage

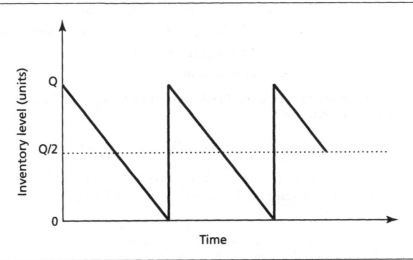

FIGURE 14.2
Inventory Costs

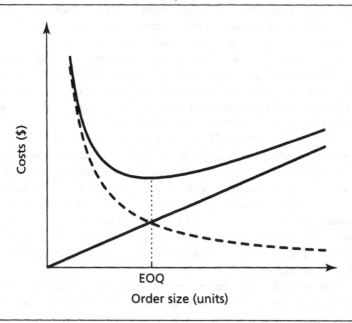

to find the optimal order size, or the economical amount to order. Ordering this quantity minimizes the total cost of inventory.[1]

The total cost of inventory depends on the carrying cost and the ordering cost. To calculate the total cost, define the variables of the model as follows:

S = annual unit sales

P = purchase cost of a unit for the firm

C = annual carrying cost as a percent of the unit's price

F = fixed cost of placing an order

Q = the quantity ordered

We can express the total cost (TC) of inventory for a year as the sum of the carrying costs and the ordering costs:

$$TC = \frac{Q}{2} \times P \times C + \frac{S}{Q} \times F$$

This expression can be interpreted as follows. The average value of the inventory over the year equals the average number of units in inventory, $Q/2$, times the purchase cost of each

---

[1] Notice that in figure 14.2 the EOQ occurs at the order size where the curves for the carrying and ordering costs intersect. It can be shown that this must always be true.

unit, P. The yearly carrying cost equals the average value of the inventory times the annual percentage cost, C, of carrying \$1 in inventory. If the firm sells S units in a year and places an order of size Q each time it orders, then it must order S/Q times per year. For example, if a department store sells 1,000 television sets in a year and each order is for 100 sets, it must order $1,000/100 = 10$ times per year. If each order costs a fixed amount, F, the ordering cost for a year must equal the number of orders per year times the cost of each order, or $(S/Q) \times F$. With the help of calculus it is possible to derive the optimal order size, EOQ, which is given in equation 14.1:

$$EOQ = \sqrt{\frac{2FS}{CP}} \tag{14.1}$$

The firm minimizes its total inventory cost by ordering EOQ units each time. As equation 14.1 shows, the EOQ increases as the fixed ordering costs and the annual sales level increase. This is because if the ordering costs increase, the firm orders less frequently, which means that it must order more units each time. By contrast, the EOQ falls as the percentage carrying cost and the purchase price increase. For example, if the carrying cost increases, the current inventory level becomes too costly for the firm, and it is then better to order less each time. Of course, it will then be necessary to order more frequently.

EXAMPLE 1

A firm expects to sell twice as many units in five years as it sells this year. By what percentage will its average inventory increase over the next five years?

Let S_0 and $EOQ_0/2$ be the sales and average inventory levels for this year. Similarly, let S_5 and $EOQ_5/2$ be the corresponding values in five years. Since $S_5 = 2S_0$, we have:

$$EOQ_5 = \sqrt{\frac{2FS}{CP}} = \sqrt{\frac{2F(2S_0)}{CP}}$$
$$= \sqrt{\frac{2FS_0}{CP}} \times \sqrt{2}$$
$$= EOQ_0 \times \sqrt{2}$$

Thus, when unit sales double, the EOQ and the average inventory increase by a factor equal to the square root of 2, or by only 41.42 percent. This is an example of **economies of scale**, since larger firms can optimally hold less inventory relative to sales than smaller firms.

EXAMPLE 2

Consider our bicycle firm that orders spokes by the case. Assume each case costs \$100. The firm uses 1,000 cases of spokes per year. The firm stores spokes in a bin, so the only carrying cost associated with the spokes is the financing cost, which is 12 percent per year. Ordering spokes costs \$75 per order. With these data, we can calculate the EOQ:

$$EOQ = \sqrt{\frac{2 \times \$75 \times 1,000}{0.12 \times \$100}}$$

Therefore, the firm should order 112 cases per order. With this order size, it orders about nine times a year (1,000/111.80 = 8.94).

As we mentioned before, the EOQ model does not itself take safety stocks into account. However, we can use the EOQ model in conjunction with safety stocks. Assume that our bicycle company wishes to have a safety stock equal to eight weeks' normal usage. This means it must order early enough so the safety stock can remain intact. Assume that the normal shipment period is two weeks.

Knowing the safety stock and the shipping time allows us to compute the order point. With 1,000 cases used per year and a safety stock equal to eight weeks usage, the safety stock would be 154 cases (1,000 × 8/52 = 153.85). To avoid using the safety stock, the firm must order two weeks before the inventory falls to the 154 case level. Equivalently, since the safety stock is eight weeks of sales, the firm should order when the total inventory is ten weeks of sales. Since the firm uses 1,000/52 = 19.23 cases per week, it should reorder when the inventory level reaches 192 cases.

Figure 14.3 shows the inventory pattern the spokes should follow. The figure reflects a safety stock of 154 cases and allows a two week lead time for receiving orders. If the

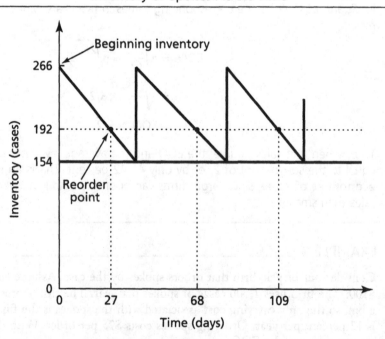

FIGURE 14.3
Inventory of Spokes Across Time

firm begins with a complete inventory of safety stock, plus an order that it just received, it will have 154 + 112 = 266 cases on hand. As it begins to use these, it must reorder two weeks before it hits the safety stock level. Since average daily sales are 1,000/365 = 2.74 cases, this occurs on day 27 at the reorder point of 192 cases. Two weeks later, the firm reaches the safety stock, but it then receives the shipment of spokes. This replenishes the inventory to 266 cases. With a policy of ordering nine times per year, the firm will order about every 40 to 41 days.

Under this policy, the firm should at all times have an inventory greater than the level of the safety stock in normal circumstances. If there are shipping delays or if the spoke maker goes on strike, there will be a delay in replenishing the inventory and the bicycle manufacturer will have to use some of the safety stock. After all, the only purpose of a safety stock is to absorb unforeseen circumstances.

BENEFITS AND COSTS OF HOLDING CASH

Holding cash generates three kinds of benefits. First, firms hold cash to pay for goods and services that they acquire. Cash held for these purposes constitutes a **transaction balance**. Without some transaction balance, the firm would have to get cash for each transaction that arose. The transaction balance acts as a pool of readily available cash and it benefits the firm by the convenience it offers.

Because running out of cash is costly, firms keep extra cash to avoid the associated penalties. Cash held for this second reason is a **precautionary balance**. Precautionary balances benefit the firm by reducing the chance of running out of cash. If managers expect prices of securities to fall, then it is better to hold cash than to hold securities. Cash held in anticipation of falling security prices is a **speculative balance**. In this case, firms essentially bet they will be better off holding cash, which does not earn a return, than holding a security that might fall in value. Firms do not normally hold the three types of cash balances in separate accounts. Instead, the point is to distinguish them as different reasons for holding cash.

Although a transaction balance is convenient and a precautionary balance affords the firm a margin of safety, holding cash does not generate an explicit monetary return. Thus, the main cost of holding cash is the lost interest that the cash would otherwise earn. The goal of cash management is to maximize the difference between the benefits and costs of holding cash. The next section presents a formal model for determining the right amount of cash to hold.

THE BAUMOL MODEL

The Baumol model relies on the exact same assumptions used for the EOQ model. In particular, it assumes that the rate of cash usage is constant and known with certainty. It is thus not surprising that the Baumol formula is a simple adaptation of the EOQ formula. The Baumol model is based on the insight that cash is a form of inventory. Just as a bicycle manufacturing firm may hold an inventory of spokes, it may also hold an inventory of cash: for the inventory model the unit is one spoke, and for the cash model it is one dollar.

Once this exact parallel is seen, the same technique used to derive an expression for the optimal inventory balance can also be used to derive the formula for the correct cash balance.

As in the EOQ model, the Baumol model assumes that the firm uses cash at a known constant rate, and in so doing it incurs holding costs. Since these costs increase with the average level of cash, focusing on this factor alone would lead the firm to hold the least amount possible. However, as the firm depletes its cash, it must acquire new cash, perhaps by liquidating some of its marketable securities. Each time the firm transacts in this way, it bears transaction costs, so it would want to transact as few times as possible during the year. This could be done by having a high cash level. As with the EOQ model, the correct balance is found by combining the holding costs and transaction costs so as to minimize the total cost of holding cash.

Assume that a firm has a maximum cash balance of C dollars. If it uses cash at a constant rate down to a level of zero cash, its average cash balance will be $C/2$ dollars. This situation is shown in figure 14.4. If the firm is able to earn a yearly rate of return r on its funds, the annual opportunity cost of holding cash can be computed as the average amount of cash held, $C/2$, times the rate of interest, r, lost because the funds were held in cash and not invested elsewhere. Therefore, the cost of holding cash over a year is $(C/2)r$.

Suppose that over a year the firm will have a total need for cash equal to T dollars. Since C dollars are acquired each time cash balances are restored, the balance will be restored T/C times per year. If the cost of acquiring the cash is F dollars, the total transaction cost for the year will be $(T/C)F$.

The Baumol model parallels the analysis for the derivation of the EOQ model. In particular, a close correspondence exists between the variables in the Baumol model and the variables in the EOQ model, as shown in table 14.3.

FIGURE 14.4
Cash Level with a Constant Rate of Usage

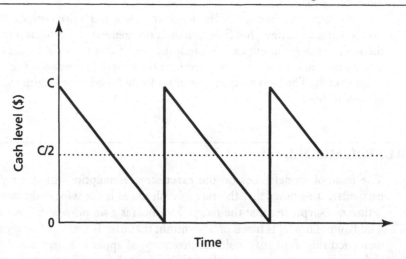

TABLE 14.3
Correspondence Between the EOQ and Baumol Models

EOQ Variable	Baumol Variable
S: annual unit sales	T: annual cash needs
F: dollar cost of each transaction	F: dollar cost of each transaction
C: carrying cost (%)	r: rate received if cash is invested
P: unit purchase cost	1: the cost of one dollar

Notice that the carrying cost of each dollar is the rate that could have been earned if the cash had been invested, say, in marketable securities. This r is an example of an **opportunity cost**. In the EOQ model, the carrying cost, C, contains not only the foregone interest rate, but also other variable costs, such as insurance.

Also notice that in the EOQ model the unit purchase cost could be $2, $10.56, or any other amount. Because of this, we used the variable P to denote the purchase cost of each unit of inventory. In the case of cash, the price of each unit is always $1.

Since we now know that the Baumol model exactly parallels the EOQ model derived previously, it follows that the correct amount of cash to hold in the firm is:

$$C^* = \sqrt{\frac{2FT}{r}} \qquad (14.2)$$

EXAMPLE 3

A firm has a total cash need of $500,000 for the coming year. The transaction cost for acquiring cash each time is $25, and the annual interest rate is 15 percent.
Find the maximum amount of cash the firm should hold, assuming it holds no safety stock.

According to the Baumol model, the amount of cash to acquire each time, which is equal to the maximum cash level the firm will hold, is:

$$C^* = \sqrt{\frac{2 \times \$25 \times \$500,000}{0.15}} = \$12,909.94$$

TECHNIQUES OF CASH MANAGEMENT

There are techniques for speeding the collection of cash and for slowing the disbursement of cash. By using these techniques, managers can conserve cash. Early collection of cash, or slow payment of cash, has important financial advantages that the cash manager must consider.

Effects of Conserving Cash

If a firm pays $1 one day later or if it collects $1 one day earlier than normal, the firm has the use of $1 for an extra day in both cases. The essential advantage of conserving cash in these ways is that the firm may invest it to earn a return. For example, if the interest rate is 12 percent and the firm collects $1 million a day early, this gives the firm a financial benefit equal to the one day's interest on that amount. In this case, it earns interest of:

$$\$1,000,000 \times \frac{0.12}{365} = \$329 \text{ per day}$$

Attention to cash management can have large benefits. For example, assume that your firm must deliver a cashier's check for $1,000,000 in five days to a distant firm. To get a cashier's check, you must actually pay the cash when the check is cut. Consider two methods of delivering the cashier's check. First, the firm could get the cashier's check today and mail it to reach the other company in five days. Second, your firm could wait five days, buy the cashier's check in the morning, and have someone fly to the receiver and deliver it personally.

If your firm hand-delivers the check, it can use the $1 million for five days. With an annual interest rate of 12 percent, the interest earned would be:

$$\$1,000,000 \times \frac{0.12}{365} \times 5 = \$1,643.84$$

This extra interest would be more than enough to pay the airline ticket and salary of the person delivering the check by hand. Therefore, that is the better practice in this scenario.

Actually, still better ways are available. Perhaps the manager should send the cashier's check by overnight mail, and save even more money. Cash management has the very practical job of finding the best way to accelerate collections and delay payments, taking all costs and benefits into consideration.

Many firms face cash management problems that are much more complex than our example. Consider a firm like Sears with several million customers all over the country mailing in payments every month. Between the date each customer buys the goods in the store and the time Sears actually receives payment, a long time passes. During this time the customer benefits by having the good, but has not yet made payment. Sears, on the other hand, has only an account receivable in its ledgers, but no cash. Figure 14.5 presents the two sides of this transaction. For Sears, this receivable stays on the books until payment for the sale reaches the firm. By contrast, the customer has the good long before paying. The time between the sale and the collection is known as the **float**. In this example, Sears has negative float, because it surrenders the good before it receives payment. By contrast, the customer has positive float, having received the good before paying.

Sears has a strong incentive to reduce the period of the float by collecting the accounts receivable early. If it can do this, it gains the use of the money that much earlier. For the customer, the float is very attractive as a result of having both the good and the use of the money that will eventually pay for it. Clearly, the customer benefits by extending the period of the float. This explains, in part, why credit cards are so popular with consumers.

For a company like Sears, it is possible to calculate the normal amount of accounts receivable. This amount depends on the average daily credit sales and the average collection period (ACP), in days, between the sale and the collection of funds. If Sears' credit sales are $10 million per day on average and the collection period is 82 days, it will have an investment in accounts receivable of $820 million:

FIGURE 14.5
Float and the Collection Process

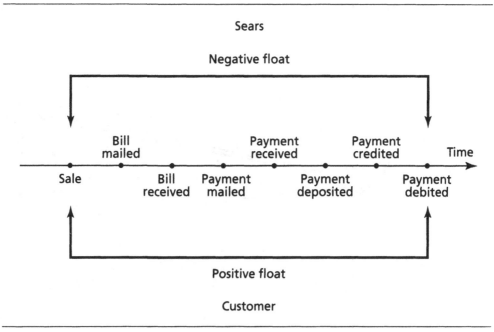

Accounts Receivable = $10,000,000 × 82 days = $820,000,000

If Sears could collect its funds tied up in accounts receivable faster, it would lower its investment in accounts receivable. The reduction in accounts receivable would be available for investment elsewhere. For example, if Sears could reduce its collection period by just three days, the new level of accounts receivable would be:

Accounts Receivable = $10,000,000 × 79 days = $790,000,000

This implies having $30 million in additional cash that could earn a return elsewhere.

Because the rewards of better cash management may be so great, well-developed techniques can improve collection and slow payments. The following section considers some of these techniques.

Concentration Banking and Lock Box Systems

In the example of Sears discussed in the previous section, one way to collect payments is to have them all mailed to the home office in Chicago. Figure 14.6 shows hypothetical mail times in days from various cities to Chicago. Concentration banking and lock box systems help reduce this period.

In **concentration banking** the firm instructs customers to mail their payments to a regional collection center rather than to the home office. This way it receives the checks sooner and therefore can begin processing the checks more quickly. Upon receipt, it

FIGURE 14.6
Mail Time to Chicago: Hypothetical Example of a Lock Box Analysis

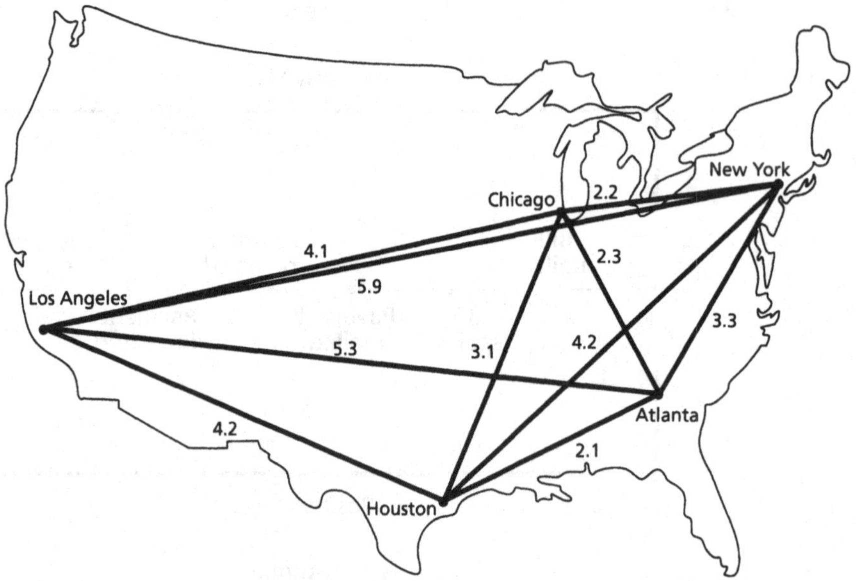

Source: K. V. Smith, *Guide to Working Capital Management,* New York: McGraw-Hill, 1979.

deposits the checks in a local bank and periodically transfers funds from there to the principal or concentration bank. It can do this electronically from one bank to another by a wire transfer, so the delay at this point of the process is negligible.

With a **lock box system,** customers mail their payments to a post office box near their homes. The firm arranges with local banks to collect the payments, credit them to a local bank account as quickly as possible, and report the transactions to the home office.

Evaluating Concentration Banking and Lock Box Systems

To see how to evaluate concentration banking or lock box cash management systems, let us continue our example of Sears. We assumed that sales average $10 million per day, that the current collection period is 82 days, and that customers make all payments to the home office in Chicago. Suppose Sears can establish a lock box system for an initial payment of $4,000,000 and a yearly fee of $1 million. This will decrease the collection period by 1.5 days. As another alternative, Sears is considering a concentration banking arrangement that requires an initial payment of $6 million and a yearly fee of $1.5 million. This more expensive alternative will cut the collection period by 2.5 days. Which system, if either, should Sears choose?

The solution depends on a direct comparison of the costs with the benefits. In both cases, the benefits are the reduction in the collection period and the freeing of cash for other uses. Since the lock box system reduces the collection period by 1.5 days, at a sales level of $10 million per day it will free $15 million for other uses. Assuming an interest rate of 12 percent, these funds can generate an annual revenue of $15,000,000 × 0.12 = $1,800,000. Similarly, the concentration banking system will free $25 million, which can produce an annual revenue of $25,000,000 × 0.12 = $3,000,000.

The annual cost of the lock box system is the foregone interest on the initial fee of $4 million plus an annual expense of $1 million, or $4,000,000 × 0.12 + $1,000,000 = $1,480,000. For the concentration banking scheme, the costs are the foregone interest on the initial fee of $6 million and a yearly expense of $1.5 million, or $6,000,000 × 0.12 + $1,500,000 = $2,220,000.

We can now compare the annual benefits and the costs of each system:

	Benefit	Cost	Net Annual Benefit
Lock Box	$1,800,000	$1,480,000	$320,000
Concentration Banking	$3,000,000	$2,220,000	$780,000

Since the concentration banking scheme gives a greater net annual benefit, the management of Sears should favor it over the lock box system.

ADVANTAGES OF DELAYING PAYMENTS

Just as collecting funds early has an advantage for a company, so does delaying payments. Both strategies let the firm use cash longer to earn a return. Therefore, most firms consciously delay payments as long as they can, without aggravating their suppliers.

Firms should never pay their debts early and, within reason, it may actually be best to pay somewhat late. There are definite costs to being a perpetual late payer, however. These costs might include a bad credit rating and suppliers' unwillingness to make shipments. Whether firms should actually pay late as a matter of policy raises practical questions of whether the savings is worth the potential damage. It also raises ethical questions about whether it is right to systematically delay rightful payments to other parties.

A common technique for delaying payments is to use banks scattered over a wide location. Assume that a firm has bank accounts in both North Carolina and Oregon. With this strategy, the firm might pay a North Carolina supplier with a check drawn on an Oregon bank, since it normally takes longer for a check sent to a distant bank to clear. Part of this strategy also suggests that very small rural banks, which tend to be somewhat slower, might be best for increasing this portion of the float.

Clearly, regulating cash flow in and out of the firm's bank accounts is a major concern. Sometimes, however, firms find themselves with more cash than they really need, in which case they generally invest the temporary excess cash in marketable securities.

THE ROLE OF MARKETABLE SECURITIES

Cash earns no explicit return, so firms should maintain only necessary cash balances. However, cash needs are sometimes difficult to predict, so firms must have a means of securing cash on short notice. Unpredictability also implies that firms sometimes have excess cash available for short-term investment.

Marketable Securities as a Substitute for Cash

The great advantage of marketable securities is that the firm can convert them into cash immediately, yet they earn a rate of interest. Because of their quick convertibility into cash, marketable securities often serve as a substitute for cash. The firm can hold minimal levels of cash and can add to cash as needed by selling marketable securities.

Some firms employ an extensive policy of substituting marketable securities for cash by the use of zero balance accounts. As the name implies, a **zero balance account** is a checking account with no balance. Each day the firm totals all checks presented for payment against the account and transfers the amount to the account by selling marketable securities. Thus, it uses the securities as a substitute for cash, because it holds all funds in this form until the moment of payment.

Temporary Investment in Marketable Securities

Although marketable securities earn a higher return than cash, they typically provide a lower return than the firm can earn through investing in its own line of business. Therefore, firms usually do not wish to invest in marketable securities on a long-term basis. However, on frequent occasions these securities can be used as a short-term investment medium.

First, sales may be unexpectedly large, generating an unexpectedly large amount of cash, so the firm can invest the excess cash in marketable securities to earn some return. Second, the firm may have seasonal fluctuations in the amount of cash available. In such instances it will have the excess amount for only a short period, so it might invest the excess cash in marketable securities. Third, firms often know in advance that they will soon need a large amount of cash, for example, to repay a bank loan. To accumulate the necessary funds before the loan repayment, they can invest the partially collected funds in marketable securities on a short-term basis.

Types of Marketable Securities

Governments, banks, and industrial corporations all issue marketable securities, so corporations use them as both an investment medium and as a source of financing. Several major types of marketable securities are discussed below.

Treasury Bills   Treasury bills, or T-bills, are obligations of the U.S. Treasury issued with maturities of one year or less. The bills have a minimum denomination of $10,000 and go up in increments of $5,000. Because the U.S. government fully guarantees their payment, T-bills have the lowest risk and the lowest yields of all marketable securities.

Commercial Paper   Commercial paper consists of short term unsecured debt of the largest and most creditworthy firms. The initial maturity cannot exceed 270 days. The issuer sells the commercial paper at a price below the promised future payment, with the difference known as the **discount**.

Bankers' Acceptances   The bankers' acceptance is a money market instrument used mainly in the financing of international trade. A bankers' acceptance is a draft against a bank ordering the bank to pay some specified amount at a future date. When the bank accepts that obligation, and stamps the draft "accepted," it creates a bankers' acceptance. The bankers' acceptance can then trade as a marketable security.

Few firms are willing to ship goods abroad on open account, as they often do domestically. Firms in two different countries may not know each other and may not have strong measures of recourse against foreign companies who default on their debt. Therefore, banks act as intermediaries. Assume that a small U.S. firm wishes to import from a foreign supplier. It is much easier for the foreign supplier to trust a respected American bank than to trust the importer. The creation of a bankers' acceptance means that the bank promises to make the specified payment to the foreign supplier. Even if the importing American firm defaults, the bank still must pay. The original debt of the American importer still remains, so bankers' acceptances are normally "two-name paper," because both the bank and the importing firm are obligated to pay as promised. Because of this, a bankers' acceptance is a very safe security.

Certificates of Deposit   Banks raise funds mostly by accepting deposits. Another important form of bank borrowing is through certificates of deposit, or CDs. CDs may be either negotiable or non-negotiable. Individual investors often hold small CDs, and these are non-negotiable. Large CDs, of $100,000 or more, are negotiable and form an important part of the money market.

Eurodollars   A Eurodollar is a dollar-denominated bank deposit held in a bank outside the United States.[2] Many foreign banks issue Eurodollar CDs to attract dollar-denominated funds, and many investors prefer Eurodollar CDs to domestic CDs since Eurodollar CDs pay a somewhat higher rate because they are generally somewhat riskier than domestic CDs.

The greater risk arises because the foreign issuing banks face less regulation than U.S. banks and thus must pay more for their funds. Since they escape the cost of tighter regulation, they are also able to pay the higher rate the market demands. To a large extent, U.S. banking regulation created the Eurodollar market. The Federal Deposit Insurance Corporation (FDIC), an arm of the U.S. government, insures virtually all bank deposit accounts in the U.S., up to a maximum of $100,000 per account. The insured banks pay for this insurance. For banks outside the United States, the insurance requirements are normally less stringent, so foreign banks can escape some of this cost and pass it on to depositors.

---

[2]In addition to Eurodollars, one sometimes hears mention of Asian dollars and Petro dollars. As defined here, these would be components of the Eurodollar market as well. Asian dollars are dollar-denominated deposits held in Asian-based banks, while Petro dollars are dollar-denominated deposits generated by oil-producing countries.

Another feature of U.S. banking regulation helping to keep the Eurodollar market in business is the imposition of reserve requirements. U.S. banks must keep a certain percentage of their liabilities in the form of non-interest earning assets, such as vault cash. The higher the reserve requirement, the more restricted the bank is in the amount of funds it can lend. Reserve requirements for U.S. banks tend to be more stringent than those imposed on banks in other countries. Consequently, the cost of operating a foreign bank is often lower than it would be for a U.S. bank. These regulatory differences create important cost differences between U.S. banks and their foreign competitors, but they also create risk differences. Due to their higher risk levels, banks taking Eurodollar deposits must pay a higher interest rate than domestic U.S. banks. However, because of the cost difference they are able to pay the higher rate and still make a profit.

Repurchase Agreements   Repurchase agreements, or "repos," arise when one party sells a security to another party with an agreement to buy it back at a specified future time and at a specified price. The difference between the sale and repurchase price defines the implicit interest rate. Repos are useful mainly for very short-term financing. In fact, most repo agreements are for just one day, and are called "overnight repos."

By buying a security with a commitment to resell it the next day at a slightly higher price, a corporation can put its excess cash to work. The desire for this kind of transaction has led to the creation of the repo market. Most of the securities used in the repo market are U.S. government securities.

One good source of information about current rates on marketable securities is the column "Money Rates," which appears daily in *The Wall Street Journal*. Figure 14.7 presents this column, which gives a good idea of the kinds of yield differences that prevail among these securities, reflecting their risk differences.

SUMMARY

This chapter first examined the management of one of the most important kinds of working capital – inventory. Inventory represents a considerable investment of funds. Depending on the type of inventory, the benefits may be the smooth running of the production process or the enhancement of sales. Ordering and carrying costs make up the total cost of the inventory.

Much of inventory management focuses on gaining information about the state of the inventory and minimizing the cost of maintaining a given level. This chapter reviewed some simple inventory management techniques as well as a formal inventory management model called the economic order quantity (EOQ) model.

The chapter also focused on the management of cash and its near substitute, marketable securities. Essentially, firms hold cash because of the great convenience it offers in making payments and avoiding default on the firm's obligations. Because cash offers no explicit return, firms try to hold as little cash as possible. The chapter presented the Baumol model for determining the optimal cash balance. In essence, this model is the same as the EOQ model, because cash is simply an inventory of money.

Since a firm can invest excess cash, it has a strong motivation to collect cash quickly and to pay it slowly. Various techniques exist to manage this cash flow, including concentration banking, lock boxes, remote banking facilities, and zero balance accounts.

FIGURE 14.7
Rates for Marketable Securities

MONEY RATES

Tuesday, March 28, 1995

The key U.S. and foreign annual interest rates below are a guide to general levels but don't always represent actual transactions.

PRIME RATE: 9%. The base rate on corporate loans posted by at least 75% of the nation's 30 largest banks.

FEDERAL FUNDS: 6³/16% high, 6% low, 6¹/16% near closing bid, 6³/16% offered. Reserves traded among commercial banks for overnight use in amounts of $1 million or more. Source: Prebon Yamane (U.S.A.) Inc.

DISCOUNT RATE: 5¹/4%. The charge on loans to depository institutions by the Federal Reserve Banks.

CALL MONEY: 7³/4%. The charge on loans to brokers on stock exchange collateral. Source: Dow Jones Telerate Inc.

COMMERCIAL PAPER placed directly by General Electric Capital Corp.: 5.95% 30 to 44 days; 5.96% 45 to 59 days; 5.99% 60 to 94 days; 6.02% 95 to 110 days; 6.07% 111 to 149 days; 6.08% 150 to 179 days; 6.10% 180 to 270 days.

COMMERCIAL PAPER: High-grade unsecured notes sold through dealers by major corporations: 6.07% 30 days; 6.09% 60 days; 6.12% 90 days.

CERTIFICATES OF DEPOSIT: 5.33% one month; 5.44% two months; 5.55% three months; 5.80% six months; 6.07% one year. Average of top rates paid by major New York banks on primary new issues of negotiable C.D.s, usually on amounts of $1 million and more. The minimum unit is $100,000. Typical rates in the secondary market: 6.10% one month; 6.21% three months; 6.40% six months.

BANKERS ACCEPTANCES: 5.99% 30 days; 6.02% 60 days; 6.05% 90 days; 6.08% 120 days; 6.11% 150 days; 6.14% 180 days. Offered rates of negotiable, bank-backed business credit instruments typically financing an import order.

LONDON LATE EURODOLLARS: 6¹/8% - 6% one month; 6³/16% - 6¹/16% two months; 6¹/4% - 6¹/8% three months; 6⁵/16% - 6³/16% four months; 6³/8% - 6¹/4% five months; 6⁷/16% - 6⁵/16% six months.

LONDON INTERBANK OFFERED RATES (LIBOR): 6¹/8% one month; 6¹/4% three months; 6⁷/16% six months; 6¹¹/16% one year. The average of interbank offered rates for dollar deposits in the London market based on quotations at five major banks. Effective rate for contracts entered into two days from date appearing at top of this column.

FOREIGN PRIME RATES: Canada 9.75%; Germany 5.05%; Japan 3%; Switzerland 5.62%; Britain 6.75%. These rate indications aren't directly comparable; lending practices vary widely by location.

TREASURY BILLS: Results of the Monday, March 27, 1995, auction of short-term U.S. government bills, sold at a discount from face value in units of $10,000 to $1 million: 5.84%, 13 weeks; 5.80%, 26 weeks.

FEDERAL HOME LOAN MORTGAGE CORP. (Freddie Mac): Posted yields on 30-year mortgage commitments. Delivery within 30 days 8.55%, 60 days 8.59%, standard conventional fixed-rate mortgages; 6.375%, 2% rate capped one-year adjustable rate mortgages. Source: Dow Jones Telerate Inc.

FEDERAL NATIONAL MORTGAGE ASSOCIATION (Fannie Mae): Posted yields on 30 year mortgage commitments (priced at par) for delivery within 30 days 8.55%, 60 days 8.61%, standard conventional fixed rate-mortgages; 7.450, 6/2 rate capped one-year adjustable rate mortgages. Source: Dow Jones Telerate Inc.

MERRILL LYNCH READY ASSETS TRUST: 5.51%. Annualized average rate of return after expenses for the past 30 days; not a forecast of future returns.

Source: *The Wall Street Journal,* March 29, 1995.

Because cash offers no explicit return, firms try to keep excess cash invested in marketable securities. This chapter also reviewed the different types of marketable securities that are available for investment, including Treasury bills, commercial paper, bankers' acceptances, certificates of deposit, Eurodollars, and repurchase agreements.

QUESTIONS

1. What are the three basic kinds of inventory?
2. Assume that your firm is a furniture manufacturer. What kinds of raw material inventories are you likely to have? What would happen to the firm if it cut its raw materials inventory to zero?
3. For the furniture manufacturer, what kinds of goods are in the work-in-process inventory? Could this type of inventory be eliminated?

4. What kinds of firms have little or no finished goods inventory?
5. What are the benefits of carrying an item in inventory?
6. What are the costs of carrying an item in inventory?
7. How do carrying costs behave as the order size increases?
8. How do ordering costs behave as the order size increases?
9. In the EOQ model, what is the value of the slope of the carrying cost line?
10. By what factor does the EOQ change if a firm's sales quadruple?
11. By what factor does the EOQ change if the unit purchase price doubles and, as a result, sales are reduced in half?
12. What are the three types of cash balances that firms hold?
13. What is the cost of holding cash as an asset?
14. In the Baumol model, by what factor does the average cash balance change if the annual cash needs, T, increase by a factor of 3?
15. Would a firm be better off to collect $100,000 in an accounts receivable one day earlier or to pay an account payable of $100,000 one day later? Is there a difference?
16. What is the difference between positive and negative float?
17. If you are responsible for cash management, would you prefer that your firm deal with a firm that has a longer or shorter collection period? Explain.
18. What is the difference between a concentration banking system and a lock box system?
19. How can marketable securities act as a substitute for cash?
20. Why are there so many different kinds of marketable securities?
21. If you had extra cash that your firm would not need for 90 days, would you consider investing it in Treasury bills or in a repurchase agreement? What factors would you need to consider?
22. There is a close correspondence between the EOQ and the Baumol models. Is this a coincidence? Explain.
23. While the EOQ and Baumol models are similar, the EOQ model considers the purchase price, P, of the inventory good, but the Baumol model does not seem to consider a corresponding variable. Is this true? Explain.
24. In the Baumol model, what is the value of the slope of the holding cost line?

PROBLEMS

Use this information to solve problems 1–12. Your firm is a microcomputer dealer, purchasing micros for $1,000 each. The cost of storing the micro in inventory is $100 per year. This does not include the financing cost of 12 percent. Placing an order costs $500, and the firm sells 900 computers per year.

1. What is the dollar cost of carrying a computer for one year?
2. What is the percentage cost of carrying a computer for one year?
3. If your firm orders 10, 50, 75, or 100 computers at a time, what will be the total ordering cost for a year's worth of sales?

4. If your firm orders 10, 50, 75, or 100 computers at a time, what will be the total carrying cost per year?

5. With an order size of 10, 50, 75, or 100 computers, what will be the total inventory cost per year?

6. From the preceding calculations, what can you determine about the best order size?

7. Graph the carrying cost of inventory relative to the order quantity for order quantities of 10, 50, 75, and 100 computers.

8. Graph the ordering cost of inventory relative to the order quantity for order quantities of 10, 50, 75, and 100 computers.

9. Graph the total cost of inventory relative to the order quantity for order quantities of 10, 50, 75, and 100 computers.

10. Using the EOQ developed in this chapter, compute the optimal order size.

11. Assume in our computer example that the ordering cost rises from $500 to $750 per order. How should that affect the economic order quantity? Compute the EOQ to confirm your hypothesis.

12. If the carrying cost drops to 10 percent, how should that affect the EOQ? Compute the EOQ to confirm your hypothesis.

13. Assume that interest rates are 12 percent and a firm collects $1 million 15 days earlier than it would otherwise. What is the value of this early collection?

14. Your firm owes $1 million to a supplier. You could pay it now or you could wait for 15 days. If interest rates are 12 percent per year, what is the value of waiting?

15. Compare your answers to the two previous problems. What does this indicate about the relative value of early collection and slow payment?

16. Firms sometimes use messengers to deliver and to collect payments. Your firm must make a payment of $500,000 in five days. Interest rates are 10 percent, and there are two ways of making the payment. First, you could mail it, but because mail times are uncertain you must mail it today to be sure it is there on time. However, you expect it to be there in two days. Second, you could wait four days and send it by overnight delivery for $20. Which should you choose? What is the expected savings of your alternative?

17. Your firm collects $10 million per year. If interest rates are 6 percent, what is the value of speeding your collections by one day?

18. Again assume that your firm collects $10 million per year and that interest rates are 6 percent. A bank is trying to sell you a cash management system. A lock box system will cost $20,000 per year, but should speed your accounts receivable by three days on average. What would be the savings (or extra cost) of adopting the lock box system?

19. With $10 million in collections per year and interest rates of 6 percent, would your firm be interested in paying $100,000 per year for a concentration banking system that would speed your collection of accounts receivable by five days? What would be the extra savings or cost?

20. Compare the lock box and concentration banking alternatives of the two previous problems. Which is preferable? Why?

21. For a large retailer, credit sales are typically $1,500,000 per day and the collection period is 31 days. What is the average level of accounts receivable?

22. Assume that you can reduce the average level of accounts receivable by $1 million for your firm and interest rates are 11 percent. What is the annual revenue that can be generated by these funds?

23. You owe $4,000 in taxes on your house, and they are due on December 31. However, if you pay in November you will receive a 1 percent discount. If you pay in October, you will receive a 2 percent discount. What specific days should you consider as possible payment dates?

24. For the house tax problem, when should you pay if you are able to earn 11 percent per year on your funds? In this case, what is the cost (or benefit) of paying in October?

25. Again, for the tax on your house, when should you pay if you can earn 15 percent per year on your funds? What is the cost of paying on the 15th of the month instead of the 31st?

26. You are a heavy credit card user, charging an average of $1,000 per month, but you always pay your monthly bill in full to avoid interest payments. Assuming you can earn 1 percent per month on your money, what would be the advantage of sending one payment ten days later than you normally do, but early enough to be on time?

27. Interest rates are 15 percent per year, and you have an account with a $500,000 balance that earns no interest. Your banker wants to talk to you about a zero balance account instead. What is the largest fee per year that you would consider for such an account?

28. Your firm uses the Baumol model to determine the optimal cash balance. The interest rate, r, is 10 percent, the fixed cost, F, of acquiring new cash is $30 per transaction, and the total annual cash needs are $2 million. Construct a table showing the holding costs, the transaction costs, and the total costs for $20,000, $25,000, ... , $45,000. Based on these numbers, give a close estimate of the maximum cash the firm should hold. Compare this estimate to the actual value found from the Baumol formula.

29. If a firm acquires $20,000 in cash each time it transacts, the holding costs are $2,000, and the transaction costs are $3,000. Under optimal conditions, find the average amount of cash, assuming the firm uses the Baumol model.

30. New York hotel queen Leona Helmsley paid the IRS $42,065,000 for personal income taxes on income she and her husband, Harry, earned in 1989. Helmsley said the IRS did not cash the check for 13 days. If interest rates at the time were 7.5 percent, how much interest did the IRS lose for procrastinating?

Chapter 15

Accounts Receivable Management

OVERVIEW

In this chapter we focus on the management of accounts receivable as we continue our discussion of techniques for managing working capital. Accounts receivable are funds owed to the firm as a result of sales not yet collected. Accounts receivable arise naturally from the conduct of the firm's business. Essentially every sale the firm makes that is not for cash gives rise to an accounts receivable. Managers must decide to whom, and under what conditions, the firm should extend credit. The management of accounts receivable includes the various collection procedures for customers who do not pay promptly.

THE MANAGEMENT OF ACCOUNTS RECEIVABLE

Any sale that a firm makes without receiving immediate payment generates an accounts receivable. In general, selling firms prefer immediate payment, but it is often impossible to avoid accounts receivable. Customary practice requires firms to ship goods and allows the customer to pay later. In such cases firms will find it very difficult to demand immediate payment. Along the same lines, allowing a customer to defer payment for some period is often necessary to secure a sale.

The total amount the firm invests in accounts receivable depends on the annual credit sales, S, and on the average collection period (ACP) as follows:

$$\text{Accounts receivable} = \frac{S}{365} \times \text{ACP} \tag{15.1}$$

For example, suppose a firm has annual credit sales of $730,000 and allows its customers to pay in 30 days. This firm must make an investment in accounts receivable equal to:

$$\text{Accounts receivable} = \frac{\$730,000}{365} \times 30 = \$2,000 \times 30 = \$60,000$$

To understand why the firm's accounts receivable investment must be $60,000, suppose the firm starts operating today. Since the firm sells $2,000 on credit every day and customers take 30 days to pay, after 30 days the firm will have a total of $60,000 in its accounts receivable. On day 31, and every day thereafter, the firm sells another $2,000 on credit, but the accounts receivable level does not increase beyond $60,000 because the first day's credit customers pay the $2,000 they owed. As a result, the new credit sales exactly offset the payment of the accounts due, and the accounts receivable level remains stable at $60,000, as long as the credit sales level does not change. This process is illustrated in figure 15.1.

Because the firm makes a significant investment by extending credit to a customer, the firm needs a credit policy to control the accounts receivable level. A **credit policy** is the set of principles that govern the extension of credit to customers. It must address three related issues. First, to whom will credit be granted? Through its **credit standards** the firm specifies the conditions that customers must meet before being granted credit. Second, for how long will credit be granted? The **credit period** is the time for which the firm grants credit. Third, what actions will be taken against customers who abuse credit? The **collections policy** is a set of guidelines that specifies the actions to take against delinquent accounts.

Credit Standards

In granting credit a firm takes a risk because there is some probability that the customer will not pay. In setting credit standards, the problem is to grant credit to the right customers, even though the firm lacks complete information about them. The initial tendency is to

FIGURE 15.1
Buildup Process for Accounts Receivable

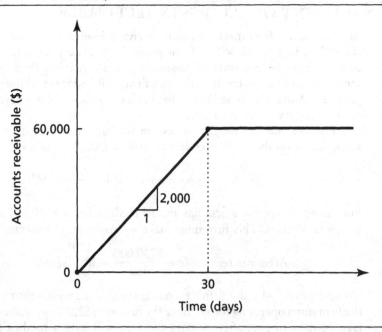

be very rigorous in applying high standards. If the firm restricts credit to those customers whom it considers absolutely safe, it will not obtain many potentially valuable customers. Such a severe policy may result in lost sales and lower profits. At the other extreme, if the firm sets its standards too loosely, it grants credit to many customers who will not pay, and it will incur losses.

As usual in finance, the problem is one of balancing the benefit of additional sales against the cost of increasing bad debts. In principle, the firm must choose standards that maximize the difference between benefits and costs. This principle is clear, but the difficult task is to find the right set of credit standards.

Of course, the firm will grant credit to some customers and deny it to others, basing this decision on the probability that the customer will or will not pay. Again, it is not necessary or even convenient to be exceedingly strict in this matter. Some firms can afford to be more lenient than others, depending on the product they sell, their cost of money, and the credit period allowed.

To understand how these variables affect the firm's decision to grant credit, consider a customer who purchases a product worth S dollars that the firm acquired for C dollars. The firm's cost of money is r percent per year, and the customer is allowed to pay T days after the purchase date. If each customer has a probability p of paying the S dollars, and probability $(1 - p)$ of not paying at all at the end of the T days, then the expected revenue at the end of the credit period is:

$$E(\text{Revenue}) = S \times p + 0 \times (1 - p) = S \times p$$

To obtain this expected revenue per customer, the firm must invest C dollars today. In addition, the firm foregoes the interest on the C dollars for the T days of the credit period. This foregone interest equals $CrT/365$. As with any investment, the firm expects the benefits of the decision to exceed its costs, that is, the following relationship must hold:

$$-C\left(1 + \frac{rT}{365}\right) + Sp > 0$$

This expression can be solved for the probability of payment, p, that is required to make the decision profitable for the firm:

$$p > \left(\frac{C}{S}\right)\left(1 + \frac{rT}{365}\right) \tag{15.2}$$

Inequality 15.2 provides valuable insight into the main factors that determine the firm's credit-granting decision. It implies that only customers deemed to have a sufficiently high probability of payment will be allowed credit. Since the right hand side of the inequality contains firm specific variables, different companies will adopt different standards. For example, inequality 15.2 states that a firm with a higher cost as a percentage of sales, C/S, will be stricter in granting credit than a firm with a lower value of C/S. This makes sense because a firm with slim profit margins cannot afford to have too many of its credit customers default. This explains why most supermarkets are reluctant to grant any credit, given that they typically have small profit margins. Similarly, inequality 15.2 implies that the higher a firm's cost of money and the greater the credit period, the tougher the firm will be in granting credit. Thus, if interest rates increase in the economy, we can expect firms to tighten credit. We also find that firms such as banks that grant credit for long periods, say between 1 and 30 years, are much more careful in evaluating their potential customers than are those firms that expect to be paid in, say, 30 days.

EXAMPLE 1

Al wants to buy a washer and dryer on credit at Sears. The combined price of the machines is $S = \$800$, and their combined cost to Sears is $C = \$500$. Sears' cost of money is $r = 12$ percent, and the credit period is $T = 90$ days. If Sears believes that Al has a 60 percent probability of paying, should he be granted the credit?

According to inequality 15.2, Sears should grant credit to any customer with a minimum probability of payment of 64.35 percent, as shown below:

$$p > \left(\frac{\$500}{\$800}\right)\left(1 + \frac{0.12 \times 90}{365}\right) = 64.35\%$$

Since Al's probability of payment does not meet this minimum standard, Sears should deny him credit.

Information and Credit Standards   We have seen that firms allow credit based on the perceived probability that the customer will pay. To estimate this probability and make better credit decisions, firms gather information on prospective credit customers. Information is costly to obtain, so firms must also weigh the benefits of gathering information against its costs. For example, magazine publishers normally grant credit to subscribers without gathering any information on their creditworthiness. Why? Because the magazine and the subscription bill are sent at about the same time, so management can discover quite quickly which customers will not pay. The only risk exposure is the cost of a few magazines. If gathering credit information on subscribers costs more than the amount the firm is risking by granting the credit, it clearly does not pay to obtain the information.

If the amounts involved are large and credit is likely to be granted repeatedly, it may be advisable for a firm to gather information about a potential customer. Standard & Poor's, a major financial publisher, specializes in obtaining and selling such data. In addition to purchasing information, firms often ask for information directly from potential customers. For instance, it is not unusual to ask a credit applicant to provide a financial statement or to complete a questionnaire.

In many cases, particularly for consumer credit, firms use a **credit scoring model**, which is a statistically based equation that predicts future payment performance. The firm asks the potential customer to provide information about age, marital status, occupation, time at last residence, time at last job, income, home ownership, phone number, and so on. Each answer contributes to a total credit score. If the score is large enough, the firm grants credit.

Analyzing Credit   Because information gathering is costly, firms should gather only as much information as necessary to establish the probability of payment with a reasonable degree of accuracy. Figure 15.2 presents an example of how to conduct credit analysis at three different levels. First, if the applicant has a good credit history, the firm may grant

FIGURE 15.2
Sequential Credit Analysis

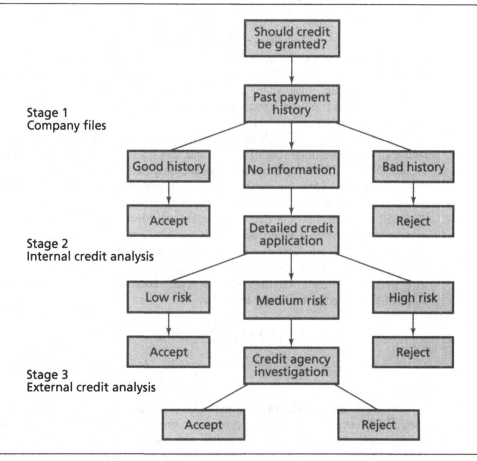

credit immediately. If there is no information on the customer, the decision requires more analysis so that the probability of payment may be estimated. With a bad credit history, the firm may reject the applicant without further ado. If there is no information, the firm may ask the applicant to fill out a detailed credit application. Once risk is assessed, the firm may accept low-risk applicants directly, reject high-risk applicants without further investigation, and decide to gather even more information on medium-risk customers, perhaps through a credit investigation by an outside agency. The firm takes this expensive step only after it exhausts less expensive means of determining the applicant's creditworthiness, and if the potential profit from the sale justifies the expense of the investigation.

The Credit Period

As part of the credit policy the firm also sets a credit period. Often the firm couples the choice of a credit period with the offer of a discount for early payment. For example, a firm may state its credit terms in the form "2/10; net 30," which means that it offers a 2 percent discount if payment is received within 10 days of the invoice date, and requires the customer to pay the full amount within 30 days if the discount option is not taken. Clearly, the firm offers the discount to induce prompt payment.

The choice of the credit period and the offer of a cash discount work together and should be chosen to give the desired effect. With credit terms of 2/10; net 30, the purchaser should pay either on day 10 and take the 2 percent discount or pay on day 30 the net amount. The selling firm offers a 2 percent discount to encourage the purchaser to pay 20 days early, but it must ask itself whether it is really worthwhile to accept 2 percent less to get the funds 20 days earlier.

Which customers are likely to pay early? To answer this question, consider a customer with a 10 percent annual cost of money that has made a credit purchase of $100 with 2/10; net 30 terms. If this customer foregoes the early payment option 10 days after purchase, it retains the use of $98 for another 20 days. By investing this $98 for another 20 days at a 10 percent annual rate, at the end of the period the customer will have $98[1 + 0.10 × (20/365)] = $98.54. Since at that time the payment must be $100, more than the amount of money the customer could make with the $98, foregoing the early payment is not a wise decision. It is not hard to see that only customers that earn a relatively high annual interest on their money should forego the early payment. In this example, all customers with a cost of money lower than 37.24 percent should take the 2 percent discount. This is seen by solving the following inequality:

$$\$98\left[1 + r\left(\frac{20}{365}\right)\right] < \$100$$

$$r < \left(\frac{2}{98}\right)\left(\frac{365}{20}\right) = 37.24\%$$

Since the vast majority of firms in the United States have a cost of money much lower than 37.24 percent, the discount provides a strong incentive for early payment. In fact, the incentive may be too strong, since it may result in an unnecessarily high cost to the firm. In this case, the cost to the firm of offering a discount for early payment is precisely 37.24 percent. In general, the annual interest rate, r, associated with credit terms of "d/n; net T" is equal to:

$$r = \left(\frac{d}{100 - d}\right)\left(\frac{365}{T - n}\right) \tag{15.3}$$

The intuition for equation 15.3 is as follows. The first term on the right-hand side represents the rate of interest the firm is giving to those customers who pay early. In the example discussed here, the 20 day rate is 2/98 = 2.04 percent. The second term represents the number of $(T - n)$ day periods contained in one year. For the example, the number of 20 day periods in a year is 365/20 = 18.25. The product of these two terms is the annual interest rate the firm pays by offering the early payment discount. Thus, in the example, the firm pays an annual interest rate of 2.04 percent × 18.25 = 37.23 percent, which is the answer we had before, save for rounding error.

In addition to the discount, the selling firm must also pay close attention to the credit period itself. Customary practice is important in choosing a credit period, as is competitive pressure within a given industry, but the seller must be aware of the cost of granting credit for differing periods.

For example, consider a company that currently offers its customers terms of 2/10; net 30 and is considering extending the terms to 2/10; net 60. With a credit period of 60 days, there are several likely effects. First, the more liberal time will attract some new customers, so the firm benefits from a sales increase. Second, the firm simultaneously incurs a cost from its present customers, because now they will wait until day 60 to pay, instead of day 30. Third, a higher proportion of customers will choose to pay the net amount instead of taking the discount by paying early because the implied rate of interest is substantially lower. For terms of 2/10; net 30, we have seen that the interest rate the firm offers is 37.24 percent. If the firm changes its terms to 2/10; net 60, the interest rate is reduced to 14.90 percent. Using equation 15.3, the calculation is:

$$r = \left(\frac{2}{98}\right)\left(\frac{365}{50}\right) = 14.90\%$$

Therefore, customers who earn rates greater than 14.90 percent will not take the discount.

COLLECTIONS POLICY

Every company will have, and should have, some difficulty with bad debt expenses. No matter how carefully the firm screens customers for creditworthiness, some bad credit risks will slip through. Furthermore, if a firm could make its credit standards so severe that it has no bad debt loss, it would be making a mistake, because it must be turning away some potentially good customers. Since some credit-granting decisions turn out to be mistakes, every firm must plan to collect late accounts.

The accounts receivable aging schedule is one technique the firm may use in determining when to proceed with collection of past due accounts. The **aging schedule** classifies accounts according to the amount of time they have been outstanding. Table 15.1 illustrates an aging schedule for a hypothetical customer.

If this customer received a credit period of 60 days, the account has $75 overdue. However, it appears that this customer, although somewhat slow in paying, may intend to pay in full, as suggested by the zero balance of any purchases made more than 90 days ago. Perhaps the firm should send a mild letter reminding the customer to pay soon. This is an inexpensive option and, in this case, it is likely to be effective.

TABLE 15.1
Aging Schedule for a Hypothetical Customer

Age (days)	Amount ($)
0–30	360
31–60	280
61–90	75
>90	0

Any collection effort is costly, so the problem is choosing the correct effort level. As the effort and expense increase, bad debt losses should decrease. In principle, the firm should incur these expenses up to the point that the benefits from the effort just equal the costs. One potential cost is driving away customers who could be profitable, even if they are slow payers.

To control expenses and to avoid antagonizing customers, firms usually employ a sequence of steps of increasing severity. These steps go from the simple letter or telephone call to the very expensive legal action.

Letters and Telephone Calls

The first action the firm usually takes to collect a late account is to send a letter. Usually the first letter is extremely polite and merely tells the customer that a payment is past due. It might even apologize in case the customer has already sent the payment. If this first step is unsuccessful, the firm sends additional mild letters. If these do not produce the desired payment, later ones adopt increasingly harsher tones, eventually confronting the customer with the possibility of a collection agency or legal action. At this point, many late customers choose to send the payment.

If letters fail to produce results, the firm may call the customer directly. Calls, particularly to individuals at their place of employment, often produce results. In general, calls are likely to be more effective for individuals than for firms. However, some laws limit the kinds of calls that can be made; for example, late-night harassment is not allowed.

Collection Agencies

Collection agencies are firms specializing in collecting overdue accounts. For a percentage of the amount they obtain, they agree to take over the attempt to collect money due. They typically use letters, telephone calls, and even personal visits. Collection agencies have a fearsome reputation with many customers. Therefore, turning an account over to a collection agency can bring quick results. Also, collection agencies can threaten to damage the late payer's credit rating. However, the firm must be aware that turning an account over to a collection agency usually means the permanent loss of a customer.

Legal Action

As a final step, the firm can employ, or threaten to employ, legal action to collect overdue accounts. Calls from a lawyer or the serving of legal papers can often bring payment from even very stubborn late payers. Legal action is essentially the final and most expensive collection technique available to the firm. Because of its expense, most firms use it only for large debts.

SUMMARY

This chapter examined the management of accounts receivable. Accounts receivable are almost certain to arise in the ordinary conduct of the firm's business. Because they represent an investment of funds and an extension of credit, these assets must be managed carefully.

In particular, the firm must develop a credit policy that includes setting credit standards, developing policies about the credit period, and employing methods to collect past due accounts.

QUESTIONS

1. If a firm has no explicit credit policy, does that mean it will have no accounts receivable?
2. What are the three components of a credit policy?
3. A manager for your company is arguing that the firm should extend credit only to those customers that are 100 percent sure to pay as promised. Is this reasonable? Explain.
4. In your firm's discussion about its new credit policy, you suggest that the firm should acquire complete information on the creditworthiness of customers seeking credit. Is this reasonable? Explain what attacks might be made on this position.
5. What is a credit scoring model? Explain how it might be used in making decisions about automobile financing.
6. If a firm expresses its credit period as 1/10; net 90, what does that mean?
7. In question 6, what is the credit period?
8. If a firm extends its credit period, but keeps everything else the same, what should happen to credit sales? What should happen to accounts receivable?
9. If the average collection period increases by 10 percent and the daily credit sales simultaneously decrease by 10 percent, what happens to the firm's total investment in accounts receivable?
10. If the average collection period increases by 10 percent and the daily credit sales simultaneously increase by 10 percent, what happens to the firm's total investment in accounts receivable?
11. If the average collection period increases by one day and the daily credit sales simultaneously decrease by $1,000, what happens to the firm's total investment in accounts receivable?
12. Explain the intuition behind equation 15.1.
13. Explain the intuition behind equation 15.3.

PROBLEMS

1. The LousyWord Corporation has annual credit sales of $2 million. The cost of its word processing software is $70, and its selling price is $230. What is LousyWord's accounts receivable level if the average collection period is 65 days?
2. The Empty Nest Corporation classifies customers according to the probability, p, that they will pay their accounts receivable. The firm sells chocolates, which carry a fat margin. In fact, the cost of chocolates is only 40 percent of the sales price. Empty Nest allows customers 90 days to pay, and has an annual

cost of money of 15 percent. To which customers, in terms of their probability of payment, should the firm deny credit?

3. Pecatoribus, Inc., determines that it will grant credit to all customers with a probability of payment of at least 70 percent. The firm earns a 35 percent contribution margin on its sales, and allows 120 days to pay. What rate of interest does the firm earn on its investments?

4. Lya's Wedding Cakes, Inc., provides 60-day credit to newlywed customers. However, believing that it is easier to collect before the honeymoon spell is over, Lya offers a 3 percent discount on the $400 cakes if payment is made 30 days after the wedding. If 40 percent of her customers pay early, and the rest pay in 60 days, what is Lya's investment in accounts receivable? Assume that Lya sells five cakes each day.

5. MicroMouse, Inc., offers credit terms of 1/10; net 30. Describe which customers will pay early, based on the customers' cost of money.

6. Chubby's Electric Supply sells on credit and 20 percent of the accounts receivable balance has an age between 0 and 30 days; 40 percent has an age between 31 and 60 days; and the rest has an age between 61 and 90 days. Given this limited information, what is your best estimate of Chubby's average collection period? Assume that daily sales are constant.

7. Lito Graph, Inc., is not sure whether to offer credit terms of 1/10; net 30 or 2/15; net 60. If Lito's objective is to entice as many customers as possible to pay early, which option should the firm choose?

8. A firm sells $1,000 on credit at the beginning of April. If it collects one fifth of this amount by the end of April, one-fifth of the remaining balance at the end of May, and so on, by what month will the $1,000 credit sales be totally collected?

9. A firm sells $1,000 on credit every day. If each customer takes 45 days to pay, how much does the firm invest in accounts receivable?

10. A firm sells $1,000 daily on credit during the first half of each month, and $2,000 daily during the second half of each month. If each customer takes 45 days to pay, describe the daily evolution of the level of accounts receivable for a typical month.

Chapter 16

Short-Term Financing

OVERVIEW

In the previous chapters focusing on working capital, we examined various kinds of assets. In this chapter, the focus turns to the various ways of financing the firm's working capital. In many cases, especially when working capital fluctuates seasonally, it is financed through short-term liabilities.

Short-term financing is important to all firms, but it becomes critically important when interest rates fluctuate. Often, short-term interest rates are lower than long-term rates, and this helps firms save money. Also, many firms have a varying need for financing and find it cheaper to use short-term financing during periods of peak demand. With such a strong need for short-term financing, it is not surprising that a wide variety of alternatives are available. Some of the opportunities arise spontaneously from the normal conduct of business, while others must be negotiated. This chapter explains how firms use short-term sources of financing.

THE RATIONALE FOR SHORT-TERM FINANCING

Historically, and particularly in recent years, interest rates have shown a strong tendency to fluctuate. Interest rates on both short-term financing sources and long-term financing sources vary together, with the former having greater volatility and generally being lower than the latter.

For a firm seeking long-term financing, corporate bonds form a major source. However, if interest rates are very high, issuing a long-term bond and promising to pay a high interest rate over that period can be expensive. Therefore, firms often use short-term financing to bridge the period of high interest rates. **Bridge financing** is the use of a short-term source to cover a temporary need.

Short-term financing also assists firms with seasonal needs. In preparation for an intense selling season, many firms build inventories beyond the normal level. After the sales period, the firms may find themselves holding an unusually high level of accounts receivable. This build-up requires extra financing until those accounts receivable are converted into cash. In retailing, for example, over 25 percent of annual sales frequently occur between Thanksgiving and Christmas. Rather than finance their pre-Christmas inventories with long-term sources, firms use short-term financing to bridge this period of high need.

Figure 16.1 schematically depicts the asset structure of a firm with fluctuating levels of working capital. At the base are the long-term assets, such as plant and equipment,

FIGURE 16.1
Firm Assets with Seasonal Fluctuations

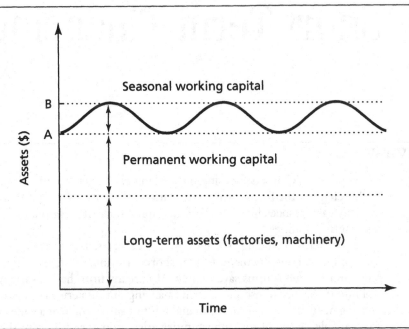

which are essentially constant through time. In addition it holds working capital, part of which is a permanent investment and is essential to the firm's operation. As we know, a certain level of cash, accounts receivable, and inventory is required for conducting normal business. The remaining working capital exhibits seasonal fluctuations and is the part that should be financed with short-term sources.

The firm must finance all of the assets shown in figure 16.1, but it has a wide variety of strategies. For example, it can choose between long-term and short-term sources. It may be tempting to use a high proportion of short-term financing because it is often cheaper, but this strategy involves risk as well. For example, if the firm uses a three-month loan, it must renew that loan every three months. This raises the possibility that the firm might eventually be unable to secure the needed funds. Further, at renewal time the loan rate may increase, resulting in unexpectedly high interest expenses for the firm. As a result of these potential problems, a major financing decision is to set the mix between short-term and long-term financing.

A very conservative policy uses long-term financing for all assets. In this case, the firm would not face the potential embarrassment of having to secure short-term financing. This policy is represented in figure 16.1 by the financing level B. A more aggressive policy, designed to achieve a greater economy in financing cost, would be to finance all seasonal fluctuations of working capital with short-term sources. In this case, the amount of long-term financing is represented by point A.

In practice, very few firms follow the conservative strategy represented by point B. The two major reasons for this are that it is too expensive, and it ignores some of the cheap short-term sources that are readily available. For example, some sources arise spontaneously from the firm's normal operations. The main question becomes how much short-term financing to use. The answer depends largely on the firm's willingness to accept risk.

TRADE CREDIT

We have already noted that accounts receivable arise spontaneously in the conduct of business, because any credit sale generates a receivable. Whenever a firm has a receivable, it is extending credit to some other party. For every receivable that one firm has, the other party has an account payable of the same amount. Just as receivables arise spontaneously, so do accounts payable.

An account payable is generated from **trade credit**, which a firm receives when it buys a good or service without immediately paying cash. Because it did not pay cash, it has the use of funds on credit from the time it receives the good until it makes final payment.

The Cost of Trade Credit

The purchasing firm receives the offer of credit for up to 30 days when the credit terms are 2/10; net 30. However, it also receives the offer of a 2 percent discount for payment within 10 days of purchase. Should the purchasing firm pay early and take the discount, or should it take the entire 30-day financing? The decision depends on the actual percentage cost of taking the financing relative to the discount and how much the firm is willing to pay for its short-term financing.

As we saw in chapter 15, the firm may take the discount and pay on day 10, or it can forego the discount and wait until day 30 to make the payment. Therefore, the firm will pay either on day 10 and take the 2 percent discount or will pay the full amount on day 30. If it pays on day 30, the firm is essentially paying 2 percent for the use of the funds between day 10 and day 30. If the full amount owed is $100, the firm has the option of using $98 for 20 days, and then paying $100. In essence, the firm receives a $98 loan for which it must pay $2 interest after 20 days. This corresponds to an interest rate of 2/98 = 2.04 percent over this 20-day period. Since there are 365/20 = 18.25 periods of 20 days in one year, the annualized cost of foregoing the discount and taking the trade credit is 37.2 percent:

$$\text{Cost of Trade Credit} = \frac{2}{100 - 2} \times \frac{365}{20} = 37.2\%$$

Unless the firm is willing to pay 37.2 percent for its short-term funds, it should take the discount and pay on the tenth day. In general, if the terms of the sale are d/n; net T, then the cost of trade credit is given by:

$$\text{Cost of Trade Credit} = \frac{d}{100 - d} \times \frac{365}{T - n} \qquad (16.1)$$

In most circumstances, taking the discount is better, unless short-term rates are very high or the firm direly needs short-term financing and is unable to secure a cheaper financing source. In any event, the manager should be aware that foregoing the discount for early payment usually carries a very high cost. We can illustrate this point by considering the following credit terms and the cost of trade credit that they imply.

Credit Terms	Annual Cost of Trade Credit
2/10; net 30	37.2%
1/10: net 30	18.4%
2/10; net 45	21.3%
2/10; net 60	14.9%

Thus far we have seen that it is always wise to pay on either the last day of the discount period or the last day of the net period. Normally, it pays to take the discount, but this decision depends on the implied cost of trade credit relative to other sources of short-term financing. One other strategy requires consideration.

Stretching Accounts Payable

Some firms may not take the prompt payment discount and not pay the net amount by the due date. They may adopt a policy of stretching accounts payable, delaying payment beyond the credit period. In effect, this is a unilateral extension of the credit period against the wishes of the selling firm.

Consider a firm that buys goods on the terms of 2/10; net 30 and pays the full amount on day 90. In doing so, it violates the credit terms offered by the supplying firm, but it receives financing for the period from day 10 to day 90 by foregoing the discount. For such a firm, the implied cost of trade credit is 9.3 percent:

$$\text{Cost of Trade Credit} = \frac{2}{100 - 2} \times \frac{365}{90 - 10} = 9.3\%$$

Financing at a cost of 9.3 percent may be very attractive, but chronically paying late is certain to irritate suppliers. In extreme cases, the supplier may refuse to ship to the offending firm or require payment before shipping. The cost of bad relations with suppliers is difficult to quantify, but it is real.

In addition to the hidden costs of irritating the supplier, a policy of stretching accounts payable raises an ethical issue. By agreeing to the shipment, the purchasing firm accepts the credit terms offered by the supplier. A policy of stretching accounts payable violates that implicit contract.

ACCRUED EXPENSES

Accrued expenses provide another source of spontaneous short-term financing. Arising from the normal conduct of business, they are expenses that have been incurred but have not been paid. One of the largest is likely to be employees' accrued wages. For an employee paid at the end of the month for work performed during that month, the firm has the use of the wages for the entire month. Assuming that an employee earns $2,000 per month, on average the firm holds $1,000 of those wages each month. With interest rates of 12 percent, the firm can earn $120 per year on this employee's accrued wages. If the firm paid this same employee a biweekly wage of $1,000, it would only hold an average of $500 in accrued wages for this individual. Then it could earn only $60 per year on the accrued wages. The pattern of accrued wages over time for monthly and biweekly payment is shown graphically in figure 16.2.

For large firms, accrued wages constitute an important source of financing. For example, a firm that has 40,000 employees paid monthly with an average salary of $2,000 per month has the use of $40 million in accrued wages, on average. If it invests this average amount over one year at an interest rate of 12 percent, it will earn $4.8 million.

FIGURE 16.2
Accrued Wages with Monthly and Biweekly Payments

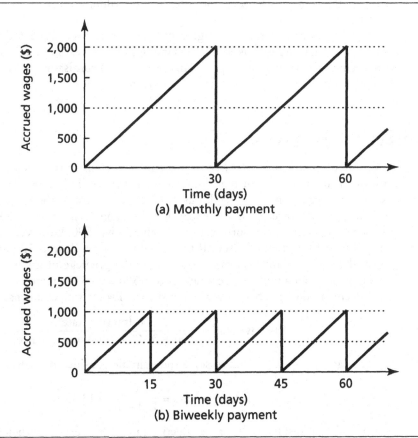

(a) Monthly payment

(b) Biweekly payment

Usually, accrued expenses are not subject to much managerial manipulation. Switching employees from biweekly to monthly pay would generate a larger amount of accrued wages, but may prove costly to the firm by irritating employees. Although these expenses confer a benefit to the firm and are a readily available source of financing, it is very difficult to increase them as a financing source.

UNSECURED SHORT-TERM BANK LOANS

An important negotiated source of short-term financing comes in the form of unsecured bank loans. An **unsecured loan** is a loan made on the good credit of the borrower, without the borrower offering any special security to the lender. By contrast, a **secured loan** is one in which the borrower gives the lender the right to seize certain assets if the borrower does not pay as promised.

To receive an unsecured loan from a bank, a firm must usually establish a good relationship with the bank by holding funds in the bank for checking and other purposes. Also, a secured loan may often precede a request for an unsecured loan. For example, the bank may finance some equipment, using the equipment itself to secure the loan. If the firm pays the loan satisfactorily, the bank may be willing to provide an unsecured loan in the future.

The borrower and the bank agree on the terms of an unsecured loan, that is, the amount, the time the loan is to be outstanding, the interest rate, and the exact payment terms. Once the two parties agree, they execute a **promissory note**, which is a legal document that specifies all the terms of the loan.

COMPENSATING BALANCES

Banks often require the borrower to maintain a portion of the loan amount on deposit with the bank in an account that does not earn interest. This deposit is a **compensating balance**. By requiring it, the bank raises the effective cost of the loan. For example, if a bank grants a borrower a one-year loan for $100 and requires that 10 percent be left as compensating balance, the borrower effectively receives $90. However, the borrower must still pay interest on the full $100. If the stated rate of the loan is 12 percent, then at the end of the year the borrower must pay $12 for the privilege of using $90 over one year. This represents an annual interest rate of $12/$90 = 13.33 percent.

In general, the effective rate of interest for a loan with a compensating balance is:

$$\text{Effective Rate} = \frac{\% \text{ Interest Rate}}{100 - \% \text{ Compensating Balance}} \qquad (16.2)$$

We can use equation 16.2 to solve the example considered earlier:

$$\text{Effective Rate} = \frac{12}{100 - 10} = 13.33\%$$

This calculation results in the same effective rate of interest found before.

THE LINE OF CREDIT

Unsecured bank loans can be an expensive source of short-term funds, so firms try to avoid them. However, they can be an extremely important source of funds when unanticipated short-term financing difficulties arise. If the need for funds is acute, most firms are glad to know that money is available.

Many firms get around the need to use bank loans by establishing a line of credit. A **line of credit** is a commitment by a bank to lend to a firm a certain amount of funds on demand. Thus the firm knows that it can borrow a given amount any time it needs. Because this is a valuable service, and because it is costly to have the funds readily available, banks charge a **commitment fee** for holding open a line of credit. Usually, the commitment fee is a percentage of the loan amount and is charged even if the customer does not borrow any money. Normally, it is in the order of 0.5 to 1 percent of the committed amount.

REVOLVING CREDIT AGREEMENTS

Often a bank extends a revolving credit agreement in which it makes some amount of funds available to the customer on a continuing basis. For example, if the line of credit under a revolving credit agreement is $1 million and the firm borrows $800,000, it still has guaranteed access to $200,000. If the firm repays $500,000, reducing its debt to $300,000, it has $700,000 available.

In most respects, this agreement is similar to bank credit cards for consumers. These cards, such as Visa and Mastercard, typically work like a revolving line of credit. The borrower cannot borrow more than the credit line limit, but is free to borrow up to that amount at any time. As the borrower repays earlier loans, more of the line of credit is available for future borrowing.

SECURED SHORT-TERM FINANCING

In addition to unsecured short-term borrowing, most firms have access to secured short-term financing. With a secured loan the borrower gives the lender a claim on some specific asset. The asset against which the lender has a claim is the **collateral** for the loan.

In some cases, the lender may actually take possession of the collateral until the borrower satisfies the terms of the loan. This is common if the collateral is transportable and can be stored, such as stocks or bonds. In other cases, legal documents provide evidence of the claim. To obtain a secured loan, a firm must be able to pledge specific collateral of obvious value. Generally, this is either receivables or inventory.

Accounts Receivable

Because of the obvious value of receivables, firms can use them as a way to get funds immediately. They can use them in two basic ways: by pledging them as collateral, or by selling them outright.

Pledging Accounts Receivable   Using accounts receivable as collateral for a loan is pledging them. To do this the firm must find a lender who can evaluate the quality of the receivables. Because the quality depends on the likelihood that the debtors will pay when promised, the lender is typically a financial institution with a credit department that can judge the risks associated with the receivables. It is helpful if the firm has had a continuing relationship with the lender, as this increases the likelihood that the lender is already familiar with the quality of the borrower's receivables.

When the borrowing firm pledges its receivables, it gives the lender a specific claim against those assets. It must also sign a promissory note, with the receivables acting as an extra guarantee that the funds will be repaid. Also, the borrower remains liable for the full payment of the loan even if it gives the receivables to the lender.

Pledging receivables can be a continuing process, with the firm presenting evidence of the receivables to the lender and receiving new funds periodically. The lender will lend only a fraction of the value of the receivables, thus ensuring that it will eventually receive full payment.

Although the lender has a claim on the receivables, ownership remains with the borrower. Only if the firm fails to pay on the loan as promised does the lender have the right to seize the collateral. Normally, a loan against the receivables is done on a **nonnotification basis**. That is, the lender does not inform the party owing the receivables that these have been pledged. If the loan is made on a **notification basis**, the lender informs the party owing the receivables that the borrowing firm has pledged the receivables, and that the borrower should send the payments directly to the lender.

Factoring Accounts Receivable   The firm can receive cash for its receivables by selling, or factoring, them. The purchaser is the **factor**, usually a financial institution. Often a bank will make a loan with the receivables as collateral or will be willing to act as a factor and buy them.

In purchasing the receivables, the factor pays some percentage of their full amount. Because the asset is a receivable, factoring typically involves both a sale of an asset and a loan. The factor receives title to the receivables and this is a transfer of an asset. Although the firm expects to collect the receivables in the future, the factor pays immediate cash to the firm. Therefore, the transaction also involves aspects of a loan. The difference between the receivables due and the amount the factor pays for them depends on the quality of the receivables, the cost the factor expects to incur in collecting the receivables, the time until the receivables are due, and the prevailing interest rate.

In a factoring arrangement, a firm can sell receivables on a **nonrecourse basis**. In this type of factoring agreement, the factor buys the receivables outright and then collects them. Failure to collect them means a loss for the factor. With a nonrecourse agreement, the factor cannot demand any payment from the firm in the event that an account receivable is not paid. Thus, the factor bears all the risk of collecting the receivables.

The firm can also sell receivables on a **recourse basis**, in which case it remains responsible for the receivables and, in effect, guarantees their collection. If the factor has difficulty collecting, it may have recourse to the firm to demand payment, so the firm continues to bear the collection risk. Naturally, because of the different risks involved, there is a difference in the price the factor is willing to pay for the receivables, depending on whether the agreement is on a recourse or nonrecourse basis.

Inventory Loans

The attractiveness of inventory as collateral for a loan depends on how much security it gives the lender. If it can be converted into cash easily, it is more valuable as collateral than a less liquid inventory. Similarly, easily transportable inventory makes better collateral than inventory that is difficult to move. Finally, if it is easy to identify and control the inventory, it also makes better collateral. Because inventories are so diverse, there are several different ways to offer inventory as collateral.

Floating Lien   A **lien** is a claim against a set of assets. With a floating lien the borrowing firm gives the lender a general claim against an entire class of assets. In inventory financing, this might include all inventory, present and future. A floating lien usually secures a loan when the items in inventory have small individual value and cannot be identified easily. It is also useful when items are moving in and out of inventory very rapidly. For example, the maker of electronic components may have thousands of circuit boards in stock which cannot be identified individually. If these circuit boards are of little value individually and are going in and out of inventory rapidly, a floating lien would be the appropriate type of security agreement.

This example contrasts with that of a highway builder with heavy equipment, such as bulldozers, that are easy to identify by their serial numbers. Furthermore, the equipment usually remains in inventory and each machine has a high value, so it is worthwhile to identify each one specifically. For the highway builder, the floating lien would not be the best security arrangement.

As these differences indicate, a floating lien is a relatively weak guarantee from the lender's point of view. If the lien is on items of relatively small individual worth, and if the items are hard to identify and easily transportable, the lender has little ability to enforce a claim on them. When possible, it is usually preferable to use another method of securing inventory as collateral.

Trust Receipts   When inventory items have serial numbers or are otherwise identifiable, the firm can use a trust receipt to guarantee a loan. A trust receipt is an agreement under which the borrower holds the goods in inventory and immediately forwards any proceeds from the sale of the inventory to the lender.

Trust receipt financing is used extensively in the automotive industry, with the manufacturer acting as a lender to the dealer. The manufacturer knows that cars bearing certain serial numbers must be on the dealer's premises, or the dealer must be forwarding funds from the sale of the car to the manufacturer. Because it is easier to inspect and enforce the collateral agreement, trust receipt financing gives the lender a better form of security for an inventory loan than does a floating lien.

Warehouse Financing   Essentially, the greater control the lender has over inventory, the better the collateral value of the inventory. We have already seen that trust receipts provide the lender with better collateral than a floating lien. Of the prevailing kinds of collateral agreements for inventory financing, warehouse financing gives the lender the best collateral. The two basic types of warehouse financing agreements are field and terminal warehousing agreements.

Under a **field warehousing agreement** the borrowing firm keeps the pledged inventory at its own warehouse, but segregates it from the other inventories. A warehouse company working for the lender manages the segregation and then issues a **warehouse receipt** to verify that the pledged inventory resides in the warehouse and is stored separately. Only after the warehouse company issues the receipt does the lender advance funds. Furthermore, the warehouse company controls the pledged inventory and will not release it to the borrower until authorized to do so by the lender.

Compared with trust receipt financing, a field warehousing agreement gives the lender better control over the collateral because it is under the control of the warehouse company that acts as an agent of the lender. One drawback to this kind of financing is the lender's additional cost incurred by hiring the warehouse company.

In a field warehousing agreement the inventory pledged for the loan is still on the borrower's premises, even if it is under control of the warehouse company. The lender can have even more control over the inventory by taking the collateral away from the borrower's premises. Under a **terminal warehousing agreement** the lender places the pledged inventory in a warehouse owned and operated by a warehousing company. Once it goes into the warehouse, the warehouse company issues a receipt certifying that the specified goods are there. The lender then issues the loan funds to the borrower. The borrower cannot move the goods from the warehouse until the lender authorizes their removal. Thus the lender secures virtually complete control over the collateral. This kind of security agreement offers the most complete protection to the lender. In comparison with a floating lien, or even a trust agreement, the terminal warehouse agreement greatly increases the lender's safety. Not surprisingly, lenders are willing to lend a greater percentage of the value of the inventory the more thoroughly they control it.

COMMERCIAL PAPER

The largest and most creditworthy industrial firms and banking firms have access to another important source of short-term financing called **commercial paper**, which is short-term debt issued by corporations in the financial marketplace. Firms back commercial paper solely by the promise of the firm to pay. To escape the requirement of registering with the Securities and Exchange Commission, the maturity of the commercial paper cannot exceed 270 days. The issuer promises to pay the holder of commercial paper a given fixed amount on a certain future date. The commercial paper sells at a discount from that promised future payment. Financial companies tend to issue most of the commercial paper. Some of the particularly big issuers of commercial paper are the finance subsidiaries of American automakers (for example, General Motors Acceptance Corporation) and the major money center banks of New York (for example, Citibank). After the debacle of Penn Central's default on its commercial paper in the early 1970s, the market has been limited to only very good credit risks.

SUMMARY

Firms have alternative financing strategies available to them in choosing the right mix between long-term and short-term financing. Conservative firms use a high proportion of long-term financing, while aggressive firms place greater reliance on short-term financing.

Whatever their attitudes toward risk, almost all firms use some short-term financing. Some sources of short-term financing arise spontaneously from the normal conduct of business. These sources are accounts payable and accrued expenses. In addition, there are negotiated sources of financing, such as secured or unsecured loans. Commercial banks are a major source of unsecured loans. Because the loans are not secured, interest rates are often higher than the stated rate due to compensating balance requirements and commitment fees.

Secured short-term financing arises from the pledging of accounts receivable or inventories. Firms can convert accounts receivable into cash by pledging them as collateral for a loan or through factoring. When they do this on a recourse basis, they continue to bear the risk of collecting receivables. To avoid that risk, firms can factor their receivables on a nonrecourse basis.

Finally, firms can use their inventories as collateral to secure loans in several ways, for example, by pledging it as collateral under various warehousing arrangements. The choice of method depends on the nature of the inventory and the amount of control the borrower is willing to surrender to the lender. Generally, the more control the borrower surrenders, the larger the amount the lender will provide, and the lower the cost to the borrower.

QUESTIONS

1. Assume that short-term rates are almost always lower than long-term rates. Would you finance your firm entirely with short-term funds? Explain.
2. Explain the purpose of using short-term financing as a bridge in periods of high interest rates.
3. If a firm has seasonal financing requirements, why doesn't it merely secure enough long-term financing to meet its total needs?
4. In the chapter, we noted that foregoing discounts usually implied that the purchasing firm would be borrowing, in effect, at a very high rate. What does this choice of credit terms say about the selling firm?
5. How do accrued expenses form a source of financing for the firm?
6. University professors are almost always paid monthly, but their salary for the academic year can be paid over nine months or over 12 months. Which would you prefer? Why?
7. For short-term financing, would you expect the interest rate to be higher or lower for secured financing in comparison to unsecured financing?
8. How should the rate of interest on a short-term secured loan vary with the kind of goods offered as collateral? Specifically, would the liquidity of the security matter?
9. How are banks able to charge a commitment fee for a line of credit even though no credit has yet been extended? Should the bank be able to get away with this? Explain.
10. Explain why a MasterCard or Visa account is a type of revolving credit agreement.

11. When one party to an agreement has more information than the other, this condition is known as one of "asymmetric information." How does this concept apply to the factoring of receivables on a nonrecourse basis?

12. Pawn shops offer a source of secured financing. Explain how you would value the different types of collateral that might be offered to you as a pawnbroker. How would the amount you would be willing to lend vary with different types of collateral?

13. Is the operation of a pawn shop more like a field warehousing or terminal warehousing agreement? Explain.

PROBLEMS

1. You are considering credit terms of 2/15; net 45. What is the rate of interest implied by these terms?

2. What if the terms are 2/15; net 90?

3. Considering problems 1 and 2, what does this show about the relationship between the length of the credit period and the cost of trade credit?

4. For a fixed credit period of 60 days and a discount period of 10 days, calculate the implied cost of trade credit for discounts of 1, 2, 3, 4, and 5 percent.

5. Prepare a graph of the implied cost of trade credit calculated in problem 4.

6. For a fixed discount of 2 percent and a discount period of 10 days, calculate the implied cost of trade credit for credit periods of 30, 60, and 90 days.

7. Graph the relationship between the cost of trade credit and the credit period as calculated in problem 6.

8. For a fixed discount of 2 percent and a fixed credit period of 90 days, calculate the cost of trade credit for discount periods of 10, 20, 30, and 60 days.

9. Graph the relationship between the cost of trade credit and the discount period as calculated in problem 8.

10. For an interest rate of 12 percent, calculate the effective rate of interest on a loan for compensating balance requirements of 5, 10, and 20 percent.

11. For a constant interest rate of 12 percent, graph the relationship between the effective rate of interest on a loan and compensating balance requirements using the calculations from problem 10.

12. For a compensating balance requirement of 10 percent, calculate the effective rate of interest on a loan with interest rates of 6, 8, 10, 12, and 15 percent.

13. For a constant compensating balance requirement of 10 percent, graph the relationship between the effective rate of interest on a loan and the interest rate using the calculations from problem 12.

14. Would you prefer a loan with a 12 percent rate of interest and a 10 percent compensating balance requirement or a loan with a 14 percent rate of interest and no compensating balance?

15. Conway Tweety needs to buy a $25,000 machine and his bank will provide the financing through a loan requiring a 10 percent compensating balance. How much money should Tweety borrow?

Chapter 17

Financial Analysis

OVERVIEW

This chapter presents the basic techniques of financial analysis. The financial manager must have current information about the firm and how it is changing. Much of this information is derived from the firm's accounting statements: the balance sheet, the income statement, and the sources and uses of funds statement. The chapter introduces two important techniques for analyzing these statements: the percentage financial report, also known as common size analysis, and financial ratio analysis.

BASIC FINANCIAL STATEMENTS

The three basic financial statements are the balance sheet, the income statement, and the sources and uses of funds statement.

The **balance sheet** presents all of the assets of the firm and claims against them at a particular moment in time. Typical assets include cash, accounts receivable, inventory, and fixed assets. Typical claims include accounts payable, bank loans, and stockholders' equity. The balance sheet is like a financial snapshot of the firm, because it shows the firm's financial condition frozen at a specific time.

The **income statement** summarizes the operation of the firm over a particular period. It reports all the income of the firm and all the costs incurred to generate it during that period. It differs from the balance sheet because it considers the flow of funds over a certain length of time, not merely the amount of funds at a particular moment. To continue our metaphor, the balance sheet might be like a particular frame from a film, but the income statement is the entire movie.

The third important financial statement is the **sources and uses of funds statement**. Its purpose is to show, over a given period, how the firm obtained its funds, and how it put those funds to work. For example, over a one-year period the firm may have obtained some funds from bank loans, some from an equity issue, and some from reducing its inventory. All of these are sources of funds. Those funds may have been used in part to buy new machinery, to increase the level of cash in the firm, and to reduce the accounts payable to suppliers. We consider each of these statements in detail in the following sections.

The Balance Sheet

The firm acquires assets using the funds provided by investors. These investors have claims against the firm, which are set against the assets. The balance sheet summarizes the amounts and kinds of assets in the firm's possession. It also shows the claims made against those assets by investors. As the name implies, the balance sheet must balance. That is, the total value of the firm's assets must equal the total value of the claims against the firm. We can state this essential fact in the following equation:

Total assets = total claims

Firms generally prepare their financial statements for the end of their fiscal year and for each quarter. The **fiscal year** is the business year, and it need not coincide with the calendar year.[1]

Table 17.1 shows a balance sheet for two consecutive years for Imaginary Products. The top portion shows the firm's assets for each year, which fall into two main categories – current and fixed assets. If these are the only types of assets, we have the relationship:

Total assets = current assets + fixed assets

A **current asset** is one the firm will convert into cash within one year in its normal operation. For example, cash is clearly a current asset. Likewise, marketable securities are current assets because they are short-term assets that the firm can sell for cash very quickly. Accounts receivable are also current assets because they are normally collected within a year. The firm's inventory is also a current asset because most firms sell a given item in inventory within one year. In equation form we have:

Current assets = cash + marketable securities + accounts receivable + inventory

Fixed assets are more permanent assets that the firm will not normally convert into cash – at least not in the short run. For example, a refinery of Mobil's or an automobile assembly plant of Chrysler's would both be fixed assets. They are typically physical assets used in the basic process of the firm's operations. The balance sheet shows their initial value, plant and equipment, minus the accumulated depreciation charged against them. In equation form:

Fixed assets = plant and equipment at cost – accumulated depreciation

The balance sheet shows fixed assets at their **historical cost**; that is, the amount actually paid for them. The historical cost typically differs from the market value or the replacement cost of the asset. The **market value** is the price at which the assets could be sold in the market today. The **replacement cost** is the cost of the assets if they were purchased new today.

The idea behind using the historical cost and subtracting the accumulated depreciation to arrive at the reported value of the fixed assets is important. If the price of an asset did not change over time, and if the depreciation charged against that asset accurately reflected the falling value of the asset due to its use and age, the asset's balance sheet value would equal its market value. However, the reported value and the market value often differ, sometimes substantially.

---

[1] Firms sometimes have good business reasons for choosing a non-calendar fiscal year. In retailing, for example, about 25 percent of sales occur in a very short period before Christmas. If a retailing firm used the calendar year as its fiscal year, it would not be able to gather all the necessary information to make a timely report of its sales. Therefore, most retailers will prefer a later ending date for the fiscal year, perhaps April 30.

TABLE 17.1
Imaginary Products – Balance Sheet
(000s omitted)

	12/31/Year 1 ($)	12/31/Year 2 ($)	Difference ($)
ASSETS			
Cash	175	210	35
Marketable securities	90	75	–15
Accounts receivable	560	520	–40
Inventory	330	670	340
CURRENT ASSETS	1,155	1,475	320
Plant and equipment	20,000	23,000	3,000
Less accum. depreciation	–7,500	–8,250	–750
TOTAL FIXED ASSETS	12,500	14,750	2,250
TOTAL ASSETS	13,655	16,225	2,570
LIABILITIES AND NET WORTH			
Accounts payable	325	390	65
Notes payable	225	530	305
Accruals	50	40	–10
Taxes payable	30	100	70
CURRENT LIABILITIES	630	1,060	430
Long-term liabilities	7,500	9,600	2,100
TOTAL LIABILITIES	8,130	10,660	2,530
Common stock			
($1 par; 1 million shares)	1,000	1,000	0
Retained earnings	4,525	4,565	40
NET WORTH	5,525	5,565	40
TOTAL LIABILITIES AND NET WORTH	13,655	16,225	2,570

The value of the assets as shown in the financial reports and in the books of the company is the **book value**. Book value and market value may differ for several reasons. Consider the case of a personal computer. If the firm pays $5,000 for the computer and depreciates it 20 percent the first year, the book value will be $4,000 after one year of use. However, if developments in computer technology have made that machine obsolete, the computer may have a market value of only $1,500. Often, technological advancements make old equipment obsolete, so the book value can exceed the market value. In this case, the book value overstates the value of an asset relative to its market value.

It may also occur that the market value exceeds the book value. For instance, accounting statements always reflect the original purchase price of land, so land is never depreciated. Its market value may increase, however, and when this happens, the book value of the land is less than its market value. In periods of high inflation, the book value of many assets can be significantly less than their market value.

A variety of individuals and firms have claims against the assets of the firm. In the balance sheet, we can divide the obligations of the firm into the claims owed to creditors, or liabilities, and to the owners of the firm, or equity. Thus, we have:

$$\text{Total claims} = \text{total liabilities} + \text{equity}$$

Liabilities are either current or long-term. **Current liabilities** are those the firm expects to pay within the next year. **Long-term liabilities** are continuing obligations the firm has undertaken that will not be completely repaid during the next year. The sum of current and long-term liabilities gives total liabilities:

$$\text{Total liabilities} = \text{current liabilities} + \text{long-term liabilities}$$

Accounts payable are current liabilities since they are short-term obligations that the firm has for goods or services it has received from others. For example, Imaginary Products may receive raw materials before paying for them. If, as normally occurs, the firm must pay within a year, the balance sheet shows those debts in the accounts payable category.

Many firms use short-term debt, usually from banks. Notes payable show the short-term debt that must be paid within the next year. Some other debts are accruals. One of the best examples of an accrual is the debt of the company to its employees. If the date of the balance sheet falls before a pay date, the firm will owe accrued salaries and wages to its employees. By the same token, firms do not pay their taxes every day, but taxes accumulate every day. Taxes payable are taxes owed but not yet paid. Summarizing, the current liability equality can be expressed as:

$$\text{Current liabilities} = \text{accounts payable} + \text{notes payable} + \text{accruals} + \text{taxes payable}$$

Long-term liabilities consist of debt and leases. If a firm has sold a 30-year bond, it has a long-term debt. Part of this debt may be due during the next year, and that portion of the debt is a current liability. Also, many firms use long-term leases, which are legal agreements to make a series of payments in exchange for the use of some asset. Thus:

$$\text{Long-term liabilities} = \text{long-term debt} + \text{leases}$$

In addition to its liabilities to parties outside the firm, the corporation has obligations to its owners. The balance sheet presents these separated into common stock and retained earnings. The common stock account reflects the stockholders' direct contribution. The retained earnings account shows the accumulated effect of the firm's earnings since its inception. Retained earnings are those funds that the firm has earned and retained for use in the business instead of paying them to the shareholders. By retaining these funds, rather than distributing them, they constitute an additional investment by the stockholders. The sum of the common stock and retained earnings constitutes the net worth, or equity:

$$\text{Net worth} = \text{common stock} + \text{retained earnings}$$

Together, the firm's liabilities and equity must equal its assets. As discussed later in this chapter, the balance sheet supplies much of the information that is critical to successful financial analysis.

The Income Statement

The income statement details the firm's revenues and expenses during a particular period. Table 17.2 presents the income statement for Imaginary Products for two consecutive periods. It begins with a report of the dollar volume of the firm's sales for the period. Subtracting the cost of goods sold from sales gives the gross profit. The cost of goods sold (COGS) reflects the direct cost associated with creating the product. For a broom manufacturer, COGS would include the cost of materials and labor that were used in making the broom. It would also include a portion of the factory costs, such as lighting for the building, maintenance, and repairs for equipment.

The gross profit is the difference between the sales and the cost of goods sold. The equation is:

$$\text{Gross profit} = \text{sales} - \text{cost of goods sold}$$

The firm must also recognize the depreciation expense to reflect the consumption of its capital and equipment. Likewise, the selling and administrative (S&A) expenses incurred by the firm also reduce profits.

After considering all sales and the costs of generating those sales, the result is the firm's **earnings before interest and taxes** (EBIT), which can be expressed as:

$$\text{EBIT} = \text{gross profit} - \text{depreciation} - \text{S\&A expenses}$$

TABLE 17.2
Imaginary Products – Income Statement
(000s omitted)

	Year 1 ($)	Year 2 ($)
Sales	19,625	25,280
Cost of goods sold	15,700	20,900
GROSS PROFIT	3,925	4,380
Depreciation	650	750
Selling and admin. expenses	2,425	2,615
EARNINGS BEFORE INTEREST AND TAXES	850	1,015
Interest expense	725	940
EARNINGS BEFORE TAXES	125	75
Taxes	47	28
NET INCOME	78	47

In addition to depreciation and S&A expenses, the firm must pay interest on its debt. Interest is normally separated from other expenses because it results from the debt-financing policies of the firm. By contrast, depreciation and selling and administrative expenses are related to operating activities. Separating interest expenses facilitates comparison among firms. For example, two firms with identical operations would have the same EBIT, even if their debt policies differed. Because of this, the EBIT is normally used when measuring operating activities.

Subtracting interest expenses from earnings before interest and taxes gives the **earnings before taxes** (EBT):

$$\text{Earnings before taxes} = \text{EBIT} - \text{interest}$$

These are the earnings subject to income taxation. Subtracting taxes from EBT gives the firm's after-tax profits, or **net income** (NI). Net income, the proverbial "bottom line," is the amount that is actually available to the owners of the firm after paying all other claimants, including the government:

$$\text{Net income} = \text{EBT} - \text{taxes}$$

The net income earned during the period is available to either reinvest in the company or to pay as a dividend to shareholders. Thus:

$$\text{Net income} = \text{retained earnings} + \text{dividends}$$

In reading an income statement, we must remember the difference between the earnings the income statement reports and the cash the firm receives. Cash flow refers to the actual payment of cash. It is very important because only actual cash gives the firm the resources to meet its obligations. If a firm sells all its goods on credit, it is possible for the firm to report large earnings for a given period even when it receives no payments. In such an extreme case, the reported earnings might be large, but the cash flow would be zero.

Although depreciation is not a cash expense, it generates cash by reducing the firm's tax bill. This is known as the **depreciation tax shield**. To illustrate, consider a firm with earnings before taxes of $4,000 after deducting a depreciation expense of $1,500. If the firm pays a 34 percent tax rate on any EBT, it pays $4,000 × 0.34 = $1,360 in taxes. If depreciation were not a deductible expense, the EBT would be $5,500 and the taxes paid in that case would be $5,500 × 0.34 = $1,870. The fact that depreciation is allowed as an expense shielded the firm from paying $510 ($1,870 − $1,360) in taxes. In general, if T is the corporate tax rate, the depreciation tax shield can be calculated directly with the following formula:

$$\text{Depreciation tax shield} = \text{depreciation} \times T$$

Using this formula in the previous example, the depreciation tax shield is $1,500 × 0.34 = $510, just as we found before.

The Sources and Uses of Funds Statement

The sources and uses of funds statement shows how the firm acquired its funds in a given period and how it used them. For example, if a firm borrows $1,000 from a bank and deposits those funds in its checking account, the loan is a source of funds that are used to increase the firm's cash account. Thus, firms may obtain funds by incurring obligations to debtholders and stockholders. Perhaps a less obvious example of a source of funds is a reduction of the firm's inventory. This is a source of funds because it generates cash for the firm. Similarly, a use of funds might be the cash purchase of a delivery truck, or a reduction in the accounts payable of the firm.

Any firm essentially has three sources and three uses of funds, as shown in table 17.3, and they fall into pairs. As a source of funds, a firm can increase a liability account. By borrowing money, for example, a firm increases the funds it has available. Decreasing a liability account is a use of funds. For example, if a firm pays an existing debt, it uses funds to reduce that liability. Accordingly, an increase in a liability is a source of funds and a decrease in a liability is a use of funds.

If a firm increases an equity account, the increased obligation is a source of funds. Likewise, if a firm decreases an equity account, perhaps by buying its own stock in the market or by paying dividends, it uses funds. Reducing an asset account, such as inventory, provides a source of funds.

Constructing a sources and uses of funds statement for one year requires balance sheets for two years. Table 17.1 provides all information necessary to construct the sources and uses of funds statement for Imaginary Products for Year 2. The right-hand column of table 17.1 presents the difference in each account from one period to the next. Using this column and the rules given in table 17.3 we can build the sources and uses of funds statement.

Table 17.4 takes all the amounts from the difference column in table 17.1 and classifies each as a source or as a use of funds. These sources and uses of funds have been ranked by dollar amount in table 17.4. For example, the two major sources of funds in year 2 for Imaginary Products were an increase in long-term liabilities ($2,100,000) and an increase in notes payable ($305,000). Imaginary Products used most of the funds to expand plant and equipment ($2,250,000), and to increase inventory ($340,000).

Note that all the information in table 17.4 comes from the balance sheets of table 17.1, with one exception. The sources and uses statement also reflects the dividend of $7,000 that Imaginary Products paid in year 2. We have seen that the net income of any corporation must go either to retained earnings or to pay dividends to the shareholders. On the balance sheets, the change in retained earnings for year 2 was $40,000. However, the income statement in table 17.2 shows that Imaginary Products earned $47,000. The dividends paid to shareholders in year 2 do not appear on the balance sheet or the income

TABLE 17.3
Sources and Uses of Funds

Sources of Funds	Uses of Funds
Increase in a liability account	Decrease in a liability account
Increase in an equity account	Decrease in an equity account
Decrease in an asset account	Increase in an asset account

TABLE 17.4
Imaginary Products – Sources and Uses of Funds Statement
(Year 2)

SOURCES OF FUNDS:	
Increase in long-term liabilities	2,100
Increase in notes payable	305
Increase in taxes payable	70
Increase in accounts payable	65
Net income from operations	47
Decrease in accounts receivable	40
Decrease in marketable securities	15
TOTAL SOURCES	2,642
USES OF FUNDS:	
Increases in fixed assets	2,250
Increase in inventory	340
Increase in cash	35
Decrease in accruals	10
Dividends paid	7
TOTAL USES	2,642

statement, but they appear on the sources and uses statement. This allows a reconciliation of the three major financial statements.[2]

FINANCIAL ANALYSIS TECHNIQUES

The remainder of this chapter explores two techniques of financial analysis. The technique of percentage financial statements allows a ready comparison of the performance of the firm over various periods. It also allows comparisons among different firms.

The ratio analysis technique investigates the firm's performance through financial ratios. A **financial ratio** is the ratio of two financial variables taken from the balance sheet or the income statement.

Percentage Financial Statements

Table 17.5 presents percentage balance sheets for the firm. We construct the percentage balance sheet by dividing each asset and liability category by the firm's total assets. At the end of year 2, for example, 90.9 percent of the firm's assets were fixed assets. The percentage balance sheet is particularly useful for identifying trends in the firm's asset and liability composition. Comparing the position of Imaginary Products at the end of the two years, we see that the relative amount of current assets increased.

---

[2] Some firms call the sources and uses of funds statement the statement of changes in financial position.

TABLE 17.5
Imaginary Products – Percentage Balance Sheet

	12/31/Year 1	12/31/Year 2
ASSETS		
Cash	1.3%	1.3%
Marketable securities	0.7	0.5
Accounts receivable	4.1	3.2
Inventory	2.4	4.1
CURRENT ASSETS	8.5	9.1
Plant and equipment	146.5	141.8
Less accum. depreciation	−55.0	−50.9
TOTAL FIXED ASSETS	91.5	90.0
TOTAL ASSETS	100.0	100.0
LIABILITIES AND NET WORTH		
Accounts payable	2.4%	2.4%
Notes payable	1.6	3.3
Accruals	0.4	0.2
Taxes payable	0.2	0.6
CURRENT LIABILITIES	4.6	6.5
Long-term liabilities	54.9	59.2
TOTAL LIABILITIES	59.5	65.7
Common stock		
($1 par; 1 million shares)	7.3	6.2
Retained earnings	33.1	28.1
NET WORTH	40.5	34.3
TOTAL LIABILITIES AND NET WORTH	100.0	100.0

At the end of year 2, Imaginary Products was financing 6.5 percent of its assets with current liabilities, compared to 4.6 percent in year 1. Also, it increased long-term liabilities substantially. Together, the increases in the relative amounts of current and long-term liabilities generated a large increase in the firm's reliance on debt. During year 2, the percentage of assets financed by some form of debt went from 59.5 percent to 65.7 percent. The relative decrease from 40.5 percent to 34.3 percent in the equity account also highlights the increasing reliance on debt financing.

A further examination of the position of Imaginary Products is possible by considering the percentage income statements of table 17.6. To prepare this statement, we express the different income statement categories as a percentage of sales. For example, in year 2 the cost of goods sold was 82.7 percent of sales.

TABLE 17.6
Imaginary Products – Percentage Income Statement
(000s omitted)

	Year 1	Year 2
Sales	100.0%	100.0%
Cost of goods sold	80.0	82.7
GROSS PROFIT	20.0	17.3
Depreciation	3.3	3.0
Selling and admin. expenses	12.4	10.3
EARNINGS BEFORE INTEREST AND TAXES	4.3	4.0
Interest expense	3.7	3.7
EARNINGS BEFORE TAXES (EBT)	0.6	0.3
Taxes	0.2	0.1
NET INCOME	0.4	0.2

Table 17.6 shows a potentially large and dangerous increase in the cost of goods sold over the two periods, from 80.0 percent to 82.7 percent. Although this change may not appear large, it dramatically affects gross profit. The 3.4 percent ([82.7 – 80.0]/80.0) relative increase in the cost of goods sold made the gross profit margin drop from 20.0 percent to 17.3 percent, a relative drop of 13.5 percent ([17.3 – 20.0]/20.0). For the financial manager analyzing the performance of Imaginary Products, this increase in COGS would be an immediate danger signal.

A second noticeable feature of the percentage income statements is the level of S&A expenses. These decreased from 12.4 percent of sales in year 1 to 10.3 percent of sales in year 2, despite the fact that their dollar amount increased. The reason for this relative reduction is that dollar sales increased even more than S&A expenses.

The percentage income statement also reveals the low profitability of Imaginary Products. For each dollar of sales, the firm earned only two-tenths of one cent on an after-tax basis in year 2. Unless these are particularly bad years, Imaginary Products could be heading for serious difficulties.

Financial Ratios

In addition to percentage financial statements, the financial manager will frequently use financial ratios to obtain an overview of some of the firm's key operating statistics. In addition, by following these measures over time the manager can detect important trends in the performance of the firm.

This section presents the major financial ratios and shows how to calculate them using the financial statements of Imaginary Products. The four major groups are liquidity, profitability, leverage, and turnover ratios.

Liquidity Ratios The two measures of liquidity managers use more widely are the current ratio and the quick ratio or acid test. The current ratio (CR) is defined by the following formula:

$$\text{Current ratio} = \frac{\text{current assets}}{\text{current liabilities}}$$

For Imaginary Products, at the end of year 2 the current ratio is $1,475/$1,060 = 1.39. The acid test is defined as follows:

$$\text{Acid test} = \frac{\text{current assets} - \text{inventory}}{\text{current liabilities}}$$

For Imaginary Products, at the end of year 2 the acid test is ($1,475 − $670)/ $1,060 = 0.76.

These two ratios measure a firm's ability to meet its current liabilities with its current assets. The greater the amount of current assets relative to current liabilities, the safer the firm will be, other things being equal.

The acid test imposes a tough measure of firm liquidity – hence its name. In some cases it is not easy to convert inventory to cash because some of the inventory may be obsolete or, in some fraudulent cases, may not even exist. Because of these potential problems, the acid test ratio removes the inventories from the calculation to see how many dollars the firm can generate from current assets to pay each dollar of current liabilities, without relying on inventory.

For Imaginary Products, the liquidity ratios are somewhat small. As a rule, many analysts think that a current ratio around 2.00 and a quick ratio of about 1.00 are appropriate for many firms. However, the best value for any of these ratios depends on the industry and the particular strategy of the firm.

These ratios are often most useful in identifying trends early, which is valuable because it allows the firm to take corrective action. For example, at the end of year 1 the current ratio for Imaginary Products was 1.83 and its quick ratio was 1.31. During year 2, both of these measures deteriorated substantially. This worsening trend is clearly dangerous and deserves managerial attention.

Profitability Ratios Three widely used accounting measures of profitability are the **profit margin** (PM), the **return on assets** (ROA), and the **return on equity** (ROE). The profit margin is calculated as follows:

$$\text{Profit margin} = \frac{\text{net income}}{\text{total sales}}$$

From the year 2 income statement, we have PM = $47/$25,280 = 0.19 percent. By almost any measure, this is a very unsatisfactory profit margin.

The return on assets ratio is given by:

$$\text{Return on assets} = \frac{\text{net income}}{\text{total assets}}$$

Using our example, this ratio is ROA = $47/$16,225 = 0.3 percent. Finally, the return on equity ratio is defined as follows:

$$\text{Return on equity} = \frac{\text{net income}}{\text{equity}}$$

For Imaginary Products we have ROE = $47/$5,565 = 0.84 percent.

Each of these profitability measures provides a slightly different gauge of a firm's operating success. The profit margin reveals how much profit a firm earns on each dollar of sales. By itself, the profit margin is not too meaningful because profit margins vary so widely by industry and by firm. For example, successful supermarkets may have small profit margins, typically in the order of 1 to 2 percent. To interpret this ratio, and most of the others discussed in this section, the manager needs to know the trend of the ratio over time for a given company, or the industry norm for the ratio in question.

By contrast with the profit margin, the ROA and the ROE both determine the rate of return on some measure of investment. The ROA determines the return on all of the assets employed by the firm and the ROE focuses only on the investment contributed by the shareholders.

The performance of Imaginary Products is dismal by all of the measures. No investor can be happy when a firm earns less than 1 percent on equity. This poor performance also means that the firm will face great difficulties in attracting any new investment capital if potential lenders believe these ratios are indicative of future performance.

Leverage Ratios   Leverage ratios calculate the extent to which a firm relies on debt. Other things being equal, a higher leverage ratio indicates a riskier firm, because the debt payments are fixed even if the earnings of the firm fluctuate. As a result, should the cash flow diminish excessively, the firm might miss its debt payments deadline, putting the firm in technical default.

Four important measures of leverage are the **times interest earned** ratio (TIE), the **debt to assets** ratio (D/A), the **debt to equity** ratio (D/E), and the **equity multiplier** (EM). The TIE is given by:

$$\text{Times interest earned} = \frac{\text{earnings before interest and taxes}}{\text{interest expense}}$$

Times interest earned is calculated using the firm's earnings before interest and taxes because these are the earnings available to pay the interest. For Imaginary Products, in year 2 the TIE is $1,015/$940 = 1.08. This means that Imaginary Products is earning only $1.08 for each $1 of interest expense it pays, which is an extremely uncomfortable margin of safety. In year 1 the TIE was 1.17, so this measure has gone from bad to worse, and the financial manager should focus on this as a matter of great urgency. Many healthy firms have TIE ratios in the order of 5 to 20.

The other leverage measures focus on the structure of the firm's long-term financing. The debt to assets ratio shows which portion of total assets the firm finances with debt:

$$\text{Debt to asset} = \frac{\text{total debt}}{\text{total assets}}$$

For Imaginary Products in year 2 we have D/A = $10,660/$16,225 = 0.657. Most manufacturing firms have debt to asset ratios between 0.30 and 0.70, so our firm uses a considerable amount of debt to finance its assets.

The debt to equity ratio shows the relationship between the firm's debt and equity financing:

$$\text{Debt to equity} = \frac{\text{total debt}}{\text{equity}}$$

In year 2, the D/E for Imaginary Products is \$10,660/\$5,565 = 1.916.

These two leverage ratios convey essentially the same information. In fact, given one, we can calculate the other. For example, a debt to asset ratio of 0.657 implies that the firm must finance 34.3 percent of its assets with equity. The ratio of debt to equity then equals 0.657/0.343, or 1.916, which is the D/E calculated above. In general, the relationship between the D/A and D/E ratios is given by:

$$\text{D/A} = \frac{\text{D/E}}{1 + \text{D/E}}$$

The final leverage ratio we consider is the equity multiplier, defined as the dollar amount of assets the firm uses for each dollar of equity:

$$\text{Equity multiplier} = \frac{\text{total assets}}{\text{equity}}$$

For Imaginary Products, in year 2 this ratio equals EM = \$16,225/\$5,565 = 2.92. Thus, for each dollar of equity, the firm has 2.92 dollars of assets. The equity multiplier can also be expressed in terms of the D/E ratio. This is easily seen by noting that total assets = debt + equity. Dividing this balance sheet identity by equity results in EM = 1 + D/E.

Turnover Ratios   The different turnover ratios measure managerial effectiveness in running the operations of the firm. Among the main ones are the **average collection period** (ACP), the **inventory turnover** ratio (ITO), and the **asset turnover** ratio (ATO). The ACP is calculated as follows:

$$\text{Average collection period} = \frac{\text{accounts receivable}}{\text{daily credit sales}}$$

In the case of Imaginary Products, the ACP in year 2 is \$520/(\$25,280/365) = 7.51 days. Notice that we are assuming that all sales are made on credit. This assumption is often necessary when the actual breakdown of total sales into cash and credit sales is not available.

The average collection period gives the average amount of time necessary to collect a credit sale. The figure of 7.51 days is extremely low for most firms that sell on credit. Either Imaginary Products is doing an extremely good job of collecting its bills or a small proportion of the firm's total sales are made on credit.

The inventory turnover ratio, which indicates how many times per year the inventory is sold or turned over, is defined as:

$$\text{Inventory turnover ratio} = \frac{\text{cost of goods sold}}{\text{inventory}}$$

Notice that the inventory turnover ratio is defined in terms of the annual cost of goods sold and not in terms of annual sales. This is because the inventory account is carried at cost, so it needs to be compared against another cost. The inventory turnover ratio for

Imaginary Products is ITO = $20,900/$670 = 31.19 times. This value is very high for most firms, since it implies that the average item was kept in inventory for only 11.70 days.

The typical problem that arises with inventory is that it may become too large when sales are slow. To control this problem, it is often useful to determine the number of days of sales that the firm holds in inventory. This days of sales in inventory (DSI) measure is essentially the reciprocal of the inventory turnover ratio, and is defined as:

$$\text{Days of sales in inventory} = \frac{\text{inventory}}{\text{daily COGS}}$$

For Imaginary Products, in year 2 we have DSI = $670/($20,900/365) = 11.70 days. This same result is obtained by reasoning that if the inventory turns over 31.19 times in 365 days, then the firm must have 365/31.19 = 11.70 days of sales in its inventory. Thus, the ITO and DSI ratios give essentially the same information.

The asset turnover ratio is given by:

$$\text{Asset turnover} = \frac{\text{sales}}{\text{assets}}$$

The ATO for Imaginary Products is $25,280/$16,225 = 1.56.

The asset turnover ratio shows how many sales dollars are generated by each dollar of assets. It therefore measures how productively the firm utilizes its assets. For Imaginary Products, the ATO of 1.56 dollars of sales per dollar of assets is quite reasonable.

It is important to notice that several of these ratios are related to one another. For example, we have already noted the relationship between the D/A and the D/E ratios, but the most important relationship of all occurs between the return on equity ratio and three of the other ratios. This important relationship is often referred to as the Du Pont equation, and is given as follows:

$$\text{ROE} = \text{PM} \times \text{ATO} \times \text{EM}$$

This relationship provides a connection between a **profitability ratio** (PM), a turnover ratio (ATO), and the equity multiplier leverage ratio (EM). It allows the financial manager to pinpoint the factors that lead to a given return on equity. For Imaginary Products, the ROE is 0.84 percent. This value can be broken down into its three components, using the values computed previously. For Imaginary Products we have 0.84% = 0.19% × 1.56 × 2.92.[3] This clearly shows that the problem with the firm's very low return on equity lies in its dismal profit margin, and not in the productivity of its assets or in its use of leverage, both of which seem adequate. This recognition should lead the financial manager to concentrate on urgently improving the firm's profit margin, perhaps by controlling expenses.

Summarizing, the preceding consideration of the percentage financial statements and the financial ratios for Imaginary Products shows that the firm faces some problems. First, the gross profit margin is extremely low. The firm is simply not earning enough on its present volume of sales to survive and prosper. If the other firms in the same industry are

---

[3] The product on the right actually gives 0.865%. The computational error is due to the rounding of each of the three ratios.

behaving similarly, the poor performance of Imaginary Industry could be due to the same factors that affect other firms. If other firms are earning a much better return on sales, problems may exist with the management of Imaginary Products. Whatever its source, the problem urgently demands strong corrective action.

The second major problem confronting Imaginary Products is the low level of liquidity, as revealed by the times interest earned ratio, the current ratio, and the acid test ratio. There is a danger that Imaginary Products could soon have difficulty meeting its debt payments. This could lead to bankruptcy and the seizure of the firm's assets by creditors.

Limitations of Ratio Analysis

All of these ratios and the technique of percentage financial statements are meaningful only in conjunction with a firm's past performance or in comparison with other firms in the industry. Also, none of these measures has a "correct" value. For example, it might seem that a higher current ratio is always better. After all, the higher the ratio, the less the risk of default. However, managing a firm to ensure a high current ratio may lead to an inefficient use of resources. For example, the firm might increase its current ratio by hoarding cash or by increasing its inventory way beyond normal levels. Since these assets by themselves do not generate any return to the firm, an exceedingly high current ratio would signal that management is too cautious, and probably underutilizing the firm's assets.

When analyzing financial statements, we should always be on the lookout for "window dressing" tactics. For example, a simple way of "improving" the firm's liquidity is to take out a long-term loan right before the end of the fiscal year, and repay it at the beginning of the next one. If the funds from the loan are kept in the form of cash, the current ratio will increase, and the ratios may not accurately reflect the true liquidity of the firm. The moral is that ratios should be viewed as part of a whole, and not just in isolation.

SUMMARY

This chapter presented the three most important types of financial statements prepared by corporations: the balance sheet, the income statement, and the sources and uses of funds statement. It also discussed some of the analytical techniques that managers can apply to understanding these statements.

The balance sheet offers a financial snapshot of the firm at a given point in time. In essence, the balance sheet summarizes all of the assets and claims against those assets, at a given moment.

The income statement reports on the revenues and expenses of a firm over a given period. The ultimate purpose of the income statement is to show the amount of income available to reward common stock owners for their investment. This is the proverbial "bottom line."

The sources and uses of funds statement reports how new funds were acquired over a given period and how they were used. For example, a bank loan may be a source of funds used to buy a new machine.

We also considered some basic techniques of financial analysis. One is to present financial statements in percentage, or common size, terms. The other major technique is ratio analysis.

With percentage financial statements, the financial manager can compare the performance of a firm in other periods or with other firms. A percentage balance sheet presents each asset and liability category as a percentage of total assets. The percentage income statement shows each revenue and expense item on the income statement as a percentage of the firm's sales.

Ratio analysis is a technique used to analyze various aspects of the firm's financial situation. We can classify financial ratios into four major groups: liquidity, profitability, leverage, and turnover ratios. Each has its application to a particular management concern.

QUESTIONS

1. How do the income statement and balance sheet differ in their summary of the events in an accounting period?
2. What are the three major financial statements?
3. Explain why the sources and uses of funds must be equal.
4. If the firm spends cash to buy inventory, how does it affect the following categories:
   a. current assets
   b. working capital
   c. the firm's current ratio
   d. the firm's acid test ratio
5. What is the difference between market value and historical cost?
6. Will book value and historical cost be identical? If so, under what circumstances?
7. Will book value always equal market value? What could cause them to diverge?
8. If a firm uses cash to pay down its accounts payable, what is the effect on the following measures:
   a. current ratio
   b. acid test ratio
   c. long-term debt
   d. retained earnings
9. You examine the income statement for a firm for two successive years and notice that the cost-of-goods sold has increased. What could explain this?
10. If VANA, Inc., has a current ratio of 0.8 and you add the same dollar amount to current assets and current liabilities, what will happen to its current ratio?
11. If VANA, Inc., has a current ratio of 1.7 and you add the same dollar amount to current assets and current liabilities, what will happen to its current ratio?
12. Elisa, Inc., has a current ratio of 1.5 and you wish to increase it to 2.0. To do so, you will add or subtract the same dollar amount to both current assets and current liabilities. By what factor must current liabilities change to accomplish this?
13. Elisa, Inc., has a current ratio of 0.5 and you wish to increase it to 0.9. To do so, you will add or subtract the same dollar amount to both current assets and current liabilities. By what factor must current liabilities change to accomplish this?

14. Is it possible to increase Elisa's current ratio from 0.5 to 1.0 by adding or subtracting the same dollar amount to both current assets and current liabilities? Explain.

PROBLEMS

Consider the balance sheets for Dismal Industries shown below and use the information contained there for problems 1–6.

Dismal Industries – Balance Sheet
(000s omitted)

	12/31/Year 1 ($)	12/31/Year 2 ($)
ASSETS		
Cash	125	100
Marketable securities	45	50
Accounts receivable	310	570
Inventory	400	200
CURRENT ASSETS	880	920
Plant and equipment	14,000	15,080
Less accumulated depreciation	5,000	5,900
TOTAL FIXED ASSETS	9,000	9,180
TOTAL ASSETS	9,880	10,100
LIABILITIES AND NET WORTH		
Accounts payable	250	325
Notes payable	225	340
Accruals	80	150
Taxes payable	70	90
CURRENT LIABILITIES	625	905
Long-term liabilities	4,500	5,000
TOTAL LIABILITIES	5,125	5,905
Common stock	1,000	1,000
Retained earnings	3,755	3,195
NET WORTH	4,755	4,195
TOTAL LIABILITIES AND NET WORTH	9,880	10,100

1. Calculate the current ratio for each year.
2. Calculate the quick ratio for each year.
3. Calculate the D/A ratio for each year.
4. Calculate the D/E ratio for each year.
5. Based on the calculations in problems 1–4, what difficulties, if any, does this firm face? What other information might be helpful for analyzing the difficulties?
6. Using the balance sheet provided here, prepare a sources and uses of funds statement like that shown in table 17.4.

Use the information from the following income statement for Dismal Industries, in conjunction with the balance sheet given earlier, to solve problems 7–14.

Dismal Industries – Income Statement
(000s omitted)

	Year 2 ($)
Sales	8,000
Cost of goods sold	6,100
GROSS PROFIT	1,900
Depreciation	900
Selling and administrative expenses	350
EARNINGS BEFORE INTEREST AND TAXES	650
Interest expense	400
EARNINGS BEFORE TAXES	250
Taxes	100
NET INCOME	150

7. Compute the firm's profit margin.
8. What is Dismal's return on assets?
9. What is Dismal's return on equity?
10. What is the times interest earned ratio?
11. What is Dismal's average daily sales?
12. What is Dismal's average collection period?
13. What is Dismal's inventory turnover ratio?
14. What is Dismal's total asset turnover ratio?
15. Recast the Dismal Industries year 2 balance sheet as a percentage statement.
16. Prepare a percentage income statement for Dismal for year 2.
17. Using the income statement for Dismal and the year 2 balance sheet, consider the following. Assume that Dismal had sales of $9 million instead of $8

million, and assume that the same percentage cost of goods sold was maintained. Prepare an income statement for Dismal that reflects those changes. In doing so, change only the items that must change.

18. Given the change in the income statement, how must the year 2 balance sheet change?

19. Go back to the income statement printed earlier, and now assume that the cost of goods sold was $7 million. Compute the new income statement based on that change.

20. What changes in Dismal's year 2 balance sheet are necessary given the new cost of goods sold presented in the preceding problem?

On January 1 of year 3, Dismal borrows $1 million on a six-month loan and issues $5 million in debt. It receives both amounts in cash. Assuming no other changes since December 31 of year 2, solve problems 21–24.

21. Compute the new current ratio.
22. Compute the new acid test ratio.
23. Compute the new D/A ratio.
24. Compute the new D/E ratio.

Dismal is planning to issue $5 million worth of stock and will receive that amount of cash, with each share having a $1 par value. The stock sells for $10 per share. Using Dismal's year 2 balance sheet as your starting point, solve problems 25–30.

25. What is the new value of common stock?
26. What is the new value of retained earnings?
27. What will Dismal's new current ratio be?
28. What will Dismal's new acid test ratio be?
29. What will Dismal's new D/A ratio be?
30. Compute Dismal's new D/E ratio.
31. Does the current ratio increase or decrease when current assets and current liabilities increase by the same dollar amount?
32. What happens to the current ratio when current assets and current liabilities increase by the same percentage?
33. A firm has just bought some inventory with cash. What effect does this transaction have on the current ratio of the firm?
34. The text provides an expression for the D/A ratio in terms of the D/E ratio. Find the expression relating the D/E in terms of the D/A ratio.
35. Show that if a firm has a positive net income and uses some debt, then its ROE will always be greater than its ROA.
36. Starting from the definition of ROE, show that ROE = PM × ATO × EM. (Hint: you can always multiply and divide any ratio by the same amount without affecting the result.)

Chapter 18

Financial Planning

OVERVIEW

Financial managers must be able to analyze the current position of their own firms as well as that of their competition. They must also plan for the company's financial future. For example, many firms seasonally build up their inventories and accounts receivable. The financial manager must anticipate these needs and seek the best financing before the funds are needed. This chapter introduces some basic financial planning techniques.

One of the worst fates that can befall a corporation is running out of cash. When this happens the firm suffers financial embarrassment, and perhaps even bankruptcy. The financial manager is responsible for planning to ensure that the firm has enough cash for its needs. A useful tool for planning future cash needs is the cash budget, and this chapter explains how to construct and use cash budgets.

Financial managers must plan for the overall financial success of the firm, so, the financial manager needs to plan for continuing profitability. Profit planning typically makes use of pro forma statements, which is just another name for projected financial statements. For example, a financial manager might prepare a pro forma balance sheet for one year in the future, which will present the firm's expected financial position at that time. This chapter explores the uses of pro forma financial statements.

THE CASH BUDGET AS A FINANCIAL PLANNING TOOL

Consider the case of Imaginary Products, first discussed in the previous chapter, with sales of $25,280,000 in year 2. Management is predicting a 7 percent increase in sales for year 3, or $27,050,000. Even if this projection is correct, if the firm offers credit, some of these sales will not yield cash until the firm collects them. Also, sales during the year have seasonal peaks and valleys; as a result, the firm's working capital level will fluctuate. Financial planning must reflect these factors to determine the evolution of cash through the year.

Not only do cash inflows fluctuate over the year, demand for cash also varies with time. For example, the balance sheet for Imaginary Products for year 2 shown in table 18.1 indicates a total of $1,060,000 in current liabilities, which the firm must pay sometime during the next year. We do not know exactly when the firm must pay them, however. For example, if all the liabilities are due on January 1 of year 3, Imaginary Products will be in deep trouble because the balance sheet shows that it has only $210,000 in cash.

In addition to problems with fluctuating levels of cash inflows and outflows, there is also the chance that the firm may not realize its plans. While the firm expects that sales will increase by 7 percent, this may not happen. Often, firms seriously overestimate their

TABLE 18.1
Imaginary Products – Balance Sheet
December 31 of Year 2
(000s omitted)

ASSETS	
Cash	210
Marketable securities	75
Accounts receivable	520
Inventory	670
CURRENT ASSETS	1,475
Plant and equipment	23,000
Less accumulated depreciation	–8,250
TOTAL FIXED ASSETS	14,750
TOTAL ASSETS	16,225
LIABILITIES AND NET WORTH	
Accounts payable	390
Notes payable	530
Accruals	40
Taxes payable	100
CURRENT LIABILITIES	1,060
Long-term liabilities	9,600
TOTAL LIABILITIES	10,660
Common stock	1,000
Retained earnings	4,565
NET WORTH	5,565
TOTAL LIABILITIES AND NET WORTH	16,225

sales for the forthcoming year. If Imaginary Products does this, it could lead to a serious cash shortfall. Therefore, the firm must also plan to have a safety stock of cash.

Planning cash requirements and taking into account the cash inflows and outflows requires a **cash budget**, which is a detailed plan for the inflows and outflows over a certain period. The firm usually prepares the cash budget for each month of the following year. Some firms use cash budgets to plan cash flows on a weekly, or even daily, basis, thus revealing the importance of cash for them.

PREPARING THE CASH BUDGET

As a first step in preparing the cash budget, the firm must estimate the sales for each period contained in the planning horizon. Table 18.2 shows the historical sales pattern

TABLE 18.2
Imaginary Products – Monthly Distribution of Sales
(000s omitted)

Month	Historical % of Sales	Actual Sales Year 2	Projected Sales Year 3
January	5	1,264.0	1,352.5
February	7	1,769.6	1,893.5
March	10	2,528.0	2,705.0
April	12	3,033.6	3,246.0
May	16	4,044.8	4,327.9
June	22	5,561.6	5,950.9
July	7	1,769.6	1,893.5
August	7	1,769.6	1,893.5
September	5	1,264.0	1,352.5
October	2	505.6	541.0
November	4	1,011.2	1,082.0
December	3	758.4	811.5

for Imaginary Products on a monthly basis and the actual monthly sales for year 2. It also shows the projected monthly sales in year 3.

As table 18.2 shows, Imaginary Products experiences a strong seasonal pattern in its sales. Sales are highest in the spring and early summer. For example, sales in June are 11 times greater than in October. This pattern might be typical of a swimsuit distributor or a firm selling patio furniture. Whatever the reason for this distribution of sales for Imaginary Products, cash inflows will be very uneven over the course of the year. The widely varying monthly sales make planning cash requirements very important.

Given the projected sales for each month, the second step in the preparation of the cash budget is to project when those sales will actually generate cash. If the firm sells on credit, there will be a delay before actually receiving the cash payment. Imaginary Products has worked with its customers for a long time and it anticipates the following distribution of payment for sales:

Payment Month	Percentage Paid
Month of sale	15
Month after sale	35
Second month after sale	50

On December 31 of year 2, when the firm is preparing its cash budget, it has not received full payment for its November and December sales. Consequently, future cash inflows from these sales will affect the cash budget for year 3. To see this more clearly, consider the actual sales of $1,011,200 made in November of year 2. According to the payment pattern shown here, the firm will capture cash for those sales as shown in table 18.3. Knowing the projected amount of sales for each month and the pattern of payment for the sales gives the financial manager enough information to budget cash receipts.

The third step is to use the projected sales and payment pattern to prepare the projected cash inflows. Table 18.4 presents the projected cash inflows for Imaginary Products for the first four months of year 3. For example, for March they are expected to be $1,746,000. This total results from collecting 15 percent of March sales, 35 percent of February sales, and 50 percent of January sales.

The fourth step is to make a schedule of disbursements. We have already observed that Imaginary Products had quite a few current liabilities at the end of year 2. The timing of the payments that the firm must make to fulfill those obligations is the crucial question for the cash budget. Table 18.5 shows the projected cash disbursements that Imaginary Products anticipates it must make during the first four months of year 3. Due to the seasonal nature of its business, it will incur increasing costs for manufacturing supplies in

TABLE 18.3

Imaginary Products – Schedule of Cash Receipts for November of Year 2 Sales

November of Year 2 Sales: $1,011,200

Cash receipts from November of Year 2 sales:

Month	% Collected	Cash Amount
November of year 2	15	$151,680
December of year 2	35	353,920
January of year 3	50	505,600

TABLE 18.4

Imaginary Products – Projected Cash Receipts from Sales
(000s omitted)

Month (Year 3)	January	February	March	April
Projected sales	1,353	1,894	2,705	3,246
Cash receipts:				
Cash sales (15%)	203	284	406	487
Collections from				
preceding month (35%)	265	474	663	947
Collections from				
two months ago (50%)	506	379	677	947
TOTAL RECEIPTS	974	1,137	1,746	2,381

TABLE 18.5
Imaginary Products – Projected Cash Disbursements
(000s omitted)

Month (Year 3)	January	February	March	April
Payments to suppliers:				
Cash	75	255	380	75
Lagged one month	60	80	435	95
Lagged two months	40	90	150	125
Wages and salaries	350	480	560	530
Rent expense	185	185	185	185
		29		
Interest payments	40	40	520	
Notes due			450	
TOTAL DISBURSEMENTS	750	1,130	2,709	1,010

the early months of the year. In addition, to prepare the goods for the heavy spring and summer selling season, it will incur increased wage expenses.

If Imaginary Products is to have any cash problems, they are likely to arise in March. Then, sales receipts are still low from the winter, but the company has high materials cost and labor expense as it prepares for the heavy selling season. In addition, March may be particularly problematic because tax payments are due in that month, along with a large interest payment. Finally, a note is also due in March. Comparing the total cash inflows and outflows for March, we see that the outflows are $963,000 ($2,709,000 – $1,746,000) more than the inflows. If Imaginary Products is to overcome this and any other cash shortfall, it must make plans in advance.

As a fifth and final step in preparing the cash budget, the firm must assemble the projected receipts and disbursements, together with the cash available at the beginning of the period. In table 18.6, for each month, line 1 shows the amount of beginning cash. For January, this is simply the amount on the balance sheet for December 31 of year 2. Line 2 shows the cash receipts the firm expects in each month (these figures are taken from table 18.4). For any given month, adding the beginning cash and the cash receipts gives the total cash available to Imaginary Products for that month, as shown in line 3.

Line 4 shows the projected monthly cash disbursements that were calculated in table 18.5. We must subtract that amount from the available cash to find the amount of cash the firm expects to have at the end of the month. This monthly ending cash is given in line 5. We carry this ending cash figure forward as the beginning amount of cash available for the next month. For example, January is expected to end with an anticipated cash balance of $434,000. This sum constitutes the beginning cash balance for February.

In addition, the firm may wish to maintain a minimum cash balance as a precaution against planning errors. Imaginary Products keeps a cash balance of at least $100,000, as indicated in line 6. Therefore, we must subtract $100,000 from the ending cash total to

TABLE 18.6
Imaginary Products – Cash Budget
(000s omitted)

Month (Year 3)	January	February	March	April
1. Beginning cash	210)	434)	441)	(522)
2. Cash receipts	974)	1,137)	1,746)	2,381)
3. Cash available	1,184)	1,571)	2,187)	1,859)
4. Cash disbursements	750)	1,130)	2,709)	1,010)
5. Ending cash	434)	441)	(522)	849)
6. Minimum cash balance	100)	100)	100)	100)
7. Excess (needed) cash	334)	341)	(622)	749)

find the excess cash, or the amount of cash the firm needs. If there is excess cash, Imaginary Products can invest these funds to earn a return for the firm; if there is not, the firm must acquire the needed cash to pay its obligations and to maintain its minimum cash balance. Any excess or shortfall of cash is shown in line 7 of table 18.6.

During January of year 3 Imaginary Products has a total of $1,184,000 available cash, out of which it expects to pay $750,000. This leaves an ending cash balance of $434,000. Out of this amount it will reserve $100,000 as a minimum cash balance for any unforeseen emergencies. This leaves an excess amount of cash of $334,000, which Imaginary Products can invest to earn more profits.

As shown in table 18.6, Imaginary Products expects to experience a cash shortfall in March. According to the cash budget, the firm needs to obtain $622,000 in cash for March. However, this is a temporary shortfall because the cash budget shows a cash surplus for April. As a consequence, Imaginary Products needs to arrange for a one month loan to cover that temporary financing need.

The cash budget is crucial in uncovering the firm's cash needs. Without it, the manager might not have foreseen the need for financing in March, and Imaginary Products might not have had enough cash to meet its debts. Failure to pay the note that came due in March could have resulted in serious consequences for its credit standing and reputation.

PRO FORMA FINANCIAL STATEMENTS

A pro forma statement is a projected financial statement that reflects current forecasts of sales and expenses. It is useful in planning the firm's operation and in anticipating its future financial position. For example, a pro forma income statement for the next year will summarize the performance of the firm if it meets the current projections of sales and expenses. A pro forma balance sheet for next year will summarize the firm's expected financial position at that time.

In addition to using these pro forma statements as forecasting tools, the firm can use them as managerial tools. If the manager prepares them based on current forecasts of sales and expenses and the result is not satisfactory, then management knows that it needs to alter its current plans to achieve a better result. This section illustrates the preparation of pro forma financial statements by continuing the example of Imaginary Products.

The Pro Forma Income Statement

With a projected 7 percent increase in sales, Imaginary Products is planning to have its sales grow from $25,280,000 in year 2 to $27,050,000 in year 3. One way of projecting future earnings and expenses is to assume that the future will resemble the past. In the pro forma income statement, this means assuming that the same ratio of expenses to sales that prevailed in the past will continue in the future. If no major changes in the firm's operations occur from one year to the next, this can be a reasonable assumption. Table 18.7 illustrates this technique, showing the actual income statement and the percentage income statement for year 2. In addition, the final column contains the projected income statement for year 3.

In this pro forma income statement, the forecasted sales are $27,050,000, reflecting the targeted 7 percent increase. The manager can construct the statement by assuming that the same operating ratios that prevailed in the past will continue in year 3. In table 18.7, the projected expense and profit items are constructed by applying the year 2 percentages shown in the middle column to the new projected sales figure of $27,050,000 for year 3.

The financial manager should be careful when applying the percentage of sales method to construct a financial income statement, because some accounts may not increase in direct proportion to sales. For example, in table 18.7 we assume that depreciation expenses in year 3 will remain at the year 2 level of $750,000. This may be a reasonable assumption if the firm operated at less than full capacity in year 2 and had no plans to purchase additional machinery in year 3. This is indeed what we will assume. An unchanging

TABLE 18.7
Imaginary Products – Actual Income Statement for Year 2
and Pro Forma Income Statement for Year 3
(000s omitted)

	Year 2 (Actual)	Year 2 (%)	Year 3 (Projected)
Sales	25,280	100.0	27,050
Cost of goods sold	20,900	82.7	22,370
GROSS PROFIT	4,380	17.3	4,680
Depreciation	750	3.0	750
Selling and administrative expenses	2,615	10.3	2,786
Interest expense	940	3.7	1,001
EARNINGS BEFORE TAXES	75	0.3	143
Taxes	28	0.1	53
NET INCOME	47	0.2	90

depreciation expense is also consistent with a linear depreciation of the fixed assets. If the firm used an accelerated depreciation method, the depreciation expense would decrease through time if the firm does not buy new equipment. The important point is that the financial planner should be aware of the actual situation of the firm so that the forecasts are as accurate as possible.

The Pro Forma Balance Sheet

Preparation of the pro forma balance sheet requires information from a variety of sources, including the previous balance sheet and the pro forma income statement. This section illustrates the preparation of a pro forma balance sheet for Imaginary Products for December 31 of year 3.

We can simplify the process by making a few practical assumptions. First, assume that Imaginary Products does not plan to issue any new common stock or long-term debt, so these accounts will not change. Second, assume that management plans to adjust the marketable securities account to make the balance sheet balance from the asset side. For example, if the firm finds itself with more cash than the amount required, it will invest the excess in marketable securities. If, on the contrary, the firm needs cash, it will have to sell some marketable securities. Also, management plans to adjust the notes payable account to allow the balance sheet to adjust from the liabilities side of the balance sheet. Using these assumptions, we can construct the pro forma balance sheet by determining the planned level for each of the remaining asset and liability accounts. We consider each of them in turn.

Cash   The cash level of the firm should increase with sales, and we assume that it increases linearly with sales. Since sales in year 3 are expected to be 7 percent greater than in year 2, the cash level should also increase by 7 percent. With a cash level of $210,000 at the end of year 2, the firm is expected to have $224,700 in cash at the end of year 3, or $225,000 rounded to the nearest thousand.

Accounts Receivable   We know that Imaginary Products collects 35 percent of its sales in the first month after the sale and 50 percent in the second month after the sale. Using this information, we can forecast the amount of receivables that the firm will have on December 31 of year 3. For sales made in November, it collects 15 percent in November and another 35 percent in December, leaving 50 percent of the receivables outstanding. Sales for November are forecasted to be $1,082,000, as shown in table 18.2, and they will generate $541,000 in receivables as of December 31. In addition, since Imaginary Products collects 15 percent of its sales in the sales month, it must have 85 percent of its December sales left as receivables at the end of the month. The projected December sales of $811,500 implies receivables of about $690,000 at the end of the month. Table 18.8 summarizes these calculations, and shows that the total level of accounts receivable expected at the end of year 3 is about $1,231,000.[1]

---

[1] Note that accounts receivable are expected to more than double during year 3. At the end of year 2, the actual level was $520,000 and it is expected to grow to $1,231,000 at the end of year 3. Such tremendous expected growth should concern the financial manager. In particular, one would expect an increase of only about 7 percent

TABLE 18.8
Calculation of Accounts Receivable Level at the End of Year 3

Sales Month	Projected Sales	% Uncollected on December 31	Contribution to Accounts Receivable
November	$1,082,000	50	1,$541,000
December	$1,811,500	85	$1,689,775
		Total:	$1,230,775
		Rounding to nearest $1,000:	$1,231,000

Inventory   Assume that the firm's inventory level increases in proportion to its sales level. With the projected 7 percent increase in sales, this means that the inventory level will increase from $670,000 in year 2 to $716,900 in year 3.[2]

Plant and Equipment   As stated previously, Imaginary Products is not planning additions to plant and equipment in year 3, so this asset category will remain at $23,000,000.

Accumulated Depreciation   The firm must depreciate assets on a fixed schedule determined when it places the assets in service. Therefore, we can project the accumulated depreciation exactly. The depreciation for year 3 will be $750,000, which matches the figure on the pro forma income statement. This gives a total accumulated depreciation of $9,000,000.

Accounts Payable   With the forecasted increase in sales, Imaginary Products expects to increase its purchases from suppliers. If it maintains its present payment policy, then the accounts payable level should increase by 7 percent. Thus, the new level of accounts payable would be 7 percent greater than $390,000, or $417,300, which we round to $417,000.

Accruals   Just as Imaginary Products expects accounts payable to increase with sales, it plans the same increase in accruals. For example, this increase in accruals would reflect the greater number of workers that the firm needs to produce the higher volume of items that it plans to sell in year 3. A 7 percent increase in accruals gives a forecasted accruals level of approximately $43,000.

---

during the year, since accounts receivable should increase linearly with sales if the average collection period is unchanged. To explain this discrepancy, we assume that the receivables collection for the end of year 2 was unusually fast.

[2] Assuming a linear relationship between sales and inventory may not be appropriate. Indeed, according to the economic ordering quantity (EOQ) model discussed in chapter 14, inventory should increase in proportion to the square root of sales. However, in the interest of simplicity, we will not account for this refinement here.

Taxes Payable   According to the pro forma income statement in table 18.7, Imaginary Products expects to owe $53,000 in taxes payable at the end of year 3.[3] This figure assumes the same tax rate as in year 2.

Retained Earnings   The pro forma income statement shows that Imaginary Products expects a net income in year 3 of $90,000, which is a very low level of earnings for a firm with such a large asset base, even though it is a substantial improvement over the net income of year 2. Nonetheless, Imaginary Products plans a cash dividend of $0.03 per share. With 1 million shares outstanding, this is a total dividend of $30,000. Because the firm must devote after-tax earnings either to dividends or to retained earnings, it plans a $60,000 increase in retained earnings, from $4,565,000 to $4,625,000.

Based on the forecasted changes in each of the asset categories, table 18.9 presents a partially completed pro forma balance sheet for December 31 of year 3. For all of the completed assets and liabilities, it shows total assets of $16,173,000 and total liabilities and net worth of $15,738,000. These numbers do not include the level of marketable securities or notes payable. Because the balance sheet must balance, the following relationship must hold:

$$\$16,173,000 + \text{Marketable Securities} = \$15,738,000 + \text{Notes Payable}$$

Equivalently, we have:

$$\text{Notes Payable} - \text{Marketable Securities} = \$435,000$$

The firm has the option of choosing any combination of the two balancing accounts, as long as their difference is $435,000. We assume that the firm prefers to have the lowest possible level of notes payable. Given this assumption, the firm will reduce its marketable securities to zero. It follows that the firm will have $435,000 in notes payable at the end of year 3. With these additional figures for marketable securities and notes payable, we can complete the pro forma balance sheet, which is presented in table 18.10.

FINANCIAL PLANNING AND PRO FORMA STATEMENTS

The pro forma balance sheet of table 18.10 reflects an improvement in the liquidity of the firm. If Imaginary Products realizes the operating plans for year 3, it will greatly increase accounts receivable, and it will repay some of its outstanding notes. These measures will increase the current ratio from 1.39 at the end of year 2 to 2.29 in year 3. Therefore, the firm will go from being very illiquid to sufficiently liquid.

From the point that we have reached in our analysis, the managers of Imaginary Products might go on to consider modifying their plans. For example, with the new liquidity figures, the managers could decide to pay even more notes, thus reducing the cash level. This would require preparing new pro forma statements to reflect those plans.

---

[3] Notice that taxes payable for year 2 are greater than the firm's income tax burden in that year. This is possible if the firm owed taxes from previous years. All the taxes due at the end of year 2 are assumed to be fully paid by the end of year 3.

TABLE 18.9
Imaginary Products – Preliminary Pro Forma Balance Sheet
for December 31 of Year 3
(000s omitted)

ASSETS	
Cash	225
Accounts receivable	1,231
Inventory	717
Marketable securities	? Balancing item + mkt. sec.
Current assets	2,173
Plant and equipment	23,000
Less accumulated depreciation	9,000
Total fixed assets	14,000
TOTAL ASSETS	16,173 + Mkt. sec.
LIABILITIES AND NET WORTH	
Accounts payable	417
Notes payable	? Balancing item
Accruals	43
Taxes payable	53
Current liabilities	513 + Notes payable
Long-term liabilities	9,600
TOTAL LIABILITIES	10,113 + Notes payable
Common stock	
($1 par; 1 million shares)	1,000
Retained earnings	4,625
NET WORTH	5,625
TOTAL LIABILITIES AND NET WORTH	15,738 + Notes payable

The essential point about planning is that the firm can use pro forma statements and the cash budget to facilitate the planning process. By making preliminary plans, and preparing pro forma statements to reflect those plans, managers can obtain insights into the effects of various alternatives.

Planning for the operation of the firm requires balancing many competing claims on the firm's resources to obtain the overall best plan. To improve the planning process, many firms are using sophisticated forecasting techniques. For example, many are using computerized financial planning models.

SUMMARY

This chapter explored some of the basic techniques of financial planning. The first of these concerned the cash budget. Every firm needs cash to survive. Failure to make a

TABLE 18.10
Imaginary Products – Pro Forma Balance Sheet for December 31 of Year 3
(000s omitted)

ASSETS	
Cash	225
Accounts receivable	1,231
Inventory	717
Marketable securities	0
Current assets	2,173
Plant and equipment	23,000
Less accumulated depreciation	9,000
Total fixed assets	14,000
TOTAL ASSETS	16,173
LIABILITIES AND NET WORTH	
Accounts payable	417
Notes payable	435
Accruals	43
Taxes payable	53
Current liabilities	948
Long-term liabilities	9,600
TOTAL LIABILITIES	10,548
Common stock	
($1 par; 1 million shares)	1,000
Retained earnings	4,625
NET WORTH	5,625
TOTAL LIABILITIES AND NET WORTH	16,173

contractually obligated payment on time means technical insolvency, which can lead to bankruptcy and the dissolution of the firm. As a consequence, firms must manage the cash account to ensure that sufficient funds are available to pay obligations.

The cash budget is essentially a plan for the cash balances of the firm over a future period. Managers use cash budgets to highlight those periods requiring additional cash and to identify those periods when the firm will generate excess cash.

The second major technique examined in this chapter was the pro forma statement. A pro forma income statement is a planned income statement for a future date. A pro forma income statement relies on a forecast of revenues and expenses and provides a plan for firm operations over the coming period. A pro forma balance sheet is a planned balance sheet for a particular date in the future. Managers usually prepare it in conjunction with the pro forma income statement.

On occasion, pro forma statements give a picture that managers do not want to see, such as deterioration of the firm's liquidity. In such cases, preparation of the pro forma statements serves to highlight problem areas requiring managerial attention and, therefore, is important in the planning process.

QUESTIONS

1. What is the difference between an income statement and a cash budget?
2. In preparing a cash budget, why does the financial manager need to know the level of sales and the collection pattern for sales?
3. Assume that you have prepared a cash budget for your firm and that you project a negative cash balance in one month. What responses are available to you?
4. Can you construct a pro forma balance sheet without a previous balance sheet? Why or why not?
5. When can you use financial ratios to guide the preparation of pro forma financial statements?
6. Can you construct a pro forma balance sheet without a pro forma income statement?
7. If a firm buys no new depreciable property during the period over which the pro forma statements are being prepared, is a pro forma income statement necessary to determine the accumulated depreciation on the pro forma balance sheet? Why or why not?
8. You are projecting next year's accounts receivable level. If the average collection period will remain the same as this year, and sales increase by 50 percent, by what percentage will accounts receivable increase?
9. You are projecting next year's accounts receivable level. If the average collection period increases from 30 to 45 days, and sales increase by 50 percent, by what percentage will accounts receivable increase?
10. You are projecting next year's accounts receivable level. If the average collection period decreases from 45 to 30 days, and sales decrease by 50 percent, by what percentage will accounts receivable decrease?
11. You are projecting next year's accounts receivable level. If the average collection period decreases from 60 to 30 days, by what percentage must sales increase for the accounts receivable level to remain unchanged?
12. You are projecting next year's accounts receivable level. If the average collection period increases from 30 to 45 days, by what percentage must sales increase so that the accounts receivable level is twice the current level?
13. You are projecting next year's inventory level, assuming that it increases in proportion to the square root of sales. If sales increase by 100 percent, by what percentage does the inventory account increase?
14. You are projecting next year's inventory level, assuming that it increases in proportion to the square root of sales. If sales decrease by 50 percent, by what percentage does the inventory account decrease?

PROBLEMS

1. Assume that sales for November are $1,500,000. Of these sales, 30 percent are for cash, 20 percent are collected the next month, 20 percent the following month, 15 percent the following month, 10 percent the next month, and 5 percent the next month. Calculate the firm's cash inflow from these sales for each month.

2. For the same firm as problem 1, assume that December sales are $1,200,000 and follow the same collection cycle. Calculate the firm's cash inflows from these sales for each month.

3. Consider the following sales pattern observed in Sales Cycles, Inc., for the past year.

January	$150,000	July	$ 80,000
February	180,000	August	70,000
March	220,000	September	110,000
April	280,000	October	130,000
May	200,000	November	120,000
June	120,000	December	150,000

If Sales Cycles makes 40 percent of its sales for cash, collects 35 percent of its sales the following month, and the final 25 percent the next month, show the cash flows generated by the sales presented here.

4. In planning for next year, Sales Cycles expects sales to be 12 percent above last year's levels shown in problem 3. Calculate the forecasted sales on a month by month basis for the next year.

5. Assume that Sales Cycles collects 60 percent of its sales in cash, 25 percent the following month, and the final 15 percent the next month. Based on the sales projected in problem 4, calculate the firm's projected cash receipts for the next year.

We met Dismal Industries in the previous chapter. Its year 2 balance sheet and income statement are presented here. We will use Dismal to develop an integrated cash budget and pro forma statements.

Dismal Industries – Balance Sheet
December 31, Year 2
(000s omitted)

ASSETS	
Cash	100
Marketable securities	50
Accounts receivable	570
Inventory	200
CURRENT ASSETS	920
Plant and equipment	15,080
Less accumulated depreciation	5,900
TOTAL FIXED ASSETS	9,180
TOTAL ASSETS	10,100

LIABILITIES AND NET WORTH

Accounts payable	325
Notes payable	340
Accruals	150
Taxes payable	90
CURRENT LIABILITIES	905
Long-term liabilities	5,000
TOTAL LIABILITIES	5,905
Common stock	1,000
Retained earnings	3,195
NET WORTH	4,195
TOTAL LIABILITIES AND NET WORTH	10,100

Dismal Industries – Income Statement
(000s omitted)

	Year 2 ($)
Sales	8,000
Cost of goods sold	6,100
GROSS PROFIT	1,900
Depreciation	900
Selling and administrative expenses	350
Interest expense	400
EARNINGS BEFORE TAXES (EBT)	250
Taxes	100
NET	150

The sales pattern for Dismal for selected months usually follows the pattern given here:

	Percentage	Actual Sales for Year 2
January	8	$640,000
February	6	480,000
March	5	400,000
November	10	800,000
December	12	960,000

Dismal expects the same percentages to be maintained in year 3, but is looking for an increase in sales of 12 percent over the year 2 level.

6. Based on the information about sales, what is Dismal's total forecasted sales in year 3?

7. Based on the information just presented, what is the forecasted level of sales for January, February, and March of year 3?

Dismal collects 50 percent of its sales in cash, 30 percent the following month, and 20 percent the next month.

8. What collections will it make in the future (after December 31 of year 2) from its year 2 sales? When will these amounts be collected?

9. For the January of year 3 sales, what portions will be collected in January, February, and March?

10. For the February of year 3 sales, what portions will be collected in February and March?

11. For the March of year 3 sales, what portion will be collected in March?

12. Calculate the total cash inflows from sales for January, February, and March, based on your answers to the four preceding questions.

13. Dismal's balance sheet shows $905,000 in current liabilities, including $325,000 in accounts payable. Dismal will pay off $25,000 of these accounts payable immediately, and the remainder will be paid evenly over the months of January, February, and March. Prepare a schedule for the first three months of year 3 showing these disbursements.

14. Dismal plans to purchase $300,000 of supplies in each month. It pays for 50 percent of these in cash, 25 percent the following month, and 25 percent the next month. Prepare a schedule for the first three months of year 3 showing the cash flows these purchases will generate.

15. Dismal must make its quarterly tax payment of $50,000 in March and must make principal payments on its notes payable of $150,000 in January and March. Prepare a schedule for the first three months of year 3 showing the cash flows these disbursements will generate.

16. Dismal will pay 60 percent of its accruals in January and 40 percent in February and will make wage payments of $150,000 in each month during the period January–March of year 3. Prepare a schedule for the first three months of year 3 showing the cash flows these payments will generate.

17. Assemble all of the cash flows from problems 13–16 into a schedule of disbursements for Dismal Industries for the first three months of year 3.

18. Assemble the completed cash receipts and disbursement schedules into a cash budget for Dismal Industries for the first three months of year 3.

19. Using the income statement for Dismal Industries printed earlier, compute a percentage income statement.

20. Assume that Dismal's sales forecast for January–March of year 3 is correct and that the same relative costs will be incurred. Using that information, and the percentage income statement prepared in problem 19, prepare a pro forma income statement for Dismal for the period January–March of year 3.

We now turn to a preparation of a pro forma balance sheet for Dismal Industries. In the problems that follow, we will use the following assumptions. Dismal is not planning to issue any common stock or long-term debt. Dismal will use the cash and marketable securities accounts, along with the notes payable account, to force the pro forma balance sheet to balance. Assume inventory will expand at the same rate as sales.

21. Calculate the amount of accounts receivable Dismal should show on its March 31, year 3, pro forma balance sheet.
22. Calculate the amount of inventory Dismal should show on its March 31, year 3, pro forma balance sheet.
23. Assuming that Dismal purchases no new plant or equipment during this period, calculate the amount of plant and equipment Dismal should show on its March 31, year 3, pro forma balance sheet.
24. Based on the pro forma income statement, what is the amount of accumulated depreciation that Dismal should show on its March 31, year 3, pro forma balance sheet?
25. Accruals should increase proportionally with sales, so what is the amount of accumulated accruals that Dismal should show on its March 31, year 3, pro forma balance sheet, assuming a sales increase of 12 percent?
26. Dismal expects taxes payable to increase by 15 percent over the pro forma period, in spite of the fact that it will be making tax payments over the period, so what amount of taxes payable should Dismal show on its March 31, year 3, pro forma balance sheet?
27. Dismal anticipates no dividend payments during the pro forma period, so what should Dismal show on its March 31, year 3, pro forma balance sheet in the retained earnings account?
28. Assuming accounts payable are $228,119.07, construct a pro forma balance sheet for Dismal Industries for March 31 of year 3, leaving cash, notes payable, and marketable securities blank for balancing.
29. Assuming no changes in marketable securities or notes payable, except for those changes in notes payable we have already considered, what is the value of the cash account?
30. If Dismal wishes to have the same ratio of cash to total assets on March 31 of year 3, as it had on December 31 of year 2, what action would you recommend?

Chapter 19

Market Efficiency

OVERVIEW

This chapter introduces the concept of an efficient market. In briefest terms, an efficient market is one that responds well and quickly to new information. The response of a market to new information is very important for market equilibrium.

While the capital asset pricing model (CAPM) introduced in chapter 9 may state what the equilibrium relationship between expected return and risk should be, the entire theory would be worthless for practical application if markets never moved toward this equilibrium. This means that there is an intimate connection between the CAPM and the efficient markets hypothesis (EMH). In fact, the CAPM and the EMH are so connected that the two ideas cannot be tested independently of one another. Tests of the EMH try to establish whether markets process new information in a way that makes prices move quickly toward the new equilibrium. But in order to evaluate that issue, there must be some conception of what the equilibrium price is. Since the specification of the equilibrium is given by the CAPM, the two theories are tied together.

In spite of the difficulties in separating the CAPM and the EMH, a number of empirical tests have been conducted that are quite revealing. Taken together, these tests provide a good indication of the adequacy of the CAPM and the efficiency of the financial markets.

In recent years, a number of controversies surrounding the CAPM have arisen. Professor Richard Roll has raised general issues concerning the potential testability of the CAPM. In addition, a number of market anomalies have been discovered that apparently violate either the CAPM or the EMH.

THE EFFICIENT MARKETS HYPOTHESIS

The **efficient markets hypothesis** is one of the central ideas in modern finance. Unfortunately, the very name is misleading, because it seems to imply that a market is efficient in the same way that a street sweeper might be efficient. Because of this potential confusion, we can speak of markets that are operationally efficient and markets that are informationally efficient. A market is **operationally efficient** if it works smoothly, with limited delays. For example, if orders can be transmitted from all parts of the world to a market very rapidly, and if those orders can be quickly executed and confirmed, then such a market will be operationally efficient.

A market may be operationally efficient, however, without being informationally efficient. An informationally efficient market is one in which market prices adjust quickly in response to new information. For our purposes, the key concept of efficiency is informational efficiency. A market is **informationally efficient** if prices in the market at all times fully reflect all information contained in some specified information set. The efficient markets hypothesis refers to this kind of informational efficiency.

As an example of how capital markets quickly incorporate new arriving information, consider the well-known case of John Sculley's arrival to Spectrum Information Technologies in late 1993, and his abrupt departure a few months later, as shown in figure 19.1. Given that Sculley had come from a successful tenure as CEO at Apple Computer, the unexpected news of his arrival at Spectrum on October 19, 1993, was greeted by investors with a sizable stock price increase. Clearly, investors were expecting Sculley's managerial skills to add value to the firm. Unfortunately, Sculley soon became disenchanted with Spectrum and rumors of the rift between Sculley and the firm's board of directors leaked, slowly eroding Spectrum's stock price. When Sculley announced his departure on February 7, 1994, the price suffered a precipitous decline. These dramatic and sudden price swings neatly illustrate the idea of an informationally efficient market.

The example illustrates that if market prices fully reflect all the information as it arrives, then prices immediately adjust to new levels in accordance with the new information. This also implies that the information cannot be used to develop a trading strategy to beat the market, as any bit of available information would already be reflected in the market prices.

FIGURE 19.1
The Effect of Sculley's Arrival and Departure on Spectrum's Stock Price

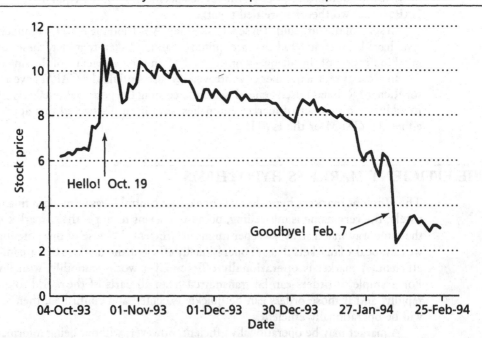

There are different versions of the market efficiency hypothesis according to the information set that is assumed to be contained in market prices. It has become traditional to distinguish three versions of the EMH.

1. weak form efficiency
2. semi-strong form efficiency
3. strong form efficiency

Each of these three versions of the EMH claims that the market is efficient with respect to a different information set.

Weak Form Efficiency

A market is weakly efficient if its prices fully reflect the information set containing all historical market data. Historical market data include the complete history of market prices, volume figures, and other similar data. If markets are weakly efficient, all such information is useless for directing a trading strategy. Analysis of this kind of information is known as **technical analysis**, so if the market is weakly efficient, technical analysis is worthless.

If the weak form version is true, then all market-related data are already reflected in security prices, and are of no further value. As a consequence, analysis of such data cannot be useful for directing a trading strategy. However, selling charts of past price movements of securities is a multi-million dollar business in the United States, and customers buy such charts largely to help them formulate better investment strategies. If the weak form version of the efficient markets hypothesis is true, such charts are worthless and the money spent on them is wasted, to the extent that the charts are to be used for improving investment performance.

The chart business is busy diversifying into home computer software that will allow personal computer owners to download price histories from a central data management source and to construct charts via the client's own computer. An immediate implication for investors that could be drawn from the truth of the weak form efficient markets hypothesis is that investment in such services is wasted money.

Semi-Strong Form Efficiency

A market is semi-strong efficient if prices in that market at all times fully reflect all public information. Public information includes all published reports, such as the firm's financial statements, newspaper reports, the financial press, and government publications and announcements. Since the semi-strong efficiency hypothesis says that market prices reflect all public information, this includes all market data as well.

If the semi-strong form of market efficiency is true, then analysis of all public information cannot profitably be used to glean additional information about market prices that is not already incorporated into those prices. This kind of inquiry is known as **fundamental analysis**. Those who believe in fundamental analysis search publicly available information on stocks in the hope of beating the market. If the semi-strong version is true, however, all of this information is already reflected in stock prices. Consequently, money spent on such analysis would bear no better results than reading tea leaves or divining the future with a crystal ball.

Strong Form Efficiency

A market is strong form efficient if its prices fully reflect all information, both public and private. Private information consists of information generated by government officials or corporate insiders that has not yet been made public. For example, members of the Federal Reserve Board often have access to private information. Imagine a meeting of the Federal Reserve Board in which new guidelines for the conduct of monetary policy are adopted. Such decisions are not revealed immediately to the public and, until the public announcement is made, Federal Reserve Board members have extremely valuable private information. Imagine also the case of an oil company that has made a major crude oil find, but has not yet announced the discovery. Before the announcement, some employees of the corporation could profitably trade by hoarding the firm's stock.

The strong form version of the efficient markets hypothesis implies that this private information is already reflected in stock prices. The most important consequence of this claim, if true, is that such privileged information could not be used to generate a trading profit that beats the market. As the name implies, the strong form efficiency claim is very strong indeed.

Currently, there are numerous laws on the books regarding the appropriate use of privileged information for securities trading. Transgressors of these laws are occasionally discovered and even imprisoned, as the Wall Street scandals of the 1980s featuring Ivan Boesky and Michael Milken have illustrated. If the strong form of the EMH is true, such laws are actually unnecessary. If markets are strongly efficient, attempts to use such information are pointless because all of this information would already be reflected in security prices. On the other hand, if the strong form of the EMH is not true, then the laws have validity and may be worthy of continued strict enforcement.

RELATIONSHIPS AMONG THE THREE FORMS OF MARKET EFFICIENCY

Figure 19.2 shows how the information sets for these three versions of the EMH are related. The weak form version of the hypothesis says that financial markets are efficient with respect to a minimum core of information, represented by the interior circle in the figure. The semi-strong form of market efficiency claims that markets reflect the minimum core of information plus all other types of public information. The strong form hypothesis says that all of the information in the large circle is reflected in market prices, including all public information, which in turn includes all market-related data.

These relationships mean that any refutation of the weak form of the efficient markets hypothesis will count against both the semi-strong and the strong versions of the hypothesis. If the market is not efficient with respect to market-related information, it cannot be efficient with respect to all public information. Likewise, if the market is not efficient with respect to market-related data, it cannot be efficient with respect to all information. So if the weak form of the efficient markets hypothesis is shown to be false, both the semi-strong and the strong form will logically be false.

The truth of the weak form of the efficient markets hypothesis is necessary for the truth of the semi-strong and strong versions. Similarly, the truth of the semi-strong version is necessary for the truth of the strong version. By contrast, if the strong form version of the EMH is true, the semi-strong and weak form versions must be true.

FIGURE 19.2
Information Sets and Different Versions of the EMH

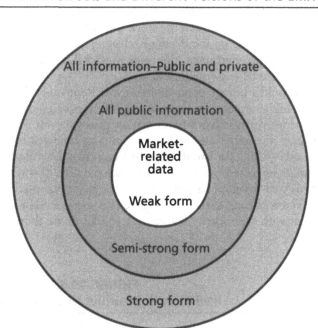

THE CAPM AND THE EFFICIENT MARKETS HYPOTHESIS

There is an intimate connection between the CAPM and the EMH. Essentially, the CAPM specifies the relationship between risk and expected return, and tests of the EMH look for situations in which that specified relationship is violated. For example, consider the fact that some stocks trade on both the New York and the Pacific Stock Exchanges, and assume for the moment that there are no transaction costs. During parts of the day, both exchanges are open and engage in active trading of the same securities. Across the country, traders follow the activity on both exchanges. Now assume that a particular stock simultaneously trades for $105 on the New York Stock Exchange and for $100 on the Pacific Exchange.

In this situation, a trader could simultaneously buy the stock on the Pacific Exchange and sell it on the New York Stock Exchange. Doing this would be riskless and would require no capital, because the transactions would be concluded at the same time. The result would be a profit of $5 per share on a riskless transaction which required no capital. Such a transaction is called an **arbitrage transaction**. Clearly, a market that allows arbitrage opportunities is performing very poorly. In a very real sense, the presence of arbitrage opportunities means that there is money lying on the ground that no one is willing to pick up.

It is also apparent that the presence of arbitrage opportunities is inconsistent with equilibrium pricing. In our example, the price differential of $5 will surely attract trader interest. The traders will buy the stock on the Pacific Exchange for $100 and sell it in New York for $105. Doing so will generate excess demand for the stock at a price of $100 on the Pacific Exchange, because everyone will want to buy the stock at that price. Likewise, everyone will be trying to sell the stock for $105 in New York, creating an excess supply. With excess demand on the Pacific Exchange, the price must rise, and with excess supply on the New York Exchange, the price must fall. In fact, only when the two prices are equal can there be any equilibrium at all.[1]

How could arbitrage opportunities exist? Remember that we have assumed that investors favor higher expected returns, all other factors being equal. If that is so, and if arbitrage opportunities persist, that implies market prices do not reflect all available information. In this case, the information that would not be reflected in the market prices is that the same good is selling for two different prices in two different markets. Also, the persistence of arbitrage opportunities would mean that the CAPM was violated.

With well-developed securities markets, most potential violations of the CAPM and the EMH are difficult to identify. Figure 19.3 shows a relationship between risk and return consistent with the security market line (SML). If we think of the line as expressing the

FIGURE 19.3
The SML with Securities Not in Equilibrium

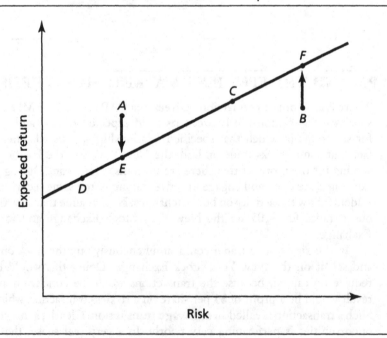

[1] If transaction costs are included, a slight difference in the price of the stock on the two exchanges could persist because the transactions costs erode the potential profits arising from the price discrepancy.

predicted trade-off between risk and return, then securities C and D are exactly consistent with the theory, while securities A and B are not.

Two explanations are possible for the behavior of securities A and B in figure 19.3. First, it could be that the market is not responding to the relevant information about securities A and B. In other words, the market may be inefficient. In a way, this is similar to the presence of continuing arbitrage opportunities discussed earlier. An investor could purchase security A and receive a greater level of return than the market should allow, given its risk. For the same level of systematic risk, the investor should only be receiving a return like that of security E. If A's returns are always above the line representing the appropriate trade-off between risk and return, then the market may be inefficient.

A second possible explanation for A being above and for B being below the prescribed level of return for their levels of risk could be that the CAPM incorrectly specifies the risk/return relationship. Perhaps expected return is not really a function of systematic risk, as measured by beta. It may be that systematic risk is not really important at all and that the CAPM is completely false. Alternatively, it may be that returns depend on other factors in addition to systematic risk and that the CAPM only gives a partial explanation of the factors that generate returns.

The most important point to note from this discussion is that attempts to test the EMH or the CAPM turn out to be tests of both theories simultaneously. As just explained, given persistent occurrences of securities like A or B, the problem could lie either with the CAPM, the EMH, or both. From our tests, we will probably not be able to tell exactly where the difficulty lies.

PERFORMANCE MEASUREMENT AND BEATING THE MARKET

Implicit in the preceding discussion of the relationship between the EMH and the CAPM is the idea that the CAPM provides a measure of normal performance. We have stressed that the CAPM expresses the equilibrium level of expected returns for a given level of risk, and that this relationship can be depicted graphically by the SML, as shown in figure 19.3.

As a consequence, any special efforts at investment analysis must focus on attempts to find securities like A or B in figure 19.3. Security A offers too much return for its level of risk, while security B offers too little. If investors could successfully identify such securities, they would want to buy securities like A and sell securities like B. The goal of investment analysis must be, therefore, to find securities that lie off the SML. An analyst who can find such securities consistently would be able to beat the market.

Since the CAPM expresses a relationship between **expected** return and risk, it can often be difficult to validate a superior performance by an analyst. In any given year, some analysts will do better than others just by chance. As a consequence, the mere report of a very good year on an investment portfolio should not impress us too much. We would want to know how much risk was involved in the particular portfolio, and we would also want to know how consistently a particular analyst had been able to turn in a good performance.

If an analyst recommends a high beta portfolio in a year when the market happens to go up, then it would be no surprise if the recommended portfolio performed well that year. However, we would rightly want to know how well this analyst's recommendations performed over a long period of time. In short, beating the market requires consistently finding securities that lie off the SML. In order for us to believe that any such analyst is truly successful, the analyst's track record must be sufficiently good and sufficiently long to make the possibility of producing such a record by chance extremely unlikely.

THE RANDOM WALK HYPOTHESIS AND MARKET EFFICIENCY

The concept of market efficiency is often linked to the random walk hypothesis. As the name implies, the **random walk hypothesis** asserts that stock returns do not follow a predictable path through time. For stock returns to follow a random walk, two important assumptions must be true. First, successive returns must be independent, so the correlation between one period's return and the next is zero. Second, the distribution of returns in all periods must be identical.

If stock returns behaved in predictable ways from one day to the next, it seems that an investor could learn the regular rules for their behavior and use that information to earn fantastic returns. For example, if a large positive return in one period is likely to be followed by a large positive return in the next period, a smart trader could buy a stock after it had a big price increase and then benefit from the next big price increase. The random walk hypothesis explicitly rules out such regular behavior, so it does not allow for the possibility of inferring future returns from knowledge of past returns.

The examination of successive returns for a single security over time focuses on **serial correlation**. For example, if a positive return in period t happens to be followed by a positive return in period $t + 1$, we could plot this pair of returns in the northeast quadrant on a pair of axes such as those shown in figure 19.4. In panel (a) of figure 19.4, the graph shows how the returns would plot if there were no correlation between the returns in one period and the next. Positive returns would sometimes be followed by positive returns, leading to a point in the northeast quadrant. However, some positive returns would be followed by a negative return in the next period. Such a pair of returns would be plotted in the southeast quadrant. If there were no correlation between returns in successive periods, the graph would be a circular cloud of points centered around the origin, as shown in panel (a).

If there were positive correlation between successive returns, the graph would appear as shown in panel (b), with most returns of one sign being followed by returns of the same sign. In this case, most points would lie in the northeast and the southwest quadrants. Similarly, if returns were negatively correlated, most of the plotted pairs of returns would lie in the southeast and the northwest quadrants, as shown in panel (c).[2]

Figure 19.5 graphs the monthly correlation of returns for the U.S. stock market for the period 1951–1994. As the graph clearly indicates, there is essentially zero correlation in the returns from one period to the next. As a consequence, this figure supports the random walk hypothesis. The reasons for this are clear from the results of another kind of test called a **runs test**.

---

[2] Even if there is no correlation between returns in one period and the next, correlations between non-contiguous periods may still exist. Empirical studies have found that such correlations are essentially zero.

FIGURE 19.4
Possible Patterns of Correlated and Uncorrelated Security Returns

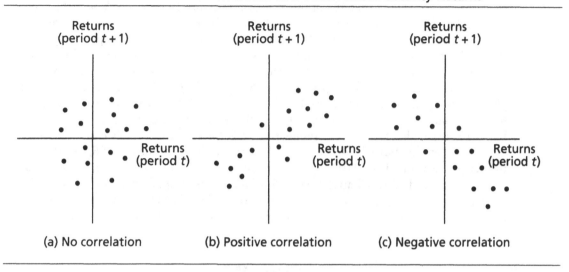

(a) No correlation   (b) Positive correlation   (c) Negative correlation

FIGURE 19.5
Serial Correlation for the U.S. Stock Market Using Monthly Returns for the Period 1951–1994

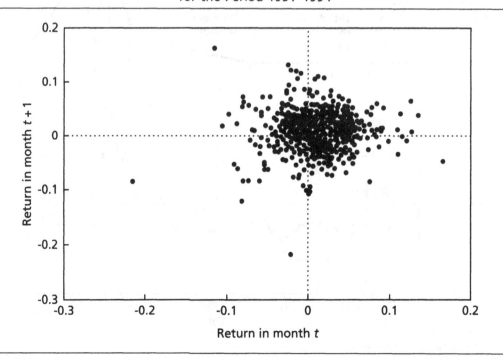

When investors look at the history of security prices, occasionally there appear to be strong trends that some analysts believe can be used to predict the future course of the stock market. A striking example of this is shown in figure 19.6, which depicts the actual level of the Dow Jones Industrial Average (DJIA) index over a 20-year period, from 1970 to 1990. Some analysts at the end of that time frame believed that the long-term trend of the DJIA strongly reflected a pattern known as the hyperwave. According to this theory, when markets are in the midst of a hyperwave, stock prices eventually return to their starting point. Notice that the hyperwave theory is very elaborate, identifying exactly seven phases of the long-term wave. Thus, based on figure 19.6, the stock market was supposed to be scheduled to return to a level of about 1,000 around 1992, thus ending the phenomenal bull market rally that began in the summer of 1982. Given the incredibly close correspondence between the stylized behavior of the hyperwave shown in the top of figure 19.6 and the actual behavior of the DJIA, gullible investors might have believed that the market was surely headed downhill after 1990. With the benefit of hindsight, we now know that quite the opposite occurred. Indeed, in direct contradiction of the hyperwave theory, the DJIA merrily continued its upward trend several years beyond 1990, achieving more than

FIGURE 19.6
The Hyperwave Theory

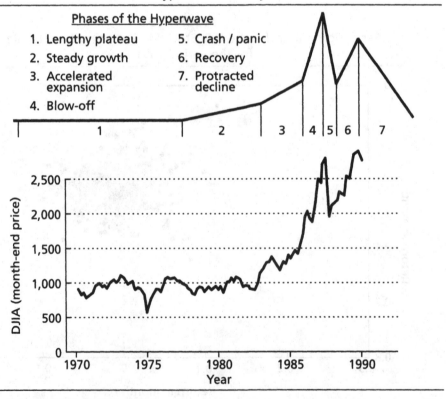

Source: Business Week, May 7, 1990, p. 134.

a 50 percent increase in the ensuing five years. Not surprisingly, we haven't heard much about the hyperwave theory since then.

THE RANDOM WALK HYPOTHESIS AND FORECASTING ABILITY

One of the strongest implications of the random walk hypothesis is that the evolution of asset prices and returns cannot be predicted. In other words, the hypothesis asserts that accurate forecasting on a consistent basis is impossible in the capital markets. Nevertheless, there appears to be a strong desire by some investors to believe that select market gurus have somehow developed the capacity to divine the future.

A striking example of purported forecasting ability is Miss Elaine Garzarelli, an investment analyst working for Lehman Brothers since 1984. Garzarelli actually predicted the stock market crash of Monday, October 19, 1987, on live television the week before it occurred. As a result, she instantly became the most famous person in Wall Street. Unfortunately, her performance since that incredible prediction has been less than stellar. Indeed, from 1988 to 1993, the fund under her management performed worse than the average fund in the market in each of those years. By the end of 1994 Miss Garzarelli was ousted from her job. The moral of this tale is that we must be careful not to ascribe exceptional predictive abilities to someone based on an isolated successful prediction.[3]

A few other interesting tales about forecasting fiascos should help establish the obvious point that accurate forecasting is extremely difficult, not only in Finance but in other disciplines as well. In August 1977 three professors from the Massachussetts Institute of Technology coded a message using an ultra-sophisticated encryption system called RSA, and offered a small prize to whoever cracked the code, an event forecasted by experts at the time to take at least 40 quadrillion years. In fact, in 1994 over 600 volunteers connected to the Internet cracked the code after only eight months of work, so the forecast was off by about forty quadrillion years.[4]

Forecasting also seems highly arduous in areas such as predicting the future success of young people. Indeed, singularly unprophetic remarks abound in this regard, to the point of being funny. Charles Darwin's father, for example, predicted that Charles "will be a disgrace to yourself & all of your family." Also, when Albert Einstein's headmaster was asked what profession young Albert should follow, he responded: "It doesn't matter; he'll never make a success of anything." Further, after a then-famous engineer visited Thomas A. Edison's laboratory, he categorically stated that he "did not think very highly of the Edison lamp and expected no great future for it."[5]

These examples, although deviating from Finance, illustrate the important point that accurate forecasting remains elusive at best. Savvy investors should be wary of any claims to the contrary.

---

[3] Imagine a swarm of financial analysts, each predicting something different every day. It is not hard to believe that some of them make accurate predictions some of the time, simply by chance.

[4] See *Scientific American*, July 1994, pp. 17–20. In case you're interested, the cipher said "The magic words are squeamish ossifrage," which were words chosen at random by the MIT professors, not expecting to see them pop up again.

[5] See Eisenberg, A., "The Art of the Scientific Insult," *Scientific American*, June 1994, p. 116.

EMPIRICAL TESTS OF EFFICIENT MARKETS

This section reviews some of the more famous efforts to test the EMH. While the EMH has been tested for many different kinds of financial markets, the most famous tests have been conducted for the stock market. As a consequence, almost all of the tests discussed here pertain to the stock market. The discussion is divided along the lines of the three versions of the EMH.

Tests of the Weak Version of the EMH

The weak version of the EMH essentially tests whether technical analysis is relevant to financial decision making. As we know, technical analysis focuses essentially on patterns of securities prices and measures of market mood or investor behavior. The strategies that focus on market mood consider matters such as the level of insider trading activity, the behavior of the odd lot trader, volume indicators, and other such non price indicators. Briefly, active net buying by corporate insiders would be a buy signal because the group with the best information is buying. The idea here is to follow the knowledgeable investors. At the other extreme, the analyst might observe the behavior of the odd lot trader. The odd lot trader is the small trader who trades shares in amounts less than a round lot, which is usually 100 shares. Odd lot trading usually incurs higher transaction costs and is the province of the market participant with little capital. After all, such traders cannot even afford a round lot. According to technical analysis, the odd lot traders are the least sophisticated traders in the market, so the **odd lot theory** suggests that one should do exactly the opposite of the odd lot traders. Heavy net buying by the odd lot trader is a sell signal to the informed trader, according to this view.[6]

The technical trading techniques that focus on price patterns have received more attention from researchers than strategies focusing on market mood, probably because they are more specific in their prescriptions for trading behavior. Following that trend in research, this section discusses three different kinds of techniques that have been employed to test for the existence of price patterns in stock prices. We have already discussed serial correlation tests, which did not indicate a violation of the EMH. We now consider runs tests and filter tests.

Runs Tests   A runs test examines the tendencies for losses or gains to be followed by further losses or gains, regardless of their size. These tests are often performed by examining a time series of returns for a security and testing whether the number of consecutive price gains or drops shows a pattern. If we let a price gain be represented by a "+" and a price drop be represented by a "−", we can depict the price movements of a security by a series of "+" and "−". For example, one possible series might be:

$$+ + + - + + + - + + + - + + + - + + + - \ldots$$

---

[6] Although it seems paradoxical, the odd lot theory really assumes that the odd lot trader is very knowledgeable, but is somehow dumb enough to *always* make the wrong decision. Why else would an analyst do exactly the opposite of the odd lot trader? This reasoning alone indicates that the validity of this theory is highly suspect, unless you really believe that, as a group, knowledgeable investors can also be consistently stupid.

If the daily price changes for a security had this pattern of three gains followed by a loss, repeated over and over, it would lead to a very simple trading strategy. We would buy the security at the close of a day with a loss; hold it for three days; and sell it at the close of the third day. Of course, we would not really expect actual price movements to follow such a rigid rule. However, if price movements followed any rule, it would be useful to know it and to form a strategy to take advantage of the regularity.

To test for this possibility, actual sequences are tested to see if they are similar to those which would be generated by chance. This is really the same as testing to determine the probability that the sequence of gains and losses could have been generated by tossing a coin. If we let heads represent a gain and tails represent a loss, what is the probability that the actual sequence under scrutiny could have been generated by flipping coins? If the sequence of gains and losses is random, then there is no information to be gleaned from trying to find patterns, just as there is no sense in trying to predict whether the next coin toss will be heads or tails by examining the result of past tosses.[7]

Table 19.1 presents the results of testing for the presence of runs in the stock market. The table shows that the number of runs in the stock market is very close to the number we would expect to find by chance. Table 19.1 shows the calculated expected number of runs of different lengths based on chance for the sample under consideration. These are shown as the expected runs. Also, the table shows the computed actual number of runs of each different length of time. With the exception of the one-day runs, there is an exact correspondence between the actual and expected number of runs. As a consequence, the evidence of runs tests is perfectly consistent with the efficient markets hypothesis. Here the situation is similar to the results in the tests for serial correlation.

Filter Rules   A filter rule has the following form:

> If the daily closing price of a security rises at least *x* percent, buy the security and hold it until its price moves down at least *x* percent from a subsequent high. At that point sell the security short and maintain the short position until the price rises at least *x* percent above a subsequent low.

TABLE 19.1
Actual and Expected Numbers of Runs of Different Lengths for Dow Jones Stocks

	1-Day Run		4-Day Run		9-Day Run		16-Day Run	
	Actual	Expected	Actual	Expected	Actual	Expected	Actual	Expected
Average number of runs	735	760	176	176	75	75	42	42

Source: E. F. Fama, "The Behavior of Stock Market Prices," E. F. Fama, *Journal of Business,* January 1965. Reprinted by permission of the University of Chicago Press.

---

[7] Some people believe that if the coin has produced, say, five consecutive heads, then a tail is more likely than a head in the very next coin toss. This is simply not true, as each toss is independent of the past, and both heads and tails are equally likely on any given toss.

Different filter rules can be specified by choosing different values for the filter x. Table 19.2 presents the results of using various filter sizes, ranging from 0.5 percent to 20 percent. As shown in the table, the filter rules could generate highly positive returns on a consistent basis, if transaction costs were ignored. These returns ranged from 11.5 percent to 4.3 percent per year. One problem with this technique is that it calls for very frequent trading. The third column of table 19.2 shows the number of transactions that would be generated by following the filter strategy. The final column shows the total returns if transactions costs are taken into account. Even assuming very low transactions costs, the apparent profits are turned to losses in almost every case. Only the 20 percent rule generates a positive return after commissions, but it is only 3 percent, and the investor could easily beat that return with a risk free bond. It appears, then, that filter rules are not able to beat the market.

In general, researchers have been unable to find any compelling evidence that technical analysis works. This does not mean that technical analysis has been proven worthless. There are many possible kinds of technical trading strategies, and to make the case against technical analysis airtight would require testing all of them. Testing technical trading rules is akin to looking for a needle in a haystack. If we look for a needle in a haystack for a long time without success, it does not mean that there is no needle, but it becomes reasonable to doubt that there really is a needle in the hay. Likewise, the continued absence of evidence in favor of technical trading rules justifies a skepticism about the value of technical analysis.

Tests of the Semi-Strong Form of the EMH

The semi-strong form of the efficient markets hypothesis maintains that security prices at all times reflect all publicly available information. This means that it should be impossible to use any public information to direct a trading strategy that earns more than the equilibrium risk-adjusted rate of return.

TABLE 19.2
Average Annual Rates of Return from Filter Rules

Value of Filter x	Return Before Commissions	Number of Transactions	Return After Commissions
0.5%	11.5%	12,500	−103.6%
1.0	5.5	8,700	−74.9
2.0	0.2	4,800	−45.2
4.0	0.1	2,000	−19.5
6.0	1.3	1,100	−9.4
8.0	1.7	700	−5.0
10.0	3.0	400	−1.4
20.0	4.3	100	3.0

Source: E. F. Fama and M. E. Blume, "Filter Rules and Stock Market Trading" *Journal of Business*, January 1966. Reprinted by permission of the University of Chicago Press.

Occasionally, firms change the number of shares outstanding by declaring a stock split or a stock dividend. A stock split occurs when a firm gives new shares for the previously outstanding shares, and thereby increases the total number of shares outstanding by 25 percent or more. If new shares are given which increase the total number of shares outstanding by less than 25 percent, the event is called a stock dividend. For example, if the investor owns 100 shares and receives 150 new shares in exchange for the old shares, there has a been a stock split, because the investor's holdings have been increased by 50 percent. Notice that a stock split or stock dividend involves no cash flow to the investor, but simply adjusts the total number of shares outstanding. Because stock dividends and stock splits differ only in their accounting treatment and have the same economic significance, we use the terms interchangeably in the discussion that follows.

Inasmuch as stock splits represent only an increase in the number of shares that each investor owns, it should not affect the total value of the firm's equity, if the market is efficient. This means that when a 2 for 1 stock split occurs, for example, the price of each new share should be 50 percent of the price of each old share, since there are now twice as many shares as before and total value is unchanged. Figure 19.7 illustrates this prediction for Boston Chicken (currently Boston Market), which made a 2 for 1 stock split on September 1, 1994. As the figure shows, the closing stock price on that day was essentially 50 percent of the closing price of the previous day, in accordance with the prediction of the efficient markets hypothesis.

FIGURE 19.7
Boston Chicken's 2 for 1 stock split

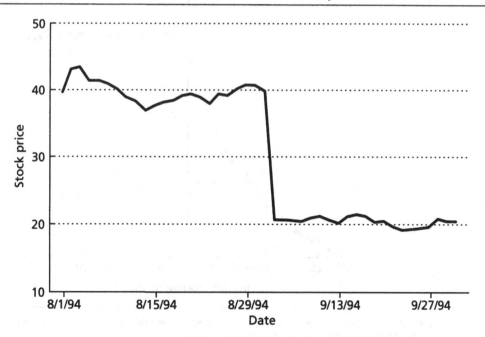

Sometimes, however, stock splits do tend to follow periods of unusually good performance by stocks, and this good performance seems to be a predictor of greater expected future earnings and dividends. Also, firms apparently use stock dividends to signal improved circumstances to the marketplace, and stock splits are often quickly followed by increases in cash dividends as well. Based on a classic study of a sample of 940 stock splits, figure 19.8 shows the risk-adjusted relative performance of the sample of stock splits taken together, relative to the market as a whole. The sample period consists of 30 months preceding and 30 months following the stock split. The rising line prior to the announcement of the split, indicated as month zero, shows that these firms, on average, did 33 percent better than other securities of comparable risk. However, by the time of the stock split, all of the relatively superior performance had been achieved. This is revealed by the fact that the line is basically flat after the announcement date. To the extent that the split was associated with good news, the market had anticipated the good news and gave no reaction to the announcement itself.

FIGURE 19.8
Average Performance for a Sample of Firms with Stock Splits

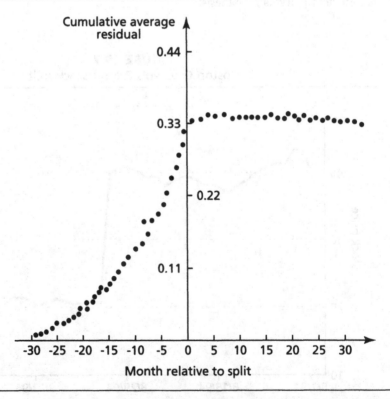

Source: E. F. Fama, L. Fisher, M. C. Jensen, and R. Roll, "The Adjustment of Stock Prices to New Information," *International Economic Review,* February 1969, pp. 1–21.

The results of this study have important implications for the efficient markets hypothesis. An investor who bought every stock that announced a stock split would not enjoy any performance that was better than the market norm, as is shown by figure 19.8. The market appears to be efficient with respect to the public information embodied in the stock split announcement. However, if the investor could find out in advance about the stock split, by obtaining privileged information, it does appear that substantial excess returns could be earned. This finding has implications for the strong form of the EMH.

Tests of the Strong Form of the EMH

If the strong form of the efficient markets hypothesis is true, no information is valuable for directing a securities investment program, because all information has already been incorporated into prices. However, the best evidence clearly indicates that the strong form of the EMH is false. Access to inside or private information can be used to generate a profit in excess of the risk-adjusted norm. This section discusses two types of tests of strong form efficiency. The first looks at the investment performance of corporate insiders and the second at the returns earned by stock market specialists. It must also be emphasized that trading on the basis of inside information is generally illegal.[8]

Corporate Insiders   Corporate insiders often have access to potentially valuable information regarding the investment prospects of their firms before the general public gets that information. This raises the possibility that officers of corporations could use that information to earn returns in excess of the risk-adjusted norm. That appears to be exactly what occurs.

There is considerable anecdotal evidence that insiders are able to make money by trading on their privileged information. Generally, these stories only come to public attention in connection with court cases. Most exciting and juicy insider trading stories probably never come to public attention, simply because the illegal trading is never detected.

In addition to anecdotal evidence, there is formal evidence as well. Corporate insiders are required to report their trading activity to the SEC within two weeks of the trade, and the SEC publishes this information in its "Official Summary of Insider Trading." Studies of this information reveal that insiders consistently earn more than would be expected in a strong form efficient market.

Market Specialists   The stock exchange specialist holds a book showing the orders awaiting execution at different prices. Also, the specialist usually holds an inventory of stocks, and may change this inventory at will. If the specialist sees a large number of buy orders at 50 when the current price lies at 55, the specialist can be fairly confident that the price will not fall below 50, at least in the short run. This kind of privileged information is very valuable, according to studies of specialists' returns. Specialists appear to average returns of about 100 percent on their invested capital, which is clearly above the risk-adjusted return. Almost all studies of strong form efficiency reach the same conclusion: securities markets are simply not strong form efficient.

---

[8] Since a 1968 ruling, corporate insiders must abstain from trading until they disclose "material" information affecting investment decisions.

Summary of Empirical Tests of the EMH

As we consider the evidence for each of the versions of the efficient markets hypothesis, it is important to remember that the research pertaining to each version is continuing. Nonetheless, there seem to be fairly stable conclusions about the validity of the weak form and strong form hypotheses. Regarding the weak form of the hypothesis, the preponderance of evidence clearly suggests efficiency. Just as clearly, the evidence also supports the view that the market is not efficient in the strong form version.

With respect to the semi-strong version of the market efficiency hypothesis, the conclusion is not as clear. While the evidence generally supports semi-strong efficiency, some studies indicate that market data are not consistent with the EMH.

MARKET ANOMALIES

In this section we discuss some important challenges that have been recently uncovered, and cast new doubts on the validity of the EMH. While not exhaustive, these anomalies illustrate the challenge that the financial researcher currently faces.[9]

The January Effect

Researchers have uncovered a monthly pattern of returns where January is, on average, the best month of the year by far. Figure 19.9 shows the historical average monthly returns for the S&P 500 index. The figure shows that January produces at least twice as much average return than any other month. Furthermore, the summer and fall months as a group have much lower returns than the winter and spring months. According to the EMH, all months should have roughly the same average return, so the January effect directly contradicts the EMH.

The Day of the Week Effect

Considerable recent attention has been devoted to the difference in daily average returns on many securities depending on which day of the week is examined. There is nothing in the CAPM or the EMH to explain why average returns on Thursdays should be different from returns on Tuesdays or Wednesdays. Nonetheless, a great deal of evidence now exists to show that returns are different depending on the day of the week. In particular, Friday returns are generally high and Monday returns (the return from Friday close to Monday close) are even negative.

These return differences are substantial and it may be possible for investors to earn a return that beats the market by timing their purchases to take advantage of these persistent differences. If so, the day of the week effect would show either that the semi-strong EMH was not true or that the CAPM was not true, or both. If the CAPM is the correct pricing

---

[9] Many market anomalies are called "effects." This has the same underlying meaning as the word "syndrome" in medicine: it means we really don't know why the situation occurs; we can only observe the symptoms.

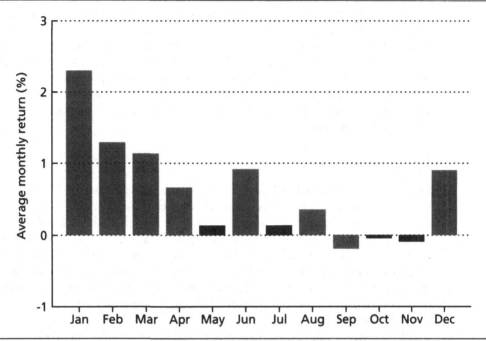

FIGURE 19.9
Average Monthly Returns for the S&P 500

relationship in the market, then the EMH must be false, because it appears that prices do not adjust correctly to reflect all available information. If the EMH is true, it seems that the CAPM must be false, because there must be additional risk factors not recognized by the CAPM to explain the differential returns depending on the day of the week.[10]

The Friday the 13th Effect

This dreadful effect, uncovered in 1987, indicates that Friday the 13th is a very bad day for investors. Indeed, the annualized average return on those days is about −36 percent. In contrast, other Fridays produce a positive average annualized return of over 43 percent.[11]

Reflecting on the fact that many tall buildings do not officially have a 13th floor, and other such apparently irrational behavior, it is perhaps not surprising that investors are not eager to trade on a Friday the 13th. Fortunately, there are never more than three such days in a calendar year, but there is always at least one.

---

[10] In particular, the CAPM would have to somehow incorporate the day of the week into the risk/return relationship.
[11] These numbers do not include the scary drop of 190 points that the Dow Jones Industrial Average index suffered on Friday, October 13, 1989. This day is now known as the date of the mini-crash.

Market Overreaction

In the mid 1980s, financial researchers were presented with a shocking result that flies in the face of the efficient markets hypothesis; namely, that portfolios that outperform the market during some "formation" period subsequently underperform relative to the market in a "test" period. Similarly, portfolios that underperform relative to the market during a "formation" period underperform relative to the market in a subsequent "test" period. In other words, this research uncovered the fact that winner portfolios become losers, and losers become winners. Since this clearly allows for a strategy to beat the market, it is totally inconsistent with the EMH. Other recent studies have uncovered overreaction in other markets as well.

Speculative Bubbles

From time to time, individuals seem to behave in ways that in hindsight seem to be extremely irrational. The greatest example of such collective folly is the tulipomania that occurred in the 17th century throughout Europe, especially in Holland.

At its height, incredible amounts were paid for a single tulip. For example, one buyer exchanged 12 acres of land for a Haarlem tulip. Another buyer paid the following for a single root of the rare species called the *Viceroy*: two lasts of wheat, four lasts of rye, four fat oxen, eight fat swine, twelve fat sheep, two hogsheads of wine, four tuns of beer, two tuns of butter, one thousand pounds of cheese, a complete bed, a suit of clothes, and a silver drinking cup.[12]

As the name implies, all speculative bubbles eventually burst. However, as in the tulipomania case, bubbles may grow for years and involve a sizable number of people who are willing to engage in collective denial, against all reason. Speculative bubbles are consistent with the **greater fool theory**. This theory states that it is perfectly appropriate to overpay for a good, if we can find a greater fool willing to pay even more.

SUMMARY

Until the last few years it has been fairly easy to summarize the evidence on the CAPM and efficient markets. Only recently have market anomalies been discovered and only recently has the CAPM come under attack. Today, we can still be quite confident that securities markets in the United States are efficient in the weak sense and that they are inefficient in the strong sense.

The assessment of semi-strong market efficiency is much more difficult. The market anomalies mentioned here may be interpreted as calling either the pricing model or the market's efficiency into question. Most researchers today probably are less certain of the truth of the semi-strong EMH than was the case a few years ago.

Faced with this uncertain situation, what should be the response of the investor? The bulk of evidence still favors semi-strong market efficiency. Further, the apparent anomalies

---

[12] For an interesting account of this and other speculative bubbles, see "Extraordinary Popular Delusions and the Madness of Crowds," by Charles Mackay, reprinted in 1980 by Harmony Books/New York.

may be entirely due to faults in our pricing models, rather than to a failure of semi-strong efficiency.

In light of the current state of knowledge, investors should behave as though they were confident that the market were efficient in the semi-strong sense. That means, first, that investors should hold a well-diversified portfolio in order to eliminate unsystematic risk. Second, in a market that is semi-strong efficient, investors should avoid paying needlessly for research of dubious value. Third, if it is not really possible to analyze public information successfully, there is little reason for active trading. A policy of active trading would be appropriate if the investor believes it is possible to identify underpriced securities. In a semi-strong efficient market, this should not be possible. Consequently, and as a fifth point, trading should be oriented toward "buy-and-hold" strategies. When trades are made, they should generally be made for liquidity reasons.

QUESTIONS

1. What is the difference between "operational efficiency" and "economic efficiency"?
2. What does it mean to say that prices "fully reflect" some body of information?
3. How are the three traditional versions of the market efficiency hypothesis distinguished?
4. Say that you have conclusive information that it is possible to beat the market by charting the past history of stock prices. Which versions of the efficient markets hypothesis would this evidence disprove? Why?
5. Assume that a worker in the U.S. Patent Office learns about new products before they are publicly announced. Might this worker be able to use this information to "beat the market"? If this worker could do so, would that conflict with the efficient markets hypothesis? If so, which versions? Why?
6. The weak form and semi-strong form of the efficient markets hypothesis imply that certain kinds of analysis of securities and prices are not useful. Explain these implications and their impact on the securities industry.
7. It is often said that the CAPM and the EMH are tested jointly. Why is this so? Would it be better to test each theory by itself? Why? Why aren't the two theories tested separately?
8. Hot Stock, Inc., is trading at this moment for $6 on the NYSE and $6.75 on the Pacific Exchange. What exact transactions would you make to earn an arbitrage profit? Assume that you will trade 100 shares. How much profit would the arbitrage strategy generate?
9. If persistent arbitrage opportunities were available, what would this imply about the CAPM? Explain.
10. Assume that an investor earned more than the S&P 500 for five years in a row. Can we conclude that this investor can beat the market? Why or why not?
11. What is the relationship between the random walk hypothesis and the efficient markets hypothesis? Is the random walk hypothesis true?
12. What is a "market anomaly" and why might it be important?

Chapter 20

Leasing

OVERVIEW

A **lease** is essentially the renting of an asset for some specified period. In leasing, the owner of the good is the **lessor**, and the party that uses the good is the **lessee**. In a lease, either the lessor or the lessee may provide maintenance for the leased good. We will focus primarily on leases in which the lessee undertakes the maintenance burden.

The lessee can either lease a good or borrow funds in the capital market and buy the good. In essence, the leasing decision is the choice of whether to lease or buy the asset. The decision depends on the after-tax cash flows associated with each alternative. Learning how to analyze these cash flows is the primary goal of this chapter.

TYPES OF LEASES

In leasing, the lessor provides the leased asset to the lessee for a specified period in exchange for a series of payments. The length of the lease, the conditions for terminating the lease before the full term, the payments, and the party responsible for maintaining the asset are all determined by negotiation. Figure 20.1 summarizes the basic differences between purchasing and leasing an asset. In a purchase, the party that will use the asset raises funds from the capital markets by issuing securities. These funds are then used to buy the asset from the manufacturer or distributor. In a lease, the lessor acquires funds from the securities markets and uses those funds to purchase the asset. The lessee acquires the use of the asset by paying a series of lease payments. The lessee can engage in an operating lease or a financial lease.

An **operating lease** typically has a term that is considerably shorter than the life of the asset and the lessee may cancel the lease with fairly short notice. At the end of the lease period, the lessor expects to be able to sell the asset or to lease it again. Therefore, the lessor is very interested in the way the lessee treats the asset during the lease. Because of this, the lessor in an operating lease usually maintains and services the leased asset. An operating lease is also known as a **maintenance** or **service lease**. Lessees usually get automobiles, computers, and office equipment through operating leases. Operating leases usually have a life of one to five years, depending on the type of asset.

The other basic kind of lease is a financial lease. In a **financial lease**, the lessee acquires an asset for a period that is close to the useful life of the asset. The lessee contracts to make a series of lease payments over the life of the lease. Usually, the lessee provides the maintenance services for the asset in a financial lease. At the end of the lease, the lessor

FIGURE 20.1
Flows of Assets and Funds in Leasing and Purchasing

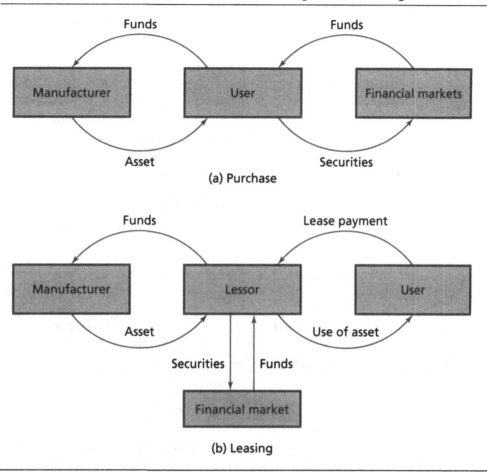

Source: Adapted from John J. Pringle and Robert S. Harris, *Essentials of Managerial Finance,* Glenview, IL: Scott, Foresman, 1984, Figure 16–1, p. 578.

owns the asset. As opposed to an operating lease, a financial lease is usually non-cancelable, so the lessee commits to the full sequence of payments.

Financial leases themselves fall into different categories, depending on how the lessor acquires the asset. The most straightforward arrangement is a direct lease. In a **direct lease**, the lessor issues equity in the financial markets and uses the funds to buy the asset. The lessor then leases the asset to the lessee. Figure 20.2 presents these arrangements graphically. In a **leveraged lease**, the lessor issues debt to raise funds to buy the asset. Panel (b) of figure 20.2 shows the flow of goods, cash, and services for a leveraged lease.

In both a direct lease and a leveraged lease, the lessor buys the asset. A third basic type of financial lease is a sale/leaseback. In a **sale/leaseback**, the lessor buys the asset

FIGURE 20.2
Flows of Assets and Funds in Alternative Types of Financial Leases

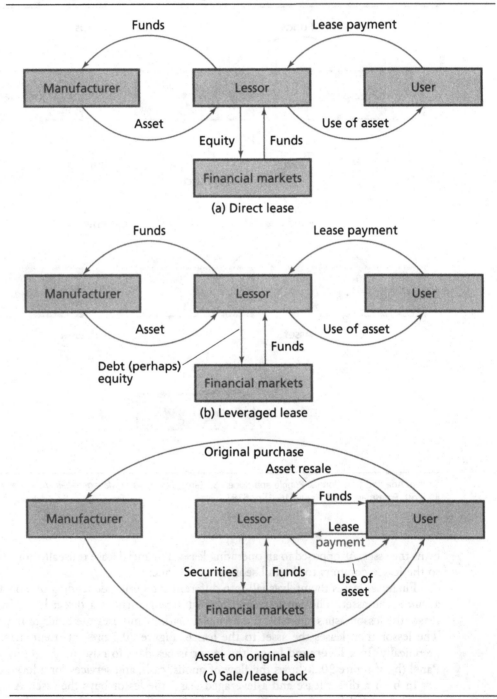

(a) Direct lease

(b) Leveraged lease

(c) Sale/lease back

from the lessee and immediately leases it back to the lessee. Panel (c) of figure 20.2 shows the flows of goods and cash for a sale/leaseback. Essentially, the lessee in a sale/leaseback arrangement retains the use of an asset it was already using. For various reasons, such as raising cash, the lessee may no longer want to own the asset, so the lessee sells the asset to the lessor and arranges to lease it back.

LEASE VERSUS OWN: THE BASIC DECISION

Some firms sell an asset and then lease that asset back from the party to whom they have just sold it. This raises an obvious question: if the firm has an asset and still needs to use it, why sell it and then lease it back? Because the sale/leaseback is so common, there must be some important reasons for it.

In the remainder of this chapter, we will focus on financial leases. The lease/buy decision is essentially a financing decision. We assume the firm has already decided to use a given asset for a certain period. Hopefully, this decision was the result of a careful capital budgeting analysis. But should the firm finance the use of that asset by buying it or leasing it? This is the lease/buy decision. The choice of leasing or buying depends on the present value of the after-tax cash flows to the user of the asset.

Evaluating Leases

To evaluate a lease versus buy decision, we need to keep two points in mind. The first concerns the principle of incremental cash flows and the second focuses on the assumptions about financial leverage.

Incremental Cash Flows To choose between leasing and buying, we need to consider only the cash flows that differ under the two alternatives. For example, whether we buy the asset or lease it under a financial lease, we still will have to pay the maintenance costs. Therefore, we can ignore the maintenance costs in evaluating the lease/buy decision. Presumably, the firm considered the maintenance costs in the original investment decision. For the financing decision, we need to consider only the incremental cash flows between the two alternatives.

The Financial Leverage Effects From our study of financial leverage, we know that the financial structure of the firm can affect firm decisions. In deciding to lease or buy, we must be sure to consider any leverage effects of one alternative relative to the other. To be sure that we evaluate the lease and buy alternatives on the same footing, we must hold the leverage effects constant.

If we lease an asset, we commit ourselves to a series of contractually obligated lease payments. These lease payments are equivalent to the promised payments on a loan. Therefore, we may regard the lease alternative as a commitment to financing the asset with 100 percent debt. To make the buy alternative comparable to the leasing alternative, we must assume that we will buy the asset with funds derived entirely from debt. This is an important point, because it allows us to evaluate the tax effects of borrowing to buy the asset.

Identifying the Relevant Cash Flows

Holding the financial leverage effects constant by assuming that we finance the purchase entirely by borrowing, which cash flows differ between the purchase and leasing alternatives? In answering this question, we must consider the various tax effects that the two financing alternatives generate. The lease requires only one cash flow, the lease payments themselves, and we must evaluate those payments on an after-tax basis.

If we buy, we can depreciate the asset, thereby gaining a depreciation tax shield. Also, if we buy the asset using debt financing, we receive some tax shields from the interest expenses. Finally, we can sell the asset at the end of its useful life for its salvage value. Table 20.1 summarizes the cash flows under the two financing alternatives.

Analyzing the Cash Flows

Suppose a firm will acquire a computer with an expected life of four years, a purchase price of $50,000, and an expected zero salvage value. The firm is in the 30 percent tax bracket and uses straight line depreciation. If the firm buys the computer, it can borrow the funds at a 12 percent rate of interest, which it would repay as an amortized loan. Alternatively, it can lease the asset for the four years by paying an annual lease payment of $15,000.

Which alternative should the firm choose? To answer this question, we must consider all the payments that the firm will make under the two alternatives. In evaluating these flows, we must consider them strictly on an after-tax basis.

If the firm buys the computer, the actual outlay for the machine will be the $50,000 cost of the machine. Because we want our evaluation to be comparable with a lease, we assume that the firm borrows the entire $50,000. Because the firm uses an amortized loan, it repays it with four equal payments. Therefore, we may analyze the loan repayment as an annuity. For four years with a discount rate of 12 percent, the annuity factor is PA(12%, 4) = 3.037. This means that the annual loan repayment will be $16,461. In addition to the loan repayment amounts themselves, we must also consider some important tax effects. First, interest on the loan payment is tax deductible, so the loan payments generate a tax shield. To calculate the tax shield in each period, we need to know which portion of the total payment is interest. Table 20.2 presents an amortization table with these calculations.

Because the loan is an amortized loan, the payment remains constant, but the interest and principal amounts vary with each payment. In the first year, for instance, the interest

TABLE 20.1
Cash Flows with Leasing and Buying

Leasing	Buying
The after-tax costs of the lease payments.	The depreciation tax shield.
	The interest payments.
	The tax shield on the interest payments.
	The principal payments on the debt.
	The salvage value.

TABLE 20.2
Amortization of the Loan

Year	Payment	Interest	Principal Repayment	Balance
0	n/a	n/a	n/a	$50,000
1	$16,461	6,000	$10,461	39,539
2	16,461	4,744	11,717	27,822
3	16,461	3,338	13,123	14,699
4	16,461	1,763	14,697	*2

*The balance does not equal zero because of rounding error.

due is $6,000 ($50,000 × 0.12), leaving $10,461 for principal repayment. As table 20.2 shows, the interest decreases each year. Therefore, the tax shield due to the interest payment also decreases. The tax shield on the interest paid equals the amount of interest times the tax rate. In the first year, for example, the tax shield from the interest payment is $1,800 ($6,000 × 0.3). We need to know these interest tax shields for each year, because they are an incremental cash flow of the decision to borrow funds and buy the computer. The second and third columns of table 20.3 show the loan payment and the interest tax shield for each of the four periods over the life of the loan. The loan payment has a negative sign, indicating that it is a cash outflow if the firm borrows and buys. The interest tax shield has a plus sign, showing the firm obtains the tax shield only if it borrows and buys.

Borrowing and buying also affect depreciation. Since depreciation is not a cash flow, it matters only because of the tax shield that it generates. For a computer costing $50,000 and zero salvage value after four years, the annual straight line depreciation expense is $12,500. The depreciation tax shield equals the depreciation expense times the tax rate, so borrowing and buying gives a depreciation tax shield of $3,750 each year. The plus signs in table 20.3 reflect this benefit of borrowing.

The firm is also able to lease the computer for a yearly fee of $15,000. Because the full amount of the lease payment is deductible as a business expense, the after-tax lease payment is $10,500 ($15,000 × 0.7). Table 20.3 shows these after-tax lease payments in

TABLE 20.3
After-Tax Cash Flows for the Borrowing and Leasing Alternatives

Year	Borrowing			Leasing
	Loan Payment	Interest Tax Shield	Depreciation Tax Shield	After-Tax Lease Payment
1	-$16,461	$1,800	$3,750	-$10,500
2	-16,461	1,423	3,750	-10,500
3	-16,461	1,001	3,750	-10,500
4	-16,461	529	3,750	-10,500

the last column. Adding all of the cash flows for the two strategies gives the total after-tax cash flows for each alternative:

Total After-Tax Cash Flows

	Period			
	1	2	3	4
Buy	−$10,911	−$11,288	−$11,710	−$12,182
Lease	−$10,500	−$10,500	−$10,500	−$10,500

The choice between these two financing methods is a choice between two series of outflows. Because these are outflows, the firm should choose the financing method that gives the lower present value of outflows when the payment streams are discounted at the firm's after-tax cost of debt. We saw that the firm could borrow for this project at 12 percent. Being in the 30 percent tax bracket means that the firm's after-tax cost of debt is 8.4 percent (12% × 0.7) Therefore, we discount the flows at this rate.

Present value of the borrow-and-buy outflows:

$$PV = \frac{-\$10,911}{1.084} + \frac{-\$11,288}{1.084^2} + \frac{-\$11,710}{1.084^3} + \frac{-\$12,182}{1.084^4} = -\$37,687$$

Present value of the lease outflows:

$$PV = \frac{-\$10,500}{1.084} + \frac{-\$10,500}{1.084^2} + \frac{-\$10,500}{1.084^3} + \frac{-\$10,500}{1.084^4} = -\$34,470$$

From these calculations, we see that the present value of the borrow-and-buy outflows is −$37,687. If we lease the computer, the present value of the outflows is −$34,470. In present value terms, leasing saves the difference in the two outflows, or $3,217. This difference is the **net benefit of leasing** (NBL).

$$NBL = PV \text{ of lease outflows} - PV \text{ of buy outflows}$$

In our example, we have:

$$NBL = -\$34,470 - (-\$37,687) = \$3,217$$

Because the NBL is positive, the firm should lease the computer rather than buy it.

As an alternative, we can find the NBL by first combining the cash flows and then discounting:

$$NBL = PV \text{ (lease outflows} - \text{buy outflows)}$$

In our example, this would result in:

$$PV = \frac{\$411}{1.084} + \frac{\$788}{1.084^2} + \frac{\$1,210}{1.084^3} + \frac{\$1,682}{1.084^4} = \$3,217$$

Not surprisingly, the NBL is $3,217, just as before. Therefore, we can use either method to calculate the NBL.

EXAMPLE

Zerlina, Inc., will acquire a fleet of 20 cars to use for five years. Each automobile costs $10,000. The firm faces a 34 percent corporate tax rate. The firm has two alternative financing sources. First, it can borrow the funds at 10 percent and buy the fleet. If it borrows, it will pay only interest each year and repay all the principal in five years. The firm will depreciate the cars over five years on a straight line basis. Alternatively, it can lease the entire fleet for $60,000 per year, including maintenance. The annual maintenance costs per vehicle would be $300. Should Zerlina lease or buy?

Step 1: Identify the after-tax cash flows

Borrow-and-Buy   If Zerlina buys the cars, it will borrow $200,000. The firm must repay this principal in full after five years. With a 10 percent rate of interest, the firm pays $20,000 in interest each year. On an after-tax basis, this is $13,200 ($20,000 × 0.66).

If it buys the fleet, it will depreciate $200,000 for five years. This gives a straight line depreciation expense of $40,000 per year. The depreciation tax shield is $13,600, which equals the depreciation expense times the tax rate ($40,000 × 0.34).

With a maintenance expense of $300 per car per year, the yearly maintenance expense is $6,000. On an after-tax basis, this would be $3,960. We must charge this maintenance expense against the borrow-and-buy alternative because the lease expense already includes maintenance. This keeps the two alternatives on an even footing. The following table specifies all of these cash flows.

Leasing   With the lease alternative, the lease payment of $60,000 includes the maintenance, and the after-tax cost of the lease payment is $39,600. The following table also shows these flows.

Borrowing

Year	Principal Payment	After-Tax Interest	Depreciation Tax Shield	Maintenance
1	—	−$13,200	$13,600	−$3,960
2	—	$−13,200	$13,600	$−3,960
3	—	$−13,200	$13,600	$−3,960
4	—	$−13,200	$13,600	$−3,960
5	−$200,000	$−13,200	$13,600	$−3,960

Leasing	
Year	After-Tax Lease Payment
1	−$39,600
2	$−39,600
3	$−39,600
4	$−39,600
5	$−39,600

Step 2: Determine NPV of Flows Under Each Alternative

Borrow-and-Buy   For each year, the total after-tax cash flows for the borrow-and-buy alternative are:

Year	Cash Flow
1	−3,560
2	−3,560
3	−3,560
4	−3,560
5	−203,560

We need to discount these cash flows at Zerlina's after-tax cost of debt. With a 10 percent borrowing cost and a 34 percent tax rate, the firm's after-tax cost of borrowing is 6.6 percent. Using these numbers results in an NPV of −$160,047.

Leasing   The NPV of the lease payments, using the cash flows found previously and an after tax discount rate of 6.6 percent, is −$164,122.

Step 3: Calculate the NBL and Decide

In present value terms, the cost of leasing exceeds the cost of borrowing and buying the fleet. Because we want to minimize the NPV of the payments, we should prefer the borrow-and-buy alternative. The net benefit of leasing for this problem is NBL = −$164,122 − (−$160,047) = −$4,075. Since the net benefit of leasing is negative, in this case leasing is a disadvantage. Therefore, Zerlina should borrow-and-buy, not lease.

HOW LEASING CREATES VALUE

Normally, the firm's financing decision does not create value, at least in perfect markets with no taxes. We saw, for example, that the capital structure of the firm is irrelevant in a world of perfect markets and zero taxes. The same was true of the dividend decision.

If markets are perfect and there are no taxes, then leasing must be a zero sum game between the lessor and the lessee. If the lease is a good deal for the lessee, it must be a bad deal for the lessor, and vice versa. In a world of perfect markets and no taxes, the choice between debt and leasing is irrelevant. However, leasing is big business, and the widespread use of leasing as a financing tool must be due to actual benefits for both the lessor and the lessee. These benefits arise either because of taxes or market imperfections.

This section shows how a leasing arrangement can reduce taxes. When the tax bill is reduced through leasing, the new wealth created by the tax savings may be divided among the lessor and the lessee. The next section considers other market imperfections that can also make leasing attractive.

To see how leasing creates tax benefits, we consider an airline that buys and operates a plane. We then determine how the cash flows differ if the airline leases the plane instead. In this example, we assume that markets are perfect except for taxes. This means that the airplane costs the same for the airline or the lessor and that the airline and the lessor have the same borrowing costs. Also, maintenance costs are the same for both parties.

The key assumption that makes leasing attractive in this situation is a difference in the tax rates between the airline and the lessor. Airline profits are extremely volatile and some airlines often lose money. If a firm has a loss in a given year, it pays no taxes in that year. Further, the firm can carry losses to subsequent years to offset future income. For example, if an airline has a $100 million dollar loss in 1994 and a $100 million profit in 1995, it will not pay taxes in either year. In 1994, it owes no tax because of its loss, and in 1995 it can offset its profits by the loss from 1994. As a result, the airline will be in the zero tax bracket in both years.

Assume a plane costs $50 million and the firm can finance it with debt at a rate of 14 percent on a term loan. The firm will only pay interest on the loan for nine years, and then make the final interest payment and repay the principal in year 10. We also assume that the full value of the plane is depreciated using the straight line method over ten years. We assume that the operating profit of the airline is zero, so the airline pays no taxes. The lessor is in the 34 percent tax bracket.

Table 20.4 sets out the after-tax cash flows resulting from the financing decision for both the airline and the lessor. These flows would be the same for years 1–9. In the tenth year, whoever owns the plane would repay the $50 million principal on the loan. We can focus on just the first nine years. The top panel of table 20.4 shows the after-tax cash flows for the airline and for the lessor, assuming the airline buys the plane. In that case, the lessor has nothing to do with the entire operation. The panel also shows that if the airline owns the plane, there is no tax collected by the government, because the airline has no profits.

If the airline owns the plane, it pays $7 million in interest each year. Because the airline has no income to shield, it cannot use the benefit of the tax shield on interest. Therefore, the airline's after-tax cost for the interest expense is the full $7 million. If the airline had positive income, the depreciation expense of $5 million would provide a tax shield as well. Since the airline has no income, it receives no depreciation tax shield. In this top panel, the lessor plays no role, so all of its cash flows are zero.

The bottom panel shows the after-tax cash flows if the airline leases. In this case, the lessor buys the plane under the same terms available to the airline. The lessor pays $7 million in interest each year. This has an after-tax cost of $4.62 million per year. In

TABLE 20.4
After-Tax Financing Flows for the Airplane

	Airline	Lessor	Tax Collection
Plane is Owned			
Depreciation tax shield	$0	$0	$0
Interest expense	−7,000,000	0	0
After-tax cash flow	−$7,000,000	$0	$0
Plane is Leased			
Depreciation tax shield	$0	$1,700,000	−$1,700,000
Interest expense	0	−4,620,000	−2,380,000
Lease payment	−6,500,000	4,290,000	$2,210,000
After-tax cash flow	−$6,500,000	+$1,370,000	−$1,870,000
Advantage from lease	$500,000	$1,370,000	−$1,870,000

addition, the lessor has a depreciation expense of $5 million. This depreciation generates a depreciation tax shield of $1.7 million. (Remember that the depreciation tax shield equals the depreciation expense times the tax rate, or $5,000,000 × 0.34 = $1,700,000.) With the leasing option, the airline makes a lease payment of $6.5 million. Again, because the airline has no income, the actual lease payment is the after-tax cost to the airline. The lessor receives the $6.5 million and pays taxes of 34 percent. This leaves the lessor with $4.29 million after-tax from the lease payment.

The decision to lease changes governmental tax collections. First, the lessor receives a depreciation tax shield of $1.7 million. Therefore, the government collects $1.7 million less than it would otherwise. Second, the interest payment of $7 million generates a tax shield of $2.38 million for the lessor. This tax shield reduces tax collections by the same amount. Finally, the lease payment is taxable. The government collects $2.21 million in taxes from this lease payment.

Summing all of the cash flows for the leasing option gives some interesting results. For each of the first nine years, the airline has an after-tax cash outflow of $6.5 million and the lessor has a $1.37 million inflow. To see the advantage of leasing in this example, we must compare the position of the airline and the lessor with and without the lease. Under the lease, the airline does not have to repay the $50 million in the tenth year. However, it pays out $1.5 million more each year under the leasing arrangement. The lease benefits the airline, because it reduces its after-tax cost of using the plane by $500,000 in each year. The lessor reaps an after-tax inflow of $1.37 million each year. Between them, the airline and the lessor have a combined benefit of $1.87 million. This exactly equals the reduction in the government's tax collections. In this example, the government provides the funds to benefit the airline and the lessor.[1]

---

[1] We did not fully consider the repayment of the $50 million principal that takes place after ten years. The ultimate feasibility of this lease depends on the value of the plane at that time.

The entire benefit for the airline and lessor arose because the two firms were in different tax brackets. In leasing, the party with the higher tax bracket will normally be the lessor. The tax shields will be more valuable the higher the tax bracket. Notice also in this example that taxes are the only market imperfection considered. Both the airline and the lessor had to pay the same price for the plane, and we assumed that the maintenance and operating costs would be the same no matter who owned the plane. We now go on to consider other kinds of market imperfections that may also give an impetus to leasing.

LEASING AND MARKET IMPERFECTIONS

In this section, we consider how market imperfections may affect the desirability of leasing. For example, assume a firm specializes in managing a fleet of trucks and assume that this specialization gives the firm a cost advantage. This advantage is a market imperfection that could make leasing a superior alternative to buying.

Convenience

Some advantages of leasing pertain to both operating and financial leases. Other advantages come to only one kind of lease. For example, if a firm needs an asset for a short time, it may be better to rent or lease the asset rather than to buy. A contractor might need a cement mixer for a particular job. The contractor might buy the mixer, use it on the job, and then sell it. However, the market for used cement mixers is imperfect, so the contractor cannot sell the mixer immediately for its true value. Because of the illiquidity of cement mixers, the firm that needs them temporarily will normally rent. This is better than getting stuck with (or in) a cement mixer.

Similarly, the fixed terms of financial leases may be very inconvenient. Imagine a firm that leases a manufacturing facility on a long-term financial lease. If technology changes, the firm might need to change the plant. However, this will be difficult if the plant is leased. The lessor may not permit the alterations, and the lessee may be unwilling to invest in making the changes anyway, since the lessor owns the plant. In either case, leasing the plant could result in a loss of efficiency.

Risk of Obsolescence

Aircraft manufacturers lease airplanes. Computer makers lease computers. The same is common for photocopier manufacturers. In these cases, the manufacturer has special expertise and knowledge about the product that make leasing more efficient than sale. Because the manufacturer has superior knowledge about the future of the industry, it may be able to bear the risk of obsolescence better than the end user of the product. In this case, the lessee makes a higher lease payment for that risk protection.

Financing Ease

For many small companies, leasing may provide an easier and more convenient way to finance than debt. For example, if a firm needs a fleet of delivery vans, the van manufacturer will almost always have a financial subsidiary that specializes in leasing the firm's products. In such a situation, a small firm may find it more convenient to deal with the manufacturer/lessor than to borrow from a bank.

For a larger firm, there may be similar advantages to leasing. In leasing high-priced items such as airplanes, the lessee can sometimes avoid the expenses associated with floating a bond issue. In other words, the legal and administrative costs of obtaining financing can be cheaper with leasing than with issuing debt. In some cases, leasing can increase liquidity. For instance, in a sale/leaseback arrangement, the lessee receives immediate cash.

Effect on Financial Statements

At one time, one of the main alleged advantages of a financial lease was its effect on the firm's financial statements. As a result of a tightening of accounting rules, firms must now show financial leases on the firm's balance sheet and treat them as liabilities. Before the passage of this rule, FASB 13, leases provided **off-balance sheet financing**, because the firm did not show the contractual obligations of a financial lease on the balance sheet. Instead, the leases appeared only in the footnotes to the annual report. This advantage may have been more illusory than real, because it is doubtful whether this stratagem fooled investors. Now, with financial leases recorded on the balance sheet, this hiding game cannot work at all.

Firms can, however, arrange leases in a way that affects reported income. For example, a firm can structure a lease with small payments now and larger payments in the future. This would give the effect of increasing current income; an effect that would only be advantageous if investors were ignorant of the real terms of the contract and were fooled by the inflated earnings figures.

SUMMARY

We began our review of leases by distinguishing operating and financial leases and noting that financial leases are really very similar to debt financing. Consequently, the choice of debt or leasing is basically a financing decision. The principle for choosing a lease or debt is to evaluate the after-tax cash flows from each alternative and to choose the one with the lower net present value of costs.

We also noted that leasing can benefit both the lessor and the lessee, particularly when the two parties have different tax rates. Other motivations for leasing arise from various other kinds of market imperfections. For instance, leasing may be more convenient than owning, it may help to avoid the risk of obsolescence, and it may make financing easier.

QUESTIONS

1. What is the difference between a financial and an operating lease?
2. What is the difference between a direct lease and a leveraged lease?
3. Explain how a sale/leaseback arrangement works.

4. Is the decision to lease or buy an investment decision, a financing decision, or both? Explain.
5. In evaluating the lease versus buy decision, why should we assume that the buy decision finances the asset with 100 percent debt?
6. "Leasing provides 100 percent debt financing." Is this claim true or false? Explain.
7. What tax benefits are typically relinquished by a firm if it leases rather than buys an asset?
8. What tax advantages does a firm acquire by leasing that it would not have if it bought an asset?
9. What is the net benefit of leasing (NBL)?
10. Explain how different tax rates between borrowers and lenders stimulate leasing.
11. Evaluate the following claim: "Leasing may create some tax advantages, but the main advantage of financial leases for the lessee is that it allows the lessee to avoid the risk of obsolescence. For example, most airlines lease planes so that they can replace them with new models as soon as they come out."

PROBLEMS

Use the following information to solve problems 1–9. Pisa Construction needs a new crane for its tower construction business. Pisa can buy one crane for $1,000,000 and depreciate it straight line over five years to a $100,000 salvage value. It can borrow at 12 percent and is in the 35 percent tax bracket. If it borrows, Pisa will pay interest only for five years and repay the loan at the end of the five years. Alternatively, Pisa could lease the crane for the same five-year period for $180,000.

1. What is the annual after-tax cost of the lease payment?
2. What is the present value of the leasing alternative cash flows?
3. With the buy alternative, what is the annual depreciation expense?
4. With the buy alternative, what is the annual depreciation tax shield?
5. With the buy alternative, what is the annual interest?
6. With the buy alternative, what is the annual after-tax interest cost?
7. Compute the total after-tax cash flows for each year for the buy alternative.
8. What is the NPV of the buy alternative's cash flows?
9. Compute the NBL of leasing.

Use the following information to solve problems 10–20. Abacus Software is a new firm that needs to furnish its offices. Abacus is in the 30 percent tax bracket. The needed furniture could be purchased for $180,000 or it could be leased. The furniture should last about four years and have zero salvage value at that time. Abacus can borrow for the furniture at 12 percent and would amortize the loan over four years. If it leases the furniture, the annual lease payment will be $40,000.

10. What is the annual payment on the loan option?
11. Make an amortization table for the loan.
12. Compute the interest tax shield for each year.

13. Compute the depreciation tax shield for each year.
14. Compute the after-tax lease payment for each year.
15. Based on the calculations that you have just made, create a table showing the principal payment, interest tax shield, depreciation tax shield, and after-tax lease payment for each year.
16. Compute the total after-tax cost of the borrow and buy alternative for each year.
17. Find the present value of the borrow-and-buy cash flows.
18. Find the present value of the leasing cash flows.
19. Compute the NBL.
20. Using the data from problems 15 and 16, combine the annual cash flows from the borrow-and-buy alternative before discounting, and then find the NBL.

Use the following information to solve problems 21–31. Deaf Leopard, a hard rock group specializing in the acoustic big band sound, has just blown its audio system out of existence. Now the group must replace the system, and its members are trying to decide whether to lease or buy. Drumbo, the group's trombonist, has suggested that the band lease the new system, since they're very likely to blow it out again. If Deaf Leopard buys an audio system, it will cost $240,000 and should last three years before it is obsolete and worthless from all the abuse. The band only knows about straight line depreciation, so they will use that technique. The band has been borrowing at 20 percent with amortized repayment and would finance its new system the same way, if it decides to buy. If it leases, the annual lease payment will be $75,000. Deaf Leopard is incorporated, and its marginal tax rate is 20 percent.

21. Evaluate Drumbo's suggestion.
22. What is the annual loan payment if Deaf Leopard buys?
23. Make an amortization table for this loan.
24. Compute the interest tax shield for each year.
25. Compute the depreciation tax shield for each year.
26. Compute the after-tax lease payment for each year.
27. Use the answers to problems 22–26 to create a table showing the principal payment, interest tax shield, depreciation tax shield, and after-tax lease payment for each year.
28. Compute the total after-tax cash flow for the borrow and buy alternative for each year.
29. Compute the present value of the borrow and buy cash flows.
30. Compute the present value of the leasing cash flows.
31. Compute the NBL.

Use the following information to solve problems 32–48. Thirty microcomputers are available at a cost of $5,000 each and are expected to last five years and to have a zero salvage value after that time. The same computers can be leased for a 5-year period with an annual fee of $28,000.

32. Your business school is planning to equip a microcomputer lab with 30 computers. The school can borrow the money for these computers at 10 percent and

pay it back with a 5-year amortized loan. The business school is tax exempt. Compute the annual payment for the loan.

33. For the business school, compute the after-tax annual payment for the loan alternative.

34. What is the after-tax cost of the lease payment for the business school?

35. For the business school, compute the after-tax present value of the borrow-and-buy cash flows.

36. For the business school, compute the after-tax present value of the leasing cash flows.

37. For the business school, compute the NBL.

38. Trumpet Castle, a struggling casino, is also considering acquiring 30 of the same computers. It can borrow at a rate of 15 percent to buy these computers and would depreciate them on a straight line basis over five years. The firm is in the 40 percent tax bracket. Compute the annual payment for the loan, assuming a five-year amortized loan.

39. For Trumpet, prepare an amortization schedule for the loan.

40. For Trumpet, compute the annual after-tax cost of the loan payment. (Remember to treat the principal and interest payments separately.)

41. For Trumpet, compute the annual depreciation expense.

42. For Trumpet, compute the annual depreciation tax shield.

43. For Trumpet, compute the after-tax cost of the lease payment.

44. For Trumpet, compute the after-tax present value of the borrow-and-buy cash flows.

45. For Trumpet, compute the after-tax present value of the lease cash flows.

46. For Trumpet, compute the NBL.

47. Consider now the difference between Trumpet and the business school. Explain the difference in the NBL for the two concerns and explain how this difference might account for the widespread use of leasing.

48. By reflecting on the problems presented so far, what can you say about how tax-exempt institutions should acquire equipment such as computers?

Use the following information to solve the remaining problems. Duck Trucks (operating with the slogan, "We never get you stuck") needs to add to its fleet of Muck Trucks for its interstate duck hauling operations. One Muck Truck costs 100,000 bucks and has a useful life of five years. If Duck purchases the truck, it will depreciate it over five years on a straight line basis. Duck can borrow the needed bucks at a 10 percent rate of interest and will pay interest only for the first four years and repay the principal in year 5. Alternatively, Duck can lease its Muck Trucks for 20,000 bucks each per year. Duck is in the 30 percent tax bracket.

49. Compute the annual interest expense for the borrow-and-buy alternative.

50. Compute the after-tax cost of the interest payments.

51. Compute the annual depreciation expense.

52. Compute the annual depreciation tax shield.

53. Create a table showing the principal repayment, after-tax interest cost, depreciation tax shield, and total after-tax cost for each year.

54. Compute the present value of the after-tax cash flows for the borrow and buy alternative.
55. Compute the after-tax cost of the annual lease payments.
56. Compute the present value of the lease alternative's cash flows.
57. Compute the NBL and determine whether Duck should lease or buy.
58. Using the data calculated in problems 54 and 56, compute the NBL by consolidating the annual after-tax cash flows before discounting.

Chapter 21

Option Valuation

OVERVIEW

One of the most exciting recent developments in finance stems from the study of options. An **option** is the right to buy or sell a particular good at a specified price for a certain length of time. In recent years, option markets have emerged which allow investors to buy and sell options on stocks, bonds, currencies, metals, and various kinds of financial indexes. In corporate finance, managers now realize that many of the firm's transactions create options of various forms.

This chapter provides an introduction to options and shows how to apply option concepts to understand the options firms create when they issue securities. The stock the firm issues, as well as its bonds, strongly resemble options. This insight has important implications for managerial behavior, showing, for example, why firms in financial straits typically engage in extremely risky projects.

Options are also important in corporate finance because of the role they play in executive compensation. As part of their compensation, executives often receive the option to buy shares of the firm at a specified price. This opportunity can have great value.

CALL AND PUT OPTIONS

There are two major classes of options: call options and put options. A **call option** gives the owner the right to buy a particular asset at a certain price, for a specified period of time. A **put option** gives the owner the right to sell a particular asset at a specified price, with that right lasting until a particular date. Although we will assume that the asset in question is a stock, it could be wheat, gold, French francs, or any other asset whose value fluctuates through time.

For every option, there is both a buyer and a seller. Clearly, these two parties have diametrically opposite beliefs about the future value of the asset underlying the option. For example, the buyer of a call option is really betting that the market value of the underlying asset will eventually surpass the exercise price of the option, since the option buyer could then buy the underlying asset for less than its market value, thus making a profit. The seller, in contrast, believes that the asset will not reach the exercise price, in which case the seller gets to keep the amount paid by the buyer.

The owner of a call option may buy an asset at the contracted price during the life of the option, but there is no obligation to do so. Likewise, the owner of a put option may sell an asset under the terms of the option contract, but there is no obligation to do so. Nevertheless, selling an option does commit the seller to specific obligations. The seller of a call option receives a payment from the buyer. In exchange for this payment, the seller of the call option must be ready to sell a given good to the owner of the call, if the owner of the call wishes. The discretion to engage in further transactions always lies with the owner (the buyer) of the option. Option sellers have no such discretion. They have obligations to perform in certain ways if the owners of the options so desire.

OPTION TERMINOLOGY

There is a great deal of special terminology associated with options and the options market. The seller of an option is also known as the **writer** of an option. The owner of the call that takes advantage of the option is said to **exercise** the option. Each option contract stipulates a price the option owner must pay to exercise the option. This price is the **exercise price** or the **striking price**.

The sale of every option involves a payment from the buyer to the seller. This payment is simply the price of the option, also called the option **premium**. If you purchase the right to buy a share of IBM at $100 and pay $25 for this right, the option premium would be $25.

Every option traded on an exchange is valid for only a limited time, usually several months. For example, an option on IBM might be valid only through next August. The option has no validity after its **expiration date** or its **maturity**.[1] This special terminology is used widely in the options market and throughout the rest of this chapter.

OPTION PRICING

One of the showcase results of research in modern finance is the pricing of options. The pricing models developed for options perform very well, and a study of these models is very useful for the trader. Unfortunately, the mathematics of option pricing is very complicated and we cannot consider it in detail here. Nonetheless, we can understand a great deal about the pricing of options without much mathematical intrigue. Prices of options on stocks without cash dividends depend upon five variables:

Stock price	S
Exercise price	E
Time until expiration	T
Volatility of the underlying stock	σ
Risk-free rate of interest	r

We can express the price of a call option as a function of these five variables using the compact notation $C(S, E, T, \sigma, r) = C$. For example, the equation:

$$C(\$120, \$100, 0.25, 0.10, 0.05) = \$22.75$$

---

[1] Options mature on the third Friday of their expiration month.

says that a call option on a stock trading at $120 per share, with an exercise price of $100, one-fourth of a year to expiration, a standard deviation of 10 percent, and a risk-free rate of 5 percent, has a price of $22.75.

The Pricing of Call Options at Expiration

By the term "at expiration" we refer to the moment just before an option expires. If the owner does not exercise the option at this time, it expires immediately and the option will have no value. Many of the complications that ordinarily affect option prices disappear when the option is about to expire.

Let us consider the value of a call option at expiration, when $T = 0$. Of course, at that time (and any other time) the stock price either exceeds the exercise price, $S > E$, or it is less than or equal to the exercise price, $S \le E$. If the stock price is less than or equal to the exercise price ($S \le E$) at expiration, the call option is worthless, and the owner of the call option should throw it away. To see why, consider a call option with an exercise price of $80 on a stock that is trading at $70. To exercise, the owner of the call option must pay $80 to receive a stock worth $70 in the market. This represents a loss of $10. In this situation, it does not pay to exercise the option and the owner will allow it to expire. Accordingly, this option has no value and its market price will be zero. Employing our notation, we have:

$$\text{If } S \le E, \text{ then } C(S, E, 0, \sigma, r) = 0$$

If at expiration the stock price exceeds the exercise price ($S > E$), then the option has a value equal to the difference between the stock price and the exercise price. The reason is that the owner of the option can make an immediate profit of $S - E$ by paying E dollars to receive the stock, and immediately selling the stock in the market for S dollars. We then have:

$$\text{If } S > E, \text{ then } C(S, E, 0, \sigma, r) = S - E$$

If this relationship did not hold, there would be an arbitrage opportunity. Arbitrage occurs when an investor can make an immediate profit without taking any risk. To see how arbitrage can occur, assume that the stock price is $50 and the exercise price is $40. If the option sells for $5, an arbitrageur would make the following trades.

Transaction	Cash Flow
Buy a call option	$–5
Exercise the option	–40
Sell the stock	50
Net Cash Flow	$5

In this case, the arbitrageur will make an immediate certain profit of $5. As long as this situation persists, the arbitrageur will continue trading as described. This is tantamount to finding a "money machine." Of course, such a situation cannot persist for more than a fleeting moment in a well-functioning market.

If the price of the call option is greater than the difference between the stock price and the exercise price, there will be another arbitrage opportunity. Continuing to use our example of a stock priced at $50 with an exercise price of $40, assume now that the call price is $15. Faced with these prices, an arbitrageur would make the following transactions.

Transaction	Cash Flow
Sell a call option	$15
Buy the stock	−50
Initial Cash Flow	−$35

The owner of this call option must then immediately exercise the option or allow it to expire. If the option owner exercises, the arbitrageur performs these additional transactions:

Transaction	Cash Flow
Deliver stock	$0
Collect exercise price	+40
Net Cash Flow	+$5

In this case, there is an immediate certain profit of $5. Alternatively, the owner of the option may allow the option to expire. Then, the arbitrageur simply sells the stock as soon as the option expires and receives $50, which is the same amount that was paid for the stock. In this case the immediate certain profit is $15, since the arbitrageur simply keeps the option premium. Again, such a situation can only last an ephemeral moment if the market is efficient.

From reflection on the situation in which the stock price is less than or equal to the exercise price and the situation in which the stock price exceeds the exercise price, we can state the first basic principle of option pricing:

$$C(S, E, 0, \sigma, r) = \max(0, S - E)$$

This expression says that at expiration, the price of a call option equals zero or the difference between the stock price and the exercise price, whichever is greater. This condition must hold at expiration to avoid arbitrage opportunities.

Option Payoffs at Expiration

We must distinguish between the option's payoff at expiration and the profit or loss that a trader incurs. Consider both a call and a put option, each having a striking price of E. Figure 21.1 shows the payoff of these options at expiration for its buyers and sellers, as a function of the stock price.

Panel (a) of figure 21.1 shows that if the stock price is less than or equal to the exercise price of E, the payoff of the call must be zero for the buyer. For stock prices above the exercise price, the call price must equal the difference between the stock price and the exercise price. The graph reflects this fact because the call option's payoff rises with a slope of 1, or a 45 degree angle, for stock prices above E. In other words, for each dollar that the stock price increases, the payoff of the call option also increases by one dollar.

The payoff at expiration for the seller of the call option is shown in figure 21.1 panel (b). The situation is exactly the opposite of the one described for the buyer. For the call option seller, the maximum payoff is zero, which occurs if the buyer does not exercise. If $S > E$, the buyer exercises the call option and the seller's payoff is equal to $S - E$, since

FIGURE 21.1
Option Payoffs at Expiration

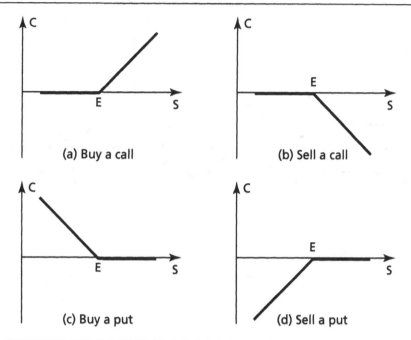

(a) Buy a call

(b) Sell a call

(c) Buy a put

(d) Sell a put

the seller must deliver to the buyer a stock worth S dollars, but only receives the exercise price of E dollars.

Panel (c) of figure 21.1 shows the payoff of a put option for the buyer. Since the buyer of a put option has the right to sell the stock at the exercise price of E, the buyer of a put benefits when the stock is worth less than E. For example, if the exercise price is $100 and the stock is worth $80 at expiration, the put owner buys the stock and exercises the option, selling for $100 the stock just purchased for $80, receiving an immediate $20 payoff in the process.

In figure 21.1 panel (d), the payoff for the seller of a put option is shown. At best, the seller's payoff is zero, but if $S < E$, the seller of the put has a negative payoff. To see this, consider a stock selling for $80 and a put option on that stock with a striking price of $100. Under these conditions, we have seen that the buyer of the put option will exercise, so the seller receives a stock which can be sold in the market for $80, but the seller must pay $100 for it, for a loss of $20.

Option Profits at Expiration

Consider now a put and a call option, each with an exercise price of $100, but now assume that each was initially bought for a price of $5. Figure 21.2 shows the profits for the buyers and sellers of these two options. Panel (a) shows the profit and loss positions for the call

FIGURE 21.2

Profits for Call and Put Options at Expiration when the Striking Price Equals $100 and the Premium is $5

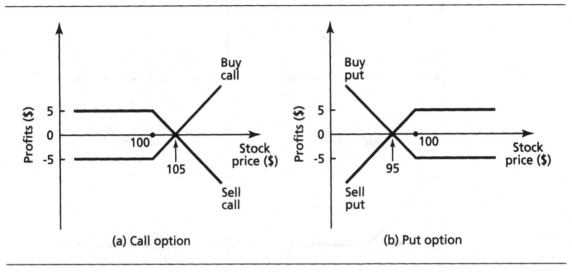

(a) Call option   (b) Put option

option buyer and seller. For any stock price less than or equal to the exercise price of $100, the call option will expire worthless and the buyer will lose the $5 paid for the call. If the stock price exceeds $100, reaching $105 say, the owner of the call will exercise the option, paying $100 for the share of stock that is worth $105. Therefore, the call owner breaks even after paying $5 for the option and the $100 to exercise it. For the call owner, any stock price less than $100 results in the loss of the total amount paid for the option. For stock prices above the exercise price, the call owner will exercise the option, but may still lose money. In this example, the stock price must exceed $105 to generate any net profit for the call owner.

For the writer of the call, the profit picture is exactly opposite from that of the call owner's. The best situation for the writer of the call is for the stock price to stay at $100 or below. In this situation, the call writer keeps the entire option premium of $5 and the call option will not be exercised by its buyer. If the stock price is $105, the owner of the call option will exercise. Upon exercise, the writer of the call must deliver shares now worth $105 and receive only $100 for them. At this point, the loss of $5 on the exercise exactly equals the $5 premium the call writer received when the option was sold, so the call writer breaks even. If the stock price is greater than $105, the call writer will have a net loss.

Notice that the buyer's profits exactly mirror the seller's losses, and vice versa, indicating that the options market is a **zero sum game**. In a zero sum game, whatever the buyer gains the seller loses, and vice versa, so the collective gains add to zero. The sum of all the gains and losses in the options market, ignoring transaction costs, will always equal zero.[2]

Figure 21.2 panel (b) shows the profit and loss positions for the put traders. If the buyer of the put pays $5 for a put with an exercise price of $100, the buyer breaks even at a stock price of $95. The writer of a put also breaks even at $95. These graphs indicate the wide variety of possible profit and loss patterns that traders may create by using the options market. Later in this chapter we will illustrate some option combination strategies.

THE PUT-CALL PARITY THEOREM

There is a definite connection between the price of a put and a call option with the same exercise price and time to maturity. To find this relationship, assume that today you buy a call option and sell a put option. If the price of the call is C and the price of the put is P, your net investment in this two-option portfolio is equal to $P - C$. At expiration, the payoff from each of the options is given by Figure 21.1 panel (a) for the purchase of a call, and by panel (d) for the sale of a put option. Since they both have the same exercise price and maturity, we can combine these two figures to find the option portfolio's payoff at expiration, as depicted in figure 21.3. This figure shows that a long call and a short put portfolio will always produce a payoff at expiration that is equal to $S - E$.

Now assume that investors are risk neutral, so they value investments based solely on their expected payoffs. Then, the value of the option portfolio must equal the present value of the expected payoffs when the options expire T years from now. We have:[3]

$$C - P = E(S_T - E)e^{-rT}$$
$$= E(S_T)e^{-rT} - Ee^{-rT}$$
$$= Se^{rT}e^{-rT} - Ee^{-rT}$$
$$= S - Ee^{-rT}$$

Notice that the expected stock price T years from now is just today's stock price compounded at the risk-free rate, r. This derivation has given us the important put-call parity theorem:

$$C = S - Ee^{-rT} + P \qquad (21.1)$$

The put-call parity theorem states that the price of a call option is equal to the difference between the current stock price and the present value of the exercise price, plus the price of a put option. Recall, however, that for the theorem to apply, both the put and the call options must be written on the same underlying stock, have the same maturity, and the same exercise price. It is because of this theorem that we can focus most of our analysis on call options, since put option properties are tied to those of call options, as equation 21.1 shows.

---

[2] Not all markets are zero sum games. The stock market is a good example since, collectively, it has historically had a positive return.

[3] Notice that we are using continuous discounting. This is customary in option theory and does not affect the results.

FIGURE 21.3

Payoff at Expiration of Buying a Call Option and Selling a Put Option

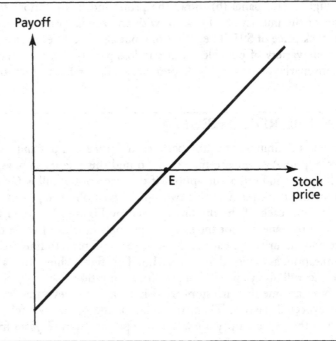

A CALL OPTION WITH A ZERO EXERCISE PRICE AND AN INFINITE TIME UNTIL EXPIRATION

A call option with a zero exercise price and an infinite time until expiration represents an extreme price and an extreme expiration date. Because of these extremes, analyzing this kind of option allows us to set boundaries on possible option prices. The owner of an option on a stock with a zero exercise price and an infinite time to maturity can surrender the option at any time without cost and receive the stock in exchange. Since the owner can transform this option into the stock costlessly, it must have a value as great as the stock itself. This allows us to state a second principle of option pricing:

$$C(S, 0, \infty, \sigma, r) = S$$

Another way to confirm this result is through equation 21.1 and figure 21.1 (c). In that figure, the payoff to a put option occurs only for stock prices below E. If E is zero the put option will never produce a positive payoff for its owner, so it must be worth nothing; that is, if $E = 0$, then $P = 0$. Using this information in equation 21.1 gives $C = S$, and the result is proven.[4]

---

[4] Notice that it is not really necessary to have an infinite maturity for this result to hold. However, the logical argument is easier to understand by making this assumption.

Together, these first two principles allow us to specify the upper and lower bounds for the possible price of a call option, which depend on the stock price, the exercise price, and the time to expiration. Figure 21.4 shows these boundaries. If the call has a zero exercise price and an infinite maturity, the call price must equal the stock price. This fact is reflected in the 45 degree line from the origin, which represents the upper bound for an option's price.

At expiration the price of the option must lie along the line running from the origin to the point at which the stock price equals the exercise price, E, and then upward at a 45 degree angle. If the stock price is less than or equal to the exercise price, the call price must be zero, as shown by the horizontal line. If the stock price exceeds the exercise price, the option must trade for a price that is equal to the difference between the stock price and the exercise price. This is represented by the 45 degree line starting at $S = E$.

Other options, such as those with time remaining until expiration and with positive exercise prices, lie in the shaded region between these two extremes. To further our understanding of option pricing, we need to consider other factors that put tighter restrictions on the permissible values of option prices.

RELATIONSHIPS BETWEEN OPTION PRICES

Numerous exercise prices and expiration dates are available for options on the same stock. Not surprisingly, there are definite relationships that these prices must bear to each other to prevent arbitrage opportunities, among them:

FIGURE 21.4
Bounds for Call Option Prices

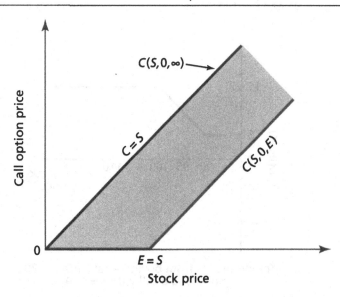

$$\text{If } E_a < E_b, \text{ then } C(S, E_a, T, \sigma, r) > C(S, E_b, T, \sigma, r)$$

This relationship says that if call options a and b are alike, except the exercise price of a is less than that of b, then the price of option a is equal to or greater than the price of option b. To see why this rule must hold, imagine a situation in which there are two options that are just alike, except the first has an exercise price of $100 and sells for $10. The second option has an exercise price of $90 and sells for $5. Panel (a) of figure 21.5 shows the profit and loss graphs for both options. The option with the $90 exercise price

FIGURE 21.5
Relationship Between Prices of Options with Different Exercise Prices

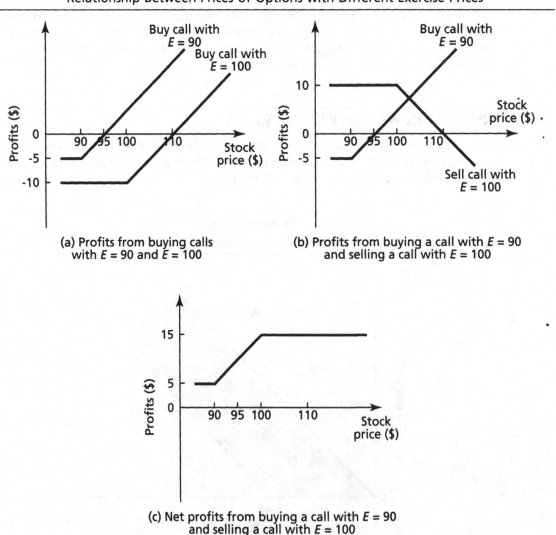

(a) Profits from buying calls
with E = 90 and E = 100

(b) Profits from buying a call with E = 90
and selling a call with E = 100

(c) Net profits from buying a call with E = 90
and selling a call with E = 100

has a much better profit and loss profile than the option with the $100 exercise price. No matter what the stock price, S, might be at expiration, the option with the $90 exercise price will perform better, because it will either produce a greater profit or suffer a smaller loss.

This price relationship is already an unsustainable result, because it represents a disequilibrium in the market. With these prices, all smart traders would want the option with the exercise price of $90, and completely neglect the option with the $100 exercise price. This would cause the price of the option with the $100 exercise price to fall to a point where investors are willing to hold it.

We can make the same point in an arbitrage context, because the profit and loss opportunities shown in figure 21.5 panel (a) create an arbitrage opportunity. Faced with these prices, the arbitrageur would simply transact as follows:

Transaction	Cash Flow
Sell the option with the $100 exercise price	$10
Buy the option with the $90 exercise price	−5
Net Cash Flow	$5

The combined position is depicted in figure 21.5 panel (b). To see why this is a good transaction to make, consider the profit and loss position on each option and on the combination of both options for various expiration stock prices, as seen in table 21.1.

For any possible stock price, there will be some profit by holding the two options. If the stock price is $90 or less, the profit will be $5 from the combined options position, plus the net cash inflow of $5 received when the position was initiated. As the stock price at expiration goes from $90 to $100, the profit rises until it reaches the maximum profit of $15 at a stock price of $100. For stock prices at expiration above $100, the profit remains at $15. Figure 21.5 panel (c) presents this result. This does not show the $5 inflow received when the trader entered the position. With the prices in the example, it is possible to trade to guarantee a total cash flow of between $10 and $20, depending on the stock price. This can be accomplished without risk or investment, so it constitutes an arbitrage. To eliminate the arbitrage opportunity, the price of the option with a striking price of $90 must be at least as large as the price of the option with the striking price of $100.

TABLE 21.1
Profit or Loss on the Option Position

Stock Price at Expiration	E = $90	E = $100	Both Combined
$80	−$5	+$10	+$5
90	−5	+10	+5
95	0	+10	+10
100	+5	+10	+15
105	+10	+5	+15
110	+15	0	+15
115	+20	−5	+15

There is another simple way to view this result. Figure 21.6 shows the payoffs of the two options with the same maturity but different exercise prices. Since call option a, with the lowest exercise price, offers at least the same payoff (zero) as option b for low stock prices and offers a strictly greater payoff for sufficiently large stock prices, option a must be more valuable than option b.

Another principle of call options refers to the expiration date: if call options a and b are alike, but option a has a greater time to expiration than option b, then option a must sell for an amount equal to or greater than option b. That is:

$$\text{If } T_a > T_b, \text{ then } C(S, T_a, E, \sigma, r) \geq C(S, T_b, E, \sigma, r)$$

Intuitively, this principle must hold because the option with the longer time until expiration gives the investor all the advantages that the option with a shorter time to expiration offers. In addition, the option that expires later also gives the investor the chance to wait longer before exercising the option. In some circumstances, that extra time to exercise the option has some value.

If the option with the longer time to expiration sold for less than the option with the shorter time to expiration, there would be an arbitrage opportunity. To conduct the arbitrage, assume that two options with a striking price of $100 are written on the same underlying stock. Let the first option have a time to expiration of six months and assume it has a price of $8. The second option has three months to expiration and a price of $10. In this situation, the arbitrageur transacts as follows:

Transaction	Cash Flow
Buy the 6-month option for $8	−$8
Sell the 3-month option for $10	+$10
Net Cash Flow	+$2

FIGURE 21.6
Payoffs for Call Options with Different Exercise Prices

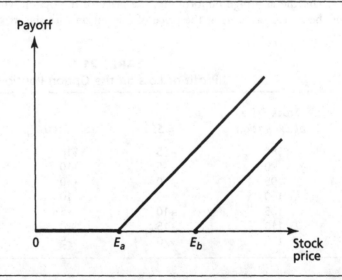

Payoff

0   E_a E_b Stock price

By buying the longer maturity option and selling the shorter maturity option, the arbitrageur receives a net cash flow of $2. However, this transaction might seem risky if the three-month option the arbitrageur sells is exercised. To see that the arbitrageur's position is secure, assume that the three-month option is exercised. In this case, the arbitrageur can simply exercise the six-month option, thus receiving the underlying stock on the six-month option. This stock received is then delivered against the exercised three-month option. Since the exercise price of both options is the same, this guarantees that the arbitrageur can keep the $2. Therefore, there will be a $2 profit no matter what happens to the stock price. Because the trader guarantees a profit without risk or investment, it is an arbitrage profit. However, as we know, this cannot be sustained for long. Generally, the option with the longer time to expiration will actually be worth more than the option with the shorter time to expiration.

We have already seen that any option must be worth at least the difference between the stock price and the exercise price $(S - E)$ at expiration. If the stock price exceeds the exercise price $(S > E)$, traders say the option is **in-the-money**. If the stock price is less than the exercise price $(S < E)$, the option is **out-of-the-money**. If the stock price equals the exercise price $(S = E)$, the option is **at-the-money**. Before expiration, an in-the-money option will normally be worth more than $S - E$. This difference, $S - E$, is the **intrinsic value** of the option, the value of the option if it is exercised immediately. Before expiration, we can expect an in-the-money option to be worth more than $S - E$ because being able to wait to exercise normally has some value. If the trader exercises an option before expiration, the trader receives only the amount $S - E$ for the option. By selling the option in the market, the trader will get the market price, which will normally exceed $S - E$. Therefore, it generally does not pay to exercise an option early.[5]

We can use equation 21.1 to see that the value of a call option will generally exceed $S - E$ before maturity. Indeed, since it is always true that $P > 0$, we have:

$$C = S - Ee^{-rT} + P$$
$$> S - Ee^{-rT}$$
$$> S - E$$

Thus, $C > S - E$.

Thus far, we have set bounds for option prices and we have established some relationships between pairs of options. We can add more restrictions to the price of a call option by now considering the impact of interest rates.

CALL OPTION PRICES AND INTEREST RATES

Assume that a stock sells for $100 and that its value will change by 10 percent in either direction over the next year. The value of a round lot of 100 shares will be either $9,000 or $11,000 in one year. Assume also that the continuously discounted risk-free rate of interest is 12 percent, that a call option on this stock has a striking price of $100 per share,

---

[5] In the case of a dividend-paying stock, this will not always be true.

and that the option expires in one year. Now construct two portfolios in the following way:

Portfolio A   100 shares of stock with a current value of $10,000.

Portfolio B   A $10,000 pure discount bond maturing in one year, with a current value of $8,869.20 = $10,000e$^{-0.12}$. This price reflects the 12 percent continuously discounted interest rate.
One option contract, with an exercise price of $100 per share, or $10,000 for the entire contract of 100 shares.

Which portfolio is more valuable, and what does this tell us about the price of the call option? In one year, the stock price for the round lot will be either $11,000 if the price goes up by 10 percent, or $9,000 if the price goes down by 10 percent. Table 21.2 shows this result for portfolio A. Portfolio B combines the bond and the call option. As table 21.2 also shows, the bond matures in one year and pays $10,000.

If the stock price rises 10 percent, the call option will be worth exactly $1,000, the difference between the stock price and the exercise price, or $S - E$. If the stock price falls 10 percent, the option expires worthless. So if the stock price falls, portfolio B will be worth $10,000 – the value received from the pure discount bond. If the stock price rises, portfolio B will be worth $11,000, $10,000 from the bond and $1,000 from the call option. Thus, if the stock price goes down, portfolio B is worth $1,000 more than portfolio A. If the stock price goes up, portfolios A and B have the same value. An investor could never do worse by holding portfolio B, but could do better. Therefore, the value of portfolio B must be at least as great as the value of portfolio A.

This tells us something very important about the price of the option. Since portfolio B is sure to perform at least as well as portfolio A, it must cost at least as much. Further, we know that the current value of portfolio A is $10,000, so the price of portfolio B must be at least $10,000. The bond in portfolio B costs $8,869.20, so the option must cost at least $1,130.80. This confirms that the value of the call option must be worth at least as

TABLE 21.2
Portfolio Values After One Year With a 10 Percent Stock Price Change

	Stock Price	
	+10%	-10%
Portfolio A		
Stock	$11,000	$9,000
Portfolio B		
Maturing bond	10,000	10,000
Call option	1,000	0

much as the stock price minus the present value of the exercise price. In our notation, it must be the case that:[6]

$$C \geq S - Ee^{-rT}$$

If the call option did not meet this condition, any investor would prefer to purchase portfolio B in the example, rather than portfolio A. Previously, we were able to say that the price of the call must be either zero or $S - E$ at expiration. The new result stating that the call price must be greater than or equal to the stock price minus the present value of the exercise price substantially tightens the bounds on the value of a call option.

As the next example shows, higher interest rates cause higher call prices, if everything else is constant. In the previous example, the continuously discounted interest rate was 12 percent, and we concluded that the price of the call option must be at least $1,130.80. For the same portfolio, imagine that the continuously discounted interest rate is 20 percent rather than 12 percent. Then, the value of the call option must be at least $1,667, as the following equation shows.

$$C \geq \$10,000 - \$10,000e^{-0.20} = \$1,812.69$$

From this line of reasoning, we can assert the following principle: other things being equal, the higher the risk-free rate of interest, the greater must be the price of a call option.

$$\text{If } r_1 > r_2, \text{ then } C(S, E, T, \sigma, r_1) > C(S, E, T, \sigma, r_2)$$

While at first this result might appear strange, it is actually quite intuitive. Indeed, for a given current stock price, S, a higher risk-free rate of interest means that the expected stock price at expiration will be greater, since the stock price is expected to grow at the risk-free rate. A higher interest rate leads to a higher stock price at maturity, and this means that the call option is worth more today.

CALL OPTION PRICES AND THE RISKINESS OF STOCKS

Surprisingly enough, the price of a call option increases as the volatility of the asset on which it is written increases. There are several ways to see this result. First, consider the payoff to the buyer of a call option, as in figure 21.1 panel (a). A higher volatility means that more extreme prices can occur, both higher and lower. Lower prices, however, will not affect the payoff (since it will be zero), but higher prices will increase the buyer's potential payoff. Therefore, the call option buyer prefers an option with an underlying asset that is as volatile as possible, other things being equal.

We can also illustrate this principle by an example. Consider a stock trading at $10,000 that will experience either a 10 percent price rise or a 10 percent price decline over the next year. As we saw in our earlier example of table 21.2, a call option on such a stock, with an exercise price of $10,000 and a risk free continuously discounted interest rate of 12 percent, would be worth at least $1,130.80. Now consider a new stock, which trades

---

[6] This inequality is also obtained from equation 21.1. Some researchers define the option's intrinsic value as the difference $S - E^{-rT}$, rather than $S - E$.

at $10,000, but that will experience either a 20 percent price increase or a 20 percent price decrease over the next year. If we focus on an option with a striking price of $10,000, what can we say about the value of the call option?

Table 21.3 repeats the scenario of the stock that will go up or down by 10 percent. We have seen that a call option of this stock must be worth at least $1,130.80 today. We also saw that if the stock price goes down in one year, the call will be worthless. If the stock price goes up 10 percent at that time, the call option will be worth $1,000. Now suppose that the stock will go up or down by 20 percent. If the stock price goes down 20 percent after one year, the call will be worthless. This is the same payoff as the call when the stock price decreased by 10 percent. If prices go up by 20 percent at the end of the year, the call will be worth $2,000, the difference between the exercise price and the stock price.

In this scenario, any investor would prefer the option whose underlying asset has a 20 percent stock price change. Therefore, the current value of the call option on the higher volatility call must equal or exceed the value of the call on the lower volatility stock.

This allows us to derive the following principle: the value of a call option increases as the riskiness of the underlying asset increases.

$$\text{If } \sigma_1 > \sigma_2, \text{ then } C(S, E, T, \sigma_1, r) > C(S, E, T, r, \sigma_2, r)$$

One of the important corollaries of this principle is that any investor holding a financial instrument that has call option features will have a strong incentive to make the underlying asset as risky as possible. As we shall discuss shortly, this insight has very crucial consequences for the stockholders of the firm, since stock behaves very much like a call option.

TABLE 21.3
Portfolio Values After One Year With a 10 Percent and a 20 Percent Stock Price Change

	Stock Price	
	+10%	−10%
Portfolio A		
Stock	$11,000	$9,000
Portfolio B		
Maturing bond	$10,000	$10,000
Call option	$1,000	0

	Stock Price	
	+20%	−20%
Portfolio A		
Stock	$12,000	$8,000
Portfolio B		
Maturing bond	$10,000	$10,000
Call option	$2,000	0

Before we engage in that discussion, however, we consider the insurance characteristic of call options in the next section.

THE INSURANCE COMPONENT OF CALL OPTIONS

In table 21.2, the call option will be worth either $1,000 or zero in one year, and the current price of that option must be at least $1,130.80. At first glance, it seems like a terrible investment to pay more than $1,000 for something that will be worth either zero or $1,000 one year from now. However, the option offers more than a simple investment opportunity, because it also contains an embedded insurance policy. We can see the insurance character of the option by comparing the payoffs from portfolio A and portfolio B. If the stock price falls by 10 percent after one year, portfolio A will be worth $9,000 and portfolio B will be worth $10,000. If the stock price rises 10 percent, both portfolios will be worth $11,000.

Holding the option ensures that the worst outcome from the investment will be $10,000. This is considerably safer than holding the stock alone. Under these circumstances it can make good sense to pay $1,130.80 or more for an option that has a maximum payoff of $1,000. Part of the benefit from holding the option portfolio is the assurance that the total payoff from the portfolio will be at least $10,000. In other words, part of the price of an option is an insurance premium against undesirable price declines.

A similar reasoning provides another explanation as to why higher risk on the underlying stock makes the option more valuable. Indeed, the riskier the stock, the more valuable will be an insurance policy against particularly bad results. Previously, we said that the price of the option must be at least as great as the stock price minus the present value of the exercise price. However, if we take into account the value of the insurance policy inherent in the option, we can say that the value of the option must be equal to the stock price minus the present value of the exercise price, plus the value of the insurance policy inherent in the option. If we denote the value of the insurance policy by I, the value of the call option is:

$$C = S - Ee^{-rT} + I \tag{21.2}$$

A direct comparison of equations 21.1 and 21.2 immediately reveals the interesting result that the value of the insurance component of a call option is exactly equal to the value of a put option written on the same stock, having the same exercise price and time to maturity. Thus, $I = P$.

THE APPLICATION OF OPTIONS TO CORPORATE FINANCE

Since its original development, scholars have applied the ideas of option pricing theory to improve our understanding of many different financial instruments. This section considers four such applications. First, the purchaser of the firm's debt essentially sells a put option to the stockholders of the firm. Second, buying equity is like buying a call option. Third, a convertible bond contains an option because the holder of the bond has the option to convert the bond to shares of stock. Fourth, we can value warrants using option pricing concepts. A warrant is essentially a long-term call option on the stock of the firm which the firm itself creates. Unlike an option, however, a warrant calls for the delivery of a new share of stock instead of an existing share. Firms often use warrants to compensate executives, and as a sweetener to encourage bond sales.

Similarity Between Bonds and Short Positions in Put Options

In option terminology, the buyer of a firm's risky bond has bought a risk-free bond and sold a put option on the firm's assets to its shareholders. To see why, consider the following example. A very simple firm with only one share of stock issues a bond for $90 that matures in one year and promises to pay $100 upon maturity. At maturity, if the firm is worth less than $100, the stockholder will not pay the bondholder. Instead, the stockholder allows the bondholder to take over the firm. Alternatively, if the firm is worth more than $100, the stockholder will pay the bondholder the $100 owed and retain full title to the firm.

Based on this analysis, figure 21.7 shows the value of the risky bond at maturity. The risky bond's value depends on the value of the entire firm. If the firm is worth less than $100, the stockholder defaults and the bondholder takes over the firm, receiving whatever it is worth. The stockholder can give the firm to the bondholder by simply defaulting on the bond payment. That is, in fact, the essence of the bankruptcy option that all stockholders have. If the firm value exceeds $100, the stockholder will pay the $100 to the bondholder and keep the firm. This means that the bondholder can never receive more than the promised amount of $100, but might receive less. As figure 21.7 shows, the value of the risky bond at maturity is exactly equal to the sum of a risk-free bond and a short position in a put option. As sellers of a put option, the bondholders are betting that the value of the firm at maturity will exceed the exercise price of the put, which is $100 in our example.

FIGURE 21.7
Value of a Bond at Maturity as a Function of the Firm's Value

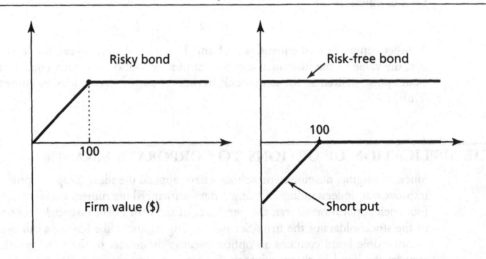

Similarity Between Stocks and Call Options

Now consider the same set of circumstances, but from the stockholder's perspective. If the value of the bond-issuing firm is less than $100, the stockholder will simply abandon the firm to the bondholder, and the stockholder will obtain no benefit from the stock. Equivalently, the stockholder will not exercise the option to pay the $100 to the bondholder. The exercise price of this call option is the $100 payment promised to the bondholder.

Consistent with this view, figure 21.8 shows the value of the share of stock as a function of the firm's value at the bond's maturity. If the firm is worth $100 or less, the stock has no value, because the bondholder has priority and will be able to claim all of the value of the firm. However, if the firm value exceeds $100, the stock has some value, because the stockholder will capture all firm value above $100. Therefore, equity is analogous to a call option on the firm, with the exercise price of the option being the payment promised to the bondholders. Indeed, figure 21.8 showing the value of equity is exactly like figure 21.1 panel (a), which shows the payoff to the buyer of a call option.

Option Pricing and Convertible Bonds

A convertible bond is a bond that gives the bondholder the option of converting the bond into stock by surrendering the bond and receiving in return a specified number of shares of common stock. The **conversion ratio** is the number of shares the bondholder receives for each bond. The **conversion price** is the price the bondholder pays for each share of stock upon conversion. It equals the market price of the convertible bond divided by the conversion ratio. The **conversion premium** is the additional amount per share of stock

FIGURE 21.8
Value of a Share at the Bond's Maturity as a Function of the Firm's Value

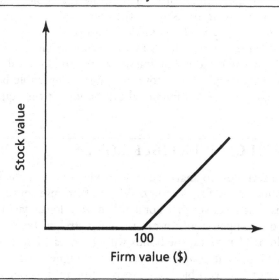

that one pays to obtain the share by converting the bond rather than by buying the stock in the marketplace.

To illustrate, consider a convertible bond with a par value of $1,000 and a market price of $940. Suppose the common stock of the issuing company trades for $40, and that the bond contract allows the bondholder to exchange the bond for 20 shares of common stock – a conversion ratio of 20. Thus, the bondholder may convert by surrendering a bond worth $940 for $800 worth of stock (20 shares worth $40 each). The conversion price of a share of stock equals $940/20 or $47. The $7 difference between the conversion price and the actual price of the stock is the conversion premium. At this point it is clearly not advisable to convert. When the bondholder converts the bonds into stock, the firm issues new stock. Therefore, there will be more shares outstanding after the conversion than before. Thus, upon conversion, a dilution of ownership in the firm occurs, because the firm must create more shares.

To see how a convertible bond is like a combination of a risky bond and a fractional call option on the equity of the firm, consider the following example. A firm issues a convertible bond today for $90. When the bond matures in one year, the firm promises to pay $100 to retire the bond. Alternatively, the owner of the convertible bond may surrender the bond at any time up to maturity in exchange for one share of stock. At the time of the issuance of the convertible bond, there was only one share of stock outstanding.

The holder of the bond has three payoff possibilities. First, at the bond's maturity, the firm may be worth less than the $100 promised payment to the bondholder. In this situation, the firm defaults and the bondholder takes over the firm. Second, the firm might be worth more than $200. In this case, the owner of the convertible bond surrenders the bond and receives one new share of stock; so after conversion the firm has two shares of stock, and each share will be worth more than $100. Third, the firm might be worth more than $100 but less than $200. In this case, the bondholder prefers to receive the promised $100 payment rather than convert. If the bondholder converts, each of the two shares would be worth less than $100, so the bondholder is better off treating the convertible bond as a straight bond. For their part, the shareholders of the firm would exercise their call option by paying the $100 to the bondholder, thus retaining title to the firm.

Figure 21.9 shows the possible values of this convertible bond as a function of the value of the firm. It also shows that this convertible bond is the sum of a risky bond and one-half of a call option. The fractional nature of the call option is reflected in the slope of 0.5 in the example. Therefore, owning a convertible bond is essentially equivalent to holding risky debt plus a fractional call option on the equity of the firm.

FINANCING WITH CONVERTIBLE BONDS

We have seen how to analyze a convertible bond as a combination of a straight bond and a call option on the firm's equity. Why do firms use convertible bonds to raise funds? One reason is that a convertible bond will have a lower yield than a corresponding straight bond. For example, if a firm can market a straight bond with an 11 percent coupon rate at a yield of 11 percent, the bonds will sell at par. For the same firm, a convertible bond with an 11 percent coupon should have a higher price, resulting in a lower yield. The purchaser of a convertible bond receives title to the same coupon stream as the purchaser

FIGURE 21.9
Value of a Convertible Bond at Maturity as a Function of the Firm's Value

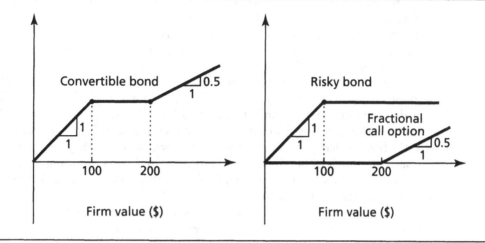

of the straight bond and, in addition, also receives an option on the firm's equity through the conversion privilege. Naturally, this option inherent in the convertible bond has value, and the price of the convertible bond will reflect this value. Equivalently, the purchaser of the convertible bond must pay not only the price of the straight bond, but also the price of the call option.

Firms also issue convertible bonds to defer issuing equity. If a firm issues a convertible bond now and the firm prospers, it may be attractive for the convertible bondholders to exercise their option and to convert the bond to stock. When they exercise, the firm issues new stock, thereby increasing the share of financing from equity and reducing the share from debt. Therefore, by issuing convertible bonds, firms can plan future changes in their capital structures. Notice, however, that the firm receives no new cash when bondholders convert a convertible bond. Instead, the firm merely exchanges bonds for stock.

Option theory shows that we should not exercise an option before expiration, except in special circumstances. The same principle holds true for the decision to convert a bond into stock. In most cases, it is wiser to wait until the last moment before expiration to exercise. Surprisingly, this is true even if the conversion price is lower than the actual price of the stock at some point before expiration, because once the option is exercised, the right to wait is gone. Usually, that right to wait on a decision has some value.

Most convertible bonds are also callable. When a firm calls a convertible bond, the bondholder must either convert the bond into stock or surrender the bond to the firm for cash.

WARRANTS

Warrants are essentially options on the firm with a very long time to expiration. Usually, firms issue warrants by attaching them to a bond to form a single package. These warrants are also usually detachable from the bond and can trade separately. For example, a bond issued this year may carry with it a warrant that expires in ten years.

The warrant allows the owner to receive a share of stock by surrendering the warrant and paying the exercise price. Thus, in virtually every respect, a warrant is just like a long-term call option on the firm's equity. In fact, the only difference is that with a warrant the firm issues a new share. By contrast, a straight call option is an option on an existing share. This is a small difference which we can ignore.

Firms issue warrants with bonds as a sweetener. Because the bond comes with a valuable warrant, it should sell at a higher price than the same straight bond alone. This means that the firm can issue the bond at a higher price and lower yield than would be possible otherwise. However, the firm surrenders the warrants, and there is no reason to believe that the bondholders pay more for the attached warrants than they are worth. As a consequence, the issuing of bonds with warrants is not really a way for the firm to get ahead. In an efficient market, the firm issuing bonds with warrants receives exactly the sum of what the two financial instruments are worth individually.

If we compare a convertible bond against a bond with a warrant attached, we can see that there are at least two important differences. Assuming that the warrant is detachable from the bond, the warrant plus bond combination is more flexible for the bondholder than a convertible bond. Remember, with a convertible bond, the bondholder must surrender the bond to receive the shares. With a warrant, the bondholder can keep the bond and surrender the warrant. Also, convertible bonds and bonds with warrants differ in their cash flows when the bondholder or warrant owner acquires the stock. We have already noted that the conversion of bonds does not generate any cash flow, but is a straightforward debt-for-stock swap. In exercising a warrant, the owner of the warrant must pay the stated exercise price. Unlike the conversion of a convertible bond, this brings new cash into the firm.

THE BLACK-SCHOLES OPTION PRICING MODEL

One of the greatest achievements of modern finance is the development of the Black-Scholes option pricing model – a mathematical model that solves for the value of a call option as a function of its five variables. The model assumes that the stock does not pay dividends and that prices follow a path through time known as a stochastic process. A **stochastic process** is a mathematical description of the evolution of some random variable, such as a stock's price, through time.

In the option pricing model (OPM), the value of a call option depends on the risk-free interest rate (r_f), the variability of the asset on which the call is written (σ), the time remaining until the option expires (T), the price of the asset on which the call is written (S), and the exercise price of the option (E). If we know the values of these five variables, we can use the OPM to calculate the theoretical price of an option.

The formula for the Black-Scholes OPM is:

$$C = S \times N(d_1) - E \times e^{-r_f T} \times N(d_2) \tag{21.3}$$

where:

$$d_1 = \frac{\ln\left(\frac{S}{E}\right) + \left(r_f + \frac{\sigma^2}{2}\right)T}{\sigma\sqrt{T}} \qquad (21.4)$$

$$d_2 = d_1 - \sigma\sqrt{T}$$

and $N(d_1)$ and $N(d_2)$ represent the cumulative probability values from the standard normal distribution for d_1 and d_2, respectively.[7] The **standard normal distribution** is a normal distribution with zero mean and unit standard deviation. Thus, $N(0) = 0.50$ because the normal distribution is symmetric around the mean. Similarly, $N(-\infty) = 0$ and $N(\infty) = 1.0$.

The cumulative probability from the standard normal distribution is the part of the OPM that takes account of the risk and allows the model to give such good results for option prices. The best way to understand the application of the model is with an example. Let us assume values for the five parameters and calculate the value for an option using the Black-Scholes model.

$$S = \$100$$

$$E = \$100$$

$$T = 1 \text{ year}$$

$$r_f = 12\%$$

$$\sigma = 10\%$$

With these values we can calculate the Black-Scholes option value. First, we calculate values for d_1 and d_2:

$$d_1 = \frac{\ln\left(\frac{100}{100}\right) + \left(0.12 + \frac{0.01}{2}\right)1}{0.1 \times 1} = 1.25$$

$$d_2 = 1.25 - 0.1 \times 1 = 1.15$$

Next, we calculate the cumulative normal probability values for d_1 and d_2. These values are the so-called z-scores taken from the standard normal probability distribution shown in figure 21.10. To calculate the cumulative normal probabilities for $d_1 = 1.25$ and $d_2 = 1.15$, we need to determine the proportion of the total area under the standard normal curve that is associated with values smaller than d_1 or d_2, respectively. We have already seen that 50 percent of the area under the standard normal distribution curve lies to the left of 0.00, because the distribution is symmetrical about its mean of 0.00. Because the standard normal probability distribution is so important and so widely used, tables of its values are included in any self-respecting statistics textbook.

The probability of drawing a value from the standard normal distribution that is less than or equal to $d_1 = 1.25$ is 0.8944. The corresponding value for $d_2 = 1.15$ is 0.8749. Thus, the two values we seek are:

---

[7] As you can see, this is not a formula for the weak of spirit. Nevertheless, there are some practical insights to be gained by analyzing it, so hang in there.

FIGURE 21.10
Normal Probability Distribution Function

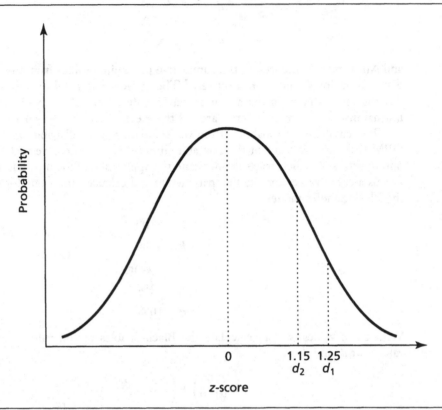

$$N(d_1) = N(1.25) = 0.8944$$
$$N(d_2) = N(1.15) = 0.8749$$

Returning to the OPM, we can now make the final calculation, using equation 21.1:

$$C = \$100 \times (0.8944) - \$100 \times e^{-0.12 \times 1} \times (0.8749) = \$11.84$$

According to the Black-Scholes OPM, the call option in this case should be worth $11.84.
Upon first acquaintance with the OPM, many people think that it is too esoteric and complicated to be useful. Nothing could be further from the truth. Of all the models in finance, the OPM is among those receiving the widest acceptance by actual investors. For example, computers on the floor of the Chicago Board Options Exchange give traders OPM prices for all options using instantaneously updated information on all of the parameters in the model. Further, most investment banking houses have staffs that specialize in options and use the OPM on a daily basis. Finally, the OPM has achieved such widespread acceptance that some calculators automatically calculate OPM values. This widespread acceptance is due in large part to the very good results of the OPM. The Black-Scholes theoretical model price is usually very close to the market price of the option. Without

doubt, the OPM contributes greatly to our understanding of option pricing and many traders find it sufficiently valuable to use it as a key tool in their trading strategies.

HEDGING WITH OPTIONS

One of the most important applications of options is their use as a hedging vehicle. Once again, the OPM gives important insights into this process. To illustrate hedging with options, let us use our original example of a stock selling at $100 and having a standard deviation of 10 percent. We saw that a call option with an exercise price of $100 and a time to expiration of one year would sell for $11.84. If the stock price suddenly rises one percent, from $100 to $101, the option price would rise to $12.73, as can be verified using the Black-Scholes equation. If the stock price and the option price are so intimately related, it should be possible to use options to offset the risk inherent in the stock.

Table 21.4 shows this possibility. Consider an original portfolio containing 8,944 shares of stock selling at $100 per share and assume that a trader sells 100 option contracts, or options on 10,000 shares, at $11.84 per option. In the table, this short position in the option is indicated by a minus sign. That entire portfolio has a value of $776,000. Now consider the effect of a 1 percent change in the price of the stock. If the stock price increases by 1 percent to $101, the shares will be worth $903,344. The price of each option will also increase from $11.84 to $12.73. Taking these two effects into account, the value of the whole portfolio will be $776,044. This is virtually identical to the original value.

On the other hand, if the stock price falls by 1 percent, each share will be worth $99. The price of each option will also fall, from $11.84 to $10.95. Taking both of these effects into account, the portfolio will then be worth $775,956. As this example indicates, the overall value of the portfolio will be nearly constant, no matter what happens to the stock price. If the stock price increases, there is an offsetting loss on the option. Likewise, if the stock price falls, there is an offsetting gain on the option.

In this example, holding 0.8944 shares of stock for each option sold short will give a perfect hedge. The value of the entire portfolio will be insensitive to any change in the stock price. How can we know exactly the right number of options to trade to give this result? The careful reader might recall the number 0.8944. When the value of this call option was calculated in the previous section, we saw that $N(d_1) = 0.8944$; it is this value

TABLE 21.4
A Hedged Portfolio

	Original Portfolio S = $100; C = $11.84	Stock Price Rises by 1%: S = $101; C = $12.73	Stock Price Falls by 1%: S = $99; C = $10.95
8,944 shares of stock	$894,400	$903,344	$885,456
A short position for options on 10,000 shares (100 contracts)	–$118,400	–$127,300	–$109,500
Total value	$776,000	$776,044	$775,956

that allows the construction of a perfect hedge in our example. The general principle can be summarized as follows:

The value of a portfolio comprised of a short position of one option and a long position of $N(d_1)$ shares of the option's underlying stock will remain constant, regardless of the fluctuations in the stock price.

Alternatively, to hedge a long position of one share in a stock, sell a number of options equal to $1/N(d_1)$. This hedge will hold for infinitesimal changes in the stock price. In the preceding example, the hedge was not quite perfect because the change in the stock price was not infinitesimal. Notice that any change in the stock price changes the value of $N(d_1)$, because d_1 depends, in part, on the stock price. This means that the hedge must be adjusted constantly as the stock price changes if it is to be kept perfect. In practice, of course, this is impossible. Nevertheless, by adjusting with some reasonable frequency, the hedge can nearly eliminate all the risk.

SUMMARY

This chapter introduced the basic principles of option pricing. First, we saw how option values at expiration depend on the price of the underlying good and the exercise price of the option. Before expiration, the price of an option depends on the time until expiration, the level of interest rates, and the riskiness of the underlying good. In examining these relationships, we also considered the prices that must prevail on comparable goods, in order to rule out arbitrage opportunities.

These principles of option pricing apply directly to the valuation of various corporate liabilities. We saw how to analyze a share of common stock as a call option on the firm, with the exercise price being the amount owed to the bondholders. Similarly, in buying a bond the owner of a bond has essentially sold a put option to the stockholders.

We also considered convertible debt, which has characteristics of both stocks and bonds. In fact, we can analyze a convertible bond using option pricing theory, which shows that a convertible bond is a combination of a short position in a put and a long position in a call on the firm's equity. We then considered bonds that contain warrants. A warrant is essentially a long-term call option on the firm's additional shares that the firm sells as a package with the bond.

QUESTIONS

1. Respond to the following claim: "Buying a call option is very dangerous because it commits the owner to purchasing a stock at a later date. At that time the stock may be undesirable. Therefore, owning a call option is a risky position."
2. "Buying a call option gives the right to acquire a stock while selling a put option means that you may buy a stock as well. Therefore the two are the same." Comment on this claim.
3. Explain the difference between the option premium and the striking price.
4. On what five factors does the value of a call option depend?

5. On what factors does the value of an option at expiration depend?
6. Why should call options be worth more, the lower the exercise price?
7. Explain why options should be priced in a way to eliminate arbitrage opportunities.
8. "I bought a call option with an exercise price of $110 on IBM when IBM was at $108 and I paid $6 per share for the option. Now the option is about to expire and IBM is trading at $112. There's no point in exercising the option, because I will wind up paying a total of $116 for the shares – $6 I already spent for the option plus the $110 exercise price." Is this line of reasoning correct? Explain.
9. Why is the options market a zero sum game?
10. Why does the value of a call option increase with interest rates?
11. Why does the value of a call option increase with the volatility of the underlying good?
12. Why is the value of a call option at expiration equal to the maximum of zero or the stock price minus the exercise price?
13. Explain how a call option includes an insurance policy.
14. Two call options are identical except that they are written on two different stocks with different risk levels. Which option will be worth more? Why?
15. Explain why owning a bond is like having a short position in a put option.
16. Why does ownership of a convertible bond have features of a call option?
17. What is the difference between a warrant and a regular call option?
18. In what sense is owning the equity of a firm like owning a call option?

PROBLEMS

1. What is the value of a call option on a share of stock if the exercise price of the call is $0 and its expiration date is infinite? Explain.
2. A call option is at expiration and has a striking price of $100. The stock on which the option is written has a market value of $103. Assume that you paid $5 for the option. What is the value of the option? Should you exercise? If you do not exercise, what is your profit or loss on the entire transaction? If you do exercise, what is your profit or loss on the entire transaction?
3. A call option is at expiration and has a striking price of $80. The stock on which the option is written has a market value of $75. Assume that you paid $8 for the option. What is the value of the option? Should you exercise? If you do not exercise, what is your profit or loss on the entire transaction? If you do exercise, what is your profit or loss on the entire transaction?
4. Two call options on the same stock have the following features. The first has an exercise price of $60, a time to expiration of three months, and a premium of $5. The second has an exercise price of $60, a time to expiration of six months, and a premium of $4. What should you do in this situation? Explain exactly, assuming that you transact for just one option. What is your profit or loss at the expiration of the nearby option if the stock is at $55, $60, or $65?
5. Assume the following: a stock is selling for $100, a call option on the stock with an exercise price of $90 is trading for $6 and matures in one month, and

the interest rate is 1 percent per month. What should you do? Explain your transactions.

6. Two call options on the same stock expire in two months. One has an exercise price of $55 and a price of $5. The other has an exercise price of $50 and a price of $4. What transactions would you make to exploit this situation?

7. Option A has an exercise price of E_a and the price of the underlying stock is S. The two corresponding values for option B are 10 percent greater than for option A. In all other respects, the two options are identical. According to the Black-Scholes model, how are the two option prices related? (For example, the price of option A might be twice the price of option B.)

8. We argued that the price of a call option with infinite maturity and zero exercise price must be equal to the stock price ($C = S$). Using the Black-Scholes model, show that for an infinite maturity option $C = S$ even if the exercise price is not zero.

9. We argued that the price of a call option at expiration should equal the difference between the stock price (S) and the option's exercise price (E), whenever $S > E$. Show this result using the Black-Scholes model.

10. Suppose the exercise price of a call option is set so that $E = S \times \exp(r_f T_0)$, where T_0 is the time to maturity when the option is written, and $\exp(x) \equiv e^x$. Using the Black-Scholes model, show that the original price of this option must equal $[2N(d_1) - 1]$ percent of the underlying stock.

11. If the stock underlying a call option is sure to maintain the same price over the life of the option, how much is the option worth?

Chapter 22

Mergers and Acquisitions

OVERVIEW

The United States has witnessed one of the largest waves of mergers in history. Firms frequently announce multi-billion dollar deals to take over another firm. At the same time, many other firms are selling portions of their businesses. This chapter develops an understanding of these phenomena and how they affect shareholder wealth. The chapter begins by exploring the terminology, methods, and the recent history of mergers.

We then consider how to evaluate a merger proposal. There are two firms in a merger – an acquiring firm and an acquired, or target, firm. Evaluation techniques fall into two categories, depending on whether the acquiring firm pays cash or stock to the owners of the target firm. The chapter then considers some motives for mergers, both those that are wise and those that are highly questionable.

The chapter concludes by examining the wealth effects of mergers on acquirers and targets. A merger always involves an exchange of assets between the shareholders of the acquiring and target firms. Does one side of the exchange benefit more, or does a merger usually constitute a fair exchange? Also, do these mergers serve the interests of society? The last sections of this chapter address these broader social concerns.

MERGER TERMINOLOGY

In a **merger** or **acquisition**, two or more firms combine to form a single independent company. In essence, one firm buys and absorbs another. The buying firm is the **acquirer** and the firm that is sold is the **acquired** or **target firm**. The merger may not change the name and operations of the target firm, but the target ceases to exist as an independent firm.

Horizontal and Vertical Mergers

We may classify most mergers as horizontal or vertical mergers. A **horizontal merger** occurs when the acquiring and target firms are in the same industry. A horizontal merger can sometimes create important economies. Usually, the acquiring firm dismisses the top management of the target firm. Also, if the firms are complementary in certain ways, the merged firm can achieve significant advantages by improving economies of scale in purchasing or distribution.

One potential problem with horizontal mergers is that they may restrict trade or result in monopolies. **Anti-trust legislation** attempts to prevent the establishment of monopolies. The Sherman Act of 1890 restricts mergers that result in a restraint of trade. The Clayton Act of 1914 limits mergers that may lessen competition or that may result in monopolies. Recent liberal interpretations by the courts, however, have allowed firms considerable freedom in completing horizontal mergers.

A **vertical merger** is a merger between two companies specializing in different parts of a given production chain. These kinds of mergers give rise to **vertical integration**, the consolidation of the production chain into one firm. Many mergers in the oil industry increase vertical integration. If we think of the oil business as consisting of exploration, refining, and distribution, we know that some firms in the oil industry might specialize in refining and some in distribution. If a refiner and distributor merge, the resulting firm brings more of the production chain within its own control. Vertical integration can provide the oil refiner with an assured outlet for its refinery products, and can provide the distributor with an assured supply of product. Some firms strive for **total integration**, the owning of all phases of the production chain, ranging from the acquisition of raw materials to the retailing of the final product.

Conglomerate Mergers

The conglomerate merger differs from both horizontal and vertical mergers. In a **conglomerate merger**, firms from unrelated industries merge. In such a merger, the merged firm achieves no operating economies, such as those that might arise from horizontal or vertical integration. Instead, the conglomerate essentially holds a portfolio of companies.

We can expect the total value of the firms after the merger will simply equal the sum of their pre-merge values. Some would argue that the combined firm is less risky than each of the separate firms, due to its greater diversification. According to this line of reasoning, the merged firm would be more valuable than the sum of the two individual firms. However, such an argument is fallacious because investors can "merge" the firms by simply buying each of the firm's stock and holding it as part of the investor's portfolio. In other words, there is no diversification benefit to the investor from a conglomerate merger.

DIVESTITURES AND SPINOFFS

Paralleling a dramatic increase in mergers, there has also been an increase in divestitures and spinoffs. In a **divestiture** or a **spinoff**, a firm disposes of some part of its operations to form a new company. The largest divestiture ever was the split-up of AT&T, in which the communications giant spun off several regional operating units in 1984.

Although the fractioning of AT&T was mandated by the courts, many companies voluntarily decide to divest part of their holdings to achieve greater operating efficiencies. This has happened with many of the financial operations of big companies such as General Motors, with its General Motors Acceptance Corporation (GMAC); and General Electric, with its General Electric Credit Corporation (GECC). These specialized companies deal only with the financing aspects of the business, and help increase sales by helping more clients obtain their products on credit.

MERGER PROCEDURES

Firms can initiate mergers in two basic ways. First, in a **negotiated takeover** the acquirer may negotiate directly with the management of the target firm. This type of merger is usually a **friendly takeover**, and the acquiring and target firms agree to a set of merger terms. A second basic type of merger is a tender offer, and this merger effort arises without any direct negotiation with the management of the target firm. In a **tender offer**, the acquiring firm approaches the shareholders directly and asks them to tender their shares to the acquiring firm. A shareholder that tenders a share promises to sell the share to the party making the tender offer at the tender price. To induce shareholders to tender their shares, the acquiring firm must offer a tender price above the current market price of the stock.

The acquiring firm chooses whether to proceed by negotiations or by making a tender offer. If the acquirer believes that the management of the target firm would not be receptive to an offer for the firm, it may make a tender offer. Firms generally prefer to negotiate. The management of the target firm may believe that the offer is not in the interest of the firm's shareholders and may reject the offer for that reason. Management may have less noble reasons for wishing to avoid a merger. We have already noted that the acquirer will often fire the managers of the target company. This fear motivates the management of the target firm to fight the takeover.

A target firm that finds itself in the grips of an acquiring firm may try to avoid the merger with that party. There are three basic strategies for avoiding a given acquirer, all with colorful names. First, the target firm may take a **poison pill**.[1] A firm takes a poison pill by taking some action that destroys the attractiveness of the firm for the acquirer. For example, firms with large amounts of cash are usually attractive takeover targets. A firm that finds itself a target may quickly dispose of its cash by buying some other firm. In fact, many companies use high leverage to make themselves less attractive as takeover targets.

A second technique for avoiding a takeover is to buy off the acquirer, paying the acquirer to cease pursuit of the target firm. Imagine a tender offer that is proceeding with an acquirer accumulating shares of the target in the marketplace. The management of the target may agree to pay the acquirer a higher than market price for the acquirer's shares. In return for this favorable price, the acquirer agrees not to pursue the target firm. This practice is known as **greenmail**. For example, Carl Icahn initiated a hostile takeover attempt on Chesebrough-Pond. The attempt ended when Chesebrough bought back Icahn's shares at the market price, but also paid $95 million, or twice book value, for a company owned by Icahn. Some observers regard this as a payoff of Icahn to drop the takeover attempt.[2]

---

[1] No doubt this name is inspired by the presumed action taken by spies when they face imminent capture by the enemy.
[2] See Colin Leinster, "Carl Icahn's Calculated Bets," *Fortune*, March 18, 1985, and "The Raiders," *Business Week*, March 4, 1985.

Another notorious case involves H. Ross Perot and General Motors. After GM acquired Perot's flagship company, Electronic Data Systems, Perot was granted a seat as a GM director. As GM's share of the auto market decreased, Perot's public chastising of GM's top management increased. Apparently, some GM directors couldn't take the heat, and negotiated with Perot to buy his shares for twice their market value, for a windfall profit to Perot in the order of $750 million – perhaps enough to finance a presidential campaign. Many smaller GM investors were outraged, since they viewed the operation as a transfer of their wealth to Perot. Table 22.1 shows other famous greenmail payoffs.

A third way that target firms wriggle off the takeover hook is by finding a white knight. A **white knight** is a third firm that acquires the target firm being pursued by the hostile acquirer. In this case, the target firm still loses its independence, but the management of the target firm may get a better deal from the white knight, or the management may be more comfortable with the operating style of the white knight.

TAX CONSEQUENCES OF MERGERS

Mergers may be either taxable or tax-free. We already noted that the target firm ceases to exist in a merger, so the shares of the target firm no longer exist. Essentially, a merger may treat the shares of the target firm as though they were sold, or as though they were exchanged for shares of the acquiring firm. If the merger treats the shares as though they were sold, then the shareholders must pay capital gains taxes on their shares. On the other hand, if the target firm's shareholders receive compensation for their shares largely in the form of shares of the acquiring firm, the merger can be tax-free. Usually if more than 50 percent of the target shareholder's compensation takes the form of shares of the acquiring firm, the merger will be tax-free.

HISTORY AND RECENT TRENDS

In the last 20 years, the number of mergers has decreased. However, their dollar value and importance in the economy increased dramatically during the 1980s. The number of announced merger attempts has fallen from a high of about 6,000 in 1969 to a range of about 2,500 per year during the 1980s. In the early years of the 1990s there was a reduced

TABLE 22.1
The Paying of Greenmail

Firm	Unwanted Shareholder	Premium Over Market Value
Blue Bell	Bass Brothers	$60.0
St. Regis	James Goldsmith	50.5
Castle & Cooke	Charles Hurwitz	14.0
Walt Disney	Saul Steinberg	60.0
Avco	Leucadia National	62.0

enthusiasm for big mergers, but in 1994 and 1995 merger activity began to increase again. The pause in merger activity during the early 1990s may have been due to the drying up of many of the traditional sources of money to conduct such massive scale transactions, as the U.S. banking industry faced a crisis in earnings and loan defaults during those years. By 1994, bank profitability had revived, and this may have helped mergers to resume. Still, the 1990s have not yet witnessed merger activity on the scale seen during the 1980s.

MOTIVES FOR MERGERS

What is the motivation for mergers? First, we noted in our discussion of horizontal and vertical mergers that mergers may create important operating efficiencies. In a horizontal merger, the new firm may have market power or economies of scale that it lacked previously. A vertical merger may reduce firm risk by securing suppliers for production inputs and outlets for the firm's final products. Both horizontal and vertical mergers may extend the scope of a superior management team over a larger enterprise.

In addition, there may be other motives for mergers, some valid and some of questionable worth. This section discusses three such motivations: the pursuit of tax benefits, the goal of portfolio diversification, and the desire to increase earnings per share.

Tax Benefits

On occasion, a merger can provide clear tax benefits. Consider a firm with a history of losses that has accumulated a large amount in tax-loss carry forwards. A **tax-loss carry forward** is an accounting loss that the firm has not been able to use to reduce taxes in the past and that it can carry forward to offset future positive income. If the firm does not anticipate positive income soon, it will not be able to use the tax shelter and the firm will lose the tax shield of the carry forwards.

Enter a profitable company in a high tax bracket. If the profitable company acquires the company with the tax losses, the combined entity can use the carry forwards of the target firm to offset the income of the acquiring company. In this situation, the merger can reduce the total sum of taxes.

Another way of making the same point is to realize that the tax-loss carry forwards have value in the merger marketplace. Thus, a chronically unprofitable company may have value just because it can provide a tax shelter through its accumulated carry forwards. Naturally, those tax losses will be most attractive to potential acquirers in the highest tax brackets.

However, if the IRS believes the parties merged solely to cut taxes, it may prohibit the use of the carry forwards. This is particularly likely to happen if the acquiring firm immediately closes the operations of the target firm. This means that firms with tax-loss carry forwards that have some decent prospects for the future are even more attractive. In this case, the new firm may allow the target firm to continue operating. At any rate, merging firms must take care to avoid the wrath of the IRS. Subject to the dangers with the IRS, tax considerations provide a rational incentive for mergers.

The EPS Game

Another incentive for mergers that was once very popular is known as the **EPS game**. Under certain conditions a merger can increase a firm's earnings per share (EPS), even without any change in the firm's operations. In the 1960s, firms found that they could dramatically increase their EPS by merging in a certain way.

We noted in our exploration of stock values that a high price-earnings (P/E) ratio is often a signal of expected future high growth rates in earnings and dividends. In the EPS game, a firm with a high P/E ratio acquires a low P/E firm and convinces the market that the new combined firm deserves the acquirer's high P/E.

Here's how it works. Consider Hype Industries, a high-growth firm in a high-tech industry. Hype has a high P/E ratio and merges with Dull Knife Corp., a low-growth, low P/E firm in a low-tech industry. The top panel of table 22.2 presents financial data for these two firms before they merge. Both firms have the same earnings, the same number of shares outstanding, and the same EPS of $3. However, because Hype is a growth firm with high future expected earnings, the market values it at a higher multiple of its actual earnings. In fact, Hype has a P/E ratio of 30, giving its shares a price of $90. By contrast, the market expects no dramatic growth in the sales of Dull Knife. Therefore, Dull Knife has a P/E ratio of only 10, for a stock price of $30.

In a merger based on an exchange of stock, Hype Industries gives one of its shares to Dull Knife and, in exchange, Dull Knife gives three shares to Hype. To acquire all 100,000 shares of Dull Knife, Hype Industries issues 33,333 new shares, making a total of 133,333 shares outstanding.

The bottom panel of table 22.2 shows the combined firm, which we will call Dull Hype. Earnings are $600,000, just the combined earnings of the two pre-merger firms. With 133,333 shares outstanding, the EPS increases to $4.50. Notice that this increase in EPS results simply from the merger. The only necessary condition for this to occur was that the P/E ratio of the shares given to Dull Knife had to be greater than the P/E ratio of Dull Knife's shares. The EPS magic is complete. Firms can create higher and higher levels of EPS just by merging.

TABLE 22.2
The EPS Game

	Earnings	Shares Outstanding	EPS	P/E Ratio	Share Price
Before the Merger					
Hype Industries	$300,000	100,000	$3.00	30	$90
Dull Knife Corp.	$300,000	100,000	$3.00	10	$30
After the Merger*					
Dull Hype	$600,000	133,333	$4.50	30	135

*In the merger, Dull Knife shareholders receive one share of Hype Industries (market value $90) for every three shares they own.

Even though we have seen how to manufacture growing EPS with mergers, there is one more feature of the merger worth exploring. If the firms can convince the market that the merged firm deserves the same high P/E ratio as the pre-merger Hype Industries, the share price of Dull Hype will go to $135. Before the merger, the market values were as follows:

	Shares	×	share price	=	firm's market value
Hype Industries	100,000	×	$90	=	$9,000,000
Dull Knife	100,000	×	$30	=	$3,000,000

This gives a total pre-merger market value of $12 million. After the merger, based on the figures of table 22.2 and the P/E ratio of 30 being applied to Dull Hype, the total market value would be $18 million, as follows:

	Shares	×	share price	=	firm's market value
Dull Hype	133,333	×	$135	=	$18,000,000

The total market value has gone up by $6 million. Thus, it appears that it is possible to manufacture $6 million of new wealth just by merging. This prospect seems too good to be true, . . . and it is.

What is really going on here? If we step back and ask ourselves what the P/E ratio of the new firm should be, it seems fairly clear that the answer should be 20, assuming that the pre-merger P/E ratios were correct. If we combine two firms with equal earnings, one of which has a P/E of 30 and the other a P/E of 10, the P/E of the new firm should be 20, unless we convince the market that the merger enhances the growth prospects of the Dull Knife side of the firm.

For a period during the 1960s, some firms seemed to convince the market that conglomerate firms could generate growth from newly acquired firms in unrelated lines of business. Accordingly, the market applied the high P/E of the acquiring firm to the earnings of the acquired low P/E firm. Looking back, this period appears to be an incredible departure from good sense. However, the market actually responded in that way. A good example is the case of Automatic Sprinkler Corporation.

Automatic Sprinkler Corporation (now called A-T-O Inc.) is a good example of how the game of manufacturing growth was actually played during the 1960s. Between 1963 and 1968, the company's sales volume rose by over 1,400 percent. This phenomenal record was due solely to acquisitions. For example, in the middle of 1967, four mergers were completed in a 25-day period. These newly acquired companies were all selling at relatively low price-earnings multiples, which helped produce a sharp growth in earnings per share. The market responded to this "growth" by bidding up the price-earnings multiple to over 50 times earnings in 1967. This boosted the price of the company's stock from about $8 per share in 1963 to $73 5/8 in 1967.[3]

In 1968, however, the EPS game ended when one of the most respected conglomerates, Litton Industries, announced a downturn in EPS. This, along with federal investigations of conglomerate merger practices, brought a selling wave of conglomerates and a general

---

[3] See Burton G. Malkiel, *A Random Walk Down Wall Street*, 2e, New York: Norton, 1981, p. 65. This book is an excellent and highly readable introduction to the stock market.

fall in P/E ratios from which conglomerates have never recovered. Table 22.3 shows the before and after picture of some of the best-known conglomerates.

With the advantage of hindsight, it is easy to see the problem. The EPS game appears to create value from nothing. By now we should be very suspicious of such illusions.[4] More fundamentally, we know that the fundamental concern of the manager should be to maximize share prices, not EPS. Of course, share price is related to the firm's income stream, so managers might attend to earnings to raise the share price. Nonetheless, when they attempt to manage earnings, it should be to increase the share price. Accordingly, an undue concentration on EPS does not benefit shareholders. Because the EPS merger game creates no real value, we may reject the desire to increase EPS as a valid reason for a merger.

CONGLOMERATE MERGERS AND PORTFOLIO DIVERSIFICATION

In addition to a desire to increase EPS, we noted that conglomerate mergers often create a portfolio of firms. Does this create a diversification benefit for mergers? The justification for this kind of merger stems directly from portfolio theory.

We have seen that it is possible to combine two risky, but poorly correlated, securities to form a portfolio that is less risky than either of the individual securities. A conglomerate merger applies the same principle to firms. A conglomerate merger might merge two firms with poorly correlated cash flows to make a portfolio of firms. In fact, we may view a conglomerate as a portfolio of firms. In a conglomerate firm, management usually allows

TABLE 22.3
Stock Valuation During and After the EPS Game

Security	1967		1969	
	High Price	Price-Earnings Multiple	Low Price	Price-Earnings Multiple
Automatic Sprinkler (A-T-O Inc.)	$73⁵/₈	51.0	$10⁷/₈	13.4
Litton Industries	120³/₈	44.1	$35	14.4
Teledyne, Inc.	*71¹/₂	53.8	$28¹/₄	14.2
Textron, Inc.	$55	24.9	$23¹/₄	10.1

*Adjusted for subsequent split.

Source: Burton G. Malkiel, *A Random Walk Down Wall Street*, New York: Norton, 1981, p. 67. Reproduced by permission of W. W. Norton & Company, Inc. Copyright © 1981, 1973 by W. W. Norton & Company, Inc.

---

[4] Perhaps the most widespread illusion is that wealth can be created by simply printing more and more money. Unfortunately, many countries continue to fall into this trap. However, rather than creating wealth, they have created runaway inflation.

the component firms to operate independently. However, the stock ownership is in the conglomerate firm itself.

Management can allow the units to operate independently because it has little to gain by operating them all together if they are in very different businesses. For example Beatrice Foods, one of the better known conglomerates, has units in both phosphate mining and Mexican food. It is difficult to imagine what advantages Beatrice can gain by operating these two units together. (Perhaps Beatrice can serve Mexican food at the mine?)

The diversification rationale for conglomerate mergers is as weak as the desire for higher EPS. The real question is whether the firm should create a diversified portfolio or whether the shareholder can do the job better. A conglomerate diversifies by actually buying and operating firms in unrelated lines of business. However, the acquisition of firms in mergers is costly. In addition, a conglomerate merger may actually interfere with the smooth operation of the acquired firm. In comparison, a stockholder can easily create a diversified portfolio of firms merely by holding the shares of diverse companies. This form of diversification is much easier, cheaper, and more flexible than actually buying and operating the companies. As a consequence, we may reject the desire for diversification as an appropriate motive for merger. Table 22.4 summarizes the valid and invalid motives for mergers.

FINANCIAL EVALUATION OF MERGERS

From our discussion of the legitimate motives for mergers, we know that we should pursue a merger only if it creates real economic value. Further, such value must come from operating efficiencies of some kind, from better access to capital markets, from the acquisi-

TABLE 22.4
Valid and Invalid Motives for Mergers

Valid	*Invalid*
Achieving economies of scale. By becoming larger, usually through a horizontal merger, a firm can achieve operating economies in purchasing raw materials and in building its distribution network. These economies of scale can also be financial, so that the new, larger firm has better access to financial markets.	**Increasing EPS.** Increasing EPS is not a valid reason for a merger or for any other financial decision. The goal of financial decisions should be to increase share price, not to manufacture EPS.
Access to resources. Through a vertical merger, a firm can often succeed in acquiring access to needed elements in the production chain, such as raw materials or distribution outlets.	**Achieving diversification.** Because shareholders can achieve diversification in the financial markets faster and more cheaply than a firm can through mergers, the desire to achieve diversification is not a valid motive for a merger.
Tax considerations. Some mergers bring clear tax benefits that can justify a merger.	

tion of more certain sources of raw materials, from obtaining better distribution outlets, from tax benefits, or from some other source that translates into improved cash flows.

In a merger, the acquirer can pay the shareholders of the target firm with cash or with the acquirer's stock. The financial evaluation of a merger is different in the two cases, and we consider each in turn.

Analysis of a Merger Through a Cash Purchase

When a proposed merger has real economic benefits, the value of the merged firm equals the value of the acquiring firm plus the value of the target firm plus the value of the merger benefit.

$$V_m = V_a + V_t + V_b \qquad (22.1)$$

where:

V_m = the value of the post-merger combined firm

V_a = the value of the pre-merger acquiring firm

V_t = the value of the pre-merger target firm

V_b = the value of the merger benefits

The value of the merger benefits, V_b, equals the present value of the additional cash flows that the merger will generate.

From the acquirer's point of view, the most it should pay for the target firm is $V_t + V_b$. If the acquirer pays more, the merger will have negative NPV. From the target firm's point of view, it should never accept anything less than V_t, its value before the merger. Also, the target should try to get as much as possible for its shareholders. From this, we can conclude that the merger price, P, must be greater than or equal to V_t and must be less than or equal to $V_t + V_b$:

$$V_t \leq P \leq V_t + V_b \qquad (22.2)$$

The price paid for the target firm, P, minus the pre-merger value of the target firm V_t, is the **merger premium**.

$$\text{Merger Premium} = P - V_t \qquad (22.3)$$

If the premium is zero, the target firm's shareholders have no incentive to sell. If the premium is too large, greater than V_b, the acquiring firm has no incentive to buy. Therefore, the merger negotiation turns on how large the merger premium will be or how the merger benefit will be split between the acquirer and the target firm.

As an example, consider firms A and T, the acquirer and target firms, respectively. Before the merger, firm A has 100,000 shares outstanding and a share price of $70, while firm B has 10,000 shares outstanding with a share price of $35. Let us also assume that the merger benefit will be $150,000. In summary, we have:

	Firm A	Firm T
Share price	$70	$35
Shares outstanding	100,000	10,000
Firm market value	$7,000,000	$350,000

In this case, the absolute minimum price acceptable to the shareholders of firm T is $35 per share. With any lower offer, the shareholders can merely sell their shares in the open market for $35 per share. Firm A cannot pay more than $50 per share. If it pays $50 per share, it receives none of the merger benefit. At any higher price, the merger has negative NPV for firm A. Accordingly, the price per share should be less than $50 and more than $35. If the parties agree on a price of $45, the premium is $10 per share, or $100,000. With a merger benefit of $150,000, $50,000 goes to firm A and firm T gets $100,000.

Thus far, we have been assuming that we know the pre-merger value of the target firm. Sometimes rumors of an impending merger circulate and the price of the target firm's shares rises in anticipation of the merger. This makes it very difficult for the acquiring firm to appraise the value of the target firm independent of the merger taking place. Also, when merger talks take place, rumors of the negotiation leak out and other potential acquirers show an interest. Competition over the target can also cause the target firm's shares to increase in price.

As an example, assume firm T has a true value of $30 per share. Also assume that its share price increased from $30 to $35 because the market anticipated a merger. Let us continue to assume that the merger benefit is $150,000. If firm A pays $45 per share when the value of shares of firm T is $30 before any merger anticipation, then the shareholders of firm T get the entire benefit. Because of the effect of merger rumors on the target firm's stock price, acquirers must be very discreet in their negotiations with potential targets. Later in this chapter we will see evidence on how the merger benefits are typically distributed between the acquirer and the target.

Analysis of a Merger Financed by Stock

When the acquirer pays the target firm's shareholders with stock of the combined firm, the analysis of merger prices becomes somewhat more complicated for two reasons. When the acquirer finances the merger by an exchange of stock, the number of the acquirer's shares increases. Second, when the acquiring firm issues new stock to the target firm's shareholders, the ownership interest of the acquiring firm's original stockholders falls.

To see the effects of the new shares and the changing ownership interest, let us use our example of firm A and firm T. Now, however, we assume the shareholders of firm T receive stock instead of cash. The ratio of share prices between the two firms is 2 ($70/$35), so we assume that shareholders in firm T receive one share in exchange for two of their shares. Firm A will issue 5,000 new shares and the post-merger firm will have 105,000 shares outstanding. The market value of the post-merger firm should equal the sum of the market values of the two pre-merger firms plus the merger benefit, or $7,500,000. After the exchange of stock, each share should be worth the market value of the combined firm divided by the number of shares outstanding, or $71.43.

Because the shareholders of firm T received one share with a pre-merger value of $70 for two of their shares worth $35 each, it appears that they received none of the merger benefit. That is not the case, however. Shareholders of firm T received 5,000 shares, and we have seen that the post-merger share price would be $71.43. As a consequence, the shareholders of firm T received a total value of $357,150, or a merger premium of $7,150.

We know that the shareholders of firm T will not accept any amount of stock that is worth less than the original $350,000 value of the firm. Also, firm A will not offer any amount of stock greater than $500,000, which is the pre-merger value of firm T plus the merger benefit. We also know from equation 22.1 that the value of the combined firm will equal the value of the pre-merger firms plus the merger benefit. If the acquirer had S_a shares outstanding originally, and issues S_n new shares to the target company's shareholders, the merged firm will have S_m shares outstanding, where $S_m = S_a + S_n$. Therefore, the price of a new share, NS, will equal:

$$NS = \frac{V_m}{S_m} = \frac{V_a + V_t + V_b}{S_a + S_n}$$ (22.4)

The total compensation received by the shareholders of firm T is equal to the new shares, S_n, times the price of those shares, NS:

$$\text{Total compensation for firm T shareholders} = S_n \times NS$$ (22.5)

We know that this compensation must lie between the pre-merger value of firm T ($350,000) and the pre-merger value of firm T plus the entire merger benefit ($500,000).

$$V_t \leq S_n \times NS \leq V_t + V_b$$

Rearranging this expression, we get:

$$\frac{V_t}{V_m} \leq \frac{S_n}{S_a + S_n} \leq \frac{V_t + V_b}{V_m}$$ (22.6)

Equation 22.6 says that the percentage of the firm owned by the shareholders of the acquired firm $[S_n/(S_a + S_n)]$ must be equal to or greater than the ratio of the pre-merger target firm to the post-merger combined firm $[V_t/V_m]$ and less than or equal to the ratio of the value of the pre-merger acquired firm plus the merger benefit to the value of the post-merger firm $[(V_t + V_b)/V_m]$.

Substituting the values from our example into this expression, we have:

$$0.04667 \leq \frac{S_n}{100,000 + S_n} \leq 0.06667$$

Worst Case for the Target Firm's Shareholders   In the worst case for the target firm's shareholders, they receive only enough shares to compensate them for the pre-merger value of their firm, with no part of the merger benefit. We can analyze the number of shares issued in this case as follows:

$$0.04667 = \frac{S_n}{100,000 + S_n}$$

$$S_n = 4,895 \text{ shares}$$

To see that this is correct, recall that the acquirer had 10,000 shares outstanding already. After the merger, there will be 104,895 shares in a firm worth $7,500,000. Therefore, each share will be worth $71.50. If the target firm's shareholders receive 4,895 of those shares, the total value received will be $350,000.

Best Case of the Target Firm's Shareholders   The best thing that can happen for the target firm's shareholders is to receive enough shares to compensate them for the pre-merger value of their firm and to allow them to capture the entire merger benefit. The number of shares issued in this situation is given by:

$$\frac{S_n}{100,000 + S_n} = 0.06667$$

$$S_n = 7,143 \text{ shares}$$

In this case, the merged firm will have 107,143 shares outstanding. The firm will have a total value of $7,500,000 and each share will be worth $70. The target firm's shareholders receive 7,143 shares, or $500,000.

From this analysis, we see that the target firm's shareholders will receive at least 4,895 shares, or they won't accept the merger offer. The most they can hope to receive is 7,143 shares, because the acquiring firm will offer no more.

WHO BENEFITS FROM MERGERS?

If a merger is economically sound, the combined firm will be more valuable than the pre-merger target and acquiring firms. In such a case, there is value to be split between the target and acquiring firms. How is that benefit divided? Does the target firm or the acquiring firm benefit? In some cases, mergers take place even when they create no benefits. In other words, one or the other of the merger partners makes a mistake. What happens to target and acquiring firms?

These issues have been studied in detail. One approach is to examine the stock returns of the target and acquiring firms around the time the intention to merge becomes public. The best technique for doing this is to see how the stock prices compare to other firms of the same risk level. Figure 22.1 shows the performance of the target firm's shares just before and just after the announcement of a merger. The vertical scale shows the average performance of the shares relative to other shares of the same risk level in the market at the same time.

If the merger news gave the acquiring firm's shareholders no benefit, the bold line would be flat all the way across at the zero percent level. The graph shows an important positive benefit for the target firm. About 20 trading days before the information becomes public, the stock price starts to move up and continues to do so until about ten days after the announcement. By this time, there is almost a 20 percent gain on these shares relative to other stocks of the same risk level. This 20 percent extra gain in 30 trading days is really spectacular.

How does this performance compare relative to the acquiring firm's shares? Figure 22.2 graphs the acquiring firm's shares and shows some, but very little, benefit for the acquiring firms. Other studies have found that the acquiring firms, on average, actually

FIGURE 22.1
Performance of the Target Firm's Shares at the Time of the Merger
Announcement

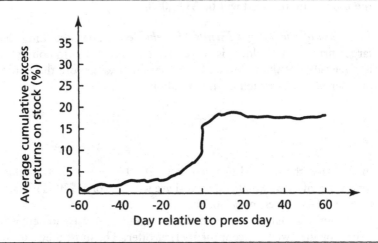

Source: P. Asquith, "Merger Bids, Uncertainty, and Stockholder Returns," *Journal of Financial Economics,*
April 1983, pp. 51–83.

FIGURE 22.2
Performance of the Acquiring Firm's Shares at the Time of the Merger
Announcement

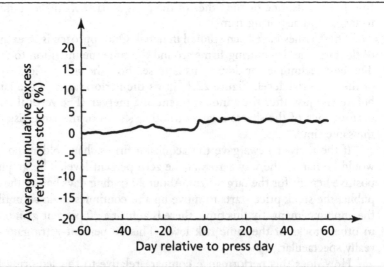

Source: P. Asquith, "Merger Bids, Uncertainty, and Stockholder Returns," *Journal of Financial Economics,*
April 1983, pp. 51–83.

lose value. However, there is still debate about whether acquiring firms gain a little or lose a little. In any case, it certainly appears that the target firms get most of the benefit from the merger.

MERGERS AND THE INTERESTS OF SOCIETY

While the target firm's shareholders appear to reap most of the merger benefit, it is still important to ask how these mergers affect society. This question is particularly important in a period of heavy merger activity. Mergers could harm the interests of society if firms became so large that they were able to wield monopoly power over their markets, allowing them to control supply and prices. In such an event, the interests of society at large would likely suffer.

SUMMARY

This chapter explored the key features of mergers. We began by introducing the special terminology of mergers and by distinguishing mergers into horizontal, vertical, and conglomerate mergers. The potentially valid motives for mergers include a desire to achieve greater economies of scale and a desire to secure a source of raw materials or an outlet for the finished product of a firm. We also examined the tax incentives that may be important in mergers and showed how they can confer real benefits. We also considered some spurious merger motives, such as the desire for EPS growth or diversification that propelled the conglomerate merger wave.

The financial evaluation of mergers differs depending on how the acquirer pays the target. The payment can take the form of cash or shares in the merged firm. In both cases we saw how to put bounds on the compensation paid to the target firm. Essentially, the compensation must be at least as great as the pre-merger value of the firm, but less than the merger benefit plus the pre-merger value of the target. Finally, we considered the allocation of the merger benefit between the acquiring and target firm and the effects of mergers on society.

QUESTIONS

1. What is the difference between a horizontal and a vertical merger?
2. If you were in charge of anti-trust enforcement, what kind of mergers would be of the greatest concern? Explain.
3. Explain why firms seek vertical integration and the role of vertical mergers in attempts to achieve this integration.
4. From an anti-trust point of view, are conglomerate mergers problematic? Explain.
5. Explain the difference between achieving diversification through a conglomerate merger and through the stock market.
6. Is a tender offer likely to be used in a friendly or an unfriendly merger attempt? Explain.

7. If you owned shares in a firm that pursued a policy of greenmail, what would you think about the management of the firm?

8. Explain why the managers of a firm might be willing to pay greenmail.

9. Why do managers try to use poison pills to avoid takeovers? How does this affect the interest of stockholders?

10. Based on the evidence presented in this chapter, do you think that stockholders need protection from merger attempts? Explain.

11. Why do managers of target firms seek white knights?

12. Explain how tax benefits can be created through mergers.

13. Are the tax benefits generated by mergers a creation of wealth for shareholders? Explain.

14. If we consider matters from the point of view of society as a whole, are the tax benefits generated by mergers a form of wealth creation? Explain.

15. In a cash purchase, what is the most that an acquiring firm should be willing to pay for a target?

16. In a cash purchase acquisition, what is the least that a target firm should accept?

17. What do we know about how merger benefits are usually distributed between the target and acquiring firm?

18. When a target is acquired by issuing stock, what happens to the ownership interest of the acquiring firm's shareholders?

PROBLEMS

Use the following information to solve problems 1–12. Iphagee Conglomerate has a P/E ratio of 27 and a stock price of $81 and one million shares outstanding. Iphagee is considering acquiring Small Fry Fisheries. Small Fry has earnings of $1 million, 100,000 shares outstanding, and a P/E ratio of 5. Iphagee will exchange two shares of Iphagee for three shares of Small Fry, and it expects the post-merger firm to keep the P/E ratio of 27.

1. What is the total market value of Small Fry?

2. What is the price per share for Small Fry?

3. How many shares of Iphagee will be outstanding after the merger?

4. Assuming that this is strictly a conglomerate merger, what will be the post-merger earnings of Iphagee?

5. Assuming that this is strictly a conglomerate merger, what should be the market value of the post-merger firm if the EPS game does not work?

6. If Iphagee is correct and the new firm keeps the P/E ratio of 27, what will be the market value of the post merger firm?

7. If the EPS game does not work, how much will the Small Fry shareholders receive for each of their shares?

8. If Iphagee is correct in its belief that the post-merger firm will have a P/E ratio of 27, how much will the Small Fry shareholders receive for each of their shares?

9. Should Small Fry accept the offer, assuming that no other offer is available?

10. If the EPS game does not work, what will happen to the value of a share of Iphagee due to the merger?

11. If the EPS game does work, and the post-merger Iphagee keeps the P/E ratio of 27, what will have happened to the value of a share of Iphagee due to the merger?

12. If the market is wise to the EPS game, what should the P/E ratio of the post-merger Iphagee be?

Use the following information to solve problems 13–20. A cattle feed lot firm, Standing Bull, is planning to buy Kansas in August, a large agribusiness concern specializing in corn production. Bull has 100,000 shares outstanding with a share price of $10. Kansas has 10,000 shares trading at $8 per share. Bull believes that the vertical integration that such a purchase will provide will give real benefits by providing a source of corn for the feed lot and a ready outlet for the corn production. Bull believes that the resulting firm should be worth $1.2 million.

13. What is the merger benefit?
14. What is the minimum price that Kansas should accept per share?
15. What is the maximum price that Bull should be willing to pay per share?
16. If Bull pays $10 per share, how is the merger benefit split between the two pre-merger firms?
17. If Bull pays $16 per share, how is the merger benefit split between the two pre-merger firms?

Consider the following additional information regarding the Kansas/Bull merger and use it to solve problems 18–20. Kansas was trading at $8 per share before any rumors began circulating about the pending merger. Now, in response to the anticipated merger, the stock of Kansas has gone up to $10 per share. Assume, further, that there are no other potential acquiring firms for Kansas.

18. In these new circumstances, what is the merger benefit?
19. In these new circumstances, what is the minimum price that Kansas should accept per share?
20. In these new circumstances, what is the maximum price that Bull should be willing to pay per share?

Use the following information to solve problems 21–28. Prune Computer has been having trouble securing a steady source of computer chips for use in its microcomputer. It is considering acquiring a chip manufacturer, Chips Away, to solve this problem. Prune has 100,000 shares outstanding at $12 per share, while Chips has 15,000 shares trading at $8 per share. Prune estimates that the post merger firm should be worth $1.5 million, and it plans to offer an exchange of shares to acquire Chips.

21. Compute the merger benefit.

22. If Prune offers two shares of Prune for three of Chips, how will the merger benefit be distributed?
23. What is the minimum number of shares that Chips should be willing to accept?
24. If the minimum number of shares is offered and accepted, how is the merger benefit distributed between the two pre-merger firms?
25. If the minimum number of shares is offered and accepted, how much of the post-merger firm will be owned by the shareholders of Chips?
26. What is the maximum number of shares that Prune should be willing to offer?
27. If the maximum number of shares is offered and accepted, how is the merger benefit distributed between the two pre-merger firms?
28. If the maximum number of shares is offered and accepted, how much of the post-merger firm will be owned by the shareholders of Chips?

Chapter 23

International Financial Management

OVERVIEW

This chapter introduces the major issues in international corporate finance. We begin by considering the different ways in which a firm can enter a foreign market – a choice that depends largely on the nature of the good and the characteristics of the market.

Every firm operating in the international environment faces problems with foreign exchange – the exchange of foreign currencies into the home currency. Generally, the firm's foreign operations earn income denominated in a foreign currency. Shareholders, however, expect payment in their home currency, so the firm must convert the foreign currency. Because the value of one currency relative to another is constantly changing, this conversion is risky. Foreign exchange risk management is one of the big issues of international financial management.

Operating in a foreign environment also creates special investment and financing difficulties. By contrast, operating abroad can give the firm access to attractive investment and financing opportunities. The chapter concludes with a brief exploration of these issues.

ENTERING A FOREIGN MARKET

A firm considering entry into a foreign market must choose one of three very different methods of doing business. First, the firm can **export** by manufacturing goods in its home country and shipping them to the foreign country. A second strategy is **licensing**. In a licensing agreement, a firm in the home country allows a firm in a foreign country to use its technology or brand name. In licensing, the foreign firm plays an essential role in the manufacturing or distribution process. The third strategy is to enter a foreign market through direct foreign investment. In **direct foreign investment** (DFI), a firm owns and operates physical capital in a foreign country. When a firm engages in direct foreign investment, we will regard it as a **multinational firm**. A single firm may use one or more of these methods, and some use all three.

Upon first examination, it appears that a firm can never profit from direct foreign investment. In comparison to a local firm, a foreign firm always faces severe disadvantages. These disadvantages arise from differences in culture, language, and knowledge of the local market. Firms engage in DFI to capture some benefit they cannot capture through exporting or licensing. The firm can capture these benefits through DFI by exploiting some imperfection in the market for an input to the firm's production process or in the market for the firm's final product. Due to these kinds of market imperfections, firms are unable to capture the full benefits of the products they have created unless they enter a foreign market through DFI. On this theory, firms engage in DFI to appropriate the potential benefits of the patents they hold or the production processes they have developed. This is the **appropriability theory**.

Some examples of the appropriability theory illustrate this line of reasoning. Today we observe U.S. electronics firms that manufacture abroad and import the finished product into the United States. Labor is an important input for these products, and labor costs are substantially higher in the U.S. than in many other countries. Firms establish their manufacturing facilities abroad to take advantage of this wage differential. Because the same unit of labor costs more in the United States than abroad, the labor market is imperfect.[1] This imperfection provides a strong incentive for firms to consider DFI. If labor costs were uniform across national boundaries, U.S. firms would manufacture locally and save the cost of importing the good into the U.S. market.

As another example, consider a firm that creates knowledge through its research program and that wants to control the new knowledge for its own benefit. Assume that this firm has developed a special production process and that it wants to produce goods for a foreign market using this process. Assume also that the firm cannot effectively export into the foreign market, perhaps due to trade barriers. In this situation, the firm has two choices. First, it can license its technology to a local firm in the foreign market. Second, it can engage itself in DFI and build and operate a plant in the foreign country. If the firm licenses the technology, it puts itself in a very risky position because the knowledge is no longer under its control. The licensee in the foreign country must learn the details of the technology to operate successfully. In this case, the licensing firm runs a considerable risk that the licensee may take the knowledge that it has gained and use it for its own benefits. While laws prohibit such a practice, they are very difficult to enforce. To avoid this danger, the firm with the advanced technology may decide to operate its own plant in the foreign country. In this example, the desire to appropriate for itself the benefits of the knowledge it created leads to DFI.

The exact combination of methods firms use to enter a foreign market depends on the specific nature of the product and the position of the firm. Firms that engage in DFI are more fully involved in the international scene than those that merely export or license. We focus on the problems of the multinational firm in the remainder of this chapter.

FOREIGN EXCHANGE

In the foreign exchange market, it is important to realize that every price, or exchange rate, that is quoted is relative. To say that one U.S. dollar is worth 2.5 deutsche marks

---

[1] We are assuming that the quality of labor, including productivity, is the same. In some cases this may not be true.

(DM) also implies that DM 1 is worth $0.40. All foreign exchange rates are related to each other as reciprocals, which is apparent in figure 23.1, showing foreign exchange quotations as they appear daily in *The Wall Street Journal*. Each set of quotations shows the rates for the current day and the preceding business day. This makes it possible to focus only on the two columns pertaining to the current quotation. The first point to notice is that the rate in one column has its reciprocal in the other column. The value of $/DM is just the reciprocal of the value of DM/$. For some countries, figure 23.1 shows only the **spot rate**, the rate at which the currency can be exchanged into dollars at the moment.

For many of our major trading partners, such as Germany, England, Japan, and Canada, there are also forward rates quoted for periods of 30, 90, and 180 days into the future. The 30-day forward rate, for example, indicates the rate at which a trader can contract

FIGURE 23.1
Foreign Exchange Quotations

CURRENCY TRADING

EXCHANGE RATES

Tuesday, March 28, 1995

The New York foreign exchange selling rates below apply to trading among banks in amounts of $1 million and more, as quoted at 3 p.m. Eastern time by Bankers Trust Co., Dow Jones Telerate Inc. and other sources. Retail transactions provide fewer units of foreign currency per dollar.

Country	U.S. $ equiv. Tues.	Mon.	Currency per U.S. $ Tues.	Mon.
Argentina (Peso)	1.00	1.00	1.00	1.00
Australia (Dollar)	.7284	.7269	1.3730	1.3758
Austria (Schilling)	.10144	.10106	9.86	9.89
Bahrain (Dinar)	2.6529	2.6528	.3769	.3770
Belgium (Franc)	.03471	.03450	28.81	28.99
Brazil (Real)	1.1013216	1.1001100	.91	.91
Britain (Pound)	1.6160	1.5960	.6188	.6266
30-Day Forward	1.6153	1.5982	.6191	.6265
90-Day Forward	1.6141	1.5951	.6195	.6269
180-Day Forward	1.6111	1.5918	.6207	.6282
Canada (Dollar)	.7129	.7149	1.4028	1.3988
30-Day Forward	.7114	.7136	1.4057	1.4013
90-Day Forward	.7090	.7115	1.4104	1.4055
180-Day Forward	.7062	.7089	1.4161	1.4107
Czech. Rep. (Koruna)				
Commercial rate	.0382848	.0380344	26.1200	26.2920
Chile (Peso)	.002454	.002454	407.55	407.55
China (Renminbi)	.118656	.118656	8.4277	8.4277
Colombia (Peso)	.001144	.001149	873.90	870.25
Denmark (Krone)	.1804	.1793	5.5445	5.5775
Ecuador (Sucre)				
Floating rate	.000415	.000413	2411.00	2419.00
Finland (Markka)	.22857	.22774	4.3750	4.3910
France (Franc)	.20419	.20206	4.8975	4.9490
30-Day Forward	.20366	.20177	4.9101	4.9561
90-Day Forward	.20295	.20121	4.9272	4.9700
180-Day Forward	.20240	.20075	4.9408	4.9813
Germany (Mark)	.7207	.7110	1.3875	1.4065
30-Day Forward	.7211	.7120	1.3867	1.4046
90-Day Forward	.7226	.7134	1.3838	1.4017
180-Day Forward	.7251	.7157	1.3790	1.3972
Greece (Drachma)	.004410	.004356	226.78	229.56
Hong King (Dollar)	.12932	.12932	7.7325	7.7330
Hungary (Forint)	.0083056	.0082597	120.4000	121.0701
India (Rupee)	.03171	.03164	31.54	31.61
Indonesia (Rupiah)	.0004481	.0004480	2231.50	2232.25
Ireland (Punt)	1.6206	1.6010	.6171	.6246
Israel (Shekel)	.3369	.3352	2.9683	2.9834

Country	U.S. $ equiv. Tues.	Mon.	Currency per U.S. $ Tues.	Mon.
Italy (Lira)	.0005898	.0005877	1695.50	1701.50
Japan (Yen)	.011249	.011179	88.90	89.45
30-Day Forward	.011288	.011222	88.59	89.11
90-Day Forward	.011375	.011303	87.92	88.47
180-Day Forward	.011512	.011434	86.86	87.46
Jordan (Dinar)	1.4493	1.4472	.6900	.6910
Kuwait (Dinar)	3.3801	3.3744	.2959	.2964
Lebanon (Pound)	.000612	.000612	1635.00	1635.00
Malaysia (Ringgit)	.3942	.3938	2.5370	2.5392
Malta (Lira)	2.8729	2.8729	.3481	.3481
Mexico (Peso)				
Floating rate	.1469508	.1486989	6.8050	6.7250
Netherland (Guilder)	.6435	.6344	1.5540	1.5763
New Zealand (Dollar)	.6512	.6489	1.5357	1.5411
Norway (Krone)	.1610	.1598	6.2100	6.2580
Pakistan (Rupee)	.0324	.0324	30.85	30.85
Peru (New Sol)	.4424	.4427	2.26	2.26
Philippines (Peso)	.03851	.03854	25.97	25.95
Poland (Zloty)	.42432210	.42553191	2.36	2.35
Portugal (Escudo)	.006841	.006776	146.18	147.58
Saudi Arabia (Riyal)	.26663	.26663	3.7504	3.7506
Singapore (Dollar)	.7052	.7042	1.4180	1.4200
Slovak Rep. (Koruna)	.0342583	.0342583	29.1900	29.1900
South Africa (Rand)	.2778	.2772	3.5992	3.6077
South Korea (Won)	.0012966	.0012998	771.25	769.35
Spain (Peseta)	.007819	.007743	127.90	129.15
Sweden (Krona)	.1366	.1378	7.3195	7.2550
Switzerland (Franc)	.8730	.8621	1.1455	1.1600
30-Day Forward	.8740	.8646	1.1442	1.1566
90-Day Forward	.8780	.8684	1.1390	1.1515
180-Day Forward	.8837	.8740	1.1316	1.1441
Taiwan (Dollar)	.038410	.038402	26.03	26.04
Thailand (Baht)	.04049	.04044	24.70	24.73
Turkey (Lira)	.0000238	.0000238	41959.02	42054.51
United Arab (Dirham)	.2723	.2723	3.6729	3.6727
Uruguay (New Peso)				
Financial	.167084	.167084	5.98	5.98
Venezuela (Bolivar)	.00589	.00589	169.78	169.78
SDR	1.54404	1.53782	.64765	.65027
ECU	1.31510	1.29940	....	....

Special Drawing Rights (SDR) are based on exchange rates for the U.S., German, British, French and Japanese currencies. Source: International Monetary Fund.

European Currency Unit (ECU) is based on a basket of community currencies.

Source: *The Wall Street Journal*, March 29, 1995.

today for the delivery of some foreign currency 30 days hence, with the actual transaction and payment taking place in 30 days.

Large banks in the U.S. and abroad comprise the main foreign exchange market. As is typical of forward markets, there is no physical location where trading takes place. Instead, banks around the world are linked electronically through their trading rooms. Such a room may have access to 60 telephone lines and five or more video quotation screens.[2] The market has no regular trading hours and is open somewhere in the world 24 hours per day. In addition to large banks, some large corporations have access to the market through their own trading rooms.

Regional banks are unlikely to have their own trading rooms. Instead, they clear their foreign exchange transactions through correspondent banks, with whom they have the appropriate arrangements. Corporations, as well as individuals, that are too small to have their own trading room engage in foreign exchange transactions through their own banks.

GEOGRAPHICAL AND CROSS-RATE ARBITRAGE

A number of pricing relationships exist in the foreign exchange market, whose violation would create an **arbitrage opportunity**, which is the opportunity to make a profit without risk or investment. The first two to be considered involve **geographical arbitrage** and **cross-rate arbitrage**.

Geographical arbitrage occurs when one currency sells for two prices in two different markets. As an example, consider a situation in which the following prices were quoted in New York and Frankfurt for the exchange rate between deutsche marks and U.S. dollars. (These are 90-day forward rates.)

New York	$/DM	0.42
Frankfurt	DM/$	2.35

The New York price, quoted as $/DM, implies a DM/$ price equal to its inverse:

$$DM/\$ = \frac{1}{0.42} = 2.381$$

In New York the DM/$ rate is 2.381, but in Frankfurt it is 2.35. This discrepancy indicates that an arbitrage opportunity exists. The example shows that to test for this, one simply takes the inverse of the price prevailing in one market and sees if it matches the price quoted in another market.

The next step is to determine the market in which a given currency is relatively cheaper. To make an arbitrage profit, the currency will be purchased in the market where it is cheap and sold in the market where it is expensive. Since a trader receives more marks per dollar in New York than in Frankfurt, the DM is cheaper in New York. To exploit this pricing difference, the trader can enter the arbitrage transactions shown in figure 23.2.

---

[2] One such trading room was featured in the film *Rollover*, starring Kris Kristofferson and Jane Fonda. In this story of international financial intrigue and panic, Kristofferson played the brilliant hard-nosed manager of the trading room, who saves the world from financial collapse.

FIGURE 23.2
Geographical Arbitrage

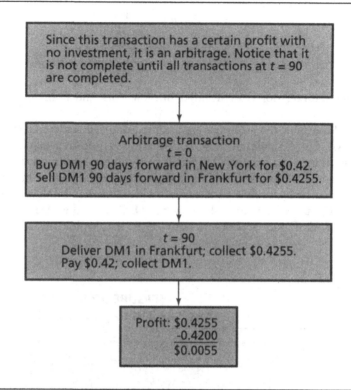

These transactions represent the exploitation of an arbitrage opportunity, since they ensure a profit with no investment. At the outset, there is no cash flow. The only cash flow involved in the transactions occurs simultaneously when the commitments initiated at time $t = 0$ are completed at time $t = 90$ days. The profit, however, was certain from the time of the initial transactions.

The second kind of arbitrage opportunity involves cross-rates. In a given market, exchange rates for currencies A and B and for currencies A and C imply an exchange rate, called a cross-rate, between currencies B and C. If the rate implied for B and C does not match the actual rate between B and C in some other market, an arbitrage opportunity exists. The cross-rate is an implicit rate, since the rate for B in terms of C will not be explicitly stated in the market. As an example, assume we observe the following rates, where SF indicates Swiss francs and all of the rates are 90-day forward rates.

New York	$/DM	0.42
	$/SF	0.49
Frankfurt	DM/SF	1.20

In New York, rates for the DM/SF or SF/DM are not stated. Not surprisingly, currency rates in the U.S. are stated in terms of dollars and traders express the value of foreign currencies in dollars, just as shown in the quotations. But the two rates shown in New York imply a cross-rate for the DM/SF:

$$DM/SF = \frac{1}{\$/DM} \times \$/SF$$

$$= \frac{1}{0.42} \times 0.49 = 1.167$$

Since the rates for DM/SF differ in New York and Frankfurt, an arbitrage opportunity exists.

To exploit the arbitrage opportunity, one can trade only the exchange rates actually shown. For example, in New York there may not be a market for DM in terms of the Swiss franc.[3] To convert DM to SF in the New York market involves two transactions, first from DM to US$, and then, from US$ to SF. To know how to trade, one must know which currency is relatively cheaper in a given market. In New York one receives DM1.167 per SF, but in Frankfurt SF1 is worth DM1.2, so the DM is cheaper in Frankfurt than New York. Figure 23.3 shows transactions that exploit this arbitrage opportunity.

FIGURE 23.3
Cross-Rate Arbitrage Transactions

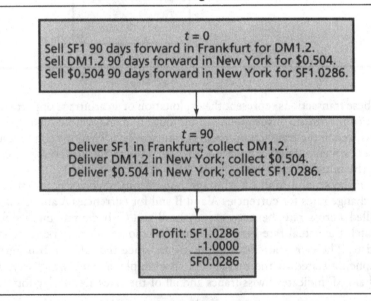

$t = 0$
Sell SF1 90 days forward in Frankfurt for DM1.2.
Sell DM1.2 90 days forward in New York for $0.504.
Sell $0.504 90 days forward in New York for SF1.0286.

$t = 90$
Deliver SF1 in Frankfurt; collect DM1.2.
Deliver DM1.2 in New York; collect $0.504.
Deliver $0.504 in New York; collect SF1.0286.

Profit: SF1.0286
       -1.0000
       SF0.0286

---

[3] Actually, in major foreign exchange centers, such as New York, some traders will make markets in the major cross-rates. For many currencies in many markets, however, there will not be a separate quotation available for cross-rates.

DETERMINANTS OF FOREIGN EXCHANGE RATES

As the fundamental factors of supply and demand determine the price of agricultural commodities, similar fundamental factors shape the exchange rate that prevails between the currencies of two countries. These factors are numerous and quite complex, with entire books being written on the subject. Consequently, the brief discussion that follows merely indicates some of the most important influences on exchange rates.

One way of thinking about currencies is to regard them as essentially similar to other assets, subject to the same basic laws of supply and demand. When a particular currency is unusually plentiful, we might expect its price to fall. Of course, the price of a given currency in terms of some other currency is merely the exchange rate between the two currencies. In foreign exchange, the flow of payments between one country and the rest of the world gives rise to the concept of a **balance of payments**. If a country's expenditures exceed its receipts, that country has a balance of payments deficit; if receipts exceed expenditures, the country has a balance of payments surplus. The balance of payments encompasses the flow of all kinds of goods and services among nations, including the movement of real goods, services, international investment, and all types of financial flows.

To understand how considerations of the balance of payments influence exchange rates, consider the following simple example. A country, Importeria, trades with other countries and always imports more goods than it exports. Therefore, there is always a net flow of real goods into Importeria. Importeria must pay for these goods in some way, so assume that its government simply prints sufficient additional currency to pay for the extra goods it imports. Such a situation cannot go on for long without causing a change in the exchange rates between Importeria and its trading partners. As the trading partners continue to send more and more goods to Importeria, they collectively have fewer and fewer real goods themselves, but have a growing supply of the currency of Importeria.

As the world's supply of Importeria's currency swells, it becomes apparent that it has only a few uses. Holders can use Importeria's currency to buy other currencies or to buy goods from Importeria. However, the accumulation of Importeria's currency continues until there is an excess supply at the prevailing exchange rate, so the value of Importeria's currency must fall. Just as Importeria cannot continually import more than it exports without the value of its currency falling, no country can continually consume more than it creates without the same result.

Fixed Exchange Rates

The kind of adjustment that a country such as Importeria might suffer in the value of its currency depends upon the kind of exchange rate system that is in effect. For most of its history, the United States has used a **fixed exchange rate**. A fixed exchange rate is a stated exchange rate between two currencies at which anyone may transact. A country such as Importeria might import more than it exports for quite some time without causing a fixed exchange rate to change. However, even fixed exchange rates are only fixed in the short run. The continual excess of imports over exports puts pressure on the value of Importeria's currency as the world's holdings of Importeria's currency continue to grow. Eventually, the fixed exchange rate between Importeria's currency and that of other nations will be adjusted. Importeria's currency will fall in value, or be **devalued**. Equivalently, the value of other currencies will increase relative to Importeria's currency, so the other currencies are **revalued**.

Under a fixed exchange rate regime, exchange rate changes occur only when a currency is under great strain to adjust to a new level. In the case of Importeria, it may seem perplexing that the value of its currency would not adjust smoothly over time as Importeria continued its program of excess imports. Rates are fixed through the intervention of the central banks of Importeria and other countries. As excess supplies of Importeria's currency accumulate in the world, central banks may use their reserves of other currencies to buy Importeria's. This buying eases the imbalance between supply and demand that would arise at the fixed level of rates. In effect, central banks sop up the excess supply of Importeria's currency, which would otherwise exist at the fixed level of exchange rates.

If the pressures against the currency of Importeria are not too severe, such action by the central banks may preserve the fixed level of exchange rates. However, the excess supply of a currency may become overwhelming. Then, central banks are unable, or unwilling, to hold all of the supplied currency. In such a situation, a country like Importeria would be forced to devalue its currency and set a new official rate of exchange. If the value of the Importeria unit of currency was one-tenth of a U.S. dollar before the devaluation, it might be reset at one-twelfth of a dollar after the devaluation. Then the procedure of trying to defend the new exchange rate level would start anew. However, if Importeria persists in its habit of importing much more than it exports, it can expect to undergo another devaluation in the foreseeable future.

One obvious, and apparently disadvantageous, feature of a fixed exchange rate system is that when changes in the exchange rates occur, they are rather large. There are, however, considerable advantages to a fixed exchange rate system. First, fixed exchange rates simplify exchange transactions. If we can count on a fixed exchange rate for the next year, we do not need to control the risk of a change in the exchange rate. Such a situation promotes international trade. Second, for multinational firms, a fully functioning fixed exchange rate system means that exchange rate fluctuations do not affect accounting income. Third, fixed exchange rates may constitute a form of discipline for economic policies by participating countries. This would be the case, since the countries would eventually realize that pursuit of certain policies leads to devaluation.

Perhaps for these reasons, and also as a signal of financial probity, the industrialized West pursued a fixed exchange rate policy from the end of World War II until 1971. Even stronger than a fixed exchange rate, the dollar was convertible into gold at a rate of $35 per ounce, in accordance with the Bretton Woods agreement. Other major currencies fixed their value in reference to the U.S. dollar. Until August 1971 the dollar remained as good as gold. At that time, faced with a weakening dollar and a soaring balance of payments deficit in the U.S., the U.S. went off the gold standard. Attempts to reestablish some semblance of a fixed rate system, notably the Smithsonian agreement of 1971, failed. March 1973 witnessed a new era in international foreign exchange. Most currencies were allowed to float, with daily fluctuations in exchange rates becoming the norm.

This new system of exchange rates, or free market, prevails today, but there are a number of important exceptions and variations that the foreign exchange trader must consider.

With the breakdown of the Bretton Woods system and the failure of the Smithsonian agreement, countries adopted a variety of exchange rate strategies. These strategies include free floats, managed or dirty floats, pegs, and joint floats.

A currency is **freely floating** if it has no system of fixed exchange rates and if the central bank of the country in question does not attempt to influence the value of the currency. Few countries have truly freely floating exchange rates, as central banks seem unable to resist the temptation to intervene. When the central bank of a country engages in market transactions to influence the exchange value of its currency, but the rate is basically a floating rate, the policy is called a **managed float** or a **dirty float**. Opposed to this floating system, a number of countries continue to use a **pegged float** as a system of exchange rates. The value of one currency might be pegged to the value of another currency that itself floats. For example, Importeria might try to maintain a fixed exchange rate with the dollar, but the dollar itself floats against most of the world's currencies. In such a situation, Importeria pegs its currency to the dollar. Pegged currencies can be pegged to a single currency or to a basket, or portfolio, of currencies.

One other policy for exchange rate management is the **joint float**. In a joint float, currencies in a particular group have a fixed exchange value in terms of each other, but the group of currencies floats in relation to other currencies outside the group. The prime example of the joint float technique comes from the European Economic Community (EEC), or European common market. The member nations formed the European Monetary System (EMS) in 1979 and created the European Currency Unit (ECU). The basic strategy of the EMS agreement is to maintain very narrowly fluctuating exchange rates among the currencies of the participating countries. The ECU is expected to increase in importance with the advent of the European unification.

In theory, a joint float system requires that the values of the currencies of the participating countries be fixed relative to one another, but float relative to external countries, such as the United States. This has important implications for speculating and hedging in all of these currencies. Recent experience has shown that some countries may be forced to devalue their currency relative to those of the group. Italy has faced the problem several times since the inception of the EMS. More recently, France has devalued several times.

MORE PRICE RELATIONSHIPS

The geographical or cross-rate arbitrage opportunities we noted before occur when foreign exchange rates are aligned improperly. The examples in figures 23.2 and 23.3 arose from a pricing discrepancy in the foreign exchange rates for a forward maturity of 90 days. Other price relationships are equally important and determine the permissible spreads that may exist between forward contracts of differing maturities. These are expressed as the interest rate parity theorem and the purchasing power parity theorem.

The Interest Rate Parity Theorem

The **interest rate parity** (IRP) theorem asserts that interest rates and exchange rates form an interconnected system. A change in interest rates will affect the exchange rate, and vice versa. The basic principle is that a trader will earn the same rate of return by investing in risk-free instruments of any currency, assuming that the proceeds from investment are converted back into the home currency by a forward contract initiated at the outset of the holding period. To illustrate interest rate parity, consider the rates of table 23.1. If interest rate parity holds, the trader must earn the same return by following either of these two strategies:

Strategy 1:   Hold an investment in the United States for 180 days.
Strategy 2:   (a) Convert funds from US$ to DM at the spot rate.
Strategy 2:   (b) Invest for 180 days in Germany, and simultaneously purchase a 180-day forward contract to convert DM into US$ at a stated exchange rate.
Strategy 2:   (c) Convert the proceeds of the investment in DM back into dollars by means of the forward contract initiated in Step (b).

If we adopt strategy 1, we could make the following transactions, assuming daily compounding. From table 23.1, the 180-day interest rate in the United States is 20 percent, so an investment of $100 in the United States for 180 days yields:

$$\$100\left(1 + \frac{0.20}{365}\right)^{180} = \$110.36$$

In strategy 2, we would first exchange $100 for marks at the spot rate of $0.42 per mark, giving us $100/0.42 = 238.10$ marks. We would then invest these marks at the German 180-day interest rate of 29.9 percent. At the end of the 180 days, the German mark proceeds are:

$$DM238.10\left(1 + \frac{0.299}{365}\right)^{180} = DM275.91$$

Simultaneous to the purchase of the marks, we engage in a 180-day forward contract, which will allow us to convert the marks into dollars at a rate of $0.40 per mark.

As the third step of strategy 2, we would arrange to convert our German mark proceeds of DM 275.91 back into dollars by using our forward contract. This would give us total dollar proceeds of:

$$DM275.91 \times 0.40 \ \$/DM = \$110.36$$

TABLE 23.1
Interest Rates and Exchange Rates to Illustrate Interest Rate Parity

		Interest Rates	
Horizon	$/DM	U.S.	Germany
Spot	0.420	n.a.	n.a.
90-days	0.405	0.19	0.2500
180-days	0.400	0.20	0.2990

The IRP theorem says that the proceeds from these two strategies must be equal. In fact, we verify that the two strategies do yield the same dollar proceeds of $110.36.

Let us now consider the same relationship, but for a 90-day horizon. Repeating the same operations as before for the new maturity gives:

Strategy 1:   Invest $100 in the United States for 90 days = $104.80.
Strategy 2:   Convert $100 to DM, invest in Germany for 90 days, and use a forward contract to convert DM into US$ after 90 days = $102.56.

Strategy 1, investing in the United States, gives a higher return than investing the $100 in Germany. This means that an arbitrage opportunity is available. It is clearly better to invest funds in the United States rather than in Germany. Figure 23.4 shows the transactions necessary to take advantage of this discrepancy. Arbitrage of this type is known as **covered interest arbitrage**, because the position in the DM investment is covered by the forward contract to convert the DM proceeds back into dollars. The transaction is a genuine arbitrage opportunity, because it makes possible a sure profit without risk and without investment.

Simply stated, interest rate parity asserts that such opportunities cannot exist in a well-functioning market. If such arbitrage opportunities did exist, money hungry traders would exploit them by making the transactions shown in figure 23.4. This exploitation would go on at a frantic pace as long as the arbitrage opportunity is available. As the arbitrageurs borrowed more and more marks, they would drive up the interest rate in Germany, and

FIGURE 23.4
Covered Interest Arbitrage

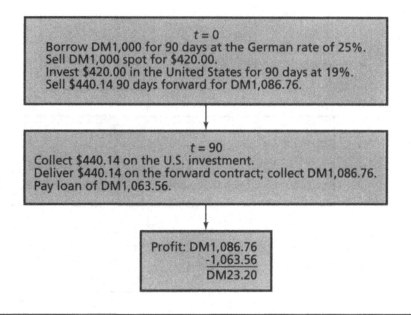

$t = 0$
Borrow DM1,000 for 90 days at the German rate of 25%.
Sell DM1,000 spot for $420.00.
Invest $420.00 in the United States for 90 days at 19%.
Sell $440.14 90 days forward for DM1,086.76.

$t = 90$
Collect $440.14 on the U.S. investment.
Deliver $440.14 on the forward contract; collect DM1,086.76.
Pay loan of DM1,063.56.

Profit: DM1,086.76
        -1,063.56
        DM23.20

as they bought bonds in the U.S., the interest rate there would be driven down. This process would stop only when there were no further arbitrage opportunities. But if no arbitrage opportunities existed, the IRP theorem would hold. Thus, the very existence of arbitrageurs ensures that the IRP theorem will hold.

The Purchasing Power Parity Theorem

Purchasing power parity is intimately tied to interest rate parity. The **purchasing power parity** (PPP) theorem asserts that the exchange rates between two currencies must be proportional to the price level of goods in the two currencies. Violations of PPP lead to arbitrage opportunities, as shown in figure 23.5. To simplify, assume that transportation and transaction costs do not exist and that there are no trade barriers between countries, such as quotas or tariffs.

Suppose the French franc is worth $0.10 and the cost of a croissant in Paris is FF1, as shown in figure 23.5. Also, a croissant sells for $0.15 in New York. This situation leads to the arbitrage opportunity that a trader can exploit by engaging in the transactions shown. The only price for a croissant in New York that is consistent with the other values is $0.10.

The intimate relationship between the purchasing power parity theorem and the interest rate parity theorem originates from the link between interest rates and inflation rates. According to the famous Fisher relationship, the nominal rate of interest is composed

FIGURE 23.5
Croissant Arbitrage

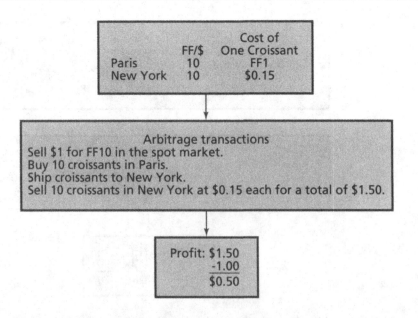

	FF/$	Cost of One Croissant
Paris	10	FF1
New York	10	$0.15

Arbitrage transactions
Sell $1 for FF10 in the spot market.
Buy 10 croissants in Paris.
Ship croissants to New York.
Sell 10 croissants in New York at $0.15 each for a total of $1.50.

Profit: $1.50
        -1.00
        $0.50

of two elements, the real rate and the expected inflation rate. We can express this relationship as follows:

$$(1 + r_n) = (1 + r_r)[1 + E(i)] \tag{23.1}$$

where, r_n is the nominal interest rate, r_r is the real rate of interest, and $E(i)$ is the expected inflation rate. Since the expected inflation equals the expected change in purchasing power, we may interpret purchasing power parity as a view about the linkage between exchange rates and relative inflation rates. Differences in nominal interest rates between two countries are probably due to differences in expected inflation. This means that interest rates, exchange rates, and inflation rates form a single integrated system.

The PPP and the Cost of a Mac Attack   Table 23.2 illustrates the PPP using the Big Mac index, a medium-rare guide to whether currencies are at their correct exchange rate. The comparison is based only on the price of a Big Mac, which has the virtue of being made locally in more than 50 countries and of tasting virtually the same from Paris to Moscow.

As table 23.2 shows, when the average price of a Big Mac (including tax) in the United States was $2.32, you would have had to fork out 391 yen in Tokyo for this gastronomic delight. Dividing the yen price by the dollar price gives an implied PPP of 169 yen/dollar, compared with an actual exchange rate of 84.2 yen/dollar at the time of the survey. So the yen appeared to be 100 percent overvalued against the dollar on PPP grounds. In other words, the Big Mac index suggests that the dollar was ready for a very substantial increase against the yen at the time the survey was made.

TABLE 23.2
The Big Mac Index

Country	Local* Price	Implied PPP[b] of the Dollar	Actual Exchange Rate 4/7/95	Over/Under Valuation of Local Currency
Australia	2.45	1.05	1.35	−22.0%
Belgium	109.00	47.00	28.40	+66.0
Britain	1.74	0.75	0.62	+21.0
Canada	2.77	1.19	1.39	−14.0
France	18.50	7.97	4.80	+66.0
Italy	4,500.00	1,940.00	1,702.00	+14.0
Japan	391.00	169.00	84.20	+100.0
Russia	8,100.00	3,491.00	4,985.00	−30.0
U.S.[c]	2.32	n.a.	n.a.	n.a.

[a]Price in local currency. Prices may vary between branches.
[b]Purchasing power parity: local price divided by price in the U.S.
[c]Average of New York, Chicago, San Francisco and Atlanta.

Source: "Big MacCurrencies," *The Economist,* April 15, 1995, p. 74.

HEDGING FOREIGN EXCHANGE RISK

Many firms, and some individuals, face foreign exchange risk. Firms that import and export, for example, often need to make commitments to buy or sell goods for delivery at some future time, with the payment to be made in a foreign currency. Likewise, multinational firms operating foreign subsidiaries receive payments from their subsidiaries in a foreign currency. A wealthy individual may plan an extended trip abroad and may be concerned about the chance that the price of a particular foreign currency might rise unexpectedly. All of these different parties are potential candidates for hedging unwanted currency risk.

Hedging Transaction Exposure

The simplest kind of example arises in the case of someone like Moncrief Snobbody, who plans a six-month trip to Switzerland. Moncrief plans to spend a considerable sum during this trip, enough to make it worthwhile to attend to the exchange rates, assumed to have the values shown on the next page. With the more distant rates lying above the nearby rates, Moncrief fears that the actual rates may be even higher in the future, so he decides to lock into the existing rates by securing the future delivery of Swiss francs for his trip at the currently available prices. Since it is currently January and he plans to depart for Switzerland in June, Moncrief buys SF250,000 180 days forward at a price of 0.5134 $/SF. He anticipates that the SF250,000 will pay for his six-month stay, as table 23.3 shows.

Hypothetical Swiss Exchange Rates in January

Spot	0.4935
Forward 90-days	0.5034
Forward 180-days	0.5134

TABLE 23.3
Moncrief Snobbody's Swiss Franc Hedge

Cash Market	Futures Market
January 12	
Moncrief plans to take a 6-month vacation in Switzerland, to begin in June, and to cost about SF250,000	Moncrief buys SF250,000 180-days forward at 0.5134 for a total cost of $128,350.
June 16	
The $/SF spot rate is now 0.5211, giving a dollar cost of $130,275 for SF250,000.	Moncrief delivers $128,350 and collects SF250,000.

Savings on the hedge: $130,275 − 128,350 = $1,925.

By June 6, Moncrief's fears have been realized, and the spot rate for the Swiss franc is now 0.5211. Moncrief, consequently, delivers $128,350 and collects his SF 250,000. Had he waited and transacted in the spot market on June 6, the SF250,000 would have cost him $130,275. By hedging his foreign exchange risk, Moncrief saved $1,925, which is enough to finance an extension of his stay in Switzerland for a day or two.

Moncrief had a pre-existing risk in the foreign exchange market, since it was already determined that he would acquire the Swiss francs. By trading in the foreign exchange market, he guaranteed a price for himself of $0.5134 per franc. Had he waited, the price he would have paid would have been higher in this example, but it just as easily could have been lower. By entering the foreign exchange market, Moncrief eliminated the uncertainty regarding the price that he would have to pay to acquire the needed francs. Of course, the foreign exchange market can be used for purposes even more serious than reducing the risk surrounding Moncrief Snobbody's Swiss vacation.

Hedging Import-Export Transactions

Consider the case of a small import-export firm that is negotiating a large purchase of Japanese watches. The Japanese executives, being notoriously tough negotiators, demand payment in yen upon delivery of the watches.[4] (If the contract had called for payment in dollars, rather than yen, the Japanese firm would bear the exchange risk.) Between the present and the delivery date there is a six-month delay. However, the price of the watches is agreed today to be yen 2,850 per watch, and the transaction will be for 15,000 watches. This means that the purchaser will have to pay yen 42,750,000 six months down the road. Hypothetical exchange rates for May 11 are given below. With the spot rate of 0.004173 dollars per yen, the purchase price for the 15,000 watches is $178,396. If we treat the forward price on May 11 as a forecast of future exchange rates, we expect the dollar to lose ground against the yen. With the 180-day forward trading at 0.004265, it seems that the actual dollar cost might be closer to $182,329. If delivery and payment occur in November, the importer might reasonably estimate his actual dollar outlay in the $182,000 range instead of the $178,000 range.

Foreign Exchange Rates for $/Yen, May 11	
Spot	0.004173
Forward 90-days	0.004200
Forward 180-days	0.004265

To avoid any worsening of his exchange position, the importer decides to hedge the transaction by trading in the foreign exchange market. Delivery is expected in November,

---

[4] It seems that rock singers can be tough negotiators, too. For a Rolling Stones concert tour of Japan in April 1995, payment was negotiated in yen, not dollars. Given that in those days the U.S. dollar fell about 20 percent against the yen in a matter of weeks, it is said that Mick Jagger and friends made a windfall profit of about $2 million.

so the importer buys yen 42,750,000 in the forward market at the forward price of 0.004265. Table 23.4 shows the transactions involved.

On November 10 the watches arrive and the importer pays dollars to obtain the yen needed for the transaction. Now the spot price for yen is 0.004285 per dollar. If the importer had waited to purchase yen, they would have cost $183,183.75 (42,750,000 × 0.004285). Because the importer hedged, the yen cost only $182,328.75. Therefore, hedging saved the importer $855. Even more importantly, using the forward market gave the importer a firmly established price for the watches.

INTERNATIONAL INVESTMENT AND FINANCING DECISIONS

In previous chapters we considered the firm's investment and financing decisions and learned techniques for making correct decisions. However, our previous discussion of these topics assumed a domestic firm operating in a domestic environment. We now consider special problems of capital budgeting and fund raising that arise in an international setting.

International Capital Budgeting

In our previous study of capital budgeting, we learned that discounted cash flow techniques provided the best way to analyze prospective investments. In particular, we noted that accepting projects with a positive NPV contributes to the wealth of the shareholders. Determining the present value of a project depends on estimating the after-tax cash flows from the project and discounting those cash flows. The discount rate must reflect the systematic risk of those cash flows.

TABLE 23.4
The Importer's Hedge

Cash Market	*Futures Market*
May 11	
The importer anticipates a need for yen 42,750,000 in November to purchase a batch of watches.	Buys yen 42,750,000 180-days forward at a price of 0.004265. This gives a total dollar commitment of $182,328.75 due in 6 months.
November 11	
The importer pays yen 42,750,000 and receives the watches.	The importer pays $182,328.75 and receives yen 42,750,000. The spot price of the yen is 0.004285.

Savings on the hedge: $183,183.75 − 182,328.75 = $855

In the international setting, the same general principles hold, but there are several special issues. Most of these special problems center around the determination and evaluation of the cash flows. The typical multinational firm consists of a parent and several subsidiary firms. A **subsidiary** is a firm owned by another firm. Usually a foreign subsidiary undertakes the foreign investment project. The subsidiary receives the cash flows from the project and the parent firm receives cash from the subsidiary.

Cash Flows of Subsidiaries versus Parent Companies

Which cash flows are relevant for the capital budgeting decision, the subsidiary's or the parent's? The two cash flows can be quite different, so the issue is of considerable practical concern. This very important issue in capital budgeting has a clear answer. The return from any project is due to the investor. Generally, the parent is the ultimate investor, because the parent provides capital to the subsidiary. In fact, it often wholly owns the subsidiary, in which case the subsidiary's cash flows are irrelevant. Only the cash flows received by the parent matter.

The Effect of Taxes

As in domestic capital budgeting, the after-tax cash flows are the flows of concern. In the international capital budgeting environment, taxation becomes quite complicated. The subsidiary often pays taxes in the foreign country and then remits the remaining proceeds to the parent. The parent must then pay taxes on these proceeds as well. Often the parent receives a tax credit for taxes paid by subsidiaries in other countries. A **tax credit** is a subtraction of some amount directly from the tax bill. For example, a $10,000 tax credit reduces the tax bill by $10,000.

Foreign versus Home Currency

If a firm takes a project in a foreign country, it almost certainly generates cash flows in the foreign currency. However, the investors in the parent normally contribute capital denominated in the parent's home currency. Which currency should the firm use to calculate the NPV of the project? For the parent, the financial managers must focus on the return they can pay to their investors. These investors are interested in changes in their own purchasing power as a result of their investment. This means that the financial manager must be concerned with the purchasing power of the investors in the parent. Because the purchasing power of these investors depends largely on the value of the home currency, the financial manager must consider the home currency cash flows that the project generates.

INTERNATIONAL FINANCING

A multinational firm often has broader financing opportunities than a strictly domestic firm. If the parent operates subsidiaries in foreign countries, the subsidiary may raise its own capital in the foreign country where it operates. Alternatively, the parent can raise capital and channel it to the subsidiary in the form of debt or equity. In addition, well-known multinational firms have access to world capital markets, as well as financial markets in their own home countries.

Without special tax considerations or other market imperfections, the firm should expect to pay the same ultimate cost for capital no matter where it is raised. As we have seen from our discussion of purchasing power and interest rate parity, the ultimate cost of funds should be the same no matter where the firm raises funds. As a general principle, we should expect the cost of financing to be independent of the country and currency in which funds are raised.

Certain factors can arise that make the cost of funds depend on where the firm raises funds. Often, foreign governments are anxious to attract DFI from abroad. DFI means more employment and tax income for the host country, so some countries actively seek DFI from multinationals. To attract DFI some countries offer special incentives to multinationals, such as special tax rules. On some occasions, host countries offer a **tax holiday**, a time during which the foreign country imposes no taxes on their operations in the host country. As another incentive, some foreign governments offer special training programs for workers in the area where a firm will invest. On other occasions, the host country provides financing for the subsidiary's operations.

SUMMARY

This chapter introduced some of the special issues that the financial manager faces upon entering the international arena. We began by considering the alternative strategies for entering a foreign market: exporting, licensing, and direct foreign investment.

No matter how a firm enters a foreign market, it confronts problems of foreign exchange. We considered how foreign exchange rates are quoted, the factors that determine exchange rates, and some arbitrage principles that govern the relationships among exchange rates, interest rates, and inflation rates. Finally, we considered special problems financial managers face in managing exchange risk, capital budgeting projects, and the firm's financing of its foreign operations.

QUESTIONS

1. How can companies enter foreign markets?
2. Why do firms engage in direct foreign investment even when faced with the disadvantages of dealing in a foreign country?
3. Explain the basic ideas of the appropriability theory.
4. Explain the imperfections in the labor market that may lead to direct foreign investment.
5. What is geographical arbitrage?
6. What is a cross-rate?
7. What is the balance of payments?
8. What is a fixed exchange rate policy?
9. What is the attraction of a fixed exchange rate policy?

10. What is the major difficulty with a fixed exchange rate policy?
11. What is the difference between freely floating rates and a dirty float?
12. Explain the basic idea of the interest rate parity theorem.
13. Explain the basic idea of the purchasing power parity theorem.
14. In international capital budgeting, which cash flows are relevant to the decision?
15. Respond to the following claim made by a financial executive of a U.S. firm:
    Interest rates in the United States today are 12 percent, but only 7 percent
    in Germany. Obviously, we can save 5 percent if we borrow in Germany.

PROBLEMS

Use the following quotations to solve problems 1–6.

| | Exchange Rates | | | | Interest Rates | |
| | New York | | Frankfurt | | | |
	$/£	$/DM	DM/£	DM/$	$	DM
Spot	1.6640	0.3879	4.3064	2.5880	—	—
30-day	1.6647	0.3887	4.2828	2.5727	10.0%	7.31%
90-day	1.6674	0.3905	4.2699	2.5608	11.0%	8.57%
180-day	1.6717	0.3935	4.2583	2.5413	12.0%	8.83%

1. Find a geographical arbitrage opportunity in these quotations.
2. Explain the exact transactions you would make to exploit the arbitrage opportunity.
3. Find a cross-rate arbitrage opportunity in these quotations.
4. Explain the exact transactions you would make to exploit the arbitrage opportunity.
5. Find a covered interest arbitrage opportunity in these quotations.
6. Explain the exact transactions you would make to exploit the arbitrage opportunity.

Use the following quotations to solve problems 7–12.

| | Foreign Currency Prices | | | | Interest Rates | | |
| | New York | | Paris | Frankfurt | U.S. | France | Germany |
	$/FF	$/DM	FF/$	DM/FF	$	FF	DM
Spot	0.10500	0.30	9.5238	0.3500			
30-day	0.10735	0.30	9.3458	0.3567	50.0%	15.00%	50.0%
90-day	0.10900	0.30	9.1743	0.3633	60.0%	37.78%	60.0%
180-day	0.11200	0.30	9.0909	0.3650	65.0%	50.20%	65.0%

7. Find a geographical arbitrage opportunity in these quotations.
8. Explain the exact transactions you would make to exploit the arbitrage opportunity.
9. Find a cross-rate arbitrage opportunity in these quotations.
10. Explain the exact transactions you would make to exploit the arbitrage opportunity.
11. Find a covered interest arbitrage opportunity in these quotations.
12. Explain the exact transactions you would make to exploit the arbitrage opportunity.
13. For his vacation, Irving buys 1,000 German marks in the forward market and pays $0.40 per mark. When Irving arrives in Berlin, the exchange rate is $0.45 per mark. How much does Irving save or lose by transacting in the forward market?
14. For her vacation, Alice buys 1,000 German marks in the forward market and pays $0.40 per mark. When she arrives in Munchen, the exchange rate is $0.38 per mark. How much does Alice save or lose by transacting in the forward market?
15. What conclusion can you draw from problems 13 and 14?

Appendix

Cumulative Standard Normal Distribution Function

	0.00	0.01	0.02	0.03	0.04	0.05	0.06	0.07	0.08	0.09
0.0	0.5000	0.5040	0.5080	0.5120	0.5160	0.5199	0.5239	0.5279	0.5319	0.5359
0.1	0.5398	0.5438	0.5478	0.5517	0.5557	0.5596	0.5636	0.5675	0.5714	0.5753
0.2	0.5793	0.5832	0.5871	0.5910	0.5948	0.5987	0.6026	0.6064	0.6103	0.6141
0.3	0.6179	0.6217	0.6255	0.6293	0.6331	0.6368	0.6406	0.6443	0.6480	0.6517
0.4	0.6554	0.6591	0.6628	0.6664	0.6700	0.6736	0.6772	0.6808	0.6844	0.6879
0.5	0.6915	0.6950	0.6985	0.7019	0.7054	0.7088	0.7123	0.7157	0.7190	0.7224
0.6	0.7257	0.7291	0.7324	0.7357	0.7389	0.7422	0.7454	0.7486	0.7517	0.7549
0.7	0.7580	0.7611	0.7642	0.7673	0.7704	0.7734	0.7764	0.7794	0.7823	0.7852
0.8	0.7881	0.7910	0.7939	0.7967	0.7995	0.8023	0.8051	0.8078	0.8106	0.8133
0.9	0.8159	0.8186	0.8212	0.8238	0.8264	0.8289	0.8315	0.8340	0.8365	0.8389
1.0	0.8413	0.8438	0.8461	0.8485	0.8508	0.8531	0.8554	0.8577	0.8599	0.8621
1.1	0.8643	0.8665	0.8686	0.8708	0.8729	0.8749	0.8770	0.8790	0.8810	0.8830
1.2	0.8849	0.8869	0.8888	0.8907	0.8925	0.8944	0.8962	0.8980	0.8997	0.9015
1.3	0.9032	0.9049	0.9066	0.9082	0.9099	0.9115	0.9131	0.9147	0.9162	0.9177
1.4	0.9192	0.9207	0.9222	0.9236	0.9251	0.9265	0.9279	0.9292	0.9306	0.9319
1.5	0.9332	0.9345	0.9357	0.9370	0.9382	0.9394	0.9406	0.9418	0.9429	0.9441
1.6	0.9452	0.9463	0.9474	0.9484	0.9495	0.9505	0.9515	0.9525	0.9535	0.9545
1.7	0.9554	0.9564	0.9573	0.9582	0.9591	0.9599	0.9608	0.9616	0.9625	0.9633
1.8	0.9641	0.9649	0.9656	0.9664	0.9671	0.9678	0.9686	0.9693	0.9699	0.9706
1.9	0.9713	0.9719	0.9726	0.9732	0.9738	0.9744	0.9750	0.9756	0.9761	0.9767
2.0	0.9772	0.9778	0.9783	0.9788	0.9793	0.9798	0.9803	0.9808	0.9812	0.9817
2.1	0.9821	0.9826	0.9830	0.9834	0.9838	0.9842	0.9846	0.9850	0.9854	0.9857
2.2	0.9861	0.9864	0.9868	0.9871	0.9875	0.9878	0.9881	0.9884	0.9887	0.9890
2.3	0.9893	0.9896	0.9898	0.9901	0.9904	0.9906	0.9909	0.9911	0.9913	0.9916
2.4	0.9918	0.9920	0.9922	0.9925	0.9927	0.9929	0.9931	0.9932	0.9934	0.9936
2.5	0.9938	0.9940	0.9941	0.9943	0.9945	0.9946	0.9948	0.9949	0.9951	0.9952
2.6	0.9953	0.9955	0.9956	0.9957	0.9959	0.9960	0.9961	0.9962	0.9963	0.9964
2.7	0.9965	0.9966	0.9967	0.9968	0.9969	0.9970	0.9971	0.9972	0.9973	0.9974
2.8	0.9974	0.9975	0.9976	0.9977	0.9977	0.9978	0.9979	0.9979	0.9980	0.9981
2.9	0.9981	0.9982	0.9982	0.9983	0.9984	0.9984	0.9985	0.9985	0.9986	0.9986
3.0	0.9987	0.9987	0.9987	0.9988	0.9988	0.9989	0.9989	0.9989	0.9990	0.9990
3.1	0.9990	0.9991	0.9991	0.9991	0.9992	0.9992	0.9992	0.9992	0.9993	0.9993
3.2	0.9993	0.9993	0.9994	0.9994	0.9994	0.9994	0.9994	0.9995	0.9995	0.9995
3.3	0.9995	0.9995	0.9995	0.9996	0.9996	0.9996	0.9996	0.9996	0.9996	0.9997
3.4	0.9997	0.9997	0.9997	0.9997	0.9997	0.9997	0.9997	0.9997	0.9997	0.9998

Present Value of $1

Periods (n)	1%	2%	3%	4%	5%	6%	7%	8%	9%	10%	11%	12%
1	0.9901	0.9804	0.9709	0.9615	0.9524	0.9434	0.9346	0.9259	0.9174	0.9091	0.9009	0.8929
2	0.9803	0.9612	0.9426	0.9246	0.9070	0.8900	0.8734	0.8573	0.8417	0.8264	0.8116	0.7972
3	0.9706	0.9423	0.9151	0.8890	0.8638	0.8396	0.8163	0.7938	0.7722	0.7513	0.7312	0.7118
4	0.9610	0.9238	0.8885	0.8548	0.8227	0.7921	0.7629	0.7350	0.7084	0.6830	0.6587	0.6355
5	0.9515	0.9057	0.8626	0.8219	0.7835	0.7473	0.7130	0.6806	0.6499	0.6209	0.5935	0.5674
6	0.9420	0.8880	0.8375	0.7903	0.7462	0.7050	0.6663	0.6302	0.5963	0.5645	0.5346	0.5066
7	0.9327	0.8706	0.8131	0.7599	0.7107	0.6651	0.6227	0.5835	0.5470	0.5132	0.4817	0.4523
8	0.9235	0.8535	0.7894	0.7307	0.6768	0.6274	0.5820	0.5403	0.5019	0.4665	0.4339	0.4039
9	0.9143	0.8368	0.7664	0.7026	0.6446	0.5919	0.5439	0.5002	0.4604	0.4241	0.3909	0.3606
10	0.9053	0.8203	0.7441	0.6756	0.6139	0.5584	0.5083	0.4632	0.4224	0.3855	0.3522	0.3220
11	0.8963	0.8043	0.7224	0.6496	0.5847	0.5268	0.4751	0.4289	0.3875	0.3505	0.3173	0.2875
12	0.8874	0.7885	0.7014	0.6246	0.5568	0.4970	0.4440	0.3971	0.3555	0.3186	0.2858	0.2567
13	0.8787	0.7730	0.6810	0.6006	0.5303	0.4688	0.4150	0.3677	0.3262	0.2897	0.2575	0.2292
14	0.8700	0.7579	0.6611	0.5775	0.5051	0.4423	0.3878	0.3405	0.2992	0.2633	0.2320	0.2046
15	0.8613	0.7430	0.6419	0.5553	0.4810	0.4173	0.3624	0.3152	0.2745	0.2394	0.2090	0.1827
16	0.8528	0.7284	0.6232	0.5339	0.4581	0.3936	0.3387	0.2919	0.2519	0.2176	0.1883	0.1631
17	0.8444	0.7142	0.6050	0.5134	0.4363	0.3714	0.3166	0.2703	0.2311	0.1978	0.1696	0.1456
18	0.8360	0.7002	0.5874	0.4936	0.4155	0.3503	0.2959	0.2502	0.2120	0.1799	0.1528	0.1300
19	0.8277	0.6864	0.5703	0.4746	0.3957	0.3305	0.2765	0.2317	0.1945	0.1635	0.1377	0.1161
20	0.8195	0.6730	0.5537	0.4564	0.3769	0.3118	0.2584	0.2145	0.1784	0.1486	0.1240	0.1037
21	0.8114	0.6598	0.5375	0.4388	0.3589	0.2942	0.2415	0.1987	0.1637	0.1351	0.1117	0.0926
22	0.8034	0.6468	0.5219	0.4220	0.3418	0.2775	0.2257	0.1839	0.1502	0.1228	0.1007	0.0826
23	0.7954	0.6342	0.5067	0.4057	0.3256	0.2618	0.2109	0.1703	0.1378	0.1117	0.0907	0.0738
24	0.7876	0.6217	0.4919	0.3901	0.3101	0.2470	0.1971	0.1577	0.1264	0.1015	0.0817	0.0659
25	0.7798	0.6095	0.4776	0.3751	0.2953	0.2330	0.1842	0.1460	0.1160	0.0923	0.0736	0.0588
26	0.7720	0.5976	0.4637	0.3607	0.2812	0.2198	0.1722	0.1352	0.1064	0.0839	0.0663	0.0525
27	0.7644	0.5859	0.4502	0.3468	0.2678	0.2074	0.1609	0.1252	0.0976	0.0763	0.0597	0.0469
28	0.7568	0.5744	0.4371	0.3335	0.2551	0.1956	0.1504	0.1159	0.0895	0.0693	0.0538	0.0419
29	0.7493	0.5631	0.4243	0.3207	0.2429	0.1846	0.1406	0.1073	0.0822	0.0630	0.0485	0.0374
30	0.7419	0.5521	0.4120	0.3083	0.2314	0.1741	0.1314	0.0994	0.0754	0.0573	0.0437	0.0334
31	0.7346	0.5412	0.4000	0.2965	0.2204	0.1643	0.1228	0.0920	0.0691	0.0521	0.0394	0.0298
32	0.7273	0.5306	0.3883	0.2851	0.2099	0.1550	0.1147	0.0852	0.0634	0.0474	0.0355	0.0266
33	0.7201	0.5202	0.3770	0.2741	0.1999	0.1462	0.1072	0.0789	0.0582	0.0431	0.0319	0.0238
34	0.7130	0.5100	0.3660	0.2636	0.1904	0.1379	0.1002	0.0730	0.0534	0.0391	0.0288	0.0212
35	0.7059	0.5000	0.3554	0.2534	0.1813	0.1301	0.0937	0.0676	0.0490	0.0356	0.0259	0.0189
36	0.6989	0.4902	0.3450	0.2437	0.1727	0.1227	0.0875	0.0626	0.0449	0.0323	0.0234	0.0169
37	0.6920	0.4806	0.3350	0.2343	0.1644	0.1158	0.0818	0.0580	0.0412	0.0294	0.0210	0.0151
38	0.6852	0.4712	0.3252	0.2253	0.1566	0.1092	0.0765	0.0537	0.0378	0.0267	0.0190	0.0135
39	0.6784	0.4619	0.3158	0.2166	0.1491	0.1031	0.0715	0.0497	0.0347	0.0243	0.0171	0.0120
40	0.6717	0.4529	0.3066	0.2083	0.1420	0.0972	0.0668	0.0460	0.0318	0.0221	0.0154	0.0107

Present Value of $1

Interest rate (r)

Periods (n)	13%	14%	15%	16%	17%	18%	19%	20%	21%	22%	23%	24%
1	0.8850	0.8772	0.8696	0.8621	0.8547	0.8475	0.8403	0.8333	0.8264	0.8197	0.8130	0.8065
2	0.7831	0.7695	0.7561	0.7432	0.7305	0.7182	0.7062	0.6944	0.6830	0.6719	0.6610	0.6504
3	0.6931	0.6750	0.6575	0.6407	0.6244	0.6086	0.5934	0.5787	0.5645	0.5507	0.5374	0.5245
4	0.6133	0.5921	0.5718	0.5523	0.5337	0.5158	0.4987	0.4823	0.4665	0.4514	0.4369	0.4230
5	0.5428	0.5194	0.4972	0.4761	0.4561	0.4371	0.4190	0.4019	0.3855	0.3700	0.3552	0.3411
6	0.4803	0.4556	0.4323	0.4104	0.3898	0.3704	0.3521	0.3349	0.3186	0.3033	0.2888	0.2751
7	0.4251	0.3996	0.3759	0.3538	0.3332	0.3139	0.2959	0.2791	0.2633	0.2486	0.2348	0.2218
8	0.3762	0.3506	0.3269	0.3050	0.2848	0.2660	0.2487	0.2326	0.2176	0.2038	0.1909	0.1789
9	0.3329	0.3075	0.2843	0.2630	0.2434	0.2255	0.2090	0.1938	0.1799	0.1670	0.1552	0.1443
10	0.2946	0.2697	0.2472	0.2267	0.2080	0.1911	0.1756	0.1615	0.1486	0.1369	0.1262	0.1164
11	0.2607	0.2366	0.2149	0.1954	0.1778	0.1619	0.1476	0.1346	0.1228	0.1122	0.1026	0.0938
12	0.2307	0.2076	0.1869	0.1685	0.1520	0.1372	0.1240	0.1122	0.1015	0.0920	0.0834	0.0757
13	0.2042	0.1821	0.1625	0.1452	0.1299	0.1163	0.1042	0.0935	0.0839	0.0754	0.0678	0.0610
14	0.1807	0.1597	0.1413	0.1252	0.1110	0.0985	0.0876	0.0779	0.0693	0.0618	0.0551	0.0492
15	0.1599	0.1401	0.1229	0.1079	0.0949	0.0835	0.0736	0.0649	0.0573	0.0507	0.0448	0.0397
16	0.1415	0.1229	0.1069	0.0930	0.0811	0.0708	0.0618	0.0541	0.0474	0.0415	0.0364	0.0320
17	0.1252	0.1078	0.0929	0.0802	0.0693	0.0600	0.0520	0.0451	0.0391	0.0340	0.0296	0.0258
18	0.1108	0.0946	0.0808	0.0691	0.0592	0.0508	0.0437	0.0376	0.0323	0.0279	0.0241	0.0208
19	0.0981	0.0829	0.0703	0.0596	0.0506	0.0431	0.0367	0.0313	0.0267	0.0229	0.0196	0.0168
20	0.0868	0.0728	0.0611	0.0514	0.0433	0.0365	0.0308	0.0261	0.0221	0.0187	0.0159	0.0135
21	0.0768	0.0638	0.0531	0.0443	0.0370	0.0309	0.0259	0.0217	0.0183	0.0154	0.0129	0.0109
22	0.0680	0.0560	0.0462	0.0382	0.0316	0.0262	0.0218	0.0181	0.0151	0.0126	0.0105	0.0088
23	0.0601	0.0491	0.0402	0.0329	0.0270	0.0222	0.0183	0.0151	0.0125	0.0103	0.0086	0.0071
24	0.0532	0.0431	0.0349	0.0284	0.0231	0.0188	0.0154	0.0126	0.0103	0.0085	0.0070	0.0057
25	0.0471	0.0378	0.0304	0.0245	0.0197	0.0160	0.0129	0.0105	0.0085	0.0069	0.0057	0.0046
26	0.0417	0.0331	0.0264	0.0211	0.0169	0.0135	0.0109	0.0087	0.0070	0.0057	0.0046	0.0037
27	0.0369	0.0291	0.0230	0.0182	0.0144	0.0115	0.0091	0.0073	0.0058	0.0047	0.0037	0.0030
28	0.0326	0.0255	0.0200	0.0157	0.0123	0.0097	0.0077	0.0061	0.0048	0.0038	0.0030	0.0024
29	0.0289	0.0224	0.0174	0.0135	0.0105	0.0082	0.0064	0.0051	0.0040	0.0031	0.0025	0.0020
30	0.0256	0.0196	0.0151	0.0116	0.0090	0.0070	0.0054	0.0042	0.0033	0.0026	0.0020	0.0016
31	0.0226	0.0172	0.0131	0.0100	0.0077	0.0059	0.0046	0.0035	0.0027	0.0021	0.0016	0.0013
32	0.0200	0.0151	0.0114	0.0087	0.0066	0.0050	0.0038	0.0029	0.0022	0.0017	0.0013	0.0010
33	0.0177	0.0132	0.0099	0.0075	0.0056	0.0042	0.0032	0.0024	0.0019	0.0014	0.0011	0.0008
34	0.0157	0.0116	0.0086	0.0064	0.0048	0.0036	0.0027	0.0020	0.0015	0.0012	0.0009	0.0007
35	0.0139	0.0102	0.0075	0.0055	0.0041	0.0030	0.0023	0.0017	0.0013	0.0009	0.0007	0.0005
36	0.0123	0.0089	0.0065	0.0048	0.0035	0.0026	0.0019	0.0014	0.0010	0.0008	0.0006	0.0004
37	0.0109	0.0078	0.0057	0.0041	0.0030	0.0022	0.0016	0.0012	0.0009	0.0006	0.0005	0.0003
38	0.0096	0.0069	0.0049	0.0036	0.0026	0.0019	0.0013	0.0010	0.0007	0.0005	0.0004	0.0003
39	0.0085	0.0060	0.0043	0.0031	0.0022	0.0016	0.0011	0.0008	0.0006	0.0004	0.0003	0.0002
40	0.0075	0.0053	0.0037	0.0026	0.0019	0.0013	0.0010	0.0007	0.0005	0.0004	0.0003	0.0002

Future Value of $1

Interest rate (r)

Periods (n)	1%	2%	3%	4%	5%	6%	7%	8%	9%	10%	11%	12%
1	1.0100	1.0200	1.0300	1.0400	1.0500	1.0600	1.0700	1.0800	1.0900	1.1000	1.1100	1.1200
2	1.0201	1.0404	1.0609	1.0816	1.1025	1.1236	1.1449	1.1664	1.1881	1.2100	1.2321	1.2544
3	1.0303	1.0612	1.0927	1.1249	1.1576	1.1910	1.2250	1.2597	1.2950	1.3310	1.3676	1.4049
4	1.0406	1.0824	1.1255	1.1699	1.2155	1.2625	1.3108	1.3605	1.4116	1.4641	1.5181	1.5735
5	1.0510	1.1041	1.1593	1.2167	1.2763	1.3382	1.4026	1.4693	1.5386	1.6105	1.6851	1.7623
6	1.0615	1.1262	1.1941	1.2653	1.3401	1.4185	1.5007	1.5869	1.6771	1.7716	1.8704	1.9738
7	1.0721	1.1487	1.2299	1.3159	1.4071	1.5036	1.6058	1.7138	1.8280	1.9487	2.0762	2.2107
8	1.0829	1.1717	1.2668	1.3686	1.4775	1.5938	1.7182	1.8509	1.9926	2.1436	2.3045	2.4760
9	1.0937	1.1951	1.3048	1.4233	1.5513	1.6895	1.8385	1.9990	2.1719	2.3579	2.5580	2.7731
10	1.1046	1.2190	1.3439	1.4802	1.6289	1.7908	1.9672	2.1589	2.3674	2.5937	2.8394	3.1058
11	1.1157	1.2434	1.3842	1.5395	1.7103	1.8983	2.1049	2.3316	2.5804	2.8531	3.1518	3.4785
12	1.1268	1.2682	1.4258	1.6010	1.7959	2.0122	2.2522	2.5182	2.8127	3.1384	3.4985	3.8960
13	1.1381	1.2936	1.4685	1.6651	1.8856	2.1329	2.4098	2.7196	3.0658	3.4523	3.8833	4.3635
14	1.1495	1.3195	1.5126	1.7317	1.9799	2.2609	2.5785	2.9372	3.3417	3.7975	4.3104	4.8871
15	1.1610	1.3459	1.5580	1.8009	2.0789	2.3966	2.7590	3.1722	3.6425	4.1772	4.7846	5.4736
16	1.1726	1.3728	1.6047	1.8730	2.1829	2.5404	2.9522	3.4259	3.9703	4.5950	5.3109	6.1304
17	1.1843	1.4002	1.6528	1.9479	2.2920	2.6928	3.1588	3.7000	4.3276	5.0545	5.8951	6.8660
18	1.1961	1.4282	1.7024	2.0258	2.4066	2.8543	3.3799	3.9960	4.7171	5.5599	6.5436	7.6900
19	1.2081	1.4568	1.7535	2.1068	2.5270	3.0256	3.6165	4.3157	5.1417	6.1159	7.2633	8.6128
20	1.2202	1.4859	1.8061	2.1911	2.6533	3.2071	3.8697	4.6610	5.6044	6.7275	8.0623	9.6463
21	1.2324	1.5157	1.8603	2.2788	2.7860	3.3996	4.1406	5.0338	6.1088	7.4002	8.9492	10.8038
22	1.2447	1.5460	1.9161	2.3699	2.9253	3.6035	4.4304	5.4365	6.6586	8.1403	9.9336	12.1003
23	1.2572	1.5769	1.9736	2.4647	3.0715	3.8197	4.7405	5.8715	7.2579	8.9543	11.0263	13.5523
24	1.2697	1.6084	2.0328	2.5633	3.2251	4.0489	5.0724	6.3412	7.9111	9.8497	12.2392	15.1786
25	1.2824	1.6406	2.0938	2.6658	3.3864	4.2919	5.4274	6.8485	8.6231	10.8347	13.5855	17.0001
26	1.2953	1.6734	2.1566	2.7725	3.5557	4.5494	5.8074	7.3964	9.3992	11.9182	15.0799	19.0401
27	1.3082	1.7069	2.2213	2.8834	3.7335	4.8223	6.2139	7.9881	10.2451	13.1100	16.7386	21.3249
28	1.3213	1.7410	2.2879	2.9987	3.9201	5.1117	6.6488	8.6271	11.1671	14.4210	18.5799	23.8839
29	1.3345	1.7758	2.3566	3.1187	4.1161	5.4184	7.1143	9.3173	12.1722	15.8631	20.6237	26.7499
30	1.3478	1.8114	2.4273	3.2434	4.3219	5.7435	7.6123	10.0627	13.2677	17.4494	22.8923	29.9599
31	1.3613	1.8476	2.5001	3.3731	4.5380	6.0881	8.1451	10.8677	14.4618	19.1943	25.4104	33.5551
32	1.3749	1.8845	2.5751	3.5081	4.7649	6.4534	8.7153	11.7371	15.7633	21.1138	28.2056	37.5817
33	1.3887	1.9222	2.6523	3.6484	5.0032	6.8406	9.3253	12.6760	17.1820	23.2252	31.3082	42.0915
34	1.4026	1.9607	2.7319	3.7943	5.2533	7.2510	9.9781	13.6901	18.7284	25.5477	34.7521	47.1425
35	1.4166	1.9999	2.8139	3.9461	5.5160	7.6861	10.6766	14.7853	20.4140	28.1024	38.5749	52.7996
36	1.4308	2.0399	2.8983	4.1039	5.7918	8.1473	11.4239	15.9682	22.2512	30.9127	42.8181	59.1356
37	1.4451	2.0807	2.9852	4.2681	6.0814	8.6361	12.2236	17.2456	24.2538	34.0039	47.5281	66.2318
38	1.4595	2.1223	3.0748	4.4388	6.3855	9.1543	13.0793	18.6253	26.4367	37.4043	52.7562	74.1797
39	1.4741	2.1647	3.1670	4.6164	6.7048	9.7035	13.9948	20.1153	28.8160	41.1448	58.5593	83.0812
40	1.4889	2.2080	3.2620	4.8010	7.0400	10.2857	14.9745	21.7245	31.4094	45.2593	65.0009	93.0510

Future Value of $1

Periods (n)	13%	14%	15%	16%	17%	18%	Interest rate (r) 19%	20%	21%	22%	23%	24%
1	1.1300	1.1400	1.1500	1.1600	1.1700	1.1800	1.1900	1.2000	1.2100	1.2200	1.2300	1.2400
2	1.2769	1.2996	1.3225	1.3456	1.3689	1.3924	1.4161	1.4400	1.4641	1.4884	1.5129	1.5376
3	1.4429	1.4815	1.5209	1.5609	1.6016	1.6430	1.6852	1.7280	1.7716	1.8158	1.8609	1.9066
4	1.6305	1.6890	1.7490	1.8106	1.8739	1.9388	2.0053	2.0736	2.1436	2.2153	2.2889	2.3642
5	1.8424	1.9254	2.0114	2.1003	2.1924	2.2878	2.3864	2.4883	2.5937	2.7027	2.8153	2.9316
6	2.0820	2.1950	2.3131	2.4364	2.5652	2.6996	2.8398	2.9860	3.1384	3.2973	3.4628	3.6352
7	2.3526	2.5023	2.6600	2.8262	3.0012	3.1855	3.3793	3.5832	3.7975	4.0227	4.2593	4.5077
8	2.6584	2.8526	3.0590	3.2784	3.5115	3.7589	4.0214	4.2998	4.5950	4.9077	5.2389	5.5895
9	3.0040	3.2519	3.5179	3.8030	4.1084	4.4355	4.7854	5.1598	5.5599	5.9874	6.4439	6.9310
10	3.3946	3.7072	4.0456	4.4114	4.8068	5.2338	5.6947	6.1917	6.7275	7.3046	7.9259	8.5944
11	3.8359	4.2262	4.6524	5.1173	5.6240	6.1759	6.7767	7.4301	8.1403	8.9117	9.7489	10.6571
12	4.3345	4.8179	5.3503	5.9360	6.5801	7.2876	8.0642	8.9161	9.8497	10.8722	11.9912	13.2148
13	4.8980	5.4924	6.1528	6.8858	7.6987	8.5994	9.5964	10.6993	11.9182	13.2641	14.7491	16.3863
14	5.5348	6.2613	7.0757	7.9875	9.0075	10.1472	11.4198	12.8392	14.4210	16.1822	18.1414	20.3191
15	6.2543	7.1379	8.1371	9.2655	10.5387	11.9737	13.5895	15.4070	17.4494	19.7423	22.3140	25.1956
16	7.0673	8.1372	9.3576	10.7480	12.3303	14.1290	16.1715	18.4884	21.1138	24.0856	27.4462	31.2426
17	7.9861	9.2765	10.7613	12.4677	14.4265	16.6722	19.2441	22.1861	25.5477	29.3844	33.7588	38.7408
18	9.0243	10.5752	12.3755	14.4625	16.8790	19.6733	22.9005	26.6233	30.9127	35.8490	41.5233	48.0386
19	10.1974	12.0557	14.2318	16.7765	19.7484	23.2144	27.2516	31.9480	37.4043	43.7358	51.0737	59.5679
20	11.5231	13.7435	16.3665	19.4608	23.1056	27.3930	32.4294	38.3376	45.2593	53.3576	62.8206	73.8641
21	13.0211	15.6676	18.8215	22.5745	27.0336	32.3238	38.5910	46.0051	54.7637	65.0963	77.2694	91.5915
22	14.7138	17.8610	21.6447	26.1864	31.6293	38.1421	45.9233	55.2061	66.2641	79.4175	95.0413	113.5735
23	16.6266	20.3616	24.8915	30.3762	37.0062	45.0076	54.6487	66.2474	80.1795	96.8894	116.9008	140.8312
24	18.7881	23.2122	28.6252	35.2364	43.2973	53.1090	65.0320	79.4968	97.0172	118.2050	143.7880	174.6306
25	21.2305	26.4619	32.9190	40.8742	50.6578	62.6686	77.3881	95.3962	117.3909	144.2101	176.8593	216.5420
26	23.9905	30.1666	37.8568	47.4141	59.2697	73.9490	92.0918	114.4755	142.0429	176.9364	217.5369	268.5121
27	27.1093	34.3899	43.5353	55.0004	69.3455	87.2598	109.5893	137.3706	171.8719	215.6424	267.5704	332.9550
28	30.6335	39.2045	50.0656	63.8004	81.1342	102.9666	130.4112	164.8447	207.9651	261.8637	329.1115	412.8642
29	34.6158	44.6931	57.5755	74.0085	94.9271	121.5005	155.1893	197.8136	251.6377	319.4737	404.8072	511.9516
30	39.1159	50.9502	66.2118	85.8499	111.0647	143.3706	184.6753	237.3763	304.4816	389.7579	497.9129	634.8199
31	44.2010	58.0832	76.1435	99.5859	129.9456	169.1774	219.7636	284.8516	368.4228	475.5046	612.4328	787.1767
32	49.9471	66.2148	87.5651	115.5196	152.0364	199.6293	261.5187	341.8219	445.7916	580.1156	753.2924	976.0991
33	56.4402	75.4849	100.6998	134.0027	177.8826	235.5625	311.2073	410.1863	539.4078	707.7411	926.5496	1,210.3629
34	63.7774	86.0528	115.8048	155.4432	208.1226	277.9638	370.3366	492.2235	652.6834	863.4441	1,139.6560	1,500.8500
35	72.0685	98.1002	133.1755	180.3141	243.5035	327.9973	440.7006	590.6682	789.7470	1,053.4018	1,401.7769	1,861.0540
36	81.4374	111.8342	153.1519	209.1643	284.8991	387.0368	524.4337	708.8019	955.5938	1,285.1502	1,724.1856	2,307.7070
37	92.0243	127.4910	176.1246	242.6306	333.3319	456.7034	624.0761	850.5622	1,156.2685	1,567.8833	2,120.7483	2,861.5567
38	103.9874	145.3397	202.5433	281.4515	389.9983	538.9100	742.6506	1,020.6747	1,399.0849	1,912.8176	2,608.5204	3,548.3303
39	117.5058	165.6873	232.9248	326.4838	456.2980	635.9139	883.7542	1,224.8096	1,692.8927	2,333.6375	3,208.4801	4,399.9295
40	132.7816	188.8835	267.8635	378.7212	533.8687	750.3783	1,051.6675	1,469.7716	2,048.4002	2,847.0378	3,946.4305	5,455.9126

Present Value of an Annuity of $1

Periods (n)	1%	2%	3%	4%	5%	6%	7%	8%	9%	10%	11%	12%
1	0.9901	0.9804	0.9709	0.9615	0.9524	0.9434	0.9346	0.9259	0.9174	0.9091	0.9009	0.8929
2	1.9704	1.9416	1.9135	1.8861	1.8594	1.8334	1.8080	1.7833	1.7591	1.7355	1.7125	1.6901
3	2.9410	2.8839	2.8286	2.7751	2.7232	2.6730	2.6243	2.5771	2.5313	2.4869	2.4437	2.4018
4	3.9020	3.8077	3.7171	3.6299	3.5460	3.4651	3.3872	3.3121	3.2397	3.1699	3.1024	3.0373
5	4.8534	4.7135	4.5797	4.4518	4.3295	4.2124	4.1002	3.9927	3.8897	3.7908	3.6959	3.6048
6	5.7955	5.6014	5.4172	5.2421	5.0757	4.9173	4.7665	4.6229	4.4859	4.3553	4.2305	4.1114
7	6.7282	6.4720	6.2303	6.0021	5.7864	5.5824	5.3893	5.2064	5.0330	4.8684	4.7122	4.5638
8	7.6517	7.3255	7.0197	6.7327	6.4632	6.2098	5.9713	5.7466	5.5348	5.3349	5.1461	4.9676
9	8.5660	8.1622	7.7861	7.4353	7.1078	6.8017	6.5152	6.2469	5.9952	5.7590	5.5370	5.3282
10	9.4713	8.9826	8.5302	8.1109	7.7217	7.3601	7.0236	6.7101	6.4177	6.1446	5.8892	5.6502
11	10.3676	9.7868	9.2526	8.7605	8.3064	7.8869	7.4987	7.1390	6.8052	6.4951	6.2065	5.9377
12	11.2551	10.5753	9.9540	9.3851	8.8633	8.3838	7.9427	7.5361	7.1607	6.8137	6.4924	6.1944
13	12.1337	11.3484	10.6350	9.9856	9.3936	8.8527	8.3577	7.9038	7.4869	7.1034	6.7499	6.4235
14	13.0037	12.1062	11.2961	10.5631	9.8986	9.2950	8.7455	8.2442	7.7862	7.3667	6.9819	6.6282
15	13.8651	12.8493	11.9379	11.1184	10.3797	9.7122	9.1079	8.5595	8.0607	7.6061	7.1909	6.8109
16	14.7179	13.5777	12.5611	11.6523	10.8378	10.1059	9.4466	8.8514	8.3126	7.8237	7.3792	6.9740
17	15.5623	14.2919	13.1661	12.1657	11.2741	10.4773	9.7632	9.1216	8.5436	8.0216	7.5488	7.1196
18	16.3983	14.9920	13.7535	12.6593	11.6896	10.8276	10.0591	9.3719	8.7556	8.2014	7.7016	7.2497
19	17.2260	15.6785	14.3238	13.1339	12.0853	11.1581	10.3356	9.6036	8.9501	8.3649	7.8393	7.3658
20	18.0456	16.3514	14.8775	13.5903	12.4622	11.4699	10.5940	9.8181	9.1285	8.5136	7.9633	7.4694
21	18.8570	17.0112	15.4150	14.0292	12.8212	11.7641	10.8355	10.0168	9.2922	8.6487	8.0751	7.5620
22	19.6604	17.6580	15.9369	14.4511	13.1630	12.0416	11.0612	10.2007	9.4424	8.7715	8.1757	7.6446
23	20.4558	18.2922	16.4436	14.8568	13.4886	12.3034	11.2722	10.3711	9.5802	8.8832	8.2664	7.7184
24	21.2434	18.9139	16.9355	15.2470	13.7986	12.5504	11.4693	10.5288	9.7066	8.9847	8.3481	7.7843
25	22.0232	19.5235	17.4131	15.6221	14.0939	12.7834	11.6536	10.6748	9.8226	9.0770	8.4217	7.8431
26	22.7952	20.1210	17.8768	15.9828	14.3752	13.0032	11.8258	10.8100	9.9290	9.1609	8.4881	7.8957
27	23.5596	20.7069	18.3270	16.3296	14.6430	13.2105	11.9867	10.9352	10.0266	9.2372	8.5478	7.9426
28	24.3164	21.2813	18.7641	16.6631	14.8981	13.4062	12.1371	11.0511	10.1161	9.3066	8.6016	7.9844
29	25.0658	21.8444	19.1885	16.9837	15.1411	13.5907	12.2777	11.1584	10.1983	9.3696	8.6501	8.0218
30	25.8077	22.3965	19.6004	17.2920	15.3725	13.7648	12.4090	11.2578	10.2737	9.4269	8.6938	8.0552
31	26.5423	22.9377	20.0004	17.5885	15.5928	13.9291	12.5318	11.3498	10.3428	9.4790	8.7331	8.0850
32	27.2696	23.4683	20.3888	17.8736	15.8027	14.0840	12.6466	11.4350	10.4062	9.5264	8.7686	8.1116
33	27.9897	23.9886	20.7658	18.1476	16.0025	14.2302	12.7538	11.5139	10.4644	9.5694	8.8005	8.1354
34	28.7027	24.4986	21.1318	18.4112	16.1929	14.3681	12.8540	11.5869	10.5178	9.6086	8.8293	8.1566
35	29.4086	24.9986	21.4872	18.6646	16.3742	14.4982	12.9477	11.6546	10.5668	9.6442	8.8552	8.1755
36	30.1075	25.4888	21.8323	18.9083	16.5469	14.6210	13.0352	11.7172	10.6118	9.6765	8.8786	8.1924
37	30.7995	25.9695	22.1672	19.1426	16.7113	14.7368	13.1170	11.7752	10.6530	9.7059	8.8996	8.2075
38	31.4847	26.4406	22.4925	19.3679	16.8679	14.8460	13.1935	11.8289	10.6908	9.7327	8.9186	8.2210
39	32.1630	26.9026	22.8082	19.5845	17.0170	14.9491	13.2649	11.8786	10.7255	9.7570	8.9357	8.2330
40	32.8347	27.3555	23.1148	19.7928	17.1591	15.0463	13.3317	11.9246	10.7574	9.7791	8.9511	8.2438

Interest rate (r)

Present Value of an Annuity of $1

Periods (n)	13%	14%	15%	16%	17%	18%	19%	20%	21%	22%	23%	24%
						Interest rate (r)						
1	0.8850	0.8772	0.8696	0.8621	0.8547	0.8475	0.8403	0.8333	0.8264	0.8197	0.8130	0.8065
2	1.6681	1.6467	1.6257	1.6052	1.5852	1.5656	1.5465	1.5278	1.5095	1.4915	1.4740	1.4568
3	2.3612	2.3216	2.2832	2.2459	2.2096	2.1743	2.1399	2.1065	2.0739	2.0422	2.0114	1.9813
4	2.9745	2.9137	2.8550	2.7982	2.7432	2.6901	2.6386	2.5887	2.5404	2.4936	2.4483	2.4043
5	3.5172	3.4331	3.3522	3.2743	3.1993	3.1272	3.0576	2.9906	2.9260	2.8636	2.8035	2.7454
6	3.9975	3.8887	3.7845	3.6847	3.5892	3.4976	3.4098	3.3255	3.2446	3.1669	3.0923	3.0205
7	4.4226	4.2883	4.1604	4.0386	3.9224	3.8115	3.7057	3.6046	3.5079	3.4155	3.3270	3.2423
8	4.7988	4.6389	4.4873	4.3436	4.2072	4.0776	3.9544	3.8372	3.7256	3.6193	3.5179	3.4212
9	5.1317	4.9464	4.7716	4.6065	4.4506	4.3030	4.1633	4.0310	3.9054	3.7863	3.6731	3.5655
10	5.4262	5.2161	5.0188	4.8332	4.6586	4.4941	4.3389	4.1925	4.0541	3.9232	3.7993	3.6819
11	5.6869	5.4527	5.2337	5.0286	4.8364	4.6560	4.4865	4.3271	4.1769	4.0354	3.9018	3.7757
12	5.9176	5.6603	5.4206	5.1971	4.9884	4.7932	4.6105	4.4392	4.2784	4.1274	3.9852	3.8514
13	6.1218	5.8424	5.5831	5.3423	5.1183	4.9095	4.7147	4.5327	4.3624	4.2028	4.0530	3.9124
14	6.3025	6.0021	5.7245	5.4675	5.2293	5.0081	4.8023	4.6106	4.4317	4.2646	4.1082	3.9616
15	6.4624	6.1422	5.8474	5.5755	5.3242	5.0916	4.8759	4.6755	4.4890	4.3152	4.1530	4.0013
16	6.6039	6.2651	5.9542	5.6685	5.4053	5.1624	4.9377	4.7296	4.5364	4.3567	4.1894	4.0333
17	6.7291	6.3729	6.0472	5.7487	5.4746	5.2223	4.9897	4.7746	4.5755	4.3908	4.2190	4.0591
18	6.8399	6.4674	6.1280	5.8178	5.5339	5.2732	5.0333	4.8122	4.6079	4.4187	4.2431	4.0799
19	6.9380	6.5504	6.1982	5.8775	5.5845	5.3162	5.0700	4.8435	4.6346	4.4415	4.2627	4.0967
20	7.0248	6.6231	6.2593	5.9288	5.6278	5.3527	5.1009	4.8696	4.6567	4.4603	4.2786	4.1103
21	7.1016	6.6870	6.3125	5.9731	5.6648	5.3837	5.1268	4.8913	4.6750	4.4756	4.2916	4.1212
22	7.1695	6.7429	6.3587	6.0113	5.6964	5.4099	5.1486	4.9094	4.6900	4.4882	4.3021	4.1300
23	7.2297	6.7921	6.3988	6.0442	5.7234	5.4321	5.1668	4.9245	4.7025	4.4985	4.3106	4.1371
24	7.2829	6.8351	6.4338	6.0726	5.7465	5.4509	5.1822	4.9371	4.7128	4.5070	4.3176	4.1428
25	7.3300	6.8729	6.4641	6.0971	5.7662	5.4669	5.1951	4.9476	4.7213	4.5139	4.3232	4.1474
26	7.3717	6.9061	6.4906	6.1182	5.7831	5.4804	5.2060	4.9563	4.7284	4.5196	4.3278	4.1511
27	7.4086	6.9352	6.5135	6.1364	5.7975	5.4919	5.2151	4.9636	4.7342	4.5243	4.3316	4.1542
28	7.4412	6.9607	6.5335	6.1520	5.8099	5.5016	5.2228	4.9697	4.7390	4.5281	4.3346	4.1566
29	7.4701	6.9830	6.5509	6.1656	5.8204	5.5098	5.2292	4.9747	4.7430	4.5312	4.3371	4.1585
30	7.4957	7.0027	6.5660	6.1772	5.8294	5.5168	5.2347	4.9789	4.7463	4.5338	4.3391	4.1601
31	7.5183	7.0199	6.5791	6.1872	5.8371	5.5227	5.2392	4.9824	4.7490	4.5359	4.3407	4.1614
32	7.5383	7.0350	6.5905	6.1959	5.8437	5.5277	5.2430	4.9854	4.7512	4.5376	4.3421	4.1624
33	7.5560	7.0482	6.6005	6.2034	5.8493	5.5320	5.2462	4.9878	4.7531	4.5390	4.3431	4.1632
34	7.5717	7.0599	6.6091	6.2098	5.8541	5.5356	5.2489	4.9898	4.7546	4.5402	4.3440	4.1639
35	7.5856	7.0700	6.6166	6.2153	5.8582	5.5386	5.2512	4.9915	4.7559	4.5411	4.3447	4.1644
36	7.5979	7.0790	6.6231	6.2201	5.8617	5.5412	5.2531	4.9929	4.7569	4.5419	4.3453	4.1649
37	7.6087	7.0868	6.6288	6.2242	5.8647	5.5434	5.2547	4.9941	4.7578	4.5426	4.3458	4.1652
38	7.6183	7.0937	6.6338	6.2278	5.8673	5.5452	5.2561	4.9951	4.7585	4.5431	4.3462	4.1655
39	7.6268	7.0997	6.6380	6.2309	5.8695	5.5468	5.2572	4.9959	4.7591	4.5435	4.3465	4.1657
40	7.6344	7.1050	6.6418	6.2335	5.8713	5.5482	5.2582	4.9966	4.7596	4.5439	4.3467	4.1659

Future Value of an Annuity of $1

Periods (n)	1%	2%	3%	4%	5%	6%	7%	8%	9%	10%	11%	12%
					Interest rate (r)							
1	1.0000	1.0000	1.0000	1.0000	1.0000	1.0000	1.0000	1.0000	1.0000	1.0000	1.0000	1.0000
2	2.0100	2.0200	2.0300	2.0400	2.0500	2.0600	2.0700	2.0800	2.0900	2.1000	2.1100	2.1200
3	3.0301	3.0604	3.0909	3.1216	3.1525	3.1836	3.2149	3.2464	3.2781	3.3100	3.3421	3.3744
4	4.0604	4.1216	4.1836	4.2465	4.3101	4.3746	4.4399	4.5061	4.5731	4.6410	4.7097	4.7793
5	5.1010	5.2040	5.3091	5.4163	5.5256	5.6371	5.7507	5.8666	5.9847	6.1051	6.2278	6.3528
6	6.1520	6.3081	6.4684	6.6330	6.8019	6.9753	7.1533	7.3359	7.5233	7.7156	7.9129	8.1152
7	7.2135	7.4343	7.6625	7.8983	8.1420	8.3938	8.6540	8.9228	9.2004	9.4872	9.7833	10.0890
8	8.2857	8.5830	8.8923	9.2142	9.5491	9.8975	10.2598	10.6366	11.0285	11.4359	11.8594	12.2997
9	9.3685	9.7546	10.1591	10.5828	11.0266	11.4913	11.9780	12.4876	13.0210	13.5795	14.1640	14.7757
10	10.4622	10.9497	11.4639	12.0061	12.5779	13.1808	13.8164	14.4866	15.1929	15.9374	16.7220	17.5487
11	11.5668	12.1687	12.8078	13.4864	14.2068	14.9716	15.7836	16.6455	17.5603	18.5312	19.5614	20.6546
12	12.6825	13.4121	14.1920	15.0258	15.9171	16.8699	17.8885	18.9771	20.1407	21.3843	22.7132	24.1331
13	13.8093	14.6803	15.6178	16.6268	17.7130	18.8821	20.1406	21.4953	22.9534	24.5227	26.2116	28.0291
14	14.9474	15.9739	17.0863	18.2919	19.5986	21.0151	22.5505	24.2149	26.0192	27.9750	30.0949	32.3926
15	16.0969	17.2934	18.5989	20.0236	21.5786	23.2760	25.1290	27.1521	29.3609	31.7725	34.4054	37.2797
16	17.2579	18.6393	20.1569	21.8245	23.6575	25.6725	27.8881	30.3243	33.0034	35.9497	39.1899	42.7533
17	18.4304	20.0121	21.7616	23.6975	25.8404	28.2129	30.8402	33.7502	36.9737	40.5447	44.5008	48.8837
18	19.6147	21.4123	23.4144	25.6454	28.1324	30.9057	33.9990	37.4502	41.3013	45.5992	50.3959	55.7497
19	20.8109	22.8406	25.1169	27.6712	30.5390	33.7600	37.3790	41.4463	46.0185	51.1591	56.9395	63.4397
20	22.0190	24.2974	26.8704	29.7781	33.0660	36.7856	40.9955	45.7620	51.1601	57.2750	64.2028	72.0524
21	23.2392	25.7833	28.6765	31.9692	35.7193	39.9927	44.8652	50.4229	56.7645	64.0025	72.2651	81.6987
22	24.4716	27.2990	30.5368	34.2480	38.5052	43.3923	49.0057	55.4568	62.8733	71.4027	81.2143	92.5026
23	25.7163	28.8450	32.4529	36.6179	41.4305	46.9958	53.4361	60.8933	69.5319	79.5430	91.1479	104.6029
24	26.9735	30.4219	34.4265	39.0826	44.5020	50.8156	58.1767	66.7648	76.7898	88.4973	102.1742	118.1552
25	28.2432	32.0303	36.4593	41.6459	47.7271	54.8645	63.2490	73.1059	84.7009	98.3471	114.4133	133.3339
26	29.5256	33.6709	38.5530	44.3117	51.1135	59.1564	68.6765	79.9544	93.3240	109.1818	127.9988	150.3339
27	30.8209	35.3443	40.7096	47.0842	54.6691	63.7058	74.4838	87.3508	102.7231	121.0999	143.0786	169.3740
28	32.1291	37.0512	42.9309	49.9676	58.4026	68.5281	80.6977	95.3388	112.9682	134.2099	159.8173	190.6989
29	33.4504	38.7922	45.2189	52.9663	62.3227	73.6398	87.3465	103.9659	124.1354	148.6309	178.3972	214.5828
30	34.7849	40.5681	47.5754	56.0849	66.4388	79.0582	94.4608	113.2832	136.3075	164.4940	199.0209	241.3327
31	36.1327	42.3794	50.0027	59.3283	70.7608	84.8017	102.0730	123.3459	149.5752	181.9434	221.9132	271.2926
32	37.4941	44.2270	52.5028	62.7015	75.2988	90.8898	110.2182	134.2135	164.0370	201.1378	247.3236	304.8477
33	38.8690	46.1116	55.0778	66.2095	80.0638	97.3432	118.9334	145.9506	179.8003	222.2515	275.5292	342.4294
34	40.2577	48.0338	57.7302	69.8579	85.0670	104.1838	128.2588	158.6267	196.9823	245.4767	306.8374	384.5210
35	41.6603	49.9945	60.4621	73.6522	90.3203	111.4348	138.2369	172.3168	215.7108	271.0244	341.5896	431.6635
36	43.0769	51.9944	63.2759	77.5983	95.8363	119.1209	148.9135	187.1021	236.1247	299.1268	380.1644	484.4631
37	44.5076	54.0343	66.1742	81.7022	101.6281	127.2681	160.3374	203.0703	258.3759	330.0395	422.9825	543.5987
38	45.9527	56.1149	69.1594	85.9703	107.7095	135.9042	172.5610	220.3159	282.6298	364.0434	470.5106	609.8305
39	47.4123	58.2372	72.2342	90.4091	114.0950	145.0585	185.6403	238.9412	309.0665	401.4478	523.2667	684.0102
40	48.8864	60.4020	75.4013	95.0255	120.7998	154.7620	199.6351	259.0565	337.8824	442.5926	581.8261	767.0914

Future Value of an Annuity of $1

Interest rate (r)

Periods (n)	13%	14%	15%	16%	17%	18%	19%	20%	21%	22%	23%	24%
1	1.0000	1.0000	1.0000	1.0000	1.0000	1.0000	1.0000	1.0000	1.0000	1.0000	1.0000	1.0000
2	2.1300	2.1400	2.1500	2.1600	2.1700	2.1800	2.1900	2.2000	2.2100	2.2200	2.2300	2.2400
3	3.4069	3.4396	3.4725	3.5056	3.5389	3.5724	3.6061	3.6400	3.6741	3.7084	3.7429	3.7776
4	4.8498	4.9211	4.9934	5.0665	5.1405	5.2154	5.2913	5.3680	5.4457	5.5242	5.6038	5.6842
5	6.4803	6.6101	6.7424	6.8771	7.0144	7.1542	7.2966	7.4416	7.5892	7.7396	7.8926	8.0484
6	8.3227	8.5355	8.7537	8.9775	9.2068	9.4420	9.6830	9.9299	10.1830	10.4423	10.7079	10.9801
7	10.4047	10.7305	11.0668	11.4139	11.7720	12.1415	12.5227	12.9159	13.3214	13.7396	14.1708	14.6153
8	12.7573	13.2328	13.7268	14.2401	14.7733	15.3270	15.9020	16.4991	17.1189	17.7623	18.4300	19.1229
9	15.4157	16.0853	16.7858	17.5185	18.2847	19.0859	19.9234	20.7989	21.7139	22.6700	23.6690	24.7125
10	18.4197	19.3373	20.3037	21.3215	22.3931	23.5213	24.7089	25.9587	27.2738	28.6574	30.1128	31.6434
11	21.8143	23.0445	24.3493	25.7329	27.1999	28.7551	30.4035	32.1504	34.0013	35.9620	38.0388	40.2379
12	25.6502	27.2707	29.0017	30.8502	32.8239	34.9311	37.1802	39.5805	42.1416	44.8737	47.7877	50.8950
13	29.9847	32.0887	34.3519	36.7862	39.4040	42.2187	45.2445	48.4966	51.9913	55.7459	59.7788	64.1097
14	34.8827	37.5811	40.5047	43.6720	47.1027	50.8180	54.8409	59.1959	63.9095	69.0100	74.5280	80.4961
15	40.4175	43.8424	47.5804	51.6595	56.1101	60.9653	66.2607	72.0351	78.3305	85.1922	92.6694	100.8151
16	46.6717	50.9804	55.7175	60.9250	66.6488	72.9390	79.8502	87.4421	95.7799	104.9345	114.9834	126.0108
17	53.7391	59.1176	65.0751	71.6730	78.9792	87.0680	96.0218	105.9306	116.8937	129.0201	142.4295	157.2534
18	61.7251	68.3941	75.8364	84.1407	93.4056	103.7403	115.2659	128.1167	142.4413	158.4045	176.1883	195.9942
19	70.7494	78.9692	88.2118	98.6032	110.2846	123.4135	138.1664	154.7400	173.3540	194.2535	217.7116	244.0328
20	80.9468	91.0249	102.4436	115.3797	130.0329	146.6280	165.4180	186.6880	210.7584	237.9893	268.7853	303.6006
21	92.4699	104.7684	118.8101	134.8405	153.1385	174.0210	197.8474	225.0256	256.0176	291.3469	331.6059	377.4648
22	105.4910	120.4360	137.6316	157.4150	180.1721	206.3448	236.4385	271.0307	310.7813	356.4432	408.8753	469.0563
23	120.2048	138.2970	159.2764	183.6014	211.8013	244.4868	282.3618	326.2369	377.0454	435.8607	503.9166	582.6298
24	136.8315	158.6586	184.1678	213.9776	248.8076	289.4945	337.0105	392.4842	457.2249	532.7501	620.8174	723.4610
25	155.6196	181.8708	212.7930	249.2140	292.1049	342.6035	402.0425	471.9811	554.2422	650.9551	764.6054	898.0916
26	176.8501	208.3327	245.7120	290.0883	342.7627	405.2721	479.4306	567.3773	671.6330	795.1653	941.4647	1,114.6336
27	200.8406	238.4993	283.5688	337.5024	402.0323	479.2211	571.5224	681.8528	813.6759	971.1016	1,159.0016	1,383.1457
28	227.9499	272.8892	327.1041	392.5028	471.3778	566.4809	681.1116	819.2233	985.5479	1,185.7440	1,426.5719	1,716.1007
29	258.5834	312.0937	377.1697	456.3032	552.5121	669.4475	811.5228	984.0680	1,193.5129	1,447.6077	1,755.6835	2,128.9648
30	293.1992	356.7868	434.7451	530.3117	647.4391	790.9480	966.7122	1,181.8816	1,445.1507	1,767.0813	2,160.4907	2,640.9164
31	332.3151	407.7370	500.9569	616.1616	758.5038	934.3186	1,151.3875	1,419.2579	1,749.6323	2,156.8392	2,658.4036	3,275.7363
32	376.5161	465.8202	577.1005	715.7475	888.4494	1,103.4960	1,371.1511	1,704.1095	2,118.0551	2,632.3439	3,270.8364	4,062.9130
33	426.4632	532.0350	664.6655	831.2671	1,040.4858	1,303.1253	1,632.6698	2,045.0964	2,563.8467	3,212.4595	4,024.1287	5,039.0122
34	482.9034	607.5199	765.3654	965.2698	1,218.3684	1,538.6878	1,943.8771	2,456.1176	3,103.2545	3,920.2006	4,950.6783	6,249.3751
35	546.6808	693.5727	881.1702	1,120.7130	1,426.4910	1,816.6516	2,314.2137	2,948.3411	3,755.9379	4,783.6447	6,090.3344	7,750.2251
36	618.7493	791.6729	1,014.3457	1,301.0270	1,669.9945	2,144.6489	2,754.9143	3,539.0094	4,545.6848	5,837.0466	7,492.1113	9,611.2791
37	700.1867	903.5071	1,167.4975	1,510.1914	1,954.8936	2,531.6857	3,279.3481	4,247.8112	5,501.2787	7,122.1968	9,216.2969	11,918.986
38	792.2110	1,030.9981	1,343.6222	1,752.8220	2,288.2255	2,988.3891	3,903.4242	5,098.3735	6,657.5472	8,690.0801	11,337.045	14,780.543
39	896.1984	1,176.3378	1,546.1655	2,034.2735	2,678.2238	3,527.2992	4,646.0748	6,119.0482	8,056.6321	10,602.898	13,945.566	18,328.873
40	1,013.7042	1,342.0251	1,779.0903	2,360.7572	3,134.5218	4,163.2130	5,529.8290	7,343.8578	9,749.5248	12,936.535	17,154.046	22,728.803

Index